POLICY FORMULATION
AND ADMINISTRATION

POLICY FORMULATION AND ADMINISTRATION

A casebook of senior management problems in business

C. Roland Christensen, A.B., D.C.S.
George Fisher Baker, Jr. Professor
of Business Administration

Norman A. Berg, S.B., D.B.A.
Professor of Business Administration

Malcolm S. Salter, A.B., D.B.A.
Professor of Business Administration

All of the
Harvard University
Graduate School of Business Administration

Eighth edition   1980

RICHARD D. IRWIN, INC.   Homewood, Illinois   60430
Irwin-Dorsey Limited   Georgetown, Ontario   L7G 4B3

ISBN 0-256-02345-X
Library of Congress Catalog Card No. 79-91633

Printed in the United States of America

1 2 3 4 5 6 7 8 9 0 A 7 6 5 4 3 2 1 0

To
GEORGE ALBERT SMITH, JR. (1905–1969)
Friend
Colleague
Teacher to all

Acknowledgments

As has been our tradition, we wish to acknowledge our thanks to all the people who have helped make possible this eighth edition of *Policy Formulation and Administration*. We are indebted to our colleagues here at the Harvard Business School, to our colleagues in other schools of business administration and in management development institutes, and to the directors of management development activities in private and public organizations in this country and throughout the world. They have been generous in helping us with the improvement of course concepts and case developments and in sharing their teaching experiences in the previous editions of our book. Changes in this eighth edition again reflect their suggestions. We are indebted also to the leaders of the organizations and their associates who have so generously contributed their time and experience to these case studies. They have shared their failures as well as their successes with all of us who study, learn, and teach in the policy area.

Case research and writing is a demanding discipline—a blend of rigorous research method and artistry of presentation. We are especially indebted to the men and women who researched and developed these case studies. Some of these cases are the products of individual efforts; others grew out of collective efforts. Some of them we have written or supervised ourselves; others have been written by our associates here and at other schools of business. We congratulate them for work well done and extend to them our gratitude for their cooperation in making this book possible.

Specifically, we thank the following colleagues for their contribution of the indicated cases: William Boulton—The Leisure Group; Robert Bruner—The Real Paper, Inc.; Ram Charan—Hawaii Best Company; Linda Elmer—Charles River Breeding Laboratories and the Dr Pepper Company; Norman Fast—Lincoln Electric Company; Tull Gearreald—Tensor Corporation; Philippe Haspeslagh—Zurn Industries; E. P. Learned—The Rose Company and The Larger Company; Leslie Levy—Note on the Soft Drink Industry in the United States; Hassell McClellan—

Sturm, Ruger and Company, Inc.; John Matthews—Pete Olson; Glenn Merry—Moleculon Research Corporation and Polaroid-Kodak; Edwin Murray—Sybron (A) (condensed); Robert Pitts—Sybron (B), (C), and (E); Elizabeth Lyman Rachal—Note on the Mechanical Writing Industry, Bic Pen Corporation and Scripto, Inc.; Bruce Scott—Midway Foods Corporation (D_2) (revised); George A. Smith, Jr.—Albert Manufacturing Company; Cheryl Suchors—Seven-Up Company; Mark Teagan—Robin Hood; and Charles Weigle—Prelude Corporation.

The text sections of this edition have been written with the objective of helping the policy student deal effectively with this book's complicated, real-life case studies. While each student will have his or her individual preferences, we would urge that section text material be read in its entirety at the beginning and end of each of the three major subdivisions of this book. This will provide a useful preview, a guide to analyze and discuss each case, and a way to review and summarize the section upon completion.

We would also like to acknowledge the special contribution of one member of our author group. Professor Norman Berg's development of the text portions of the eighth edition marks a major step forward in the continuing evolution of this casebook. We believe both students and instructors will find the text sections helpful in their study and discussion of these policy cases. What he has achieved is to combine the general manager's analytic task of formulating strategies for accomplishment with the critical policy process tasks of implementing that strategy and providing the vital leadership ingredient.

We are also grateful to the administrative officers of the Harvard Graduate School of Business Administration for their continuing encouragement of this effort. Dean Lawrence Fouraker, Dean John McArthur, and Audrey Barrett, Assistant Director of Case Services, have been most supportive. Madeleine Healy, Dyanne Holdman, and Eve Bamford have been most helpful in administrative and editorial contributions.

We wish again to pay tribute and acknowledge our great debt to George Albert Smith, Jr., who passed away October 12, 1969. Professor Smith was "The Pioneer" in the development of the Business Policy field. His influence continues in the thousands of students with whom he worked, in the countless teachers and researchers developed under his personal supervision, and in the concepts and ideas expressed and used in this edition. He personally influenced and taught each of the present authors of this text. We hope to honor him by the continuing development of his ideas and by this book.

C. Roland Christensen
Norman A. Berg
Malcolm S. Salter

Contents

Introduction

The purposes of this eighth edition of *Policy Formulation and Administration* are essentially the same as those of the previous editions. The book provides both text and a selection of cases that can assist men and women preparing for a career in business administration to become acquainted with the opportunities and challenges confronting the senior manager of a firm. This material also provides significant opportunities for learning for middle managers and senior managers enrolled in university or corporate management development programs.

The educational objectives of this edition are the same as for earlier editions. Its orientation is managerial. It seeks to encourage the development of leadership skills. Men and women who can "take charge" of organizations are a scarce resource. The hope of the authors is that the study of these situations may encourage interest in general management skills and may provide an opportunity for academic practice of skills requisite to this organization position via discussion of selected case problems.

Specifically, the study and discussion of these cases, and the accompanying text, offer opportunities:

1. To learn about the functions, roles, and skills of senior management; the perspective of general management.
2. To develop skill in envisaging goals; to delineate the functions and activities that must be performed to achieve the goals; and to determine what functional strategies are needed for goal achievement.
3. To become familiar with "risk" and its place in general management thinking.
4. To learn to identify—and to attract to a business—personnel with the requisite technical and emotional abilities and to build them into a thinking, living, acting organization.
5. To develop the ability to divide the work of a firm into logical and understandable assignments, with limitations of authority and, at the same time, provisions for individual decision-making powers and opportunities for cooperation.

6. To learn to set standards for measuring performance.
7. To understand how to provide motivation for the members of the management group so they will apply their skills (which the organization needs) and in doing so find nutriment for their own needs—both economic and ethical.
8. To gain insight, self-confidence, imagination, and the ability to furnish leadership to the organization. Coupled with leadership is the willingness to take ultimate responsibility not only for the results of one's own decisions but also for the results of the decisions and actions of all to whom the leader has delegated authority.
9. To anticipate and accept the responsibilities of the leader and those of the organization to the various sectors of society that are affected by the organization's actions: the investor, the worker, the supplier, the community, and the country.

This casebook invites both instructor and student to enter into a process of policy formulation and administration. This process, as will become apparent from class discussion, depends upon a melding of intellectual and administrative skills. For example, identifying problems that affect the long-term position of the firm calls for the ability to select and relate disparate bits of information so that an inclusive statement of key problems can be made. Making such a statement requires, however, more than the intellectual skill of analyzing environmental trends and data on internal corporate operations. It also requires the ability to articulate problems in such a way that suggests actionable alternatives that can be submitted to careful evaluation. This ability reflects what we can call an administrative sense. Similarly, setting objectives and formulating a plan of action require both the sense of what is needed and what will work.

The cases presented in this book are not meant to stand alone. They are not traditional research documents which describe important aspects of policy formulation and administration. Nor are they studies which suggest how policy should be formulated and administered by top corporate executives. Rather the cases have been designed to provide the raw material for students to work out for themselves, under the guidance of a trained instructor, what policies are appropriate for particular firms. It is intended that a course based upon these cases will help the student develop an analytical approach to broad business policy problems.

Each case in this book describes an actual situation as of the time the case was written. To preserve confidentiality, fictitious names have been used in some instances, and sometimes the geographical locations have been changed. Only on rare occasions has the industry been changed or the size of the company materially altered. Almost always the case contains information about the industry and its competitive conditions; some historical background about the company itself; financial and statistical data;

information about products and production, and marketing methods and facilities; the organization plan; and executive personnel. These cases are the raw materials that permit simulation in the classroom of the actual discussions carried on informally among managers and in board and committee rooms.

In the tradition of earlier editions, this volume contains a selection of "seasoned" cases used in previous editions as well as a selection of new cases not heretofore published. We have also selected cases from a wide variety of corporate organizations, ranging in size from the small, new enterprise to the large and very complex conglomerate organization. In addition to cases covering problems of the overall enterprises, we have included, in this edition, some cases focusing on the problems of the individual manager as he attempts to survive and to influence his organization.

It has been our experience and the experience of many other instructors that, by using cases such as these, teacher and students together can create "ways of thinking," "ways of feeling," and "ways of doing" that accelerate tremendously both intellectual growth and emotional development.

The questions or problems in the cases and their solutions

At the top level, an executive does not have any "all-wise" adviser to identify what problem or problems he or she should be watching or working on at a particular time—that must be decided personally. And there is no reference book to look into, no infallible aid to give *the* solution. The executive must, nevertheless, find *some* solution, some workable solution. This is done by the use of experience and the exercise of judgment, usually after discussion and consultation with others. And neither before a decision is made, nor after, can the executive be absolutely sure what action is *right* or *best*.

The administrator must be willing and able to work in a climate of uncertainty, which is often uncomfortable. He or she must accept the responsibility for reaching decisions under time pressure, on the basis of limited facts, and in the face of many unknowns. Imperfect, the administrator must work with people who also are imperfect. Almost always, some associates or other parties involved will disagree, and their disagreement and their views should be taken into account. The administrator is in the usually lonesome situation of being the possessor of ultimate responsibility. He or she inevitably will make some mistakes. If experienced and mature, the administrator will expect this and will allow for it, but will hope to reach wise decisions most of the time. The administrator who succeeds in doing that is a successful business leader.

This clearly suggests that the cases do not include any "official" or "demonstrably correct" answers. We do not have either "official" questions or "approved" solutions. It is part of the student's task, as it is part of an executive's task, to discover questions and to distinguish the important from the unimportant. In some instances, we do not agree among ourselves as to exactly what the most fundamental problems or opportunities are; and in still more instances we do not agree on the best possible course of action. If we did, we would question the reality of our cases and perhaps also the quality and integrity of our own views. Complicated business situations such as are presented here are episodes taken out of business life. Since we are all different people, with our own special backgrounds and experiences, we will attach to these problems at least somewhat differing interpretations and envision somewhat differing or substantially differing solutions or courses of action.

We do have our own ideas about each of the cases we are offering; so do our colleagues who use them. In some instances, we hold our views with strong conviction. In others, we are much less sure of what we think. And we change our views from time to time. So we certainly do not feel that we *know* what should be done in each of the situations presented. The value of the cases in the classroom lies in their discussion, not in the giving or finding of an "authoritative" answer.

Organization and philosophy of the book

This edition contains the basic organizational features of its predecessor efforts with some modifications. We have divided the book into three major subsections: Policy formulation; Policy administration; and Policy formulation and administration in diversified firms.

This plan with its selected distribution of cases can give you as students a sense of the atmosphere in which top-level executives work and can make real to you the individuals in top management, with their range of human frailties and strengths. It also will make clear to you that managers must work through and depend on other people; that they must engage in much routine work; that virtually all they can be sure of is change and the unexpected. You will learn also that policy formulation is not always a formal process; that there often is a discrepancy between stated policy and policy as practiced; that much policy making is done (and should be done) at fairly low levels in organizations; and that effective authority or leadership is not conferred from above but is earned and awarded from below.

As you progress in your study of the cases, many other important things will become clear. For example, you will be disabused of any idea that the executive discovers and solves one problem at a time. On the contrary, he or she deals with many problems concurrently, each at a different stage of development. Furthermore, the route of travel from sizeup, through planning, organizing, putting plans into action and control, to reappraisal, is not a straight line. The route is much more like a circle. Even in dealing with one problem, the administrator goes around the circle many times and, as we have said, is busy with many circles. The executive's job is never really finished.

Preparing a case for class

The question of how students should prepare a case for class has been put to us many times by our own students and also by people studying and teaching these cases elsewhere. Actually, the question is often phrased: "What is the *best* way to prepare a case?" That one we cannot answer, inasmuch as we do not think there is any *best* way. There are, no doubt, many good and useful ways. Each of us must develop the methods that serve us best. Moreover, we all must change our approach somewhat to deal with each new situation. And each case is a new situation. So there is no formula, no basic pattern that we can pass on. We can, at most, make a few overall observations and then try to detail some specific suggestions.

We recommend, with the qualifications just stated, the following to the student: we suggest you first read the case through to get a general impression of what it is about, how it seems to come out, and what kinds of information it contains. We think there is a real advantage in doing this first reading a day or two before the time when you must do your thorough and final preparation. There is a value in having the general situation in mind in time to mull it over, both consciously and subconsciously, for a while. That is true of any important problem one has to deal with—in school, in business, anywhere.

For the second reading, we suggest you take the time to proceed slowly and carefully, studying the tables and exhibits and making notes as you go. Perhaps some headings will occur to you under which you want to summarize what you believe are especially pertinent factors. Perhaps, however, when you feel you are about at the end of your preparation, it will be well to ask: "Have I worked this thing through to the point where, if I really had a chance to talk to the persons responsible for this company, I could (1) talk intelligently with them about their company and their job in managing it; (2) show them why the main issues I have distilled out as a result of my analysis are really of first importance; and (3) give them a coordinated program of action that would be practical and would have a reasonable chance to succeed?"

We urge students, if possible, to discuss the cases with one another while preparing them. Managers in business discuss their problems with other key people. But be sure you do your own independent work and independent thinking. Do not be too stubborn to recognize a better idea than your own, but be sure you really understand and believe in it before you adopt it.

One more observation. Not infrequently, students express the wish for more information than is in a case; they feel they cannot make a decision without more facts. Do not hide behind that bogeyman. For one thing, business leaders never have all the facts they would like to have. And, as far as the cases are concerned, they all contain enough information to enable you to decide and recommend something sensible. Be sure you learn how to use, and do use, all the information you have.

The dimensions of general management

The focus of this volume is on the functions, roles, and skills of the general manager. One of our authors, M. S. Salter, concludes that there are five basic dimensions to the job of the general manager:

1. Supervising current operations.
2. Planning for future operations.
3. Designing and administering decision-making structures.
4. Developing human resources and capabilities.
5. Representing and holding an organization responsible to its various constituencies.

The most immediate concern of the general manager is supervising current operations. This normally involves setting goals and targets for various functional departments and product divisions, and periodically reviewing performance against preestablished goals. Sometimes operating goals and policies need to be modified by the general manager (and his associates) as changes in the environment suggest courses of action different from those currently being followed by various parts of the organization. Both the review of current performance and the reassessment of current operating goals and policies require a flow of relevant, reliable, and timely information. Overseeing this activity is an important aspect of the general manager's operating concerns.

Perhaps the most critical aspect of supervising current operations is the occasional need to intervene in disputes over operating problems where those closest to the situation cannot reach agreement on appropriate courses of action. Here the task of the general manager is to identify or extract the relevant policy issues and suggest action that reflects his view of appropriate policy. This intervention must be done selectively and in ways which do not permanently upset established methods for resolving problems at lower levels of management. If every crisis were to be brought to the general manager's desk for resolution, most of his time would be taken up with managing a myriad of small crises which would detract from careful attention to other important general management tasks, such as planning for future operations.

Planning for future operations is paid lip service more often than practiced. In part, this is due to the fact that many general managers perceive the payoff of comprehensive forward planning as being quite low. For those who are guiding companies which have dominant positions in relatively stable, low growth markets, there is the tendency to accept projections of past experience as solid bases for estimating future resource needs. General managers of relatively weak companies, occupying subordinate roles in either growing or stable markets, also tend to invest lightly in future-oriented planning since their tendency is to "wait for the breaks" and scramble as fast as possible when opportunities present themselves. The greatest incentive to invest heavily in comprehensive forward planning is for general managers of companies with dominant positions in dynamic growth markets. Here the costs of losing that position of dominance can be very high. However, it is companies without dominant market positions which can often profit the most from comprehensive forward planning since it is the principal means of organizing the development of competitive strength over time. A large majority of companies fall into this category.

Planning for future operations involves making informed judgments about what opportunities and risks will face the company in the future, and identifying alternate means of either exploiting these opportunities or accommodating these risks.

In addition to supervising current operations and planning future strategies, every general manager inevitably becomes preoccupied with forging an organizational structure that fits the company's needs and unique characteristics. In its most basic sense, this structure is primarily a decision-making apparatus. Differences among organization structures result from different ways of allocating decision-making authority and responsibility to administrative subunits and to individuals within these subunits. An organization structure thus defines the locus of decision-making responsibilities and identifies who will make which decisions under normal conditions. At operating levels of management, departmental or product-oriented structures typically provide the basic models for each company's organizational format. At the top policy levels of management, collectives of executives from key operating posts are often asked to review recommendations and approve decisions made at the departmental or product division levels.

General managers must determine which decision-making structure best suits their current and future needs. They must also reinforce its effectiveness by communicating clearly and directly what is expected from each decision maker. Performance measurement and reward systems typically have an important role to play in this effort. Designing and administering these systems is thus another important aspect of the general manager's job.

An additional responsibility of general management is the development of human capabilities and resources appropriate to the organization's present and future needs. The general manager must analyze both current operations and future plans in order to judge how many persons with what kinds of experience and competences are required. Once these needs are identified, the general manager must ensure that realistic plans are implemented to provide adequate human resources at all organizational levels when they are needed.

As straightforward as this sounds, there is perhaps no aspect of general management that is left so much to chance as manpower planning. Recruitment, staffing, job rotation, and training are often handled on an *ad hoc* basis rather than studied in advance. A common result of this practice is an unsystematic scramble for people, on the one hand, and career blockages, on the other, as companies experience shifting manpower needs. For general managers who proclaim that their organizations' past successes are due to the high quality of personnel, there can be no greater irony than finding that their organizations are equipped with inadequate personnel resources for the future or staffed with persons who face few opportunities for increased growth and development.

Apart from the administrative aspects of manpower planning, the development of an organization's human capabilities rests in large measure on the commitment of individuals to stretch themselves beyond their known limits. The reinforcement of this commitment (and morale) is the most subtle task of general management. While each successful general manager develops his own approach, a common characteristic shared by many organization leaders is the ability to institutionalize those values and articulate those objectives critical to the organization's success. Few groups of individuals—either inside or outside the business world—have been able to maintain their effectiveness without the leadership of those who can both represent and guide the development of the group's goals and values. This requirement is virtually universal; fulfilling this requirement is unquestionably the general manager's most difficult responsibility.

A final responsibility of general managers is representing their organizations to the world at large. One way of describing the external environment of companies and other purposive organizations is in terms of evolving coalitions of interests and power. These coalitions can be semipermanent alliances, as in the case of joint ventures between companies. They can also be extremely fluid coalitions which have coherence around certain issues and little coherence around other issues. A company's relations with labor unions and industry associations are cases in point. In these coalitions there are elements of both cooperation and controversy, and relations between parties are typically fluid and sometimes volatile. Relations between companies and various levels of government can have these characteristics as well. In this context the general manager has a dual responsibility. First, he must defend the integrity of his organization in these shifting coalitions and lobby for its interests. Second, where contracts, government regulation, and other aspects of law are involved, he must be cognizant of the rules of law and take personal responsibility for ensuring compliance with these rules.

The basic dilemma of the general manager concerns what emphasis to give these tasks and responsibilities at any one time. A primary objective of this book is to provide the student of policy with case and text material whereby he or she can practice and develop the necessary attitudes and skills to deal with that basic dilemma.

Outside reading

While the text and cases in this book make up the subject matter of a complete course, an instructor may wish to assign outside readings which reinforce the concepts brought out in class discussion. Several works, in particular, are relevant to the cases presented in this book:

Andrews, Kenneth R. *The Concept of Corporate Strategy.* Homewood, Ill.: Dow Jones-Irwin, 1979.

Ansoff, H. Igor. *Corporate Strategy.* New York: McGraw-Hill Book Co., 1965.

Chandler, Alfred D. *Strategy and Structure.* Cambridge, Mass.: The M.I.T. Press, 1969.

Levinson, Harry. *The Great Jackass Fallacy.* Boston: Division of Research, Harvard Business School, 1975.

Sloan, Alfred P. *My Years at General Motors.* Garden City, N.Y.: Doubleday & Co., Inc., 1972.

Zaleznik, Abraham. *Human Dilemmas of Leadership.* New York: Harper & Row, Publishers, 1966.

The work by Andrews provides a good overview of the range of policy problems which will be addressed in this casebook. Zaleznik's book complements Andrews by shedding light on the human problems of top-level decision makers. The works of Ansoff, Zaleznik, and Sloan are particularly relevant to Part one of the book, while the Chandler study will provide an important perspective for looking at the cases presented in Part three. Professor Levinson's study is of primary value in relationship to the issues raised in Part two.

Each instructor, of course, will be able to add to this list. In doing so, the relevant criteria for selection should be whether a given work sharpens the focus of policy problems or helps students of administration broaden their perspective in analyzing the cases presented for study.

Quite apart from course-specific readings, there is a world of literature relevant to the study of policy formulation and administration. Biographies and autobiographies offer a rich account of policy formulation and decision making. Similarly, history and political science present innumerable opportunities to study the evolution of policy and organization. Accounts as diverse as those on the administrative organization set up in France by Napoleon in the 18th century, the development of the railroads in the 19th century, and the path of the social revolutions in the 20th century all offer clues about how organizational leaders manage their affairs.

part one

POLICY
FORMULATION

chapter

1

Policy formulation: An overview

The general manager of a company, or a major subunit thereof, is the person primarily responsible for the performance of the human, physical, and monetary assets entrusted to his/her[1] care. Those responsibilities are broad and numerous, the tasks often difficult, and the skills required varied indeed. It is a role in which few students of business administration have had direct experience, one to which many aspire, and one which often takes many years to reach. Though the responsibilities are great and the hours seldom short, it is a job which can be highly rewarding to the individual, both in economic terms and in the personal satisfaction that comes from running your own show and from successfully meeting both the intellectual and administrative challenges of the job.

Although some of the readers of this book may not aspire to become general managers, and others may assume that role only after years of gaining experience in a functional field or a staff capacity, we believe all those who plan to work in any purposive organization can benefit greatly from an exposure to the problems and responsibilities of the general manager, distant though they may be. The knowledge, skills, and attitudes required of the successful general manager are not gained overnight, and early exposure to the nature of the job is beneficial in enabling you to seek and interpret experience which will improve your abilities as a general manager. In addition, a better understanding of the job of the general manager is useful to those subordinates who seek to help managers with their job.

We shall not burden you with any detailed checklists of the content of a general manager's job, but instead hope you will find more useful an observation by one of our authors, C. R. Christensen, that the good general manager needs the rare ability "to lead effectively organizations whose complexities he can never fully understand, where his capacity to control directly the human and physical forces comprising that organization is se-

---

[1] In this text, masculine pronouns alone will sometimes be used instead of the more accurate dual form because of simplicity of presentation.

4

verely limited, and where he must make or review and assume ultimate responsibility for present decisions which commit concretely major resources for a fluid and unknown future."

In Part I of this book we invite you to join with us in exploring one major aspect of the general manager's job, that of the formulation of corporate policy or strategy. Since the purpose of the book is to help you enlarge the background of knowledge, improve the skills, and develop the attitudes that will make you a better manager (*and* subordinate), we ask you to attempt to understand and adopt the position of the involved general manager in each of the cases. At times you will be asked to assume *you* are the "person on the spot"; at times you will be asked to *advise* the manager—either as a subordinate or as a consultant. In any event, it is essential for you to establish the habit of asking yourself "What strategic actions would *I* take or advise in *this* situation?" and then deal with the uncertainties, conflicts, constraints, unknowns, and ambiguities as best you can—just as the practicing general manager must do. The cases in Part I of this book have been selected and designed to enable you to focus primarily on this strategy formulation aspect of the general manager's job.

Your primary emphasis should be on the identification and solution of the specific problems as you find them in the cases, and not on expository writings about various aspects of the general manager's task in general. For this reason, we will make little reference to the abundance of literature on the general manager's job in this text beyond the background readings given in the preface. You will have read much before undertaking this course; and the principal task before you is to draw upon the background readings your instructor may suggest, as well as materials and techniques with which you are already familiar, to assist you in the solution of the problems found in these specific cases. Your objective should be to develop an understanding of an approach to the analysis and solution of the problems of the general manager via the study of a series of specific cases, not to learn what various authors may say about general classes of problems.

We should also note that in Part I of this book, which focuses on the formulation of corporate strategy, we will be concentrating largely on the single-business company or the business (division) level of the diversified company. We will be concerned with developing your ability to identify, evaluate, and recommend a strategy which is primarily for a single principal product and identifiable industry. In Part III of this book, dealing with the diversified company, we will deal with the far more complex task of strategy formulation and implementation at the corporate level of the multibusiness company. We do this not because most companies are single-business companies—about 85 percent of the *Fortune* 500 companies are decidedly multibusiness in nature—but because the task of strategy formulation can best be learned by looking at the single-business situation first.

WHAT DO WE MEAN BY "STRATEGY"?

If we are to ask you to read hundreds of pages and spend many hours trying to improve your skills as a strategist, it is surely not unreasonable for you to be concerned at this point with defining "strategy." We all know that it is generally useful to define our terms, and indeed it is important to attempt to do so with regard to the concept of strategy. It has been our experience, however, that precise and exact definitions are neither desirable nor possible. Unlike many terms used in the more exact sciences, there is no way one can quantify or measure the overall concept of strategy. Many aspects of a statement of strategy, to be sure, can and should be expressed in quantitative terms, as, for example, earnings or growth goals, but it is no more possible to assign a number to a strategy than it is to the health of an individual. That a definition precise enough to enable quantitative measurement—a key step in many of the advances in the physical sciences—neither exists nor seems likely to occur should neither discourage nor detain us.

It is more useful to focus instead on what a statement of corporate strategy should encompass, proceeding in large part from a consideration of the purposes the development and explicit statement of a strategy can serve for an organization:

a. To improve the ability of the firm to select appropriate basic, long-term objectives for itself, and
b. To develop the means by which these objectives can be achieved.

It then becomes possible to suggest the elements that should commonly be included in a statement of strategy in order to accomplish the above purposes.

Selection of objectives

One major component of the statement of strategy is the selection of the longer term basic objectives of the total enterprise or major business unit. These might include such items as desirable levels of growth, profits, and risk; broad definitions of the industries or products the company intends to engage in; and, if possible, something which captures the somewhat intangible "character" of the enterprise. The important point to emphasize is that the general manager has both the responsibility for and some ability to influence the longer term basic objectives of the firm. These are seldom fixed either by law, practice, or edict. We think it will be more fruitful for you to attempt to discover in the specific companies described in the cases what these objectives seem to be, and what they might be, rather than attempt to define exactly what the term objectives should include in all cases.

Our definition of strategy, though common to business, is therefore unlike that used by most military writers. The military definition most often accepts an objective or a goal as fixed and often imposed by a higher authority, and views a strategy as a means of achieving that objective. The general manager has the additional task of selecting appropriate objectives for the firm. The manager must be concerned with not only how to achieve an objective but also with what the objective should be.

As you discover in a number of the cases which follow, the determination of these longer term objectives can be both important and difficult. Objectives that turn out to be too high in terms of growth or profits can have severely damaging effects on an otherwise healthy business because of the pressures they create to change the basic nature of the business or to take excessive risks. On the other hand, objectives which are too low in view of the opportunities open to the firm and its own resources will be less challenging to the members of the firm, and will likely result in reduced economic performance. More important for the longer run, it may also cause an unnecessary loss of market position and competitive strength. Few firms would admit publicly to objectives as modest as simply "keeping up with our industry," or with the overall growth in GNP, but that does not automatically make the substitution of higher growth or profit objectives either wise or attainable.

We should note at this point that such objectives as "grow as fast as possible" or "maximize the earnings per share" or "maximize the long-run value of the common shareholder's interest," useful though they may be to the economist or social scientist seeking to perfect models of the firm or of the economy, are seldom a solution to the above difficulties. Without considerable elaboration, they do little more than point a direction. They communicate little about the acceptable level of risk or the character of the business, for example, and provide even less help in the task of translating a strategy into terms which will have meaning to the managers and employees of the business as they go about their work.

Achievement of objectives

A second major purpose of a strategy is to develop and make explicit the means by which the firm can achieve the objectives it has selected. An examination of those objectives will lead to an identification of the factors that are likely to play a role in their achievement, and therefore those factors that should receive explicit attention. Since there is almost invariably a strong economic element in the objectives firms establish for themselves, a statement of strategy should include some attention to those items that are likely to affect, in a major way, the economic performance of the company.

A statement of strategy should include something about the nature of the products, not only in the literal terms of what the product is called and is made of but of what service it provides the consumer. What, if anything, is distinctive about the product or service? Is it high or low quality, relatively high or low volume, designed for a broad market or a selected portion of the market, and is it rapidly changing or relatively stable? Are we emphasizing function or fashion? Do we offer a limited line or a full line? How important is advertising and promotion to the product or service provided? How, if at all, can our product be distinguished from present and potential competing products or services? The particular dimensions selected for describing the product will vary with the product. It is important, however, that you find a way to move beyond the label of "autos" or "handguns" or "ball-point pens" to a more detailed product description.

The means of financing the enterprise is important, not only with respect to the present but even more so with regard to the way in which future requirements will be met. Growth requires increased assets, which can only come from internal sources (primarily retained earnings) or external sources. In qualitative terms, what degree of risk is acceptable? More specifically, what maximum proportion of debt can we get and will we tolerate in the capital structure, what level of dividends do we want to pay, and with what certainty, and how willing are we to risk having to sell stock at depressed prices, sell a portion of the assets, or even be forced to merge with another company if things do not work out as planned? In simple terms, balancing growth and profit objectives with financial requirements and the concomitant risks of reduction of control or, in extreme cases, loss of job, forces one to think about the relative importance one attaches to sleeping well as opposed to eating well.

In addition to the nature of the product or service and the means by which we will finance the business, it is important to know specifically how the product or service will be provided. Are we a manufacturer, or primarily an assembler of purchased parts? To what extent have we integrated backwards to provide for our own sources of supply or raw materials—as in the case of steel producers owning coal and iron ore mines—and to what extent have we integrated forward to control our channels of distribution, as in the case of Massey-Ferguson establishing some of its own farm equipment dealers? To what extent do we seek and need to take advantage of economies of scale in manufacturing via standard products, high volume, long production runs, and few locations, or are we a more specialized, lower volume, and higher cost manufacturer?

Included in a statement of corporate strategy should be some attention to the policies to be followed in the major functional departments of the company to the extent these have not been covered elsewhere. In view of our objectives and the basis we have chosen for achieving them, do we give balanced attention to the various functional areas, or do we favor some over others? What, if anything, is distinctive or unusual about our research and development department, our manufacturing operations, our financial controls, our marketing department, or our personnel policies? There is no one best way to operate any of these functions, and the challenge for the general manager is to establish policies for the major functional areas so that they are consistent with each other and contribute to the achievement of the overall objectives of the company. As you examine the operations of Prelude Corporation, or Sturm, Ruger & Company, Inc., or BIC Pen, for example, what is the role and importance of the marketing, manufacturing, and research and development functions in each of these companies? Given the nature of their products and the manner in which they have chosen to compete, what should these functions be doing in each case? Just as important, what can the companies afford? If you want to devote more resources to one area, where will they come from?

STATEMENT OF STRATEGY

A statement of strategy, then, should convey both what a company is trying to achieve and how it hopes to achieve it. The plan for achievement should include attention to the important factors influencing that achievement, as mentioned, and it should specify what major steps are to be taken, in what rough time frame, by whom, what resources will be required, and how the resources will be obtained. It should communicate, in as tangible a way as possible, just how this particular company has chosen to compete in the marketplace. Frequently, this means attention and thought to the issue of how to compete against larger competitors with greater resources and greater potential for economies of scale in R&D, manufacturing, marketing, or management.

We have thus far focused primarily on the purpose and content of a statement of corporate strategy, and have said very little about how one might move from simply identifying the strategy of a company to evaluating it and making recommendations for changes. Developing and explaining an approach to this which you can apply to the case situations is the principal purpose of the next several chapters. Before turning to this main task, however, there are several other items which warrant our attention at this point.

THE GENERAL MANAGER AND STRATEGY FORMULATION

Does strategy make a difference? Of course it does. We are completely convinced, on the basis of our own experience as well as our broader exposure to a great many practicing business executives, that the choice of the products and markets in which to compete, and the basis for competing in them, is of crucial importance to a company. That proposition may be difficult to prove because of the myriad of variables that affect company performance, including the catchall "luck." It is certainly far more difficult to find either evidence or logic that would support the opposite position, however, that the choice of markets and ways to compete in them is of no consequence to a company. We would therefore strongly encourage you, as you study the cases in this book, to do for yourself what an experienced and highly successful group vice president of a major diversified industrial company has told us is the first thing he does when he takes over the responsibility for a new division, often in a business in which he has had no previous experience. He develops, along with the division management, an explicit, brief statement of what the current strategy of the division is before making any attempts to evaluate or change their strategy.

It does not follow from the above, of course, that the task of leading the organization in the implementation of that strategy, to which we shall turn in Part II, is of less importance. Clearly, skill and success at both is helpful to the overall success of the firm. The music that results comes from both the violin and the violinist, and if either is poor, the results suffer.

Responsibility for and participation in the strategy formulation process is therefore a key responsibility of the general manager. That participation is essential not only because the outcome is important to the company but also because the general manager brings both a perspective and a level of authority to the task that is likely to result in a better strategy as well as better acceptance of the strategy within the organization. Responsibility for and participation in does not mean, of course, that the general manager has to do all of the work; for anything but the smallest or simplest business, that would result in superficial analysis. What it does mean, in our judgment, is that the general manager of any company, no matter how large, clearly must understand the key problems and opportunities facing the company, enlist the help of line managers and staff and perhaps outsiders in collecting and analyzing the information needed and in developing possible courses of action, and then visibly support the choices made. Staff and subordinate assistance is helpful and often essential, but without the involvement and commitment of the general manager to the results, the staff work is likely to be ineffective. The single greatest hazard facing both the professional corporate planner and the company whose chief executive turns too much of the task of developing the corporate strategy over to the long-range planning department is that the resulting 200-page five-year plan, which may by all objective standards be an excellent plan, will gather dust rather than precipitate action.

In the next several chapters, then, we will turn to the task facing the general manager in the development of strategy for the firm.

2

An approach to strategy formulation

The strategy of the firm at any particular time is the product of a wide range of factors, including history, happenstance, oversight, external forces, and the conscious efforts of management to influence that strategy. It is our experience that both practicing general managers as well as their advisors and those aspiring to that role can make their efforts to influence corporate strategy more efffective by the conscious use of a conceptual scheme or framework of analysis to assist them in the task.

The problem of formulating strategy for a firm can be complex in the extreme in terms of the number of variables which should be taken into account, the difficulty of obtaining reliable estimates for many of those variables, and the judgment required in predicting how the variables will interact with and influence each other as well as the overall performance of the firm. The variables include technical, economic, political, and social factors, and in addition require judgments to be made about some of these items for many years ahead in uncertain environments. Some may be willing to venture firm opinions on short notice about the strategy Chrysler should have adopted in order to avoid their financial debacle of 1979, for example, or how electric utility companies should respond to environmental regulations, high capital costs, rapidly rising fuel and plant costs, and increasing consumer opposition so as to generate enough profits to ensure that the large amounts of capital they will need in the next decades will somehow be forthcoming. In attempting to develop answers to such problems, however, all but the few true geniuses among us will find some sort of general framework or approach useful, if not essential.

We would like to suggest to you an approach to analysis which is simple to state, of wide applicability, but which still requires thoughtfulness, practice, and hard work to apply effectively. It has evolved over several decades as a result of the research, teaching, and consulting activities of the authors as well as a large number of our colleagues in the Business Policy course at the Harvard Business School. Professor Kenneth Andrews has been the most

articulate of those involved in this development, and the authors all acknowledge the great contributions made by him in bringing order and
common sense to a still-evolving framework of analysis.[1]

The approach we suggest is designed to help you simplify a complex task
so that you can deal with it more effectively. It is not a model that would
meet the standards of our academic colleagues in the natural sciences or
those with strong interests in quantitative methods, as neither the individual elements of the model nor the relationships among them can be usefully
quantified. We would welcome such an advance, but to our knowledge, no
such comprehensive "strategy formulation model" useful to general managers exists. What we do propose is an approach which will encourage disciplined attention to several major areas of importance by the practicing
general manager faced with the real-life task of formulating and evaluating
the corporate strategy of the firm.

The approach we have found both general enough to be applicable in a
wide number of situations as well as specific enough to be useful in individual and unique situations consists of considering the strategy of a company
to be influenced by the interaction of four main areas:

Formulation of strategy

Corporate environment ⎫
Corporate resources   ⎪
                       ⎬ ↔   Corporate strategy
Management values   ⎪
Corporate responsibilities ⎭

The process of analysis consists of an assessment of the relevant facts and
trends occurring within each of these major areas, a judgment of the ways in
which these areas will or can be made to influence each other, and the
creative development of a strategy suited to the unique situation of the particular company. We cannot emphasize strongly enough nor frequently
enough the notion of fit, the need for the strategy to build on what is unique
to the particular situation with regard to all of the important factors and the
ways in which they complement each other.

A strategy should allow for the trends in the company's environment, including the actions of competitors; take advantage of the resources and
minimize the weaknesses of the company; allow for the personal values and
aspirations relevant to the company of those managers who are in a position
to influence the company; and make provision for what the company either
wants to do or should do in view of what may be expected of it beyond economic performance by the broader society of which it is a part.

---

[1] See, for example, *The Concept of Corporate Strategy*, rev. ed. (Homewood, Ill.: Dow
Jones–Irwin, 1980). © 1980 by Richard D. Irwin, Inc.

As you proceed to identify, evaluate, and recommend changes in the strategies of the companies described in the following pages, it may be useful to keep in mind the three deceptively simple questions you are trying to answer with regard to each unique situation that you study:

1. Where are we now?
2. Where do we want to go?
3. How do we get there?

The approach described above will help you arrive at reasoned answers to the above questions, but not in a mechanical or deterministic way; it provides neither checklists nor "yes-no" questions. It is our experience that such seeming expedients make it less rather than more likely that the creative job that needs to be done will take place.

Neither does the approach ensure that you will arrive at a demonstrably "right" answer, but that is a reflection of the difficulties of formulating strategy in real life as opposed to strategies for competing in a computer simulation model or a chess game. No approach of which we are aware does guarantee the "right" answer; experienced and intelligent executives will often disagree in difficult strategic situations. If systematically and carefully followed, however, the approach will result in the logic and assumptions underlying strategic recommendations becoming more explicit and clear to all. This, in turn, has several significant benefits:

1. It permits a more detailed and reasoned examination or "dissection" of the basis for differing strategic recommendations for the same situation. The quality of the assumptions and the logic as well as the choices being made with regard to levels of risk, profits, growth, and so on, can more readily be isolated and discussed. To say that an approach does not guarantee a single, "right" answer is not to say that some strategic recommendations will not, upon examination, be judged by most to be of higher quality than others.

2. Because the entire process of strategy formulation is made more explicit, improving one's skills at that process becomes easier. Intuitive approaches by experienced and skillful business people may result in brilliant strategies, but such intuitive abilities are not easy to acquire, either by birth or practice. Although some of the most difficult and important decisions business people must make involve a substantial combination of intuition, creativity, inspiration, artistry, and judgment, students as well as executives benefit from expanding rather than reducing the explicit and analytical portion of the strategy formulation process and improving their skills at that portion through practice. Because strategic decisions by their very nature are not made frequently, are seldom made by aspiring executives early in their careers, and often require the passage of many years or even decades before their wisdom and quality can be evaluated, practice and skill in

making strategic decisions are not easy to come by. Breaking down the process of making those decisions and participating, when possible, in that process as junior members of management facilitates the development of the skills and experience that will be crucial to the successful performance of that key aspect of the job of the general manager.

3. An evaluation of both the strategy itself as well as the progress of the organization in carrying out that strategy is made easier if the strategy formulation process and the underlying logic and assumptions are made explicit. Conditions change, unforeseen obstacles as well as opportunities arise, and progress inevitably exceeds hopes and plans in some respects and falls short in others. Periodic reevaluation of progress as well as of the strategy itself is essential, both to provide guidance to the manager in leading the organization in the implementation of strategy—a topic with which we shall be more concerned in Part II—and in making whatever changes seem necessary in the strategy itself.

In discussing the steps to go through in formulating a corporate strategy, apart from other aspects of the general manager's job, we run two risks that should be addressed at the outset. First, strategic problems in practice seldom appear, nor are they addressed, in isolation of the problems associated with implementing that strategy within the organization. Policy formulation and administration are intertwined in real life, and the effective manager must constantly move back and forth between the tasks of the ongoing administration of the existing strategy and the continual examination and reassessment of that strategy.

We deliberately begin this book with cases that permit—perhaps even require—that your primary concern be with the evaluation and formulation of strategy rather than the ongoing administration of that strategy for two reasons: developing skills in the formulation of strategy can best take place by means of some concentration on that portion of the general manager's job, and even the most experienced general manager can best make progress by concentrating first on one and then on another aspect of the job. Even though many of one's problems are interrelated, one cannot work effectively on everything at once. Neither can we present everything at once in a text or series of cases, and we have chosen to concentrate on problems of strategy formulation in Part I of this book. Just because we do so, we hope you will not forget that policy formulation and administration, although separable mental activities, are clearly interrelated in practice.

The cases in Part II include more problems and information pertaining to the administration or implementation of the strategy of the company, and many of those cases will provide you with ample opportunity to develop your skills at both the formulation and implementation of strategy in relation to each other. At a minimum, the need to tailor the approach to administration to the requirements created by the strategy of the company will become clear. The cases in Part III, all of which deal with managing the diversified firm, will from the outset require balanced attention to both strategy formulation and implementation.

The second risk we incur in discussing the strategy formulation process is in giving the impression that it is a sequential, "one-time through" procedure in which one can in turn analyze the environment, assess the strengths and weaknesses of the company, ascertain the values and aspirations of the management, allow for social expectations, and produce strategic recommendations which will be good for some substantial period of time. Such a procedure has two characteristics which do not correspond with practice, or at least with good practice, in two important respects: each major factor must be investigated in relation to the others, and the process is a never-ending one. The basic nature of the strategy will hopefully remain constant over substantial periods of time, but changing industry conditions, company performance, and competitive moves make continual examination and adjustment of the competitive posture essential. The major strategic evaluations and adjustments take place during the annual planning cycle in most companies, to be sure, but in the better companies there is constant attention to the need to make adjustments between the annual planning periods as well as thorough examination, rather than mechanical updating, during the annual planning effort.

Just because we discuss the formulation of strategy before devoting much attention to its implementation and discuss discrete elements of the formulation process in sequential fashion, then, we nevertheless hope you will not lose sight of the fact that strategy formulation in reality can better be described as a continuous process, separable from but not independent of the ongoing administrative problems and characteristics of the company. It is a process of continual examination and adjustment of interrelated elements, not a series of discrete puzzles to be solved in sequence independently of each other.

We will turn in the next chapters to more detailed suggestions as to how you might begin trying to apply the approach just described to the specific case situations which follow.

chapter
3

Strategy formulation and corporate environment

The importance of looking at the competitive environment of a company should not require any elaboration. The issue is not whether to look, but what to look at, how to predict what is likely to happen, or can be made to happen, and what effect these happenings might have on our business. The *environment* is listed first in the approach to strategy formulation that we encourage you to use, but that is a matter of choice rather than necessity. It could be investigated after a thorough examination of the strengths and weaknesses of the company, for example, but we have found that in most cases it is better to proceed from a broad investigation of the industry in which a firm competes to a more detailed examination of the firm itself.

WHAT IS "OUR INDUSTRY"?

By the environment we generally mean all of those factors external to the company which do, or could, have an important influence on the performance of the company. The first problem arises in determining how to define what we will look at so that the task can be accomplished by ordinary mortals in the course of all of the other demands on their time and thoughts. It is true but of little help to observe that the world increasingly is becoming one large interrelated system in which happenings anywhere may impact upon any business. It is also true, however, that often events and developments take place which are not apparent in the everyday course of business which may nevertheless have a significant impact on us. The environment consists of a spectrum of events, some immediately observable and obviously important, and some with such low probability of impact on us that we can safely ignore them in order to deal more effectively with what we can perceive and comprehend. It is essential to recognize that limits must be drawn, that the limits must be defined in terms of the specific company and its strategy and products, not just a general notion of the industry, and that we must strike a balance between the risks of lost opportunities as well as unseen threats that may come from defining the limits too narrowly and the intellectual paralysis that accompanies the attempt to include everything.

The principal reason for defining an industry in operational terms for each specific company situation you encounter is the need to identify both present and potential competitive products and services, principal competitors, and the important factors affecting both the demand for the products and services of that industry and the operations of the companies that meet this demand. Those questions arise in the first cases and become more difficult as you proceed to the cases on the mechanical writing industry and BIC Pen; the soft-drink industry, Dr Pepper, and Seven-Up; and Polaroid-Kodak and the Tensor Corporation. In the Polaroid-Kodak case, for example, you will want to think about what difference it makes to the presidents of Polaroid and of Kodak as to how they define their industries and when they consider each other as competitors. When a young and small Polaroid was offering an instant print of lower quality and at a higher price than conventional prints by the huge and well-established Kodak, were the companies really competitors? At what point did instant photography compete significantly for the same consumer dollar, as is clearly the case by the time of the introduction of an instant camera by Kodak in 1976? How one defines the industry has a major influence on the size and growth of the market, who your competitors are, and what trends and developments then become relevant, and the possible opportunities for the company.

INDUSTRY ECONOMIC PERFORMANCE

After you have defined an industry sufficiently well to identify competitive products and services and the companies that provide them, you will want to investigate the economic performance of the industry. What is the approximate size of the market, at what rate has it been growing, what is the average level of profitability of the industry, and how much do these vary from year to year?

The general level of profitability within an industry is obviously of interest, and these levels vary both among industries and over time within an industry. From the point of view of the general manager, the most important figures are likely to be the return on stockholders' equity and the return on investment.

One reason the size of the market is important is because the volume of business reasonably obtainable clearly has implications for the investment that can be undertaken to enter or compete in that market. A small market cannot justify high research, advertising, or capital expenditures no matter how successful the efforts are; conversely, a large market potential may justify, if the company wishes to try, large investments. Indeed, large markets often attract large investments and therefore large companies, a fact of which most small companies are well aware.

Another reason for concern with size is that many companies prefer not to bother with ventures which are unlikely to grow large enough to have a significant effect on the overall operations of the company even if successful. Small companies often justify seeking specialized market niches for this very reason—in the hope that larger companies will not find it worthwhile to do battle over small markets. Tensor, you will note as you study Case 13, explicitly made this judgment with regard to the potential entry of giants like Westinghouse and General Electric into the small market for hi-intensity lamps.

The growth of the market is important for a number of reasons. Foremost, of course, is that a growing market may provide sufficient opportunity for all of the competitors to achieve satisfactory rates of growth from the expanding market rather than from each other. Company growth secured from an expanding market rather than at the expense of an embattled competitor is likely to be both more profitable and more pleasant.

High industry growth does not necessarily indicate high industry profits or opportunity for any individual company, however. More important is the balance between the capacity of the industry and the demand for its products. High-growth industries where capacity exceeds demand, and particularly where strong competitors are determined to increase market share, can be thoroughly unattractive in terms of current profits. Sometimes the slumps last only a few years, as in the case of semiconductors or pocket calculators; sometimes the reduced levels can last for many years, as in the case of the basic chemical industry and the fertilizer industry. Few would seek out low-growth industries except for very special reasons, but high growth is no guarantee of high profits.

In many cases, detailed and complete industry figures abound, as for example in the case of the American automobile industry. Production and sales by manufacturer, by model, and by state are readily available and frequently reported, sometimes by weekly periods. In smaller and less mature industries or product lines the statistics may be very difficult to come by, as in the case of hi-intensity lamps and metal tennis racquets, as you will discover in the Tensor case. Sometimes production and sales figures are more readily available than profit figures; sometimes the opposite is true. In some industries you will practically be suffocated by statistics; in others you may find the lack of reliable data on market size, growth, and profitability frustrating. General managers share your difficulties and frustrations, and have learned to do the best they can with the data available. We encourage you to do the same with the data in the cases, and neither avoid reasoned judgments based on the data available nor flee to the library in search of more statistics.

The key question, of course, is what is likely to happen in the future, not what occurred in the past, but knowledge of what has happened to date provides the essential base for looking ahead. Industry economic statistics are but a starting point and a background for the rest of your analysis; sometimes they raise as many questions as they answer. An investigation of the characteristics of the industry such as we suggest in the next section may help explain the performance trends of some industries, and may also help you in forming judgments as to possible competitive strategies for companies within the industry.

INDUSTRY CHARACTERISTICS

The field of industrial organization, a specialty within the economics profession, seeks to explain much of the behavior and economic performance of an industry in terms of the structural characteristics of that industry. Those of you who have some familiarity with the concepts and findings of that field of study may find some useful applications of them here. Our objectives are more limited and more situational, namely, to suggest some of the kinds of questions about various industries that you might want to ask yourself for the purpose of understanding "how the industry works." We will be less interested in whether high industry profit ratios are associated with high industry concentration ratios, for example, than in the implications of industry dominance by a few large companies for the strategies of all the companies in the industry.

As you seek to gain an understanding of the characteristics of the industries in which the companies you will be studying compete, you will find it useful to seek data on the following broad categories:

1. What is the distribution of size of firms (or divisions of firms) with which we compete, and where do we rank? Are there many firms of somewhat equal size, or is the industry characterized by a few very large companies, with consequent large market shares, and then a large number of smaller ones? What are the strategies of firms large enough and strong enough to affect the smaller firms in the industry? Is there a single market leader which tolerates the existence of smaller firms as long as they do not try to expand too aggressively, or are there two giants battling each other for market share, using price as a competitive weapon? Endless combinations are possible, each with different implications for other firms in the industry.

2. What economies of scale are available to firms in the industry? The concept of economy of scale has played a large role in both the development of theory and the empirical research of economists interested in the firm. By economies of scale we mean simply a reduction in the costs of a unit of output that is made possible by an increase in the scale of operations and the accompanying investment. Economies of scale are thought of as occurring most commonly in production facilities, but they can be achieved in many areas. Large companies can generally obtain both debt and equity

funds more cheaply from the capital markets than can small companies; large research and development facilities for some purposes may be much more efficient than smaller ones; national advertising campaigns are cheaper in terms of unit costs than local campaigns; expenditures for management salaries and corporate overhead generally need not increase at the same rate as sales, and so on. Industries vary widely in the areas in which significant economies of scale, and therefore possible competitive advantage, can be achieved; and it is essential for a company to select its own strategy accordingly. What are the advantages of large size, and how can we capitalize on them if we are large and minimize their effects on us if we are small?

3. Are there significant barriers to entry which either protect us or adversely affect our ability to move in other directions? A barrier to entry may be considered as the minimum ante required to enter the game, or the minimum investment required to compete in the mainstream of the industry. Some industries are characterized by low barriers to entry—for example, tool and die shops serving the automotive industry, plastic injection molding manufacturers, garment manufacturers, and so on. Some have high barriers to entry, for a variety of reasons—basic steel, the major oil companies, pharmaceutical companies, and so on. The barriers may consist of the minimum investment required in productive facilities, in the distribution system, in research and development and patents, in advertising expenditures and consumer brand identification, among other things. Industries with low barriers to entry tend to be characterized by many small firms and relatively high turnover of firms; the opposite tends to be true for industries with high barriers to entry.

4. What is important about the financial and operating characteristics of the industry, and how are these likely to influence competitive decisions and strategies? In some industries the combination of high capital and therefore fixed costs in relation to variable costs, a production process which either must or can easily be continuous, and a largely undifferentiated product result in pressures to operate at full capacity regardless of demand, with consequent wide swings in prices and profits. The manufacture of paper, basic chemicals, and steel would be in this category, for example, whereas the manufacture of handguns by Sturm, Ruger & Company, Inc. would not. What operating financial ratios are typical of the industry—items such as amount of increased working capital and fixed assets required to support increased sales, the contribution of each incremental sales dollar to these needs, and so on? What are the implications in relation to the financial condition, profitability, and growth goals of the individual company? To what extent does it seem to be desirable or necessary to invest in either forward or backward integration, with the consequent increase in assets required to support the same end sales to the consumer? Many items such as these will have implications on the strategic alterna-

tives available to a company and the strategic responses it is likely to receive from competitors.

PIMS AND THE EXPERIENCE CURVE

Two major approaches which seek to provide guidance to the strategist with regard to a number of the factors just discussed merit mention at this time. The first of these is the PIMS study, and the second is the notion of the experience curve.

One goal of many business practitioners as well as researchers has been to "quantify the variables that affect the profitability" of a business. It is an objective disarmingly easy to state, but one which has eluded the efforts of most who have tried to do so. The most ambitious attempt to accomplish this was undertaken by the General Electric Corporation in the early 1960s as a proprietary strategic planning technique. The effort was later transferred to the Marketing Science Institute, an independent research organization, and expanded considerably in its scope. Known as PIMS (for *Profit Impact on Market Strategy*), the project has collected data from 800 businesses supplied by 100 companies. Working with a very large number of variables such as market share, degree of capital intensity, R&D and marketing expenditures as a percent of sales, and so on, the researchers have concluded that 37 variables can explain 80 percent of the observed variation in the profitability of the many businesses studied. Of all the variables, market share is most strongly correlated with profitability.

The application of these findings requires both considerable data and great caution, however, especially with regard to the definition of the product, relevant costs, and the market. In addition, there is the very considerable difficulty of moving from correlations to cause and effect, and then to the operational questions for the manager of how to change the strategy to "cause" the desired "effect." To put the question perhaps a bit too simply, even if high market share is significantly correlated with high profits, and furthermore thought to be a cause of rather than a result of high profits and other factors, how does a company with low market share obtain a high market share?

The findings stemming from the PIMS research can generate many interesting questions for the strategist, even though their application requires care and the approach is not without a number of strong critics. Two articles which outline the promise of the PIMS approach are noted in the footnote below.[1]

Another approach which has gained considerable publicity within the

---

[1] Sidney Schoeffler, Robert D. Buzzell, and Donald F. Heany, "Impact of Strategic Planning on Profit Performance," *Harvard Business Review*, March–April 1974; and Robert D. Buzzell, Bradley T. Gale, and Ralph R. M. Sultan, "Market Share—A Key to Profitability," *Harvard Business Review*, January–February 1975.

last decade or so is that of the reduction in costs which arises as a consequence of the effects of the experience curve, as developed and popularized by the Boston Consulting Group. Simply put, it is the observation that in many cases the unit costs of production are a function of the *accumulated* production of that item, not the present scale of operations, and that these costs will decline (adjusted for inflation and changes in the cost of purchased goods and services) as the total amount of production of that item increases. The notion of the cost reduction arising from accumulated experience, then, is in some ways a bridge between the economist's concept of economy of scale based on current absolute size and the effects of the learning curve studied by every industrial engineer and applied to the production scheduling since World War II of complex assembly products such as airplanes and ships.

The proponents of the experience curve claim that it is a much more important and pervasive phenomenon than simply the reduction in direct labor-hours that can be predicted by learning curve theory as a result of production workers becoming familiar with repetitive operations, and that the maximum advantage will be retained only by good managements which use their experience to continue improving their operations and to stay ahead of their competitors with less accumulated experience. A strategy built upon the need to have the greatest accumulated production experience so as to have the lowest costs in the industry would result in having the highest market share, and would not be inconsistent with one of the findings of the PIMS project. In addition, proponents of the experience curve argue that it is essential to obtain this high market share early in order to have the greatest accumulated experience and therefore the lowest costs in the industry. Therefore market share leadership should be obtained at almost any cost, since it will ensure eventual high cash flow and profitability.

Just as with the PIMS approach, considerable care needs to be taken with regard to the application of experience curve concepts to the specific situation. Examples can be found where aggressive pricing strategies based on the desire to take market leadership early and the assumption that costs will eventually decline to an acceptable proportion of prices have been successful for some companies. Texas Instruments in semiconductors and pocket calculators is perhaps the best-known example. It should be apparent, though, that if two strong companies decide to follow this basic strategy, a long and very costly battle for market share can make the battle not worth winning. In addition, the issue of the economies of scale of the single plant are not addressed directly by the proponents of the experience curve, and neither is the issue of the impact of new equipment or new manufacturing technology in the hands of a competitor, regardless of the scale of the plant. Neither is the issue of the importance of competitive strategies other than low-cost production, such marketing expertise, product innovation, and so on. Even if it seems that the logic of experience curve analysis leads you to recommend becoming the company with the greatest accumulated experience in whatever product the company happens to make, you will need to go on to specify a strategy which will enable the company in question to achieve that position. The more you believe in the applicability of the experience curve, the more important it will be to achieve this position, but the more difficult it will also be to achieve if there is already someone in the industry with greater accumulated experience.

Just as with the PIMS approach, experience curve analysis can suggest many interesting questions for the strategist. Two writings which present both the basic approach and some of the limitations of that approach are noted in the footnote below.[2]

Both the PIMS data and experience curve analysis lead to a number of important hypotheses concerning the allocation of funds by the corporate level of a diversified company to the various business units comprising the company. We will examine these portfolio planning models, as they are called, in Part III of this book.

FACTORS AFFECTING GROWTH AND PROFITS

Next, you may find it useful to try to identify the major factors which affect the growth and profitability of the industry, what trends are occurring, and which of these factors are susceptible to some control. Some of these factors will be common to many industries—consumer disposable income or level of capital goods expenditures, for example—but many will be unique to a given industry. They will encompass consumer tastes as well as finances; technical development, both within and outside the industry and country; economic trends; political developments; and social trends or pressures. They will be of varying importance, depending upon the industry. Interest rates have little effect on the demand for automobile replacement parts, for example, but for a mortgage banker or anyone associated with or affected by the home construction industry, the level of interest (and therefore mortgage) rates is crucial. The political decisions that created extensive price controls for several years in the early 1970s affected some companies more than others. For example, the sale of large quantities of wheat to Russia at about the same time, which also resulted in unprecedented increases in the prices of domestic wheat, caused the bankruptcy of many of the smaller baking companies, but were of little consequence to many other segments of the food business.

With regard to the major factors affecting a particular industry, we are often much more interested in the trends they are likely to follow than in their current level. In some cases, predicting the trends may be both diffi-

---

[2] Note on the "Use of Experience Curves in Competitive Decision Making," Harvard Business School, Case No. 9-175-174; and William K. Abernathy and Kenneth Wayne, "Limits of the Learning Curve," *Harvard Business Review*, September–October 1974.

cult and uncertain; in other cases, even a child can predict the direction, if not the magnitude and timing, of the changes that are likely to occur. It does not require an advanced degree to conclude, for example, that in most cases the amount of government regulation is going to increase, that raw materials will become more expensive, that wage and fringe benefit costs per hour are likely to increase, and that the rate of technological change will continue to increase. Whether real (inflation adjusted) disposable (after-tax) income will also increase, as has long been the trend, is now much more debated. The key still is to predict what these changes may mean for a specific company, when either the threats or opportunities are likely to become significant, and even more important, what the company can do to benefit by, rather than be harmed by, the changes that are coming.

COMPETITIVE STRATEGIES

An industry can be thought of as much like the forest pond so frequently described by the naturalist—full of all sorts of animals and plants, many competing for the same limited supplies of sunlight and food, some mutually supportive, some feeding on others, some gaining in prominence or power at times, and some disappearing from the scene. In spite of the activity there is a reasonable stability and balance until some new animal comes along, or some other change in the environment occurs. A company in an industry is subject to similar forces—a variety of competitors, many larger and stronger, some with different strategies for capturing "our" sources of revenue; unexpected disturbances in the form of new technical developments, government regulations, economic slumps, credit restraints, or raw material shortages—the list is endless.

The questions you can ask and the data you can seek to help you understand the working of an industry are limited only by your own ingenuity and energy. The objective is to provide a basis for forming judgments about what opportunities and threats are likely to exist for the specific company with which you are concerned in the years ahead, and to use this as a basis for developing some strategic alternatives.

It is likely to be useful to determine which individual companies have done well in the industry and which ones have done poorly. More important, how do you explain their performance—both good and bad—and what can you learn and perhaps adopt from their experiences? Five or ten years from now, what do you think the most successful companies in the industry will look like? What will be the cause of the downfall of the least successful? How can we develop a strategy that will serve our longer term objectives? Before we can go further with developing specific recommendations, it is necessary to undertake a more detailed analysis of the company itself, a task to which we turn in the next chapter.

chapter

4

Strategy formulation and corporate resources

COMPANY STRENGTHS AND WEAKNESSES

A corporate strategy has to be designed to fit the needs and capabilities of a specific company, not a typical company. Your strategic recommendations will need to be based not only upon your analysis of the industry but upon the problems, opportunities, resources, and aspirations of a given company in the industry. Furthermore, the challenge is to develop a clear understanding of what the unique or distinctive competences of the company are, or can be, that will enable it to capitalize on the opportunities and minimize the threats in its competitive environment. The notion of fit is important. The creation of a strategy which matches corporate resources with opportunity should be your objective, and this may be completely different than simply attempting to duplicate the strengths of your competitors so that you may do battle with them on the same basis. David attacked Goliath with a slingshot, not with brute force. For example, it may very well be that strong dealer relations constitute a significant advantage in some industries, as with Kodak in the consumer photographic market. It may also be, however, that it is more sensible to compete with Kodak in other ways than trying to duplicate their dealer strengths. Your evaluation of Polaroid's strategy will surely include an examination of this issue. One needs not only to assess strengths and weaknesses relative to competitors but also look for strategies which will enable the company to turn relative strengths into true competitive advantages.

In this section we would like to give you some suggestions that may help you in identifying the present position of the company, evaluating that position in view of the conditions and trends in the industry, and developing some strategic recommendations that you feel are appropriate to the situation. We have not yet discussed the values and aspirations of the management or the expectations of society as they affect the determination of

24

strategy, and you would surely want to consider these before proposing changes in strategy for the company. We will discuss these areas in more detail in the next chapters, and will at this point turn our attention from the task of understanding the external world as it affects the company—the environment—to the internal world of the company itself.

Present position

Your first task is to gain an understanding of what the company is, how it works, what its strategy is, and what may be major problems or opportunities. We cannot emphasize too strongly the need for constant attention to facts before conclusions at this point, in spite of the desirability of forming some tentative conclusions early in your analysis in order to direct your attention to data and issues that may be important. The ability to make this evaluation or size up of a company is a key skill of the successful general manager, consultant, or company financial advisor. It is not unlike the diagnostic skills of the experienced medical doctor, who must first determine what ails the patient before prescribing a cure. In our experience, it is something at which experienced executives often show an uncanny skill and speed, an ability more akin to intuition or a sixth sense. You can achieve similar results, although not as quickly, through thoughtful analysis of selected portions of the data present in the cases. The least useful approach, in our view, is the mechanical manipulation of all of the available data, devoting equal attention to all areas. In each of the cases you study, you should attempt to make educated guesses as soon as possible as to the areas most worthy of investigation, and then pursue them. They will not all turn out to be fruitful, but we believe it will be more useful and educational for you to focus your attention on a series of areas in this manner rather than routinely complete a checklist.

As much as we would like to discourage you from the mechanical use of a checklist, however, we would like to suggest that there are a number of major areas you will invariably want to at least skim, if the information is available, to see if there appear to be grounds for more detailed investigation.

Financial analysis

Early in any strategic evaluation of a company you will surely want to investigate the financial information on the company available to you for whatever leads it may provide with regard to present or potential problem areas or constraints. Many of your strategic recommendations are likely to require the expenditure of money, and recommendations arrived at without attention to the problems of financing them are likely to be of little value. Even more important, you will not find it easy to justify recommendations which do not take account of a current financial crisis, no matter how admirable those recommendations might be for the longer term.

You will want to peruse the profit and loss statements for clues as to what is happening to the business. What is the level of, and trend in, dollar profits, earnings per share, return on equity, costs, and margins? How do they compare with industry figures, if they are available?

A similar investigation of the balance sheet is appropriate and, together with the information you have gleaned from the profit and loss statements, this may lead you to areas of possible problems. You will particularly want to check the level of and trends in the current ratio, working capital, and the debt/capitalization ratio to see if the firm appears to be in or headed for short-term financial difficulties. Some notion of the cash flow available from profits and depreciation as well as the possible sources of cash from debt or sale of equity, if need be, will be useful to have. The possible number of items and ratios to look at is large, but the experienced manager has generally developed an ability to skim a large number of items efficiently, focusing on those which may, in combination with other bits of information, signal problems. Some of the most important and perceptive analysis can consist of simple arithmetic and the combination of data from various sources, and not the sophisticated manipulation of data which often seems so deceptively appealing to perform. You do not need a computer terminal, or even an electronic pocket calculator, to draw the important conclusions obtainable from the financial statements of the Prelude Corporation and of Sturm, Ruger & Company, Inc., for example. Without those conclusions, however, you will find yourself on tenuous ground when it comes to defending whatever strategic recommendations you put forth on those companies.

Products and organizational resources

On the more qualitative side, you will want to investigate, to the extent the data are available, the principal products, their technology, and the state of the research and development efforts supporting them; the position and reputation of these products in the market, as well as the marketing organization itself; the physical facilities of the company with regard to age and efficiency as well as capacity to serve the projected demands to be placed upon them; and most important, the nature of the human resources of the company. Quantitative data may be available and useful for some of these items; qualitative assessments will have to suffice for many. Are there any crises or major efforts occurring in any of these areas? Is the company undergoing a transition in several of these areas at once which may compound their task? Occasionally small but successful companies, for example, find themselves faced with the need to move from entrepreneurial to more professional management at the same time that significant sources of new financing must be found to support a new generation of products, which in turn will require new or greatly expanded plant facilities. Each of these transitions can pose a significant but surmountable challenge all by itself; occurring together, they may prove too much for most managements.

You should do your best to determine, by product line or major line of business if possible, where the assets of the company are invested, profits in relation to assets by product lines, and what may be expected by product line in terms of sales, profits, and requirements of assets and people. Almost every company can break down its products or services into categories with different production requirements or performance characteristics. Before making recommendations to the company you will want to ascertain, as best you can, just where the company has committed, or plans to commit, its assets, and what their important sources of profits are.

As you progress through your analysis, you should now be coming to the point where you feel more confident of proposing some tentative strategic recommendations that will take into account your investigation of the industry, your evaluation of the present position and problems of the company, and the distinctive strengths on which the company may build. No company can be best at everything, and remedying competitive weaknesses or relative disadvantages takes time, money, and effort. The challenge is to devise a strategy which builds upon the present or readily achievable strengths and minimizes the effects of the areas in which we suffer from competitive disadvantages.

What are our strengths and weaknesses?

One of the most difficult but important tasks a general manager faces is the determination of just what the distinctive strengths (*and* weaknesses) are of the organization. The determination of these is both an intellectual and emotional challenge, and disseminating and acting upon that determination is likely to be a significant administrative challenge as well. One of our students stated the problem quite perceptively when he compared it to trying to "be in a parade and on the reviewing stand at the same time." You will no doubt find the task easier from the more detached viewpoint of a student than the involved role of the practicing general manager, but it is a task worth your serious attention.

It may be difficult for a manager to accurately identify those aspects in which a company does have distinct advantage over its competitors; it is difficult and perhaps unpleasant to identify those areas in which the company is at a distinct disadvantage, especially if the areas concern people currently a part of the organization. It is even more difficult for a subordinate to suggest some of these areas of weakness; in altogether too many organizations such statements are interpreted as indicating disloyalty, lack of "team spirit," or lack of understanding and true appreciation of the "fine qualities that made this company great."

Such judgments need to be made because a strategy which is not based on an awareness of the strengths and weaknesses of a company relative to its competitors can very easily lead to difficulties. Competitive success comes from the ability to do better than your competition in one or more tasks, or combination of tasks, that contribute to success—lower manufacturing costs, more effective advertising, better R&D, a stronger distribution system, better overall coordination, superior product strategy, or whatever. The fact is, however, that every company in an industry does *not* have the best, or hardest working, or most experienced, or loyal management team; does *not* offer the best quality or the highest value; is *not* the leader in product development; does *not* have the lowest cost manufacturing facilities, and so on. Strategies which ignore these realities are not likely to be productive. Neither are strategies which blindly attack competitors on their strong points. Strategies which recognize the weaknesses as well as the distinctive strengths of the company, and seek to find a creative match of these strengths with the characteristics of competitors and opportunities in the environment, are much more likely to be successful.

5

Strategy formulation and management values

We have thus far discussed strategy formulation as a matching of opportunities and threats in the environment and the strengths and weaknesses of the company itself to achieve economic goals. A strategy based on such factors may be called an economic strategy, even though it takes into account far more than just the economic aspects of the environment of the company. It is economic in the sense that it presumes the objectives of the management are overwhelmingly economic in nature. The process is commonly thought of as one which should be objective and rational, although with ample room for different conclusions based on different judgments about critical factors affecting the strategy. The process is complex, but nonetheless the product of reasoned analysis by managers who are assumed not to let their own values interfere with their professional analysis any more than medical doctors would let their personal values influence diagnosis or treatment of a patient. Although strategies may differ, the goal is presumed to be long-term profit maximization within the law, largely uninfluenced by the personal preferences of the managers involved.

It is of course useful to simplify reality, both for purposes of teaching and research. We cannot talk about everything at once, and it makes little sense to talk about the impact of the values, aspirations, or assumptions of management on the strategy of the company until we have discussed the economic factors both within and outside of the company that influence that strategy strongly. In addition, there are considerable advantages to making the assumption that firms are—or at least should be—primarily economic units, all seeking the common goals of maximizing the long-run value of the common stockholders' equity in a rational and analytical manner. It simplifies greatly the development of economic models of firms and industries and their role in the wider national economy.

The everyday observations of all of us, however, should be sufficient reminder that the personal values and the assumptions about what is desirable and possible of those with power within the organization have an influence on the longer term objectives, the strategies, and the everyday working environment of the organization. In order to understand the strategy of a company, why the company has evolved as it has, as well as what kinds of recommendations might be acceptable to the management, it is essential to think about the values of the managers involved. What kind of people are they? How have the beliefs and assumptions they hold influenced the company? How much would your possible strategic recommendations run counter to these, and how strong would your case have to be to convince them to change to accommodate your suggestions? And why, if it is the influence of personal values that are critical, are your values better than those of someone else?

The distinction between the effect of personal values on management decisions and actions taken under the general heading of corporate responsibility, discussed in Chapter 6, is not precise. Happily, it need not be. For some, the desire to use corporate resources to help society, or segments of it, achieve goals which can only remotely be justified as being in the economic interests of that company's shareholders in the foreseeable future is a strongly held personal value. We will discuss these issues subsequently. In this chapter we will focus more on the impact of a variety of other personal values on the strategy and everyday operation of the corporation.

A WIDESPREAD PHENOMENON

Evidence of the impact of personal values on the character of a business is everywhere. As you study the Moleculon Research Corporation, for example, ask yourself how large a role the background and values of Arthur Obermayer have played in the development of that company, and what limitations they might place on recommendations stemming from an economic analysis of the company, its problems, and its opportunities.

In The Leisure Group, Inc. you will find a company quite different than Moleculon in terms of attitudes toward growth and acceptable levels of company and personal risk. In that case two young entrepreneurs with impressive educational and work backgrounds were able to borrow, on the basis of only an $8,000 investment of their own, another $550,000 to enable them to start buying companies in the "leisure industry." In only seven years they increased the sales to $58 million by an aggressive acquisition program and extensive restructuring of the companies they bought, all the while operating with a highly leveraged financial position. They unfortunately lost $30 million as well as a bit of credibility in the seventh year, but their enthusiasm for growth continued undiminished. That the character of both The Leisure Group and Moleculon were strongly influenced by the values and aspirations brought to the situation by the founders seems indisputable, as does the conclusion that the values of managers vary widely.

The values of management affect far more than just decisions concerning the more traditional goals for growth and risk. You will find in the Tensor Corporation an outspoken manager, Jay Monroe, with much more on his mind than just earning a return for the stockholders of his publicly held company in the traditional way. That his personal values and goals affect his business decisions greatly will be obvious; whether this influence is appropriate for the president of a publicly held company, and how to influence his behavior in the event you should like to, are among the more difficult and interesting questions you will be dealing with in that case.

In Midway Foods Corporation the influence of the owner-president on the criteria to be applied in a promotion decision involving a middle-level manager in a small, privately held company is both clear and controversial. The manager being considered for promotion is a prosegregationist; the president is a liberal and a long-time antisegregationist. The issue is not competence to do the job or management potential, but the person's views, which are fundamentally different than some strongly held personal views of the president. Should we encourage the president to ignore such extraneous factors, should we accept his reservations and perhaps opposition as regrettable but understandable, or should we encourage him to stand firm in his opposition on the grounds that any executive team has to be close working and cohesive in order to be effective, and to make promotions which may make that team less effective is simply poor management? From a purely economic standpoint, can a large organization be built and managed within the constraints the president seeks to impose in this case?

WHAT ARE THE DESIRABLE LIMITS?

The Tensor and Midway cases not only demonstrate the influence of the personal values of the management on both the strategy and the everyday operations of the firm but also raise the issue of the type and degree of influence by the manager that is both wise from the standpoint of the economic well-being of the company and fair from the standpoint of those affected by the decisions, our own sense of values, and those of the broader society. Consider, for example, the following quote from an outstanding classic on management, *The Functions of the Executive* by Chester Barnard, who at the time of writing (1938) had long experience as president of the New Jersey Bell Telephone Company:

"Fitness"
... in all the good organizations I have observed the most careful attention is paid to it [the informal executive organization]. ...

The general method of maintaining an informal executive organization is so to operate and to select and promote executives that a general condition of compatibility of personnel is maintained. Perhaps often and certainly occasionally men cannot be promoted or selected, or even must be relieved, because they cannot function, because they "do not fit," where there is no question of formal competence. This question of "fitness" involves such matters as education, experience, age, sex, personal distinctions, prestige, race, nationality, faith, politics, sectional antecedents; and such very specific personal traits as manners, speech, personal appearance, etc. It goes by few if any rules. . . . It represents in its best sense the political aspects of personal relationship in formal organization . . . it is certainly of major importance in all organization. . . .[1]

Do these observations seem reasonable to you in terms of today's practices and beliefs? If you attempt to make the very important distinction between the "what is" and the "what should be" in the world, to what extent do his observations still describe the reality, if not your ideal? You will want to explore what degree of influence would be appropriate, and on what kinds of issues, and whether the size of the company or the form of ownership—public or private—is important.

We should beware of the temptation to believe that the values of the managers are a factor and need be considered only in smaller companies. Have not the founders and managers put their personal imprint on companies like Polaroid-Kodak and The Lincoln Electric Company, both of which you will study later in this book? Or on IBM and Xerox? Indeed, at least a part of the success of many of our outstanding companies can be attributed to the strong personal values of their founders concerning products and ways of doing business.

We should also note that the personal values of those in a position of influence can be important in all types of organized activity—law firms, the government, the military, labor, and religious organizations. An interesting recent legal case involved the prestigious New York law firm of Cravath, Swaine & Moore. The plaintiff charged Cravath with violating Title VII of the Civil Rights Act of 1964 for allegedly denying him partnership in the firm because he was a Catholic and of Italian heritage. Cravath denied the charges, and also argued that the law did not apply to partnership selections, and that interference in the partnership selection process would violate the firm's First Amendment right of association. As part of the case for the plaintiff, it was argued that law firms, even though partnerships, certainly are a business and provide employment to their members. In addition, a survey of the 20 largest law firms in New York City revealed that of the 912 partners listed, only 15 had Italian surnames, and only 62 had graduated from Catholic law schools.

That some of the factors mentioned by Barnard exist in contemporary organizations seems apparent. The degree to which they should influence

---

[1] Chester Barnard, *The Functions of the Executive* (Cambridge: Harvard University Press, 1960), p. 224.

managerial decisions, the remedy to be applied in cases where you think the influence inappropriate, and the way in which you will let your own personal values influence your decisions when you are in a position of responsibility are issues to be explored.

We should also be careful to note that the relationship between the personal values of the manager and the strategy and operations of the company can result in a significant impact on the manager as well as the company. This is clearly demonstrated, for example, by the resignation of the president of Holiday Inns, Inc., a company with revenues of $1.3 billion, in 1977. It was reported in *The Wall Street Journal* that when the company approved its first venture into casino gambling, a proposal to build and operate a $55 million hotel-casino in Atlantic City, New Jersey, Mr. Clymer, the president, chose to take early retirement. A company executive stated the board felt that it was simply a prudent business decision, and that hotel casinos were a logical extension of their current business. Mr. Clymer, who had long opposed casino gambling in the company's hotels, said that personal and religious reasons prompted him to ask for early retirement. "This is a personal conviction not involving the financial or business aspects of the industry," he stated. "The great concern in my heart is that some may erroneously read into this action a silent judgment of those who have reached a different conclusion. . . . This most certainly isn't the case."

SUMMARY

We raise the issue of the impact of the personal values and aspirations of the management on the organization because our concern is with the administration of real enterprises involving real people, with all of the complications that entails. The values of the managers on a variety of dimensions—technology, products, ways of doing business, acceptable growth and profit goals, acceptable levels of risk, criteria for promotion, and so on—exert an influence in all organizations. These influences may enhance or hinder the attainment of purely economic goals, and they may also have an effect on all those who have some dealings with the company.

In taking these personal values into account, you should attempt to:

1. Recognize, as best you can, the extent to which certain practices or decisions are, or have been, influenced by the personal values of someone in a position of power and responsibility.
2. Assess how important these practices or decisions are with regard to the economic well-being of the company.
3. Come to some judgment about the appropriateness of the values themselves and the degree to which the manager has let personal values, quite apart from economic considerations, affect professional decisions.
4. Structure and present your recommendations so that a person in power,

who may have quite different values than you do, will nevertheless be moved to action along the lines you recommend.

Management, of course, does not "own" the corporation. The law is clear on the responsibilities of the management to manage the company in the interests of the shareholders, which has uniformly been interpreted to be the pursuit of primarily economic objectives. Management, does, however, have very considerable leeway in practice with regard to how they shall achieve these economic objectives. To assist you in developing some standards by which you might judge the actions both of others and of yourself when you are in a position to influence an organization, we would like to suggest the following questions:

1. Have you allowed for a reasonable input from others in the organization, and from the groups or individuals that might be affected by your decision?
2. Would you be willing to acknowledge publicly both your beliefs and the extent to which they have influenced your decisions?
3. Do you honestly feel that your decisions or actions are fair to the groups involved, according to reasonably accepted standards of fairness? Would you object to being treated in that way yourself?

We can only judge the values of others in relation to our own standards or those of a broader society, and the question of what is appropriate or better is an unavoidable one. We shall deal more in the next chapter with the issues of what society, or vocal segments of society, expect of businesses in addition to the traditional role of providing employment, goods and services, and a return to the suppliers of capital.

chapter

6

Strategy formulation and corporate responsibility

The fourth major influence on the formulation of corporate strategy that you should take into account is that of corporate responsibility.

The concept of corporate responsibility is not well defined, either in theory or practice. The terms "social responsibility" or "public expectations" are sometimes used as well, and we will take these all to signify an important area of concern for the manager interested both in the economic well-being of his company and the role that it plays in the broader society.

It is apparent that business firms are increasingly being held responsible for far more than the direct economic consequences for their shareholders of the decisions they make and the activities they undertake. Because of the overwhelming importance in the non-Socialist countries of the role of private enterprise in the furnishing of employment and the utilization of productive assets to provide goods and services, society has a legitimate interest in the manner in which these activities are carried out.

It may be useful to think of the many types of claims on and criticisms of the corporation that come under the broad heading of corporate responsibility as falling into five rough categories:

1. Those items which are largely a consequence of the manufacturing process itself. Many of our most serious pollution problems are in this category, as would be worker health and safety conditions related to the job.
2. Those items related to the sale and use of the product, which can also include pollution and safety aspects, as in the case of automobiles, but also would include such items as marketing practices and adverse effects, as with liquor and cigarettes.
3. Vacation, medical, insurance, and retirement benefits and practices which affect primarily the existing employees, but which increasingly are being viewed as proper for external regulation rather than a subject

to be resolved in the process of bargaining over conditions of employment.

4. Actions which a company could take which would affect individuals largely outside of the company and independent of the nature of the product or its manufacture: building or expanding plants in the inner cities or ghetto areas; the hiring, training, and promotion of the disadvantaged (although this can clearly affect existing employees as well); contributions of money and/or time to charitable or educational activities; and participation in urban rehabilitation programs.

5. Actions in which the ethical practices, and not necessarily the results of the practices, are the primary concern: policies on expense accounts and entertainment, bribes and illegal contributions, deceptive marketing practices, investment in undesirable activities or areas, and so on.

The above is of course only a partial list; you may wish to add items that you think should be on it, or items that it is apparent others feel are a responsibility of the corporation.

Neither are the categories mutually exclusive; many items can be placed in several categories. The categories do tend to present different kinds of problems and opportunities from the viewpoint of the manager, however; and we will look later at some specific examples of issues that have been much in the news in the last several years.

We will use the term "corporate responsibility," then, to cover the activities of the corporation that are seen by others as having a sufficient economic or social impact on the broader society, or segments of it, to justify the use of outside (in the sense of nonmanagement) influence, or ultimately law or regulation, to affect these decisions. The influence may come via the traditional legal attempts to place resolutions on the proxy statements for vote at annual stockholders meetings, or by means of the myriad ways of persuasion, publicity, and pressure open in a free society to individuals and groups with a cause. Ultimately, change may be compelled via law and regulation if those espousing the cause can muster the arguments and the power to achieve their goals through legislative channels, as Ralph Nader, for example, has been so successful in accomplishing.

Responsibility for the resolution of matters affecting the public interest ultimately falls upon the general manager of the enterprise.

The issue of corporate responsibility actually breaks down into two basic questions: the *legitimacy* of the power held by corporate executives and the *proper exercise* of that power. Questions concerning the legitimacy of the power derive from the fact that executives are neither selected by nor accountable to the broader community, even though their actions affect that community significantly. We will turn to this issue later in the chapter. The proper exercise of the power held, totally apart from the means by which that power is achieved, is perhaps the more common concern of those seeking to influence the corporation. If one is dissatisfied with the exercise of the power, it is of course natural to attack the legitimacy of that power as well, and the issues do become thoroughly intertwined in practice. The broad question you will have to answer remains: "To whom am I responsible, and for what?" Corporate executives have very substantial power over the allocation of resources in the pursuit of economic, as well as other, goals. The exercise of the power cannot be avoided; decisions have to be made on issues such as product quality and characteristics, plant location, hiring and promotion policies, and so on, which affect a large number of people. There have been some attempts to categorize the groups affected by the corporation's decisions as "stakeholders" (in addition to the traditional shareholders): employees, the local community, minorities, suppliers, customers, and so on. The purpose of such a classification is to facilitate identifying the impact of the corporation's decisions on various stakeholders as well as to explore means by which the various groups affected by the corporation's actions can gain a voice in the decisions.

EXERCISE OF POWER

We will turn next to the question of what is a "proper exercise" of the power you will have as a general manager. Unfortunately, there is little in the way of theory to provide you with guidance for the above question. Both legal and economic theory in essence state that "The Social Responsibility of Business Is to Increase Its Profits," as Milton Friedman has argued so well in an article with the above title. Most of us, however, would regard that as less than we personally would like to see companies do, less than almost all segments of society expect of companies, and less than would be in the best interests of the broader corporate community, even though it might benefit the individual firm in the short run. It is also less than might be wise for the company to undertake on its own, long before the public brings pressure to bear, in order to minimize the chances of legislation and regulation which could have been avoided by means of foresight on the part of management.

The dilemma, of course, is that the possible claims are endless, the resources and skills are limited, and neither the theory for what should be undertaken nor the mechanism by which conflicts can be resolved are clear. To complicate the matter further, managers do have a responsibility for the health and survival of the firm in purely economic terms, and pursuing those goals in most companies can fully occupy the manager's time and abilities. Indeed, in the economist's ideal world of perfect competition, no manager or company would have the excess resources or time to pursue anything other than profit maximization under the law. It is apparent, however, that the more business is perceived as pursuing that classical goal, the more it is subject to criticism from those who expect it to do more for society.

The range of issues for which business has been criticized either for not doing enough or for doing the wrong thing is long. Not all claims and complaints can be heeded, but neither, for reasons of both wisdom and morality, can all be ignored. A strident criticism of hiring policies is akin to a genteel request for contributions to the local symphony in that they both represent an expectation, or at least hope, of what the corporation will do that it may not be required to do, and which it might find difficult to justify purely in terms of its own short-term economic interests. Improving opportunities for the disadvantaged or raising the cultural level of the community may both benefit the company in the long run, but those can also be argued as the proper concern of the broader community, not individual segments of it. For the manager, the issue is to decide what could and should be done about such claims. What constitutes the proper exercise of power in the specific case?

CURRENT PROBLEMS

To help you develop guidelines and an approach where so little theory or accepted rationale exists, it might be useful to consider some typical issues that have been much in the news in recent years.

You will discover as you study the Sturm, Ruger & Company, Inc., case that the founder, principal owner, and manager of the company is intensely proud of his accomplishments. In giving his views on the company, William Ruger states:

> ... I think it's a perfect picture of a model company. It has made money honestly, provided for its employees, advanced the technology of the industry, and continued to grow and be profitable. ... I like my job and am proud of what I'm doing. I'm proud of this company. ...

It will not require much additional study to also discover that the principal business of Sturm, Ruger is the design, manufacture, and distribution of high-quality handguns, and that the company is an acknowledged leader in its field. In view of the problems caused by the widespread ownership of handguns in the United States, is there justification for considering this company to be irresponsible with regard to the occasional tragic consequences of the widespread possession of its products, or products like them supplied by other manufacturers?

Ownership of handguns in the United States on both an absolute and per capita basis far exceeds that of any other country. The number of handguns in circulation has been estimated at around 50 million, and the number is alleged by critics to be growing at an increasing rate. Our rate of homicide by means of guns is also the highest in the world. Public opinion polls generally support more restrictions on handguns, often by a wide margin, and especially in and around the larger urban centers of the country. Law enforcement officials are generally much in favor of stricter controls.

Opposition to increased controls has been very effectively voiced by various groups, however, including the National Rifle Association; most veterans' groups, hunters, the general public in the less-populated midwestern and western states where urban crime is not as much of a problem; and many who resist further incursion by the government into what they consider their private affairs, and particularly their "right to bear arms." The outcome has been few if any increased restrictions since the death of Robert Kennedy by means of a handgun in 1968 gave rise to much of the recent concern.

Is Mr. Ruger a model business executive, operating a very successful company completely within the law and in an ethical manner, or is his company to be criticized for not living up to its responsibilities? If you do wish to criticize him, what other manufacturers of legal products would you also criticize, and why?

To move to a more widespread problem: Pollution of the environment, both in the manufacturing process and by the product in use, has received much attention in the last decade or so. Companies have been much criticized for their actions in not anticipating the problems and acting on their own, rather than waiting for, and often opposing, legislation. In their defense, companies have pointed to the substantial costs that are involved in remedying many pollution problems, and have argued that no company in a competitive economy can afford to spend much more money than its competitors, either on capital costs or operating costs, without suffering a disadvantage. And the costs are in fact substantial. It has been estimated, for example, that the paper industry would have to devote about 21 percent of its total capital spending to meet pollution standards during the mid-70s, and that the petroleum, iron and steel, and nonferrous metal industries would have to devote about 15 percent to 18 percent of their capital budgets for the same purpose.

Executives have also been quick to point out that in spite of the great increase in regulations and federal agencies, they have often had to plan under such uncertainty as to the applicable standards and available technologies that the only prudent choice would be to delay capital commitments as long as possible. That their claims with regard to the growth of regulations and regulators are true seem evident in view of the fact that as early as 1970, when the first Earth Day was celebrated, there were 26 quasi-governmental bodies, 14 interagency committees, and 90 separate federal programs dealing with the environment.

By the end of the 1970s, evidence was widespread that the complexity and uncertainty as well as the substance of regulation related to the protection of the environment were causing significant delays in new projects. Planning cycles seemed to be stretching beyond ten years for major projects such as pipelines and power plants. The uncertainties concerning nuclear plants were such that some experts were predicting there would not be any more planned because of the lead times and uncertainties that existed. A major oil terminal and pipeline to the Southwest widely acknowledged as being essential to make efficient use of the oil arriving from Alaska had finally been abandoned by its sponsors in 1979 after many years of trying to receive the necessary permits from the many governmental units involved. At that point the administration, caught in the midst of the worst oil shortage since the 1973 Arab oil embargo, announced plans to create a new federal agency that could "cut through the red tape" for such essential energy projects as the pipeline.

Few would argue that our method of dealing with our environmental problems has been ideal, but there is little common agreement on what better solutions might be. Many regard the laws and regulations as a necessary way to counter the "irresponsibility" of corporations. That practices which we do not now condone existed, and would likely have continued to exist if laws had not been passed, is clear. It is also important to note that the standards of what is acceptable have changed considerably, partly because of the much greater knowledge that we now have about the harmful effects on the environment of a variety of industrial substances and wastes, and partly because we have set higher health and aesthetic standards for our society in recent years. The regulations arose because individual companies did not, and individually perhaps could not, meet the expectations of society with regard to environmental protection. Were the regulations inevitable, or could more responsible leadership on the part of businesses or business executives have made a difference?

It is not necessary to provide detailed examples of each of the many types of issues that may arise under the umbrella of corporate responsibilities. There is much discussion of these issues in the press, and much that is unique to the specific situation. The purpose of giving a few examples here is simply to point out the variety as well as the complexity of the problems general managers face in this broad area. Public concern with the ethical level of business practice for its own sake, however, rather than primarily because of the results of that behavior, has increased greatly in recent years, and warrants some further exploration.

Two such examples of corporate behavior that have received much attention in recent years would be corporate investment abroad, and particularly in South Africa, and "Improper Corporate Payments Abroad," now covered by the Foreign Corrupt Practices Act of 1977.

Because of the apartheid policies of the South African government, there has in recent years been a very considerable criticism of American companies with investments in South Africa. Strong external pressures have been brought to bear on companies to divest themselves of these holdings on the grounds that such investments help to perpetuate a morally corrupt regime. The nature of the investments is generally not an issue, nor is the question of whether the employment practices of the American subsidiary are better than South African law or custom would dictate. Neither are the arguments that the employment and training made possible by that investment is important in the short run for South Africa's blacks, and that it may contribute to the long-run improvement of the society, seen as persuasive. Although the critics hope that the withdrawal would impose a hardship on the South African regime, the essential element of much of the criticism seems to be that the investment is simply morally wrong. To withdraw and to let someone else—South African or third country interests—own and operate those facilities is seen as preferable to permitting American investments to remain within the country.

Some managers, as a result of conscience as well as pressure, spent a great deal of time dealing with this question. Managements may have traditionally considered that their investment decisions in foreign countries should be determined largely by their own business judgment and the applicable national laws or guidelines, but it has become apparent that significant and vocal segments of the public consider it a legitimate concern of theirs as well. One company which devoted significant top executive time to deal with this question, for example, was Polaroid, a highly successful company you will study later in this book with reference to their strategic battle with Kodak in instant photography. And Polaroid found themselves deeply involved in spite of the fact that it was commonly acknowledged that they would rank high on any list of "socially responsible" corporations, based on their operations in this country, and that their South African investments were minimal in terms of their overall business.

Other companies with more substantial investments in fixed assets, or with a more important share of their revenues in South Africa, were both more vulnerable to criticism and in a more difficult position in the event they did decide to withdraw. Even university investment committees became involved as a result of widespread attempts to persuade universities to eliminate from their investment portfolios the securities of any companies doing business in South Africa. Policies on investments in South Africa, as well as the broader question of whether to invest in companies that came under criticism for the level of their corporate responsibility, were developed and widely debated.

FOREIGN CORRUPT PRACTICES ACT

The enactment of the Foreign Corrupt Practices Act in December of 1977 seems also to have stemmed in good part from a concern with the morality of the practices proscribed, and not just the direct consequences of the practices on American consumers or citizens.

In the course of the investigations of the Watergate scandal in the Nixon

42

administration, it became evident that the Committee to Re-Elect the President (CREEP) had obtained substantial amounts of money from sources either illegal, unreported, or both. Further investigations uncovered a considerable number of corporate contributions for political purposes, clearly against existing laws. Critics alleged these were simply bribes offered by corporations to politicians in order to influence legislation and secure favors.

Corporations often said these contributions were demanded or expected of them as a condition for gaining business or not losing business with federal and state governments, and numerous reports of repeated and insistent solicitation for corporate contributions by high administration officials were reported.

Extensive investigations and much highly critical publicity followed, and more than 300 corporations were eventually implicated. There were a number of stockholder suits to force the executives involved to repay to the corporation from their own resources the illegal contributions from corporate funds that they had made. Many of these created a serious financial burden as well as personal trauma for the executives involved. Considerable personal legal costs were incurred by many individuals, and in addition there were a number of prosecutions and convictions of corporations and executives for having violated the law, although the penalities were generally modest fines ($5,000 or less).

Since hundreds of corporations were involved in thousands of individual cases of illegal contributions, there were presumably also many hundreds of individuals who allegedly received the contributions who could also be in violation of the same law. For example, the lobbyist for only one of the companies found guilty of extensive illegal contributions identified under oath 117 senators or candidates for the Senate and about a score of contenders for governor that had received illegal contributions from his company, surely one of the worst offenders. He added in his deposition that the representatives who had received illegal gifts were too numerous to identify with precision.

Leon Jaworski, the Special Prosecutor during the period, pointed out that the law required that the recipient either knew of the corporate source of political contribution or received such money in the "reckless disregard" of whether the source was a corporation or not. He noted that their investigations had demonstrated the virtual impossibility of proving such knowledge by the recipient, since the contributions were usually made in cash "from your friends at the X company." As a result, it appears that there were only about two successful prosecutions of politicians for accepting illegal corporate contributions, and they were facilitated by guilty pleas.

The Senate itself seemed to show considerably less enthusiasm in assisting the efforts of the Special Prosecutor and others in investigating recipients of illegal contributions than in condemning those who made the contributions. In spite of evidence that the private law office of the then Senate Minority Leader had demanded and received semiannual payments of $5,000 from one of the companies for a number of years (the company's lobbyist testified under oath a total of $100,000 had been paid), the Senate Ethics Committee refused to call witnesses in the matter, refused to open the senator's sealed financial records on file, and refused to turn over any information to the Internal Revenue Service. It also voted to drop its investigation of about two dozen other senators alleged to have received payments from the same company. Further complicating the efforts of prosecution by the Justice Department, Congress at about the same time shortened the statute of limitations for knowingly accepting corporate gifts, or for failing to disclose gifts, from the existing five years to three years, which placed a number of the alleged offenses beyond reach.

That the political contributions made by corporations were both illegal and improper is clear. That most of those who received the contributions escaped virtually unscathed, both in the eyes of the public as well as in penalties imposed by law, seems equally clear. Regrettable though the double standard of conduct and justice may seem, the important lesson to be drawn from the episode is not that business may have been treated unfairly but that as a business executive you will need to conduct your affairs so as to avoid not only illegal practices, as these undeniably were, but also practices which may at a later date be viewed as morally wrong. That others may not be equally condemned will be of little comfort and no defense.

What led to the passage of the Foreign Corrupt Practices Act, however, was the further discovery that substantial amounts of money—in the millions of dollars for many companies—had been paid to foreign government officials over the years in efforts to secure business. In our usual sense of the word, many of these payments would be called bribes. They were justified by the companies which had paid them as being necessary to obtain the business because of the demands of the local governmental officials and the existence of foreign competitors ready to pay the bribes, as well as by the undisputed fact that the practice of bribing officials had been widespread for centuries in many of the countries involved. The payments were denounced by those concerned with the morality of the practice as well as those concerned by the poor example this set for the rest of the world by the world's leading proponent of the free enterprise system. A strict law establishing severe criminal penalties for individuals caught violating the law, as well as substantial fines for both individuals and companies, was the result. Included in the law was a section charging management with the responsibility for establishing internal controls to prevent violations of the law. Both management and the outside auditors have become responsible under the law for seeing to it that the internal controls are satisfactory, and it appears that management, the auditors, and the directors (and especially the audit committee of the board of directors) may incur individual liability if transgressions occur and the control systems are considered, on subsequent investigation, to have been insufficient. This liability can occur, it should be noted, totally apart from the direct involvement on the part of the manager, auditor, or director in the particular violation.

The supporters of this controversial law see it as essential in improving the image of capitalism, and particularly American capitalism, in the rest of the world. They also point to the basic immorality of paying bribes to secure favors, totally apart from the issue of what others may think of the practice. In addition, they make the irrefutable argument that the citizens in a country in which officials in power have the opportunity to enrich themselves by means of bribes incorporated into the price of the products the government buys are hardly being well served by their rulers.

The critics of the bill, on the other hand, consider it unduly restrictive with regard to its definition of payments that are illegal, as well as an impractical and unjustified attempt to impose the American standard of morality on cultures where seeking and accepting bribes has been a practice for centuries, and is likely to continue regardless of what we desire or legislate. In addition, they point out that the products and services we are selling are generally available from countries such as England, France, Germany, and Japan, among others, and that these countries have shown a remarkable lack of enthusiasm for developing international standards or for enforcing provisions such as ours on their own companies. As a result, it is argued, we are losing a significant amount of business at a time when we can ill afford it in terms of the serious balance of payments deficits the country is incurring, in large part because of the enormous increase in oil prices since 1973.

The principal reason for looking briefly at the history of the Foreign Corrupt Practices Act is not to enable you to debate the merits of the Act but to point out how rapidly practices which the business community once thought were not a major concern of the broader society can become the subject of public scrutiny, disapproval, and legislation. Some companies managed to avoid most of the practices proscribed by the act long before its enactment on the grounds that for either moral or economic reasons (or both) they simply did not want to engage in the kind of business that required the payment of bribes, domestically or abroad. Companies that were not as strict in their standards before it became a legal requirement helped bring about the considerable public criticism of business that developed at this time, and no doubt helped bring about a political climate that resulted in the passage of the act.

In addition, many of these companies also found it necessary to spend considerable amounts of money and time conducting internal investigations and negotiating with the SEC concerning the amount of disclosure that would be required in public filings concerning their reliance on "improper corporate payments abroad," as the practice was delicately called, to secure business. Several years before the passage of the act the SEC held that such practices constituted a material fact for an investor with regard to his evaluation of the integrity of the management and therefore the merits of the company as an investment, and therefore would have to be disclosed. If the payments by the company had been entered as tax-deductible business expenses, however, disclosure of payments that would be considered bribes then created the possibility of prosecution for tax fraud by the Internal Revenue Service—a criminal violation—on the grounds that bribes are not deductible for tax purposes. This problem arose, it might be noted, even though foreign bribes—or even domestic, for that matter—were not generally against the law at the time.

Just as with the question of the procedures by which our society has handled the problem of protection of the environment, one could raise the question of whether there is not a better way to improve certain business practices that no one ever defended as being desirable and that many felt were distasteful, if not immoral, although perhaps a necessary evil. The practices brought considerable discredit on business in general and caused expense and embarrassment for individual managers in a remarkably short time.

COSTS OF CORPORATE ACTIONS

You should beware of arguments seeking to avoid the dilemma caused by the fact that actions taken in the name of corporate responsibilities to help the broader society often cost money, and perhaps require the time and talents of busy executives. Some things you may want to do, and perhaps you feel you should do, may be difficult to honestly justify in terms of the demonstrable economic interests of any *individual* company. Although an individual may benefit greatly from the contributions others have made to The American Cancer Society or the Salvation Army or the local YMCA or private universities, it does not follow, regrettably, that it is in the best economic interest of any single individual to contribute. So it is for some of the choices companies must make. How much responsibility does a company have to establish a plant in a ghetto area if the economic analysis and experiences of others show this to be a doubtful decision on economic grounds? What charitable and educational contributions should a company make, and why?

Some of the actions and consequent economic costs will be incidental to the mainstream activities of the business and limited in their impact on the performance of the business. Other problems, such as reducing the harmful emissions in automobile exhaust gases, entailed much more drastic economic consequences. In this case the improvements desired not only required expenditures in the hundreds of millions of dollars for the necessary research and development work and manufacturing facilities but resulted in automobiles which were more expensive to buy, more expensive to operate, both for fuel and maintenance, and had poorer performance than earlier models. The entire package was neither a financial nor a marketing department's dream, and it is easy to see why individual companies did not take the lead in reducing harmful exhaust emissions. It is equally easy to point out that if anyone were in a position to anticipate the clearly unpleasant and harmful consequences of uncontrolled emissions in large urban areas such as Los Angeles and New York City, it should have been the larger automobile companies. Perhaps if they had assumed responsibility for calling attention to a problem that was bound to occur, they could have contributed to some form of industry solution earlier instead of being seen much later as obstacles to a solution imposed via a stringent law and a consequent adversary relationship with still another government agency.

Another example of the problem of incurring significant short-run costs for the individual company would be with regard to the safety characteristics of automobiles. Most safety features such as collapsible steering columns, seat belts, air bags, safety glass, or improved crash protection add more to the price of the car than most consumers would prefer to pay. In addition, many of these advances have required considerable investment in tooling and machinery, and are feasible only if built into all the models offered, and not as individual options. If the manufacturer chooses to add to the cost of his product by building in features that increase the cost above that of his competitors, but the extra features are not perceived as being worth the extra cost by the customer, the manufacturer who chooses to be "socially responsible" is likely to suffer in the marketplace.

POLICING CORPORATE BEHAVIOR

A greatly complicating factor for business in comparison with professions such as law and medicine is that the broader business community has virtually no control over the behavior of the individual company and/or management that chooses to act in a grossly irresponsible manner, even though within the letter of the law. Indeed, it can be observed that unscrupulous practices on the part of one competitor not only go unpunished by the business community but sometimes result in pressure on others to reduce their standards as well.

The more established professions such as law and medicine have a clear advantage over business with regard to policing both the ethics and competence of their members. Standards for admission to the practice of the profession as well as standards of conduct for members have been developed by the professions themselves and are legally enforceable. In view of the frequency with which members of the Bar have been involved either as principals or advisors in some of the public and business scandals that have occurred, however, it is not clear that the legal profession has much grounds for criticizing the behavior of business executives.

At the level of policing distinctly harmful behavior on the part of those few who might follow that path in the pursuit of their own interests, it is often argued that the only effective course is industry or governmental regulation. The passage of the Securities and Exchange Act almost 50 years ago probably did more to eliminate certain abuses in the securities industry than 50 years of preaching by the more responsible moral members of the community would have accomplished. Few of us, however, would like to see regulation as the only means by which corporations can be influenced to use their broader powers responsibly.

INDIVIDUAL BEHAVIOR

The question of just how education can increase your awareness of the ethical issues and choices that you and others will face as managers, and hopefully provide you with a framework and a set of values which will result in behavior most people would regard as responsible, remains.

Based on our experience, simply reading about ethical choices in the abstract, divorced from specific situations, is unlikely to change behavior. Neither, unfortunately, is preaching. What a person considers ethical behavior is influenced strongly by the church, the schools, the family, and peers during childhood and early adolescence. If children have found that highly aggressive behavior, perhaps accompanied by minor chiseling or outright deception, has been a fruitful strategy, it is unlikely that the preachings of a professor will change their ideas of how to "Look Out for #1" when they get out in the real world.

We believe it will be most useful for you to put yourself in the position of the manager, with all of its competing demands and pressures and constraints, and to develop and defend your position before your peers. What degree of freedom do you have to do what you feel is right and desirable, and how can you create opportunities and new strategies or policies that will enable you to best meet all these competing demands? How can you be more foresighted than some managers have been and anticipate what needs to be and should be done before it becomes a crisis? We have found it is most useful for you to state and defend your position to peers who think you are not being responsible enough as well as those who think you are doing more than either wisdom or morality would require. Values and sensitivity to ethical issues develop and change but slowly, but they seem to us to be influenced more by the need to articulate and defend them than by being told what they should be.

SOCIETY AND CORPORATE RESPONSIBILITY

It is important to remember that private enterprise exists only by the consent of society, and that the "rights" business has with regard to making decisions in its own interest can be abridged or modified by means of our democratic process. If enough people become convinced that a company should not be allowed to reduce employment in a given area without extensive consultation with local authorities and the payment of very substantial termination costs, as is the case in many European countries, such laws will be enacted. If enough people become convinced that business would serve society's interests better under a plan of federal, rather than state, chartering of corporations, with perhaps labor and government representatives on the boards of directors of larger companies, that too will happen.

The difficult decisions for the manager are not with respect to behavior covered by law or regulation, even though they may have been matters that once were at the discretion of business. By far the more difficult questions involve those things a manager wants to do because they seem right—in a moral, personal, and ethical sense. The problem is to perceive what usefully can be done that is not required to be done to contribute to the broader goals of society, and to undertake in good faith early those things that society may later feel business was remiss in not undertaking. And while doing all of this, you will have to remember that your primary responsibility as a general manager is to maintain the economic health. Actions undertaken for reasons of corporate responsibility that severely affect the economic capacity of the enterprise to furnish employment and provide goods and services are not likely to be a net benefit to the society, let alone the shareholders.

Two trends seem evident. First, the public is coming to expect more and more of business enterprises than the traditional economic role that they have played in the past. Even though business may not be the cause of many of the shortcomings of our society, their resources are increasingly being viewed as available to help solve problems such as those of the disadvantaged minorities, the decaying cities, and the protection of the environment.

Second, it is clear that matters that once could be decided by managements based largely on their own personal values and sense of fairness have in many cases become regarded by the public as a responsibility of the corporation, and these in turn have become the subject of law or regulation in instances where it has been felt corporations were not living up to their responsibilities. In a sense, many of our laws and regulations can be considered the result of someone not living up to the responsibilities society thinks appropriate.

LEGITIMACY OF POWER

In the preceding pages we have been concerned primarily with the proper exercise of corporate power, as seen as the broader public or significant segments of it, as opposed to the legitimacy of that power. No solution has as yet been found to the basic dilemma argued by Carl Kaysen that corporate power is irresponsible, not necessarily because of the exercise of that power in any specific decisions or the motives of management but because those affected greatly by those decisions—employees, the community, and even the stockholders—very often have little or no real voice in the making of those decisions. There have been many attempts to remedy this situation, with attempts to influence management via the media, university investment policies, shareholders meetings, and so on being perhaps the most common and most visible. That most of these are in Kaysen's sense still irresponsible should be evident; the problem of legitimacy remains.

A more fundamental approach to the problem of corporate governance and therefore the legitimacy of the power that corporations have has been underway for some time by the Securities and Exchange Commission and others with regard to their attempts to change the composition of boards of directors to include more members "independent of management." Some plans include provision for the election or appointment of directors to represent special interests such as "the community" or "the public," or "the employees," but these proposals have incurred considerable opposition on legal, philosophical, and practical grounds. The SEC has been aggressively expanding the responsibilities and personal liabilities of the directors for corporate misdeeds, however; and this trend will surely continue.

TO WHOM AM I RESPONSIBLE, AND FOR WHAT?

The manager cannot avoid facing the basic question "To whom am I responsible, and for what?" If you decide no one other than stockholders in terms of economic performance, even though within the requirements of the law, you will be doing less than most of us personally would like to do, and less than could be expected of any healthy corporation. If you listen to and follow all who would put a claim on the company's resources and skills, the result is sure to be disastrous for the economic well-being of the company.

For the present, and even for the foreseeable future, there is no theory that will help you make decisions with regard to corporate responsibilities that would satisfy both those who cling to traditional legal and economic doctrines as well as those who view the corporation as an instrument of society, available to help society achieve much more than the traditional economic goals. To help you achieve a proper balance in these matters is one of the goals of a professional education. We believe a strategy which does not make any allowance for the pressures that exist and will be brought to bear in the broad field of corporate responsibility, as it pertains to that particular company, industry, or community, runs the risk of being deficient by purely economic standards. More important, we feel it may not take advantage of the opportunities private enterprise does have to make a contribution to the quality of life beyond what is required by current law, practice, or the threat of proposed legislation. If management is to have any valid claim to being a profession, its members need to develop a set of personal standards and attitudes regarded as worthy by the broader society. Knowledge and skills and techniques directed at achieving economic goals—which are so much easier to teach and to learn—will not alone equip you to make the decisions in the area of corporate responsibilities that you will ultimately have to decide for yourself. To attempt to do good while also doing well is neither an illegal nor unattainable goal.

The job of the general
manager: Perspective,
function, role, and skills

**POLICY
FORMULATION**

Moleculon Research Corporation

INTRODUCTION

It was March 1975 and Dr. Arthur Obermayer, president, founder, and majority stockholder of Moleculon Research Corporation, sat in his office thinking over the decisions he faced. For more than two years since the invention of his company's product Poroplastic® (essentially a solid plastic material composed, in fact, mostly of a liquid carried in a submicroscopic spongelike structure: see Exhibit 1), Art's goal had been to find a commercial use for his product.

Because Poroplastic was thought by Art to possess a number of useful attributes, for example, the ability to shrink controllably and thus allow for the sustained release of various compounds, the initial marketing effort at Moleculon had concentrated on the drug, cosmetic and toiletry, and pesticide industries. In each of these cases the ability of Poroplastic to release active compounds either in bursts or over long periods of time appeared to answer almost classic needs for products with unique, and genuine, marketing characteristics (see Exhibit 2).

More recently it had been discovered that Poroplastic produced in powder form (that is, beads) could be made to appear to change its state. For example, a powderlike formulation rubbed on the skin would appear to liquefy as the user applied it. In this form Poroplastic was being marketed under the name Sustrelle®.

Within a few months, as a result of a 20-month, $453,000 research and development contract from the Electric Utility Research Foundation (EURF), an organization funded by U.S. utility companies and cable manufacturers, Moleculon would begin producing significant quantities of Poroplastic sheet material in a pilot plant located on the third floor of Moleculon's building, a 50-year-old, roomy structure located close to the Massachusetts Institute of Technology in Cambridge, Massachusetts. The machinery, now being delivered, would be capable of producing up to 1

53

EXHIBIT 1
Description and properties of Poroplastic

General description

Poroplastic sheet material (Sustrelle is the product in bead or powder form) is a plastic. Unlike most plastics, Poroplastic is composed of an open structure (it would look a great deal like a common sponge if greatly magnified) which can be filled with a variety of materials, for example, water, oil, and other compounds which are in solution in these and other liquids.

Noteworthy properties

1. Poroplastic, which gives up its liquid phase, that is, when water or some other liquid evaporates or leaves it, shrinks irreversibly. The shrinkage which takes place can be from 70 percent to 98 percent of the original size.
2. The size of the pores or open spaces in the sponge is very small. Normally their size ranges from 10 to 250 angstroms (about 0.00000004 to 0.000001 inches) in diameter. This range of sizes is useful for trapping the molecules which make up flavors, fragrances, and the active compounds in drugs.
3. Poroplastic has the ability to repel water and attract oil. This means that oil-impregnated Poroplastic can be made very stable, while water-impregnated forms tend to be unstable.
4. Poroplastic has good resistance to acids and bases.
5. The material is quite flexible, particularly when filled with a liquid phase.
6. Deterioration from thermal environmental changes is minimal, except at extreme temperatures.

Source: Company promotional materials.

EXHIBIT 2
List of potential applications for Poroplastic

Cosmetic and toiletries industry

Principally, Poroplastic can be used as a fragrance extender (to make fragrances last longer) in the following products: perfumes, colognes, toilet water, dusting powder, bath oils, makeup base, face powder, body talc, emollients, hand lotion, antiperspirants, deodorants, hair rinses, dressings, conditioners, shampoos, hair sprays, baby products, toilet soap, shaving cream, shaving lotions, toothpaste, mouthwash, suntan lotions and creams, sunburn medications, acne remedies, dandruff preparations, rash medications, and foot powders and deodorants.

Drug and medical industry

As a controlled-release additive and for medical diagnostic applications, Poroplastic can be used in the following products: bandages and burn dressings, topical analgesics, conformable skin electrodes, ultrafiltration membranes, dialysis and hemodialysis membranes, column chromatography packing medium, electro-

EXHIBIT 2 (continued)

phoresis medium, enzyme sensors, immunoassay and radioimmunoassay vehicle, and delivery of ingestible or implantable topical pharmaceuticals.

Industrial and miscellaneous

Utilizing numerous qualities, Poroplastic can be used in the following products and concepts: pesticides, air fresheners, insect repellents, detergents, disinfectants, cleaners, filters, electrical insulation, self-tightening tapes, polymer alloys, battery separators, capacitors, liquid crystal thermometers and displays, self-lubricating washers and bearings, pen cartridges, catalyst matrices, contact curing adhesives, and treated copy papers.

N.B.: In most applications the percentage of Poroplastic or Sustrelle would constitute from 1 percent to 15 percent of the final product weight.
Source: Company promotional materials.

million square feet per year of Poroplastic sheet for use in the research program, which was designed to test the feasibility of using oil-impregnated Poroplastic as a replacement for the oil-impregnated kraft paper then in use for insulating high-voltage, underground power cables.

Although the potential profit from this use of Poroplastic was negligible because of the contractual arrangement between EURF and Moleculon, it would be, nevertheless, a stunning technological advance. The industry had sought, for almost a century, a viable substitute for the kraft paper-based technology. More important, because the actual needs of the research program were far below the capacity of the machine being built (about 1 or 2 percent of the estimated annual capacity), Moleculon had arranged with EURF that any amount above that required for research would be available to Moleculon for sale to noncompeting users. Moleculon would, of course, have to pay for raw materials and personnel when producing Poroplastic for its own account.

Art's problem at this point was that to date the most promising applications appeared to be for his product in the Sustrelle, or bead, form. Specifically, a number of large chewing gum producers (International Macher, Torus Industries, and American Dent-All) were all tantalized by Sustrelle's ability to extend the flavor and fragrance of their gums from the normal five minutes to more than half an hour. Also, several large national consumer goods companies which were considering marketing a chewing gum were gaining interest in this exciting means of differentiating their entries to the market. Last, yet another prominent company was exploring the use of Sustrelle in its popular after-bath talcum powder product to extend the shelf life of the fragrance additive.

Although sample quantities of Sustrelle were being produced regularly in a small room on the third floor of Moleculon's building, the process in use was quite wasteful, resulting in a cost for Sustrelle of more than twice that thought possible in a larger plant. To avoid the cost of building a facility devoted exclusively to the production of Sustrelle (Art's estimate for this was about $100,000), several alternatives had been explored. The first, and most obvious, had been to try to perfect a means of chopping up the Poroplastic sheet. This had been proven to be an impossibility.

A second approach was to expand the current method and, hopefully, increase the yield. Yield was important in the production of Sustrelle and directly influenced by the proportions of various solvents which could be recycled. The current method allowed only a small proportion of the solvents to be recycled. While it had been discovered that production could be increased from the current 25,000 pounds-per-year capacity, at a cost of $10,000 for each additional 25,000 pounds of capacity, no increase in yield had as yet been attainable in laboratory tests, which had been extensive.

Yet another approach had been to ask three of the very largest chemical companies if they would be interested in taking out a license to produce Sustrelle. These firms, however, had been unanimous in their lack of interest for quantities under "several million pounds per year"—regardless of the financial aspects of the contract.

As a last resort Art had undertaken negotiating with potential users of Sustrelle with the hope that they might be willing to finance the construction of a plant. As with the EURF contract, his goal had been to secure for Moleculon the right to sell to noncompeting users any excess output from such a plant. To date only one potential user had expressed any interest at all in an arrangement of this type.

Art was concerned with how he could find a use for the excess Poroplastic sheet capacity he would soon have, as well as a lower cost source of supply for Sustrelle. In addition, Moleculon itself was changing rapidly as a consequence of his decision in 1968 to change his government-contract research firm into a product-oriented company, as described below. The depth and extent of all the changes made or needed in personnel, organization, finance, and production seemed, at this point, almost endless.

HISTORY OF MOLECULON

Art Obermayer received his Ph.D. in chemistry from MIT in 1956. In late 1960 he decided that his job at Tracer Lab, his second since graduation, had become too mechanical. As an administrator for government contracts Art felt that, in his own words, "I spent 99 percent of my time filling out forms for the government"; he yearned for the chance to become involved with the technical and managerial aspects of more than just one radiation monitoring program after another. Within two months Art left Tracer Lab.

Moleculon Research Corporation began operations in January 1961 with two initial goals: conducting laboratory research for the federal government under contracts (a business Art felt he knew all too well), and searching for a unique product that would at some point provide the basis for the conversion of Moleculon into a manufacturing enterprise. It was Art's hope that the latter objective would provide him with some of the motivation that had become so elusive in recent years.

In Moleculon's first year revenues were only $1,800 from a single consulting contract; the loss after taxes came to $13,200, largely the result of the cost of writing and submitting proposals for various government contracts. Art supplied all the firm's capital and, aside from his own full-time dedication to the company, all other employees were part time (friends, graduate students, etc.)

In 1962 Moleculon received its first government contract (relating to radiation monitoring) for $45,000; in its second year of operation Moleculon made a small profit.

By 1968 the company employed 35 people and reported contract revenues of $568,581 and an aftertax profit of $43,206. Growth from 1962 to 1968 had been steady and always positive and predictable, averaging about 50 percent per year. Also in these years several interesting products were developed: a radiation-sensing plastic, a fuel-cell membrane, and a flame retardant for textiles. In the case of the radiation-sensing plastic, the product had seemed so interesting that High Voltage Engineering, a Route 128 high-technology firm, purchased 20 percent of Moleculon, and was given a seat on the board of directors. But within a short time it was felt that the actual market for the plastic would be more limited than originally envisioned, as the clamor for household A-bomb shelters died down. Nothing further happened with the product.

The fuel-cell membrane, which was more efficient than any on the market, also suffered from limited mass appeal. Although fuel cells were highly efficient converters of chemical to electrical energy, and the membrane is the most critical determinant of this efficiency, the usual fuel is a combination of pure hydrogen and oxygen gases. Both pose difficult storage and safety problems. At one point while the product was still being considered, however, General Electric stopped production of a material critical to Moleculon's membrane, and this dealt the product its final blow.

The textile flame retardant, developed in 1968, was the product of a slightly different organizational setup at Moleculon. Previous to 1968, Larry Nichols, a Harvard-trained Ph.D. chemist who had joined the company in 1962 as a technical vice president, worked alone in the laboratory on all the company's product research, which he also directed. In 1968, however, John Healy, a retired executive from Monsanto, came to Moleculon. John's career at Monsanto had carried him from the research laboratory to his final position as a vice president in the marketing department. John came to Moleculon at Art's request to help with the problem of finding a suitable new product. The flame retardant, although discovered by Larry

Nichols, was the first product at Moleculon to receive a comprehensive marketing evaluation by an experienced individual within the firm. Although it was decided that Moleculon would not pursue the product for various nonmarketing reasons, Art's exposure to John Healy's approach to the problems of the marketing-research interface had a lasting effect. Art realized that this aspect of new product development would be a critical factor in any product Moleculon developed.

A CHANGE IN POLICY IS MADE

In mid-1968 Art Obermayer made a conscious decision to change the direction of his company. He decided that from that time on, Moleculon would not solicit government contracts, particularly those coming from the Department of Defense. Art commented on this decision:

> I was unhappy with our dependence on military contracts both from a business and a personal point of view. The government contracts primarily involved testing, development, and evaluation in the nuclear weapons program. We were selling services rather than a product. Before we finished one contract, we had to scramble for the next one. The most effective salespeople were the same technical people who were required to perform on the contracts. There were usually periods of feast or famine as we took our chances on new proposals being accepted, and there was very little real security for our personnel. We desperately wanted to develop a commercial product upon which we could build a stable business.
>
> In a personal way I could take little pride in our work. I had many doubts about the morality and utility to the country of our nuclear weapons measurements. But it wasn't that easy to get out of the rut. Dedicated people within the company were trying to build up the military business because their jobs depended upon our success in this. How could I tell the head of our physics department, a man with a wife and seven children to support, that he was to be laid off because we wouldn't accept the kind of business he could generate and perform profitably on? My answer was to head in new directions, but not by breaking the military bond with radical surgery.
>
> During the next two years our military contracts decreased rapidly, not only because of our own desires but also because of a shift in government policy. Certain cutbacks in military funding meant that government-run laboratories like Sandia and Lawrence Radiation Laboratories pulled a lot of contracts in-house in an attempt to save their own necks. Also, other programs were being taken over by the National Science Foundation (NSF), and their traditional clientele is the university. They (NSF) always show a preference for academia and provide little opportunity for contract support at profit-making companies.

By mid-1970 Moleculon had lost all but two of its government contracts and was down to five employees. Art continued:

We thought about cashing in our chips at that point. We had made about $250,000 by 1970 and had all of it in marketable securities. We own this building. But we decided that it was important to continue, to try and find the kind of product that would take us where we wanted to go. And, of course, the contracts didn't stop completely. . . . So we kept going. During the next few years we received enough commercial product development contracts to remain in business and operate with a nominal profit. The commercial contracts had the added advantage that they made us think in terms of raw material costs, processing costs, and competitive advantages. These factors were rarely in our minds when conducting research for the government.

POROPLASTIC IS INVENTED

Late in January 1973, Art had just returned from lunch with two of his company's bankers. Art realized that their comments on his company's need to develop and market a product had been all too timely. As he began to settle in behind his desk, Larry Nichols appeared in the doorway of the office.

"Art, I have something I'd like to show you." Art nodded and Larry approached the desk, as he had so many times before, carrying a small piece of plasticlike material in one hand.

"Grip the edges and pull it until it begins to stretch." As Art pulled, small beads of liquid formed on the surface of the sample.

"It's 85 percent water and shrinks to one-eighth size when it dries." Art tightened his grip on the material and could feel the cooling effect resulting from the evaporation of water from the surface. It also seemed a bit slippery, no doubt as a result of its absorption of the natural oils on his fingertips.

The period from January to May 1973 was one of intense experimentation at Moleculon. As with all patentable ideas, it was extremely important to extend both the possible formulations and end uses into every conceivable direction so that the broadest possible protection could be obtained. On May 23, 1973, the patent application was filed with 61 claims.

On November 5, 1974, the U.S. Patent Office granted U.S. Patent 3,846,-404 to Larry D. Nichols, inventor, and Moleculon Research Corporation, assignee, for a "process of preparing gelled cellulose triacetate products and the products produced thereby."

The marketing effort begins

In June 1973 Peter Magie, a Harvard economics major with sales and marketing experience, was hired to become the vice president of Moleculon's Poroplastic Division. (See Exhibit 3 for the company's organizational structure.)

Peter Magie's experience prior to joining Moleculon had centered on starting a company with his brother to manufacture and market specialty lubricants. A highly successful enterprise that was sold to a large company for cash, Peter's company was, in so many ways, identical to what Moleculon was trying to be. Peter commented on the task he encountered upon arriving at Moleculon:

It was a great challenge, something I had wanted to get back to again. After we, my brother and I, sold out we went separate ways with a lot of cash. I became interested in sports, tennis and skating really, and built this huge complex just outside of Boston. I used to spend 20 hours a day at that place . . . did that for over a year. Then, one day, my partner decided he needed his money back and went to the bank and took it, all of it. Well, it had been more than a year of screaming kids, mothers, guys trying to bribe their way onto the courts at lunch time . . . all those ice skates. One day I woke up and I just couldn't face it. I've never been back there . . . only my lawyer really knows what happened, and he won't even tell me!

So when I heard about Art and Moleculon and Poroplastic I was more than ready to take up where I had left off . . . in marketing. We had trouble in the beginning, trying to understand what our customers' requirements might be. For example, we had approached the research people in our three primary target markets—drugs, cosmetics and toiletries, and pesticides. We sent out 1,000 direct-mail pieces to companies in these industries and got back over 350 responses requesting more information. This was all great until we discovered that in cosmetics and toiletries it's the marketing people who call the shots. R&D in these companies is almost purely a quality control function . . . and the marketing people expect you to come in there with the product, the package, the whole thing ready to go. We can do some of these things, but not very many at $5,000 a presentation.

Then we realized that for Sustrelle to become an accepted additive in drugs would take maybe five years of testing, FDA approval, and $20,000 for *each* potential application. So there we were with the market which could bear the highest price for our product taking too long for us to recoup our investment.

Also, in pesticides it became obvious that we were awfully high in price for these people. You just can't add a $5-a-pound product like Sustrelle to a 50-cents-a-pound fertilizer or pesticide and expect to have people banging down the door.

So then we had to go back to the cosmetic and toiletries companies and try to interest their marketing people . . . without stepping on the toes of the research people, and without spending a lot of money in the process.

In spite of all this I'm still confident that we will be much larger than we are now. I'd like to be on the road then . . . taking orders for 50-gallon drums to be drop-shipped from one of our plants.

OTHER CHANGES TAKE PLACE

By the beginning of 1975, as the marketing effort continued, other areas of the company were being more directly affected by the Poroplastic effort.

In January, Lloyd Gilson, an M.B.A. with a chemical engineering degree, was hired to supervise the construction and operation of the EURF pilot plant. As shown in Exhibit 3, six other people were added or transferred from other areas of the company to assist Lloyd with his work. Lloyd commented on the production aspect of Moleculon's future:

> Art hired me as soon as the ink was dry on the EURF contract. He can't wait to see Poroplastic being rolled up and sent off to EURF for testing.
>
> My reason for coming here was not just because of salary, even though we are well paid. My real reason is so that I can have a chance to perform. I love production. Right now we make a lot of batch-runs for some of our private contracts, but soon that machine over there will be turning out

EXHIBIT 3
Organizational chart, March 1975

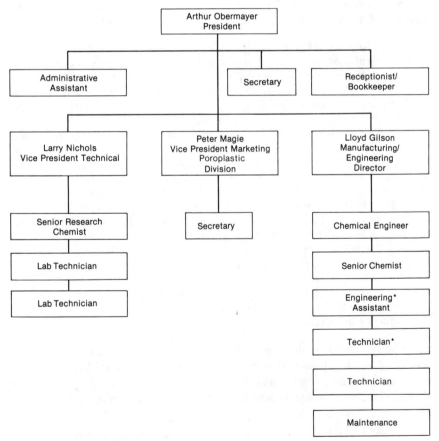

* Added at the time Gilson was hired.
Source: Company records.

Poroplastic sheet for EURF and others. My dream is a new plant, out on Route 128 or 495.[1] At some point we have to get out of this building. We don't even have a loading dock. I had to break out a 12-by-12-foot section of that wall and rent a crane to get the EURF machinery up here. Right now in production we spend a lot of time just moving materials around, and we still make money on every job. But with a new plant it would be even better.

I'm confident that five years from now, when we're doing $5 million a year or so, this will be the research facility for Larry and some of the others, but that most of us will be out on 128 in our production plant.

Another change had taken place in Moleculon's research department. Early in 1975 Art had decided that henceforth no research at Moleculon on Poroplastic was to be of the open-ended type; that is, each investigation in the laboratory now had to have a definable goal, such as a response to the specific request or needs of a potential customer, or to improve any existing desirable characteristics of either form of the product. Art's message to Larry Nichols was clear, if not loud. Larry commented on this change:

With contract research my job was 100 percent creative scientist. It's different now. My administrative functions occupy a significant proportion of my time. I used to come in here and spend the first hour and a half of each day familiarizing myself with the work I would be concentrating on that day—reviewing the data, thinking. The rest of my day was spent solving the problems themselves in the lab.

Now when I come in, I still get to spend the first hour or so reviewing things, but quite often now someone will come in and ask me if they should try this or that, or if the report is ready, or the data, or the samples, or to chat about a packaging idea for the staff meeting. We have weekly staff meetings now. By the end of the day, not every day of course, it's possible that I'm still in here, in my office rather than in the lab where I belong. I used to think that if I was operating at 50 percent efficiency it was a miracle. Now if I hit 25 percent it *is* a miracle.

You might say the atmosphere around here is frenetic now. We have so much information coming in, from marketing in particular, that it's very difficult to make decisions that we can stick with. But I'm sure it will all work out; at least we seem to be learning from our mistakes. Five years from now I'll be in my lab doing what I do best—just research. Art and the others will be running the company.

Although no one ever referred to it, Moleculon's financial situation (see Exhibit 4) was not such that it could be totally ignored. Within a few months Moleculon's last government contract would be completed; and thus, after almost seven years of benign neglect, that phase of the com-

---

[1] Circumferential highways around Boston where many firms had built new plants.

EXHIBIT 4

MOLECULON RESEARCH CORPORATION
Income Statement and Balance Sheet
(Period Ending 12/31/74)

Income:
From service fees	$110,659
From other sources	20,886
Total income	$131,545

Costs and expenses:
Direct costs of service fees	$ 36,333
Overhead and administrative expenses	97,906
Product development costs	88,812
Total costs and expenses	$223,051

Net income (loss) before taxes	$ (91,506)
Provision for (refund of) taxes	(31,416)
Net income after taxes	$ (60,090)

Earnings per common share, in cents	(30)

Assets

Current assets:
Cash	$ 4,409
Marketable securities, at cost	138,138
Accounts receivable	12,653
Refundable income taxes	31,416
Unbilled costs and fees	1,581
Notes and other receivables	4,128
Prepared expenses and deposits	1,370
Total current assets	$193,695

Fixed assets:
Property, plant, and equipment	$ 85,208
Less: Accumulated depreciation	69,893
Net property, plant, and equipment	$ 15,315

Other assets:
Investment, at cost	2,300
Total assets	$211,310

Liabilities and Stockholders' Equity

Current liabilities:
Accounts payable	$ 14,139
Accruals	5,748
Payroll taxes payable	2,537
Total current liabilities	$ 22,424

Stockholders' equity:
Common stock	$ 18,000
Capital in excess of par value	34,168
Retained earnings	136,718
Total stockholders' equity	188,886
Total liabilities and stockholders' equity	$211,310

Source: Company records.

pany's history would come to a close. While private contracts were still being sought and obtained with some regularity, management time for this purpose was scarce.[2] Including EURF, the total value of all contracts in progress in March 1975 was about $550,000.

Chewing gum

As stated previously, a number of companies had become interested in the potential of Sustrelle to extend flavor and fragrance life in chewing gum. More specifically, Torus Industries had been among the respondents to the direct-mail promotional effort of April 1974. By June of that year, Torus, the smallest of the three leading chewing gum manufacturers, had contracted with an independent laboratory to test for flavor extension in its products. The laboratory's initial findings, from data collected using Torus' Sucre-Dent brand gum (a sugarless gum utilizing saccharin as the active sweetening agent, along with a spearmint flavor), had been that chewing gum which normally exhibited a flavor life of from 3 to 5 minutes (a common figure) could, with the addition of Sustrelle, have this limit extended to about 20 to 40 minutes.

Armed with these results, Moleculon approached the two largest chewing gum manufacturers, International Macher (with 47 percent of the U.S. market) and American Dent-All (with 33 percent of the U.S. market). In 1974 the total U.S. market for chewing gum was $575 million in factory sales, while the world market was about twice this figure. About 85 percent of the market consisted of conventional gums, that is, stick types, while the other 15 percent was composed of ball, bubble, medicated, and other specialty types.

By September 1974 Moleculon was attempting to reach some kind of preliminary agreement with at least one of the three majors, but was always put off by requests for more time for "technical analysis." By late November International Macher contacted Moleculon to say that, in their opinion, Sustrelle didn't perform satisfactorily and that they were no longer interested. When contacted shortly after this, both Torus and American said they would still require more time for analysis.

Convinced that the research people at International were not familiar enough with the methods necessary for successful preparation of Sustrelle gums (International's last new product from the R&D labs appeared in 1908), Moleculon undertook gum manufacturing on its own. By the end of January 1975 large batches of Sustrelle gum were being produced. Art commented on this period:

---

[2] As with most nongovernment contracts, EURF and the others resulted in about half the contract value being paid out for materials, supplies, and subcontracts. For most contracts, progress payments were made monthly.

We found that making a superior gum was quite easy. Most gums are about 24 percent bolus (chewing gum base),[3] 75 percent water-soluble fillers,[4] and about 1 percent flavor, saccharin, BHT, and so on. Most fillers are sugar and corn syrup, or, in the case of sugarless gums, sorbitol and mannitol—low-calorie replacements for the sugar types.

We discovered that most manufacturers have, as their greatest concern, the cost of the flavor. Peppermint, while the most common, is also the most expensive at about $15 per pound in a pure oil formulation. In extending flavor life Sustrelle allows for two important changes: first, you can reduce the amount of flavoring required for an acceptable product; and second, you can avoid the problems of an overly intense flavor perception during the initial chew period.

But we also discovered that manufacturers were so cost conscious that it was easy to make a superior product simply by varying the existing ingredients.[5] It is our feeling that their greatest interest would be in using Sustrelle to reduce the required amount of flavoring even further.

It was helpful to have these understandings when talking with the people (national consumer goods companies) who seemed serious about making a product of their own.

Still, by the end of January 1975, there were no definite plans on the part of any of the five remaining firms for using Sustrelle. To help the firms make their decisions, Moleculon wrote a letter to each explaining, or implying, that one large company (unspecified) was moving quite close to an exclusive agreement with Moleculon. Torus Industries wrote back within a week saying that they were no longer interested. The other four, led by one which sent a telegram, all asked for more time for testing. Moleculon responded to these requests by informing everyone that "due to circumstances" the deadline would be extended for two months. It was now the beginning of March, and no further communications had taken place between Moleculon and its prospects.

Talcum powder

In late February, Art had held his last meeting, one in a continuing series, with Hayes & Smith, the large firm interested in using Sustrelle in its after-bath talc product.[6] H&S was the only firm to date which exhibited any interest in a financing arrangement with regard to a Sustrelle plant. Negotiations had reached a point at which Art felt he should offer to sell to H&S at variable cost, that is, $1.03 per pound in a large plant, if they would finance the 250,000-pound-per-year plant envisioned.

However elusive the details which might eventually be worked out, it

[3] About 35 cents per pound.

[4] Most fillers cost about 25 cents per pound.

[5] Most gums have a retail price of between $2.50 and $5.00 per pound.

[6] Talc products retail for $2.50 per pound; bulk talc costs 24 cents per pound.

was clear that H&S was very excited by Sustrelle. Art was concerned that the plant might be owned, in part, by his customer, but far more concerned with his need to have Sustrelle in bulk manufacture.

SUMMARY

Art wondered what his next move should be with the companies interested in Sustrelle chewing gum. The data on his desk from gum assessment sheets (see Exhibit 5) was over 3 inches high and looked ever more

EXHIBIT 5

GUM ASSESSMENT SHEET

Gum number _____ - _____ Other identifying notes _____
            Notebook no.   Page no.

                                         _____

Made by _____ Date ____/____/____

Formulation:

    _____ % Bolus

    _____ % 10-X sugar

    _____ % Corn syrup

    _____ % Minted Sustrelle, batch no. _____ - _____, assay _____ %

    _____ % Saccharine Sustrelle, batch no. _____, assay _____ %

Other production notes: _____

Test report:

Clock time	Minutes	Mint	Saccharine	Comments

Test scale: (0) none; (1) unacceptably weak; (2) weak but OK; (3) moderate; (4) strong but OK; (5) too strong.

Note: Use "+" or "−" to indicate intermediate values.

FDA approval code CFR21-121.2514

Source: Company records.

promising. On the other hand, H&S seemed so willing to continue talking about the Sustrelle plant that Art wondered if he should press forward on that issue first.

But there were other issues that Art felt required further analysis, too. A recent development, largely the result of the looming Poroplastic sheet capacity, had been the idea of making a room air-freshener strip. Should Peter be devoting more time to this potential product? Should Larry pursue it in the lab? And yet another use for Sustrelle was envisioned in the solid deodorant market. Here products like Mitchum's, made from 50-cents-a-pound aluminum chlorohydrate paste, were retailing for about $30 per pound and up. Should Larry and Peter concentrate more on this application?

Most important, Art was concerned about where his company was really going; was it on the way to becoming a true manufacturing enterprise, or would it be necessary to backtrack for a few years to gain strength?

The casewriter asked Art what he thought Moleculon would, or should, be in five to ten years, and how it might get there. Art responded:

> Sales should be over $10 million a year, or considerably in excess of this. Our product line would be Poroplastic and Sustrelle sold in bulk to industrial users for use in their products. I also see some contract R&D work, maybe $500,000 per year regardless of what total sales come out to. There's also the possibility that we would have our own consumer product using Poroplastic or Sustrelle, but this would happen later. R&D inside Moleculon would break down into corporate and contract, each about the same size, with the former devoted to applied research on Poroplastic and Sustrelle almost exclusively.
>
> Our key variable for success will be emphasizing marketing, making marketing a top-management function.

The casewriter then asked Larry Nichols the same question. Larry responded:

> Well, I'm not into finance, so I really can't come up with a defensible estimate, but as a guess I'd say at least several million in sales, enough for us to be self-supporting. Of course, if we really are successful, then $8 to $10 million or $80 to $100 million would be more like it. Our product line would be industrial materials—Poroplastic, Sustrelle, and some newer things we're working on. Also, there would be some contract research. My department would be about five or six people, devoting most of our time to corporate research, a lesser amount to contract work.
>
> Our key variable for success is finding real needs for Poroplastic and Sustrelle.

The casewriter then asked Peter Magie the same question. Peter's response was as follows:

> From $2 to $4 million a year—realistically, 10 percent of this from contract research, the other 90 percent from industrial sales of Poroplastic and

Sustrelle to about a dozen customers. R&D should be in a separate facility from the production plant.

How will we get there? By shifting the emphasis in Moleculon from research to *sales*.

The casewriter then spoke with Dr. Pascal Levesque, president of High Voltage Engineering and board member of Moleculon, who commented:

They *should* be a $10-million-a-year chemical specialty products company in five years, but without a commitment to get there they will be the same. They are pursuing a fine technology, but they are having too much fun. This interferes with, prevents if you will, the ability to be committed to growth.

What they need to do is to *decide* to do it. This will make everything else fall into place.

Prelude Corporation

In June 1972 Prelude Corporation could look back on 12 years of pioneering in the newly developed offshore segment of the Northern lobster fishing industry (see Appendix). Having accounted for 16 percent of the offshore poundage landed in 1971, this Massachusetts company ranked as the largest single lobster producer in North America. Joseph S. Gaziano, president since 1969, looked forward to a still more dominant position and, in the long run, to further vertical integration beyond what he had already introduced:

> Basically, we're trying to revolutionize the lobster industry by applying management and technology to what has been an 18th-century cottage industry heretofore. Other companies have become giants by restructuring such commodity businesses as crab, tuna, avocados, celery, and chicken; we want to become the Procter & Gamble of the lobster business. Until we opened up the offshore resource there was no way to bring about this revolution, but now the chance is there. Furthermore, the technology and money required to fish offshore are so great that the little guy can't make out; the risks are too great. The fishing industry now is just like the automobile industry was 60 years ago; 100 companies are going to come and go, but we'll be the General Motors.
>
> We have toyed with the idea of establishing a restaurant chain featuring the Prelude lobster, similar to Black Angus or Red Coach (local chains which offer only a small selection of beef as their fare), but have never really gotten serious about it. We find we have enough to manage now. The Deep Deep and Wickford distribution systems, which we purchased in the past fiscal year, have given us some vertical integration.

As Mr. Gaziano voiced these expectations, Prelude hopefully saw itself as starting to recover from a recent precipitous and unexplained decline in its per-trip catch (Exhibit 1). This decline had plunged the company back into the red for the fiscal year ending in April (Exhibit 2) and had raised the specter of depletion of the offshore lobster population by pollution or overfishing. Mr. Gaziano viewed these possibilities as bleak, but discounted them:

The vessels we have are especially designed and constructed for our lobster gear and couldn't be used for any other purpose without costly refitting. I suppose we could go south into the Caribbean for crawfish or go after finfish that are amenable to the longline techniques. We could even use the vessels for research, laying cables, or as oil-survey ships. Practically speaking, if someone said tomorrow that we couldn't sell lobsters due to mercury content or some other reason, I guess we would be forced to close the doors. However, I foresee this risk as minimal. Certainly it is possible, but there are no studies or indications that this is at all a likely occurrence.[1]

HISTORY

Prelude's predecessor company had been organized in 1960 to develop techniques for deep-sea lobster fishing. Its founder was an ordained minister, the Rev. William D. Whipple, and its name reflected Mrs. Whipple's profession—music. In the course of raising money for a company that was never in the black until 1971, Rev. Whipple had incorporated in 1966 and had arranged a private placement of 140,000 shares (58 percent of the total). This brought in $350,000, which was supplemented by debt. Late in 1968, when Rev. Whipple felt ready to start commercial operations, prospects for growth plus creditor pressure led to additional financing, some of it completed before the end of the go-go market in 1969:

Date	Financing	Amount
February 1969	250,000 common shares at $8.50	$2,125,000 gross
September 1969*	10% senior (John Hancock Insurance Co.) .	500,000
September 1969	40,000 rights at $6.75 (John Hancock).....	270,000
June 1970	50,000 common shares at $3 (private placement)	150,000

*This financing became necessary when an expected government subsidy for fishing fleets failed to materialize.

Also during 1969, Rev. Whipple agreed to bring in Mr. Gaziano as president, and to have him put together a professional management team. The purchase of two 101-foot trawlers for $1,585,000 completed Prelude's makeready, and the year ending April 30, 1971 brought operating earnings of $273,000 from a lobster catch of 1.1 million pounds.

Spurred by this success, Prelude purchased two more ships of 96 feet and

---

[1] In support of his belief that depletion of the resource was unlikely, Mr. Gaziano employed a widely used argument—namely, that the average weight of offshore lobsters caught was holding steady at about 2½ pounds (with a range of 1–11 pounds or more), a fact taken to indicate that the more mature lobsters were not being fished at a rate higher than their natural replacement.

EXHIBIT 1
Average monthly company landings per trip (as percentage of fiscal 1971 average)

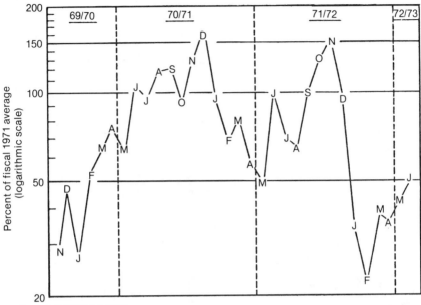

Source: Company records.

125 feet for $1,118,000 and acquired two nearby subsidiaries in the lobster distribution business. The latter were the Wickford Shellfish Company and the distribution segment of Deep Deep Ocean Products. These would, it was hoped, reduce price fluctuations and raise margins by reducing Prelude's dependence on independent wholesalers. In the three fiscal years prior to their purchase, Wickford had had two nominal profits and one nominal loss. Deep Deep had suffered significant losses, but these were laid by management chiefly to Deep Deep's operation of three ships which Prelude did not buy—although it agreed to market their catch.[2] Prelude saw both firms as competently managed but beset by inability to raise enough capital to finance their rapidly expanding sales which were as follows:

	($000)			
	1969	1970	1971	1972
Wickford (years ending February 28)	—	$ 870	$1,000	$1,600
Deep Deep (years ending December 31)	$950	1,623	1,414	—

---

[2] By June 1972 one of these ships had been sold.

EXHIBIT 2

PRELUDE CORPORATION
Statement of Operations and Accumulated Deficit, 1967–1972
($000)

			Year ended April 30			
	1967	1968	1969	1970	1971	1972 (consolidated)*
Net sales	$ 128	$ 176	$ 152	$ 371	$1,511	$ 3,064
Costs and expenses:						
Vessel operations	$ 108	$ 161	$ 225	$ 445	$ 832	$ 1,175
Purchased seafood					—	1,062
Depreciation	22	23	21	68	135	253
Selling, general, and administrative†	53	90	193	249	271	265
Total costs and expenses	$ 183	$ 274	$ 439	$ 762	$1,238	$ 3,055
Income (loss) from operations	$ (55)	$ (98)	$ (287)	$ (391)	$ 273	$ 9
Other income (expenses)	—	(1)	(69)	(21)	(107)	(157)
Income (loss) before income taxes and extraordinary items	$ (55)	$ (99)	$ (356)	$ (412)	$ 166	$ (148)
Provision for income taxes					84	—
Income (loss) before extraordinary items	$ (55)	$ (99)	$ (356)	$ (412)	$ 82	$ (148)
Extraordinary items:						
Write-down of vessels				(133)		
Credit arising from carry-forward of operating losses					72	
Net income (loss)	$ (55)	$ (99)	$ (356)	$ (545)	$ 154	$ (148)
Accumulated deficit at beginning of year	—	(55)	(154)	(510)	1,055	(901)
Accumulated deficit at end of year	$ (55)	$(154)	$(510)	$(1,055)	$ (901)	$(1,049)
Income (loss) per share of common stock assuming full dilution	$(0.23)	$(0.41)	$(1.25)	$ (1.15)	$ 0.28	$ (0.27)
Shares assumed outstanding	240	240	285	474	550	550

*Includes the results of subsidiary operations from November 1, 1971, on.
†Includes all operating costs incurred after landing, such as vehicle operations, salaries of delivery and restaurant personnel, and tank maintenance, as well as executive salaries and general overhead.
Source: Company records.

Both Prelude's new ships (which began fishing in July 1971 and January 1972) and its acquisitions (effected in December and January) led to additional financing:

Date	Financing	Amount
April 1971	Two ships mortgages consolidated at 1 percent above prime	$1,200,000
December 1971	Paid 17,500 common shares, valued at $7* for Wickford, plus cash	122,000 170,000
January 1972	Paid 22,845 common shares valued at $7 for Deep Deep distribution, plus assumption of certain liabilities	—

*According to the terms of sale, if the former owner should sell his or her stock at less than $6.50 a share, the company would pay the difference.

Still another episode in Prelude's history deserves mention because of the worldwide attention it received. In the spring of 1971, Prelude became the focus of a well-publicized international incident involving the United States and Russia. Early in the year, ships of the Russian commercial fishing fleet had caused the loss of more than $70,000 of Prelude's gear by dragging fishing nets over the bottom on which Prelude's traps were resting, clearly marked by buoys and radar reflectors. Such fixed gear had legal right-of-way, so Mr. Gaziano not only sued the Russian government for $177,000 in actual damages plus $266,000 in punitive damages but also caused a Soviet merchant ship to be attached in San Francisco. The actual out-of-court settlement was for only $89,000, but it was hailed as a precedent in commercial relations between the two countries. (See Exhibit 3 for Prelude's balance sheets for years 1971 and 1972.)

PRELUDE IN 1972

In mid-1972, Prelude was organized primarily along functional lines, with departments for operations, engineering, research, and finance and administration. Distribution functions were divided among the Deep Deep and Wickford subsidiaries (see Exhibits 4 and 5).

Operations

Fishing. Fishing operations and the logistics involved in landing and distributing the lobster catch were under the direction of Robert E. (Gene) White, age 33, vice president, operations. Prelude's four ships operated year-round on a two-week cycle, ten days fishing and four days in port for unloading and resupply. Each ship carried a crew of ten: captain, mate, en-

EXHIBIT 3

PRELUDE CORPORATION
Balance Sheet
($000)

	April 30	
	1971	1972 (consolidated)
Assets		
Current assets:		
Cash and marketable securities	$ 460	$ 253
Accounts receivable	22	243
Lobster and seafood inventories	13	62
Trapping supplies	158	323
Prepaid expenses	55	108
Total current assets	$ 708	$ 989
Fixed assets	$2,743	$3,471
Less: Accumulated depreciation	189	420
Total fixed assets	$2,554	$3,051
Goodwill	—	315
Total assets	$3,262	$4,355
Liabilities and Stockholders' Equity		
Current liabilities:		
Notes payable	$ —	$ 350
Current portion of long-term debt	79	270
Accounts payable	107	257
Accrued taxes and expenses	46	75
Total current liabilities	$ 232	$ 952
Long-term debt	$1,616	$1,857
Stockholders' equity:		
Common stock:		
Authorized—1,100,000 shares		
Issued and outstanding—569,985 shares in 1972, 530,000 shares in 1971	$ 265	$ 285
Additional paid-in capital	2,065	2,325
Accumulated deficit	(901)	(1,049)
	$1,429	$1,561
Less 6,200 treasury shares	15	15
Total stockholders' equity	$1,414	$1,546
Total liabilities and stockholders' equity	$3,262	$4,355

Source, Company records.

gineer, cook, and six deckhands. After a 12-hour steam to the offshore lobster grounds, the crew would begin hauling pots 12 hours a day (see Appendix). When the lobsters were brought up and removed from the pots, their claws would be pegged with a red plastic peg which displayed the Prelude brand, and then they would be stored in the hold. The empty

EXHIBIT 4
Organization chart

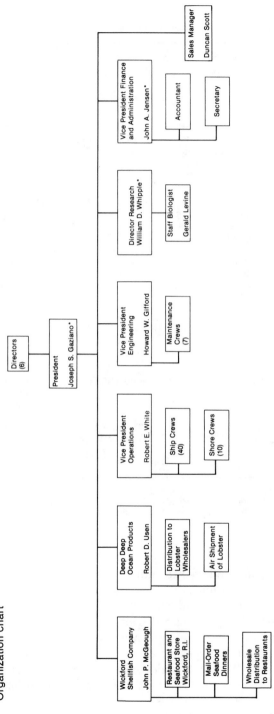

* Indicates director of corporation.
( ) Indicates number of personnel involved.
Source: Company records.

EXHIBIT 5
Personal data on officers and management personnel

	Joseph S. Gaziano	John A. Jensen	W. D. Whipple
Title(s)	Director, president, CEO	Director, VP finance and administration	Director, director of research
Age	36	33	41
Education	MIT, BSEE, 1956 AMP programs: Harbridge House Sloan School	Babson Institute: BS/BA, 1962 MBA, 1963	Princeton, BA, 1953; Boston University School of Theology, STB *cum laude,* 1958
Previous experience	Raytheon Co., 1962–67, rising to manager, Major Space Systems Allied Research Associates, Engineering and Systems Division, 1967–69, VP and GM	U.S. Army, September 1963–February 1964 Price, Waterhouse & Co., 1964–June 1968	Owner of charter yacht business, 1954–58 Inventor and innovator in the area of fishing equipment, especially for deep-water lobster fishing, 1958–59
Date of entry	January 1969, executive VP	June 1968	Founded predecessor company, 1960
Office(s) held . . .	President	VP, June 1970; director, September 1971	President, 1960–69

Note: The three outside directors were Chester A. Barrett, chairman, Merchants National Bank of New Bedford; Joshua M. Berman, partner Goodwin, Proctor and Hoar; Robert F. Goldhamer, vice president and vice chairman of the executive committee, Kidder, Peabody and Co.
Source: Company data.

trap would be rebaited and stacked until the line was ready to be played out again for three days of fishing.

Whether the trawl was relaid where it had been, or in another location, was a decision made by the captain, depending very much on how the catch was running. In any event, the captain was charged with bringing in as many pounds of lobster as possible on each trip, an amount which could vary tremendously. Although Prelude's ships averaged about 20,000 pounds per trip, the results of a single trip could range from 4,000 to 40,000 pounds. (An indication of the variation in the size of the catch can be obtained from Exhibit 1.) In Mr. Gaziano's words:

Howard W. Gifford	Robert E. White	John P. McGeough	Robert D. Usen
Vice president engineering	Vice president operations	President, Wickford Shellfish Co., Inc.	President, Deep Deep Ocean Products, Inc.
37	33	31	42
New Bedford Institute of Technology, BS	U.S. Navy Nuclear Sub School	Providence College, BS, 1962	Tufts University, BA
Electric Boat Division of General Dynamics, rising to supervisor in mechanical engineering department	U.S. Navy, 1960–69, rising to 1/C Engineman; held technical assignments, including mechanical inspection, systems, and machinery testing	Former professional football player; increased sales of Wickford almost tenfold in the five years prior to its acquisition	Over 15 years' experience in several family-owned seafood businesses, including Tabby Cat Food Company; as president had expanded this to $25 million sales volume prior to its sale Founded Deep Deep in 1968
May 1969	March 1969	December 1971	January 1972
VP. September 1971	Vice president	President of subsidiary	President of subsidiary

The biggest problem in the production process is the variability in the size of the catch. It is not like a manufacturing business. The size of the catch is uncertain. There is no proven way of forecasting where the lobsters will be on a given day. Mating habits, weather, and so on, are some of the many variables which determine the size of the catch. Black magic is used by the captains to find lobsters. Presently, it is an art, not a science. Actually, it is on a trial-and-error basis. If one canyon is not producing, the skipper moves to another location.

Work force. Along with dispatching and supplying the vessels, Mr. White was responsible for staffing both the ships and Prelude's truck fleet and storage facility. These operations used 50 people who were engaged in manning the ships or moving lobster. Because Prelude was located in Westport Point, these workers were nonunion. In nearby New Bedford, where the larger portion of the fishing industry was located, unions were a predominant force. Unlike most others in the fishing industry, who were required by the union to pay their crews a straight percentage of the catch, Prelude paid a base salary plus a sum of 20 cents a pound on everything over 25,000 pounds, to be divided among the crew on a pro rata basis. Mr. White commented on some of the problems with people:

> The fisherman is an independent worker. He is always in demand and has a job waiting at his beck and call. His reputation stays with him, although references are not easy to evaluate. Since there is "always a ship leaving," he does not hesitate to tell his boss to "get screwed" if he is unhappy about something. How do you get a reference on somebody who has told his last three bosses to "get screwed?" So we end up hiring them and taking a chance based on their informal reputation, which I get from my sources in the industry. We spin our wheels on quite a few. We attempt to hire experienced fishermen, but 20 percent of our crews are bank tellers and "potato farmers" who want to try something more exciting and more financially rewarding. We start the experienced fishermen at $225 per week and the layman at $150. If the latter pans out after two or three trips, he goes to $225, also.
>
> The cook is one of the most important men on the ship. If I get a bad cook, morale goes to hell. Most ship cooks are drunks—it is just a question of whether they are good drunks or bad drunks. I try to have at least one crewman on each ship with welding expertise. This avoids having to return to shore to make minor repairs. Engineers are hard to get—their education allows them to earn good money on shore and avoid the hard sea duty. Lobstering is a hard and demanding job. Guys over 40 break up after several trips.

Logistics.   Since the inlet leading to Prelude's headquarters in Westport Point was not deep enough for the draft of the four ships, the company rented 225 feet of pier space at the State Pier in Fall River, about 15 miles away. Here the vessels tied up for unloading, maintenance, and resupply. The company owned and maintained a fleet of refrigerated trucks with which to transport the catch. After a returning ship had docked, the mesh baskets of pegged lobsters were lifted out of the hold and into these trucks. If the catch had already been sold, the truck, driven by a member of the shore crew, began its delivery rounds immediately.

If there was an excess, however, or if it was desired to hold the catch for better prices, then the truck would make the 20-minute run to Westport Point, where the lobsters would be transferred to the Prelude holding tank. This tank, built during 1968 and 1969 at a cost of $250,000, was capable of holding 125,000 pounds of lobster in seawater cooled to 42° F. The tank was designed around an experimental system aimed at reducing handling costs by keeping the lobster in mesh baskets aboard ship and stacking these baskets in the storage tank. The system had not worked out well in practice, however, since one dead lobster could cause the loss of 10 percent to 15 percent of its tankmates within a 24-hour period. As a result, the baskets had to be hauled out and culled regularly. Prelude management felt that if they did expand their holding capacity it would be with conventional three-tier tanks which, even though they required more space and lobster handling, could be culled more efficiently and could be built for only $1 per pound of storage capacity. Security measures, both at the holding tank and on the trucks, were important since lobster was a readily marketable commodity at any roadside stand.

Engineering

Engineering activities at Prelude were under the direction of Howard W. Gifford, age 37, vice president, engineering. These activities included the maintenance and procurement of vessels and equipment, as well as the development of gear, and so on.

Maintenance.   With each ship representing an investment of over $500,000 and subject to continual stress at sea, maintenance was an important and continual activity. This work was carried out by a seven-person maintenance department located at the pier in Fall River. Available there were complete facilities for the welding and machinery necessary to overhaul and repair a ship's engines, life-support equipment, and trap-handling gear. Additionally, this crew performed periodic preventative maintenance on the holding tank at Westport Point. This life-support system was particularly important since its failure, if full, would result in the loss of 125,000 pounds of lobster. Mr. Gifford was responsible for the hiring and firing of the maintenance personnel. Also, even though the ships' engineers were under the operational command of Mr. White, Mr. Gifford was responsible for their technical direction.

Purchase of ships and gear.   Mr. Gifford was responsible for evaluating potential vessels for use as fishing platforms; writing the specifications for their conversion; and initiating, supervising, and approving their fitting out. In all these activities Mr. Gifford worked closely with Rev. Whipple in improving designs. Mr. Gifford also spent considerable time working with manufacturers' representatives on developing improved refrigeration technology for the life-support systems. The corrosive nature of the seawater, coupled with the lobster's sensitivity to trace amounts of certain metals which were traditionally used for refrigeration systems, made this a difficult area.

Research

Rev. Whipple, age 41, held the title of director of research. Since 1958 he had devoted a major portion of his time to commercial fishing and to developing a number of improvements and innovations in its equipment. Among these were a hydraulic power block and various rigging and hauling devices related to high-speed handling of deep-water lobster trapping systems.[3] Rev. Whipple was constantly evaluating the operational design of the ships' fishing gear and experimenting with ways to improve it. A qualified captain himself, Rev. Whipple would often take a ship out when a captain was sick or missing for some reason. In any case, he was generally aboard the vessel whenever there was a new idea to be tried out, a frequent occurrence.

In an effort to enhance their knowledge about the habits of the lobster, Prelude's management had recently hired a marine biologist. Mr. Gaziano remarked as follows regarding research on the "product":

> We knew a lot about management and lobster fishing when we started, but we didn't know a damn thing about the lobster. We hired Jerry (a marine biologist) to give us some expertise in this area. He started with the task of accumulating all the data he could find on the lobster. It turned out nobody really knows a heck of a lot about them. He has three current projects. One is to set up a lobster-rearing facility downstairs (corporate headquarters) and see what we can learn from that. The second project is to help us figure out what to do with the crabs we catch in our traps along with the lobsters. They are highly perishable and only bring 25 cents per pound. There is not much market for them, but since we haul them in from the sea in quantities equal to or greater than the lobsters, we would like to exploit the resource. And last, we've chartered a little research sub. Jerry's going to spend five days on the bottom seeing what really goes on down there. It's going to cost us $25,000, but we will have information that no one else has.

Marketing

Prior to the acquisition of Wickford and Deep Deep late in fiscal 1971, Prelude sold most of its catch directly to wholesale lobster dealers in large lots, usually an entire shipload. As a result, the number of transactions was limited, and Mr. Gaziano was able to handle the telephone negotiations himself. He commented on the bargaining process as follows:

> The distributor knows when you have a large catch. He may say, "You have 30,000 pounds—well, we don't really want any today," and thereby drive down the price. Even with our large holding capacity we have been caught in this situation. There are no long-term, fixed-price contracts. It is cutthroat haggling to a great degree. We are really in the commodity trading business—buy and then sell at a profit; there is very little value added.

With the acquisition of Wickford and Deep Deep, each of which owned a variety of trucks and sorting tanks of 50,000 pounds capacity, marketing arrangements had changed. The original plan was for the two acquisitions

---

[3] Although the company held design patents on certain of these mechanisms, management stated that the patents were no protection against competitors using similar but not identical equipment.

combined to handle some three fourths of Prelude's catch, although, in line with the intent to treat all three entities as profit centers, each could sell or buy where it got the best price. In any event, the Wickford and Deep Deep acquisitions happened to coincide with the precipitous drop in lobster catches, so all of Prelude's lobsters were sold "inside" during the first half of 1972.

Wickford, located in North Kingston, Rhode Island, had brought Prelude a business in live lobsters (about 70 percent of sales) and in other types of seafood, including other shellfish and frozen-fish products. It distributed these products in various ways. It had a combined retail seafood store and restaurant located in its hometown, which accounted for 30 percent of its sales; it had a mail-order business in prepackaged clam and lobster dinners; and it operated a wholesale business in a market area that extended along the Eastern seaboard south to Pennsylvania. Customers were restaurants and small dealers, whom it reached by making four delivery runs a week, locally, and to Pennsylvania, Connecticut, New York, and New Jersey.

Deep Deep, located in Boston, Massachusetts, brought Prelude a business that consisted of distributing lobsters to dealers and restaurants in New England, New York, the Midwest, West, and South, the latter three markets being served by air shipments. Deep Deep's major accounts, however, were wholesalers serving restaurants in New York City. Shipments to these accounts had to be made by common carrier, since Prelude's nonunion drivers could not gain safe access to the city's highly organized Fulton Fish Market.

Critical to selling all accounts of both companies was knowing who wanted to buy what, where, when, and at what offered price. Contacts were a marketer's paramount asset in the lobster trade. Prelude's management believed that John P. McGeough, former owner of Wickford, and Robert D. Usen, founder and ex-president of Deep Deep, were highly qualified in this regard, basing this opinion partly on a three-week cross-country trip that the financial vice president had made with Mr. Usen prior to the Deep Deep acquisition.

Both Messrs. Usen and McGeough had agreed to follow their companies into Prelude, where they continued to serve as presidents of the two subsidiaries. Here the compensation of each would be based primarily on the total profit of his unit. Although the decline in the lobster catch had prevented a full-scale testing of the two companies' performance, Prelude management indicated that their expectations had been largely fulfilled to date.

Besides bringing in Mr. Usen and Mr. McGeough, Mr. Gaziano had staffed marketing with a new sales manager, hired in November 1971. This was Duncan Scott, who had been on the road since his arrival, "cold calling" potential new distributor and restaurant accounts, and visiting old ones. Any business Mr. Scott turned up was referred to either Wickford or Deep Deep.

In still another marketing move in the spring of 1971, $15,000 had been invested in advertising on two Boston radio stations, WBZ and WHDH. This advertising was aimed at raising the ultimate consumer's awareness of Prelude's offshore lobster. Mr. Gaziano outlined the rationale behind this program:

> We are trying to establish brand identification for the Prelude lobster. We want people to ask for Prelude lobster—not just lobster—similar to the Chiquita banana strategy. Toward this end we have used radio advertising and promotional devices in the form of handouts and red plastic lobster pegs with the Prelude name etched on them. The handouts are put in our lobster shipping boxes, and Scott leaves them wherever he goes. We plan to start direct mailings. But our radio advertising was ill timed in that we didn't follow up soon enough with sales calls, and our catches were not large enough to satisfy the demand we created.

Finance and administration

John A. Jensen, age 33, was in charge of the financial affairs of the company. In the past he had been responsible for shepherding the financial transactions required to raise needed capital. Mr. Jensen kept close tabs on the day-to-day state of affairs, maintaining an eight-week cash flow projection which he revised weekly, monitoring the daily transactions of the subsidiaries, and monitoring accounts receivable. (Restaurants and their suppliers were notoriously slow payers.)

His most current concern was centered around providing the funds needed to finance the two new ships which were planned for 1973. Exhibit 6 shows the projected income statement assuming the two new ships were added. The cost of the two vessels was estimated at $1.3 million, of which all but $300,000 could be mortgaged. Additionally, Mr. Jensen and Mr. Gaziano were concerned about the impact of interest charges on net income, interest being the main component of the fairly substantial figure carried in the operating statement as "other" income and expense (Exhibits 2 and 6). They felt that they needed a reduction in short-term debt of between $200,-000 and $450,000 to clean up their balance sheet and reduce interest charges.

The company's underwriter had prepared a prospectus proposing a private placement of 100,000 to 150,000 shares of stock at $5 per share in order to secure the needed funds. Unfortunately, the release of the prospectus in March 1972 coincided with drop in the catch and the issue had had to be withdrawn.

OUTLOOK FOR THE FUTURE

By the summer of 1972, Prelude had weathered the downturn of fishing catches which had so far occurred that year. The company's boats had been

EXHIBIT 6

PRELUDE CORPORATION
Projected Statement of Operations
($000)

| | For years ending April 30 | | |
	Actual 1972	Projected 1973	Projected 1974
Sales:*			
Prelude	n.a.	$2,656	$3,990
Wickford†	n.a.	1,250	1,360
Deep Deep†	n.a.	850	840
Total sales	$3,064	$4,756	$6,190
Costs and expenses:			
Vessel operations.....................	$1,175	$1,464	$2,146
Purchased seafood	1,062	1,420	1,316
Depreciation	253	312	362
Selling, general, and administrative	565	780	1,014
Total costs and expenses	$3,005	$3,976	$5,108
Income (loss) from operations	$ 9	$ 780	$1,082
Other income (expense)‡	(157)	(123)	(180)
Income (loss) before income taxes	$ (148)	$ 657	$ 902
Provision for income taxes	—	338	464
Income (loss) before extraordinary items ..	$ (148)	$ 319	$ 438
Extraordinary credit from operating loss carry-forward.........................	—	272	347
Net income	$ (148)	$ 591	$ 785

n.a. = not available.
    * Assumes that fishing conditions parallel those of May 1970–January 1972; that two new ships for a total of six begin fishing in fiscal 1974; that sales of the subsidiaries continue at mid-1972 levels; and that Prelude receives a price per pound of $1.33, with 25 percent of its sales to outsiders.
    † Assumes that the subsidiaries will handle 75 percent of sales reported by the parent.
    ‡ Primarily interest expense.

Sources and Uses of Funds
($000)

| | For years ending April 30 | |
	1973	1974
Uses of funds:		
Increase in fixed assets (new vessels)	$ 300	$ —
Increase in current assets (32% of sales)	531	460
Reduction in note payable	350	—
Reduction in long-term debt	370	270
Total uses of funds	$1,451	$ 730
Sources of funds:		
Increase in accounts payable (11% of sales)	$ 191	$ 157
Net operating income	319	438
Anticipated operating loss carry-forward	272	347
Depreciation......................................	312	362
Total sources of funds	$1,094	$1,304
Funds needed (surplus)	$ 357	$ (574)

Source: Company records.

able to bring in enough lobster to meet its $198,000 per month cash flow break-even (including the subsidiaries).

Break-even costs were divided as follows:

Vessel operations	$120,000	S,G&A	$23,000
Selling	42,000	Taxes, interest	13,000

In terms of break-even per trip, this monthly $198,000 (which excluded depreciation of about $25,000) worked out to about $22,000. The break-even catch in pounds varied, of course, with the price attainable in the market. In the spring of 1972 it ran about 8,000 pounds a trip, since the wholesale price of select lobster had risen to more than $3 per pound during some of this period.

Although the lobster catch had recently risen (Exhibit 1), no one knew when or whether it would return to normal. On the one hand, industry optimists argued that the scare condition was only a transient event and that there were still "plenty of lobsters out there for everybody." On the other hand, industry pessimists, championed by federal fishery officials, raised doubts about the long-term viability of the resource and were calling for some form of management to sustain the yields.

Competition

Even under managed conditions, Prelude's leaders expected the company to survive if not to prosper—barring total disappearance of the off-shore lobster. They felt that they had the staying power to outlast the one-boat competitors who had come in on a shoestring, and, further, that they had an edge of experience and success which would enable them to outdistance the newer and better capitalized multiboat competitors. Chief among these had been Deep Deep; Mr. Usen had had three new boats fishing out of Boston since 1968 but had not been able to make them pay. He was presently operating two of these boats under a separate company but selling his catch at market price to Prelude and attempting to dispose of the fleet. A second established competitor, MATCO, which fished five boats off the Virginia coast, was also reported to be in financial trouble, having been dragged under by its allegedly overextended parent, Marine International Corporation. Although three other firms were putting three to five boats each out to sea, Mr. Gaziano was not particularly worried about the threat they presented. He summed up his feelings as follows:

> This is going to be one hell of an interesting summer (1972). We're going to have some new boats out there, each backed by some rich Johnny who is fascinated by the sex appeal of lobstering. They're going to find out the hard way how much it really costs to pot fish offshore. We have got a real shakeout coming.

In management's eyes a more real threat was that Prelude itself would be taken over by a larger company. Although there were no blocks of stock large enough to make for an easy takeover, the depressed state of Prelude's stock made a tender bid not unlikely.[4] For example, Mr. Jensen had heard a speech in which a spokesman for a West Coast seafood firm with 1971 sales of $25 million had stated:

> We are, then, a seafood company. And we want to remain a seafood company. The potential in utilizing the rich harvest of the sea is enough to keep any company of our size busy for as long into the future as we care to look.
>
> Already we are expanding from a solid base in the Pacific salmon industry into a much broader segment of the total spectrum of Alaskan and Northwestern fisheries. But we do not see ourselves as confined to Alaska and the Pacific Northwest. Rather we are interested in fisheries virtually anywhere on the globe if we can find a way to enter them in a sound and profitable manner. And, yes, we are constantly looking for acquisitions which could expand and complement our activities in the seafood industry.[5]

Expansion and diversification

With the acquisition of Wickford and Deep Deep, Prelude had achieved integration all the way through to the consumer, and management was considering expanding this chain in several ways. One way would be to develop more restaurant/lobster stores similar to the one in North Kingston. Another way would be to enlarge on the branding program already underway. One California firm, Foster Farms, Inc., had been very successful with branding its fresh chickens and placing them in supermarkets.

A third alternative entailed broadening the product base by marketing other types of seafood that could be purchased outside and then resold through the company's distribution system. Flounder, trout, clams, and oysters were among the types of gourmet seafood products bought by restaurants in much the same way as lobster was.

Processing and marketing crab meat was another possibility, but somewhat remote. Canning crab meat required a multimillion-dollar investment in centrifuging equipment and a continuous supply of crab meat. Although Prelude did catch a lot of crabs, they could not be stored together with lob-

---

[4] In June 1972 the bid price of Prelude's stock was in the range of $2¼–$3. Five brokers made an over-the-counter market in the 530,000 shares outstanding. Of these, Rev. Whipple held 92,400; a prominent Boston family, 70,000; Mr. Usen, 22,845; and Mr. McGeough, 17,500. The balance of the holdings were widely fragmented, with no individual or institution owning more than 15,000 shares. No other officer or employee held more than a few thousand shares, although this group as a whole held qualified options granted at prices of $6.50 to $9.00 on 53,500 shares.

[5] Larry M. Kaner, vice president, Whitney-Fidalgo Seafoods, Inc. Speech to Boston Security Analysts, February 9, 1971.

sters, and furthermore, the catch was sporadic. There was, however, a minority small business company in New Bedford which was using government funds to develop a crab processing plant, and Prelude was watching this development with interest.

Nor were Mr. Gaziano's interests entirely confined to seafood. Previously, the company had looked at the possibility of acquiring a manufacturer of small boats, but had been beaten out by the CML Group, Inc. In any event, Mr. Gaziano did feel that any future expansion or acquisition efforts should be seaward oriented, once the present difficulties were resolved.

APPENDIX

Appendix on the lobster industry

Having graced the Pilgrims' first Thanksgiving, the Northern lobster remained a U.S. gourmet delicacy, demand for which was growing abroad. Supply had not kept pace, however, even though the U.S. market drew 80 percent to 90 percent of the Canada-landed catch, thereby roughly doubling poundage available for domestic consumption and export.

From a 1960 peak of 73.2 million pounds liveweight, supply had dropped to 56.5 million pounds in 1967 but rose again thereafter, partly owing to the success of new techniques of offshore fishing (Exhibit 7).

EXHIBIT 7
Total U.S. supplies of Northern lobster (liveweight in millions of pounds)

	1968	1969	1970	1971
U.S. landed	32.6	33.8	34.2	33.3
Imports*	31.3	31.6	30.2	34.5
Total	63.9	65.4	64.3	67.9

* Converted to liveweight equivalent.
Source: National Marine Fisheries Service.

Shortage had sent prices rising even faster than general inflation, and in 1971 the 33.3-million-pound, U.S.-landed catch brought fishermen $35.1 million in sales, making lobsters the second most valuable single species (after Gulf shrimp) in the $643 million fishing industry.

The resource

The Northern lobster inhabited the chilly waters of the North Atlantic from Newfoundland to North Carolina. Two populations had been observed, one in the shallow water from Canada's Maritimes south to New Jersey, the other further out, usually in the deep, cold canyons of the continental shelf from Massachusetts to the Carolinas. During the spring and fall the latter population migrated, and could thus sometimes be found crawling across the flats of the shelf. Estimated weights and numbers for "legal-sized" (legally fishable) lobsters in the two populations were as follows:

Population	Total weight (millions of lbs.)	Annual replenishment (millions of lbs.)	Number (millions)	Weight average (lbs.)
Inshore	25–31	15–20 est.	20–25	1 ¼
Offshore	100–120	25 est.	25–30	4

Besides fluctuating from year to year, lobster catch rates were seasonal, being lowest in the winter when lobsters and fishermen were least active, and highest in October and May. Since demand was highest in midsummer (shore-dinner time), prices rose then, giving dealers a motive to buy and hold lobsters in enclosed tidal pools until values increased.

Harvesting the resource

Inshore fishing.   Inshore and offshore lobster fishing differed in technique, the inshore method being much the same in the 1970s as in the 1840s. A 30-foot boat, manned by its owner and a relative, could manage 300–800 lath traps or pots, sinking each at depths of less than 30 fathoms, and hauling it up with a power winch to empty, bait, and toss overboard again.

By 1971 some 8,000 individuals were engaged in inshore lobster fishing, and a million pots were being used. Fishing was so intensive that government sources estimated that 90 percent of the legal-sized inshore lobster population was caught every year. Of this total, some 70 percent was delivered to ports in Maine. Optimum investment for entering this trade was estimated at $8,000–$10,000, but anyone could enter who had a few used traps, an outboard motorboat, and a license.

Offshore fishing.   Only after World War II were feasible methods devised for fishing the offshore lobster population, and only in the late 1950s did the industry start significant growth. By 1968 two techniques were being used: trawling and potting on long lines.

Trawling involved scooping up migrating lobsters from the offshore flats by dragging weighted nets along the bottom. With the government pointing the way on methods, catches rose quickly, fluctuating around 5.5 million pounds a year in 1965–71, but ranging between 3.9 million in 1966 and 7.1 million in 1970.

Attractive features of offshore trawling included the absence of competition from Canada and Maine (where it was illegal to land the catch), relatively modest manning requirements compared with other types of fishing, and the low investment needed to equip a boat for switching back and forth from ground fish to lobsters. Increasingly unattractive features included overcrowding, loss of expensive gear when nets were dragged across the rising number of offshore pots, and injuries to the catch which might render 50–70 percent of it unsalable. Thus, government sources believed that this industry segment would level off at 100–130 boats.

Offshore lobster potting started with experiments to develop gear for trapping lobsters in the deep canyons of the continental shelf, where government researchers reported a year-round abundance. Prominent among the first experimenters was Prelude's Rev. Whipple, who finally settled on a method that entailed a mile-long line, buoyed and anchored at each end, to which 50–75 weighted traps were attached by four-foot wires. Keys to his system were gears strong enough to haul the heavy line, and also a special clip to permit the automatic attachment and detachment of the traps as the ship steamed along.

In 1970 this technique proved its worth when Prelude landed nearly all of the 1.5 million pounds attributed to offshore potting in the first statistics to segregate this figure. In 1971 the offshore potting catch rose to 2.3 million pounds, but this was shared by a growing number of competitors, lured in part by Prelude's success. By mid-1972, 92 vessels were fishing 50,000 offshore pots, nearly half of which had come into service during the previous six months.

Such an influx brought technical problems. These included loss of gear when one's boat line was laid across another's, or when the lines were cut by boats pursuing finfish. Crowding, too, was a problem in the canyons, with the result that some pot lines had been set upon the flats, where they ruined the offshore trawlers' nets and motivated trawlers to retaliate.

Costs varied widely for putting a vessel into offshore lobster potting, some vessels having been converted from dragging to potting for as little as $50,000, whereas Prelude's fourth ship came to almost $600,000, including both cost of the hull and conversion.

Regulation

Lobstering was a regulated trade, the regulations being set by the states, the federal government, and international conventions. Thus, to protect the resource, all states except North Carolina and Virginia set a minimum size for a landable lobster, and most states forbade the harvesting of egg-bearing females. To protect the consumer, the federal government required all lobsters to be alive when sold, and forbade U.S. ships to process them at sea. To govern fishing rights, nations had agreed not to fish within 12 miles of one another's coasts, and most had signed an international convention establishing a court-enforced code of conduct for vessels.

One clause in this code, of special interest to lobstermen, gave right-of-way to fixed equipment, such as pot lines. This requirement tended, however, to be ignored by ships in hot pursuit of finfish, particularly, lobstermen believed, by foreign ships. In any event, losses were frequent and significant. One incident alone could damage or destroy several trap lines costing about $7,000 each and thereby put a one-boat operation out of business. Lobstermen vociferously complained, but the U.S. Coast Guard lacked enough patrol boats for adequate policing. New England members of Congress, however, had been persuaded to sponsor a bill in the amount of $500,-000 to reimburse fishermen for cumulative gear losses.

In other future plans, the federal government was pressing the states to enact uniform and more stringent laws for resource protection within the three-mile limit, which was the area of state jurisdiction. To protect the resource farther out, the federal government might take several steps, from imposing a federal license requirement to extending the 12-mile limit to a highly controversial 200 miles. What fishermen favored was bringing foreign as well as domestic deep-sea lobstermen under federal control, an objective that could be accomplished by officially declaring lobsters to be "creatures of the shelf" as opposed to "free-swimming" fish.

How urgent it might be to take protective action on the offshore resource was not clear. Reported removal of 14 million pounds[6] by all takers was well below the 25 million pounds a year that government biologists estimated could be removed without depleting the resource, but no one knew how many pounds were being taken out unreported or how many were maimed and killed through fishing operations. One highly placed official admitted, "it would not be at all unreasonable to speculate that as much as 25 million pounds might be being removed."

Handling and transport

Unlike inshore lobstermen, offshore lobstermen making ten-day runs required refrigerated tanks to hold their catch, not just barrels and some seaweed for moisture. Once delivered to the dock, most lobsters again went into holding: perhaps for a few days in a dockside car or floating tank, then for a few months in a pound or tidal pool, and then for a few more days in a

---

[6] In 1972 U.S. offshore trawling and potting reported 5.7 million and 2.3 million pounds, respectively; foreign lobstermen about 5 million; and U.S. ground fish fishermen about 1 million.

dealer's sorting and culling tank. In total, cars, pounds, and dealers' tanks in the Northeast could accommodate an estimated 7 million pounds.

With the advent of refrigeration and lightweight packing containers, shipments by rail or truck posed no problem, and shipment by air could carry Northern lobsters to far-distant points.

Over the years, consumers had come to expect their lobsters live. Weak and dying lobsters could be culled and cooked, then canned and frozen, but despite high prices these operations barely recovered their costs, so dealers pressed suppliers for a high-quality catch.

Aquaculture

Although worked on for some time, techniques to supplement lobster fishing by farming remained undeveloped in 1972. Progress had been made, however, especially on the biological side. Lobsters had been developed to breed in captivity, and experiments had been started to breed selectively for fast growth, bright color, two crusher claws, and high meat content. Already, lobsters had been grown to 1-pound size in two years, compared with

EXHIBIT 8

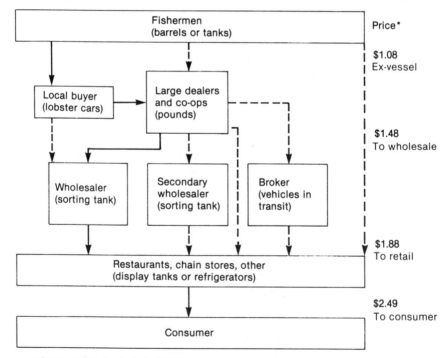

* Casewriter's estimate, typical 1971 price per pound.

six years in the wild. And lobsters had been grown to half-pound size in six to seven months, with tails bigger than any commercially available shrimp.

The big problem lay with engineering the life-support system. Depending on investment in development and plant, the start of commercial operations was put at two to five years away by the best-known authority in lobster hatchery.

Marketing the resource

Channels. As indicated by solid lines on Exhibit 8, lobsters typically moved from the fishermen's barrel or tank to a local buyer with a lobster car or so, who then sold to a larger dealer operating a lobster pound. From there, the lobsters passed to a primary wholesaler, who sold to a retail outlet—most likely to a restaurant, since about 80 percent of all lobsters reached the consumer that way. Lobsters could pass to the retailer in several alternate ways, however, as indicated by dotted lines on Exhibit 8. These could either add or eliminate a step.

Price. As indicated by the price data on Exhibit 8, prices more than doubled between the fisherman and the consumer, with retailers (largely restaurants) accounting for the biggest rise. The estimated price figures shown conceal wide seasonal variations, as well as variations for different weights of lobsters, and a steep year-to-year uptrend (see Exhibit 9).

EXHIBIT 9
Liveweight wholesale prices per pound, Fulton Fish Market, New York City

	"Chix" 1⅛ lbs.	"Quarters" 1¼ lbs.	"Duces" 2 lbs.
1970:			
High	$1.85	$1.88	$1.89
Low	1.24	1.34	1.36
1971:			
High	2.06	2.14	2.66
Low	1.45	1.46	1.47

Source: National Marine Fisheries Service, *Shellfish Situation and Outlook, Annual Review, 1971.*

Two major market segments combined to yield the aggregate statistics given in Exhibit 10. Restaurants and fancy seafood stores, which favored "select" (1½–2½-pound lobsters), had a relatively constant demand, so that prices sometimes reached astronomical levels. Supermarkets and volume restaurants had a price-sensitive demand and tended to drop out of the picture when prices went above a certain level. When prices were low, how-

EXHIBIT 10

Weighted-average annual price per pound paid to Maine fishermen

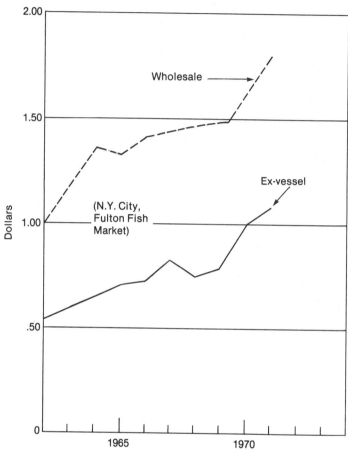

ever, chains tended to buy for promotions, thus helping to stabilize the market.

Competition among distributors. Companies of varying types and sizes were engaged in lobster distribution, and they competed fiercely to handle the limited supply on a price basis favorable to themselves.

Two of the largest entities in the business were J. Hook and Bay State, both of Boston, who together handled an estimated 30 million pounds a year. Despite their size, they might find themselves outbid by "small lotters," who were able to sell crate lots in Europe for twice what their large competitors were getting from a high-volume restaurant account.

Hook and Bay State operated quite differently, thus illustrating the wide variety of ways that entities in lobster distribution could be linked together or combined. Bay State specialized in furnishing the restaurant trade with sorted lobster at a stable year-round price, which might be above or below the current market. While it had preferred to confine itself to a wholesale function, it had recently been forced to enter the dealer function of running a pound in order to secure its sources of supply. In contrast, Hook maintained only a skeleton staff year-round, but geared up when the market was good to provide tremendous quantities of case lots of unsorted lobsters to secondary wholesalers. Hook also brokered a large volume to chains.

case 3

Sturm, Ruger & Company, Inc.*

Founded in 1949, Sturm, Ruger & Company, Inc., had sales of $19.5 million in 1973 and was an acknowledged leader in the design and manufacture of quality target shooting and hunting firearms. At its headquarters in Southport, Connecticut, and a manufacturing facility in Newport, New Hampshire, the company produced both handguns and long-guns for consumers in the United States, Canada, and some foreign countries. Over the period 1968–73, sales and earnings had increased at compound rates of 16.6 percent and 13.8 percent, respectively, and net profit margins had averaged 14.7 percent for the same period. (For additional financial information, see Exhibits 1, 2, and 3.)

In September 1974, as he assessed the future for his company, William Ruger, president and chairman of the board, reflected on the performance of Sturm, Ruger & Company:

> I think of this company as a composite whole, or picture, which includes design, customers, employees, engineering, and manufacturing. It is a picture that I have painted, and I think it's a perfect picture of a model company. It has made money honestly, provided for its employees, advanced the technology of the industry, and continued to grow and be profitable. If anything, these are the standards by which a company should be judged. The most important of all these criteria is that we have been profitable, and that's been a plus for everyone involved. But deep down inside, it also makes me feel very good to know that we've designed some damn beautiful firearms.

Even as Mr. Ruger reflected on the past performance of Sturm, Ruger, he was concerned with developing and implementing the appropriate strategy to ensure the continued viability of his company in the face of potentially adverse legislation and economic circumstances. As the company's product

---

* This case was made possible by the cooperation of Sturm, Ruger & Company, Inc.

EXHIBIT 1
Profit and loss data for the years 1949–1973

Year	Net sales		Cost of goods sold		Gross profit		Selling	General and administrative	Total		Other inc.	Profit before taxes		Taxes		Net profit	
	Amount	%	Amount	%	Amount	%	amount	amount	amount	%	(exp.)	Amount	%	Amount	%	Amount	%
1949	$ 29	100	$ 35	—	$ (6)	—	$ 7	$ 9	$ 16	—	$ (1)	$ (22)	—	$ —	—	$ (23)	—
1950	206	100	125	60.7	81	39.3	13	23	36	17.5	(1)	44	21.4	6	3.0	38	18.4
1951	368	100	214	58.2	154	41.8	33	39	72	19.5	(3)	79	21.5	42	11.4	37	10.1
1952	427	100	240	56.3	187	43.7	45	42	87	20.4	1	101	23.6	59	13.8	41	9.8
1953	535	100	303	56.6	232	43.4	51	44	95	17.9	—	137	25.5	87	16.3	49	9.2
1954	802	100	460	57.4	342	42.6	60	46	106	13.2	—	236	29.4	122	15.2	114	14.2
1955	1,297	100	786	60.6	511	39.4	83	73	156	12.0	(2)	353	27.2	188	14.5	165	12.7
1956	1,849	100	960	51.9	889	48.1	107	79	186	10.1	(2)	701	37.9	374	20.1	327	17.7
1957	2,509	100	1,293	51.5	1,216	48.5	144	92	236	9.4	5	985	39.2	525	20.9	460	18.3
1958	2,562	100	1,341	52.3	1,221	47.7	167	101	268	10.4	4	957	37.4	509	19.9	448	17.5
1959	2,938	100	1,493	50.8	1,445	49.2	182	141	323	11.0	8	1,130	38.4	602	20.5	527	17.9
1960	2,742	100	1,536	56.0	1,206	44.0	215	162	377	13.8	10	839	30.6	446	16.3	393	14.3
1961	2,581	100	1,491	57.8	1,090	42.2	298	97	395	15.3	(33)	662	25.6	357	13.8	305	11.8
1962	3,474	100	2,098	60.4	1,376	39.6	286	87	373	10.7	(29)	974	28.0	526	15.1	448	12.9
1963	3,713	100	2,176	58.6	1,536	41.4	312	112	424	11.4	(12)	1,100	29.7	591	15.9	509	13.7
1964	4,121	100	2,478	60.1	1,643	39.9	343	107	450	10.9	(54)	1,139	27.6	587	14.2	551	13.4
1965	5,797	100	3,319	57.2	2,478	42.8	354	183	534	9.2	36	1,980	34.2	980	16.9	1,001	17.3
1966	6,023	100	3,490	57.9	2,533	42.1	370	196	566	9.4	63	2,030	33.7	997	16.5	1,003	17.2
1967	7,595	100	4,359	57.4	3,236	42.6	447	228	675	8.9	69	2,630	34.6	1,268	16.7	1,362	17.9
1968	9,068	100	5,364	59.1	3,704	40.9	515	283	798	8.8	63	2,969	32.7	1,568	17.3	1,401	15.4
1969	11,090	100	5,968	53.8	5,122	46.2	631	315	946	8.5	30	4,206	37.9	2,246	20.2	1,960	17.7
1970	12,789	100	6,956	54.4	5,833	45.6	886	296	1,182	9.2	27	4,678	36.6	2,452	19.2	2,226	17.4
1971	13,318	100	9,064	68.1	4,254	31.9	1,050	347	1,397	10.4	45	2,902	21.8	1,440	10.8	1,462	11.0
1972	16,183	100	10,510	65.0	5,673	35.0	1,151	407	1,558	9.6	107	4,222	26.1	2,093	12.9	2,129	13.2
1973	19,542	100	12,643	64.7	6,899	35.3	1,325	490	1,815	9.3	343	5,426	27.8	2,752	14.1	2,674	13.7

Source: Company reports.

EXHIBIT 2

STURM, RUGER & COMPANY, INC.
Consolidated Balance Sheets

	December 31	
	1973	1972
Assets		
Current assets:		
Cash and certificates of deposit		
(1973—$4,300,000; 1972—$4,025,000) ..	$ 6,315,337	$ 5,565,565
Trade receivables, less allowance		
(1973—$25,000; 1972—$5,000)..........	1,050,576	1,228,826
Inventories:		
Finished products	$ 709,981	$ 435,105
Materials, supplies, and products in process	5,314,740	4,548,979
Total inventories	$ 6,024,721	$ 4,984,084
Prepaid expenses	110,294	56,340
Total current assets	$13,500,928	$11,834,815
Property, plant, and equipment:		
Land and improvements	$ 405,298	$ 319,583
Buildings......................................	2,479,145	2,092,641
Machinery and equipment	3,413,030	2,806,755
Dies and tools	1,689,500	1,403,350
	$ 7,986,973	$ 6,622,329
Less: Allowances for depreciation	3,595,523	2,996,907
Total property, plant, and equipment ...	$ 4,391,450	$ 3,625,422
Other assets:		
Deferred federal income taxes	$	$ 216,600
Cash value of life insurance	115,175	108,359
Miscellaneous accounts	158,045	136,161
Total other assets......................	$ 273,220	$ 461,120
Total assets	$18,165,598	$15,921,357
Liabilities and Stockholders' Equity		
Current liabilities:		
Trade accounts payable	$ 390,506	$ 252,463
Employee compensation	276,883	220,674
Taxes, other than income taxes	100,134	99,433
Pension plan	92,400	93,900
Federal and state income taxes	971,603	983,357
Total current liabilities	$ 1,831,526	$ 1,649,827
Deferred federal income taxes	48,700	—
Stockholders' equity:		
Common stock, par value $1 a share:		
Authorized—3,500,000 shares.		
Issued and outstanding—1,651,320 shares .	$ 1,651,320	$ 1,651,320
Retained earnings	14,634,052	12,620,210
Total stockholders' equity	$16,285,372	$14,271,530
Total liabilities and stockholders' equity	$18,165,598	$15,921,357

Source: Company annual reports.

EXHIBIT 3

Financial and statistical highlights

Highlights	1950	1955	1960	1965	1970	1973
Net sales ($000)	$ 206	$ 1,297	$ 2,742	$ 5,797	$ 12,789	$ 19,542
Net income after taxes ($000)	38	165	393	1,001	2,226	2,674
Net income as percent of sales	18.4%	12.7%	14.3%	17.3%	17.4%	13.7%
Return on total assets	53.5%	39.4%	19.3%	23.2%	19.6%	14.7%
Number of units sold	9,147	42,589	71,111	157,827	271,040	391,863
Average sales price per unit	22.52	30.45	38.56	36.73	47.18	49.87
Average profit per unit	4.15	3.87	5.53	6.34	8.21	6.82
Total number of employees	27	62	104	153	380	694
Square feet of manufacturing space	2,220	6,844	23,192	58,129	96,714	134,000

Supplemental data	Sales	Gross profit	Total selling, general and administrative	Profit before taxes	Net profit
Growth rates:					
1959–69	13.8%	13.5%	11.4%	13.8%	13.8%
1969–73	15.2	7.7	13.9	6.6	8.1
1972–73	20.8	21.6	16.5	28.5	25.6

Per share data	Earnings	Dividends	Price range
1969	$1.19	$0.18	$15½–$10½
1970	1.35	0.20	15 – 8¾
1971	0.89	0.20	23¼ – 10
1972	1.29	0.225	18¼ – 10¼
1973	1.62	0.30	12 – 6½

Source: Company reports.

mix was approximately two-thirds handguns, Mr. Ruger believed enactment of handgun control legislation could have a significant impact on the company's future. Although he had not completely rejected the possibility of diversifying outside of the gun industry, he had tentatively decided to prepare the company for the impact of potential handgun control laws by adding police handguns and army rifles to his product line, and shifting the product mix toward long-guns.[1]

As Mr. Ruger pondered the appropriateness of this strategy, he was also concerned with questions of greater utilization of the company's overall skills and resources, its organizational strengths and needs, and his future role in the company.

THE GUN INDUSTRY

Structure and competition

The firearms industry was one of the oldest industries in the United States, dating back to 1798. The industry consisted of four major segments: handguns, long-arms, ammunition, and accessories. Firearms were usually divided into three categories: handguns, rifles, and shotguns.

Until fairly recently, public data on the U.S. gun industry were extremely scarce as there were no central reporting agency and many of the producing companies were privately owned.

Approximate figures for firearms sales in millions in 1973, however, were reported by the Bureau of Alcohol, Tobacco, and Firearms as shown in Exhibit 4.

In the handgun segment of the industry, the Colt Firearms Division of Colt Industries, Smith and Wesson (a division of Bangor Punta) and Sturm, Ruger & Company were the acknowledged leaders in sales. In long-guns, Remington Arms and the Winchester–Western Division of Olin Corporation were generally acknowledged as the industry leaders, followed by Savage Arms and Marlin Firearms; Winchester–Western and Remington were believed to each have approximately 24 percent of the total market share.[2]

In ammunition sales an estimated 90 percent of the market was thought to be controlled by Winchester, Remington, and Federal Cartridge Company, a privately held company.[3]

---

[1] Handguns, rifles, and shotguns were the three common types of civilian small arms. Handguns included both revolvers (cartridge chambers in a rotating cylinder separate from the barrel) and pistols (single chamber contiguous with the barrel) designed to be fired with one hand. Rifles and shotguns were classified as long-guns because of their longer barrels.

[2] Source: Industry data and Sporting Arms and Ammunition Manufacturers' Institute.

[3] Source: Sporting Arms and Ammunition Manufacturers' Institute.

EXHIBIT 4

Wholesale shipments of firearms and ammunition

	1973		1972	
	Millions	*Percent of total*	*Millions*	*Percent of total*
Pistols and revolvers	$ 86.6	21.5	$ 75.8	21
Rifles and shotguns	142.4	35.4	122.6	33.9
Ammunition	173.5	43.1	162.8	45.1
Total..................	$402.5	100	$361.2	100

Source: Tax records of U.S. Treasury Department—Bureau of Alcohol, Tobacco, and Firearms.

Markets and uses

The primary uses for sporting firearms were for hunting and target shooting. However, many recent sales were believed to have been motivated by fear, generally of possible burglaries, assaults, and other people with guns.

Some industry observers estimated the number of firearms in civilian hands in the United States to be in excess of 90 million.[4] Studies done for the National Commission on Violence in the late 1960s also indicated that nearly 50 percent of the approximately 60 million U.S. households owned one or more firearms (see Exhibits 5 and 6). Production by domestic manu-

EXHIBIT 5

Firearms introduced into the U.S. civilian market (1899–1968) (in millions for every ten-year period)

Period	*Rifles*	*Shotguns*	*Handguns*	*Total*
1899–1948 (average)	4.7	3.2	2.7	10.6
1949–1958	6.4	9.4	4.2	20.0
1959–1968	9.6	9.4	10.2	29.2
Accumulated total ..	39.5	34.9	27.9	102.3

Source: Staff report to National Commission on Causes and Prevention of Violence.

facturers for private sale in the United States had shown a growth trend which reflected the rising demand for guns (see Exhibit 7). For fiscal year 1973, domestic and foreign gun makers produced approximately 5.7 million firearms for nonmilitary U.S. consumption; of this amount roughly 38 percent were handguns (see Exhibit 8).

---

[4] Source: Staff report to National Commission on Causes and Prevention of Violence, 1969.

EXHIBIT 6

A. Percentage of U.S. households with firearms by city size

	Rural	Towns	Suburbs	Large cities
Handguns	19	22	16	21
Rifles	42	29	25	21
Shotguns	53	36	26	18

B. Percentage of U.S. households owning firearms by region

	East	South	Midwest	West	Total U.S.
Handguns	15	18	20	29	20
Rifles	22	35	26	36	29
Shotguns	18	42	40	29	33
Any firearms*	33	59	51	49	49

* Any firearm = households having any firearm at all.
Source: 1968 Harris Poll.

EXHIBIT 7
Annual growth of domestic firearms production

	Handguns (percent)	Rifles (percent)	Shotguns (percent)	Total all firearms (percent)
1960–65	7	11.0	9.8	9.3
1965–68	23	11.8	8.7	14.3
1960–68	13	11.2	9.4	11.2

Source: Staff report to National Commission on Causes and Prevention of Violence.

In addition to hunting and target shooting, law enforcement officers and collectors constituted a significant market for guns.

Despite its growth, many observers believed the industry faced an extremely paradoxical and potentially restrictive set of environmental conditions. As described by David Gumpert of *The Wall Street Journal:*

> On the one hand, there's growing pressure to limit or outlaw entirely the private ownership of firearms. And even without legal restrictions, gun makers fear that a growing public aversion to hunting—derisively attributed by some in the industry as a "Bambi complex"—is undermining a major source of their business. At the same time, population pressures are reducing the amount of hunting land available, discouraging hunters.[5]

Gun control legislation

The question of gun control was one which evoked considerable emotional debate from both opponents and proponents of gun control laws. It

[5] *The Wall Street Journal*, May 1, 1972.

EXHIBIT 8
Firearms available for U.S. domestic consumption in 1973* (000 units)

	Total domestic production	– Exports	+ Imports	= Total available for U.S. consumption
Pistols and revolvers	1,734	95	559	2,198
Rifles	1,830	124	195	1,901
Shotguns	1,280	60	420	1,640
Total	4,844	279	1,174	5,739

* Based on fiscal year July 1, 1972–June 30, 1973.
Source: U.S. Treasury Department—Bureau of Alcohol, Tobacco, and Firearms.

involved such prominent individuals and organizations as Senator Edward Kennedy and Mayor Richard Daley of Chicago, on one side, and the National Rifle Association and the National Shooting Sports Foundation on the side opposing gun controls.

Although some proposed legislation was aimed at controlling all firearms, the majority was geared to curtailing the sale and dissemination of so-called Saturday Night Specials, small, concealable handguns costing $10 to $25. Many established gun manufacturers felt that these cheap handguns should be controlled as they gave the industry a bad name and were thought to be of no use for other than killing or wounding a human being. William Ruger noted:

> Often the handguns made abroad are contemptible contraptions and are unreliable and dangerous. It's the importation and assembly of these guns that has caused such adverse public reaction and led to enactment of some of the existing gun control laws.

Opponents of gun control laws stressed the constitutional right of individuals to own firearms for hunting and sporting purposes. Led by the National Rifle Association, with about one million members, opponents of gun controls consisted of a vocal and well-disciplined group of gun manufacturers, sellers, and sportsmen who used their weapons for hunting and target shooting, not for killing people.

Still, the relationship of guns and violence in the United States had provided considerable fuel for the actions of those who pushed for strong federal and state control of firearms. Many of the most outspoken proponents of gun control laws attempted to substantiate their views with data which cited the role of firearms in criminal activity (see Exhibit 9).

In spite of the controversy over gun control legislation, gun sales were expected to continue to grow. These expectations, combined with the profitability of the industry, led some public officials to make statements that

EXHIBIT 9
Crime and firearms data

Type of crime	Number of crimes	Percent involving firearms
Murder	19,510	67*
Armed robbery	252,570	63
Aggravated assault	416,270	26

* The data also indicated that approximately 6,928 murders, or 35.5 percent of the total murders, involved handguns.
   Source: 1973 Uniform Crime Reports—FBI, September 6, 1974; Crime Index Totals—Year of 1973.

many in the industry felt were rather radical and emotional. For example, Representative John M. Murphy of New York was quoted as saying:

> Manufacturers and sellers who consider only profit divorce themselves completely from the final results of their activity. There's just no conscience on the part of these people.[6]

HISTORY OF STURM, RUGER & COMPANY, INC.

Beginnings

Founded in 1949, Sturm, Ruger & Company, Inc., owed its existence principally to the gun designs, engineering skills, and interests of William B. Ruger, Sr. In his early childhood, Mr. Ruger had developed an interest in guns which led to the eventual founding of Sturm, Ruger. As described by Mr. Ruger:

> My interest in firearms actually began when my father taught me to hold a rifle to my shoulder when I was eight or nine years old. He had a duck hunters' lodge out on Long Island, and many times he would take me out and let me shoot. These experiences stimulated my initial interest in guns. For my 11th birthday, I received a .22 rifle of my own. Mechanically, the rifle was particularly appealing to me; the fact that it could fire a bullet so fast, and hit a target so far off, was fascinating.
>
> Also, one of the reasons I eventually went into the firearms business was because I liked the life-style the gun seemed to symbolize: the rugged, early western frontier and the outdoor sportsman. In combination with that was a driving interest in machinery and design.
>
> As a boy, I used to go to the library and look at a book on steamboat designs and dream of making one myself. I hung around gun stores and I gained an insight into the design, mechanisms, and engineering of guns. This led me to try to design one of my own. This was a tremendous chal-

---

[6] *The Wall Street Journal,* May 19, 1972.

lenge for me. In view of all the limitations, finding a way of making things you want is perhaps the greatest of challenges.

You know, there are two kinds of boys: those that like baseball and those that like guns; I liked guns. When I was about 14 years old, I saw an article in a magazine about a machine gun and I was awed by the simplicity of the technology, although the machine gun was really a leap forward in technology. A machine gun design played a very important role in my later life.

Although his childhood experience laid the foundation, Mr. Ruger did not become actively involved in the gun industry until 1937. After attending the University of North Carolina for two years, Mr. Ruger took a job with the War Department as a draftsman in the Springfield Armory. Although he had developed several gun designs, Mr. Ruger had had no formal training as a draftsman. He explained:

At the time, I was 22 and really wasn't a very good draftsman. In fact, until the War Department job, I had never been inside a real drafting room. I worked there for a while but didn't stay long. When the War Department made an invitation for drawings for a new machine gun, I submitted one I had done. On the strength of that design, I got a job with the Auto Ordnance Corporation, for whom I worked all during the war. Auto Ordnance, now McGuire Industries, was famous for the Thompson submachine gun. While working for Auto Ordnance, I was one of the youngest people working and developing a real perspective on gun design.

Mr. Ruger went on to describe the events leading to the founding of Sturm, Ruger & Company, Inc.:

I left Auto Ordnance Corporation in 1945 and was still interested in a company of my own. For about three years, I tried to make a go of a little machine shop making small parts. It began losing money and finally went into receivership in 1948. Later that same year, Alexander Sturm came to me and offered to finance me in a new company to manufacture an automatic target pistol I had designed. This .22 pistol looked something like a German Luger. The design of the gun led to low production costs, which enabled us to have a cost advantage of about 20 percent less than the then competitive models of Colt and High Standard. With the $50,000 provided by Alex Sturm, we went into production. Although this gun had some technical improvements, and we would not have survived if we had not had a price advantage, since we didn't have the reputation that Colt and other gun makers had.

Another important factor was timing. People had suddenly begun to become involved in hobbies and specialty interests. The war was over, the depression was over, and it was an entirely new atmosphere. In effect, the company's start couldn't have occurred at a more opportune time economically.

Priced at $37.50 (retail), this target pistol proved to be a tremendous success. In 1950 the company had net sales of $206,000 and net profits of $38,-

000 for a net return on sales of 18.4 percent. The company sold approximately 9,147 guns in 1950.

1950–1960

With the death of Alexander Sturm in 1951, complete responsibility for the business fell on Mr. Ruger. Over the next ten years, Mr. Ruger continued to add new handguns to his product mix. By 1961 the Sturm, Ruger product line consisted of the following small arms: the original automatic pistol, still at $37.50; a single-action .22 Western style six-gun at $54.50 to $75.50; a Blackhawk line single-action revolver, introduced in 1955 for big caliber cartridges, at $87.50 to $116; and the Bearcat .22 single-action revolver at $49.50. By 1960 sales had risen to $2.7 million and net income totaled $393,000. Mr. Ruger commented:

> After the first target pistol, our next product was a single-action Western style six-gun. This gun was the kind that the shooter had to cock the hammer after each shot. For some reason, Colt had abandoned this product, although there was a demand for it. They saw their primary market as the police and law enforcement. I thought they were out of touch with the market. I was a gun and shooting enthusiast, however, and was completely familiar with the market. I knew this gun would sell.

Mr. Ruger's calibration of the market potential proved accurate, and the company sold thousands of the handguns. According to the vice president of marketing, Edward P. Nolan, "Some were even bought by people who buckled on a six-gun to watch television Westerns."

Growth and product line expansion

In 1961, with sales of its handguns approximately $2.6 million, Mr. Ruger broadened the company's product line by introducing a hunting rifle called the Deerstalker. Mr. Ruger described the development of this rifle:

> We had developed the Blackhawk revolver for the .44 magnum cartridge, which is the most powerful handgun cartridge made. As a result of the revolver, we had acquired a reputation for having the best revolver for the .44 magnum. As a hunter, I thought the .44 cartridge would make an excellent deer rifle and would appeal to hunters. There was no market research, just a gut feel that it would sell and that selling only handguns would limit the company's growth.

Enjoying considerable success with this long-gun, Sturm, Ruger added additional rifles to its product line. By 1971 the company manufactured four rifles, priced from $56.50 to $265, and six handguns, priced from $47.50 to $125.[7] Most of the company's success during this period was attributed to

---

[7] Retail price.

the intuitive approach and design skills of Mr. Ruger. One writer in *Outdoor Life,* a leading magazine for hunters and fishermen, wrote:

> Bill Ruger, the president of the Sturm, Ruger Company which manufactures the Ruger firearms, has a number of things going for him. Among them he is a gun nut of the first order, a guy with a sentimental love of guns for their own sake. He is also a firearms designer who can look at a blueprint of a gun mechanism, visualize the gun, see how it works, and know how it should be manufactured.
>
> He is attuned to the same wave-length as a considerable part of the gun-loving, gun-buying public, and he has always felt that if he was interested in and liked a certain design that enough gun buyers would feel the same way to make the manufacture profitable. He is also fortunate in that he is for all practical purposes the Sturm, Ruger Company and he has no board of directors on his neck to second-guess him.
>
> Ruger's initial success, the one that put him in business and financed other ventures in the field, was the .22 automatic pistol, which was shrewdly designed for reliable functioning, simple manufacture, and eye appeal. His next success was a single-action .22 rimfire caliber revolver. In outward appearance it was the spitting image of the old Colt Frontier revolver.
>
> At the time Ruger began manufacture of his single action it was generally believed in the trade that the single-action revolver was dead beyond recall. When Ruger showed me the prototype of his .22 single action and asked me how I thought it would go I told him I thought it would sell like mad. Some straws were then in the wind. One was that a single-action Colt in good condition was bringing from four to six times the price it had brought new before the war.
>
> Another was that movies and the infant TV were leaning heavily on horse operas and that in such exciting dramas the single-action revolver is a prop of prime importance.
>
> Like many a gun nut Ruger had always admired the appearance of the ... single action. I'm quite sure that Ruger made no consumer surveys, didn't consult his dealers and failed to test the market. If Ruger had a genius with a Ph.D. from the Harvard School of Business Administration doing market research and chained to a desk in a back room somewhere, I am sure the guy fainted when Ruger told him what he had in mind.[8]

Diversification effort

Again reflecting Mr. Ruger's interests and skills as an engineer, the company in 1965 initiated an attempt to diversify into the automobile business. At Mr. Ruger's direction, the company undertook to design and build a working prototype of a luxury sportscar similar to the British-made 1929, 4.5 liter Bentley. The intent was to sell these cars on a limited basis, at a price of approximately $12,000–$13,000 per car.

---

[8] Jack O'Connor, *Outdoor Life,* 1967.

The Ruger Tourer was designed to be a sports-touring car with a soft top and body styling of the 1929 vintage Bentley, but with a modern power plant and structural mechanics. The car was to be equipped with a 427 V–8 Ford racer motor, sophisticated Monroe shocks, Bendix brakes, and a double-walled fiberglass body (see Exhibit 10).

In interviews with the casewriter, Mr. Ruger and Mr. Nolan, vice president, marketing, described the rationale and events leading to the company's efforts in this area. Mr. Ruger explained:

> I've always been interested in cars and motorcycles since I was young. I've tinkered around with a number of cars, including Jaguars, Rolls Royces, and Ferraris. In the process, I noticed that there was a lot of overlap between guns and cars among purchasers. I felt that a well-known reputation for quality and engineering design in guns would be useful in selling a particular type of car; hopefully, the name Ruger would correlate the two. I also felt I had some insight into what people would like to have in cars. I thought we could come up with a beautifully engineered car that we could sell at a profit.

Mr. Nolan indicated the automotive project was in line with Mr.Ruger's skills and interests in engineering and design which had made the company successful in guns.

> Bill had a love for engineering and design in everything, particularly cars. When we used to go to lunch and I would stop for gas, Bill would get out and look underneath the cars on the racks. After he bought one Bentley, I remembered he set up a guy in a garage to work on it. We would go to lunch and then stop by the garage afterwards; Cal always kept a second slide board, and before you knew it, Bill had his coat off and was banging around underneath the car and talking about it for hours with Cal. I started taking work with me to lunch because I knew we would wind up at the garage.

Two prototypes of the Ruger Tourer were built at a cost of approximately $400,000 for design and development. Those prototypes were displayed at various auto shows, including the New York Automobile Show, and received the attention of several widely read car magazines. In the December 1970 issue of *Motor Trend,* a feature article discussed the Ruger car and the man behind it:

> Bill Ruger won't fit on anybody's bar-chart, nor will his car jibe with any bean-counter's forecast of what's happening in the world of personal transportation. He's made a fortune designing and building firearms that combine the elements of nostalgia, classical good taste and faultless function with reasonable price—and he's flown in the face of doubting "experts" and conventional wisdom at every stage of his upward climb. Therefore, it's no surprise that he's decided to build and sell a car that combines these same principles, despite the doubts and chuckling disapproval of entrenched automotive nay-sayers.

EXHIBIT 10

". . . when cars and car makers seem to be tumbling off assembly-lines with a desperate dreary sameness, a kind of cookie-cutter uniformity, a little outrageous automotive non-conformity may be just what the doctor ordered."

It was a Bentley Vanden Plas that provided the inspiration for the Ruger Tourer. The body is double-walled fiberglass reinforced at stress and attachment points with bonded-in steel pieces. The floor, battery box are molded in as well.

Source: Reprinted from December 1970 *Motor Trends*.

Bill Ruger, then, is not of the common herd. He is the product of another time, a different environment. He is more like the merchant-princes of the Italian Renaissance or the go-getter nobility of Victoria's reign than today's interchangeable captains of industry. His collections of art and antique arms are remarkable, and he has steeped himself in history and the classical lore of the gentle folk.

It's been remarked that nothing of redeeming social value has ever been devised in committee, and Ruger's success would seem to bear this out. His firm, Sturm, Ruger & Company recently went public and now has a proper board of directors and all the other trappings of a modern manufacturing concern. What's more, there are a number of Ruger heirs and relations scattered through the company's hierarchy. Yet one cannot visit either of his two factories—one in Southport, Connecticut, and the other in Newport, New Hampshire—without the feeling that the company and all its products are cast exclusively in the image of William B. Ruger himself. Ayn Rand would have loved him.

In this sense, one is reminded forcefully of other, similar business enterprises headed by the likes of Ettore Bugatti and Enzo Ferrari. Ruger resembles Bugatti in the way his products are so profoundly influenced by his personal tastes and enthusiasms, and he's like Ferrari in that he's been able to make it pay handsomely.

He has owned a fair fleet of exotic automobiles over the years, and though his automotive buying habits have been quite catholic—spanning the distance from a Pontiac GTO or a Plymouth Hemi to classic Bentley and Rolls-Royces, salted liberally with Jaguars and MGs and God knows what else—his true loves are more sharply defined. For instance, right now he owns three Ferraris, a Land Rover, a Mercedes-Benz 6.3 sedan (for his wife) and a 4.5 liter Bentley Vanden Plas tourer built in 1929.

Over the eight-year period from 1965–73, the company attempted to assess the realistic potential for the Ruger car. These efforts included the preparation of an extremely comprehensive and detailed production and financial plan by Ernst and Ernst.[9] However, in 1974 the following statement appeared in the company's 1973 annual report:

> In previous reports, I have mentioned the company's automotive project with great pride and enthusiasm. During the past year we have been reassessing our position in connection with this project. After weighing all the alternatives, in view particularly of the current stringent requirements for antipollution devices and the marked trend for compact, high mileage per gallon automobiles, it was reluctantly decided to abandon this project. This is a substantial disappointment in view of the time and money expended, but our decision is undoubtedly correct.

Mr. Ruger commented to the casewriter:

> I really felt this car would sell, but unfortunately we got a very ambiguous market reception. Then there was also a mechanical problem in the steering which caused the car to drift. This blasted some confidence in the car. We finally decided to abandon the program in 1973.

---

[9] This plan projected required sales of approximately 180 cars per year for the company to show a profit on automobile business.

STURM, RUGER & COMPANY, INC., IN 1974

Product policy

In 1974 Sturm, Ruger manufactured several basic models of pistols, revolvers, and rifles for a variety of sporting purposes. In addition to its sporting guns, police revolvers were added to the company's product line in 1969. A program was also underway to develop and manufacture shotguns and a carbine for law enforcement and military use.

The keynotes of Mr. Ruger's product policy were design quality and purchaser utility. Mr. Ruger emphasized that his guns "appealed primarily to hunters and sportsmen who demanded exceptional performance." In the 1973 annual report to stockholders, Mr. Ruger elaborated on this subject:

> The demand for our entire range of firearms continues to be highly gratifying. These products which have achieved market leadership continue to grow in popularity, while our newer products appear to be rapidly gaining the recognition we hoped for.
>
> Our products are engineered and produced to the highest possible standards of quality and performance. It is, therefore, not surprising that we have a growing share of the market for firearms, and that we have enthusiastic supporters among all categories of users. Our identification with quality manufacturing and unique engineering capability is the result of 20 years of constant effort.

All of the company's guns were sold under the name "Ruger," and while they were not subject to annual design change, the company's policy was to strive for product improvements. Many of the guns were available in varying models for different cartridge calibers, ranging from .22 caliber to .44 magnum and .458 magnum. Some were also manufactured in such special finishes as stainless steel to appeal to particular market segments or geographic areas, for example, gun collectors, performers, and/or to individuals in areas where heat and humidity were a problem.

Handguns.   Pistols and revolvers accounted for approximately 62 percent of the company's sales in 1973 (see Exhibit 11). In total, 248,337 units were sold for an average manufacturer's price of $48.85 in 1973. Distributor pricing ranged from $34.80 to $84.95. The basic retail prices ranged from $61.75 for a standard target pistol to $152.50 for a Security-Six Stainless Steel Magnum.

Rifles.   Rifles and carbines accounted for roughly 34 percent of the company's 1973 sales. The company sold 143,526 of the four basic models in 1973. Prices to distributors ranged from $40.93 to $148.02. The basic retail price ranged from $66 for a .22 rifle to $265 for a Number One Single Shot Rifle (see Exhibit 12).

In addition to guns, Sturm, Ruger also sold component parts and accessories for and with its guns. These included extra revolver cylinders, maga-

EXHIBIT 11

	Product breakdown				
	1969 ($000)	1970 ($000)	1971 ($000)	1972 ($000)	1973 ($000)
Handguns:					
Sales	$7,768	$9,375	$8,813	$10,621	$12,132
Percent total sales	70%	73%	66%	66%	62%
Income before taxes	$3,464	$4,002	$3,283	$ 3,501	$ 3,995
Percent total income before taxes	82%	86%	113%	83%	74%
Rifles:					
Sales	$3,062	$3,074	$3,896	$ 4,913	$ 6,618
Percent total sales	28%	24%	29%	30%	34%
Income before taxes	$ 611	$ 527	$ (538)	$ 431	$ 1,058
Percent total income before taxes	15%	11%	(19%)	10%	19%
Parts and service:					
Sales	$ 260	$ 340	$ 609	$ 649	$ 791
Percent total sales	2%	3%	5%	4%	4%
Income before taxes	$ 132	$ 149	$ 158	$ 290	$ 382
Percent total income before taxes	3%	3%	6%	7%	7%

STURM, RUGER & COMPANY, INC.
Pine Tree Castings Division
Profit and Loss Statement

	Six months ended June 30, 1973	Six months ended June 30, 1974
Net sales	$2,101,459	$2,304,409
Cost of goods sold	930,513	1,104,264
Operating profit	$1,170,946	$1,200,145
Expenses:		
Selling	$ 10,938	$ 16,611
General and administrative	11,460	13,542
Total expenses	22,398	$ 30,153
Income (loss) before taxes	$1,148,548	$1,169,992

zines for selected rifles and pistols, telescope mounting rings, and panels for handguns. Sales of these accessories and related services accounted for approximately 4 percent of total revenues and amounted to $791,128 in 1973.

Marketing

Sturm, Ruger competed, through one or more of its various models, with the active domestic and foreign arms industry. Most of its competitors, such as Colt, Remington, Savage, and Winchester, were older, larger, and better known, but Mr. Ruger stressed that his company sought to compete by con-

EXHIBIT 12

Models and prices of Ruger firearms*

	Suggested retail price list	Dealer price (tax inc.)	Net distributor price	Distributor price (fed. tax inc.)

Pistols:

1. Standard model: This was the company's original product and was designed for target shooting and small game hunting.

Lowest priced model	$61.75	$46.93	$34.80	$38.28
Highest priced model	66.90	50.84	37.70	41.47

Mark 1 target model: A refined version of the standard model and was intended for formal, competitive target shooting.

Lowest priced model	$78.50	$59.66	$44.24	$48.66
Highest priced model	83.45	63.42	47.03	51.73

Revolvers:

3. New model super Single-Six: Designed in 1952, it was modeled after the .45 caliber Colt Army model of 1873 and was intended to capture the flavor of the Old West. Intended for use as an informal target or hunting gun, the Single-Six was the most expensive single-action .22 on the market. When sold with an extra cylinder for the use of .22 magnum cartridge, it was called the Single-Six Convertible.

Lowest priced model	$ 92.25	$ 71.30	$53.34	$58.55
Highest priced model	143.85	111.20	83.00	91.30

4. New model Blackhawk: Blackhawk revolvers were essentially enlarged Single-Six revolvers and were made for the most powerful handgun cartridge available, such as the .357 magnum, the .44 magnum, .41 magnum, and the .30 caliber cartridge. These guns were intended for informal target shooting and hunting.

Lowest priced model	$119.75	$ 91.01	$67.49	$74.24
Highest priced model	148.50	112.86	83.69	92.06

5. Security-Six—Double Action: These weapons were designed for police and law enforcement use.

Lowest priced model	$102.00	$ 77.52	$57.49	$63.24
Highest priced model	152.50	115.90	85.95	94.55

6. Speed-Six—Double Action: A smaller, lighter revolver, the Speed-Six was intended for use in police work.

Lowest priced model	$102.00	$77.52	$57.49	$63.24
Highest priced model	120.00	91.20	67.63	74.39

7. Old Army (Cap & Ball): This firearm was intended for target shooting and hunting.

Lowest priced model	$125.00	$ 95.00	$70.45	$77.50
Highest priced model	140.00	106.40	78.90	86.79

Rifles:

8. Model 10/22: Purported to be one of the most popular .22 rifles on the market, the 10/22 was intended for use in informal target shooting and small game hunting.

Lowest priced model	$66.00	$49.50	$36.87	$40.93
Highest priced model	77.50	56.58	42.18	46.82

9. Model .44 carbine: A short, light self-loading firearm, the .44 magnum carbine was designed particularly for deer hunting in heavily wooded areas.

EXHIBIT 12 (continued)

	Suggested retail price list	Dealer price (tax inc.)	Net distributor price	Distributor price (fed. tax inc.)
Lowest priced model	$131.56	$ 99.94	$73.44	$81.52
Highest priced model	134.50	102.22	75.12	83.38

10. M77 bolt action: The M77 was designed primarily for large game hunting.

Lowest priced model	$193.00	$144.75	$107.79	$119.65
Highest priced model	278.30	208.73	155.43	172.53

11. Single-shot rifle: Conceived as a luxury product, the single shot was a high-powered rifle meeting a wide range of requirements including hunting and target shooting.

Lowest priced model	$165.00	$123.75	$ 92.16	$102.30
Highest priced model	265.00	198.75	148.02	164.30

---

* Prices shown are for highest priced and lowest priced guns of each model. Other models with variations such as longer barrels, walnut panels, or stainless steel were available at prices within the two price limits.
Source: Company's distributor price list.

centrating on limited lines of high-quality products and building in unique qualities into his guns. Although Mr. Ruger believed that pricing was often competitive, he indicated that price was not a major factor for many of his guns:

> Some of our models are price competitive, but many have unique qualities which enable us to get a premium price. For example, in our single-shot rifle, we have no major competitors, so competitive pricing is not a prime factor and we peg the price up considerably more than we do with a high volume product like our 10/22.

The company sold its products throughout the United States, Canada, and several other countries. Management, however, estimated that foreign sales represented less than 10 percent of the company's business. According to Mr. Ruger, foreign sales had considerable potential in spite of the company's relatively small share of foreign sales. As he explained:

> In foreign markets, we are almost unknown, although foreign governments and law enforcement groups prefer American revolvers. To my knowledge, there is no quality revolver made in Europe, so there is little foreign competition. Primary competition in foreign markets would come from Smith and Wesson, which is selling a lot of revolvers abroad and is quite well known.

Sales of the company's product were promoted by advertising in national magazines and assorted firearms specialty magazines, for example, *Outdoor Life*, the *Rifleman*, and *Field and Stream*. Mr. Nolan, vice president, marketing, indicated that approximately $250,000 was spent on advertising in 1973 to keep the ultimate consumer familiar with Ruger guns.

Because the company's firearms were used primarily for hunting and target shooting, sales records indicated that sales tended to be highest in nonurban areas and in the Southeast and Southwest. Rifle sales were greatest in the period from July to November in anticipation of the fall hunting seasons, while handgun sales were fairly constant throughout the year. A one-year warranty against defective materials and workmanship were extended to retail purchasers of all its products. Through 1973, Sturm, Ruger had not been required to expend material amounts of money as a result of warranty claims. Mr. Nolan commented:

> We emphasize service and quality, and there is a place in this industry for a company with good service. We also make a better product, and at a better price than the competition.

Mr. Nolan, who had joined the company in 1956 when the company's sales approximated $1.8 million, went on to state:

> Year in and year out, the market for guns is pretty static. I would estimate that the total market for guns is about 15 million people. If we are to grow in this static market, we have to win some market share away from competition.
>
> Because of this static market, I think our future is definitely in long-guns. In fact, our sales ratio has begun to change slightly; for the first six months of 1974 ending in June, our sales mix was roughly 54 percent handguns versus 46 percent for rifles, compared to a ratio of about 64 percent for handguns the previous year. That's a major shift. Keep in mind our total sales were up.

Distribution and sales

Distribution of the company's products was accomplished through a group of approximately 160 wholesale distributors in 43 states. These distributors varied in size from an organization with 1 salesperson in the field to an organization with over 300 salespersons calling on retailers. Approximately 48 percent of the distributors were hardware specialists, 26 percent were sporting goods distributors, and the remaining 26 percent were composed of firearms specialty distributors and chain stores. These distributors supplied several thousand retailers. The company did not sell directly to retailers nor to the ultimate user, directly or by mail order. No salespersons or field representatives were employed by the company. Contact with the distributors was maintained by correspondence, telephone, and personal visits by company executives.

At the beginning of each year, Sturm, Ruger requested "firm" annual orders from its distributors, although the company usually allowed them to reasonably adjust their orders throughout the year. At the end of the year, Sturm, Ruger canceled all outstanding unfilled orders and asked the distributors to place new orders. The company's outstanding unfilled orders from dealers/distributors on March 1, 1974, were $37,651,000 as compared to approximately $21,599,000 on March 1, 1973. Management indicated that the company would be able to produce and ship a large part of these orders during 1974, but not all. It was also management's belief that 10 percent to 15 percent of these orders were inflated as customers wanted to ensure receiving an adequate supply of Ruger guns.

New markets

Mr. Ruger had decided to develop several new products for new markets in light of several environmental and market trends. In 1969 the company had introduced a revolver designed for law enforcement use (Exhibit 13). Development and marketing of a shotgun and a police/military firearm was also underway, with the latter two products scheduled for introduction in 1974. The shotgun was expected to retail at about $400 with roughly 60 percent going to Sturm, Ruger. John Kingsley, executive vice president, indicated that the company had high hopes for its shotgun and that as many as 50,000 units might be sold over a two- to three-year period after initial introduction. Mr. Ruger indicated that the marketing of the police revolver posed some new problems for the company. He stated:

> We put out our first police revolver in the late 1960s. Ed Nolan had come to me and said "Let's put out one." We did so, but it's just starting to become a significant contributor to our sales. The cost of the product is high so that the product is less profitable. The police revolver line presently constitutes less than 10 percent of our business.
>
> We have to approach the law enforcement market and government market differently than we do the consumer market. With consumers, you are involved with many buyers, with many different tastes, often looking for unique and new products. In the law enforcement and government market, we have to deal with purchasing agents who want items they are familiar with. They are not interested in new and innovative products. These markets, however, can produce large sales. Our strategy will have to be to seek an opportunity to see technical purchasers and attempt to familiarize them with our guns before bids are given out. Then when we submit a bid, our products won't be new to the purchasing agent.

Development of these products had also been influenced by some concern with the possible threat of gun control legislation. Mr. Ruger discussed his concerns:

> There is a lot of talk about gun controls, but the real question is whether laws will make it more difficult for individuals to own firearms. Unfortunately, the trend is for people to be more and more supervised by government, which is a personal abbreviation of personal liberties. There's an old saying that "a country that would pass a law like Prohibition can't be trusted." Democracy, I'm afraid, is an unpredictable beast. All of this has

EXHIBIT 13

RUGER®
SECURITY-SIX®
DOUBLE ACTION REVOLVER

CROSS SECTION VIEW

FIELD-STRIPPED VIEW

STURM, RUGER & CO., INC.
Southport, Connecticut, U.S.A.

© 1972 - STURM, RUGER & CO., INC.

given rise to a slight fear on my part that we might be legislated out of business. Enactment of laws like those *requiring* people to fasten seat belts before they can drive their cars suggests that a bureaucratic process might develop a restriction on firearms.

I still regard firearms legislation as remote. People do want the right to defend themselves, and they have a right, a God-given right, to do so. Still, we have begun to diversify our product line so that the focus of gun control will not completely dominate our sales. We have moved rather quickly but carefully to develop the shotgun and the Mini 14, which is a Ruger version of the Army M14 rifle. What we want to do is have our long-guns successful but have our handguns continue to grow. Therefore, if our handgun business were lost, it would cause some problem to shrink this company, but we would still have a strong position in long-guns.

Mr. Nolan also commented on this issue:

Legislation would have definite impact on our industry, but as long as we continue to make a quality product, the world will still want our guns.

Overall, I am very optimistic and realistic about our future growth and rate of growth. We are still young and unknown by millions of people who buy guns. We're young and ambitious, and we make decisions our large and lethargic competitors can't make because of committees. They also don't innovate or have a Bill Ruger.

We can march into areas that companies already make guns for, because if Bill Ruger makes it, everyone knows it will be good. We're presently making a film about Bill because when Bill has finished designing, he will have contributed more to the state of the art and exceeded the productivity of John Browning or any other gun designer.

Mr. Ruger also stated:

We have done nothing to frustrate gun control laws other than to testify against some which purported to control guns but also abbreviated the right of citizens to own guns. Unfortunately, most of these proposals don't have an effective screening mechanism to differentiate between the criminal and the responsible citizen. As a shooter, I also oppose proposals that would give local police chiefs discretionary authority on the issuance of firearm permits; they are simply not trained to do this and end up denying permits to everyone.

Research and development

During fiscal 1973, Sturm, Ruger spent approximately $146,664 on material research activities relating to the development of new products and the improvements of existing products. Approximately four employees engaged in research and development activities, but it was generally acknowledged that Mr. Ruger was an integral part of the company's design, engineering, and research activities. All work was conducted under his personal supervision. Research expenditures were charged to expense in the year incurred.

Mr. Kingsley, executive vice president, indicated "that R&D had generally been less than 2 percent of sales."

Primarily through Mr. Ruger's efforts, the company owned approximately 20 patents and trademarks. Management indicated that none of these patents were considered basic to any important product or manufacturing process of the company.

Production and manufacturing

Manufacturing of the company's guns took place in its plant facilities in Southport, Connecticut, and Newport, New Hampshire. The Southport plant contained approximately 33,000 square feet on the ground floor, of which approximately 26,000 square feet was devoted to manufacturing operations and the balance was used for office, shipping, and warehousing facilities. The plant was located on a 2⅓-acre site near the Connecticut Turnpike. During 1970 a second story was added, giving approximately 2,-200 square feet of office and design space.

In a tour of the Southport headquarters and plant, the casewriter observed that the plant appeared to be fully utilized. Many offices looked out onto the shop floor, which was clean, well organized, and crowded. There appeared to be little room for expansion unless the employee parking lot was eliminated.

The Newport plant, located on 8½ acres of land, contained approximately 114,000 square feet, of which approximately 6,000 square feet was office, shipping, and warehouse space. Approximately 40,000 square feet of the building was occupied by the company's Pine Tree Castings Division which manufactured steel investment castings. Approximately 4 acres of land had been acquired in the rear of the plant for expansion, and an additional 60,000 square foot manufacturing plant was scheduled for completion by the end of 1974 to handle expected demand for the shotgun and other new products.

Many of the parts used in the company's products were readily available from several outside suppliers. The company purchased a great majority of its rifle barrels, but equipment to produce a portion of this requirement had been installed at the Newport plant, and some barrels were produced there. The company produced its own walnut and other wood stocks in its woodshop in the New Hampshire plant. The wood used was purchased from several domestic suppliers.

Mr. Ruger indicated that the company's production methods and facilities were probably the equal of any in the industry. He was supported in this assertion by an article in *The Wall Street Journal* which described Sturm, Ruger's manufacturing operation:

> Production methods have also changed relatively little over the years, remaining highly dependent on hand labor with little automation. The gun

industry "has tended to be a little slower than other industries to change," says William Ruger, president of Sturm, Ruger.

Indeed, there isn't even a moving assembly line in Ruger's Southport plant. In one area, machinists and other technicians turn out gun frames and other parts. Elsewhere, men seated at tables spread out batches of parts and assemble them into complete revolvers. In a small room off to one side, the weapons are test-fired on a miniature target range by two men wearing soundproof earmuffs.[10]

The Pine Tree Castings Division, formerly a subsidiary, produced high-quality steel investment castings for use in the firm's guns. Although 90 percent of the division's output was consumed by Sturm, Ruger, management felt that Pine Tree had the capability to develop substantial outside business. One view was expressed by Mr. Kingsley:

> Our Pine Tree operation is an excellent opportunity for diversification. This operation makes plumbing valves, firearms components, and metal pieces of all sizes and shapes. Although only 10 percent of Pine Tree's output presently goes to the outside, I would like to see Pine Tree do 50 percent of its sales with outside customers.
>
> Although coordination and integration is somewhat of a current problem, I don't think a major management restructuring will be required to expand Pine Tree's operation. However, our management structure is pretty thin now. Bill's philosophy has always been to have as low overhead as possible and try to put as much personnel as possible on the production side.

Mr. Ruger also commented:

> Our Pine Tree Castings Division offers a range of diversification possibilities. It can manufacture plumbing valves, high-strength metal parts, bits for bridles, and hardware for saddles. Boats, for example, also have created a demand for equipment made of stainless steel and investment castings.
>
> The big question with our Pine Tree situation is the need to develop a strong marketing and sales organization. We currently use sales reps, and our outside orders are rather informal. In fact, it's basically a New England market. In the long run we are going to have to develop a national sales force if we are going to build a substantial outside market for Pine Tree. We might even have local sales offices or even go the route of having multiple plants.

Finance

The initial financing of Sturm, Ruger & Company, Inc., had been $50,-000 provided by Alexander Sturm. By year-end fiscal 1973, retained earnings accumulated throughout the years had built the net worth to $16,285,372.

---

[10] *The Wall Street Journal,* May 31, 1972.

In September 1974, Sturm, Ruger had approximately 900 stockholders as a result of a public offering in 1969. This public offering resulted in the sale of a total of 330,264 shares to the public at a price of $14 per share, with net proceeds to the selling stockholders of $13.05 per share. Mr. Ruger sold 264,000 shares, and the daughter of his deceased partner sold 66,264 shares. As explained by Mr. Ruger, the decision to make a public offering in 1969 was influenced by other alternatives.

> In 1968 I was approached by a major conglomerate who offered me $28 million for the company. At that time I owned 1,320,000 shares, or about 80 percent of the outstanding shares; the other 20 percent was owned by Joanna Sturm. I considered this offer, which was basically a stock deal, and would have been based on bottom line and volumes performance for a specified period, but the alternative was to go public. I chose the latter alternative since it enabled me personally to diversify my assets. After the public offering, I didn't have all my own eggs in one basket and I was still free to operate the company with my own philosophy.

As of September 18, 1974, the company's stock was traded in the over-the-counter (OTC) market at a selling price of 6¾ bid, 7¾ asked.[11] Mr. Ruger owned approximately 906,000 shares out of a total of 1,651,320 shares outstanding; an additional 50,000 shares were owned by William Ruger, Jr.

Commenting on the company's financial posture, Mr. Kingsley noted:

> We've been fortunate to not have to use any outside financing, and in the future we plan to finance our expansion internally. A key to this will be our ability to manage our inventories more judiciously. I think, however, we can grow and still maintain our net profit margins at about 15 percent of sales.

Personnel

In 1973 the company employed approximately 250 persons in its Southport plant, 356 in the Newport plant, and 88 in its Pine Tree Castings Division. Approximately six of the individuals at the Southport headquarters and three at the Newport facility were listed as "executive."

None of the employees of the company or of Pine Tree were represented by a labor union, although a union drive had been attempted during the summer of 1974. The scheduled elections were never held. Mr. Ruger commented on the company's labor relations policies:

> On three occasions, unions have tried to organize our shop. I must admit, I've always felt that if a union came in, I would take it personally, as it would mean I had been a little foolish and had done something wrong. I've

---

[11] *The Wall Street Journal*, September 19, 1974.

always felt that men should work hard and be paid well without the need for a union.

We just had a union drive, but the union backed down before the election. Our campaign against the union was not really a campaign; it was sort of a review of our labor relations in the past. We basically argued that we have a proven record.

Management and organization

Although no organization chart existed, the casewriter learned that the key managers and executives at the Southport headquarters reported directly to Mr. Ruger; these included the executive vice president, the vice president of marketing, and the vice president of manufacturing of the Southport operation. Also reporting directly to Mr. Ruger were the vice presidents of sales for the Pine Tree Castings Division and of manufacturing at the Newport plant. Mr. Ruger and other members of management indicated that he deeply involved himself in all aspects of the company's operations.

The executive vice president, John Kingsley, had joined the company in 1971 after serving as a consultant to Mr. Ruger. Mr. Ruger indicated that Mr. Kingsley, a Harvard MBA, and former investment banker and a CPA, was brought in to help bolster the company's management structure, particularly in finance and planning. He added:

> John came in at a particularly necessary time as Walter Berger, our secretary and controller, was retiring. However, we were also a public company by then, and we needed to do things a little more openly and improve our reporting to the public. In addition to his title of executive vice president, John is primarily responsible for financial matters.

Other members of management included Edward Nolan, vice president of marketing, who had joined the company in 1956. Prior to coming to Sturm, Ruger, Mr. Nolan had been a district sales manager with Winchester. William B. Ruger, Jr., was also employed in the firm. He had formerly been the vice president of manufacturing at the Southport plant, and was now involved in other areas of the company. Mr. Ruger commented:

> Bill, Jr., now has more of a planning function in the company. This gives him an overview which he should have as he may eventually be president. My son-in-law, Steve Vogel, is also with us, and is responsible for developing government sales.

Mr. Kingsley, 42 years old, and William Ruger, Jr., 34, were both directors of the company. Other directors included William B. Ruger, Sr.; Townsend Hornor, first vice president of White, Weld and Co., Inc.; Frank L. McCann, president of Mohawk Aluminum Corporation; Norman K. Parsells, a senior partner of Marsh, Day & Calhoun; Richard Kilcullen, member of Bathe, Fowler, Lidstone, Jaffin, Pierie & Kheel; Lester A. Casler, partner of Little & Casler; and Hale Seagraves, former partner of Pennie, Edmonds, Morton, Taylor & Adams.

A VIEW TOWARD THE FUTURE

As Mr. Ruger articulated the future opportunities and potential problems for his company in 1974, he commented on the start of the company and his philosophy. When the casewriter asked what had contributed to the success of his company, Mr. Ruger replied as follows:

> I think my being extremely familiar and identifying with gun enthusiasts, hunters, and sportsmen has been one very important factor. This was our market, and I have been fortunate to design guns that appealed to their technical and esthetic needs. But I've often thought about another very important factor over the years. At the time I started this company, my confidence was shaken. Everything I had tried had failed. I wasn't sure I had the qualities to be an entrepreneur. As I look back, I was perfectly qualified. I had a mix of interest, experience, and health. In my first business, I think I failed because I didn't think everything through. I had focused on the creative side of the business and not enough on the management side; both have to be of interest if you want to succeed.
>
> You've also got to love money to be an entrepreneur. My uncle, who was on the wealthy side of my family, used to say: "The way you keep score is by how much money you make. When you see a successful company, making money, it means they are making something that people want."

Mr. Ruger indicated, however, that environmental and market circumstances posed entirely new and different problems than had been encountered by the company in the past. The most immediate threat to the company's principal business appeared to be the various pending gun laws. Mr. Ruger voiced his views and concerns as follows:

> Unfortunately, politicians and newspapers who are talking about this issue don't have any knowledge of what they are talking about. Of course I think there should be some controls of maniacs and irresponsible people getting guns, but as I told the governor of New Hampshire, people should be licensed, not guns. Unfortunately, you have people like some of the editors on the *Boston Globe* who have personal biases, but their views are not universal beliefs. I and quite a few other people believe that there is some truth in those bumper stickers that say, "If guns are outlawed, only outlaws will have guns." Besides, if people didn't have guns, they would use sticks, stones, or some other instrument to injure others.

In light of these concerns, Mr. Ruger felt that broadening the company's base of products and achieving some measure of diversification was in order. Diversification, however, as seen by both Mr. Ruger and Mr. Kingsley, required some relationship to the company's skills and resources. Mr. Kingsley commented:

> We have looked at a few acquisitions; for example, we recently looked at an instrument company with sales of a little over $1 million and net profits at about 10 percent. We decided not to follow through, however. If we eventually do purchase another company, it will have to have a sound and strong management team. I don't rule out some potential acquisitions, but I don't see us becoming a mini conglomerate.
>
> Still, diversification is an issue for us. Bill considers the new Mini 14 and shotguns to be a part of our diversification. I think he's right, but I don't think the marketplace will ever change the multiple on our stock because we develop a new gun. I would basically like to see us with an earnings tripod: (1) guns; (2) castings from Pine Tree; and (3) some other type of operations, preferably metal manufacturing. I don't, for example, see us in fast foods.

Mr. Ruger also discussed the issue of acquisitions:

> We have taken a concentrated look at a few companies but have never seen one that would be perfect for us. Our drive to diversify has been compromised by our need to exploit the businesses that we are in. It dawned on me during the car project that we needed to spend more time on the gun industry.

In looking at the company's future organizational needs, Mr. Kingsley made the following observations:

> A key question is whether this company can be transformed from an extension of a man to a professionally managed company. Bill has been 100 percent responsible for the success of the company, and whether the company will ever reach the point where Bill Ruger is not the most important factor is an open question. With our new guns, Bill thinks that our sales will exceed $40 million in the near future. The biggest problem thus will be to take a step up the growth curve, and do so profitably.

Mr. Ruger, in speaking of the future, expressed the following thoughts:

> Although we've done extremely well in guns, the gun industry won't grow dramatically. Hunting never was a mass sport. One man needs a lot of land to wander over and that land is getting pretty scarce. Technology won't influence the industry much, either, as technical innovations in this industry are few. Our own growth in guns will have to result from continually seeking increased market share, but that becomes more difficult as you get larger.
>
> Over the long run, however, I would like to bring the company up to a point where it's well established in all areas of the gun business, including government business. I would also like to see Pine Tree with an established outside market and a good management structure. If we get much bigger, I would also like to see a little more vertical integration.

Overall, I would like to remain essentially the same company, but with twice our present sales. There might be a unique event, such as a merger with a big company, but I like my job and am proud of what I'm doing. I'm proud of this company. I think a job or a career should always have a tie-in with your interests. I could never understand how anyone could make a career of working for Procter & Gamble selling soap. With this company, I feel like an artist or writer; just because you've painted a good picture or written a good book you don't stop. It's the interest that counts. However (pointing to a picture on the wall behind him that showed barrels overflowing with dollar bills), when I get too involved in my work, that picture is there to remind me of what I'm here for.

section 2

Establishing
objectives and
formulating strategies
for accomplishment

POLICY
FORMULATION

case 4

Note on the mechanical writing instrument industry

> Competition in this industry is fierce. Materials and labor costs keep rising, and prices keep falling. The situation is a terrible headache, but new companies keep appearing because it's a high-growth market. They're willing to take the risk. As long as there is one firm making it, they think they can, too.
>
> MR. FRANK KING
> Executive Vice President
> Writing Instrument Manufacturers Association

The mechanical writing instrument industry involved the manufacture and sale of four basic product types: fountain pens, ball-point pens, soft-tip pens,[1] and mechanical pencils, and their component parts.[2] Each product was introduced in the marketplace to meet a new and specific writing need, rather than to replace an existing product. The fountain pen, for example, was traditionally used in signing documents and letters, while the ball-point pen was used in making carbon copies, the soft-tip pen in marking and underlining, and the mechanical pencils in working with figures.

In 1973 approximately 200 companies were engaged in the manufacture and sale of mechanical writing instruments, of which 131 made refillable ball-point pens, 102 nonrefillable ball-point pens, 22 ordinary fountain pens, 16 cartridge-filled fountain pens, 78 thick-line markers, 99 fine-line porous pens, and 85 mechanical pencils. It was uncommon for firms to manufacture all of the four basic product types. Most firms competed selectively in the industry on the basis of (1) product type—fountain pen, ball-point pen, soft-tip pen, and mechanical pencil; (2) price range—low (< 50 cents), medium (50 cents–$1), and high (> $1); and (3) market—retail, commercial, advertising/specialty, premium, export, government, and military.

---

[1] *Soft-tip pens* were defined as broad-line felt-tip markers and fine-line porous-point pens.

[2] Wooden pencils were customarily considered as a separate industry, the nonmechanical writing instrument industry. The 1973 annual growth rate in manufacturers' dollar sales was 2 percent.

HISTORY OF MECHANICAL WRITING INSTRUMENTS

Product evolution

The first writing instruments had their origins lost in antiquity but could be traced through drawings and crude messages smeared with natural-colored ore by a finger or scratched by a sharpened stone fragment onto cave walls. The first known instrument, the stylus, appeared around 3400 B.C., and was used to make impressions on wax and clay tablets. About 300 B.C., the Egyptians invented papyrus, the forerunner of modern paper and the standard medium for carrying the written word, which marked the beginning of the development of more sophisticated writing tools. Graphite, the main ingredient in the modern-day pencil, was introduced around 1400 A.D., the first fountain pen around 1650 A.D., and the mechanical pencil at the turn of the 20th century. The ball-point pen was introduced in 1945, the soft-tip pen in the mid-1960s, and the combination pen in 1969.[3] Proposed future writing instrument products are presented in the Appendix to this case.

Product life cycle

Mechanical writing instrument product types tended to follow these similar life cycle patterns in the marketplace:

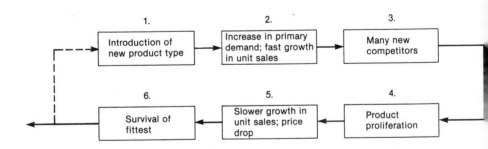

The one exception to this pattern was the fountain pen, whose average price increased relative to a decline in unit sales. As industry prices began to polarize into the high- and low-price ranges, the low-price/high-volume manufacturers tended to drop their fountain pen lines, which left only the high-price/low-volume manufacturers competing in that market.

Exhibits 1 to 5 present information on manufacturers' dollar sales, unit

---

[3] The combination pen had a rotating carbide ball point, which wrote with the flow of a marker using water-based ink, had the hard feel and carbon-making feature of a ball-point pen, and the overall feel and writing effect of a fountain pen.

EXHIBIT 1

Manufacturer's sales in dollars—by product

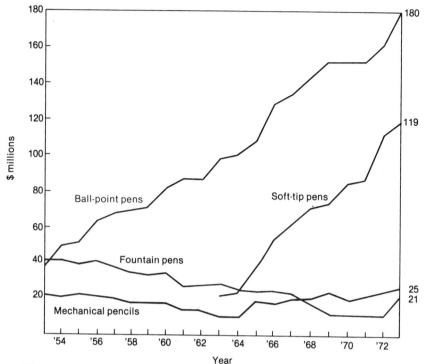

* Desk and pen sets not included.
Source: Writing Instrument Manufacturers Association.

sales, and average prices by product from 1954 through 1973. During that period, total dollar sales increased from $117.1 million to $353.3 million, total unit sales from 261.7 million to 2,342.4 million, and the average writing instrument price decreased from 45 cents to 15 cents.

The price war

The price war in the mechanical writing instrument industry began in the early 1960s with the overwhelming success of the BIC 19-cent stick pen. It was BIC Pen Corporation's objective "to place a generic name (BIC) on all the cheap no-name ball-point pens in the industry."[4] Using heavy advertising, BIC created the concept of the disposable pen as well as quantity selling in multipacks. By stimulating primary demand, BIC encouraged many other firms to enter the low-priced ball-point pen market, which rep-

---

[4] No-name products were those which were not advertised and were marketed at retail prices far below the comparable, inexpensive, nationally advertised products.

EXHIBIT 2
Unit sales—by product

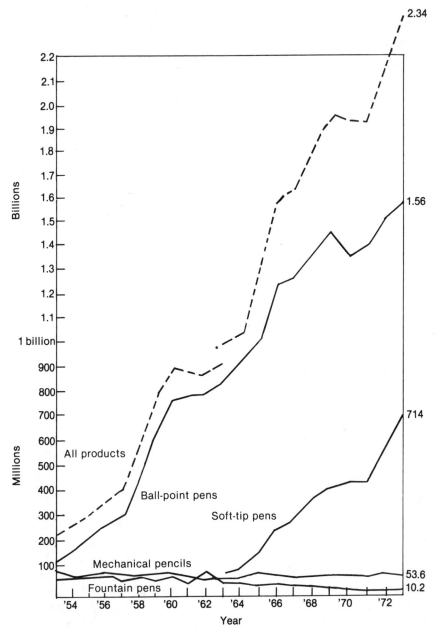

* Unit sales line for "All products" adjusted in 1963 to include soft-tip pens.
Source: Writing Instrument Manufacturers Association.

EXHIBIT 3
Average price—by product

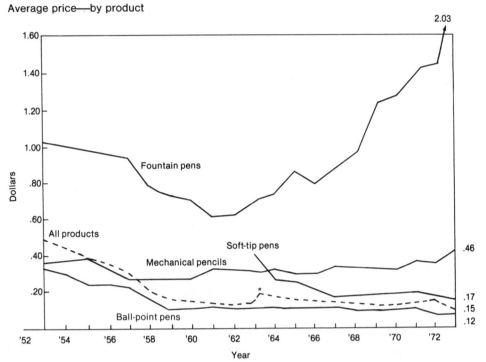

* All-product line adjusted in 1963 to include calculation for soft-tip pens.
Source: Writing Instrument Manufacturers Association.

resented the fastest growing segment of the mechanical writing instrument industry at the time. Several well-established writing instrument manufacturers, namely A. T. Cross, Sheaffer, and Parker, chose not to follow suit and continued to position their products in the high-price segment, where margins rather than sheer volume could be relied upon to produce profits.

The price war history repeated itself with soft-tip pens in the early 1970s. By 1973 industry officials believed that ball-point pen prices had fallen as far as they would go, although soft-tip pen prices were still dropping. The price wars were thought to be manufacturer imposed, particularly by high-volume producers such as BIC, rather than consumer influenced, which accounted for the fact that prices in the low-price market segment were never raised despite inflation. Almost all porous-point pens and 93 percent of all ball-point pens retailed for less than $1 each in 1973.

The competition

No single manufacturer dominated the mechanical writing instrument industry in 1973. Rather, individual manufacturers dominated specific in-

EXHIBIT 4

Mechanical writing instrument industry statistics
(dollars and units in millions)

	Estimated number of units shipped	Estimated total $ value at factory prices (exclusive of tax)	Estimated number of units shipped	Estimated total $ value at factory prices (exclusive of tax)
	1954		1955	
Fountain pens	40.3	$ 41.7	40.8	$ 40.2
Ball-point pens	162.0	48.9	210.7	50.6
Mechanical pencils	57.6	22.0	55.8	22.5
Desk and dip-pen sets	1.8	4.5	2.3	4.8
	261.7	$117.1	309.6	$118.1
	1959		1960	
Fountain pens	44.3	$ 33.5	48.7	$ 35.1
Ball-point pens	657.2	71.0	761.9	81.6
Soft-tip pens*				
Mechanical pencils	63.8	18.8	60.1	18.7
Desk and dip-pen sets	8.1	5.0	4.1	3.7
	773.5	$128.3	874.8	$139.1
	1964		1965	
Fountain pens	33.1	$ 25.4	27.8	$ 24.2
Ball-point pens†	914.7	100.7	1,051.5	106.8
Refillable				
Nonrefillable				
Soft-tip pens*	86.5	22.8		
Markers (thick line)			75.2	22.1
Porous-point pens			82.5	15.2
Mechanical pencils	47.2	16.0	64.0	18.9
Desk and dip-pen sets	2.2	3.3	10.7	5.0
	1,083.7	$168.2	1,311.7	$192.2
	1969		1970	
Fountain pens	12.3	$ 16.0	10.2	$ 15.2
Ball-point pens:				
Refillable	761.3	94.1	685.5	92.7
Nonrefillable	686.3	58.7	700.3	59.8
Markers (thick line)	116.8	26.8	105.1	25.4
Porous-point pens	304.1	50.3	334.5	58.9
Mechanical pencils	65.5	22.3	57.8	20.1
Desk and dip-pen sets	7.2	10.3	5.6	7.0
	1,953.5	$278.5	1,899.0	$279.1

* No sales breakdown until 1965.
† No sales breakdown until 1967.
Source: Annual estimates compiled by Writing Instrument Manufacturers Association.

Estimated number of units shipped	Estimated total $ value at factory prices (exclusive of tax)	Estimated number of units shipped	Estimated total $ value at factory prices (exclusive of tax)	Estimated number of units shipped	Estimated total $ value at factory prices (exclusive of tax)
1956		1957		1958	
42.8	$ 41.5	40.9	$ 38.2	44.9	$ 35.0
265.9	63.5	300.5	67.7	485.6	65.0
64.0	21.8	67.8	20.7	64.6	18.9
3.2	6.2	2.9	6.5	2.5	4.1
375.9	$133.0	412.1	$133.1	597.6	$123.0
1961		1962		1963	
43.9	$ 28.1	46.4	$ 29.6	37.7	$ 27.8
775.2	86.1	779.3	85.7	846.2	97.8
				55.0	21.7
45.1	15.1	45.1	15.0	50.7	15.5
3.2	2.6	2.9	3.0	1.3	2.8
867.4	$131.9	873.7	$133.3	990.9	$165.6
1966		1967		1968	
29.7	$ 24.2	25.7	$ 22.9	17.6	$ 17.4
1,217.2	126.4				
		662.2	80.6	725.0	89.6
		577.4	52.0	623.6	53.4
79.6	24.2	103.0	26.2	123.5	28.8
169.6	28.8	195.0	34.9	253.4	41.9
61.4	18.2	56.4	20.4	55.9	20.1
3.0	4.6	3.3	4.4	6.1	9.7
1,560.5	$226.4	1,623.0	$241.4	1,805.1	$260.9
1971		1972		1973	
10.1	$ 14.7	9.8	$ 15.3	10.2	$ 20.8
670.3	90.9	729.8	99.2	738.6	110.5
720.4	61.4	760.3	64.6	821.8	69.8
102.2	25.0	120.3	29.5	209.4	33.7
344.5	60.7	475.9	80.8	504.5	85.7
55.7	21.5	59.5	22.9	53.6	24.9
3.7	6.5	4.1	7.1	4.3	7.9
1,906.9	$280.7	2,159.7	$319.4	2,342.4	$353.3

dustry segments, which were identified by product type, price range, and market. In most cases, purchases were made on the basis of individual products, rather than on the basis of a manufacturer's complete product line.

Industry market shares were subject to wide fluctuation. Those innovative firms which had made an early entry into newly discovered markets, and had subsequently supported their new products with heavy national advertising, tended to become the dominant forces in those markets. BIC Pen, for example, dominated all markets in low-priced ball-point pens, as did Gillette in fine-line porous-point pens. Exhibit 6 presents the 1973 primary corporate focus of major writing instrument competitors, with respect to product line, market, product price range, advertising program, and new products.

Manufacturers felt that success depended heavily upon the strength of their financial resources, which was reflected in their marketing and distribution programs as well as upon their ability to be innovative. Advertising, packaging, and distribution costs combined were estimated to average close to 100 percent of the manufacturer's unit cost of low-priced products. Manufacturers unable to sustain those costs in all markets tended either to position their products in the retail market as no-name brands or to concentrate the bulk of their resources in specific market segments.

INDUSTRY STRUCTURE

Manufacturers

There were two types of writing instrument firms: assemblers (70 percent) and producers (30 percent).

The *assemblers* were typically small, privately held, product specialists which sold their products by direct mail on a special order basis to the three most price-sensitive markets: commercial, advertising/specialty, and premium. To become an assembler required very little capital investment, manufacturing expertise, or marketing know-how, which accounted for the large number of assemblers and the fact that they tended to come and go. Assemblers bought writing instrument components from suppliers, which were then assembled and packaged for sale. Competition was based heavily on price, and product promotions were common.

Producers tended to be larger firms, some publicly held, which sold their products to all markets with special emphasis on the retail. Competition centered around the strength of their distribution networks (number of outlets reached and distributor loyalties) and national advertising programs. Producers manufactured most of their own component parts before assembling and packaging products. Their operations were characterized as capital intensive and precision oriented. It was not uncommon for some producers to manufacture certain products and to import others.

EXHIBIT 5
Annual growth rate (percent)

Product line	1969	1970	1971	1972	1973	5-year average	1973* Unit sales	1973* $ sales	1973* Average price
Fountain pens	(29.8)	(17.8)	(0.6)	(3.1)	4.7	(9.3)	0.4	6.2	$2.03
Mechanical pens	17.2	(11.8)	(3.6)	6.8	(9.9)	(0.3)	2.3	7.2	0.46
Ball-point pens	7.3	(4.3)	0.3	7.1	4.7	3.8	66.7	52.3	0.12
Refillables	5.0	(10.0)	(2.2)	8.9	1.2	1.0	31.5	32.0	0.15
Nonrefillables	10.0	2.0	2.9	5.5	8.1	6.8	35.2	20.3	0.09
Soft-tip pens	11.7	4.5	1.6	33.5	19.7	14.2	30.6	34.3	0.17
Broad-line markers	(5.4)	(10.0)	(2.7)	17.7	74.0	14.7	9.0	9.8	0.16
Porous-point pens	20.0	10.0	3.0	38.1	6.0	15.4	21.6	24.5	0.17
Total industry	10.8	(2.7)	1.0	13.3	8.4	6.2	100.0	100.0	$0.15

* Excludes desk and dip-pen sets.

Source: Writing Instrument Manufacturers Association.

EXHIBIT 6
1973 primary corporate focus

Writing instrument firms	Product line	Market	Price range	Ad program	Newest product
BIC	bp, pp	All	Low	Consumer (TV)	Disposable lighter
Berol	wp, bp	Commercial	Middle, low	Trade	Combination pen
Cross (A.T.)	mp, bp	Retail	High	Consumer (mags)	Luxury pp
Gillette	bp, pp	All	High, low	75%—consumer (TV); 25%—trade	Disposable lighter
Lindy	bp	Retail	Low	Consumer (mags); formerly trade	Disposable lighter
Magic Marker	bp, pp, bm	All	Low	Consumer (all media) trade	pp
Pentel	pp, bm	All	Low, middle	Consumer (TV); formerly trade	Combination pen
Parker	fp	Retail	High	Consumer (mags)	Luxury pp
Scripto	mp, bp, pp	Retail, advertising/specialty	Low	Consumer (TV, mags); formerly trade	Disposable lighter
Sheaffer	fp	Retail	High	Consumer (mags)	Luxury pp
Venus Esterbrook	Full line	All	Low, middle	60%—trade; 40%—consumer (mags)	Technical drafting products

Abbreviations:
bp = ball point pens.
bm = broad-tip markers.
fp = fountain pens.
mp = mechanical pencils.
pp = fine-line porous-point pens.
wp = wooden pencils.
Source: Case researcher's interviews with the corporate marketing personnel.

Distribution

Company sales forces. A typical producer used three types of sales forces: regular, specialized, and detail (optional).

The *regular sales force* made direct sales to large retail chains and discount houses, and indirect sales through specialized distributors to smaller retail stores and commercial supply outlets.

The *specialized sales force* made direct sales to the government, military, export, and premium markets, and indirect sales through advertising/specialty distributors to the advertising/specialty market.

Some firms added a *detail sales force* to work at the retail level, taking orders and arranging displays. Smaller firms relied more heavily on indirect selling than did the larger firms, which could afford to cover the cost of direct selling to large accounts.

Specialized distributors. Specialized distributors (wholesalers) first appeared in the writing instrument industry when manufacturers came to realize that they could no longer handle an enormous number of accounts on their own. They carried a multitude of products and were not captive to any one manufacturer. Their sales function was one of showing promotional items and order taking, for which they received a 15 percent margin off the retail price. In most cases, they assumed ownership of inventories. Along with the percentage markup, their own sales forces often received promotional monies (pm's), which were tied to major manufacturer's promotions at the retail level.

Distributors assisted dealers and retailers by providing an inventory management service that guaranteed replacement of faulty merchandise, better product selection, and faster inventory turnover.[5] "A better return on investment" became their key selling tool, which was supported by fair and attractive margins (40 percent off retail price) and frequent sales calls.

The late 1960s marked the beginning of an industry shift in distribution patterns in the retail market (largest market)—away from indirect selling via specialized distributors to small, independent retail outlets, towards direct selling to large national chains and discount houses. The turn sparked embitterment on the part of distributors, who felt that they were not only being abandoned by the very firms which had influenced their creation but were also being victimized by manufacturers' price-cutting actions affecting margins on the business which they still had. By 1973 approximately 60 percent of the dollar volume in the retail market represented direct sales from the manufacturers to mass-merchandise outlets.

---

[5] Dealers were office products stationers in the commercial market. Retailers were over-the-counter marketers in the retail market.

Markets

In 1973 manufacturers' dollar shipments by market segment were estimated by industry sources to be retail (50 percent), commercial (20 percent), advertising/specialty (16 percent), export (9 percent), premium (4 percent), and military and government (1 percent).

Retail market. The retail market represented by far the highest concentration of manufacturers' dollar sales (50 percent) in the mechanical writing instrument industry in 1973. The only instrument which was selling better in another market was the fountain pen, of which 63.6 percent of its dollar volume was sold overseas. Drugstores were the highest volume retail outlet for writing instruments, capturing over 33 percent of the industry's total dollar retail sales, and one out of every two ball-point pen sales. Grocery stores were the smallest with 3 percent of the retail sales. Specialized distributors (tobacco, drug, and sundries) sold products to small chains and independent stores, while large chains and discount houses bought writing instruments direct from manufacturers.

Retailers selected product lines based primarily on product quality and reputation of the manufacturer. National advertising support was believed to be important for boosting retail sales, particulary in the low-priced items.

A survey of retail customers conducted by the researcher indicated the following consumer purchase priorities: (1) function, (2) quality, (3) price, (4) style, and (5) packaging. It was generally felt that—

Products were selected for specific purposes.

Low-priced items tended to be impulse purchases often bought in quantities, while higher priced instruments were planned purchases bought individually.

Prices which varied (a few cents in the low-price range) among fairly undifferentiated products *did not* sway selection of a preferred brand.

Consumers associated generic names with particular products which had been heavily advertised, such as Flair for porous-point pens, and Cross for mechanical pencils.

Commercial market. The commercial market represented 20 percent of the total manufacturers' dollar shipments in 1973. Manufacturers' sales were made primarily through office supply distributors to dealers (commercial stationers) whose customers were corporate purchasing agents and students. Distributor/dealer loyalties were common in the commercial market, and were built up over the years on the basis of good account service, good quality merchandise, and attractive product offerings (at least one type at each price point). Commercial sales were heavily concentrated in the low-price range (< 50 cents).

As in the retail market, quality was considered the most important factor affecting a purchase decision by the dealer in the commercial market. However, price was more critical to the dealer than to the retailer because companies were interested in obtaining cost savings through bulk buying, whereas retail customers took personal pride in selecting their merchandise and were often willing to pay a premium for the products of their choice.

Advertising/specialty market. Sales in the advertising/specialty market represented 16 percent of manufacturers' dollar shipments in 1973. Purchasers tended to be organizations requesting inexpensive products on which to stamp advertisements. Price was the most important factor affecting a purchase decision. Orders were placed through advertising/specialty distributors and filled by a specialized company sales force. Approximately 70 percent of the 200 writing instrument firms were engaged in the advertising/specialty business, many of whom were assemblers.

Premium market. The premium market represented approximately 4 percent of manufacturers' total sales in 1973. Competitors included nonwriting instrument firms, as well as writing instrument companies, that (1) could meet the price objectives of the purchaser and (2) could offer products acceptable as giveaway promotional items for other products.

Other markets. In 1973 export sales represented 9 percent of the total manufacturers' sales. The rising trend in export sales was attributed to (1) the lowering of tariffs on imported products in foreign countries and (2) the increased activities of firms which held licenses or ran operations abroad. The average prices of writing instruments sold abroad were markedly lower than the average retail prices in the United States since so much of the cost in the domestic market was tied up in distribution, advertising, and packaging. Heavy U.S. import taxes (about 2 cents per unit) on writing instruments continued to bar entry of low-priced foreign-made products into the United States on a large scale.

The military and government markets combined represented only 1 percent of manufacturers' unit sales in 1973.

CIGARETTE LIGHTERS

By 1973 many mechanical writing instrument companies had entered the cigarette lighter business as a means of product-line diversification and yet another way to capitalize on their production expertise and market contacts. Although the two classes of products were functionally unrelated, their manufacturing processes, distribution patterns, and product life cycles bore striking similarities. The only major differences centered around market appeal, susceptibility to government regulation, and import trends.

Lighter/writer similarities

Product life cycle. Cigarette lighter product and price patterns almost exactly paralleled those of mechanical writing instruments—only a decade later. Until the late 1960s competition among dominant cigarette lighter companies was concentrated almost exclusively in regular refillable lighter products selling in the middle price range ($2–$12). Following the introduction of an inexpensive disposable lighter by Garrity Industries in 1967, and an expensive electronic lighter by Maruman in 1970, sales of cigarette lighters began to polarize by price and product: disposables at < $2 and electronics at > $12, leaving the backbone of the business, regular refillable lighters, in a vulnerable position with respect to sales prospects.

Distribution patterns. Cigarette lighters were sold direct from the manufacturer, or indirect, through specialized distributors, to writing instrument markets. In 1973 there were 175,000 retail outlets in the United States marketing cigarette lighters. Grocery stores represented the largest number (45–50 percent) of lighter sales. Of all cigarette lighters retailed, 75–80 percent were for less than $6.95. Like writing instruments, lighter sales were slightly seasonal, with the heaviest concentration occurring around the holidays. Distributors' margins off retail price generally ran between 15 percent and 25 percent, increasing proportionately with the price of the product. Retailer margins were 40 percent off retail price.

Manufacturing process. Cigarette lighter production required the same basic technology as that of mechanical writing instruments: plastics injection molding of parts, followed by a precision assembly process. The average mechanical writing instrument consisted of 7 parts and could be produced in a matter of minutes, whereas the average lighter had 21 parts and required a three-day production schedule because of "cure time" (a 24-hour wait between lamination of the subassemblies and filling the fuel reservoir).

The porous-point pen and liquid fuel lighter operated on the same basic principle: The tank of the porous-point pen held ink; the tank of the lighter held lighter fluid. The nib of the porous-point pen was analogous to the wick of the lighter. Both drew the fluid out of their respective tanks by capillary action.

Lighter/writer differences

Import trends. Unlike mechanical writing instruments, many cigarette lighters, particularly the disposables (70 percent), were imported into the United States for sale by domestic firms, which felt that the 25 percent duty fee on a foreign manufacturer's product was less than the additional amount required for direct labor costs in the United States. An added attraction was the quick access gained to a fast-growth market opportunity. In 1972, 45 percent of the lighters sold in the United States represented foreign imports, versus 36 percent in 1965. Japan was by far the largest supplier in every class of imported lighters (54.5 percent overall), with the exception of disposable butane lighters, 71 percent of which were imported from France.

Government regulation.   Until 1973 most cigarette lighter regulation related to the transportation of lighters containing flammable fuel. However, in 1973 the Consumer Products Safety Commission was given the authority to evaluate the quality of consumer products and enforce stringent safety standards. Cigarette lighters, particularly the inexpensive imports, were likely to be subject to CPSC attack if they lacked a flame adjuster (controlled height) or constant flame length regulator (controlled duration).[6] Although they were ranked 38th on the CPSC list in terms of severity of accidents, mechanical writing instruments were considered less hazardous. They were represented in Washington, D.C., by an industry trade association, the Writing Instrument Manufacturers Association, while lighters were not.

Market appeal.   Writing instruments appealed to a much broader consumer base than cigarette lighters did. All persons of all age groups were considered potential users of writing instruments, whereas cigarette lighter users were mostly smokers or campers.

Industry trends

Cigarette smoking.   During 1972 domestic consumption of cigarettes rose slightly from the previous year's level, which had reversed a four-year downtrend. Americans, including those at home and those abroad in the armed forces, consumed 565 billion cigarettes, or 2 percent above the prior year's level. Annual consumption per adult of 4,040 cigarettes (202 packs) remained about the same, which was 7 percent below the 1963 peak.

There were three principal reasons for the rise in cigarette consumption in 1972:

Increased concentration of the American population in the heaviest smokers' age group (25–39), which was 18.4 percent in 1972 and forecast to be 20 percent by 1975 and 22.9 percent by 1980.

Minimal cigarette price boosts, which had not affected the demand for cigarettes.

A decrease in the influence of antismoking campaigns after medical research evidence linking cigarette smoking to serious disease was termed inconclusive.

Cigarette lighter sales.   Cigarette lighter dollar sales in the United States were estimated to be $153 million in 1973. Compared to a 5.1 percent drop in per capita cigarette consumption, lighter sales had nearly doubled since 1965. Industry sources attributed the sudden sales surge to (1) the advent of disposable lighters and (2) an increased consumer awareness of

---

[6] The $1.29 disposable lighter by Rogers was the first disposable lighter to be recalled because of a flame adjuster problem (fall 1973).

cigarette lighters as the result of new and vigorous advertising campaigns (see Exhibit 7).

EXHIBIT 7
Cigarette lighter retail dollar sales ($ millions)

	1965	1966	1967	1968	1969	1970	1971	1972	1973 (est.)
Total lighters	$72.6	$85.9	$90.2	$94.3	$94.9	$98.1	$106.9	$115.0	$153.0

Source: Case researcher's estimates based on trend and company interviews and unpublished figures from the *Drug Topics* magazine research group (1972).

Product types

There were three basic lighter product types: (1) disposable, (2) regular refillable, and (3) electronic. These types could be further differentiated by (1) price range—low (< $2), medium ($2–$12), and high (> $12); (2) style—compact, pocket, or table; (3) fuel type—butane gas or naphtha liquid fuel; (4) consumer purpose—refillable or disposable; and (5) starter mechanism—wick, flint, quartz crystals, or battery (see Exhibit 8).

EXHIBIT 8
Cigarette lighter differentiation

Product type	Price range	Starter mechanism	Fuel	Style	Consumer Purpose
Disposable	< $2	Flint	Butane gas	Compact	Disposable
Regular refillable ...	Mostly $2–$12	Flint	Butane gas (90%)	Compact, table, pocket	Refillable
	Some > $12	Wick	Naphtha (10%)		
Electronic	> $12	Quartz crystals, battery	Butane gas	Pocket, table	Refillable

Disposable lighters. Disposable butane lighters represented the faster growing segment in the cigarette lighter industry, accounting for 35 percent of total lighter unit sales in 1973 (Exhibit 9).

Disposable lighters were introduced in the United States in 1967 by Garrity Industries, Inc. They earned immediate consumer acceptance due to their low price and no-reflint/no-refill feature. They appealed for the most part to match users, an untapped end-user market within the lighter industry, and to regular refillable lighter users who were tired of losing personal lighters and wished to trade down to the inexpensive line. Like inexpensive

EXHIBIT 9
Disposable lighter retail sales ($ millions)

	1971	1972	1973	1975 (est.)
Dollar sales	$18	$36	$50	$120
Unit sales	13	21	40	100

Source: Trade estimates.

mechanical writing instruments, disposable lighters were considered impulse purchase items that had to be backed with heavy consumer advertising support and sold in mass-merchandise channels.

The success of the disposable lighter in the American market caused a chain reaction among mechanical writing instrument firms which had been seeking to diversify into related product lines. Most firms entered the cigarette lighter business as distributors of foreign-made models. Some intended to eventually set up domestic manufacturing operations of their own.

In 1973 there were three clear contenders for industry dominance in the disposable butane lighter business: Gillette, BIC, and Garrity Industries, with Scripto running a distant fourth. Gillette introduced a $1.49 French-made product called "Cricket," in 1972 , through mass-merchandise channels, and used heavy consumer advertising. It planned to manufacture lighters domestically by 1973. BIC followed a similar plan one year hence with its $1.49 BIC Butane. Garrity Industries distributed its $1.49 Dispoz-a-lite in smoke shops, hotel stands, and drugstores, and used trade advertising. Scripto introduced its 98-cent Japanese-made Catch 98 in 1973 through independent retailers and used no consumer advertising. It planned to introduce a family of disposable lighters in 1974.

Regular refillable lighters. By 1973 cigarette lighter sales had grown rapidly at the inexpensive and luxury price ends of the market. Victimized by this trend was the regular refillable lighter, the mainstay of the lighter business, 95 percent of whose sales were concentrated in the middle-price range. Industry sources attributed the slow decay of the middle-price segment to three factors.[7]

1. Style changes in lighters, which reflected the growing consumer interest in either more decorative luxury lighters or more functional disposables.
2. A trade-down to disposable lighters by the former purchaser of the refillable butane lighter, who became tired of losing refilling lighters.
3. The trend towards distribution through mass-merchandise outlets, where profitability depended upon high-volume turnover of inexpensive prod-

---

[7] Industry sources believed that sales patterns for regular refillables would have been much worse, had it not been for the support of the advertising/specialty market in the middle-price range.

ucts, away from independent retail outlets, where most regular refillable lighters were sold.

For years three companies had dominated the regular refillable lighter market: Ronson, Zippo, and Scripto. Together they produced two thirds of the 1973 sales in that product segment. Industry sources believed that of the three, Zippo would be the least affected by the product/price polarization trend, as Zippo had developed long-time customer loyalties with its high-quality product, which held a lifetime guarantee. Ronson had lost market share by moving to higher priced regular refillable lighters and decreasing its advertising support of its products. Scripto lacked the advertising and marketing strength necessary to support its lower priced regular refillable lighters against the competition from disposable lighters.

Electronic lighters. Electronic lighters represented less than 2 percent of the total cigarette lighter unit sales in 1973. They required no flint or wick, as their flames were produced, electronically, by the striking together of ceramic quartz crystals, or with a battery. As luxury gift items, they were sold exclusively in department and jewelry stores and were priced above $12. Electronic lighters were new to the American market in 1973, and had not yet earned wide consumer acceptance—due in part to a lack of consumer awareness of their existence, and in part to the fact that consumers had traditionally thought of lighters as functional, rather than as highly decorative jewellike products.

The leading distributors of electronic lighters in 1973 were Maruman, Dunhill, Colibri, Crown, and Consul. All electronic lighters were imported either from Europe or from the Far East. As was the case with disposables, a number of companies, such as Scripto and Ronson, had introduced electronic lighters in order to expand their product lines and to take advantage of sales opportunities in a high-growth segment of the cigarette lighter market.

APPENDIX

Mechanical writing instruments of the future

Multicolor blending. A pen that will provide many colors, shades, and hues with a simple push of a button or twist of the cap to blend inks. Colors can be darkened, lightened, changed by interaction of inks—an artist's palette within a pen barrel.

Variable-tip marker. For Jekyll-and-Hyde writers who must switch from the fine lines used for underlining to the bold strokes of a package address, they will have to go no further than this soft-tip pen. Three point sizes—fine, medium, broad—can be included in the barrel and are as easily interchangeable as a push on the cap top.

Computerized writing.   Enables the most modern businesses to keep the personal touch alive in the computer age. Personalized notes will be produced on a large scale by programming individual handwriting into the memory. It will write any message fed into the computer in exact duplication of the handwriting.

Dictating pen.   "What you say is what you get." A pen that is able to translate spoken messages into your own style of handwriting.

The permanent writer.   Pen carries its own 100-year ink supply and never needs replacement.

Multitip pen.   A ball-point, soft-tip, marker, and fountain pen—all in the same writing instrument. For workers with four jobs at once and no time to hunt up or change their writing instrument.

Multipointed mechanical pencil.   Soft, medium, and hard pencil points all encased in one unit for ease in switching from one job to another—without searching through pencil boxes or desk drawers.

Self-destruct ink.   For keeping those hush-hush secrets really secret. This ink disappears after 48 hours, leaving no trace of important information that is written "For Your Eyes Only."

Radio transmitting writing instruments.   Write down your message at one location and it is transmitted to another miles away and written down—without connection.

Homing device.   This device will transmit a short sound beam so that you can keep tabs on your mislaid writing instruments. Great for big offices with absentminded "borrowers."

Power writing.   The conversion of atomic power into a writing ink. Lines will be burned into paper by converting light, neutrons, or other power sources in the barrel of the writing instruments.

Source: *Office Products*, May 22, 1972.

BIC Pen Corporation (A)

Described by an economic observer as "one of the classic success stories in American business," the BIC Pen Corporation was widely acknowledged as a leader in the mechanical writing instrument industry in 1973. "The success was dramatic," the observer had said, "because it was achieved from the residue of a deficit-ridden predecessor company, over a short period ..., in the extremely competitive, low price sector of the industry. 'BIC' had become a generic name for inexpensive ball-point pens."

Robert Adler, president of BIC, was extremely proud of the firm's success, which he attributed to "numerous and good management decisions based 40 percent on science and 60 percent on intuition." BIC had reported its first profit in 1964 based on net sales of $6.2 million. Over the following nine years, net sales increased at a compounded rate of 28.2 percent and the weighted-average aftertax profit as a percentage of net sales was 13.2 percent. (See Exhibits 1 to 3 for a summary of financial data from 1964–73.)

Until 1972 BIC concentrated exclusively on the design, manufacture, and distribution of a complete line of inexpensive ball-point pen products. The most successful pen was the 19-cent Crystal, which accounted for over 40 percent of BIC's unit sales in ball-point pens and about 15 percent of industry unit sales in ball-point pens in 1972. That same year, BIC expanded its writing instrument product line to include a fine-line porous-point pen. In 1973 it added a disposable cigarette lighter.

COMPANY HISTORY

The name "Waterman" meant a writing instrument since Louis Waterman invented the first practical fountain pen in 1875. For many years, the Waterman Pen Company led the world in the manufacture of fountain pens. But in the late 1950s, when the shift to ball-point pens swept the United States, the Waterman company continued to concentrate on its fountain pen line, and its performance slipped substantially.

EXHIBIT 1
Financial highlights 1964–1973

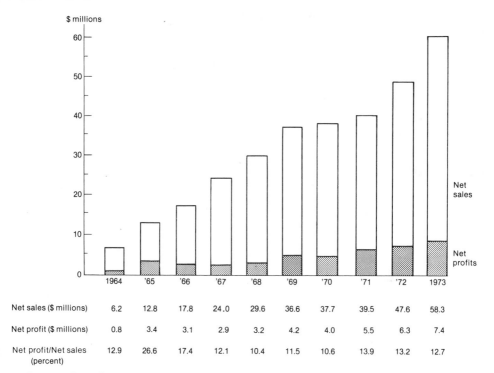

	1964	'65	'66	'67	'68	'69	'70	'71	'72	1973
Net sales ($ millions)	6.2	12.8	17.8	24.0	29.6	36.6	37.7	39.5	47.6	58.3
Net profit ($ millions)	0.8	3.4	3.1	2.9	3.2	4.2	4.0	5.5	6.3	7.4
Net profit/Net sales (percent)	12.9	26.6	17.4	12.1	10.4	11.5	10.6	13.9	13.2	12.7

Source: BIC Pen Corporation annual report, 1973.

In 1958 Marcel Bich, a French businessman well established as a leading European pen maker, bought the facilities, trademark, and patent rights of the ailing Waterman company, which then became the Waterman–BIC Pen Corporation. Believing strongly that the ball-point pen was the writing instrument of the future, M. Bich established the objective of becoming the leading firm in the low-price disposable ball-point pen industry. To obtain that position, management proposed the use of forceful consumer advertising and mass-distribution policies.

At the time of M. Bich's purchase of Waterman, ball-point pens constituted only 8 percent of Waterman's unit sales. By 1964, however, all fountain pen and ink products had been eliminated, and most sales came from the 19-cent stick-type ball-point pen. The conversion process was costly, as reflected in the five years of deficits (1959–63). BIC reached its turning point in 1964, marked by the national success of its Crystal pen.

From 1964 through 1973 the company expanded its ball-point pen line to include 12 models of retractable and nonretractable pens offered in varying point sizes, ink colors, and barrel colors at retail prices between 19 cents

EXHIBIT 2

BIC PEN CORPORATION
Consolidated Financial Statements
For the Years Ended December 31, 1973, and 1972
($000)

Consolidated Statement of Income

	1973	1972
Net sales	$58,326	$47,571
Cost of goods sold	26,564	19,892
Gross profit	$31,762	$27,679
Selling, advertising, and general and administrative expenses	17,191	15,248
Profit from operations	$14,571	$12,431
Other income	589	269
Total profit from operations	$15,159	$12,700
Other deductions	327	196
Income before income taxes	$14,787	$12,504
Provision for income taxes	7,357	6,240
Net income	$ 7,430	$ 6,264
Earnings per share	$1.15	$1.00

Consolidated Statement of Retained Earnings

	1973	1972
Balance—beginning of year	$11,683	$10,262
Net income	7,430	6,264
Total	$19,113	$16,526
Dividends:		
Cash:		
Common shares	$ 1,750	$ 1,603
Preferred shares		
Total cash	$ 1,750	$ 1,603
Common shares		3,240
Total dividends	$ 1,750	$ 4,843
Balance—end of year	$17,363	$11,683

Source: BIC Pen Corporation annual report, 1973.

and $1. A 29-cent fine-line porous-point pen was added in 1972, and a $1.49 disposable butane cigarette lighter in 1973. In addition to product-line expansion, BIC established a 100 percent-owned operation in Canada (1967), joint ventures in Japan (1972) and Mexico (1973), and a distributor arrangement with a firm in Panama (1973).

On May 1, 1971, the company changed its name to the BIC Pen Corporation. The Waterman trademark was subsequently sold to a Zurich firm, and BIC went public with an offering of 655,000 shares of common stock listed at $25 per share on the American Stock Exchange. In 1973 BIC's parent company, Société Bic, S.A., held 62 percent of the BIC stock.

EXHIBIT 3

BIC PEN CORPORATION
Consolidated Financial Statements
December 31, 1973, and 1972
($000)

Consolidated Balance Sheet

	1973	1972
Assets		
Current assets:		
Cash	$ 683	$ 919
Certificates of deposit and short-term investments—at cost, which approximates market	8,955	10,000
Receivables—trade and other (net of allowance for doubtful accounts, 1973—$143,000, 1972—$102,000)	9,445	8,042
Inventories	9,787	6,299
Deposits and prepaid expenses	644	633
Total current assets	$29,514	$25,893
Property, plant, and equipment—at cost (net of accumulated depreciation, 1973—$9,687,000, 1972—$7,091,000) .	15,156	9,687
Investments and other assets	1,790	1,329
Total assets	$46,460	$36,909
Liabilities and Shareholders' Equity		
Current liabilities:		
Notes payable—banks................................	$ 21	—
Construction loan payable (due March 21, 1974)	560	—
Accounts payable—trade	3,872	$ 1,245
Mortgage payable	62	58
Accrued liabilities:		
Federal and state income taxes	1,231	815
Pension plan.......................................	306	265
Other	488	402
Total current liabilities	$ 6,540	$ 2,785
Deferred liabilities	$ 361	$ 275
Mortgage payable.......................................	$ 459	$ 520
Minority interest*	$ 91	—
Shareholders' equity:		
Common shares	$ 6,480	$ 6,480
Capital surplus	15,166	15,166
Retained earnings	17,363	11,683
Total shareholders' equity	$39,009	$33,329
Total liabilities and shareholders' equity	$46,460	$36,909

*Mexican subsidiary is 80 percent owned.
Source: BIC Pen Corporation annual report, 1973.

MEN OF INFLUENCE

Marcel Bich

Marcel Bich has been described as having done for ball-point pens what Henry Ford did for cars—produce a cheap but serviceable model.

In 1945, Bich and his friend Edouard Buffard pooled their wealth—all of $1,000—and started making ball point refills in an old factory near Paris. Soon it occurred to Bich that a disposable pen that needed no refills would be more to the point. What his country needed, as Bich saw it, was a good 10¢ pen. Today the cheapest throwaway Bic sells for close to that in France—about 7¢. In the United States the same pen retails for 19¢, and it is the biggest seller on the market. . . .

Marcel Bich is a stubborn, opinionated entrepreneur who inherited his title from his forebears in the predominantly French-speaking Val D'Aoste region of northern Italy. He abhors technocrats, computers, and borrowing money. At 58, he attributes his business successes to his refusal to listen to almost anyone's advice but his own. Bich says that his philosophy has been to "concentrate on one product, used by everyone every day." Now, however, he is moving toward diversification. A disposable Bic cigarette lighter that gives 3,000 lights is being test marketed in Sweden; if it proves out, Bich plans to sell it for less than 90¢. . . .

In the United States, Bich is best known for his fiasco in the 1970 America's Cup Race: His sloop *France*, which he captained, got lost in the fog off Newport. He speaks in aquatic terms even when describing his company:"We just try to stick close to reality, like a surfer to his board. We don't lean forward or backward too far or too fast. We ride the wave at the right moment."[1]

Société Bic, S.A., was known as a "one-man empire" which in 1972 accounted for a third of the ball-point pen sales worldwide and included full operations in 19 countries. M. Bich's personal holdings were estimated to be worth about $200 million. "The only way he could control his empire," BIC's treasurer Alexander Alexiades had said, "was to have certain rules and guidelines. All Société Bic companies were quite autonomous once they had become consistent with his philosophies."

Bic Pen Corporation had been characterized as the "jewel in M. Bich's crown." In the firm's early years, M. Bich had provided much of the machinery, production techniques, and supplies from the French parent company. By 1973 the only substantial business exchange which still remained between the two firms was in research and development. One of the few visible signs of the American company's European heritage was the Renaissance artwork which M. Bich had hung in BIC's reception and board rooms.

---

[1] "Going Bananas over BIC," *Time*, December 18, 1972, p. 93.

Robert Adler

In 1955, the day after Connecticut's Naugatuck River raged out of control and flooded the countryside, Mr. Adler reported to work at the old Waterman Pen Company as a newly hired junior accountant fresh out of Pennsylvania's Wharton School of Finance. Instead of being shown to his desk and calculating machine, he was handed a shovel and ordered to help clean out the mud which had collected in the plant during the flood. Nine years later, at the age of 31, he became president of the Waterman–BIC Pen Corporation, which under his leadership became the largest ball-point pen manufacturer and distributor in North America.

Mr. Adler was described by a business associate as "a president who liked to be totally familiar with and completely immersed in every area of his company's operations, one who felt that he should never quash his instincts with an overdependency on numbers and facts alone . . . a shirt-sleeved president who made it his personal concern to know intimately every facet of the BIC marketing and manufacturing process, including highly technical matters involving complex moulding equipment, advanced production techniques, merchandising, advertising, and sales . . . a do-it-yourself investigator-president who regularly made the rounds of the plant, keeping himself available at all times."

Mr. Adler had stated that he personally selected his colleagues on the basis that they demonstrated aggressiveness and an unswerving belief and conviction that they were serving a company that produced the world's finest writing instruments—products of exceptional quality and value. "A businessman is born, not made," he said, "and education can only enhance and refine what already exists." He attributed much of BIC's success to the fact that in the firm's early years he had consciously hired persons who were unfamiliar with the industry and who therefore did not question BIC's ability to succeed by selling an inexpensive ball-point pen via extensive advertising. He emphasized the importance of his own role in determining BIC's performance by stating:

> A lot of decisions are easy because there is only one way to go. Sometimes you're lucky and sometimes, no matter what, you'll get the same outcome. A president gets paid to make decisions. That's his big job. What's important once a decision is made is to make sure that it comes out right. The decision is not so important; it's the outcome. A president must say to himself: "I will now make my decision successful."

WRITING INSTRUMENT PRODUCT LINE

The BIC Pen Corporation manufactured and sold inexpensive writing instruments in a variety of shapes: stick or pocket pen; ink colors, 1–10;

point sizes, medium or fine; and retail prices, 19 cents to $1. All retractable pens were produced in a pocket pen shape; all nonretractables in a stick shape.

The most successful product, the Crystal, accounted for over 40 percent of all ball-point pen units sold in North America. Its sister product, the 25-cent Fine Point Pen, which differed from the Crystal only in point size, accounted for over 15 percent of all ball-point pen units sold.

In 1973 writing instruments accounted for approximately 90 percent of BIC's consolidated net sales. Nonretractable pens accounted for 80 percent of the writing instrument unit sales, retractable pens for 6 percent, fine-line porous-point pens for 12 percent, and refills for 2 percent.

Exhibit 4 presents the 1973 BIC writing instrument product line.

EXHIBIT 4
1973 writing instrument product line

Product Name	Ink colors	Point sizes	Retail price
Ball-point pens:			
Nonretractable/nonrefillable:			
Crystal	4	m	$0.19
Fine Point	4	f	0.25
Reproduction	4	m	0.25
Eraser	4	m,f	0.25
Deluxe Eraser	4	m,f	0.29
Deluxe	4	m	0.39
Accountant	4	f	0.49
Retractable/refillable:			
Clic	4	m,f	0.49
Two-color pen	2	m,f	0.69
Four-color pen	4	m,f	0.98
Citation	1	m	1.00
Retractable/nonrefillable:			
Pocket pen	3	m	0.29
Fine-line porous-point pen:			
BIC Banana	10	m,f	0.29

Source: Corporate records.

Nonretractable/nonrefillable ball-point pens

The Crystal, a nonretractable/nonrefillable ball-point pen, was introduced on the market in 1959 at a retail price of 29 cents. As the first product of the newly formed Waterman–BIC Pen Corporation, the BIC Crystal was intended to become a "brand name replacement for all no-name,[2] disposable pens in a market where no dominant competitor existed." Its retail

---

[2] No-name products were those which were not advertised and were marketed at retail prices far below the comparable, inexpensive, national advertised products.

price was dropped to 19 cents in 1961. In commenting on the success of the Crystal, Jack Paige, vice president of marketing, remarked:

> We built this company on the 19-cent pen. In 1961 it was selling for 19 cents, and in 1973 it is still 19 cents. One third of all retail sales are from the 19-cent stick. It's a highly profitable business. We've found ways to become more efficient and still maintain our profitability.

Between 1961 and 1968, BIC expanded its nonretractable ball-point pen line to include six other models of varying point sizes, ink colors, and usages. Nonretractables were priced from 19 cents to 49 cents.

Retractable/refillable ball-point pens

In 1968 BIC introduced its first retractable/refillable ball-point pen, the 49-cent Clic.[3] Management felt that the Clic would (1) improve the overall corporate profit margin; (2) enable the company to sell merchandise in multipacks (quantity selling in one package), such as school specials; and (3) increase distribution—as some retail outlets, particularly those not dependent on BIC for their profits, had been reluctant to sell the 19-cent and 25-cent pens.

Following the Clic, four other retractable ball-point pens were added to the BIC product line. Three imported French pens—the 98-cent 4-color pen (1971), the 69-cent 2-color pen (1972), and $1 Citation pen (1973)—were introduced to "upgrade ball-point pen sales." The 29-cent pocket pen, the only nonrefillable pen in the retractable line, was added to "expand primary demand for ball-point pens."[4]

Fine-line porous-point pens

In April 1972, BIC introduced its first nonball-point pen product, the 29-cent BIC Banana, which was a fine-line porous-point pen produced in a stick shape. Mr. Paige commented on the Banana decision as follows:

> The development of the concept of entering the porous-point pen market was not a sudden decision. Our philosophy was simply that as soon as we had a porous-point pen that would reflect BIC quality and could be mass marketed at a popular price that anybody could afford, we would then move into that business.
>
> For openers, we were faced with a couple of major problems. First we

---

[3] In retractable pens, industry sales volume in dollars was concentrated in the high-priced products and in units in the no-name brands.

[4] Despite a major introductory campaign ($1.5 million spent on advertising), sales in the pocket pen were "disappointing," according to one company spokesperson. He attributed the poor results to styling problems and a lack of room for new products in a market with a declining sales growth rate.

were a late entry and the market was dominated by a 49-cent strong brand name of good quality that had a 50 percent market share. Maybe for some companies that stark statistic would have been enough not to enter. However, at BIC there is an aggressive attitude about marketing. That attitude manifested itself a year and one-half ago when we began plotting our sales course for the introduction of this new product. (BIC spent $3 million on advertising the BIC Banana in 1972.) We took the attitude that we weren't going to be squeezed into that remaining 50 percent share that the leading brand left for the rest of the field. Our plan was to expand the consumer market for this type of writing instrument—to make it grow. In a larger market, we felt we would have the opportunity to build a franchise that would give us a substantial share.

In reviewing the same product decision, Mr. Alexiades said:

In 1966 we saw the product opportunity for the soft-tip pen, but Marcel Bich owned 90 percent of the company, and we had a difficult time convincing him that this was the right approach. He thought that the soft-tip pen was a passing thing and that it was impractical because it wouldn't write through carbon. But we're in a carbon society, and there's no logical explanation for the consumer. However, M. Bich's philosophy changed. Years ago, he only wanted to sell ball-point pens. He's now interested in inexpensive, disposable, mass-produced items. He has the marketing know-how, the distribution, the name.

We saw that the porous-point pen was not a fad so we got in, perhaps a little late, but at least we entered an expanding portion of the market. The growth rate of ball-point pen sales had leveled off. If we didn't enter the porous-point pen market, it would have been difficult to grow since we're so dominant in the industry. We knew that the only way to grow was through product-line diversification or acquisition.

Our objective is to become the largest producer of fine-line porous-point pens. We are in ball-point pens. It might be difficult because Gillette's Flair has been there for five years. Papermate brand is not a no-name brand with no resources like those which we initially attacked in the ball-point pen market.

A competitor commented on the market entry of the BIC Banana:

Many people associated BIC with the ball-point pen. BIC had a difficult time because people thought that the Banana was a ball point. It's a stick shape and looks like a ball point. They don't have that problem with the lighter (1973) because it is a different looking product altogether. BIC hasn't done well with the Banana against the Flair. After all, who could enter the stick pen market now and do well against BIC? But at least BIC broke the price point (49 cents) with its 29-cent point which softened the retail and commercial markets. Maybe they'll get smart and get out.

THE MARKETS

Mr. Adler's philosophy had always been "to sell BIC products wherever there was a doorknob." Consistent with that view, marketing efforts had been focused on all writing instrument markets, with special emphasis placed on the "four key sales volume opportunities"—the retail, commercial, ad/specialty, and premium markets, which represented about 90 percent of the dollar sales volume in the writing instrument industry in 1973. The other three markets—government, military, and export—accounted for the remaining 10 percent. In 1973 the Writing Instrument Manufacturers Association estimated total industry sales at $353.3 million.

Retail market

The retail market, or over-the-counter market, was the largest mechanical writing instrument market, accounting for over 50 percent, or $176.6 million, of the total industry dollar sales in 1973. Of significance in the retail market was the growing trend away from indirect selling through retail distributors to independent stores toward direct selling from the manufacturers to mass-merchandise outlets.

Since the national success of the 19-cent Crystal pen in 1964, BIC had completely dominated the ball-point pen segment of the retail market. By the end of 1973, BIC held a 66 percent share of that segment, followed by Gillette with 15 percent and Lindy with 5 percent. In fine-line porous-point pens, Gillette was the front runner with a 35 percent share followed by BIC with 22 percent, Magic Marker with 8 percent, and Pentel with 5 percent.

Management attributed BIC's successful penetration of the retail market to its aggressive marketing and distribution policies, as well as to the low price and high quality of its products.

Commercial market

The commercial market, or office supply market, was the second largest mechanical writing instrument market, accounting for about 20 percent, or $70.6 million, of total industry sales in 1973. Selling in the commercial market was primarily handled through commercial distributors, who channeled products from the manufacturers to office supply dealers, who in turn sold to commercial customers. Large office supply dealers bought directly from manufacturers and used distributors to fill in inventory gaps.

At the end of 1973, management estimated that the leading market shareholders in ball-point pens in the commercial market were BIC with 50 percent, followed by Berol with 18 percent, and Gillette with 5 percent. In fine-line porous-point pens, it was estimated that Gillette held a 40 percent share; Berol, 25 percent; Pentel, 10 percent, and BIC, 4.5 percent.

In commenting on BIC's 4.5 percent market share in fine-line porous-point pens, Mr. Adler said:

> We have had difficulty in the commercial market because that market is conditioned to something like the Flair, Pentel, or Berol porous pens which

sell for 49 cents and allow good margins to the distributors. The model which BIC manufactures does not compete head on with Flair. Ours is a stick model; theirs is a pocket model. Because of the design of the product, it's difficult to get a certain percentage of the market. The Flair product costs twice as much to manufacture (has a clip, etc.). The 29-cent Write-Brothers also has a clip. For us, we're a long way from being number one. To get into the porous-pen business, we had to use the stick model. Our problem is that the distributors do not want to push the Banana because they have a 49-cent market. Naturally, they make less on a 29-cent model. It will take time.

Ad/specialty and premium markets

The ad/specialty and premium markets together accounted for approximately 20 percent or $70.6 million of the total industry dollar sales volume in 1973.

Ad/specialty sales referred to special orders made through specialized distributors for products imprinted with a slogan or organization name. Competition in the ad/specialty market was based heavily on price which accounted for the strength of the no-name brands in that market. BIC held close to a 5 percent share in the ad/specialty market in 1973.

A "premium" was defined as a free promotional item which was attached to another product in order to promote the sale of that product. Premium sales were made through distributors or direct from the manufacturer to customer. As in the ad/specialty market, competition was based upon price. Unlike that market, it was also based upon brand recognition and included a broader base of product types, not just writing instruments. Although it was a small market, management considered BIC's participation in the premium market as important in "reinforcing the firm's dominant position in the pen business." BIC held close to a 100 percent market share among writing instrument firms in the premium market in 1973.

THE COMPETITION

In 1973 approximately 200 firms were engaged in the manufacture and sale of mechanical writing instruments in the United States. Most firms competed selectively in the industry on the basis of (1) product type— fountain pen, mechanical pencil, ball-point pen, or soft-tip pen; (2) price range—high (>$1), medium (50 cents to $1), and low (<50 cents); and (3) market—retail, commercial, ad/specialty, premium, military, government, and export. Strong advertising programs and mass-distribution networks were considered critical for national success.

In management's view, BIC had four major writing instrument competitors: Berol, Gillette, Lindy, and Pentel.[5] The five firms competed at price points with similar products (see Exhibit 5).

The Berol, Lindy, and Pentel corporations were well known for product innovation. In 1973 the Berol Corporation, best known for its drafting products, particularly for its Eagle brand pencils, was the second firm to introduce the rolling writer combination pen, a pen which performed like a regular fountain pen, yet could write through carbons. Lindy Pen Corporation had earned its reputation as an early entrant into new markets, yet lacked the advertising strength to back the sale of its new products. Lindy introduced a 39-cent stick pen prior to the introduction of the BIC Crystal in 1959, a fine-line porous-point pen in 1969, and a disposable lighter in 1970. Pentel Corporation had earned the reputation of "revolutionizing the U.S. mechanical writing instrument industry" with the introduction of the soft-tip pen in 1964 and the rolling writer combination pen in 1969. Like Lindy, it lacked the resources to support heavy advertising and mass distribution programs.

EXHIBIT 5
1973 selected product lines

Product type	BIC	Berol	Gillette		Lindy	Pentel
			Paper Mate	Write-Bros.		
Ball-point pens:						
Retractable:						
Refillable	$0.49	$0.29	$0.98	—	$1.00	$2.98
	0.69	0.39	1.50			5.00
	0.98	0.49	1.98			7.00
	1.00	0.59	3.95			8.50
		1.49	5.00			
			5.95			
Nonrefillable	0.29			$0.39		0.79
Nonretractable	0.19	0.19		0.19	0.19–	
	0.25	0.25			0.59	
		0.29				
		0.39				
Fine-line porous-point pens	0.29	0.29	0.49	0.29	0.59	0.29
		0.49	0.98			0.35
			1.95			0.49

Source: Corporate records.

---

[5] The Magic Marker Corporation was considered a strong competitor in fine-line porous-point pens with four models selling from 19 cents to 49 cents and comprising an estimated 8 percent share of the retail market. However, Magic Marker was best known for its broad-tip markers (ten models, from 39 cents to $1.29). Its ball-point pen products were sold strictly as no-name brands.

158

Gillette

The Gillette Company was considered BIC's major competitor in all writing instrument products. The comparative performance in writing instruments for the two firms from 1968–73 is shown in Exhibit 6.

EXHIBIT 6
Comparative performance in writing instruments (consolidated statements)

	1968	1969	1970	1971	1972	1973
BIC:						
Net sales ($ millions)	$29.6	$36.6	$37.7	$39.5	$47.6	$52.4
Net income ($ millions)	3.2	4.2	4.0	5.5	6.3	7.3 (est.)
Net income/sales	10.8%	11.7%	10.6%	13.9%	13.2%	14.0% (est.)
Net sales/total assets*	—	—	1.6	1.4	1.3	1.3
Total assets/total equity	—	—	1.3	1.2	1.1	1.2
Gillette (Paper Mate Division):						
Net sales ($ millions)	$33.2	$36.5	$47.0	$51.1	$60.9	$74.5
Net income ($ millions)	2.5	3.3	3.3	2.5	3.0	4.3
Net income/sales	4.5%	9.0%	7.0%	4.9%	4.9%	5.8%
Net sales/total assets*	1.4	1.4	1.3	1.3	1.3	1.3
Total assets/total equity	1.8	1.8	1.8	1.9	2.0	2.1

*Estimated total assets allocated to writing instruments.
Source: Corporate 10-K reports.

In 1973 Gillette competed in the high-price market with its Paper Mate products and in the low-price market with its Write-Brothers products. The Paper Mate ball-point pens had been the mainstay of its writing instrument business since the early 1950s. In the late 1960s, management at Gillette "recognized the potential of Pentel's new soft-tip pens." Backed by a large research and development capability, a well-known corporate name, and advertising and distribution strength, Gillette set out to capture that market with a fine-line porous-point pen called "Flair," which retailed in three models from 40 cents to $1.95. In 1972 Gillette created the Write-Brothers products: a 39-cent retractable ball-point pen, a 29-cent fine-line porous-point pen, and a 19-cent nonretractable ball-point pen, in order "to take advantage of growth opportunities in the low-price end of the mechanical writing instrument market." The Write-Brothers name was selected to prevent confusion on the part of consumers who had associated the Paper Mate name with high-priced ball-point pen products and middle- to high-priced Flair products.

Retail market share patterns for BIC and Gillette are shown in Exhibit 7. (The BIC Banana was introduced in May of 1972 and the Write-Brothers products in July of 1972.)

Over the five-year period 1969–73, BIC and Gillette made the advertising expenditures on writing instruments shown in Exhibit 8.

EXHIBIT 7
Bimonthly retail market share patterns (units)

	Jan.–Feb.	Mar.–Apr.	May–June	July–Aug.	Sept.–Oct.	Nov.–Dec.	Jan.–Feb.	Mar.–Apr.	May–June	July–Aug.	Sept.–Oct.	Nov.–Dec.
			(1972)							(1973)		
Ball-point pens:												
Total BIC	66%	67%	65%	65%	66%	65%	67%	66%	65%	66%	68%	66%
$0.19 Crystal	36%	35%	34%	33%	31%	31%	32%	32%	31%	31%	31%	31%
0.25 Fine Point	12	14	13	13	11	13	13	12	13	13	11	12
0.29 Pocket pen	—	1	2	2	3	3	3	3	3	2	2	2
0.49 Accountant	8	7	7	8	9	7	8	7	8	8	10	9
0.49 Clic	8	8	7	7	9	8	8	8	7	8	9	7
Other	2	2	2	2	3	3	3	4	3	4	5	5
Total Gillette	8%	8%	9%	13%	13%	13%	13%	15%	15%	14%	14%	15%
$0.19 W-B	—%	—%	—%	3%	3%	3%	4%	6%	5%	5%	5%	5%
0.39 W-B	—	—	1	2	2	2	2	2	2	2	2	2
0.98 Retractable	4	4	4	4	4	4	4	4	4	4	4	4
Other	4	4	4	4	4	4	3	3	4	3	3	4
Lindy	7%	7%	8%	7%	6%	7%	6%	6%	6%	5%	5%	5%
Other	19	18	18	15	15	15	14	13	14	15	13	14
Total	100%	100%	100%	100%	100%	100%	100%	100%	100%	100%	100%	100%
Fine-line porous-point pens:												
BIC	—	—	5%	11%	15%	16%	16%	19%	19%	20%	23%	22%
Total Gillette	49%	46%	45%	43%	43%	40%	39%	37%	36%	37%	35%	35%
$0.49 Flair	45%	43%	41%	36%	34%	33%	32%	30%	30%	30%	28%	29%
0.49 Hotliner	2	2	1	1	1	1	1	1	1	2	1	1
0.29 W-B	—	—	2	5	7	5	5	5	5	5	5	4
Other	2	1	1	1	1	1	1	1	—	—	1	1
Lindy	5%	5%	4%	4%	4%	4%	3%	3%	2%	2%	2%	2%
Magic Marker	—	—	—	—	—	—	6	6	7	8	9	8
Pentel	9	9	9	7	7	7	7	6	6	5	4	5
Other	37	40	37	35	31	33	29	29	30	28	27	28
Total	100%	100%	100%	100%	100%	100%	100%	100%	100%	100%	100%	100%

Source: Corporate records.

160

EXHIBIT 8
Writing instrument advertising budget estimates ($ millions)

	1969	1970	1971	1972	1973
Gillette	$1.9	$4.0	$6.0	$8.5	$9.0
BIC	3.6	4.0	4.3	7.0	6.8

Source: Case researcher's estimates derived from corporate records, interviews with company officials, and journal articles.

In commenting on advertising programs and the BIC/Gillette competition in general, David Furman, advertising director at BIC, said:

> Our stategy has been to emphasize profit, and therefore look for the mass market. Gillette has said: "Let's make the most money and not worry about the size of the market." Gillette had a nice profitable business with Flair. It kept Paper Mate alive. But they can't stay alive with one-dollar-plus pens. We expanded the market so now their unit sales are up. The philosophy of Gillette has been to spend heavily to develop the product, then let the products decay and spend on new product development. Their unit sales continue to go up but their loss of market share is considerable.

COMPANY POLICIES AND STRUCTURE

Mr. Adler had sometimes described his company as a car with four equally important wheels—sales, manufacturing, finance, and advertising—all of which had to be synchronized in order for the car to accelerate and sustain itself at high speed. That car, he claimed, had equal responsibility to its stockholders, employees, and customers. It followed, therefore, that management's attention should be focused on achieving a good return on investment, which Mr. Adler felt was derived by improving (1) productivity (unit production per hour), (2) efficiency in production (cost savings methods), and (3) quality control standards and checks.

Finance

In the spring of 1971, BIC Pen effected a recapitalization which resulted in an aggregate number of 3.03 million outstanding common shares, 87 percent of which were owned by Société Bic, S.A., 3 percent by M. Bich, 9 percent by Mr. Adler, and 1 percent by other officers and directors (stock bonuses.[6] On September 15 of that year, 655,000 of those common shares were offered to the public at $25 per share, resulting in a new capital structure of 67 percent of the shares owned by Société Bic, S.A., 3 percent by

---

[6] Four million common shares were authorized.

M. Bich, 7 percent by Mr. Adler, 1 percent by other officers, and 22 percent by the public. Proceeds from the public offering after underwriting discounts and commissions amounted to $15.4 million. On July 27, 1972, M. Bich exercised his warrants for the purchase of 210,000 shares of common stock at $25 per share, totaling $5.25 million, which BIC received in cash. That same day, the company declared a 2-for-1 share split in the form of a 100 percent share dividend of 3.24 million shares, $1 par value, which resulted in the transference of $3.24 million from retained earnings to common stock. At the end of 1972, 6.48 million shares were outstanding of the 10 million shares authorized in June of 1972; none of the 1 million authorized shares of preferred stock had been issued.

Since 1967 the company paid cash dividends as shown in Exhibit 9.

EXHIBIT 9
BIC Pen Corporation dividend payment history

	1967	1968	1969	1970	1971	1972	1973
Consolidated net income ($ millions)	$2.862	$3.231	$4.233	$4.033	$5.546	$6.264	$7.430
Dividends ($ millions)	2.591	—	1.175	1.166	1.319	1.603	1.750
Adjusted net dividend/ share*	0.43	—	0.19	0.19	0.22	0.26	0.27
Stock price range*	—	—	—	—	12¼–18	16¼–37	11⅝–32½

* After giving retroactive effect to a 2-for-1 share split in 1972.
Source: BIC Pen Corporation annual report, 1973.

Regarding dividend policy, Mr. Alexiades said:

> When we were a private firm, there was no dividend policy. Dividends were only given when declared by M. Bich. In 1969 when we knew that we would be going public, we tried to establish a policy to find the proper relationship between earnings and dividends. Twenty to twenty-five percent of earnings seemed like a good target policy. Now we're having trouble increasing our dividends, due to government guidelines, although we would like to increase the payout in accordance with our rise in earnings.

The purchase of the original BIC plant from the Norden Company in 1963 was financed with a 5¾ percent mortgage loan from Connecticut General, payable in monthly installments of $7,749 (principal and interest) until January 1, 1981.[7] The three plant expansions—$1 million for 110,000 square feet in 1965, $1.8 million for 100,000 square feet in 1969, and $5–$6 million for 275,000 square feet in 1973—were financed through short-term loans

---

[7] The loan had not been paid off by 1973 because of its low interest rate.

and cash on hand. Regarding the 1973 expansion, Mr. Alexiades said: "We decided to use our own cash so that if something develops in 1974 or 1975, such as an acquisition or new product opportunity, we can always fall back on our credit rating."[8]

In keeping with BIC's informal organizational structure, management used no formalized budgets. "We use goals, not budgets. We just keep surprising ourselves with our performance," said Mr. Alexiades, "although perhaps as we mature, we will need a more structured arrangement."

BIC was known in the New Haven area for its attractive compensation plan. It was Mr. Adler's belief that good people would be attracted by good pay. Plant workers received the highest hourly rates in the area ($4.53 base rate for the average grade level of work). All employees were invited to participate in a stock purchase plan whereby up to 10 percent of their salaries could be used to purchase stock at a 10 percent discount from the market price, with BIC assuming the brokerage commission cost. Executives participated in a bonus plan which Mr. Adler described as follows:

> We have a unique bonus system which I'm sure the Harvard Business School would think is crazy. Each year I take a percentage of profits before tax and give 40 percent to sales, 40 percent to manufacturing, and 20 percent to the treasurer to be divided up among executives in each area. Each department head keeps some for himself and gives the rest away. We never want bonuses to be thought of as salaries because they would lose their effect. So we change the bonus day each year so that it always comes as a pleasant surprise, something to look forward to.

Manufacturing

Manufacturing had emphasized the development over the years of a totally integrated, highly automated production process capable of mass producing high-quality units at a very low cost. Except for the metal clips, rings, and plungers, all components—even the ink—were produced in the Milford plant. Société Bic had supplied the basic production technology, machinery, and research and development.[9] Some raw materials, particularly the brass, were still imported from France.

The U.S. energy crisis posed a major threat to BIC in 1973. Polystyrene, the key raw material used in making pens, was a petroleum derivative. Mr. Adler commented on the shortage of plastic:

> We've reached a point in our economy where it's become more difficult to produce than sell. I mean I have this big new plant out there [pointing to

---

[8] BIC borrowed on a seasonal basis to meet working capital needs, using bank lines of credit ($15.5 million available; maximum borrowed was $10.6 million in 1970.)

[9] BIC Pen Corporation spent $30,368, $15,254, and $128,553 on R&D in 1971, 1972, and 1973, respectively.

the new $5–$6 million addition] and I may not be able to produce any products. I have to worry about the overhead. I'm reluctant to substitute materials.

I predict that in 1974 polystyrene will cost more than double what it costs in 1973, which is 15 cents per pound. It represents about 10 percent of the manufacturing cost of the ball-point stick pen.

The production process consisted of three stages: (1) manufacture of parts, (2) assembly of parts, and (3) packaging. Porous pens (4 parts) were the simplest instrument to manufacture followed by ball-point pens (7 parts) and lighters (21 parts). Some parts, such as nonretractable pen barrels, were interchangeable, which built flexibility into the production process. Production rates were steady throughout the year, while inventory buildups were seasonal. In mid-1973 BIC was producing on average about 2.5 million ball-point pen units per day and 0.5 million porous pens per day, which was close to plant capacity.

Management felt that production costs were substantially controlled by the strict enforcement of a quality control system. One fourth of the plant's employees participated in quality control checks at each stage of the production process, which was precision oriented, involving tolerances as close as $0.0002\pm$. Charles Matjouranis, director of manufacturing, had stated that it was his job to search for cost-savings programs which would protect profit margins on products. He said:

> We are in the automation business. Because of our large volume, one tenth of 1 cent in savings turns out to be enormous. Labor and raw materials costs keep increasing, but we buy supplies in volume and manufacture products in volume. One advantage of the high-volume business is that you can get the best equipment and amortize it entirely over a short period of time (four to five months). I'm always looking for new equipment. If I see a cost-savings machine, I can buy it. I'm not constrained by money.

In 1973 there were 700 persons working at BIC in Milford, of which 625 were production personnel represented by the United Rubber Workers Union under a three-year contract. Management considered its relations with employees as excellent and maintained that BIC offered the best hourly rates, fringe benefits, and work environment in the area. Weekly meetings between supervisors and factory workers were held to air grievances. Workers were treated on a first-name basis, and were encouraged to develop pride in their jobs by understanding production technicalities and participating in the quality control program and production shift competition. Most assembly-line workers were women. At least 40 percent of the factory workers had been with BIC for over ten years, and 60 percent to 65 percent for over five years. Despite increased automation, very few layoffs had occurred because workers were able to be retained for other positions to compensate for the increase in production unit volume. Over 50 percent of the workers had performed more than one job.

Marketing and sales

In admiring his BIC ring studded with six diamonds, each representing an achieved sales goal, Ron Shaw, national sales manager, remarked:

> It's almost a dream story here. When I started with the company in 1961 as an assistant zone manager, we were selling 8 million units a year. We now sell 2.5 million units a day. Everyone said: one, we couldn't sell 5,000 feet of writing in one unit and succeed; two, we couldn't have the biggest sales force in the writing instrument industry and make money; and three, we couldn't advertise a 19-cent pen on TV and make money. Well, we did and we're number one!

Distribution. The BIC products were sold in the retail and commercial markets by 120 company salespeople who called on approximately 10,000 accounts. Those accounts represented large retailers, such as chains, as well as wholesale distributors. Through those 10,000 accounts, BIC achieved distribution for its products in approximately 200,000 retail outlets, of which 12,000 were commercial supply stores. In addition, the salespeople called on 20,000 independent retail accounts which were considered important in the marketplace. In the case of those accounts, the BIC salespeople merely filled orders for the distributors. A specialized BIC sales force sold ad/specialty orders to ad/specialty distributors and most premium orders directly to corporate customers.

The backbone of BIC's customer business had originally been the mom and pop stores. They had initially resisted selling BIC pens, but were later forced to trade up from the no-name products once BIC had become a popular selling brand. As product distribution patterns moved away from indirect selling towards more direct selling to large chains and discount houses, the mass merchandisers became eager to carry BIC products, which had earned a reputation for fast turnover, heavy advertising support, and brand recognition. In 1973 BIC did 60 percent of its sales volume through distributors and 40 percent through direct sales channels.

Pricing policy. BIC had never raised the original retail prices of any of its products. Management, therefore, placed a great deal of importance on retail price selection and product cost management. Advertising expenses generally ran 15 percent of the manufacturer's selling price; the combined costs of packaging and distribution approximated 20 percent to 30 percent of the manufacturer's selling price. The distributor's profit margin was 15 percent off the listed retail price; the indirect retail buyer's was 40 percent; and the direct retail buyer's was 55 percent. Regarding pricing policy, Mr. Adler said:

> If I increase my price, I help my competition. The marketplace, not ourselves, dictates the price. We must see what people are willing to pay. You must sell as cheaply as possible to get the volume.

Customary marketing tools. In a speech made before the Dallas Athletic Club in September 1972, Mr. Paige remarked: "We're in the *idea* business. Selling is an idea. Many people have products but we have ideas."

BIC used four basic marketing tools to sell its "ideas": (1) advertising, (2) point-of-purchase displays, (3) packaging forms, and (4) trade and consumer promotions. Management felt that the only way to enter a new market was to be innovative either by (a) introducing a new product, (b) creating a new market segment, or (c) using unique merchandising techniques designed specifically for that market. The BIC salespeople were known to be aggressive.[10] Products were always introduced on a regional rollout basis with the entry into each new region attempted only after market saturation had been achieved successfully in the prior region.

Advertising was considered the most important element of the BIC marketing program. Company research had shown that seven out of ten writing instruments sold were impulse purchase items. With that knowledge, management felt that widespread distribution of a generic name product line was essential for success. It was further felt that retailers and commercial stationers preferred to carry nationally advertised brands.

BIC used TV advertising, "the cheapest medium when counting heads," almost exclusively. In 1973 BIC added advertising in *T.V. Guide* and the Sunday supplements "in order to reach more women, the biggest purchasers of writing instruments."

In keeping with the belief that merchandising techniques should be designed differently for each product and market, BIC varied its TV commercials substantially, depending upon the intended product usage, time of entry into the market, and demographic interest. Each advertising message was designed to be simple and to communicate *one* idea at a time. Exhibit 10 presents examples of four different themes: (1) BIC has a lighter (BIC Butane), (2) BIC's products are durable (Crystal), (3) BIC has coloring instruments for children (Ink Crayons[11]), and (4) BIC offers a "new and fun way to write" (BIC Banana).

Another marketing tool was the *point-of-purchase display*. Mr. Paige remarked:

> Merchandise well displayed is half sold, particularly on a low consumer interest item. Displays must be designed to fit every retail requirement because, for example, what's good for Woolworth's may not be good for the corner drugstore.

Packaging was considered another form of advertising. "We want to make the 19-cent pen look like a $1 pen," Mr. Paige had said. BIC was one

---

[10] On average, assistant zone managers earned $12,000 and zone managers earned $22,-000 a year. Compensation consisted of a base salary plus commission.

[11] Ink Crayons consisted of a multipack of BIC Banana pens in an array of ink colors.

EXHIBIT 10
Television advertising themes

BIC BUTANE	BIC CRYSTAL	BIC INK CRAYONS	BIC BANANA
"For $1.49 and thousands of lights, it's a Pretty Good Lighter. BIC Butane."	"Dear BIC . . . You're probably not going to believe this but...."	"You can't write with blueberries, but you can write with a BIC Banana, the new porous tip pen."	"BIC Banana Ink Crayons. In ten bright colors. The only fruit you can draw with."

Source: BIC Pen Corporation annual report, 1972.

of the first firms to use the concept of multipacks. Packaging forms were changed as much as six times a year. Regarding packaging and *promotions,* Mr. Alexiades commented:

> We've created a demand for constant innovation, excitement in the marketplace. Many people say that's the reason for BIC's success. We change the manner in which we sell (blister packs,[12] multipacks, gift

---

[12] Blister packs were product packages which were designed to be displayed on pegboards.

packages), which makes our merchandise turn and keeps our name in front of the wholesaler and retailer all of the time. The consumer remembers us because we offer a true value. The retailer and dealer remember us because they receive special incentive offers, free merchandise, and promotional monies, plus their merchandise turns.

Organizational structure

Throughout its 15-year history, the BIC organizational structure had remained small and simple. (See Exhibit 11 for the 1973 organizational chart.) In 1973 the average tenure (since 1958) of the six key executive officers was 13 years. At least 40 percent of the factory workers had been at BIC for over ten years. Several of the managers commented on the BIC environment:

> We try to run this company as a family organization. We don't try to run it as a General Motors. We've been very successful with this concept. It's a closely knit management group—very informal. Decisions are made immediately. A young guy comes here. He sees that we (management) exist. We understand him. He gets his decisions immediately. We try to get him to join the family. Inside of two to three years, if he's not in the family, he won't work out.
>
> Robert Adler
> President

> Part of the success of management is our ability to communicate with one another. We're trying to remain the same. It's one of the regrets that growth has to bring in departments and department heads, but we're trying to maintain a minimum.
>
> Alexander Alexiades
> Treasurer

> We have few managers, but the best. One real good one is better than two average.
>
> Charles Matjouranis
> Manufacturing director

> This company does not believe in assistants. Philosophically, we try to stay away from any bureaucracy. There are no politics involved here, no knifing, no backbiting. Part is a function of size. Everybody knows his place and area of responsibility. We don't want to break from that.
>
> David Furman
> Advertising director

> We promote from within. We recognize the abilities of our own people.
> Ron Shaw
> National sales manager

EXHIBIT 11
1973 internal organizational chart.

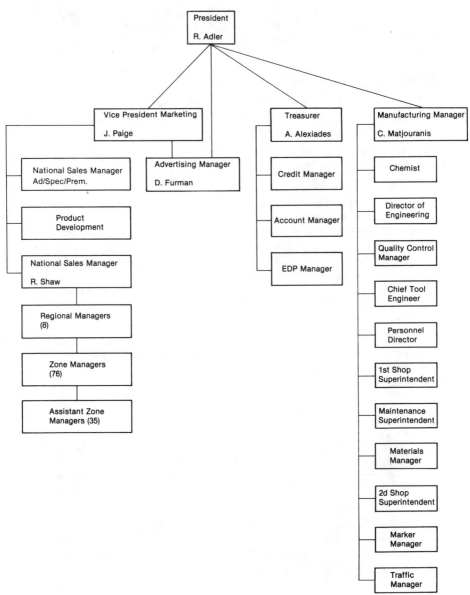

Source: Corporate records.

THE BIC BUTANE DISPOSABLE CIGARETTE LIGHTER

The lighter decision

In March 1973 BIC Pen Corporation introduced its first nonwriting instrument product, the BIC Butane disposable lighter, at a retail price of $1.49. Management viewed the BIC Butane as a logical extension of its current product line as it was inexpensive, disposable, of high quality, and able to be mass produced and distributed through most writing instrument trade channels, especially retail. It differed from writing instruments in that it required 21 rather than the basic 7 assembly parts, more precise manufacturing, and was subject to strict governmental standards. Mr. Furman made the following statement regarding BIC's decision to enter the disposable lighter business:

> For years we were in the high-level, profitability trap. We had had it as far as that market would go. The Banana was the first break out from the trap and now the lighter. We utilize our strengths, but we're no longer a writing instrument company. We're in the expansion stage where writing instruments are a base from which we are expanding. We're using the skills we've gained and are applying them to any kind of mass-produced product.

Introductory campaign

The decision to sell a disposable lighter dated back to 1971 when Marcel Bich purchased Flaminaire, a French lighter company, with the objective of marketing a substitute for matches in Europe. Matches had never been free in Europe, and for that reason disposable lighter sales had been very successful there far before they caught on in the United States. The BIC Butane was imported from Flaminaire but was scheduled to be produced at the Milford plant on a highly automated production line by March 1974.

The BIC Butane was introduced first in the Southwest, where management claimed it had captured a 32 percent retail market share by year's end. Management expected its national retail market share of 16 percent to rise to 25 percent when the product reached full national distribution in February of 1974. The regional rollout was backed with a $1 million advertising campaign. A $3 million campaign was planned for 1974. Lighter sales approximated 10 percent of BIC's consolidated net sales in 1973. An industry source estimated their pretax margin at 15–21 percent.

The cigarette lighter industry

Lighters were categorized in three basic product classes: disposables, regular refillables, and electronics. Disposable lighters contained butane gas; electronic lighters contained butane gas or a battery; regular refillable lighters contained either butane gas (90 percent) or liquid fuel (10 percent).

There were three basic price categories: <$2 (all disposables), $2–$12 (most regular refillables), and >$12 (all electronics and fancy regular refillables). It was estimated that from 75 percent to 80 percent of all cigarette lighters sold in 1972 were priced below $6.95 at retail.

Cigarette lighter sales in the middle-price range had begun to fall off in the early 1970s. As a replacement for matches, disposable lighters had expanded the primary demand for lighters and represented the major growth opportunity in the U.S. lighter industry (Exhibit 12).

EXHIBIT 12
U.S. cigarette lighter retail sales (dollars and units in millions)

	1969	1970	1971	1972	1973 (est.)
Total lighters ($)	$94.9	$98.1	$106.9	$115.0	$153.0
Disposables ($)	n.a.	8.5	18.0	36.0	50.0
Units (#)	—	—	13	21	40

n.a. = not available.
Source: Case researcher's estimates based on trade and company interviews and unpublished figures from the *Drug Topics* magazine research group (1972).

Major competitors

By 1973 many firms, particularly manufacturers of writing instruments, had entered the disposable lighter business. Most firms served as distributors of foreign-made products, many of which were reputed by trade sources to be of questionable quality. As with writing instruments, BIC's management believed that industry success was heavily dependent on the strength of a

EXHIBIT 13
1973 major competitors in disposable lighters

	BIC	Gillette	Garrity	Scripto*
Market entry (year)	1973	1972	1967	1972
Product	BIC Butane	Cricket	Dispoz-a-lite	Catch 98
Price	$1.49	$1.49	$1.49	$0.98
Product produced in ...	France (→1973); U.S. (after)	France (→mid 1973); Puerto Rico (after)	France	Japan
Ad $ Strategy (1973) ..	Consumer	Consumer (¾), trade (¼)	Trade	None
Distribution emphasis*	Mass/chains	Mass/chains	Smoke shops, hotel stands, drugstores	Independent retailers

*In 1974 Scripto planned to raise the price of the Catch 98 to $1.19, add another Japanese disposable lighter at the $1.39 price point, and produce a $1.69 disposable lighter in its Atlanta plant.
Source: Casewriter's interviews with corporate marketing managers.

firm's advertising program and distribution network, although most firms did well initially due to the excessive demand for disposable lighters relative to the available supply.

There were three clear contenders for industry dominance in the disposable lighter business: Gillette, Garrity Industries, and BIC, with Scripto a distant fourth. Gillette's Cricket lighter was the leading market shareholder, accounting for one third of all disposable lighter sales in 1973 (Exhibit 13).

In speculating on the future of the BIC Butane lighter, Mr. Paige stated:

> We think that the disposable butane will cannibalize every low-priced lighter. BIC, Dispoz-a-lite and Cricket will do 90 percent of the business in 1973. Cricket advertises extensively. BIC will compete with Cricket at the $1.49 price point. BIC and Cricket will dominate the industry in the future. The cheaper disposables of lesser quality will only sustain themselves.

case 6

BIC Pen Corporation (B)

News release: January 11, 1974

BIC Pen Corporation, which has specialized successfully in mass-marketing consumer products, soon will introduce a new product which it will distribute in the $1.3 billion retail pantyhose market, Robert P. Adler, president, disclosed today.

"The sale of pantyhose is for BIC a further expansion into other mass-produced disposable consumer products," Mr. Adler said. "Because of BIC's strong reputation for value, and our ability to merchandise successfully to the consumer through more than 200,000 retail outlets, we believe our new pantyhose product will be well received in this marketplace."

THE WOMEN'S HOSIERY INDUSTRY

Hosiery had always been the most rapidly consumable apparel item in a woman's wardrobe. For years the women's hosiery industry had been stable in unit sales and repetitive in product offerings. Many low-profile brands were sold in a wide range of sizes and typical colors. The business "kicked up its heels" in the late 60s with the advent of the convenience product pantyhose and miniskirts. Hosiery became a fashion item, costing as much as $10 a pair, depending upon style, texture, color, and brand name. Prosperity did not last, however; and by 1973 the $2 billion women's hosiery business was characterized as "having to run faster to stay in the same place." The market had become plagued by an uncertainty in consumer demand, sagging profits, price battles, distribution changes, and the rising fashion trend of women's pants. Hosiery makers claimed that women had begun to go without hose or to wear ripped stockings under pants (see Exhibit 1).

The pantyhose market

As an attempt to interject some life into the stable pantyhose market, the three big hosiery makers—Hanes Corporation, Kayser-Roth Corporation,

172

EXHIBIT 1
U.S. women's hosiery industry trends

	1964	1965	1966	1967	1968	1969	1970	1971	1972	1973
Numbers of—										
Companies	645	609	576	579	574	530	502	471	457	390
Plants	828	782	750	746	741	734	699	665	604	521
Annual per capita consumption:										
Pantyhose	—	—	—	—	2.3	9.0	13.3	11.0	12.7	11.7
Stockings	14.8	15.7	17.3	19.5	18.1	12.7	6.3	4.2	3.1	2.5
Knee-highs, anklets	0.1	0.1	0.1	0.1	0.1	0.1	0.1	0.3	0.6	1.2
Total consumption	14.9	15.8	17.4	19.6	20.5	21.8	19.7	15.5	16.4	15.5

Source: National Association of Hosiery Manufacturers.

and Burlington Industries—launched an unprecedented $33 million promotional campaign in 1973. They cast aside their established merchandising techniques and began pushing new, low-priced pantyhose in supermarkets. The firms adopted catchy brand names and used dramatic advertising campaigns centering around "trendy" packaging. Their assumption was that women would buy more pantyhose if the products were cheaper, more accessible, and more attractively displayed than before. No longer were branded products available exclusively in department or specialty stores at $3 a pair; rather they could be purchased at every corner market for 99 cents to $1.39. As a result, pantyhose sales in food outlets rose from 5 percent in 1968 to 28 percent of the industry pantyhose sales in 1973, with analysts predicting a 50 percent share by 1975. Despite the surge in supermarket buying, sales of pantyhose declined by 7 percent in 1973.

The private label business represented 50 percent of the hosiery sales in food stores in 1973, with some labels selling as low as 39 cents a pair. The supermarket invasion by known brands—"L'eggs" by Hanes, "Activ" by Burlington, and "No-Nonsense" by Kayser-Roth—resulted in a general upgrading in the quality of the private label brands and an expansion of the branded lines to cover additional market segments, such as pantyhose in large sizes for heavier women and pantyhose for less than $1 for price-conscious women.

In describing pantyhose purchase behavior, one industry source said:

> Generally, all women are interested in quality, price, fit, and availability, but purchasers do tend to fall into three basic categories: (1) women who think that all hosiery is the same and therefore look for the lowest price; (2) women who feel that an extremely low price implies inferior quality; and (3) women who switch off between high and low prices, depending upon their needs.

L'eggs was the largest selling brand name in 1973 with a 9 percent dollar volume share of the total hosiery market. The idea for L'eggs was born out of the recognition that no high-quality name brand dominated the highly fractionated pantyhose market; nor was one available at a reasonable price (< $2) at convenience locations (supermarkets). The L'eggs integrated marketing program centered around the theme, "Our L'eggs fit your legs," and the distinctive egg-shaped package. The L'eggs direct selling approach leaned heavily on a platoon of 1,000 young delivery women clad in hot pants and traveling their appointed routes in distinctive white vans. Their task was to restock flashy "L'eggs Boutiques" in supermarkets and drug chains. L'eggs retail sales rose from $9 million in 1970 to $110 million in 1973. Hanes spent $20 million on their promotion in 1972 and $13 million in 1973.

Activ and No-Nonsense pantyhose were priced at 99 cents a pair, in contrast with L'eggs at $1.39.[1] Both brands were backed by $10 million promotional campaigns in 1973. The "Activ Girls" competed with the "L'eggs Ladies." Similarly clad and driving red vans, they also sold products on consignment. Besides supermarkets, Activ pantyhose appeared in outlets serviced by tobacco distributors, thus supporting Burlington's motto: "Activs are everywhere." Kayser-Roth shunned the distribution system favored by the other two hosiery makers and delivered its No-Nonsense brand-name pantyhose to food brokers at supermarket warehouses. The No-Nonsense approach—without vans, hot pants, and comely delivery women—allowed the retailers a 45 percent profit margin, compared with the 35 percent return guaranteed by Hanes and Burlington.

THE PANTYHOSE DECISION

David Furman, advertising director, commented on BIC's entry into the pantyhose business:

> The hosiery industry used to be dominated by manufacturing, not marketing, companies. L'eggs was the first attempt to change that. The success of L'eggs and other industry leaders has depended on an extremely expensive direct selling distribution system which is good for large-volume outlets but is not feasible for smaller stores or local advertising. BIC intends to use its usual jobbers and make it profitable for them to act as middlemen and garner the independent stores.
>
> Nearly all companies deal primarily with pantyhose as a fashion item. The market is moving away from the fashion emphasis, which cannot be successful in food stores. BIC will address the fit problem by using the slogan: "It fits there, it fits everywhere"; hence the name—Fannyhose. Ours is a utility story as it was with ball-point pens.

---

[1] Hanes introduced First-to-Last pantyhose at 99 cents a pair to counter the price competition from Activ and No-Nonsense pantyhose.

In introducing Fannyhose to the trade, management used the theme of "taking a simple idea and making it pay off." The quality product was priced at $1.39, came in two sizes and three colors, and was packaged in a compact little can with a see-through top. The advertising program centered around the "better fit" concept, as was illustrated in animated television commercials and Sunday supplements. Product promotions included cents-off coupons and free samples.

In contrast with its major competitors, BIC planned to act as a distributor of pantyhose, rather than as a manufacturer/distributor, and to establish a specialized sales force to sell the product direct or through distributors to its wide variety of writing instrument retail accounts. BIC's supplier was DIM, S.A., one of France's largest hoisery makers ($100 million in sales), which M. Bich bought control of in 1973. Mr. Furman called the BIC plan "a brilliant stroke around L'eggs. Theirs is a fixed sytem—low profits, no risk, fixed price. We add promotional profits by passing on to the trade the money we've saved by avoiding the need for our own service crews."

BIC's investors react

An article appearing in the February 4, 1974, edition of *The Wall Street Journal* described the reaction of the investment community to BIC's entry into the pantyhose business. One analyst cited several obstacles which BIC faced in its new venture, namely: (1) the limited pricing flexibility which BIC would have because of import duty costs[2] and (2) the fact that BIC had not been particularly strong in supermarkets. Another analyst took a more positive view, citing the recent market price decline in the BIC stock to "investors' questions over the competitive nature of the pantyhose business without understanding the philosophy of BIC—to produce inexpensive disposable consumer products once there is an established market for them and to use its widespread marketing system to become a powerful force in the industry." A third analyst predicted a bright future for BIC in the pantyhose business because of its "access to materials through Société Bic, its reputation for high-quality products, its well-developed distribution system, and its commitment to marketing, rather than to manufacturing, pantyhose."

---

[2] Duty fees averaged 33 percent per unit. One analyst speculated that the pretax margin on Fannyhose was 15 percent.

case 7

Scripto, Inc.

In January 1974 Herbert "Bo" Sams, president of Scripto, Inc., an Atlanta-based mechanical writing instrument and cigarette lighter company, was reviewing the performance of the Atlanta Division which accounted for 64 percent of the firm's total revenues in 1973. Mr. Sams was conducting his review with an awareness of his decision made in 1971 to rebuild Scripto's writing instrument business. Regarding that decision, he had stated:

> Sometimes I wake up at three o'clock in the morning wondering if that was the right decision. Would it have been better to get out of the writing instrument business and consolidate the cigarette lighter operation? All the numbers said to get out of writing instruments, and we were certainly more profitable in lighters. But people had always thought of us as a writing instrument company. They associated the Scripto name with pens and mechanical pencils. Our name was our biggest strength. So we decided to reestablish Scripto as a meaningful factor in the mechanical writing instrument industry.

This case study traces the history of Scripto, Inc., by presidential era from its inception in 1923 through 1973. It focuses on the operations and decision problems of the Atlanta Division which manufactured and /or distributed mechanical pencils, fine-line porous-point pens, ball-point pens, and three types of cigarette lighters—disposable, regular refillable, and electronic—in the domestic and foreign markets. Exhibits 1 and 2 present the consolidated financial statements by presidential era from 1963 to 1973.

CORPORATE HISTORY BY PRESIDENTIAL ERAS

Harold Hirsch (1923–1939)

Scripto, Inc., was established as a manufacturer of mechanical pencils in Atlanta, Georgia, in 1923. The idea for Scripto was conceived by the then only independent pencil lead manufacturer in the United States, Monie Ferst, who wanted to prevent the Germans from recapturing the U.S. lead

176

and eraser market which they had held before World War I. Rather than seek government aid to restrict German imports, Mr. Ferst decided to create his own market for leads and erasers by mass producing a quality mechanical pencil which would sell for 25 cents or less and thus appeal to the American mass market.[1] The product earned immediate market acceptance and industry dominance in its product class, although thousands of pencils had to be given away to distributors and retailers initially to overcome the disbelief that a quality mechanical pencil could be produced and sold so inexpensively. Under the leadership of its first president, Harold Hirsch, Scripto reached its break-even point in sales in 1930, whereupon the price of the mechanical pencil was dropped from 25 cents to 10 cents and maintained at that level through World War II.

Eugene Stern and E. P. Rogers (1940–1946)

During World War II, two interim presidents, Eugene Stern and E. P. Rogers, managed the firm. Scripto remained a one-product firm relying heavily upon M. A. Ferst, Ltd., Mr. Ferst's company, for its lead and eraser supply. The manufacture of mechanical pencils was halted only temporarily during the war when Scripto adapted its precision manufacturing operation to the production of ordnance materials for the U.S. government.

James Carmichael (1947–1963)

In 1947 Jimmy Carmichael, following an unsuccessful bid for the Georgia governorship against Eugene Talmadge, was selected by Mr. Ferst as the new president of Scripto, Inc. His stated objectives were twofold: (1) to develop Scripto into a full-line mechanical writing instrument manufacturing firm and (2) to make Scripto the largest manufacturer of mechanical writing instruments in the world. Over his 17 years as president, Scripto in fact achieved the first objective, but not the second.

A full line of mechanical writing instruments. Mr. Carmichael's principal objective was to expand the Scripto product line by adding other mechanical writing instruments. His first step was to take advantage of the demand in the U.S. market for the new ball-point pen which had been introduced by Reynolds in 1946 at a retail price of $15. As it had successfully done with the mechanical pencil, Scripto set out to prove that a quality ball-point pen could be produced and sold inexpensively. The ball-point pen was introduced on the market in 1947 at a retail price of 25 cents and, like the mechanical pencil, earned immediate market acceptance.

By 1952 Scripto was known as a full-line writing instrument manufac-

---

[1] Mechanical pencils on the market at the time were only of fair quality and were sold exclusively as gift items priced well over $1.

EXHIBIT 1

SCRIPTO, INC.
Consolidated Income Statements by Presidential Eras

	Carmichael		Singer	
	1963	1964	1965	1966
Net sales:				
Dollars	$26,344,306	$25,237,265	$36,664,054	$33,494,076
Percent	100.0	100.0	100.0	100.0
Cost of goods sold	54.4	58.8	63.8	57.7
Gross profit	45.6	41.2	36.2	42.3
Expenses:				
Selling and administrative	32.3	34.4	28.0	30.4
Interest (net)	0.4	0.4	0.7	0.4
Other (net)	0.9	0.6	0.2	0.8
Total expenses	33.6	35.4	28.9	31.6
Profit before tax	12.0	5.8	7.3	10.7
Provision for income tax	6.2	2.7	3.1	4.9
Net income (loss) before				
extraordinary item	5.8	3.1	4.2	5.8
Extraordinary item	—	—	—	(2.4)*
Net income	5.8	3.1	4.2	3.4
Ratio analysis:				
Net sales/total assets	1.5	1.5	1.5	1.5
Net income (before extraordinary				
items)/total assets	8.7	5.7	6.9	8.6
Net income (before extraordinary				
items)/net worth	12.4	6.5	12.6	14.3
Depreciation/net sales	3.7	3.4	3.3	2.9
Dividend payout	51.2	98.0	48.3	41.8
Investment in plant and				
equipment/net sales	3.7	5.2	5.7	8.7

*$793,000 lost on discounted carpet operations.
†Losses: (1) start-up costs for Canadian subsidiary ($264,000); and (2) losses on product lines, abandonment of properties. Gains: (1) reevaluation of currencies ($55,000), (2) sale of properties ($730,000), and (3) tax-loss carry-forward credit ($170,000).
‡Losses: Sale of product lines, abandonment of properties ($105,000). Gains: (1) sale of properties ($105,000), (2) tax-loss carry-forward credit ($60,000).
§Gains: Tax-loss carry-forward ($89,000).
Source: Scripto, Inc. annual reports.

turer in the low-price market. Fountain pens had been introduced at retail prices of $1.00 and $3.50; the ball-point pen line was expanded to include models retailing at 29 cents, 39 cents, and $1.00; a $1.00 mechanical pencil was added, as well as a matching fountain pen and pencil set retailing for $5.00. All products were supported by heavy consumer advertising and dealer promotion programs.

Cigarette lighters: A new business. In 1957 Scripto introduced its first

	Ferst		Harris		Sams		
	1967	1968	1969	1970	1971	1972	1973
	$30,462,424	$30,914,857	$31,229,304	$31,928,975	$30,979,108	$28,378,819	$31,154,608
	100.0	100.0	100.0	100.0	100.0	100.0	100.0
	60.7	65.9	72.1	71.0	72.8	71.2	70.6
	39.3	34.1	27.9	29.0	27.2	28.8	29.4
	34.0	31.7	32.9	31.9	25.4	25.4	23.1
	0.6	0.6	0.8	1.3	1.3	0.9	1.0
	0.3	1.3	0.2	—	0.4	0.4	1.4
	34.9	33.6	33.9	33.2	27.1	26.7	25.5
	4.4	0.5	(6.0)	(4.2)	0.1	2.1	3.9
	2.1	1.1	(2.2)	(0.8)	1.5	1.5	2.5
	2.3	(0.6)	(3.8)	(3.4)	(1.4)	0.6	1.4
	—	—	—	—	1.5†	0.2‡	0.3§
	2.3	(0.6)	(3.8)	(3.4)	0.1	0.8	1.7
	1.4	1.5	1.3	1.3	1.4	1.5	1.4
	3.2	(0.8)	(5.0)	(4.2)	(3.1)	1.0	2.0
	5.3	(1.3)	(9.7)	(9.6)	(6.2)	1.6	3.6
	3.0	3.0	3.5	2.9	3.1	2.3	2.2
	114.0	—	—	—	—	—	—
	4.7	3.2	3.1	3.9	2.7	3.2	2.7

nonwriting instrument product, a naphtha fuel lighter called the Vu-lighter, which derived its name from the fact that its liquid fuel supply was visible. Although it was well known that Mr. Ferst, founder of Scripto and then chairman of the board, had always wanted to add a cigarette lighter to the product line, Scripto had not been consciously seeking product-line diversification into nonwriting instruments. Rather, it came across an available opportunity in 1954 to rescue a small cigarette lighter firm in Missouri which was experiencing production and quality control problems. At the time, Scripto was selling its writing instrument products exclusively to the retail and ad/specialty markets, both of which were well suited for the distribution of the Vu-lighter because the same sales force and distributors could be used. The company was purchased in 1954 for a nominal price. The lighter was subsequently redesigned at an investment of $1 million and then rein-

EXHIBIT 2

Income Statements
SCRIPTO, INC.
Consolidated Balance Sheets by Presidential Eras

	Carmichael		Singer	
	1963	1964	1965	1966
Total assets ($)	$17,570,967	$17,168,506	$24,155,764	$22,700,251
Assets (%)	100.0	100.0	100.0	100.0
Current assets:				
Cash	5.5	6.0	4.3	5.3
Accounts receivable	32.8	29.4	30.0	32.6
Inventory	27.9	27.6	34.3	26.3
Total current assets	66.2	63.0	68.6	64.2
Property, plant, and equipment (net)	31.1	34.4	29.4	30.0
Investments in affiliates...........	—	—	—	4.2*
Prepaid expenses................				0.8
	2.7	2.6	2.0	
Other assets				0.8
Liabilities (%)...................	100.0	100.0	100.0	100.0
Current liabilities:				
Notes payable	1.7	1.5	8.3	2.2
Accounts payable	4.5	6.5	7.5	6.4
Accrued taxes	4.0	3.4	3.3	2.7
Accrued liabilities	6.0	4.8	4.7	5.6
Total current liabilities	16.2	16.2	23.8	16.9
Long-term debt	13.2	11.3	20.8	22.2
Deferred income taxes	—	—	0.9	1.2
Minority interest	—	—	—	—
Stockholders' equity:				
Common stock	7.5	7.6	5.7	6.1
Paid-in surplus	18.3	18.7	14.4	15.3
Retained earnings	44.8	46.0	36.2	40.0
(Treasury stock)...............	—	—	(1.8)	(1.7)

* Acquisition of Modern Carpet Industries, pooling of interests.
† 7½ percent cumulative preferred stock issued by the Irish subsidiary to a bank ($316,000).
‡ Joint ventures between (1) Wilkinson Sword and Scripto, Inc., in Scripto (Eng), Ltd., and Scripto Industries (Shannon, Ireland), Ltd.; and (2) Scripto, Inc., and Scripto de Mexico.
Source: Scripto, Inc., annual reports.

troduced on the market in 1957 selling at $3.95 for the regular size; and in 1960, $4.50 and $5.00 for the compact models.

International expansion. Mr. Carmichael's second objective was to develop Scripto, Inc., into the largest mechanical writing instrument manufacturing firm in the world. In the early 1950s he felt that the growth of Scripto's business outside of the United States was being curtailed by high tariffs imposed on U.S.-made products and a shortage of dollars abroad. He concluded, therefore, that owning and operating manufacturing subsid-

	Ferst		Harris		Sams	
1967	1968	1969	1970	1971	1972	1973
$22,556,707	$21,180,588	$23,428,666	$25,210,155	$22,295,681	$18,946,674	$21,705,004
100.0	100.0	100.0	100.0	100.0	100.0	100.0
5.5	6.4	4.3	8.6	5.7	5.0	2.0
26.7	27.1	31.5	27.6	30.7	31.2	30.9
30.6	28.3	31.3	31.5	29.1	28.8	37.8
62.8	61.8	67.1	67.7	67.6	65.0	70.7
31.4	31.4	27.1	25.8	24.5	22.9	22.0
3.2	5.5	4.2	4.1	4.4	8.5‡	5.5
1.5	0.7	0.7	1.1	1.2	1.0	1.4
1.1	0.6	0.9	1.3	4.4	2.6	0.4
100.0	100.0	100.0	100.0	100.0	100.0	100.0
5.5	2.8	14.8	23.4	15.0	16.1	23.7
6.0	6.6	8.3	9.2	8.3	3.9	7.6
1.9	1.0	6.3	7.2	9.7	9.8	8.0
4.7	5.0					
18.1	15.4	29.4	39.8	38.0	29.8	39.3
20.7	20.2	16.9	14.0	14.1	8.3	4.5
1.5	1.7	1.5	0.3	1.0	1.2	0.8
—	—	—	1.2†	1.4	—	—
6.1	6.5	6.1	5.6	6.5	7.6	6.7
15.4	16.4	15.3	14.2	16.6	19.2	17.0
39.9	41.6	32.6	26.0	29.5	36.0	33.8
(1.7)	(1.8)	(1.8)	(1.1)	(2.1)	(2.1)	(2.1)

iaries abroad was more desirable than exporting American-made products to foreign countries. In 1957 Scripto was reorganized into a corporate group, which managed all domestic and foreign subsidiaries, and a domestic group, which managed the Atlanta operation. By the time that Mr. Carmichael resigned for health reasons in 1963, Scripto had either established or purchased foreign operations in Canada (1950), the United Kingdom (1955), Southern Rhodesia (1955), Australia (1957), Mexico (1959), New Zealand (1959), and Colombia (1959). All were 100 percent owned by Scripto with the exception of Colombia, which became a licensing agreement. The purchases and operation of the foreign subsidiaries were funded in three ways: through internally generated funds, long-term debt, and a $2.5 million common stock issue in 1956 at $7 per share.

Scripto's response to a changing market. In 1957 domestic sales began to slip for the first time in Scripto's history. Mr. Carmichael attributed the performance setback to two factors: (1) an oncoming recession in the United States and (2) the gradual shift from an overdemand to an oversupply of products in the mechanical writing instrument market. From that year on to the end of his presidential term (1963), Mr. Carmichael responded to the squeeze on Scripto's profit margins by—

Implementing a stringent across-the-board cost-cutting program.

Upgrading the Scripto product line to higher priced writing instruments (> $1) with the objective of eventual dominance in the higher priced gift item field. (Ball-point pens retailing at $1.98 and $2.95 were added plus an innovative Tilt-tip pen [$1.95] which featured accurate performance when held at any angle.)

Acquiring three domestic subsidiaries (Burnham Products Corporation, Broadway Pen Corporation, and Austin Metal Products, Inc.) in 1959 in order to strengthen Scripto's position in the ad/specialty market where very inexpensive, unbranded pens were sold.

Revamping the foreign manufacturing operations, particularly in the United Kingdom, with the objective of improving Scripto's competitive position in the Common Market countries where the price war had become even more severe than in the United States.

Making heavy expenditures in the research and development of new markets and products.

During Mr. Carmichael's final six years at Scripto, the firm's market share in writing instruments slipped from 16 percent (ranked second to Paper Mate) to less than 10 percent (ranked fifth behind Paper Mate, Waterman–BIC Pen, Parker Pen, and Sheaffer). Performance results are shown in Exhibit 3.

Mr. Carmichael retired in 1963. Despite his own assessment of the factors affecting Scripto's performance during his final years, some company officials believed that those factors were not entirely of external origin. Both Mr. Ferst and Mr. Carmichael had had serious health problems. Mr. Carmichael had been seriously injured in a car accident in his early teens and

EXHIBIT 3
Financial performance, 1958–1963 ($000)

	1958	1959	1960	1961	1962	1963
Consolidated net sales ...	$22,639	$23,106	$21,001	$21,156	$25,750	$26,344
Consolidated PAT	1,433	1,080	653	1,150	1,706	1,536
PAT/sales (%)	6.5	4.7	3.1	5.4	6.6	5.8

Source: Scripto, Inc., annual reports, 1958–63.

had been on crutches or in a wheelchair ever since. Scripto had assumed the cost of his medical expenses. In addition to his disability, Mr. Carmichael had held many civic obligations which kept him away from the day-to-day operation of the company. In an article appearing in *Business Week* magazine, one company executive remarked:

> The most dangerous time in a company's existence is when things are going well. Lax habits and bad decision-making are hidden by the success of the moment. Jimmy (Carmichael) was paternalistic, so that jobs that were poorly done and decisions that were poorly made tended to be overlooked and condoned. What happened was that an organization was allowed to build up over a period of years that was lax in work habits and in accepting the necessity of getting the job done.[2]

Carl Singer (September 1964–July 1967)

In September 1964 Carl Singer, former president of the Chicago-based Sealy Mattress Company, became president of Scripto, Inc. Found by an executive search firm and representing the first top-management change at Scripto in 17 years, Mr. Singer was described by his colleagues as "a man of action from a marketing background who saw Scripto's problems with a sense of urgency." Assessing the morale at Scripto as very low, Mr. Singer described his task as one of "complete changeover and repositioning," which he planned to carry out in two stages: Stage I was to focus on cost-cutting measures to improve profit margins which had been Mr. Carmichael's objective, and Stage II was to focus on revenue-generating activities, primarily in foreign markets.

Stage 1: Cost cutting (1964–1966).   Mr. Singer felt that Scripto's most immediate problem was the inadequacy of its production facilities. The decline in profit margins, he felt, underscored the need to trim costs by modernizing manufacturing facilities, both in Atlanta and overseas. Scripto's Atlanta plant had fallen into a state of disrepair. A plan was developed to rehabilitate the existing manufacturing facilities (a group of three-story buildings near downtown Atlanta) as well as to build a new plant on newly acquired land outside of Atlanta which would double production capacity. Production improvements were also made on existing facilities in Mexico, Canada, and the United Kingdom, as it was Mr. Singer's objective to continue the worldwide expansion envisioned by Mr. Ferst, Scripto's founder, who had died in 1965.

In 1965, $2.1 million was spent on plant and equipment improvements, and in 1966, another $2.9 million. To finance the improvements and to provide additional working capital, Mr. Singer negotiated a $5 million, 15-year

---

[2] "Rewriting the Script for Scripto," *Business Week*, December 17, 1966, p. 171.

loan at 5.45 percent interest with the Metropolitan Life Insurance Company. A portion of the proceeds was used to retire a $2.3 million balance in previous long-term Metropolitan loans. The new agreement allowed Scripto to take revolving short-term bank loans, providing the total did not exceed $2 million in any 60-day period each year.

A second problem which Mr. Singer faced was how to deal with the low morale of Scripto's employees. He increased the size of the total employee work force from 2,500 to 2,900 to prepare for the expected increase in unit production in Atlanta; he drew the control of subsidiary operations more closely to management in the Atlanta Division; and he made substantial reassignments and redefined responsibilities at the top-management level. As the result of a six-week labor dispute, factory workers became unionized (International Chemical Workers Union), much to the opposition of a number of Scripto's managers, some of whom subsequently resigned or were replaced.

In keeping with his "repositioning" theme, Mr. Singer took steps during Stage I to move Scripto in two product directions: (1) to higher priced writing instruments and (2) to wholly new product areas unrelated to writing instruments. This objective was to increase profit margins and to lessen the risk of concentration in one or two industries. At the time when Mr. Singer became president of Scripto, the company was in the process of installing highly automated equipment in its manufacturing facilities that would enable high-volume production of low-priced products. Mr. Singer reversed that process in the belief that "low-margin products were uneconomical to produce and sell." He began phasing out products such as inexpensive ball-point pens and fountain pens. Two "dramatically new" product lines were introduced: (1) butane (gas) lighters retailing at $4.95 and (2) fiber-tip pens retailing at 39 cents.

Aside from the move to higher priced writing instruments and lighters, Mr. Singer set in gear a large-scale product diversification program which he carried out either through internally generated research and development or through company acquisitions. Three new products were under internal development: a thermo-fax copier machine, a wide-angle lens camera, and a special butane lighter (Vu-tane). The copier machine was intended to gain a better foothold in the commercial (office supply) market where Scripto's sales had been practically nonexistent. The copier made transparencies to be used as audiovisual aids and was to be marketed at a retail price of $250 by a separate sales force through a separate distribution network (A. B. Dick and Heyer Corporation). The wide-angle lens camera was a personal research interest of a long-time Scripto employee, for which he had received between $1 and $1.5 million in R&D funds. While no suitable direct application had been found during the lengthy time of its development, management believed that the camera would be of interest to the

U.S. military in reconnaissance missions or for underwater photography. The Vu-tane lighter was to become Scripto's first entry into the plastic-encased butane lighter field at a price point of well under $5.

Two acquisitions were made during Stage I. In 1965 Scripto issued 143,-000 shares of its stock in exchange for all of the stock of Modern Carpet Industries, a leading privately owned carpet manufacturing firm. The carpet line was compatible with Mr. Singer's background in home furnishings, and he was attracted by "its outstanding organization and position in the fast-growing tufted carpet industry, which was considered to be the most volatile segment of the multibillion dollar home furnishings field." Following the acquisition, management devoted a great deal of time and money to enlarging, modernizing, and adding equipment to MCI. The second acquisition was Florence Ceramics Company, a Pasadena-based firm which produced imprinted ceramic products, such as ash trays. Mr. Singer described the ceramic products "as naturals for Scripto's retail outlets and ad/specialty activities."

Stage II: Revenue generation (1966–1967). Mr. Singer's master "repositioning" plan proved a little too grandiose; and Stage II, which dealt with his long-range objective of revenue growth, hardly met with implementation before his departure from Scripto in July of 1967. During his final months with the firm, Mr. Singer continued to introduce higher priced writing instruments ($1.00 and $1.95 ball-point pens and a $1.00 refillable fiber-tip pen) as he had intended, but his visions for the production area and his favorite project, Modern Carpet Industries, fell flat. Construction was delayed on the new Atlanta plant "for economic reasons." MCI was sold in 1966 because "it no longer fit into the redefined long-range growth projections for Scripto."[3] The employee base was reduced in number from 2,900 to 2,700.

Robert H. Ferst (August 1967–March 1968)

In August 1967 Robert Ferst, president of M. A. Ferst, Scripto's graphite and eraser subsidiary, replaced Mr. Singer as an interim president of Scripto, Inc. Company sales revenues had slumped to $30.46 million by the end of that year, returning $716,000 in net profits. Mr. Ferst attributed the poor performance to necessary write-offs to obsolete and excess inventories which had accumulated because of major product changeovers, as well as to currency devaluations on foreign markets.

While only at the helm for eight months, Mr. Ferst saw his mission as twofold: (1) to continue the cost-cutting program which dated back to the Carmichael days; and (2) to focus his attention on marketing the Scripto

---

[3] Scripto retained a 35 percent investment in the acquiring company, Modern Carpet Industries, Inc. The sale represented a $793,000 loss to Scripto, Inc.

products aggressively, with specific aim at consumer acceptance, an area which he felt had been neglected over the years. New systems of inventory controls were implemented. Drastic cost-control measures were enforced. Dividend payments were halted for the first time since Scripto's public offering in 1956 in order to conserve working capital for development and promotion of new and diversified products. Plans to proceed on the construction of a new Atlanta plant were again postponed. Higher priced butane lighters ($7.95–$16.95) were added to the cigarette lighter product line to follow the continuing emphasis on higher priced products with sizable profit margins. Independent design consultants were employed to restyle all products as an attempt to attract new consumers, particularly the younger generation and the adult gift buyers. Mr. Ferst resigned in March of 1968.

Arthur Harris (April 1968–March 1971)

In April 1968 Arthur Harris signed a five-year contract to become president of Scripto, Inc., with the option to terminate after three years. Mr. Harris came to Scripto from the Mead Paper Company where he had been head of its packaging division for many years. He was a fellow Atlantan and personal friend of the Ferst family who owned approximately 43 percent of the Scripto stock and controlled the executive committee of Scripto's board of directors.

Mr. Harris's three-year term as head of Scripto was characterized by change on all fronts—in organizational structure, international activities, marketing and sales programs, and product policies, with the overall objective "to reposition Scripto at the point of sale." One Scripto executive described Mr. Harris as "brilliant, strong-willed, and even dictatorial" in his attempt to turn the company around.

1968: Corporate overhaul. In 1968 Mr. Harris introduced substantial changes in the areas of (1) corporate organization, (2) marketing programs, and (3) product policies. His first step involved a complete overhaul of both domestic and foreign organizations. In Atlanta he reassigned existing personnel and added new personnel to develop second echelon depth. Attempts were made to revitalize foreign subsidiaries: in Mexico, new top management was added; in Canada, top management was also changed as well as the entire organizational structure; and in the United Kingdom, plans were made to relocate the plant in Ireland. A second step was to revamp marketing and sales programs which involved—

Complete realignment of sales territories in the United States.

Implementation of a new incentive method of compensation.

Installation of a sophisticated electronic data system for market research and forecasting.

Introduction of a new advertising scheme to tie merchandising more closely to point-of-purchase displays.

Addition of a special detail sales force at the retail level.

Development of an entirely new approach to marketing for the subsidiaries in South Africa, Rhodesia, New Zealand, and Modern Carpet Industries, Inc.

The third step was to "reevaluate all Scripto products." Many old products reappeared in new designs and colors. Three new products—the thermal copier, wide-angle lens camera, and Vu-tane lighter, all of which had been under development since 1964—were given deadlines for launching. A network of distributors and dealers was formed to sell the copier, an appropriate market for the wide-angle lens camera was still being sought, and the Vu-tane lighter was scheduled to be introduced on the market in 1969.

Despite his efforts, Scripto reported a net loss of $173,000 in 1968 based on net sales of $30.915 million. Mr. Harris summed up the performance results by calling the year one of "evaluation and appraisal." He attributed the losses to tax-loss carry-backs which could no longer be applied for tax purposes against foreign losses ($364,000 in 1968) as well as to inventory write-offs.[4]

1969: A wave of new products. Mr. Harris looked to 1969 as a year to "capitalize on conclusions drawn in 1968 and to continue to reposition Scripto at the point of sale." However, despite an increase in sales revenues to $31.2 million, Scripto reported an even greater net loss ($1.183 million) than the year before. Management attributed the losses to the costs and expenses related to the introduction of new products and the elimination of other products, all of which exceeded $1.6 million before tax credits. In that year the Vu-tane lighter ($3.95), Scripto-fax copier ($250), a thin-line mechanical pencil (49 cents), and fiber-tip ink crayons (in England) along with many new packages, particularly blister cards, were introduced.[5] In a letter to stockholders, Mr. Harris emphasized the importance of "keeping Scripto's identity as the only nationally advertised company with a *complete* line of writing instruments to meet almost any writing need in price ranges to fit anyone's budget."

Scripto acquired the Butane Match Corporation of America in 1969, which added a 98-cent refillable butane lighter (Butane Match) to its product line. The net assets of BMC were acquired in a pooling of interests transaction for an exchange of 66,000 shares of restricted Scripto stock at $1.23 per share for accounting purposes, and an additional 62,500 shares contingent upon BMC's future earnings.

---

[4] Inventories were reduced by approximately $900,000 during that year.

[5] Blister cards were product packages which could be hung on a pegboard for display purposes, and were designed to protect the retailer against pilferage.

In contrast to his predecessors, Mr. Harris began to shift the corporate focus in 1969 from international activities to those centered around the U.S. operation. The Mexican operation, upon its reorganization in 1968, was turned into a joint venture with Novaro, publishers of *Time* magazine in Mexico. The South African and Rhodesian operations were turned into licensing agreements, and the English plant was moved to Ireland where its operations would be free from British taxation.

1970: Demise of a vision. Mr. Harris's third and final year at Scripto, Inc., again produced a substantial earnings loss ($1.075 million) due to the condition of the economy and to heavy advertising and promotion commitments. Sales of the Scripto copier were minimal, and Florence Ceramics once again proved unprofitable. Renewed plans to relocate the Atlanta facilities were again termed financially infeasible and were finally abandoned. Scripto exchanged its 35 percent common stock investment and all previous advances to Modern Carpet Industries, Inc., for convertible preferred stock ($436,000 liquidation preference) in a newly formed parent company, Modern Holdings, Inc., and for an unsecured note receivable ($464,000) payable over five years. The New Zealand subsidiary was turned into a licensing arrangement.

Mr. Harris resigned in March of 1971. In his statement to stockholders, he remarked that he had met his principal objectives—"to form an aggressive and capable management team, eliminate unnecessary costs, and streamline operations in general." His future intention was to reside in Europe and spend a portion of his time as a special consultant to Scripto on the sale of Scripto products in the Common Market countries and on new product development.

Herbert "Bo" Sams (April 1971——)

On April 1, 1971, Herbert "Bo" Sams was elevated to the presidency of Scripto, Inc., from the position of vice president and general manager of the Atlanta Division which he had held since 1969. A veteran of Scripto for 35 years, most of which was spent in the manufacturing area, Mr. Sams had known Scripto in its heyday as well as the depths of poor performance.[6] It was at the latter point that he found himself in 1971. With that recognition, he set out to rebuild a company which had digressed far from its original business at the expense of an overall declining market share in writing instruments and fluctuating operating results.

Mr. Sams envisioned his mission as twofold: (1) to stop the company-wide losses which implied a disciplined approach to cost cutting in the European, Atlanta, and Canadian operations; and (2) to develop a long-range

---

[6] Mr. Sams had worked at Scripto, Inc., during his college days and had joined the firm upon his graduation from Georgia Institute of Technology in textile engineering in 1936.

plan for the Atlanta Division which would clearly define the corporate business and eliminate those products and activities which were not consistent with that plan. It was the latter decision which, in part, was unclear to "Bo" Sams. He considered two courses of action: (1) to abandon the writing instrument business altogether and rebuild Scripto–Atlanta solely as a cigarette lighter company; or (2) to reestablish Scripto–Atlanta as a viable competitor in the U.S. writing instrument business, as well as to continue in cigarette lighters. He chose the latter.

Stage I: A short-range profitability plan. In the 1970 annual report, Mr. Sams named profitability as his immediate goal, with special attention to be given to the three greatest loss-producing areas: the Atlanta Division and the Canadian and English subsidiaries.

Atlanta Division. When Mr. Sams became general manager of the Atlanta Division in 1969, the division had reported a net loss of $1.5–$2.0 million for that year.[7] John Tucker, vice president of finance,[8] assessed the problems in Atlanta:

> Scripto's performance in the early 1970s could not be blamed upon current decisions because it had its roots a decade before. The company had felt that the writing instrument market was locked up in the United States so we had decided to look elsewhere. We had illusions of grandeur which marked the beginning of problems because the U.S. market had not been developed properly. BIC came along, and Scripto's attitude was to laugh. Whoever thought that people would buy such a cheap and ugly stick pen? So we chose to go international and later learned that we were not powerful enough. All that time, the Atlanta Division was neglected. The company grew fat with people, and sales did not justify the advertising dollars spent. We didn't have the marketing capability to see if our products were right. And it seemed that every time there were problems, we cut out our research effort and capital expenditures program.

To eliminate the losses in Atlanta, Mr. Sams outlined a six-point program aimed at creating "a leaner organization with a new disciplined approach to marketing." His objectives were the following:

To build an aggressive, sound, and talented management team (see Exhibit 12).

To eliminate several unprofitable product variations.

To place a new emphasis on accurate sales forecasting.

To orient Scripto's market research toward better identification of consumer needs.

To improve the computerized accounting procedures to give faster, more accurate accounting and better inventory control.

---

[7] The Atlanta Division reported a $404,925 before-tax loss in 1972.

[8] Mr. Tucker was described by a colleague as "Mr. Sams' right-hand man. He adds front-office continuity to the team."

190

To reduce costs by lowering overhead and streamlining the manufacturing process.

Canada and the United Kingdom. Aside from the Atlanta Division, the Canadian and British operations represented the major sources of losses to Scripto in the late 1960s. Over the five-year period 1966–71, the Canadian operation produced roughly $500,000 in cumulative net losses. In 1972 Scripto entered a business partnership with the John A. Huston Company in Canada, in which the latter contracted to manufacture and market Scripto products while Scripto, Inc., supplied component parts and the Scripto name. The Canadian operation broke even in 1972 on revenues of $600,000 and was expected to break even again in 1973.

EXHIBIT 4

SCRIPTO, INC.
Consolidated Income Statement

	1973	1972
Net sales	$31,154,608	$28,378,819
Costs and expenses		
Cost of sales	$22,006,870	$20,192,819
Selling and admininstrative expenses	7,202,628	7,004,770
Interest expense, net	301,075	241,562
Equity in loss of foreign companies	192,267	157,971
Provision for losses on investments and long-term notes receivable	219,751	200,000
Other (income) expense, net	19,441	(18,943)
Total costs and expenses	$29,942,032	$27,777,653
Income before income taxes and extraordinary items	$ 1,212,576	$ 601,160
Provision for income taxes	779,000	420,000
Income before extraordinary items	$ 433,576	$ 181,166
Extraordinary items, net of applicable income taxes	89,648	$ 58,301
Net income	$ 523,224	$ 239,467
Per share:		
Income before extraordinary items	$0.15	$0.06
Extraordinary items	0.03	0.02
Net income	$0.18	$0.08

Source: Scripto. Inc., annual report, 1973.

The British operation faced a crunch in 1970. Scripto sold its run-down English plant and moved its facilities to Ireland where income from operations was tax free and government grants were readily available for equipment purchases. Despite those benefits, however, the English skilled labor refused to move to Ireland. The subsidiary reported a $1 million net loss in 1971. In 1972 Scripto, Inc., sold 55 percent of its equity in Scripto Pens,

Ltd. (England), and Scripto Industries (Shannon), Ltd., to Wilkinson Sword, Ltd., for which it received $1.1 million and the option to return to a 50–50 deal after five years. Scripto, Inc., continued to supervise the British manufacturing operation while Wilkinson assumed the marketing responsibility. By year's end, the British operation had cut its net losses to $0.5 million, in 1973 to $175,000, and a small profit was predicted for 1974.

Butane Match Corporation of America. In 1972 Scripto, Inc., arranged to sell the business of its wholly owned subsidiary, Butane Match Corporation of America, and certain related patent rights. Contrary to management's expectations, sales of the 98-cent refillable butane ligher ($644,000 in 1972) had been minimal. Due to the buyer's subsequent inability to meet the financial requirements of the sale, Scripto chose to reacquire Butane Match in September of 1973.

Atlanta property. During 1971 the holder of the 5.45 percent long-term note agreed to purchase Scripto's undeveloped property in Atlanta for a specified amount, subject to a third party's option to acquire the property at a higher price. The sale was recorded in 1971, and an extraordinary gain of $407,000, net of applicable income taxes, was included. In 1972 the third party exercised its option to purchase the property; an additional $104,768 net gain was included in the 1972 extraordinary item.

Further eliminations. In 1971 Scripto sold its ceramic products firm, the French operation, and the thermal copier product rights, whose combined contribution to profits had been only marginal. The decline of $1 million in sales revenues for that year was attributed to the elimination of those three revenue-generating activities, as well as to limited production at the new Irish plant facility.

Stage II: A return to the basic business in Atlanta. Management shifted its attention and allocation of resources in 1972 to the task of achieving its long-range objective: the realization of prominence by Scripto in the U.S. mechanical writing instrument industry. Over the previous 15 years and five presidential terms, profitability achieved through cost reduction, particularly in the manufacturing operation, had been the primary concern. The new focus in 1972 became the generation of revenues through the use of aggressive marketing programs, and product-line positioning, in the fastest growth segments of the writing instrument and lighter industries.

Product line. In 1973 management described Scripto, Inc., as "a full-line manufacturing company in mechanical writing instruments and cigarette lighters." The company reported 0.62 percent of the industry's dollar sales in ball-point pens, 0.34 percent in markers, 13.2 percent in mechanical pencils, 2.4 percent in porous-point pens, and 10.7 percent in cigarette lighters. Exhibit 5 presents the major consumer products which were manufactured and/or distributed by the Atlanta Division from 1965 to 1973. Exhibit 13 presents a sales breakdown by product line in the Atlanta Division from 1965 to 1973.

EXHIBIT 5
Atlanta Division 1973 major consumer product line*

	Price	Number of models	Production location	Production capacity (millions of units per year)	1973 Production rate (percent capacity)
Writing instruments:					
Ball-point pens:					
Retractable	$0.39, $0.98	2	Atlanta	15	28
Nonretractable (nonrefillables) ...	$0.19, $0.25	2	Burnham	>50	60–70
Porous-point pens ..	$0.19, $0.49	6	Atlanta	40–50	About 100%
Mechanical pencils:					
Regular	$0.39, $0.49, $1.29	5	Atlanta	25	75
Marking	$0.49	2	Atlanta	15–20	75
Cigarette lighters:					
Disposables (butane) ..	$0.98	1	Japan	Purchased	—
Regular refillables:					
Match (butane) ...	$0.98	1	Atlanta	4.5	50
Butane	$3.95–$14.95	10	Atlanta	6	90
Naphtha	$4.95–$5.95	2	Atlanta	6–7	100
Electronic	$17.95–$29.95	10	Japan	Purchased	—

* Ball-point pen refills, leads, erasers, lighter fuel, and no-name brand pens were manufactured and distributed by other U.S. subsidiaries.

Mechanical writing instruments. In 1972 Scripto introduced two inexpensive writing instruments: the 19-cent "Superpen" (a stick model ball-point pen), and the "19¢er" (a disposable fiber-tip pen). It was management's hope that the Superpen would provide a reentry point for Scripto in the commercial market and that the 19¢er, as a price competitor and quality instrument, would revitalize Scripto's overall position in the mechanical writing instrument industry. Scripto's competitive action was explained in an article appearing in *Distribution Executive*, as follows:

Scripto, Inc., back in the black last year after three years in the red, is taking an aggressive new posture in writing instruments to increase its profitability.

The Atlanta-based manufacturer, always a factor in writing instruments, has for some time given primary emphasis to its cigarette lighters.

"With the growth of our lighter business, which is substantial, we tended to neglect our writing instruments somewhat," says Marketing Vice President George L. Curran. "It was an easy thing to do. We were making money on lighters and the company in general was profiting. Then we suddenly awakened to the fact that, though we had both a name and adequate production facilities for writing instruments, we had not been active in this field for a long time."

To regain its former position of prominence in writing instruments,

Scripto is going after BIC's market with its new 19¢ Superpen and it's challenging Paper Mate's 49¢ Flair with a new 19¢ fiber tip pen.

Scripto, though it has had entries in both these markets, hasn't been a real contender in either. Of the two, the one it's most interested in developing is the fiber tip. In fact, its objective seems to be to become to the fiber tip business what BIC has become to the ball point business.

"Basically," says Curran, "the fiber tip has been a 49¢ market. What we're doing is positioning ourselves as the BIC of the fiber tip line."

In explaining why Scripto is marketing a fiber tip that's 30¢ lower than the popular price level, Curran mentions that the growth of the ball point market coincided with the gradual price reduction from the initial $12.50 to the present 19¢. The market, which had been a few hundred thousand units in the early Fifties, is now something like 1.8 billion units.

"As late as ten years ago," he says, "everybody felt that $1.00 was the popular pen and 49¢ was the inexpensive pen. Then BIC proved that 19¢ was a lot more popular.

EXHIBIT 6

SCRIPTO, INC.
Consolidated Balance Sheet

Assets	1973	1972
Current Assets:		
Cash	$ 432,354	$ 941,659
Receivables, less reserves of $545,963 in		
1973 and $418,649 in 1972	6,704,883	5,902,845
Inventories:		
Raw materials and supplies	3,585,031	2,029,475
Work in process	3,720,943	2,627,531
Finished goods	895,120	791,571
	$ 8,201,094	$ 5,448,577
Prepaid expenses	318,633	184,554
Total current assets	$15,656,964	$12,477,635
Property, plant, and equipment, at cost:		
Land	$ 633,220	633,220
Buildings.................................	2,246,016	2,216,530
Machinery and equipment	9,972,760	8,995,502
	$12,851,996	$11,845,252
Less: Accumulated depreciation	8,086,531	7,511,753
Total property, plant, and equipment	$ 4,765,465	$ 4,333,499
Investments:		
Equity in net assets of and advances to jointly		
owned foreign companies	$ 1,199,666	$ 1,408,247
Modern Holdings, Inc.:		
Investment in preferred stock less reserve of		
$436,000	—	—
Note receivable	—	200,000
Total investments	$ 1,199,666	$ 1,608,247
Other assets	82,909	527,293
Total assets	$21,705,004	$18,946,674

EXHIBIT 6 (continued)

Liabilities and Stockholders' Investment

Current liabilities:

Notes payable	$ 4,520,000	$ 2,447,154
Accounts payable	1,659,834	734,555
Accrued liabilities	1,613,978	1,534,213
Income taxes payable	131,934	331,659
Long-term debt due within one year	611,776	605,440
Total current liabilities	$ 8,537,522	$ 5,653,021
Long-term debt due after one year:		
5.45% term loan	$ 965,620	$ 1,565,620
Other	9,485	10,880
Total long-term debt	$ 975,105	$ 1,576,500
Deferred income taxes	179,000	227,000
Commitments and contingent liabilities:		
Stockholders' investment:		
Common stock 50¢ par value; authorized 5		
million shares, issued 2,891,200 shares	1,445,600	1,445,600
Paid-in surplus	3,693,459	3,693,459
Retained earnings	7,342,453	6,819,229
	$12,481,512	$11,958,288
Less:		
Treasury stock, at cost (42,520 shares)	$ 320,935	$ 320,935
Notes receivable from officers and employees		
for stock issued	147,200	147,200
	$ 468,135	$ 468,135
Total stockholders' investment	$12,013,377	$11,490,153
	$21,705,004	$18,946,674

Source: 1973 Scripto, Inc., annual report.

"So, we're trying to repeat this phenomenon in fiber tips. We're bringing the fiber tip into line for more purchases, for an ultimately higher volume of sales." ...

"Frankly," Mr. Sams says, "we're challenging our major competition head on...."[9]

At the end of 1973 the three competitors—BIC, Gillette, and Scripto—held the retail market shares shown in Exhibit 7.

During 1962–73 the three firms made the consumer advertising expenditures on writing instruments shown in Exhibit 8.

Cigarette lighters. For years, three companies—Ronson, Scripto, and Zippo—dominated the regular refillable lighter market, which represented two thirds of the total industry sales in lighters in 1973 (see Exhibit 9).

In 1973 cigarette lighter sales were rapidly increasing in the disposable (<$2) and electronic (>$12) lighter market segments. Sales in the regular refillable ($2–$12) segment had begun to level off. Industry sources believed

---

[9] "Scripto Taking on the Giants," *Distribution Executive,* March 1972, p. 12.

EXHIBIT 7
1973 comparative retail market shares (units)

	Gillette	BIC	Scripto
19-cent nonretractable ball-point pen:			
Price	$0.19	$0.19	$0.19
Market share (%)	5	31	<1
Fine-line porous pens:			
Price	$0.29, $0.49	$0.29	$0.19, $0.49
Market share (%)	352	22	3
All ball-point pens:			
Price	$0.19–$0.98	$0.19–$1.00	$0.19–$0.98
Market share (%)	15	66	2

Source: Corporate records.

EXHIBIT 8
Consumer advertising expenditures on writing instruments* ($000)

	BIC	Gillette	Scripto			BIC	Gillette	Scripto
1962.......	$ —	$ 146	$ 634		1968.......	$4,194	$3,346	$ 209
1963.......	132	165	736		1969.......	3,626	1,900	56
1964.......	285	126	413		1970.......	3,968	4,033	153
1965.......	654	61	536		1971.......	5,000	6,000	1,800
1966.......	943	61	1,449		1972.......	6,900	8,500	650
1967.......	3,071	2,720	766		1973.......	7,000	9,000	545

* Network TV, spot TV, consumer magazines.
Source: Corporate records.

EXHIBIT 9
1973 regular refillable lighter retail sales ($000)

	Estimated lighter sales	Percent of share	Estimated fuel and accessory sales	Percent of share	Estimated total sales	Percent of share
Ronson	$16,672	16.5	$26,676	78.0	$43,348	32.1
Scripto	18,339	18.2	3,335	9.7	21,674	16.1
Zippo	31,678	31.4	1,667	4.9	33,345	24.7
Estimated total market	100,809	100	34,235	100	135,044	100

Source: Corporate records.

that Zippo would be the least affected by the polarization trend. Zippo had built up long-time customer loyalties based on the high quality of its metal lighters, which held a lifetime guarantee. Ronson had lost market share to Scripto and Zippo when it moved to higher priced regular refillable lighters in the early 1970s and simultaneously cut back on its advertising support. It was felt that Scripto lacked advertising and marketing strength, and its lower priced regular refillable lighters faced keen competition from the inexpensive disposable lighters which were new to the marketplace. Additions to its regular refillable product line were largely responsible for its dramatic growth (32 percent) in lighter sales in 1972.

Scripto became a full-line cigarette lighter firm during 1973 upon the introduction of its "Catch 98" disposable lighter and its series of "Piezo" electronic lighters. The Japanese-made Catch 98 retailed at 98 cents. Management stated that the Catch 98 had captured a 10 percent share of the disposable lighter market and represented 24 percent of Scripto's dollar sales in cigarette lighters in 1973. A tobacco distributor commented on the Catch 98:

> Disposable lighers are not a perfect product yet. In the expansion stage of the market, lighters of questionable quality can be sold when they can't be sold in later stages. The Catch 98 is not the same quality as the Cricket, BIC Butane, or Dispoz-a-lite, which sell at $1.49. It has a smaller fuel reservoir and no pressure wick.

The Japanese-made Piezo series lighters ranged between $17.95–$29.95 in retail price and were sold in jewelry outlets. Their sales were minimal in 1973.

Problems facing Scripto. In an interview with the case researcher in October of 1973, Mr. Sams stated that there were four major problems facing Scripto at that time:

1. Potential embitterment on the part of independent distributors who felt that Scripto was going to abandon them in favor of direct selling to mass-merchandise outlets.
2. Uncertainty as to the availability and price of plastic because of the current worldwide energy shortage.
3. Limitation of financial resources due in part to loan covenant restrictions placed on future borrowing and, in part, to a shortage of internally generated cash.
4. Rising vocalism and absenteeism among the labor force in the Atlanta plant.

Disgruntled distributors. Management's intention to emphasize direct selling to mass-merchandise outlets added to the frustrations of distributors who had relied heavily on the Scripto business over the years and who had already become disenchanted with the firm's marketing and sales programs in recent years. In a survey conducted by Scripto in 1971, distributors complained that the company salespeople were unaggressive and made infrequent sales calls, that deals and promotions were unattractive because they required high minimum orders to get full discounts, that the product line was too broad, and that the products received very little advertising support. Generally, they felt that Scripto was a me-too company which had

EXHIBIT 10
Consumer advertising expenditures on cigarette lighters ($000)

	Ronson	Scripto	Zippo		Ronson	Scripto	Zippo
1966	$432.7	$ 8.6	$729.0	1970	$378.0	$1,006.0	$692.7
1967	634.8	533.3	799.6	1971	164.0	175.3	409.8
1968	554.0	312.0	804.7	1972	419.2	8.2	470.9
1969	422.8	317.3	709.6	1973	261.7	0.0	480.5

Source: Leading National Advertisers, Inc.

concentrated too long on cigarette lighters and had neglected its writing instrument business.[10]

In 1973 approximately 58 percent of Scripto's dollar sales in writing instruments and 81 percent in lighters were concentrated in the retail market, 16 percent and 1 percent, respectively, in the commercial market, and 10 percent and 7 percent, respectively, in the ad/specialty market. The remaining sales were distributed among the firm's minor markets. Despite the direct selling trend, Scripto had continued to rely on indirect selling through its distributors.

EXHIBIT 11
Atlanta Division dollar shipments (percentages)

	Writing instruments		Cigarette lighters	
	1972	1973	1972	1973
Regular sales:*				
Direct	11	15	21	26
Indirect	60	71	66	66
Specialized sales:†				
Direct	12	5	5	2
Indirect	17	9	8	6
Total sales	100	100	100	100

* Retail and commercial sales.
† Ad/specialty, premium, government sales, and so forth.
Source: Corporate records.

Mr. Sams commented on Scripto's position:

> Scripto had been devoted to the drug and tobacco distributors for many years and did not change as the market did because we were protecting those distributors. Now we must change, and the specialized distributors whose businesses are rapidly declining feel that they may be jilted.

---

[10] One manager stated that the salespeople were responsible for the shift to lighters because the sales commissions were more attractive on cigarette lighters than on writing instruments in years past.

The increasing price of plastic. Due to a serious worldwide fuel shortage in 1973, industries which relied heavily on oil-based supplies were predicting a rise in the price of plastics in 1974 and possible production cutbacks in the event of plastics shortages. Cigarette lighter and writing instrument firms, which used metal rather than plastic as their primary raw material, owned their own refineries, or imported products from countries that were looked upon with favor by the Arabs, were likely to be less directly affected by the energy crisis. Scripto, whose products were made primarily from plastic, was predicting at worst a 20 percent production cutback in its Atlanta plant.

Financial limitations. At the end of 1973, approximately $1.6 million remained outstanding on the original 5.45 percent long-term loan of $5 million negotiated in 1965 with Metropolitan Life Insurance Company. The loan agreement, amended in 1972, required a $600,000 principal plus interest payment at the end of 1974 and 1975 with a balloon payment of $366,000 in 1976. Provisions under the loan agreement required the U.S. and Canadian companies to maintain a minimum net working capital balance of $6.5 million, limited short-term borrowings to $3 million until April of 1974, and prevented dividend payments to stockholders or additional advances to foreign subsidiaries. During 1972 Scripto applied $959,380 from the sale of certain properties to payment of loan principal.

In 1973 there were approximately 2.8 million shares of Scripto common stock outstanding of which 43 percent was controlled by the Ferst family. No dividends had been paid on outstanding stock since 1967.

Work force attitudes. In 1973 the absenteeism rate of plant workers ran as high as 7 percent. Mr. Sams had said, "Morale is improving. It was at ground zero in 1971." Absenteeism had never forced an operations shutdown, but production efficiency was always severely damaged.

Management attributed the labor problems primarily to a "change in social attitudes in the United States" but also to the available work force pool within Atlanta itself. About 60 percent of the work force had been with Scripto for over ten years, and it was believed that those workers felt a sense of loyalty to the company and to their jobs. Absenteeism problems prevailed among the remaining 40 percent who in management's judgment tended to be the younger workers, many of whom were hired from the small group of unemployed persons (2.8 percent of the total work force) in Atlanta in 1973.

The work force was composed primarily of black women. About 60 percent to 70 percent of the male workers were black. Management stated that racial tension existed among black assembly-line workers and white supervisors, but tension was greater between black supervisors and black assembly-line workers who resented the supervisors for their professional advancement. Base salaries ranged from $2.25–$2.60 per hour (unskilled work) to $4.00 (skilled work).

Factory conditions were felt by some managers to contribute to worker dissatisfaction on the job. The plant facility consisted of a group of old three-story buildings five minutes from downtown Atlanta. The manufacturing areas were noisy (workers were supplied with ear plugs and eye glasses for protection against noise levels above 85 decibels, flying debris, and sparks), dirty, and hot (no air conditioning). Production rates were machine paced. The work was seasonal, and layoffs were a common occurrence.

MR. SAMS LOOKS TO THE FUTURE

Mr. Sams viewed his role as that of a major policy maker. Consistent with that view, he had great faith in the capabilities of his management team to oversee the day-to-day operation of the business and to implement his decisions. As president, he felt that he had made three key decisions: (1) to cut the losses in Atlanta, Canada, and Britain; (2) to reemphasize the writing instrument business; and (3) to introduce such products as the 19¢er porous-point pen and the Catch 98 disposable lighter, which would compete in the high-growth areas of the market.

EXHIBIT 12
1973 top management—Atlanta Division

Name	Title	Years at Scripto	Job(s) prior to Scripto	Expertise
"Bo" Sams	President	37	—	Manufacturing
John Tucker	Executive vice president	4	Controller (Kelsey-Hayes Tools); accountant, Touche Ross	Accounting
Jack Bozarth	Vice president marketing	½	Marketing manager, consumer products division of Gulf & Western	Marketing
Morton Chaber	Vice president manufacturing	4	Vice president of manufacturing at Ronson; vice president of manufacturing at Revlon	Manufacturing
George Dinnerman	Vice president sales	3	Vice president of marketing at Ronson	Sales
Bill Black	Vice president national accounts	8	Sales director at Timex	Sales
Roberta Haynes	Assistant vice president sales and marketing	10	Army Services	Administration
John Dolan	Controller	1	Accountant at Price Waterhouse	Accounting

Management outlined the 1974 sales objectives for the Atlanta Division as follows:

To increase dollar sales in writing instruments by 10 percent and cigarette lighters by 5 percent using proven promotions and programs.

To increase distribution of the basic product line with current chain customers, and to develop new chain customers, with special emphasis placed on writing instruments.

To concentrate sales attention on the products with the greatest potential, that is, disposable lighters, broad-tip markers, and porous-point pens.

Sales objectives.   Plans to achieve the 1974 sales growth objectives for writing instruments and cigarette lighters centered around a reorganization of the sales organization in the Atlanta Division. Specifically, the commercial stationery division was to become a specialized sales operation in which all sales would be handled through 11 manufacturer's representatives in lieu of the 2,000 distributors which it had used in the past. Direct retail sales would be handled by a national accounts manager working with 75–100 large chain accounts, and by 17 company salesmen and 14 manufacturer's representatives working with the 150 small chain accounts in the northeast, central, southern, and western divisions. Indirect retail sales would be made through 4,500 specialized retail distributors and 40 food brokers. Scripto would use its five specialized company salesmen to sell to the 1,344 ad/specialty distributors and would sell direct to the other markets. A detail force of 35 women would be used at the retail level. Exhibits 12 and 14 present the new organizational charts.

Chain store expansion.   In 1973 Scripto sold 15 percent of its writing instruments and 26 percent of its cigarette lighters direct to chain store accounts. Management hoped to increase chain store sales by at least 10 percent and 5 percent, respectively, in 1974, by assigning district managers and detail salespersons to handle all national and regional chain accounts and divisional sales managers to coordinate those activities.

New products.   Management planned to concentrate on rapidly growing segments of the writing instrument and cigarette lighter markets in 1974. A family of disposable lighters selling at retail prices of $1.19, $1.39 and $1.69 would be introduced. The $1.69 lighter would be manufactured at full capacity (10 million units per year) in the Atlanta plant. The $1.39 lighter would be imported from Japan. The $1.19 product was the former Catch 98 at 98 cents. The 19¢er porous-point pen would be repositioned at the point of sale to provoke greater impulse purchases. The 49-cent porous-point pen would be aggressively marketed in the commercial market. Scripto was testing a finer point porous pen with a harder tip which would write through carbons. Scripto planned to introduce a better canister

EXHIBIT 13
Atlanta Division sales, 1965–1973

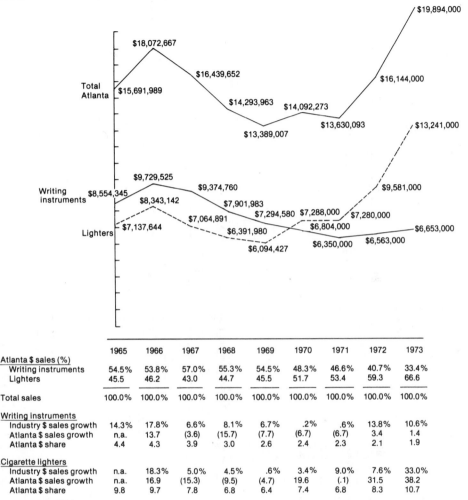

	1965	1966	1967	1968	1969	1970	1971	1972	1973
Atlanta $ sales (%)									
Writing instruments	54.5%	53.8%	57.0%	55.3%	54.5%	48.3%	46.6%	40.7%	33.4%
Lighters	45.5	46.2	43.0	44.7	45.5	51.7	53.4	59.3	66.6
Total sales	100.0%	100.0%	100.0%	100.0%	100.0%	100.0%	100.0%	100.0%	100.0%
Writing instruments									
Industry $ sales growth	14.3%	17.8%	6.6%	8.1%	6.7%	.2%	.6%	13.8%	10.6%
Atlanta $ sales growth	n.a.	13.7	(3.6)	(15.7)	(7.7)	(6.7)	(6.7)	3.4	1.4
Atlanta $ share	4.4	4.3	3.9	3.0	2.6	2.4	2.3	2.1	1.9
Cigarette lighters									
Industry $ sales growth	n.a.	18.3%	5.0%	4.5%	.6%	3.4%	9.0%	7.6%	33.0%
Atlanta $ sales growth	n.a.	16.9	(15.3)	(9.5)	(4.7)	19.6	(.1)	31.5	38.2
Atlanta $ share	9.8	9.7	7.8	6.8	6.4	7.4	6.8	8.3	10.7

n.a.-not available.
Sources: Scripto, Inc., annual reports and Writing Instrument Manufacturers Association.

marker in 1974, which management claimed could be differentiated from competitors' products.

An allocation of $1.6 million was planned for the 1974 advertising program which was to cover all products at the trade and consumer levels. Scripto intended to use two themes: (1) Scripto (products) works and (2) Scripto (company) is alive and well.

Jack Bozarth, vice president marketing, summed up Scripto's position in 1974 as follows:

EXHIBIT 14
1974 organizational chart—Atlanta Division

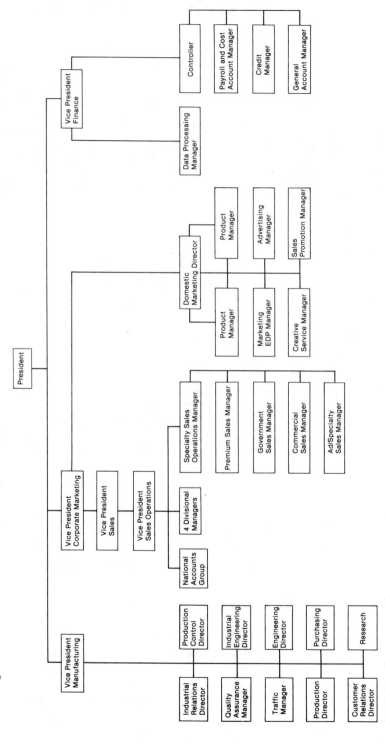

Source: Company records.

Scripto is in a different position than anyone else in the industry. We're the only full-line writing instrument supplier left. Whether they know it or not, BIC is the stick, Paper Mate is the Flair, Magic Marker is the canister marker.

For the first time, Scripto is going with the industry. We're competing in the growth areas but are protected by our full line. Right or wrong, it will be interesting to see how the industry goes.

case 8

Note on the soft drink industry in the United States

"The soft drink is one of the greatest of American traditions," commented a reporter, "really far more American than apple pie (which originated in France) or hot dogs (which are of German extraction). The soft drink was born and raised in the U.S. of A., and most of us were born and raised with soft drinks—or soda pop for those of western heritage."

Some might well object to this nationalistic interpretation since naturally carbonated water was used as medicine by the ancient Greeks and soft drinks had been commercially available in Europe for years. Yet clearly the American consumer has had a long love affair with "soda pop." In 1974 total soft drink sales were over $7.8 billion at wholesale and per person consumption was over 429 eight-ounce containers per year. And the romance has been of long duration; buoyed by population and real income growth, per capita consumption doubled from 1962 to 1973. Soft drink case sales rose from 1,668 million to 3,772 million during that period moving from 16 percent of total beverage consumption in 1960 to almost 25 percent in 1973. This sales growth brought prosperous days to concentrate makers, bottlers, and retail organizations.

In 1974 and 1975 industry growth patterns changed, with case sales and per capita consumption remaining approximately level. Had the bloom disappeared from the rose—or should we ask, had the "fizzle disappeared and the soda pop gone flat?" Industry analysts seemed to agree that the 7 to 8 percent annual unit growth rates of the past were probably no longer possible. But what next? One analyst noted, "The industry is in a period when sales will basically plateau." Maxwell Associates, a consulting firm, predicted 3 to 4 percent sales growth in 1976. But these modestly enthusiastic future predictions by analysts did not seem to deter the competitive ambitions of the industry's leading firms. Each of the top five companies, according to Standard & Poor's 1976 Beverage Industry Reports, had clear-cut expansion goals. "Dr Pepper expects to continue to grow at two to three times the industry rate and is confident of being number three in national sales in the not too distant future. Pepsi hopes to extend its string of 52 consecutive months of market share gain, and, nevertheless, Coke expects to continue to gain market share on a total product basis." The president of the Seven-Up Company, on another occasion, announced, "We really believe and we're seriously dedicated to the point of view that 7UP can and should be the number one selling soft drink in the United States."

In addition to this development, the industry was confronted with pressure from private environmental groups and increasing interest on the part of regulatory agencies in its operations. Private environmental groups and federal and state agencies were attempting to find ways of limiting the use of nonreturnable containers. Governmental concerns about health forced the industry to drop cyclamates as a substitute for sugar in diet drinks, and government antitrust concerns had resulted in legal action against the franchise system—regarded by many company executives as important to the industry's success.

Commenting on the overall scene, one corporate officer queried, "Where is this industry going? I'm not sure! Competition is getting worse. Nothing seems to stay pinned down—franchising, distribution, ingredients, and packaging are all 'up for grabs.' One competitive development has already started. Billboard advertising has always had a 'product message,' but now they are being directed to a 'cents per ounce' price theme. Food stores will become a battlefield." This note explores the soft drink segment of the U.S. beverage industry; as such it gives but limited attention to the international market and to other beverages such as coffee, tea, chocolate, milk, bottled waters, juices, and alcoholic drinks. In sequence, the note will cover six areas: the product—past success and current situation, industry structure and participants, key industry functional strategies, new competitors—the intruders, the industry's critics, and future market directions—a cloudy crystal ball.

In studying this note, the reader should keep in mind the complexity of the territory being described and the simplicity of this map. He or she will note that some of these data are not comparable, that experts sometimes derive diametrically opposite conclusions from common data, and that some very useful data were simply not available. Any judgments made, by necessity, must be tentative.

PRODUCT

Soft drinks, or nonalcoholic carbonated beverages, consist of a flavoring base such as cola, a sweetener, water, and carbonation. Most soft drinks are consumed cold, and the product has a seasonal sales pattern, peaking in hot summer months.

Originating in a Philadelphia apothecary shop, soft drinks were first sold primarily through drugstore soda fountains where flavors and carbonated water would be mixed for immediate sale to an on-premise customer. This early association with apothecaries and drugstores gave soft drinks a medicinal association which still prevailed, to some degree, in the 70s. The executive vice president of Seven-Up commented, "There was a group for whom our green bottle had almost medicinal or therapeutic overtones, the thing to take when you had the flu and the doctor told you to take a lot of liquid."[1]

The development of manually operated filling and bottling machines in the mid-1800s encouraged the establishment of thousands of local bottling works. Each of these supplied carbonated beverages to its nearby market under a variety of brand names, which the researcher found fascinating: Cardinal Necter, Queer, Marrowfood, Creme Puncho, Peach Bounce, Muscadine Thrill, Wami, and Egg Soda—the latter coming in an egg-shaped bottle.[2]

In 1884 Hires Root Beer advertised in *Harper's Magazine*. The trade name Dr Pepper was copyrighted in 1885, followed by Coca-Cola in 1886. Brad's Drink, which became Pepsi-Cola, appeared in 1886. The predecessor company of Seven-Up was formed in 1906 (7UP was introduced in 1920), and the predecessor company of Royal Crown appeared in 1924 and introduced Royal Crown Cola in 1935.

In 1976 regular soft drinks came in a variety of flavors with cola accounting for 58 percent of the market. Most of these used sugar or sugar plus high fructose corn syrup as a sweetener; diet drinks (15 percent of the market) used a noncolor artificial sweetener, in 1976, usually saccharin. Diet drinks in most cases carried related brand names, for example, Diet Pepsi, Sugar Free Dr Pepper; but in some cases they were promoted under different brands, for example, Tab (Coca-Cola) and Diet-Rite Cola (Royal Crown). National brands accounted for approximately 67 percent of the U.S. market in 1975 (see Exhibits 1 and 2).

The industry's past success

The soft drink industry had enjoyed consistent and substantial growth over a period of several decades; per capita consumption had increased from 17.5 gallons in 1960 to 31.6 gallons in 1974, an increase of 65 percent. Soft drinks, a Boston physician decried, are "cradle to grave. We wean babies to Coke and serve 7UP to the geriatrics ward." A casualty in the gallonage race was water.

Four primary factors, the researchers believed, had contributed significantly to this success: the growth in disposable income, marketing innova-

---

[1] "Can Uncola Make Cola Cry Uncle?" *The Grocery Manufacturer*, June 1972, p. 82.
[2] Dudley Lynch, "Dr Pepper Takes on Coke," *D Magazine* (Dallas/Ft. Worth), September 1975.

EXHIBIT 1
Market share by flavor

Flavors:	1971	1972	1973	1974	1975	1976 (Est.)
Regular cola	52.0%	51.5%	51.0%	51.0%	50.0%	50.5%
Diet cola	5.6	6.0	6.2	6.6	7.3	7.8
Total cola	57.6%	57.5%	57.2%	57.6%	58.0%	58.3%
Regular lemon-lime	11.4%	11.3%	11.4%	11.3%	11.0%	10.9%
Sugar free lemon-lime	0.6	0.7	0.8	1.2	1.7	2.0
Total lemon-lime	12.0%	12.0%	12.2%	12.5%	12.7%	12.9%
Regular orange	4.8%	4.7%	4.6%	4.4%	3.9%	3.6%
Regular root beer	4.4	4.4	4.0	3.9	4.1	4.2
Dr Pepper and Mr. PiBB	3.9%	4.3%	5.0%	5.2%	5.7%	6.0%
Diet Dr Pepper and Mr. PiBB	0.2	0.4	0.5	0.7	0.9	1.2
Total Pepper	4.1%	4.7%	5.5%	5.9%	6.6%	7.2%
Ginger ale, tonic, carbonated water, and soda	4.4	4.6	4.7	4.8	4.9	5.0
All other (regular grape, Mountain Dew, chocolate, black cherry, etc.)	9.6	9.0	8.3	7.4	6.0	4.8
All other diet, diet orange, and root beer	2.9	3.0	3.4	3.6	3.8	4.0
Total regular drinks	90.6%	89.8%	89.0%	87.9%	86.2%	85.0%
Total diet drinks	9.4%	10.2%	11.0%	12.1%	13.8%	15.0%
Total	100.0%	100.0%	100.0%	100.0%	100.0%	100.0%

Source: J. C. Frazzano, Oppenheimer & Co., *Beverage World*, February 1977, p. 8.

tions, packaging developments, and the industry's competitive culture (see Exhibits 3, 4 and 5).

In commenting on the first factor, Emanuel Goldman of Sanford Bernstein and Company noted:

> The work that I've done clearly indicates that the industry is most sensitive to real disposable personal income ... when real DPI was pumping along at about 3.5 to 4.0 percent growth rate in real terms, soft drink gallonage was growing at some faster rate.... Similarly, during recessionary periods, 1954 and 1958, for example, the recession of '60 to '61, and the recession of mid-'74 to mid-'75, there was a definite softness, with a decline in soft drink volume in the mid-year to mid-year periods.[3]

Second, corporate executives stressed the importance of marketing to the industry's past accomplishments. W. W. Clements, chairman of the Dr Pepper Company, noted:

> This industry has several characteristics that place it somewhere in between true service industries and purely manufacturing industries. It, in

[3] "The Beverage Industry," *The Wall Street Transcript*, May 24, 1976, pp. 43, 766.

EXHIBIT 2
Top ten soft drink brands 1966–1975

| | 1966 | | 1970 | | 1975 |
Brand	Percent share of market	Brand	Percent share of market	Brand	Percent share of market
Coke	27.6	Coke	34.8	Coke	26.2
Pepsi	16.1	Pepsi	14.2	Pepsi	17.4
7UP	6.4	7UP	5.8	7UP	6.6
Royal Crown Cola	3.8	Royal Crown	3.5	Dr Pepper	4.9
Dr Pepper	2.4	Dr Pepper	3.4	Royal Crown	3.4
Diet Pepsi	1.9	Sprite (Coke)	2.3	Sprite (Coke)	2.6
Diet-Rite Cola (Royal Crown)	1.6	Diet-Rite Cola (Royal Crown)	1.8	Tab (Coke)	2.6
Sprite	1.5	Fresca (Coke)	1.4	Diet Pepsi	1.7
Tab	1.4	Canada Dry Ginger Ale	1.1	Mountain Dew (Pepsi)	1.3
Mountain Dew (Pepsi)	1.4	Diet Pepsi	0.9	Canada Dry	1.2
	64.1	Tab (Coke)	0.9		66.7
			70.0		

Source: Maxwell *Consumer Service Reports on the Soft Drink Industry*, February 23, 1976; used with the permission of the Dr Pepper Company.

EXHIBIT 3

Historic per capita soft drink consumption and wholesale sales levels, selected years

Year	Wholesale sales ($ millions)	Cases (192 ounces) (millions)	Per capita (8-ounce containers)
1859	$ 1.4	2.8	2.2
1929	214	272	53.1
1950	877	1,002	158.0
1960	1,698	1,477	192.0
1970	4,800	3,097	362.8
1972	5,684	3,541	406.4
1973	6,223	3,772	429.6
1974	7,827	3,798	429.4

Source: National Soft Drink Association, 1975.

EXHIBIT 4

U.S. beverage consumption, 1960–1974

	1960 gallons per capita	1964 gallons per capita	1970 gallons per capita	1974 gallons per capita	Percent increase (decrease) 1964–74	1975 gallons per capita
Coffee	40.2	39.2	35.5	32.8	(15)	31.6
Soft drinks	17.5	19.1	27.0	31.6	65	31.4
Milk	28.0	25.9	25.0	25.9	(7)	24.5
Beer	15.4	16.0	18.5	21.3	33	21.6
Tea	6.0	6.2	6.9	7.6	23	7.4
Juices	4.0	3.2	4.8	5.7	78	6.1
Distilled spirits	1.3	1.4	1.8	2.0	43	2.0
Wine	n.a.	1.0	6.3	1.7	70	1.7
Total	112.4	112.4	125.8	126.9		126.3

Imputed water consumption: 1966, 67.3 gallons per capita; 1975, 56.7 gallons per capita.

n.a. = not available.
Sources: Maxwell *Consumer Services for 1960–1974*, used with permission of Dr Pepper Co. The 1975 data from *Advertising Age*.

addition, does not qualify as an industry relying to any great extent on engineering development or research. The sophisticated part of the soft drink industry is the marketing area.[4]

Since the 1930s, industry operations had been substantially influenced by the competitive struggle between Coke and Pepsi. Pepsi, during that era, began to challenge the industry giant with a series of marketing innovations. In 1939 Pepsi used the first singing radio commercial: "Pepsi-Cola hits the spot. Twelve full ounces that's a lot. Twice as much for a nickel too.

[4] Unpublished speech to Thunderbird School of International Management, June 8, 1972.

EXHIBIT 5
Disposable income and soft drink industry growth

Year	Disposable personal income ($ billions)	Percent Increase	Constant $ D.P.I. ($ billions)	Percent Increase	Soft drink industry percent increase
1972	$795.1	6.9	$579.0	4.3	5.6
1971	744.3	8.0	544.7	4.1	8.3
1970	689.5	8.8	533.2	3.9	6.3
1969	634.0	7.3	513.6	2.9	4.9
1968	591.0	8.2	499.0	4.6	12.1
1965	473.2	8.0	435.0	6.6	8.0
1963	404.6	5.1	381.3	3.9	7.0
1961	364.4	4.1	350.7	3.1	3.2
1959	337.3	5.8	330.0	4.4	0.0

Source: Based on Bureau of the Census data, 1973.

Pepsi-Cola is the drink for you." In 1942 reporter Robert Scheer noted that a survey showed this jingle to be the best-known tune in the United States—ahead of the Star-Spangled Banner. In 1976 most soft drink companies were heavy investors in all kinds of worldwide consumer advertising. To his dismay, Scheer found a soft drink sign greeting visitors as they climbed the steps to the apadana to view the magnificent ruins of Persepolis in Iran.

Pepsi also began to systematically survey changing life styles and relate its marketing program to that moving target.

> Pepsi being a modern corporation takes its cultural contributions seriously and all of the execs ... are quite aware that they have never been in the business of simply selling a product but rather a way of life. Throughout the years of Pepsi-Coke rivalry, the arena has always been in the packaging and sales effort and not the concentrate, which has stayed the same while the companies' fortunes have gone up and down. It was, therefore, not the taste that mattered but rather how the public was taught to perceive it. The same stuff could be "light," "sociable," a healthful tonic— it could make you "stay young and fair and debonair" and gets you into The Pepsi Generation. This magic is worked for a concentrate that is basically the same for all of the colas and the much-guarded secrets can be obtained from a flavor chemist's handbook.[5]

Industry innovations in packaging were also credited with increasing soft drink consumption. Developments occurred on many fronts: the introduction of soft drinks in cans and nonreturnable bottles, which encouraged increased out-of-the-home consumption; the introduction of new types of carrying containers, for example, the six-pack beverage package; and an in-

---

[5] "The Doctrine of Multinational Sell," Robert Scheer, *Esquire*, April 1975, pp. 163–65.

crease in number of sizes of bottles and cans. Between 1960 and 1975, available package sizes had increased from two to ten sizes ranging from 6½ to 64 ounces, plus 1- and 2-liter sizes. One executive estimated that 24 ounces and larger packages accounted for over 30 percent of all soft drinks sold for home consumption in 1975.

EXHIBIT 6
Soft drink package types, 1960–1975

	1960	1965	1970	1975
Returnable bottles	94%	83%	46%	34%
Nonreturnable bottles	2	5	25	31
Cans	4	12	29	35

Sources: *Soft Drink Annual Manual,* 1971–1972, *Beverage Industry,* 3/19/76, and NSDA Sales Survey, 1960.

A final factor impacting industry growth was the corporate "climate" of the leading soft drink firms. As described by business journalists, it seemed to be a mixture of general management leadership style, a concept of business competition as a "war game" and a set of corporate values which emphasized belief in your product, volume growth, market share improvement, and by all means "beat the competition and sell that drink." The latter goal was neatly summarized by a vice president who, speaking at the prospect of the Bamboo Curtain coming down, said "There are 800 million gullets in China and I want to see a_____in every one of them."

Long dominated by "Mother Coke," the soft drink industry's recent competitive posture had been substantially influenced by two men—Donald Kendall, president of Pepsi-Cola, and W. W. Clements, president of Dr Pepper. Robert Scheer characterized Mr. Kendall and Pepsi's corporate "ambience" as follows:

> In ten years' time Don Kendall was to kick, pull, and make a bumbling, small one-product company into a modern multinational conglomerate giant. One of his first acts was to begin plans for the new world headquarters. The Purchase, New York, world headquarters of PepsiCo is on one hundred forty-one acres of choice Westchester property, sullied by not a single Pepsi-Cola sign. An "elegant modern" seven-building complex designed by Edward Durrell Stone is focused on an imported-cobblestone courtyard. Five thousand new trees (thirty-eight varieties), it is said, remind Kendall of his native Washington State and, as a somewhat personal touch, there is jet d'eau in the lake which shoots up eighty feet whenever Kendall pushes a button on his desk.
>
> I asked Kendall for his opinion of John Kenneth Galbraith's theory that corporations, being large planning units, could simply plan to have lower levels of growth. I might just as well have advocated bisexual love. "No Growth! What?" It was the same disbelief that I found when I put the

question to the other execs—like telling a missionary that the number of converts doesn't matter.[6]

W. W. Clements's aggressive leadership of Dr Pepper illustrated the "war game" characteristic of the industry. President of a company with profits amounting to but one twentieth of Coke's, Mr. Clements's campaign to expand Dr Pepper's sales was described in part by Dudley Lynch:

> One crisp November morning in 1969 Woodrow Wilson "Foots" Clements and his team of executives stepped into a cab outside New York's Waldorf-Astoria Hotel. Mission: To pull off what some would call the biggest coup in soft drink history. Clements and his Dr Pepper executives, representing an easy-going beverage which had stayed home in Texas and minded its own business for 85 years, headed over to the 34th Street offices of Coca-Cola Bottling Company of New York, the world's largest distributor of soft drink's Goliath: Coca-Cola. Objective: to convince Coca-Cola of New York to bottle Dr Pepper. Seven months later the arrangements were completed.
>
> Dr Pepper's invasion of Coke's independent bottlers didn't go unnoticed at Coke's parent company headquarters, 310 North Avenue, Atlanta. Amidst Dr Pepper's campaign to sign up Coke bottlers came the New York coup, followed two years later by Dr Pepper's signing, in Mother Coke's backyard, of Coke's independent Atlanta bottler. Now the Coca-Cola parent company would take guests through the Atlanta bottling works and find themselves walking along halls bedecked with Dr Pepper signs. That was too much. "What Dr Pepper doesn't understand," suggests an Atlanta observer, "is the insult involved. What Dr Pepper did to Coke is something you just don't do to Coca-Cola—at least that's the way Coke views things. . . ."
>
> Adding to the insult was Dr Pepper's foray two years ago into Japan, a market that in 1973 produced 19 percent of Coke's worldwide profits. Dr Pepper signed a joint venture, with yes, you guessed it, Tokyo Coca-Cola Bottling Company, to introduce Dr Pepper to Japan. . . . Jumping into Japan was like waving a red flag, says Richard McStay, formerly research director at Atlanta's Irby & Co. "To Coke, Japan is motherhood, virginity, apple pie or anything you want to call it."[7]

An additional industry characteristic should be noted: market characteristics for soft drinks varied substantially by region. The highest per capita consumption according to industry analysts was in the South and Southwest. The popularity of diet drinks, flavor, packaging, and retail outlet preferences also varied by region (see Exhibit 7). Historically, soft drink companies had originated in the South, and in 1976 four out of the top five firms had their headquarters in the South and Southwest.

---

[6] "The Doctrine of Multinationals," *Esquire*, April 1975, p. 126.

[7] "Dr Pepper Takes on Coke," *D Magazine* (*Dallas/Ft. Worth*), September 1975, p. 61.

EXHIBIT 7
Regional variations in the soft drink market

	North-east	East Central	West Central	South	South-west	Western	Pacific
Diet	13%	8%	9%	11%	13%	14%	
Flavors:							
Cola	30	47	55	42	53	41	
Lemon-lime	16	17	19	10	18	20	
Package sizes:							
10 and 12 ounce	37	60	58	56	51	54	
Over 24 ounces	40	16	18	16	22	20	
Package type:*							
Returnable bottles	20	50	41	53	46	48	
Nonreturnable bottles	38	9	25	13	10	18	
Cans	33	22	24	27	30	24	
Fountain	9	10	10	7	15	11	
Outlets:*							
Food stores	70	54	72	60	54	73	
Restaurants, bars	10	13	6	6	21	8	
Service stations	5	12	10	12	10	8	

* Percent of packaged volume.
Source: *Soft Drinks,* December 1974.

The early 70s market

In the early 70s soft drink sales plateaued: Per capita consumption was 31.9 gallons in 1973, 31.6 in 1974, and 31.4 gallons in 1975. Among industry analysts interviewed, there seemed to be general agreement that two critical factors at least partially explained this development: the 1974–75 decline in real disposable income and the approximately 50 percent retail price increase created by cost increases—primarily sugar (see Exhibit 8).

EXHIBIT 8
Cola carbonated drink consumer price indexes (1967 = 100)

Date	CPI	Change from previous year
January 1973	129.7	1.5
January 1974	136.5	5.2
July 1974	165.6	25.9
January 1975	203.3	48.9
July 1975	197.6	19.4
January 1976 (est.)	193.2	−4.9

Source: U.S. Bureau of Labor Statistics.

One analyst, commenting on the 1975 situation, said:

From what I can tell, based on quarter-to-quarter changes in real income, generally soft drink consumption varies around those changes, but more dramatically. For example, in a bottlers survey that I completed, in the February–March period a year ago, when real income was down close to five percent, soft drink consumption was off seven or eight percent. Generally, when real income is growing on an annual basis at four to five percent, similar to the 10 years ending in December of '73, soft drink consumption was growing at a rate of about 7.8 percent compounded.[8]

The implications of price trends and consumer routines were viewed somewhat differently by another investigator:

> Sometime late in 1974, Andy Pearson (President of PepsiCo) made the statement that before PepsiCo's soft drink unit volume declined, soft drink bottling prices advanced by 54 percent. By that time, which was at the end of 1974, we did have real income starting to decline, and we had prices up 50 or 55 percent or whatever. So you did have the worst of two worlds, and I think this was one of the most important things that could happen to the soft drink industry because they realized that they had an enormous amount of pricing flexibility, and that volume was not impacted to any significant degree.[9]

INDUSTRY STRUCTURE AND PARTICIPANTS

There were four major participants involved in the soft drink industry: concentrate producers; soft drink bottling and distribution companies; retailers—primarily food stores, restaurants, and vending machine operators; and packaging and raw material suppliers. This industry classification system was imprecise with some firms operating in more than one category. Exhibit 9 gives the researcher's overview of the industry, with estimates, where available, as to the dollar amounts of 1974 intersector transactions.

Concentrate producers

In 1975 there were approximately 56 concentrate producing and marketing firms in the United States. Major firms sold flavoring concentrate or syrup (concentrate plus sugar) to independent, franchised bottlers. Large concentrate firms might have from 300 to 800 separate franchise operations.

The concentrate sector was dominated by the "Big Six": Coca-Cola, PepsiCo, Seven-Up, Dr Pepper, Royal Crown, and Canada Dry (see Exhibit 10). Each of these firms served the U.S. markets and, in some instances, sold in international markets. Each had created a valuable consumer franchise by substantial and continuous brand, promotional, advertising, and marketing programs. Three members of the Big Six had achieved substantial diversification from their original product lines: Coca-Cola into noncola

---

[8] *The Wall Street Transcript*, May 24, 1976, Mr. J. C. Frazzano, pp. 43, 766.
[9] Ibid., pp. 43, 767.

EXHIBIT 9

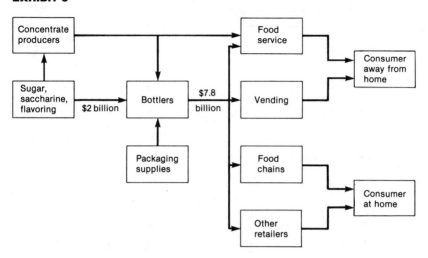

beverages and PepsiCo and Royal Crown into nonbeverage lines. Canada Dry (division of Norton-Simon), Seven-Up and Dr Pepper had remained primarily soft drink specialists.

The second group of concentrate producers (see Exhibit 11) included smaller, independent national firms such as Dad's Root Beer (1.2 percent of 1975 market) and Squirt (0.8 percent of the market) as well as product divisions of larger companies, such as A&W Root Beer, a division of United Brands. These firms had geographically scattered representation often with smaller, less competitive bottlers. In addition, regional firms, such as Faygo in Michigan, produced a wide variety of regular and diet drinks in what the industry called flavor lines, for example, orange, strawberry, and grape. A decreasing share of market was controlled by small, local bottlers.

Two other competitive factors were the private label brands of local and

EXHIBIT 10
Big Six sales net profit and product breakdown, 1975 ($000)

	Sales	Net profits	Major product lines
Coca-Cola	$2,872,000	$239,304	Beverages
PepsiCo	2,300,000	104,600	Beverages, $1,035,000; food, $805,000; sporting goods, $230,000; transportation, $207,000
Royal Crown	257,451	13,294	Beverages, $159,000; citrus products, $43,000; home furnishings, $55,000
Seven-Up	213,623	20,341	Beverages and flavors
Canada Dry*	180,032	13,861	Ginger ale, mixers, and standard flavor line
Dr Pepper	138,250	11,904	Beverages

* Division of Norton-Simon; 1975 overall sales of $2,443,027.
Source: Company records.

EXHIBIT 11
Industry participants' percentage of market

	1966	1972	1975
The Big Six:			
Coke	33.4	34.7	35.3
PepsiCo	20.4	19.8	21.1
Seven-Up	6.9	7.2	7.6
Dr Pepper	2.7	3.8	5.5
Royal Crown	6.9	6.0	5.4
Canada Dry	4.2	3.6	3.4
Total	74.5	75.1	78.3
Small nationals and regionals:*			
Total	7.5	11.5	11.9
Supermarket private labels:			
Total	0.2	2.4	1.1
Shasta	0.9	1.9	2.5
All others (small, local firms)	16.9	9.1	6.2
Total cases (millions)	2,910	3,675	4,460

* Includes operations such as Hires, Orange Crush, Cott's, Dad's Root Beer, Squirt, Schweppes, Moxie-Monarch, Nugrape, A&W Root Beer, No-Cal, Faygo, White Rock.
Source: Data compiled from trade sources by the Dr Pepper Company.

national food chains and the products of the Shasta Beverage Division of the Consolidated Foods Corporation. Private labels had been on the competitive scene for many years. One trade source estimated that national brands sold in 1975 for about 2 cents per ounce (12-ounce can) while private labels sold for 1 to 1.2 cents per ounce. *Beverage Industry* in commenting about the current position of "Store Brands" noted "chain executives surveyed noted a significant decline in gross margins in private label soft drinks, currently about 21–22 percent. It was high as 27 percent before current price increases. When warehouse costs (5–7 percent) are deducted from gross, the net profit is below that earned on national brands."[10] Typically, private brands were produced by nearby bottlers or contract canning companies.

Shasta, a subsidiary of Consolidated Foods (1976 sales of $2,754 billion— net income $89,453 million; soft drink and food division $239.3 million— pretax income of $17.2 million) produced standard flavors with diet drinks making up approximately 50 percent of overall sales. Sales were made to large purchasers, such as food stores, airlines, and government departments, with the bulk of the product being delivered directly to customer warehouses.

The Coca-Cola Company of Atlanta, Georgia, was number one among concentrate producers in terms of marketing franchise, sales, profit, share of

---

[10] *Beverage Industry 1975–76 Annual Manual*, p. 38.

market, and financial strength. Coke's 1975 balance sheet listed cash and marketable securities of $148 million, long-term debt of $9 million, and deferred taxes, capital stock, and surplus of $1.25 billion. Analysts estimated that Coke's international sales were growing more rapidly than domestic; the company had been the pioneer in international soft drink operations. Originally, and for decades, a specialist in cola drinks, Coke introduced a line of flavor drinks—Fanta orange and grape; Sprite, a lemon-lime drink; Mr. PiBB, a cherry cola drink; and diet drinks—Tab and Fresca. In the 1960s Coke added Minute Maid orange juice, instant tea and coffee, and bottled spring water.

PepsiCo of Purchase, New York, was the second largest company in the industry with 1975 sales approximating 80 percent of Coca-Cola's and its net profit 44 percent of Coke's. PepsiCo was involved in four major domestic product areas plus international operations. Its principal soft drinks were regular and diet Pepsi-Cola, Mountain Dew, and a new product Pepsi Light (a semidiet, combination cola and lemon-lime drink). PepsiCo's food division was the leading snack food, for example, potato and corn-based products, producer in the United States with its own route delivery system. Two smaller divisions were involved in sporting goods and intercity truck transportation.

The 7UP brand was the third largest selling soft drink in the world; its product specialty was a lemon-lime drink sold in both regular and diet formula. Seven-Up, located in St. Louis, Missouri, dominated that flavor with an estimated 60 percent share of market, outselling the next product—Sprite—by three to one. Since 1968 the brand had grown about 7 percent annually versus an average 5½ percent for the industry. In 1970 the company began a modest acquisition program.

Dr Pepper, of Dallas, Texas, the fourth largest selling brand, shared with Seven-Up the record of having the industry's highest earnings growth rate from 1968 to 1975—18 percent. Its share of market had moved from 2.7 percent in 1966 to 5.5 percent in 1975. Company operations were concentrated in the North American market with Dr Pepper, in regular and diet formulas, comprising 99 percent of company sales. Dr Pepper, a unique fruit-based flavor, had only one direct competitor—Mr. PiBB. Company gallonage growth rates had been historically targeted by management at 15 percent, but industry analysts did not believe that objective had been reached in 1974 and in 1975 were estimating future gallonage growth of 10 percent.

Royal Crown Cola of Atlanta, Georgia, was the fifth largest selling brand (1975 market share—4.2 percent for regular and diet Royal Crown Cola plus 1.2 percent market share for associated flavor lines). Royal Crown had been a leader in the introduction of diet cola drinks, and its market share in that product segment originally equaled or exceeded Coca-Cola's. Originally a soft drink specialist, Royal Crown began to diversify in 1969 and

1970 into home furnishings and into the processing of citrus fruits and juices. In 1976 the company announced the acquisitions of Arby's, a roast beef sandwich, fast-food chain, headquartered in Youngstown, Ohio.

Soft drink bottling and distribution companies

Franchise owners were granted, without cost, in perpetuity, the exclusive right to bottle and distribute a concentrate company's line of branded soft drinks as long as conditions of the franchise agreement were met. Key elements in the franchise involved maintaining product quality standards, bottling facilities, distribution and marketing programs within a franchise territory, not selling product to organizations that might transship to another franchised territory, and a willingness not to handle a directly competitive brand, for example, a bottler could not bottle both Coca-Cola and Royal Crown Cola.

A Pepsi-Cola franchise owner could, however, handle a noncompetitive brand such as Dr Pepper—a product type not produced by PepsiCo.[11] Also, a franchise owner might elect not to handle one of PepsiCo's secondary brands, for example, Teem, a lemon-lime drink, and instead bottle and distribute 7UP, the leading lemon-lime brand. A franchisee might also take on a minor line such as Dad's Root Beer or Squirt, a citrus-flavored drink. In addition, if the territory were too small to support both a bottling and canning line, the franchisee could purchase canned products from other sources.

The franchise system was originally developed to achieve local delivery economics and to enable concentrate companies to obtain intensive market coverage at minimum capital investment. In 1975 the sector was still dominated, numerically, by family owned and operated firms despite a 42 percent decline since 1960 in the number of plants operating. Approximately 60 percent of these bottlers (1971) were located in cities with a population of 50,000 or less. An industry observer commented, "Local bottlers and the concentrate manufacturers are in a family relationship. It sounds corny, but it's true. Coke is the best example; they really try to watch out for the small bottlers. Some of them are run by the third generation of a family." (See Exhibit 12.)

The bottler segment of the industry could be divided into four major sectors. First were privately owned, usually small, bottlers such as Coca-Cola Bottling Company of Annapolis; it serviced 1,335 accounts and had sales of $1.1 million. Some of the larger of these franchisees, located in small metropolitan districts, had achieved substantial growth by buying up franchise operators in contiguous areas and by an aggressive policy of taking on

---

[11] A court decision in 1962 interpreted franchise bottler agreements to allow a bottler to sell noncompeting brands.

EXHIBIT 12

U.S. bottling plant distribution by sales category, 1972

Annual sales per plant	Number of plants	Change in number of plants since 1971	Percent of total bottler sales
Over $10 million	124	48%	26.6
$5–10 million	129	50	19.4
$3–5 million	226	13	19.2
$2–3 million	360	56	12.2
$500,000–$1 million	539	−4	9.1
$300,000–$500,000	393	−21	3.3
$100,000–$300,000	582	−24	2.9
Under $100,000	321	−19	0.6
Unclassified	51		
Total	2,725	−4.9%	

Source: Bureau of Census data.

secondary brands such as Dr Pepper or 7UP. The average sales of a bottling plant in 1973 were just over $2 million.

The second sector included large, publicly owned, multibrand firms, based in major metropolitan districts. Coca-Cola Bottling of New York, for example, bottled and distributed Coke, Dr Pepper, and minor soft drink brands and other beverages in a five-state area from multiplant sites. The company had also expanded operations into wine and the manufacture of coolers (see Exhibit 13). One analyst estimated that the pretax return on assets for three large publicly owned bottlers (1968–72) was 19.2 percent versus 30.3 percent for Coke, 16.4 percent for PepsiCo, and 46.8 percent for Dr Pepper.

EXHIBIT 13

Comparative sales of six largest publicly owned bottlers, 1974

Bottlers	Sales ($ millions)	Bottlers	Sales ($ millions)
Coca-Cola Bottling, Los Angeles	$702	ME-1	$220
Coca-Cola Bottling, New York	645	Pep-Com	168
Associated Coca-Cola Bottlers	558	General Cinema Bottling Division	157

Bottling operations of conglomerate companies such as Beatrice Foods and Borden comprised the third sector. These firms not only owned large bottling operations but in some cases minor concentrate manufacturers. Industry experts predicted that both the publicly held bottlers and the conglomerates would continue to grow in part via the acquisition of other franchise operations.

Seven of the eight largest concentrate companies owned some bottling operations. Coca-Cola owned and operated bottling facilities in Chicago, San Francisco, Seattle, Oakland, San Jose, Baltimore, and Boston. PepsiCo packaged approximately 20 percent of its domestic gallonage in company-owned plants. Senior management spokespersons for the concentrate companies unanimously supported the existing franchise system, and the presidents of Coca-Cola and Dr Pepper had taken public positions that their firms did not want to own any more bottling operations.

In surveying developments in the franchise bottling field, an industry spokesman states:

> The overall effects of the market developments since 1945 can be identified as these: (1) The increased power of retail chains strengthened the popularity of franchising through the emphasis on national brands. (2) Availability of the one-way container enabled the easy market entry of store-owned brands as well as national and regionally shipped brands, and further strengthened the retail market position of chains as soft drink outlets. (3) Larger market spheres for many bottlers were brought about by the growth of urban centers, necessitating greater capital requirements and redefinition of territories. These needs were met by a high degree of mergers, sales and other interindustry ownership transactions. (4) High growth rate of product volume began to attract "outside" money for the first time in the industry's history and companies not previously identified with soft drinks began entry into the industry. Availability of this new capital assisted the industry in its accommodation to newly dimensioned markets. (5) The one-way container brought substantial influence on the price of the product in the market. In 1950 the retail price was the same as it was in 1887, approximately a nickel a glass, but as a growing share of product moved to single use packages, the cost of soft drinks has inevitably reflected the higher cost of packaging.[12]

Federal Trade commission officials, however, took a critical view of these developments asserting they had resulted in high industry concentration levels and in the companies' ability to raise prices substantially:

> Because such large firms engage in soft drink bottling, high concentration levels exist in this industry. The 24 largest Coca-Cola bottlers serve nearly 61% of the United States population and account for approximately 24% of the total soft drink sales. The 10 largest Pepsi bottlers serve 48% of the population and account for almost 8% of total soft drink sales. The 12 largest Seven-Up franchisees, two of which are also two of the top Pepsi franchisees, serve 41% of the population. Approximately 40 bottlers account for more than one-third of total soft drink sales.

---

[12] Statement of president of the National Soft Drink Association before the Subcommittee on Antitrust and Monopoly Legislation, August 8, 1972.

However, the relevant measure of concentration in the soft drink industry is the concentration in local markets. Local markets, not national markets, are the locus of competition in soft drink bottling as territorial restrictions confine bottlers to competing in local markets. To put it simply, bottlers compete on the local level, not on the national level, and concentration of sales among local bottlers is quite high. According to the Bureau of Census, in 1963, the four largest bottlers in nine large metropolitan areas had, on the average, 68% of the market. This high concentration level among bottlers at the local level parallels the high concentration level of the four largest syrup manufacturers who share about 70% of the national market. Thus, a similar concentration level would naturally exist at the local level since bottlers' sales reflect, to a great extent, the market share of the brands they sell.

One reason for the high level concentration among bottlers is the extent to which bottlers produce products of several syrup manufacturers. For example, in New York City, both Coca-Cola and Dr Pepper products are marketed by Coca-Cola Bottling Co. of New York. Certainly, there can be no real competition between these brands bottled by a common bottler as a firm is not going to engage in price competition with itself. In 1970, of the 1,654 bottlers of products of the eight largest syrup manufacturers, 738 bottled products of more than one such manufacturer. Because of the large number of bottlers who bottle more than one brand, effective competition between different brands does not exist.

The high concentration among bottlers in local markets is reflected by the ease at which they have been able to increase prices in recent years. In this regard, it should be noted that for the period 1959–70, Bureau of Labor Statistics data indicates the wholesale price of cola soft drinks, which account for about 60% of the soft drink industry, has increased by 65%. Similarly, the Consumer Price Index records a 64% price increase in cola soft drink prices. This 64% rise in cola soft drink prices on the Consumer Price Index is a much faster price rise than the 33% price rise for all food prices during the period 1959–1970.[13]

Retailers

Industry analysts typically assigned soft drinks to three retail market segments: packaged goods sold via food stores; vending machines; and the fountain trade, the latter subdivided into two areas—restaurants and fast-food chains. A fourth category—the institutional market (e.g., hospitals and industrial plants)—was assigned in some cases to the vending section, in other statistical surveys to the fountain trade. Because of this, market share estimates varied substantially from one to another analyst's survey.

In 1975 Oppenheimer & Co. Inc., estimated food stores sales at approxi-

---

[13] Statement of Mr. Alan Ward, Director of Bureau of Competition, Federal Trade Commission. Hearings before the Subcommittee on Antitrust and Monopoly, 92d Congress, part 1, pp 223–24.

mately 55–60 percent, vending at 10 percent and fountain at 30–35 percent. Another analyst estimated, respectively, 50 percent, 20 percent, and 30 percent. But all agreed that food stores were still the dominant market. In 1900, 70 percent of soft drinks were consumed on the premises of the vendors and 30 percent at home. In the 50s and 60s the amount of products sold via food stores increased to 70 percent of the total market. The food store market was dominated by Pepsi-Cola and Coca-Cola with Pepsi having a modest share-of-the-market advantage. Some analysts believed Pepsi had a significant long-run strategic advantage over Coke, however, because of its major position in the snack food field.

Food stores sold $2.6 billion worth of soft drinks in 1975, making them the single largest retail outlet for soft drinks and accounting for approximately 55 percent of the cases sold that year. Case sales had increased steadily between 1960 and 1973 when industry marketing efforts had been concentrated on the take-home market segment. Food stores' share of total soft drink sales, however, had declined from 70 percent in 1960 to 60 percent in 1970, and were expected to decline further to 50 percent by 1980. Supermarkets had been the site of most national brand, soft drink competitive battles during the early 1970s.

Food retailers' sales of $131 billion in 1974 ranked them as one of the nation's largest businesses; supermarket chains played an important role in the industry, accounting for only 10 percent of stores but 45 percent of total sales. The three largest supermarket chains and their respective 1974 sales were Safeway, $8.19 billion; A&P, $7.03 billion; and Kroger, $4.78 billion. Many independent supermarkets were members of large cooperative buying groups or voluntary wholesaler groups which provided distribution economies of scale and staff services.

Soft drinks were of major interest to supermarkets since their 22 percent gross margin was one of the highest for any grocery items and the category achieved high turnover. In 1974 the average supermarket carried over 100 different brands and sizes of soft drinks which generated $2.3 billion in total sales and $503 million in gross margin. Product shelf space allocations by chain store management directly correlated with market share. In 1975 canned soft drinks maintained their position among the top ten grocery product volume leaders.

The 1960s had been a period of rapid growth and prosperity for supermarkets, but the future looked less promising for the 70s and early 80s. Predictions of things to come by supermarket executives included little growth in real per capita food expenditures and little population growth. They anticipated increasing price competition, a rapid decline in the number of supermarkets operated, and increasing pressure for operating efficiencies, including more automated warehouses and full truckload delivery systems.

Another development in food retailing was the rapid growth of convenience stores (1967 estimated sales of $6.2 billion with estimated $1.6 billion of beverage sales). These stores were relatively small, had limited stock, long operating hours patterns, and serviced a local community area. Many soft drink bottlers viewed these expanding outlets as a prime sales opportunity. An executive of the Dr Pepper Company noted that selling to convenience stores was very different from supermarket selling. He noted, "The loss-leader approach commonly used in supermarkets was unworkable, whereas tie-in and theme promotions did seem effective. Convenience stores show a noticeable trend in selling sandwiches and other prepared-on-the-premise food items and therefore offer beverage tie-in possibilities."[14]

Vending machines, manufactured to serve a variety of containers from cans to bottles to paper cups, were employed to service the single-drink market. Costing the bottler between $800 to $1,000, these machines blanketed locations such as service stations, small stores, and sports arenas. An estimated 1.7 million machines were in operation in 1975, and some corporate executives believe this to be a mature or even potentially declining market sector. Coke was experimenting with the installation of small RE-FRESH office units. These units vended drinks at 10 cents a cup in private and public offices. Coke hoped to have 20,000 units in place by 1976.

Some bottlers, whose distributor salespeople originally serviced only soft drink machines, were expanding into the full-line vending business—including foods, candy, and cigarettes. Such firms could then contract to serve a factory or a public institution where a bank of vending machines had replaced the traditional cafeteria arrangement.

The fountain trade subdivided into two segments: the traditional restaurant, specialty restaurant, and coffee shops market; and fast-food operations. Americans seemed to be in the midst of a major shift toward "eating out," and the primary beneficiary seemed to have been chain operations. An observer noted, "Many independent full-service/atmosphere restaurants have been forced to close in recent years. . . . In contrast, chain operations in the coffee shop, specialty, and fast-food areas have expanded rapidly with the greatest growth coming from multisite operations in the fast-food segment. According to the U.S. Department of Commerce and A. D. Little, total personal consumption for food and beverages spent in fast-food outlets grew from about $400 million in 1960 to over $13 billion in 1976."

Fast-food chains operated with corporate owned (one fourth) and through franchise arrangements (three fourths) with the percentage of franchises gradually declining as franchisers purchased their own large franchise operation. Analysts noted further that "the top seven firms, McDonald's, Kentucky Fried Chicken, A&W Root Beer, International Dairy Queen, Tastee Freeze, Burger King, and Pizza Hut accounted for 47

---

[14] *Beverage World*, January 1977, p. 36.

percent of all fast-food units and 46 percent of sales. While fast-food chains dominate the fast-food segment they do not dominate the entire restaurant industry; the top 35 chains still accounted for only one quarter of total domestic eating and drinking industry sales. McDonald's, the largest independent, accounted for 3 percent of total food service sales (1975 sales of $2.616 billion). Burger Chef (General Foods) and Kentucky Fried Chicken (Heublein) were divisions of larger firms."

Suppliers

In 1975 the soft drink industry purchased approximately $4 billion of raw material ingredients and packaging supplies. This included approximately $1.7 billion for sugar, $200 million for high fructose corn syrup, $5 million for saccharin, $408 million for flavorings, $1 billion for cans, over $750 million for glass containers, and $127 million for closures and cartons. The soft drink industry accounted for 23 percent of the sugar consumed in the United States, 70 percent of the saccharin, and was one of the largest customers for companies such as Continental Can, and Crown Cork and Seal.

Sugar prices were vulnerable to major short-term price fluctuations in response to small changes in demand, since 96–97 percent of world production was sold under long-term contracts. In 1974 and 1975, increasing world demand and poor crop yields pushed prices as high as 75 cents per pound, compared to 2 cents to 9 cents per pound between 1950 and 1973. Recent sugar price increases prompted the use of high fructose corn syrup (HFCS) which at 20 cents per pound was 10–15 percent less expensive than sugar for equivalent sweetening power. By 1975 most major concentrate producers, except Coca-Cola and PepsiCo, had authorized their bottlers to use a 50/50 or 75/25 sugar/HFCS mixture, but actual usage was modest due to limited high fructose production capacity. Capacity was not expected to be adequate to meet demand until 1980. Saccharin was the primary artificial sweetener used in diet soft drinks, with approximately 2 million pounds purchased in 1974 at $2.40 per pound from one domestic producer.

Glass containers accounted for a substantial percentage of all soft drink packages used in 1974. Sales to the soft drink industry accounted for approximately 23 percent of the $5 billion glass container market in 1976. There were two dominant glass container manufacturers: Libbey-Owens (1975 packaging material sales, $1,400 million) and Anchor Hocking (1975 sales, $411 million).

Five can companies accounted for 98 percent of the cans sold to the soft drink industry with American Can Company (1974 sales, $2.7 billion) and Continental Can Company (1974 sales, over $3 billion) accounting for over 50 percent of the market. Crown Cork and Seal, National Can Company, and Reynolds Aluminum were the other major participants.

Packaging manufacturers, while typically dominant in one packaging

EXHIBIT 14

Soft drink bottlers operating income and expense ratios as percent of net sales, 1973

	Top 10 Percent in Net Operating Income	All Units	Under $1,000	$1,000 to $3,000	$3,001 to $6,000	$6,001 to $10,000
Cost of sales:						
Materials	13.11	17.32	15.63	16.72	16.76	14.83
Packaging expense	10.61	12.55	4.30	9.93	17.69	15.36
Plant labor	4.14	4.83	5.89	4.85	4.87	4.36
Indirect	3.44	4.07	3.90	3.90	3.99	4.12
Total	31.30	38.77	29.72	35.40	43.31	38.67
Contract purchase (finished beverages) ..	26.70	24.52	32.92	28.23	19.48	25.46
Total cost of sales	58.00	63.29	62.64	63.63	62.79	64.13
Gross profit	42.00	36.71	37.36	36.37	37.21	35.87
Total other operating income	3.36	2.15	2.26	2.53	1.98	1.67
Gross operating income	45.36	38.86	39.62	38.90	39.19	37.54
Operating expenses:						
Warehousing	1.69	2.81	1.93	3.22	1.95	1.77
Selling	19.70	21.12	20.76	20.67	21.56	22.43
Administrative	5.89	7.97	12.03	7.84	7.52	7.72
Total operating expenses	27.28	31.90	34.72	31.73	31.03	31.92
Net operating income	18.08	6.96	4.90	7.17	8.16	5.62

Source: National Soft Drinks Association 1973 financial survey.

technology, often engaged in the manufacture and sale of multiple types of packaging, for example, both glass and plastic. These manufacturers carried on most of the packaging research and development for the soft drink industry. A recent improvement in the popular, large-size glass containers (all one-way packages) was a clear or semiclear plastic coating which reduced breakage and required less glass, therefore reducing package weight and distribution costs. In 1976 Owens-Illinois "Plastic-Shield" coated 33 percent of the 28- and 32-ounce bottles and 50 percent of the 48- and 64-ounce bottles which it produced.

KEY INDUSTRY FUNCTIONAL STRATEGIES

Marketing

"In this industry the key strategic function has been marketing—that includes advertising, promotion, packaging, and distribution," an analyst commented. "Finance, so far, hasn't been limiting; and with one exception, the concentrate people are in very conservative positions. Production hasn't been that critical, but changing logistics and possible changes in product technology make it increasingly important. And don't forget there are three teams playing in this game—concentrate producers, bottlers, and the government. Their interests are different, and it makes the game complicated."

Soft drinks were inexpensive, frequently purchased products often consumed on impulse by a broad spectrum of the population. According to Standard & Poor's, in 1975, 90 percent of U.S. teenagers consumed at least seven soft drinks per week, 74 percent of young adults consumed that many, and 43 percent of the population over 50 drank one soft drink a day. Efforts to increase consumer awareness, achieve extensive availability, and appeal to consumer desires for product variety and user convenience involved the joint participation of both concentrate producers and bottlers.

Large, national concentrate producers did overall market research and planning, determined advertising and promotion themes, introduced new container sizes and materials, and developed and tested products. They financed national advertising, staff and development services, and paid part of the cost of local advertising and promotion of new packages and products.

Bottlers worked with national concentrate representatives to determine the advertising media, promotion themes, product mix, package mix, and price points to most effectively meet the particular consumer preferences, distribution channels, and competitive situations of their local market area. The bottlers were responsible for day-to-day implementation of the marketing plan. They usually paid about 50 percent of the cost of local advertising and promotion, and most of the costs of new packing and vending and dispensing equipment. Local cooperative advertising and promotion budgets were usually based on both concentrate producers and bottlers contributing a fixed amount per gallon of product sold in the territory.

Marketing strategies for local and regional companies and minor national brands generally followed a pattern of sales through food stores; few had vending machine exposure and few received much media advertising support. Local and regional firms usually concentrated on flavor lines and competed on a price basis. Minor national brands "piggybacked" on the franchise bottlers of the top six concentrate manufacturers. Schweppes and Canada Dry competed primarily as premium priced "mixers" for use with alcoholic drinks.

An industry marketing executive commented that the seven critical ingredients for industry success were advertising, availability, promotion, packaging, pricing, personal selling, and new product introduction.

Advertising. Consumer advertising was a critical element in selling soft drinks and accounted for a large proportion of concentrate producers' annual marketing budgets. Exhibit 15 indicates amounts spent on national media alone by the largest advertisers between 1960 and 1975. Most national brand advertising was directed toward achieving or maintaining consumer "top of mind" awareness. The emergence of 7UP as an aggressively advertised soft drink brand with its "Uncola" theme was considered to be an industry advertising success story. The initial Uncola campaign relied heavily on 60-second spots on network television. Later billboards, newspapers, radio commercials, and prime-time television spots were used. Between 1966 and 1976, 7UP case sales increased from 200 million to 340 million.

Industry executives anticipated increasing competition in the advertising arena in 1976. According to *Beverage Industry:*

> With another no-growth year just ended, the major thrust in advertising is coming from those companies who have seen their individual market shares increase at the expense of both the best known brands and the regional or private label soft drinks. Because of this, the key word for this year is product identity, and ad agencies across the country are turning out television and radio spots designed to leave the consumer with an indelible memory of their clients' product.

Availability. An ornithologist does not need a laboratory full of measuring instruments to prove that geese are migrating; rare will be the reader who has not, in the previous week, had several soft drinks, consumed in a variety of places. A researcher walking down a city street provided ample evidence of the industry's merchandising impact: soft drinks were available at 12 locations (including a funeral parlor for an undesignated clientele); men and women, young and old, black and white were observed consuming their favorite beverage; several hundred cans provided typical big city litter; and 64 soft drink advertisements "decorated" one four-block street section.

Soft drink availability accomplished three objectives for soft drink marketers. It provided a safe, cold, palatable drink almost anywhere people became thirsty. Second, point-of-sale advertising in hundreds of thousands of locations contributed to brand awareness. Finally, extensive availability was an important sampling device which helped to create and maintain consumer flavor preferences. Several industry sources stated that Coca-Cola dominated the cold, single-drink market. In some regions of the country, however, other brands had achieved substantial single-drink availability; Pepsi in the Midwest, for example, and Dr Pepper in the Southwest and parts of the Southeast.

In food stores and supermarkets the major national brands vied with local and regional brands and the stores' own private label soft drinks to best appeal to the consumer's varying degree of thirst (6 ounces to 64 ounces), the size of the consumer's family (single bottles, 6-ounce cartons, 8-can packs), budget, weight consciousness, desire for convenience, and

EXHIBIT 15

Soft drink advertising expenditures for selected brands ($ millions)

	1960	1968	1970	1971	1972	1973	1974	1975
Coca-Cola:	$4,423							
Coke	3,837	$19,092	$20,243	$18,664	$17,965	$24,108	$22,122	$20,261
Fresca		—	3,861	4,317	2,862	2,590	2,545	2,381
Sprite		2,500	1,063	1,198	1,835	1,738	2,463	2,601
Tab		6,162	3,443	4,248	3,814	5,435	5,278	6,496
Fanta		800	470	396		392	147	74
Dr Pepper:	27							
Regular		2,950	4,098	4,945	4,082	5,363	5,402	4,872
Diet		244	24	285	687	1,208	1,759	1,548
PepsiCo:	3,148							
Pepsi		16,512	15,939	17,797	15,268	13,520	14,856	14,995
Diet Pepsi		1,465	4,034	4,593	4,254	4,321	4,139	3,673
Teem		41	22	10	—	—	—	61
Mountain Dew		796	263	148	162	350	635	2,577
Pepsi Light								918
7UP:	2,229							
Regular		8,993	11,496	13,169	12,835	10,438	10,437	10,180
Diet		2,242	576	1,481	1,725	2,398	1,967	3,255
Norton-Simon:	313							
Canada Dry		5,790	6,659	8,528	6,139	5,503	4,859	5,213
Barrelhead Root Beer						239	561	1,314
R. C. Cola:	1,003							
Regular		2,980	3,082	4,779	4,230	4,885	5,695	10,509
Diet Rite		4,961	2,303	3,095	2,472	2,351	2,131	3,497
Shasta							2,324	2,828

Sources: Abstracted from *Advertising Age* and company reports.

ecological concern (returnable, resealable bottles, cans, nonreturnable glass containers).

Sales promotion.   Recent point-of-sale promotional activity focused primarily on increasing packaged product sales through food stores. Consequently, most of the interaction took place between the bottlers, food retailers, and the consumers. Executives noted that usually the larger the size of display and shelf-space allocations and the greater the frequency of appearances in weekly food store newspaper advertising, the faster a particular soft drink brand sold. Thus, a wide variety of programs fell under the general category of promotions in the competition for consumers' and retailers' attention. They included installing point-of-sale signs, obtaining special end-of-aisle or high-visibility display areas, providing special permanent display racks and in-store refrigerated coolers. One industry source estimated that bottlers spent as much or more money on promotions as on advertising. Another industry participant estimated that bottlers annually spent the equivalent of 2–3 percent of sales on advertising and promotion efforts, or $100–$150 million in 1975.

Packaging.   "The proliferation of packaging has led to wider availability, particularly in vendors, to greater consumer convenience, and to increased consumption," an industry analyst commented. "The explosion in larger size packages has also increased gallonage sales. The grocery store consumer usually buys the same number of bottles or cartons of soft drinks each week. The more ounces each of those bottles or cartons hold, the more ounces go home with the consumer each trip. That's why the new plastic bottles are going to give such a boost to gallonage sales. The bottles themselves are smaller and lighter, so more containers can be put in a carton at the same weight. But the big ones create shelf shortage problems too! Look at the soft drink aisles in your supermarket; they have cases of gallon bottles stacked all over the place."

In addition to increasing total consumption of soft drinks by getting more product in the consumer's refrigerator, each new container size or material provided the opportunity to increase a brand's supermarket shelf "facings." Packaging variety also gave price choices within and among brands. Generally, soft drinks in larger size containers cost the consumer less per glass because packaging accounted for a lower proportion of total raw materials cost. The consumer also paid a lower price per ounce for beverages in returnable containers since the container cost was amortized over ten or more fillings.

The most frequently purchased container sizes in the early 70s were 10- and 12-ounce containers with 58 percent of unit sales; followed by 16-ounce containers, 20 percent; 24 ounces and larger, 16 percent; and 6–9 ounces, 6 percent. The 10- and 12-ounce *cans* accounted for 38 percent of unit sales, one-way *bottles* accounted for 28 percent, and returnable *bottles* for 34 percent. According to one analyst:

> Packaging innovations are usually led by the companies who have the most money. This is a me-too industry—once one company brings out something new, the others aren't far behind. Coke was the first with the plastic bottle, but Pepsi was first with the 64-ounce size and 7UP with the liter bottle. Royal Crown was the first company to come out with cans, but it took Coke and Pepsi to really put that package on the map.

In 1976 one new packaging innovation was already in the market testing stage—plastic bottles. The introduction by Coca-Cola of 32-ounce plastic bottles in the Providence, Rhode Island, market had been described as "successful," capturing over 50 percent of that particular Coke bottler's entire product mix. Over the years plastics may be adding 1 percent a year to industry growth, one analyst concluded.

Plastic pouches and plastic "bags" encased in a corrugated paper box were being used in the wine and fruit juice industry. Mirolite, a plastic pouch wrapped in a paper sleeve, was manufactured by ICI in England. When European soft drink producers first adopted the package they had to reformulate some of their high carbonation drinks to retain their original flavor and lower carbonation level.

Can manufacturers were developing lighter, two-piece tin and aluminum cans, and nonreturnable bottle manufacturers were marketing lighter and stronger bottles. "Weight's important in this game—you are shipping water and metal around. You can't do much with the water but you sure try to cut down container weight. With the trend toward bigger bottles (64-ounce) you get difficult-to-handle products."

Pricing. Retail prices for soft drinks varied substantially by geographic region of the country, by container type, by channel of distribution, and a host of other factors such as local manufacturing costs, retailer markups, and degree of competition. For example, food retailers rarely achieved more than a 25 percent margin, while fountain retailers often achieved 65 percent to 75 percent gross margin of soft drinks. Exhibit 16 shows the range of average retail soft drink prices by regions for 1964–72, and their steady increase over the period.

Some industry analysts believed that the market for soft drinks was relatively price inelastic. They also believed that even greater pricing flexibility existed at the concentrate producer's level because concentrate cost accounted for such a low proportion of finished product cost, 4 percent in the case of Coca-Cola, and comparable amounts for other producers' soft drinks. Seven-Up was the only concentrate producer yet to put the theory to a major test. According to one analyst, Seven-Up increased its concentrate prices 11 percent in October 1974 and 25 percent the following June. The company apparently quelled bottler resistance to the second price hike by promising to spend more money on advertising and local promotion.

EXHIBIT 16

Retail pricing trends of fruit-flavored soft drinks by region, 1964–1972
(per 72-ounce carton)

Region	1964	1965	1966	1967	1968	1969	1970	1971	1972
Northeast	56.8¢	54.7¢	55.2¢	59.0¢	63.5¢	64.7¢	69.8¢	75.4¢	75.4¢
South	n.a.	n.a.	n.a.	n.a.	55.0	58.7	59.7	63.1	64.4
Midwest	54.7	57.6	59.5	60.4	62.8	70.2	74.9	77.2	75.6
West	63.0	64.2	63.9	64.2	69.5	72.3	81.4	83.3	84.4
All regions	53.4	53.6	54.8	57.0	60.5	63.1	69.1	72.6	72.7

n.a. = not available.
Sources: Bureau of Labor Statistics, and *Beverage Industry*, July 28, 1972. The 1972 figures as of March of that year.

Personal selling. Concentrate producers employed two types of selling organizations: bottler-oriented sales personnel and fountain salespersons. Concentrate producers' bottler sales personnel worked with franchised bottler management to tailor national brand plans to the individual requirements of the local market area. Franchised bottlers were independent business people so the persuasiveness of the concentrate producers' salesperson as marketing consultant was important. However, the salesperson did not have to rely completely on charm or intimidation: incentives such as cooperative advertising and promotion funds were available.

Some concentrate producers, including Coca-Cola, Seven-Up, and Dr Pepper, maintained their own sales organizations to sell fountain syrup directly to retailers. Pepsi-Cola and other producers relied primarily on their franchised bottlers and independent jobbers to sell to fountain outlets. Most fountain retailers carried a maximum of four different brands because standard dispensers were equipped to handle but four flavor lines. Thus, the main task of concentrate producers' fountain sales personnel was first convincing the franchise chain's home office to approve the inclusion of their brand on the list of products which the local franchisee might use. Later they might help bottlers or jobbers sell individual retailers on carrying company products. Fountain sales personnel were also responsible for placing point-of-sale advertising and implementing cooperative advertising and promotion programs. The syrup producer or supplier also provided the retailer dispenser maintenance and repair services, usually free of charge.

New product introduction. New product introductions had played a relatively minor role in the marketing of soft drinks. Companies infrequently did introduce new brands, usually for a variation in the formulation of an old standard flavor, for example, Pepsi's introduction of Teem—a lemon-lime drink. Exactly what constituted a "new" soft drink product was difficult for industry executives to define. One type of product innovation involved introduction of a new flavor, such as Cott's diet mint; another, a new combination such as cherry-flavored chocolate drinks. One firm had recently introduced a chocolate-flavored, high-protein health drink into several foreign markets. However, 7UP, first marketed in 1920, and Dr Pepper, first sold in 1885, were the only flavors outside of cola which had achieved major national brand status.

Most industry observers did agree that diet beverages were a new product category. First introduced in the early 1960s, diet drinks had achieved a 15 percent market share in 1969. When the Food and Drug Administration banned cyclamates as an artificial sweetener, sales dropped precipitously to 6.7 percent of the market in 1970. By 1976, diet beverages again accounted for 15 percent of industry sales and were the fastest growing product category. One bottler characterized Coke's introduction of Fresca, its citrus-flavored diet drink, as the most successful new product introduction in which he had ever participated. "I gave Fresca away to every one of my outlets in quantities amounting to 20 percent of each outlet's monthly 12-ounce Coke sales. When Coke wants to move in—they *move in.*"

Pepsi Light, Pepsi-Cola's reduced-sugar, cola-plus-lemon was, in the view of some analysts, the major new product of the 70s. The drink used some artificial sweeteners while still containing only half the sugar (and half the calories) of regular cola. At the end of 1975, Pepsi Light was in selected markets covering about 50 percent of the U.S. population; national advertising expenditures had already reached close to a million dollars.

The Pepsi challenge. One example of the increasing competitiveness among major national brand soft drink producers was the major advertising campaign begun by Pepsi-Cola in April 1974, in Dallas, which declared, "Nationwide, more Coca-Cola drinkers prefer Pepsi than the taste of Coca-Cola." *The New York Times* described the genius of the campaign in an article on July 5, 1976.

> . . . research had indicated that more than half the Coke drinkers who participated in a blind test of Pepsi and Coke preferred the taste of Pepsi. . . . So Pepsi decided to launch a "challenge" campaign in a marketing area where it had been weak: Dallas and Fort Worth.

In Dallas, over nine months of heavy advertising and price promotions by both cola producers resulted in a small increase in market share for Coke, approximately 30 percent at the end of the period, and almost a doubling in market share for Pepsi, from 7 percent to 14 percent. Retail soft drink prices had fallen to almost half their pre-challenge prices, and the two colas had increased their combined market shares from 36 percent to over 44 percent at the expense of the smaller competing brands, especially Dr Pepper. The challenge, and the competitive reaction, had spread to other cities by the summer of 1976, including San Antonio, Corpus Christi, New York City, and Los Angeles.

Distribution

The soft drink industry had achieved both extensive distribution of major national brands and a substantial degree of control over the distribution process itself, compared to other nonperishable food products. Exhibit 14 gives some information on distribution costs; they are included in the category—selling. A key element in the distribution process, especially for food stores and vending machines, was the franchised bottler's sales force.

The franchised bottler's sales force comprised driver salespeople who combined both delivery and sales functions. Each morning route salespeople left the plant with trucks full of the soft drink assortment they expected customers to buy that day. The route salespeople stocked the customers' shelves directly from their mobile inventory, often handling billing and collections on the spot. They were usually compensated with a percentage of sales commission, and their check sometimes came directly from the concentrate producer rather than the bottler.

In recent years, however, some bottlers had begun to use "presold, bulk delivery" techniques with large supermarket accounts. An advance salesperson called on the store and took orders and the product was delivered the next day, via large vans holding up to 2,000 cases. Large carts, each holding up to 40 to 70 cases, were wheeled into the store's warehouse area. The next day the bottler's merchandising staff arrived and personally stocked the store's shelves. Supermarket owners approved of the system because it improved the store's receiving and stocking efficiency; bottlers estimated they saved about 10 cents per case delivery cost.

In-store merchandising, whether carried out by a route salesperson or a separate merchandising force, was considered crucial to maintaining high sales levels. An executive of the New York Coca-Cola Bottling Company explained:

> Unlike other businesses where the product comes through a warehouse and is at the mercy of whatever the supplier may want to do with it, or even comes through a food broker who does not have the kind of service dedication that exists in the soft drink business, the soft drink business is service dependent. So the man who goes in there (a) rotates the stock, (b) is in a constant battle for shelf space, both in terms of quality and quantity; he is trying to get it on the shelf in the best possible place, (c) in terms of helping the dealer, (d) in terms of pricing, we believe even if our price is on the high side, it is important to have it marked, clearly marked, (e) in terms of promotion or special display that needs to be built, to be sure that it is properly in place.[15]

---

[15] Kuhn, Loeb summary of *Federal Trade Commission Hearings in the matter of Coca-Cola et al.*, May 19–23, 1975, p. 50.

EXHIBIT 17

Consumption of soft drinks (selected years)

	1966		1970		1971	
	Million cases	Percent of market	Million cases	Percent of market	Million cases	Percent of market
Coca-Cola Co.:						
Coca-Cola	806.0	27.7	1,045.0	28.4	1,040.0	27.1
Sprite	43.0	1.5	65.0	1.8	71.0	1.8
Tab	42.0	1.4	49.0	1.3	66.0	1.7
Mr. PiBB	—	—	—	—	—	—
Fresca	33.0	1.1	46.0	1.3	52.0	1.3
Others	48.0	1.7	71.0	1.9	85.0	2.1
Total	972.0	33.4	1,276.0	34.7	1,344.0	34.0
PepsiCo, Inc.:						
Pepsi-Cola	470.0	16.1	625.0	17.0	687.0	17.4
Diet Pepsi	55.0	1.9	40.0	1.1	52.0	1.3
Mountain Dew	40.0	1.4	34.0	0.9	35.7	0.9
Teem	15.0	0.5	14.0	0.4	14.0	0.4
Pepsi Light	—	—	—	—	—	—
Others	15.0	0.5	15.0	0.4	15.0	0.4
Total	595.0	20.4	728.0	19.8	803.7	20.4
Seven-Up Co.:						
7UP	185.0	6.4	257.6	7.0	271.4	6.9
Sugar Free 7UP ...	13.0	0.4	6.5	0.1	8.4	0.2
Howdy flavors	2.0	0.1	3.0	0.1	2.3	—
Total	200.0	6.9	267.1	7.2	282.1	7.1
Royal Crown Cola Co.:						
Royal Crown	110.0	3.8	142.0	3.8	153.0	3.9
Diet Rite Cola	48.0	1.6	36.0	1.0	42.0	1.0
Nehi and others	43.0	1.5	45.0	1.2	46.0	1.2
Total	201.0	6.9	223.0	6.0	241.0	6.1
Dr Pepper:						
Regular Dr Pepper	79.0	2.4	135.2	3.7	147.7	3.7
Sugar Free Dr Pepper	8.0	0.2	5.0	0.1	7.2	0.2
Total	87.0	2.6	140.2	3.8	154.9	3.9

Source: *Beverage World*, April 2, 1976, p. 28; based on data supplied by John R. Maxwell, Jr., Wheat First Securities, Inc.

The efficient management of this route delivery system was a major determinant of bottler profitability and required efficient routing and skill in matching inventory load to customer demand. Five to ten percent of a bottler's accounts represented 20 percent to 45 percent of their total volume. Many of the smaller accounts, particularly those under five cases per stop, were marginally profitable at best and were serviced as a form of advertising through product availability and as an aid in keeping total plant volume above the break-even level. To support this extensive route delivery

1972		1973		1974		1975		1974-75
Million cases	Percent of market	Million cases	Percent of market	Million cases	Percent of market	Million cases	Percent of market	Percent change
1,125.0	26.8	1,190.0	26.7	1,180.0	26.5	1,170.0	26.2	−0.8
81.0	1.9	95.0	2.1	105.0	2.4	115.3	2.6	+9.8
85.0	2.0	97.0	2.2	100.0	2.2	115.0	2.6	+15.0
5.0	0.1	15.0	0.3	23.0	0.5	37.5	0.8	+63.0
48.0	1.2	44.0	1.0	38.0	0.9	35.0	0.8	−7.9
95.0	2.3	100.0	2.3	100.0	2.2	100.0	2.3	—
1,439.0	34.3	1,541.0	34.6	1,546.0	34.7	1,572.8	35.3	+1.7
735.0	17.5	777.4	17.4	780.0	17.5	778.0	17.4	−0.3
58.0	1.4	60.3	1.4	68.0	1.5	75.0	1.7	+10.3
35.0	0.8	42.0	0.9	47.0	1.0	56.0	1.3	+19.1
14.0	0.3	14.8	0.3	14.0	0.3	13.5	0.3	−3.6
—	—	—	—	—	—	2.0	0.1	—
15.0	0.4	16.0	0.4	15.8	0.4	15.0	0.3	−5.1
857.0	20.4	910.0	20.4	924.8	20.7	939.5	21.1	+1.6
289.6	6.9	317.7	7.1	311.3	7.0	295.5	6.6	−5.1
10.1	0.2	12.7	0.3	27.3	0.6	43.6	1.0	+59.7
1.8	0.1	1.4	—	1.5	—	1.4	—	−6.6
301.5	7.2	331.8	7.4	340.1	7.6	340.5	7.6	+0.1
165.0	3.9	165.0	3.9	150.0	3.4	153.0	3.4	+2.0
44.0	1.0	42.0	0.9	34.0	0.8	36.0	0.8	+5.9
49.0	1.2	53.0	1.2	56.0	1.2	51.0	1.2	−8.9
258.0	6.1	268.0	6.0	240.0	5.4	240.0	5.4	—
180.0	4.3	208.7	4.7	216.0	4.8	217.0	4.9	+.005
11.0	0.3	14.8	0.3	18.0	0.4	28.0	0.6	+55.0
101.0	4.6	223.5	5.0	234.0	5.2	245.0	5.5	+4.7

system, the industry supported the nation's largest private trucking fleet, second only to the U.S. Post Office.

Changing marketing and distribution patterns

The researchers noted several industry trends which they believed would influence concentrate company-bottler relationships and which would impact local bottler marketing and distribution patterns.

First, new cooperative relationships would be needed to handle sales to the expanding fast-food market. Food stores' share of market had been decreasing while sales to fast-food chains had increased from 20 percent (1960) to 25 percent (1970) to 30–35 percent (1975). Of the restaurant and food service market, sales to the fountain/fast-foods market, in contrast to food stores, required different sales and promotional techniques and organizational arrangements.

Second, local bottlers increasingly were dealing with chains which served market areas larger than an individual bottler's territory. A chain promotional campaign might necessitate the coordination of several franchise bottlers, a concentrate company's advertising manager, and the chain buying staff.

Third, during the 1950s, bottlers typically handled only one concentrate company's product line. Beginning in the early 60s and spurred by Dr Pepper's aggressive campaign to sign up Coke and Pepsi bottlers, bottlers were increasingly managing multibrand operations. A Pepsi bottler might, for example, handle 7UP and Dr Pepper.

Finally, there appeared to be basic changes evolving in local bottler profit economics. Bottling executives testified that profit margins had been declining as a consequence of packaging proliferation and increased ingredient and operating costs and that their business was becoming more capital intensive as larger plants, larger sales volume, and larger market areas were needed to achieve cost economies. Smaller bottlers often lacked the capital to buy a bottling line ($250,000) or lacked a market large enough to break even on a canning-type operation ($2 million in sales). Some bottlers, to deal with this situation, had developed cooperative canning and distribution facilities with nearby bottlers holding similar franchises. A Dr Pepper executive commented that Coca-Cola and PepsiCo had been urging their franchised bottlers to cooperate among themselves for the last eight to ten years, while this was a relatively new policy at Dr Pepper. The most extreme illustration of this trend so far had occurred in Charlotte, North Carolina, where a dozen Coke bottlers had closed down their separate production facilities and opened a central plant ringed by a number of distribution centers. Warehousing and order filling took place at the distribution center from which bottlers served their traditional territories.

Production

Production operations in the soft drink industry were divided between concentrate producers and bottlers. Quality control was one area where branded concentrate producers exercised influence over bottlers' and canners' production activities. Quality control required meeting plant, equipment, and process sanitation standards, as well as standards for product composition. Product composition standards covered the proportion of flavoring, sugar, and water in the drink, degree of carbonation, taste, and appearance. Quality control violations were one of the few grounds on which concentrate companies could revoke a bottler's franchise rights.

Concentrate and syrup production were simple processes involving little investment in plant or equipment and a low labor component. One analyst estimated that the Coca-Cola Company could double its syrup-producing capacity with a $200,000 capital investment. The concentrate process itself involved mixing fruit extracts and other liquefied natural and artificial flavorings with water and sugar in large vats. The resulting concentrate was shipped to bottlers and canners. Concentrate contained only a small proportion of the sugar needed in the finished drink and was more economical to ship; consequently, one or two concentrate factories might efficiently serve bottlers all over the United States.

Franchise companies which produced concentrate shifted the bulk of sugar purchasing requirements onto their franchised bottlers. Coke was the only major company to produce and ship syrup rather than concentrates. Coke maintained 22 regional syrup production centers to minimize the high costs of shipping. It partially handled the problem of sugar purchasing risks by charging its bottlers a syrup price which fluctuated depending on average quarterly sugar prices.

Soft drink bottling was also a simple, nonlabor-intensive, manufacturing process, although it was more capital intensive than concentrate production. One source estimated that bottlers' total investment in plant, equipment, supplies, and distribution vehicles was close to $2 billion in 1975. The researcher estimated that approximately 30 percent of that $2 billion represented investment in plant (manufacturing and warehousing space) and 10 percent was in machinery and equipment.

Depending on its age, filling equipment currently in use in the industry ranged in capacity from 100 to 1,000 bottles per minute. Bottle washing, filling, and packing equipment had limited flexibility in terms of the range of container sizes and materials it could handle. Consequently, a bottler producing the full-size range of 6 to 64 ounces might require two or three lines.

Much of the industry's canned product was produced by large bottlers, by contract canners, and by concentrate company-owned canning lines because of the scale of capital investment required. Cans were lighter and easier to handle than bottles of comparable capacity, so canning production could be more easily centralized than bottling. The Coca-Cola Company was, in terms of capital investment, the most forward-integrated producer. Its canning operations were carried out by a wholly owned subsidiary called Canner for Coca-Cola Bottlers, Inc. (CCCB). CCCB put the bottling companies' syrup in cans for a fee at six different locations. The company's depreciated investment in canning plant was $21 million in 1975. CCCB accounted for approximately 1 percent of Coke's pretax profits in 1974, and 42 percent of its output went to company-owned bottling plants serving 14 percent of the U.S. population, and 38 percent went to independent franchised bottlers.[16]

NEW COMPETITORS—THE INTRUDERS

"Concentrate production is a license to steal," an industry analyst remarked. "The industry is bound to attract competitive interest." While other industry observers did not agree with the "extremity" of this judgment, they did agree that the industry was most profitable. They noted that compound earnings growth among the industry leaders ranged from 10.5 percent to 16.8 percent and ROI capital ranged from 12.3 percent to 25.4 percent for the five-year period ending in 1974.

In 1976 old players were experimenting with new games and new players were joining the battle. Cash-and-carry chains were making their appearance in the United States and Canada. Shasta Beverages, with a different concept of distribution, was moving from a regional to a national basis; beverage powders were expanding in sales volume; and rumors of significant new technological developments were "bubbling," in trade circles.

Cash-and-carry franchise outlets

The original cash-and-carry concept combined soft drink bottling and retailing functions in a single company. Independent bottlers, whose proprietary brands were being pushed out of supermarkets by national brands, sold their beverages at reduced markups from their own plant or at a separate retail store. While data were difficult to obtain, some industry observers estimated that cash-and-carry sales accounted for between 2 percent and 10 percent of packaged soft drink sales, depending on the region in the United States, and a higher percentage in Canada.

In the early 1970s, local bottlers' interest in cash-and-carry operations accelerated as two firms—Towne Club and Pop Shoppes—developed a franchise system of operations for theat market. Towne Club, formerly an independent bottler, owned and operated 40 sales outlets in the metropolitan Detroit area, supplying these operations from a central bottling facility. In addition, Towne Club had franchises in six other metropolitan areas in five states with over 100 outlets.

Pop Shoppes, a Canadian operation, opened its first State-side operation in Phoenix, Arixona, in 1972. In 1976 the company had 24 factory plants in the United States and 25 in Canada supplying approximately 400 retail outlets. Both firms planned major further expansion; and in 1975, Pop Shoppes' major Canadian competitor, Pick-A-Pop, sold a 50 percent inter-

---

[16] Mr. Ogden, Coca-Cola Company, quoted in summary of and excerpts from the *Hearing before the Federal Trade Commission.* Kuhn, Loeb summary, May 5–9, 1975, p 1E.

est to Moxie Industries, an Atlanta-based concentrate producer. That firm immediately began franchising operations in the western United States.

Pop Shoppes, for example, provided a franchised store owner with site selection tips, marketing plans, advertising and co-op promotion plans, and training programs. Typically, the independent bottler would open a sales outlet at the bottling plant and expand to other retail sites later. Sales strategy was based on low prices (approximately 50 percent of supermarket prices), only returnable bottles, limited numbers of bottle sizes, a complete flavor range (25–32) from colas to fruit flavors, and fast, quick service. All sales were in case lots, and one of the two persons operating the shop managed the cash register while the other stocked floor displays and helped customers load their cars.

Shasta beverages

Shasta soft drinks were produced and distributed by the Shasta Beverage Division of Consolidated Foods, located in Chicago, Illinois. Consolidated operated in a number of food-related areas: sugar refining, meat packing, convenience food stores, institutional and volume feeding operations, and restaurants; some of its well-known brand names included Sara Lee frozen foods and Popsicles.

Shasta's competitive posture differed substantially from other industry participants. Its soft drinks were not sold via franchised bottlers but were sold directly by the company to buyers who operated their own warehouse facilities. Shasta produced 20 standard flavors, in both diet and conventional formulations, primarily in steel cans (80 percent), but also in 28-ounce and 64-ounce nonreturnable bottles. Product was manufactured in 21 plants, each of which also had warehouse distribution facilities; and in some cases was distributed in Shasta's own trucks, in truckload lots, to large-volume customers.

A 250–300 persons sales force worked with large chain store personnel assisting them with product display, pricing, and promotion. The company gave discounts off list price to chains with the view that the chains would pass that lowered price on to the consumer. More than 80 percent of Shasta's business was to food stores; the company did not attempt to sell the single-service market. Shasta did not impose a geographic limit on its wholesale purchasers. They could resell Shasta products in whatever area they liked. Retail prices were established locally; Shasta beverages were generally sold at higher prices than private labels, but lower than national brand prices.

Since 1960 Shasta (sales $6 million) had gone from regional to national distribution and had achieved a 2.5 percent share of the U.S. market with estimated 1976 sales of over $200 million. The company's 1976 annual report reported that Shasta had initiated price reductions and had increased promotional expenditure. Pretax income increased 13 percent in fiscal 1976.

"POWDERS—A $600 million stir in the soft drink market"

So headlined the lead article in *Beverage World*, reporting that "mix-it-yourself" drinks were enjoying extraordinary sales success with a 50 percent sales gain in 1974, another 50 percent sales gain in 1975, and predictions for 1976 being similarly optimistic.

> Beverage powders, for years dismissed as "kid stuff" and virtually ignored by most beverage manufacturers, are fast making their presence felt in the market. There are no specific figures indicating that powdered beverages are cutting drastically into carbonated soft drink volume, but their tremendous sales growth, sparked by consumer resistance to higher-priced carbonated drinks . . . clearly shows that powder manufacturers are capturing a share of the carbonated soft drink market.[17]

In 1976 finished beverage powder gallonage was estimated to be 1.2 billion, about 20 percent of the approximately 6.3 billion gallons of soft drinks expected to be purchased that year.

Beverage syrups and powders had been on the market for almost 50 years. Originally sold as fruit drinks, they offered the homemaker the advantages of low price and carrying convenience. And, in addition, they provided the fountain and institutional market a colorful visual advertising display—a large, glass container with a jet spray of constantly moving, brightly colored juice. In recent years, bottle syrups for home use had declined in sales importance and, therefore, in amount of supermarket shelf space. Beverage mixes came in five basic flavors, and trade sources estimated consumer preferences as (1) lemonade, (2) grape, (3) orange, (4) strawberry, and (5) cherry. Mixes came with sugar, without sugar, and in Pillsbury's new entry "Squoze" a sugar-plus-artificial-sweetener formula that contained half the regular calories, and they were packaged in compact containers with lower per ounce prices for the consumer. Mixes were also available in envelopes or packets (60 percent of market), ranging from 1 to 3 ounces to 12 ounces (retail price 99 cents) and the kitchen-type canisters (40 percent of the market) from 24 to 45 ounces ($3.19 retail).

A random series of interviews with housewives in Boston supermarkets could be summarized by the following:

> I've quit buying the bottled stuff. These mixes are cheaper, they allow me to regulate the amount of sugar the kids get, they don't break my back carrying them to the kitchen from the car, and it cuts down the trip to the dump. My daughter says they are ecologically superior.

---

[17] John D. Stacey, *Beverage World*, March 1976, p. 30.

Three major food marketing companies dominated the grocery trade mix business in 1976: General Foods' Kool-Aid (40 percent of the market), Borden's Wyler's (40 percent), and Pillsbury's Funny Face and Squoze (10 percent). Each of these firms had substantial marketing skill and distributive capacity. Most employed broad-scale couponing, free premiums, special price offers, and display assistance to the supermarket. All of the companies allocated significant advertising dollar support to these products; Kool-Aid spent $7.6 million in 1974, while Wyler's allocated $1.9 million. One industry source noted that the companies spent $17 million in 1974 and estimated they would spend $30 million in 1975 on beverage powder advertising.

In April 1976, RJR Foods (a division of the former Reynolds Tobacco Company) announced its entry into the field with a powdered mix version of its single-strength, canned, Hawaiian Punch drink. The company allocated $6 million in advertising funds for the first-year introduction. "The consumer shifted away from single-strength fruit juices for economy reasons," a company spokesperson said. "What kept them from totally switching back again as sugar prices came back down was that they discovered manufacturers had vastly improved the quality since they had last tried it as kids."[18]

By 1976 other companies were testing the mix market. A&P and Kroger were leaders in introducing their own private label mixes. This decision had been spurred by the major success of "canister" packaging which gave the retailer a bigger "ticket-price" item to promote. Coca-Cola Foods Division had been test marketing fruit-flavored powders under its Hi-C (a canned single-strength juice line) for almost a year in Florida and Michigan.

There seemed to be some consensus in the trade that the boom in powders had been permanently influenced by what sales executives referred to as "product repositioning." Promotion had moved from selling "kids' " to a "family" drink. Advertising was changed to highlight *soft drink* mixes as opposed to fruit drink syrup and powders and shifted from a seasonal to a year-round promotional program. Attractive new display racks were installed next to, or near, the soft drink shelf space in food stores. Natural flavors were substituted for artificial flavors, and powder packages were supplied to the consumers in an increased number of sizes. In predicting the future, an industry expert noted:

> Beverages powders by their nature probably will accelerate the thrust toward fruit and citrus flavors and possibly affect carbonated soft drink flavor favorites. In view of the popularity of fruit flavors with young consumers, it poses the question of how much this might change future adult soft drink flavor preferences.[19]

---

[18] "The Mix-It-Yourself Boom," *Business Week*, May 17, 1976, p. 56.

[19] John D. Stacey, *Beverage World*, March 1976, p. 35.

In addition to a $400 million, 1976 consumer market, the trade sold an estimated $250 million to the food service and institutional feeding market. Of the over 100 companies operating in this field, General Foods led with 15 percent of the volume, followed by Nestle (11 percent), Wyler's (10 percent), and Standard Brands (7 percent).

> This market is both huge and unseen. . . . While public eating places offer opportunities for promoting beverage brands, the institutional market (plants, hospitals, etc.) is often controlled by dieticians. Many such institutions do not serve carbonated beverages, preferring to serve beverages made from powders or syrups. In these outlets, powders compete with syrups . . . buyers frequently switch to the cheapest one.[20]

Product technology

In the course of interviews with industry executives, the researchers heard infrequent references to possible, upcoming technological changes. It was difficult, however, to obtain any definitive information about the specifics of these possible developments or their future impact on the industry. In some overseas markets, an old product—the siphon bottle—was again being pushed as a way of manufacturing carbonated drinks in the home. Another source noted that one firm was experimenting with the sale of packages of carbonated ice cubes and syrup.

A number of references were made to the possible entrance of General Foods and Procter & Gamble into the field. The alleged P&G entry basis would be a self-carbonating product—probably a coating on the bottom of a cup—which would effervesce with the addition of water and syrup. Some observers believed P&G already had patents on such a product. Procter & Gamble's interest, they stated further, was the fact that soft drinks commanded an average of 120 linear feet of chain store shelf space versus 100 for detergents and 45 for coffee; also that soft drink sales per square foot of shelf space were almost twice that of coffee or detergents.

THE INDUSTRY'S CRITICS

"We are under attack on a number of fronts," an industry executive stated, "but our critical concerns are health issues, the bottle and can disposal problems, and antitrust action to break up the franchise system. In some ways the first area is the most difficult with which to deal. Our critics range from government agencies to consumer, health-oriented, private pressure groups, to individual technical critics with strong interest in the safety of specific drugs or the nutritional value of certain ingredients. And the impact of government edict can be disastrous. Do you recall the 1969

---

[20] Ibid., p. 35.

cyclamate ban; it almost liquidated Royal Crown—they had specialized in diet drinks with sugar substitutes."

Questions as to the public health record of the industry centered on two key-related issues: first, the more general question as to the nutritional contribution—or danger—of soft drinks on American eating patterns; and, second, on the safety or hazards posed by product ingredients, for example, sugar, caffeine, and chemical additives.

A dietician in a veteran's hospital commented:

> World War I vets are strictly meat and potatoes men. World War II and Korean vets like a more balanced, varied diet. But Vietnam veterans don't eat meals at all. They don't eat breakfast . . . and in the morning they start getting hungry and begin munching hamburgers, hot dogs, French fries, and soft drinks. They'd probably eat every meal at McDonald's if they could.[21]

Nutritional experts engage in lengthy public debates about the dietary wisdom of these "fast-food" eating habits and of possible dangers in the consumption of large quantities of soft drinks.

With per capita soft drink consumption substantially over 400 8-ounce containers, some nutrition experts questioned the wisdom of ingesting high quantities of sugar into the human body. Dr. Jean Mayer, president of Tufts University, was a strong proponent of this point of view. In a June 20, 1976, *New York Times Magazine* article entitled "The Bitter Truth about Sugar," he stated that "purveyors of health foods and natural foods are unanimous in their statements that white sugar is toxic and . . . there is a strong suspicion that a large sugar intake may be causally related to diabetes." An equally well-respected expert, Dr. Frederick J. Stare, chairman of the Department of Nutrition at Harvard University, took a diametrically opposite position: "There are hazards in foods but they don't come from sugar or additives; they come from eating (and drinking) too much and lack of elementary principles of sanitation."[22]

The Food and Drug Administration in 1969 had banned the use of cyclamates as a sugar substitute in diet soft drinks, alleging that research evidence indicated that it would cause bladder cancer in rats. In 1976 the FDA again ruled against the use of cyclamates, noting that there were "unresolved questions about the product's potential for causing cancer, its effects on growth and reproduction, and the possibility that it might damage chromosomes, the basic genetic apparatus."

In October 1976 Senator Gaylord Nelson, a consistent critic of the Food and Drug Administration, charged that a report by the General Accounting Office "shows that the FDA actually violated the law by allowing continued

---

[21] *Prevention Magazine*, November 1971, p. 30.

[22] *New York Times Magazine*, Letters section, July 18, 1976.

use of saccharin without making final determination of safety."[23] The FDA allowed the use of saccharin for more than four years on a "temporary basis." Saccharin was believed to be the industry's only practical alternative to cyclamates. The most serious circumstance would be if both sweeteners were banned. Drink reformulation would be possible if an approved, non-caloric sweetener could be developed. The risk was that the consumer might or might not like the new taste. The introduction and major success of Diet Dr Pepper and Diet 7UP had occurred during the time saccharin took the place of cyclamates.

In 1976, as a part of its review of several hundred food additives—the so-called GRAS list (Generally Recognized as Safe)—the FDA was reviewing the safety status of caffeine. A "split" report, released by the department, indicated that some members believed it was "prudent to assume" there might be a potential health hazard, particularly for children because cola drinks might expose them to daily caffeine in their period of brain growth and development. A 12-ounce cola drink contains two thirds the caffeine found in a cup of coffee.

The 1970s had witnessed a steady acceleration in criticism of the industry for its part in "trash pollution." Senators Hatfield, Javits, McGovern, Packwood, and Stafford introduced a bill in February of 1975 "to prohibit the introduction into interstate commerce of nonreturnable beverage containers." While this bill failed to pass, beginning in September 1975, "throwaways" were banned from federal installations and national parks by administrative order.

On the state level, a ban on throwaways was in force in Vermont and Oregon where proponents stated it had reduced can and bottle litter along the roads by 75 percent. Industry spokespersons disagreed with this finding. In the November 1976 elections, four states—Colorado, Massachusetts, Maine and Michigan—had proposals for mandatory deposits on bottles and cans for voter consideration. The Maine plan called for a 5-cent deposit on bottles used by several firms, a 10-cent deposit on bottles used by one firm only; deposits were also required on beverage cans. In addition, efforts were being made to ban the use of pull-top lids for beverage cans. The editor of the industry's leading trade magazine commented:

> The beverage industries and the United States of America still survive this kind of misdirected, simplistic, well-intentioned, but really dumb legislation. It is not what mandatory deposit bills will do to individual bottlers that matters so much as the potentially disruptive effect they could have on the over-all market picture. Such legislation, for example, might go a long way toward helping the food processing industry in its current effort to position various packs and sizes of powders, concentrates, fruit juices, and fruit flavored drinks as *soft drinks* in both the consumer's mind and in the

---

[23] *The New York Times*, Wednesday, October 26, 1976, p. 40.

supermarket. This will have a lot more impact than the development of franchise cash and carry soft drink chains, which are in place and ready to reap the benefits of mandatory deposit legislation in many key states.

Most soft drink bottlers are in no position to either fight or join such a shift in products, packaging, sales, and marketing. And there is no evidence so far that the parent companies are going to respond directly to the threat. Everyone knows that a 4-oz. pouch is no match for a 64-oz. bottle. Right?[24]

Industry executives generally believed that the major costs of a nonreturnable ban, if such legislation were to be widely enacted, would fall on the franchised bottler. One New England–area Dr Pepper bottler commented:

> Excluding the construction of new plant and warehouse space, I would need over $1 million to convert back to returnable bottles. I would need new filling and handling equipment, more delivery trucks and route people to handle the double volume, and money to convert vending machines. The working capital invested in bottle float alone would be tremendous: each 6½ ounce bottle costs 12 cents, and I sell 3 million 24-bottle cases per year.

As an alternative to forced deposit systems and nonreturnable bans, the industry supported a group called the National Center for Resource Recovery, Inc. The group was a cooperative effort involving the federal government and packaging manufacturers whose objective would be to fund profit-making ventures to reclaim all of a municipality's solid waste, 6 percent of which would be reclaimable as energy. Pilot projects were already under way in St. Louis, New Orleans, and Macon, Georgia. Should the project expand to the national level, its initial funding might come from a tax on packaging manufacturers.

A third major regulatory uncertainty concerned Federal Trade Commission action to substantially modify the industry's franchise bottler system. In 1971 the FTC cited the eight major concentrate producers, charging their exclusive territorial agreements were anticompetitive. In what some observers described as a "counterattack," the beverage industry pressed Congress for legislative approval of the exclusive territorial franchise system. The industry's bill came close to passing in 1972, but failed. Industry efforts to gain congressional support of their position continued in 1976. In 1975 FTC Administrative Law Judge J. P. Dufresne ruled that territorial provisions in franchise agreements did not unreasonably restrain trade but resulted in greater rather than lessened competition. The FTC appealed this decision and hearings continued into 1976.

The franchise controversy was covered in the business press, was a popular topic area in industry and company publications, and was investigated by the Senate Subcommittee on Antitrust and Monopoly in the summer and fall of 1972. Thousands of pages of data resulted. The researcher has at-

---

[24] "The Editor's Notebook," *Beverage World,* July 1976, p. 8.

tempted to summarize the critical arguments for both government and industry; chances for error or omission, however, are substantial.

The franchise system, pioneered by Coca-Cola, authorizes a bottler to manufacture, distribute, price, and sell a soft drink only in a designated territory. In summary, the FTC alleged that this exclusive franchise territory system kept soft drink prices artificially high and prevented intrabrand price competition. The specific charge stated:

> Respondent's contracts, agreements, acts, practices, and method of competition aforesaid have had, and may continue to have, the effect of lessening competition in the advertising, merchandising, offering for sale, and sale of premix and postmix syrups and soft drink products, deprive, and may continue to deprive, the public of the benefits of competition ... in methods of competition and unfair acts or practices, in commerce, in violation of Section 5 of the Federal Trade Commission Act.

The complaint ordered franchise companies to "cease and desist" from entering into agreements which prevented bottlers from selling products to any type of customer in any location, from restricting the location of the bottler's place of business, and from refusing to sell concentrate to or otherwise penalizing a bottler for selling outside his territory or selling to central warehousing customers. In the words of one industry executive, "The FTC was gung-ho to sink us, and it was frightening."

In a more philosophical vein, the counsel to the Senate subcommittee stated that committee's interest in the question:

> Isn't it inevitable that in this industry there is going to be change from the status quo in order to accommodate modern technology and modes of distribution trends, and if there is, shouldn't the shift in business be determined by the marketplace without having erected artificial restraints which in large part permits the parent company to determine who is going to stay in business and who is not going to stay in business?

At the hearings, a number of witnesses, many of whom operated small bottling operations, testified in opposition to the FTC complaint. They argued that breaking down the franchise system would (1) drive many small bottlers, particularly those near large metropolitan areas, out of business; (2) would reduce product availability because large bottlers wouldn't want to service small customers; (3) would reduce local advertising and promotion funds; (4) would increase the power of chain stores to push their own private labels; (5) the era of returnable bottles would end since chain stores would not want to handle them and door-to-door delivery and pickup would diminish; and (6) soft drink prices would not drop.

Ms. Alice Brady, of Kuhn, Loeb & Co., summarized the FTC charges and the industry's rebuttal as follows:

> The marketing structure of the soft-drink industry, as described by the Coca-Cola bottlers who have testified to date, has remained practically un-

changed for almost 70 years. This structure has depended on substantial capital investment by individual entrepreneurs, whose willingness to invest in the industry was closely tied to the contractual promise of territorial exclusivity. Under the umbrella thus provided, the individual bottling organizations have been encouraged to develop their markets to the fullest extent possible, serving all potential customers in each area at a uniform price, regardless of account size ... territorial protection has enabled (in fact, forced) the small bottler to place his products in virtually every conceivable outlet, thereby achieving a total fluid volume that would be otherwise unattainable ... removal of the territorial umbrella would probably cause industry-wide contraction in the number of bottling companies, package and brand varieties, and accounts served. In addition, a multi-tiered pricing structure would be the likely result, with the probability of higher average unit price. Ineluctably tied to the foregoing would be a decline in total consumption of soft-drink gallonage.[25]

The Federal Trade Commission views were summarized by Alan S. Ward, director of the Bureau of Competition, before the Senate committee.[26] He stressed three points:

In summary, territorial restrictions in the soft drink industry have actually contributed to the decline in the number of bottlers. Small bottlers have been denied the opportunity of expanding their sales and growing to efficient size, and, thereby, to continue to do business in this industry. Consequently, they have been induced to leave the industry. If the territorial restrictions are removed, small bottlers will be given an opportunity to expand their operations to the point at which they can support an efficient plant.

Ending territorial restrictions will neither cause the end of service to small customers nor force them to pay higher prices. Many small soft drink buyers currently purchase other food products from wholesalers who operate warehouses. Such wholesalers will provide soft drinks to small stores along with other food products. Indeed, it may be cheaper for these small stores to depend on one source for all their food product needs rather than having to split their business as currently must be done.

The end of territorial restrictions will not have the drastic effect on ecology predicted by some bottlers. First, more and more consumers are demanding nonreusable containers and this trend would be expected to continue regardless of whether territorial restrictions are eliminated or maintained. Second, chain grocers handle the products demanded by consumers and handle returnables if consumers wish these products.

An industry analyst agreed with some of Mr. Ward's conclusions, stating:

Warehouse distribution is coming. A "drop" to a vending outlet or Mom or Pop store costs 45 cents. The average delivery cost per case is 35 cents,

---

[25] Summary of and excerpts from the *Hearing before the Federal Trade Commission in the matter of Coca-Cola Company et al.*, May 19–23, 1975, pp. 1792–2468.

[26] *Hearings before the Subcommittee on Antitrust and Monopoly*, 92d Congress, part I, p. 225.

but the cost for the warehouse delivery is but 15 cents. Major concentrate producers and the consumer would benefit from warehouse deliveries via a reduction in national brand prices. The current franchised bottler system is the main deterrent to warehouse delivery, and this is because of the relatively small size of a franchise territory. Franchise territories were originally defined when there was a single 6½-ounce returnable package, and small territories were very efficient for handling this type of distribution. Now, with package and flavor proliferation and the big increase in one-way bottles, traditional franchise territories are inefficient. Smaller territories were also advantageous to the concentrate companies because they could increase consumption with total availability and pushed their bottlers to service vending machines and small outlets. Now, with the increase in transportation costs, bottlers realize they're losing money on those small stops, but they need them for volume.

Not all franchise owners were in sympathy with the "industry" position taken at the Subcommittee hearings. A critical view of the franchise system was outlined by Mr. John M. Alden, president of the Royal Crown Bottling Corporation of Denver, Colorado, in ten pages of committee testimony. Excerpts from his testimony follow:

What protections do territorial restrictions provide, then, if there is not sufficient business in a franchise area to support a costly, modern and efficient plant? The concentrate houses know this. They have had game plans and programs, which they are implementing ... they definitely plan to concentrate the industry with major production centers and major distribution centers.

This concept in itself, put to work, eliminates a lot of small bottlers. At best, it permits that little bottler to become a distributor, and just a distributor. What does that have to do with territorial restrictions?

We think it is only a matter of time before supermarket purchases of soft drinks will have to be totally serviced, at the central warehouse. We are also convinced that every major concentrate house, in the confines of their own offices, agrees. The strategy question is, what the hell do we do about it?

At the moment concentrate houses are frozen with a lot of franchise agreements. If all the franchise contracts could be washed out tomorrow, I believe the major concentrate companies would happily go ahead and operate unburdened, free of small bottlers. But, at this hour, the courts are honoring the validity of the bottlers' trademark licensing agreements.

They may say, "This man has paid for this franchise. You just can't throw him out the window. He has some equity in it." And if you add it up, and laminated all these sums of money, this involves sums of money too big for even the largest concentrate houses in the country to pay off on. Therefore, another strategy and alternate must be developed.

Every major concentrate house has already set targets and time schedules for the consolidation of production and distribution of their major brands concentrated in major trading areas where the food-store warehouses are located. The clue is in the hurried efforts during the past year to structure production centers and distribution enclaves in major marketing areas, and the emphasis there is on the warehouse profile rather than the old geographical county lines on which franchise areas were crudely structured. In other words, the concentrate houses are "getting on the ball" so territorial restrictions can be ignored if they are still in effect. To me, it looks like an adaptation of the cartel system used by European corporate giants to divide the world market among themselves. I think we now have in this country a version of the cartel method of allocating markets areas, which will end up being shared by not more than 100 or 200 major bottler-canner companies, at most, and any remaining bottlers, still alive, will be doing yeoman's work as distributors for the key bottler and canning operations in the hands of a few giants.

As one of the few voices in the soft drink industry to speak up for elimination of territorial restrictions, I do so fully aware of continued harassment, and possible additional reprisal actions and economic sanctions that may be initiated against my operation by concentrate house interests.[27]

Senior officers of the concentrate firms unanimously and strongly publicly backed the franchise system. W. W. Clements, president of the Dr Pepper Company, testified to the same committee about the dangers in the government's suit, noting:

> The small independent bottler would be a thing of the past. Dr Pepper would be forced into owning and operating a great number of bottling plants throughout the United States. . . . This would happen in varying degrees to other brands. However, the larger companies with greater resources would have a tremendous advantage. The industry would end up with a very few large bottling companies, and they would all be owned by large companies, such as franchise companies, public-owned companies, and food chains.

Predictions of the future varied by market segment. With regard to diet drinks an analyst stated:

> There is real potential to create new markets and increase consumption in diet beverages. Company advertising and promotional activities are very effective in increasing soft drink consumption, but advertising expenditures for diet drinks have been disproportionately low. Most companies are one product companies, even Coke. They never needed diet drink sales or secondary flavors before, and were never very successful with them. Coke grew at 6.5 percent per year on sales of regular Coke alone. No company except Seven-Up has been very aggressive with their diet brands, especially the colas. They've been scared stiff to heavily promote diet brands because they thought they would lose brand loyalty and brand identity for their main products. Now the major companies can't meet their growth objectives with their flagship brands.

---

[27] Ibid., pp. 370–80.

A number of analysts were optimistic about the fountain market; one made the following comments:

> Fountain, or on-premise sales in food service outlets, is the only growth area left in the domestic soft drink industry, and it belongs to Coke. The growth of fast-food chains has been responsible for the rapid growth of sales in this area, and the chains' continued rapid growth will continue at 6–8 percent per year for the next five to seven years.
>
> The fountain business is very different. The retailer buys syrup from an independent jobber or directly from the concentrate manufacturer. Most bottlers did not sell fountain syrup. The syrup is mixed with carbonated water by a dispenser at the point of purchase. There are 5–6,000 independent jobbers who have no territorial limitations on their sales areas. For most jobbers, soft drinks are loss leaders, for example, Martin Brauer distributes Coke syrup to McDonald's at only pennies per gallon.
>
> Coke dominates the fountain market. Seventeen percent of its total domestic gallonage is sold through fast-food chains, and an additional 16 percent is sold through other types of food service outlets, such as restaurants and ice cream shops. Pepsi was late in entering the fountain sales part of the business and has a very convoluted distribution structure. Franchised Pepsi bottlers formulate syrup or purchase it from the company, then sell it to jobbers who, in turn, sell to retail outlets. Consequently, only 15 percent of Pepsi's total gallonage is from on-premise sales, and the proportion will probably diminish in the future. The only major chain to carry Pepsi is Burger King.

Another analyst commenting on Coke's competitive position stated:

> Intensified brand and price competition in the 1977–80 period would be unlikely to dent Coca-Cola's dominant position in the fountain or vending markets. About one-half of Coke's domestic fountain installations are owned by the Coca-Cola Co., and major restaurant chains are unlikely to switch allegiance. A longer term concern, albeit premature, is the possibility of backward integration into soft drinks by a restaurant chain to develop an additional and significant profit center. McDonald's Corp. currently accounts for an estimated 10 percent of Coca-Cola's fountain volume or 3 percent of Coke's domestic syrup gallonage, has a captive and expanding customer base, and has become increasingly new-product oriented.[28]

Other analysts estimated Coke's share of the fountain market as close to 80 percent, but they expected competition to increase as Dr Pepper and Seven-Up made increased fountain sales a major objective of growth strategies. "The picture spells competition, challenge, and, bluntly, we must also gain share from the competition to meet our new sales objectives," a Seven-Up executive remarked to a *Beverage World* editor in April 1976.

---

[28] Paine, Webber, Jackson, and Curtis, "Soft Drink and Beer—Midyear, 1976 Review."

Two analysts commented on the future of the vending machine market:

> In the past, the percent of sales through vending was higher, but the energy shortage hit vending hard. Also, prices in vendors only change in fixed increments, for example, 5 cents or 10 cents and price changes are slow to catch up with rising distribution costs. In the last year or so, vending has become more profitable due to price increases, and all the concentrate companies are trying to increase their participation in the vending market.

> Bottle, can, and cup vending account for approximately 20 percent of soft drink sales in the United States today, but it's a declining area. For independent soft drink bottlers, the vending part of their business just keeps the public aware of their products. But now, distribution costs are rising so fast that I see zero or a net decrease of 1.5 percent in industry sales through vending outlets.

A prediction as to the future of the third major market segment—food stores—was made by another analyst:

> In the last few years, the total number of food stores has been declining, and there has been a net contraction of shelf space for soft drinks. Sales growth through the industry's most important outlet will be at most 1 or 2 percent per year.

FUTURE MARKET DIRECTIONS—A CLOUDY CRYSTAL BALL

> Where is this industry going in the next decade? I wish I knew the answer. Just skim the trade press and you get a feel for the jet pace of this game. Coke is test marketing a health drink called Samson! Implications? Washington is in on every issue. If franchising breaks down, this industry may go the way beer has—just a dozen major firms. Two more good-sized franchise operations have just been purchased by conglomerates.

> Did you see that West German health officials have removed cyclamates and saccharin from the cancer-producing agents list, and they are both available for use in soft drinks? Our FDA won't release cyclamates! And the international market's fascinating: Schweppes is moving into the USSR and Shasta into Canada. We are even getting new products—Nestle and Lipton are pushing canned tea. They are big internationally, too, and already are in fruit drinks abroad.

> OK, Professor, what's *your* answer? What's coming up, when, and what does it mean for me?

case 9

The Dr Pepper Company

The Dr Pepper Company of Dallas, Texas, manufactured, distributed, and marketed concentrate for a unique fruit flavored soft drink called Dr Pepper. "It's a corporate Horatio Alger story," an industry observer noted. "And a lot of the credit goes to the marketing abilities of its president; he is one of the best in the United States."

Since 1962 the company had been growing at two to three times the industry rate while it maintained a net return on investment of approximately 24 percent. During the past decade Dr Pepper had displaced Canada Dry Ginger Ale and Royal Crown Cola to move from the sixth to the fourth largest selling soft drink in the United States (see Exhibits 1 and 2).

Senior management attributed much of the company's success to two key factors: the strength of the Dr Pepper bottler network and the "uniqueness" and "goodness" of their soft drink. In the past decade the company had established a national network of franchised bottlers spreading the distribution of Dr Pepper from its regional southwestern base to the entire United States. "If there's one secret to the success we've had, it's the strength of our bottling organization," an executive stated. Senior management devoted much of their time to cultivating effective bottler-company relations. For despite the successful franchising of 100 percent of the U.S. market, product availability in 1976 was only 70 percent; some bottlers did not fully service their franchise territory. Management noted, too, that one of their continuing challenges was to get the multibrand bottler (who might also bottle Coke, Pepsi-Cola, or 7UP) to allocate the necessary amount of time, money, and effort to effectively distribute Dr Pepper.

Heralded in company promotional efforts as either a "misunderstood drink" or as the "most original soft drink ever," the uniqueness of Dr Pepper's flavor was cited as a second major corporate strength by company managers. The difficult to describe flavor had what management described as consumer "staying power"; once a customer sampled and liked Dr Pepper, s/he became a constant user and could consume many bottles each day.

EXHIBIT 1

THE DR PEPPER COMPANY
Consolidated Statements of Earnings and Retained Earnings, 1970–1975

	1970	1971	1972	1973	1974	1975
Net sales	$57,449,749	$63,622,653	$77,396,257	$98,918,466	$128,299,707	$138,250,075
Cost of sales	27,428,675	29,787,613	37,310,346	50,791,111	74,659,678	77,831,275
Gross profit	$30,021,074	$33,835,040	$40,085,911	$48,127,355	$ 53,640,029	$ 60,418,800
Administrative, marketing, and general expenses	19,835,343	21,991,585	25,402,094	31,262,480	36,297,111	37,702,958
Operating profit	$10,185,731	$11,843,455	$14,683,817	$16,864,875	$ 17,342,918	$ 22,715,842
Other income	899,051	894,811	842,982	1,502,848	1,121,634	414,588
Earnings before income taxes	$11,084,782	$12,738,266	$15,526,799	$18,367,723	$ 18,464,552	$ 23,130,430
Federal and state income taxes	5,455,761	5,966,125	7,424,580	8,632,223	8,562,853	11,226,295
Net earnings	$ 5,629,021	$ 6,772,141	$ 8,102,219	$ 9,735,500	$ 9,901,694	$ 11,904,135
Retained earnings at beginning of year	15,518,210	18,239,639	21,398,131	26,016,511	31,452,612	36,006,705
Dividends paid	$21,147,231	$25,011,780	$29,500,350	$35,752,011	$ 41,354,311	$ 47,910,840
	2,907,592	3,613,649	3,878,553	4,299,399	5,347,606	6,018,782
Retained earnings at end of year	$18,239,639	$21,398,131	$25,621,797	$31,452,612	$ 36,006,705	$ 41,892,058
Earnings per share	$0.61	$0.73	$0.43*	$0.51	$0.52	$0.62
Dividends per share	$0.31½	$0.39	$0.20⁴⁄₅*	$0.22¾	$0.28	$0.31½

* 1972, 2-for-1 stock split.

Dr Pepper was the only noncola product ever to achieve per capita consumption of 100 or more bottles per year in many key markets.

Dr Pepper's success, however, had not gone unappreciated—executives of major bottling firms spoke in extremely complimentary terms of the firm's record—or unchallenged by competitors. In 1972 Coca-Cola introduced Mr. PiBB, a new soft drink which, to many, tasted remarkably like Dr Pepper. This was not Coke's first competitive entry into this flavor field; they had previously test marketed two drinks, Texas Stepper and Chime, but neither succeeded commercially. A common industry interpretation was that Coke introduced Mr. PiBB to provide its bottlers with a product which they could sell to the Dr Pepper taste market. Dudley Lynch, a business journalist, commented:

> Predictably, Coke discouraged any thoughts that Mr. PiBB was aimed at Dr Pepper. "I haven't tasted Dr Pepper myself," said a Coke spokesman blandly, "so I wouldn't know how similar Mr. PiBB is to it. I don't think it was meant to compete with Dr Pepper—as far as I know Coke just felt there was a market for this kind of soft drink." Curiously enough Coke decided to test its new soft drink in Waco, birthplace of Dr Pepper, where more Dr Peppers are consumed than any other drink.[1]

The completion of Dr Pepper's national franchising program and its resultant almost 5.5 percent share of the 1975 soft drink market, some industry executives believed, had given the company both new status as well as a new competitive position. "They are playing in a different ball game now—against the big boys. And that game is getting rough, with an increasingly rough competitive battle between Coke and Pepsi-Cola. They are like two bull elephants locked in combat; it's dangerous to be in the same ring."

There did not seem to be much doubt that the U.S. soft drink industry was becoming increasingly complex and competitive (see Note on the United States Soft Drink Industry). The immediate, visible manifestation of this increased competitive circumstance in 1976 was an outbreak of retail price cutting in certain southwestern markets—Dallas and Ft. Worth—as well as a national, stepped-up, aggressive Coke versus Pepsi-Cola advertising program in which competitors' advertising claims were attacked in sometimes "savage" ways.

Labeled by *Time* magazine as a "likeable Lilliputian," Dr Pepper's total sales were only two thirds of Coca-Cola's 1975 net profits. But competing with billion-dollar giants did not seem to concern Dr Pepper senior management. The company announced an objective of making Dr Pepper America's number one soft drink with projected nationwide market shares of 10 percent in 1980 and 15 percent in 1985. Projected sales and earnings growth were targeted at 15 to 20 percent a year.

---

[1] Dudley Lynch, "Dr Pepper Takes on Coke," *D Magazine* (*Dallas/Ft. Worth*), September 1975, p. 60.

COMPANY HISTORY

Dr Pepper's historical background would provide any novelist with all of the ingredients of an exciting corporate drama. Formulated by an unknown fountain clerk, named after his girl friend's physician father to help "gain her hand," the drink came to the attention of R. L. Lazenby, a chemist. First dispensed at the Old Corner Drug Store in Waco, Texas, in 1885, it came on this local market approximately at the same time Coca-Cola was being introduced in the state of Georgia.

The early history of the company was characterized by family management, modest growth into contiguous territories, and a product reputation which combined a refreshment and a medicinal product mission. From the early 1920s well into the 1950s, the company was under the leadership of Mr. J. B. O'Hara, who was responsible for the transfer of company headquarters from Waco to Dallas and for the introduction of a bottlers' franchise program in 1926. Prior to that time Dr Pepper had been shipped to surrounding towns by Wells-Fargo Express. The company's advertising featured, as a trademark, an iron anvil, bordered by braided grain with the headline—DR PEPPER'S PHOSFERRATES—Wheat and Iron.

While family management and influence continued (in 1975 Mrs. O'Hara was the company's second largest shareholder) two critical developments occurred in the late 1950s. In 1956 Mr. W. R. Parker, a former General Foods Corporation executive, joined Dr Pepper and brought to the company a variety of modern marketing and advertising promotion techniques. He was assisted in this effort by Mr. W. W. Clements, who was named vice president of marketing in 1957. Their task was a formidable one. Dr Pepper's growth during the 30s and 40s had been modest; company marketing and management practices were conservative, and company bottlers tended to serve moderate-sized towns and rural areas, primarily in the southern areas of the United States.

The second critical development was legal in character. In 1962 the Pepsi-Cola Company sued Dr Pepper for alleged trademark infringement over Dr Pepper's use of the word "pep." Pepsi-Cola won the suit; however, Dr Pepper countersued, and the result was the ruling that Dr Pepper was not a cola drink but a unique and separate flavor. This judgment, later reaffirmed by the Food and Drug Administration, marked a turning point in the company's history. Coke and Pepsi-Cola franchised bottlers, the most powerful in the industry, could now also bottle Dr Pepper without violating their cola franchise. A company officer summarized the development as follows:

> Traditionally, up until about this time period, bottling companies produced under one basic franchise agreement. For example, there was a bottling company producing Coca-Cola and its flavor line—Fanta; another bottling company producing Pepsi-Cola and the Pepsi-Cola flavor line; and

EXHIBIT 2

THE DR PEPPER COMPANY
Consolidated Balance Sheets, 1970–1975

Assets	1970	1971	1972	1973	1974	1975
Current assets:						
Cash	$10,760,891	$11,818,371	$15,778,158	$ 872,776	$ 364,141	$ 145,276
Marketable securities	—	—	—	18,147,335	4,790,445	21,676,451
Receivables:						
Trade accounts	2,907,310	3,746,097	4,106,580	5,369,462	7,509,935	7,137,317
Other notes and accounts	972,108	930,663	1,162,725	1,310,362	1,605,048	452,976
Inventories (FIFO):	1,906,624	2,155,307				
Finished products			1,267,301	1,469,919	2,046,557	2,152,623
Raw materials and supplies	—	—	1,162,371	1,584,520	3,682,058	2,209,723
Prepaid expenses	1,046,045	1,844,082	2,235,984	3,314,330	3,548,258	1,990,119
Total current assets	$17,592,983	$20,494,520	$25,713,119	$32,068,704	$23,546,442	$35,764,485
Marketable securities held for investment	$ 470,656	$ 1,153,352	$ 1,519,251	$ 1,779,325	$ 8,156,618	$ 5,573,586
Notes receivable and other investments					1,260,829	738,243

Property, plant, and equipment:

Land	$ 4,027,325	$ 4,546,716	$ 4,615,832	$ 5,753,104	$ 1,951,050	$ 1,951,050
Buildings and improvements	8,237,902	8,922,629	10,531,118	14,446,416	6,102,342	6,385,146
Machinery, equipment, and furniture					16,478,513	18,126,276
	$12,265,227	$13,469,345	$15,146,950	$20,199,520	$24,531,905	$26,462,472
Less: Accumulated depreciation	5,249,478	5,594,253	6,535,564	8,902,926	9,171,248	10,421,632
Net property, plant, and equipment	$ 7,015,749	$ 7,875,092	$ 8,611,386	$11,296,594	$15,360,657	$16,040,840
Formulas, trademarks, and goodwill	272,910	272,910	272,910	272,910	270,910	270,910
Total assets	$25,352,298	$29,795,874	$36,116,666	$45,417,533	$48,595,456	$58,388,064

Liabilities and Stockholders' Equity

Current liabilities:						
Accounts payable and accrued expenses	$ 2,859,195	$ 3,537,896	$ 3,412,671	$ 6,006,509	$ 4,884,550	$ 6,321,455
Federal and state income taxes	715,455	996,987	1,551,370	1,240,930	73,469	2,505,819
Total current liabilities	$ 3,574,650	$ 4,534,883	$ 4,964,041	$ 7,247,439	$ 4,958,019	$ 8,827,274
Stockholders' equity:						
Common stock without par value	$ 3,538,009	$ 3,862,860	$ 5,530,828	$ 6,717,482	$ 7,630,732	$ 7,668,732
Retained earnings	18,239,639	21,398,131	25,621,797	31,452,612	36,006,705	41,892,058
Total stockholders' equity	$21,777,648	$25,260,991	$31,152,625	$38,170,094	$43,637,437	$49,560,790
Total liabilities and stockholders' equity	$25,352,298	$29,795,874	$36,116,666	$45,417,533	$48,595,456	$58,388,064

a Seven-Up bottling company producing that product. Included among the bottling companies would perhaps be a Dr Pepper company. These Dr Pepper bottlers inherently would be the ones least financially able and equipped to make a major effort at market penetration in competition with the entrenched and well-established and financed cola companies. With the court decision ruling that Dr Pepper was not a cola, the Dr Pepper Company legally was in a position to solicit franchise agreements with the strongest of the cola-producing bottling companies in any geographical area.

By 1962 the company had entered a phase of rapid growth which brought company sales from $17 million to $138 million in 1975 and an even more rapid profit expansion. This expansion program was climaxed by Dr Pepper's introduction to the New York City area market in 1970.

One crisp November morning in 1969 Woodrow Wilson "Foots" Clements and his team of executives stepped into a cab outside New York's Waldorf-Astoria Hotel. Mission: To pull off what some would call the biggest coup in soft drink history. Clements and his Dr Pepper executives, representing an easy-going beverage which had stayed home in Texas and minded its own business for 85 years, headed over to the 34th Street offices of Coca-Cola Bottling Company of New York, the world's largest distributor of soft drink's Goliath—Coca-Cola. Objective: To convince Coca-Cola of New York to bottle Dr Pepper, load it on Coke trucks, and sell America's "most misunderstood" soft drink to 20 million New Yorkers.

Seven months later Millard[2] and Clements shook hands. New York Coke would bottle Dr Pepper. After 85 years Dr Pepper hit the big time, beginning a fascinating David and Goliath battle that in five years has brought Dr Pepper headlines and stirred the ire of Coca-Cola, whose dominance of the soft drink market is even greater than General Motors' dominance of the auto industry.[3]

By 1973 domestic franchising was virtually 100 percent complete and Dr Pepper made its first major move into the international market. It introduced Dr Pepper in Japan via a franchise agreement with the Tokyo Coca-Cola Bottling Company, Ltd.

Central to this period of growth and profit was the leadership of W. W. Clements, who became executive vice president in 1967, president and chief executive officer in 1970, and chairman of the board, president, and chief executive officer in March 1974. In 1976 Mr. Clements noted enthusiastically, "We have just started. The potential is tremendous." Some evidence of that potential was detailed in a *Fortune* magazine article:

Consumption of Dr Pepper remains heavily concentrated in the areas where the drink traditionally has been popular. Five southwestern states with 10 percent of the nation's population account for 37 percent of the

---

[2] Coca-Cola of New York's president.

[3] "Dr Pepper Takes on Coke," pp. 59–60.

company's gallonage, while at the other extreme, nine northeastern states with 24 percent of the population account for a mere 6 percent.

The strongest market of all, appropriately enough, is Waco, the old home town, where Dr Pepper outsells Coca-Cola and Pepsi-Cola combined. The 95,326 citizens of Waco drink more Dr Pepper than the 1,512,893 citizens of Detroit. If the rest of the country were to rise to even half of Waco's per capita consumption of over 250 bottles a year, Dr Pepper's domestic revenues would approach $1.5 billion. That kind of formulation may seem starry-eyed to outsiders, but it is taken quite seriously at Dr Pepper headquarters.[4]

PRODUCT

Dr Pepper was a carbonated, soft drink made of 23 flavorings, plus some phosphoric acid, caffeine, and caramel color. Its exact formulation was a closely guarded company secret. Dr Pepper was unique among soft drinks on two dimensions: its palatibility when served hot or cold and its basic flavor. The unique Dr Pepper flavor was summarized in the following company advertising message:

> Dr Pepper is different from any brand of soft drink. It is not a cola, nor a root beer, nor any single flavor, but a blend of 23 flavors. As most customers say ... THERE IS NOTHING LIKE DR PEPPER!!! IT'S DISTINCTIVELY DIFFERENT.

The drink's uniqueness, however, created promotional challenges for the company. Dr Pepper's unusual flavor was an acquired taste for many people and required repeated trial before acceptance. One bottler estimated that it required eight bottles of the beverage in two weeks to turn a potential customer into a regular Dr Pepper drinker.

Moreover, numerous consumer misconceptions about Dr Pepper inhibited its acceptance, especially outside of the South and Southwest. Its caramel coloring led some to expect a cola, others thought it made of prune juice or pepper sauce, while its name led others to believe it was a medicinal drink.

A diet Dr Pepper was introduced in 1962. Sales increased steadily until 1969, when sales stopped because of the ban on the use of cyclamates as artificial sweeteners. Reformulated to use saccharin as the sweetener, sales of Sugar Free Dr Pepper increased from 7.2 million cases in 1971 (0.2 percent of the market) to 18 million cases in 1974 (0.4 percent of the market) and 28 million cases in 1975 (0.6 percent of the total market). The increase in sales from 1974 to 1975 was 55.6 percent, outpacing the total diet drink market which increased by only 16.8 percent. Company executives attributed

---

[4] A. M. Lewis, "What Happened When Dr Pepper Began Thinking Big," *Fortune*, December 1973, p. 128.

Sugar Free's spectacular competitive performance to its ability to mask saccharin's bitter aftertaste better than cola drinks and to the first Sugar Free advertising campaign initiated in 1974.

In the mid-1960s Dr Pepper had attempted to broaden its product line with a sophisticated ginger flavored soft drink from Sweden called Pomac. Initial market introductions were not successful due to improper "positioning" and inadequate advertising and promotion support, according to Mr. Clements, and the product was withdrawn by 1967.

Regular Dr Pepper remained the company's leading product in 1976, accounting for 85 percent of unit sales in 1975. Regular Dr Pepper sales had grown steadily over the past decade with market share doubling from 2.4 percent in 1966 to 4.9 percent in 1975. Sugar Free accounted for 14 percent of sales, while the company's flavor lines Salute, Waco, and Hustle together accounted for 1 percent. Salute and Waco were six standard soft drink flavors manufactured only as a service to Dr Pepper bottlers who needed a wider range of product to service multiflavor vending machines and soda fountain dispensers. No sales, advertising, or promotion efforts were expended on them. Hustle was a skim-milk based, high protein, vitamin and mineral fortified, controlled calorie drink distributed primarily to athletic teams.

A FIRST VISIT WITH PRESIDENT WOODROW WILSON CLEMENTS

"Sure, I can take you there. It's 5523 Mockingbird Lane, and they have a beautiful building and I'll bet at least nine acres of beautiful park land. They're a Dallas company, you know, and we are proud of them. My kids drink Dr Pepper by the case. You folks have it up North?"

At corporate headquarters the researchers were introduced to a ritual which was later repeated in every office visited. "Welcome! We are pleased to have you here. Would you like a Dr Pepper? It's a great drink." While consuming their hot Dr Pepper, the Yankee guests were given a tour, starting with a visit to a replica of the Old Corner Drug Store of Waco, Texas, a quick look at the concentrate production facilities, and a walk through various offices. The atmosphere was informal, and the researchers sensed an atmosphere of warmth and good spirits.

"Let's go to Foots's office now; he asked about you. Everybody calls him Foots, by the way; there's a great story behind that nickname and he ought to tell you about it."

Mr. Clements's office was large, deeply carpeted, and with the help of green decorative plants seemed to subdivide into three areas: a large conference table section, a conversation-oriented cluster of modern Knoll chairs with throw rugs accenting the soft wall and chair colors and Mr. Clements's desk area. Mr. Clements's desk, backed by a massive office chair, was flanked by two large lamps and a super-polished brass spittoon. Two telephones, pictures of grandchildren, and a tray of marbles were evident on the desk top. The adjacent walls were covered with personal memorabilia, organizational memberships, and the Distinguished Salesman Award given by the Sales Executive Club. An antique clock and abstract painting completed the decor.

Lighting up an ever-present cigar, Mr. Clements welcomed the researchers, ordered them another Dr Pepper, and expressed his full support for the case research. Sipping a Dr Pepper, he observed:

This is a wonderful company, and I have been with them since I started as a route salesman in Tuscaloosa, Alabama, in 1935. You will meet some fine people.

As to my nickname, well, I'll be glad to tell you. There's about 49 different versions of it—but the *real* facts are my feet just grew up before I did and I had rather small legs and I played football rather young and my feet in those days were turned that way. So when I was playing football with the football pants just reaching my knees and those big feet, and not too graceful, why that's where I picked up the nickname. I was not sensitive about my given name but just felt like it was, you know, a name that everybody says, "Well, you're named after the President—Woodrow Wilson—you're a Democrat." My mom wanted me to be President, by the way. So since my schooldays I've always used my nickname. I send my Christmas card out in footprint form, and everybody calls me Foots. When I became president, an executive suggested that I might want to go to using my real name—it was a little more sophisticated. I said no—I *got* here using the nickname Foots and I'm going to continue to use the nickname Foots. Now of course I sign my checks differently—but everything else is Foots.

Let me try to give you a first start at understanding Dr Pepper. We have a small number of company-owned bottling plants and a can operation. The latter is located in Dallas and produces canned Dr Pepper for the markets that can be economically served from that location—about 150 miles. It services bottlers who do not have canning abilities. We also have a fountain operation which sells syrup to theaters, fast-food chains, or to vendors at major sports facilities. Finally and most important is our franchise bottler operation. It is responsible for the sale of concentrate and syrup to franchise bottlers.

We have a different philosophy than Coke and Pepsi-Cola. We consider ourselves as in the franchise business and not in the bottling business. Now we do own Waco, Dallas, Ft. Worth, and San Antonio. We took over a plant in San Angelo but sold it later. We bought Ft. Worth three years ago because we felt Ft. Worth and Dallas are really one market. We feel that operating a plant does give us a chance to learn a great deal, to try out programs and experiment. We then take these programs to our franchise bottler, and he makes the final decision.

We've been successful. But we still have only about 6 percent market share. In this part of the country we may have as high as 30 or 40 percent; in New York City, we will have 1 percent; in Boston, 1/10 of 1 percent. Our problem there is to get the right bottler and enthuse him and train his people in marketing fundamentals.

I was frustrated during part of 1974 when things began to waver a bit. I knew the bottlers needed some stimulation and needed some inspiration and I had seven echelons between me and the bottler. So I came back and restated the basic fundamentals to my own people and to my bottlers. I had less than 25 people out of my top 200 that had been in their present position more than five years. I never make a speech now that I don't hammer at those fundamental marketing precepts.

You might be interested in these excerpts from my opening speech to the 1975 Dr Pepper Bottler Meeting:

> We have been working hard in getting our own people fully aware of the correct way to market Dr Pepper. The difference is in building a business on an original flavor with a distinctive taste, and a name that is a misnomer, from doing business with a flavor that is well known and a name that identifies that flavor.
>
> Now, what is our program? There isn't any one answer, but there is one absolute and rigid criterion for every market. Every program for every market must be built around and with the complete utilization of the basic fundamentals—not just one—but all five. J. C. Penney once said they don't rewrite the Bible every Sunday; the same applies to these basic fundamentals.
>
> **Perfect product:** We are selling taste and building a business on an original flavor with a unique taste. The products must taste right when they're consumed.
>
> **Distribution and availability:** Even though Dr Pepper now has theoretical national distribution, as all the United States is under franchise, we have poor distribution in far too many markets—and much room for improvement in every market. We are weak in the most important segment of the market—single-drink accounts. There isn't any way you can build a high per capita on Dr Pepper in any market without concentrating on the single-drink outlets. We must never forget we are building a business on a unique drink—and it is much easier to get them to try one drink than a 6-pack—or 8 pack—or a 32-, 48-, or 64-ounce bottle.
>
> **Sampling:** The need for sampling is obvious. And **point-of-sale advertising** still performs the same important function in the basic fundamentals it always has.
>
> **Media advertising:** I am not going to dwell on this—not because I don't think it is important, because I recognize the important and productive part it plays in building a consumer franchise and a profitable Dr Pepper volume—and if there is anything all of us are oversold on, it is media advertising.

Following Foots's suggestions, the researchers decided just to study the marketing aspects of Dr Pepper, then examine in sequence manufacturing, research and development, finance, the impact of federal regulations on company operations, international operations, and finally review briefly the formal organization structure of the company.

COMPETITION

"Basically," a senior executive said, "we compete for space in the consumer's stomach, for space on the retailers' shelves, and for the time and attention for our multibrand bottlers. Competition is the name of the game, and marketing is the key player." All company officers seemed marketing oriented, all had almost a "messianic belief" in the goodness of their product, and all "believed" in the Dr Pepper Company and its potential. Marketing seemed to be as much a state of mind at Dr Pepper as basic techniques.

In its "tummy" competition, Dr Pepper obviously competed with all liquid refreshments, but its primary competitors were other soft drinks—particularly cola products. Company executives believed that a balanced package of advertising, point-of-sale promotion, extensive distribution, competitive packaging, and pricing tailored to specific franchise market areas was the key to success.

Recent competitive action by PepsiCo provided dramatic evidence of the intensity of competition between Dr Pepper and the major colas. Labeled the "Pepsi Challenge," the Pepsi-Cola Company introduced a major share of market campaign in Dallas in mid-April 1974. At that time industry observers estimated Dr Pepper's share of market was 25 percent, Coke's was 28.6 percent, and Pepsi's was 7.6 percent. After ten months of vigorous advertising effort and extensive price-off promotions (cola prices were slashed to one third their normal level), Pepsi had increased its market share to fourteen percent, Coke had increased to 30.5 percent, and Dr Pepper had declined to 20 percent. Responding to Coke and Pepsi "would have been degrading to our product," said vice president Bruce Conner.

Dr Pepper was the dominant factor in its flavor type as was 7UP in the lemon-lime category. Dr Pepper's only direct flavor competitor was Coca-Cola's Mr. PiBB. First introduced in 1972, just after Dr Pepper had successfully franchised many Coca-Cola bottlers, Mr. PiBB simulated the taste of Dr Pepper and had received extensive marketing support in areas where Dr Pepper was popular. Sales of Mr. PiBB had grown from 5 million cases in the year of its introduction to 37.5 million cases in 1975, representing an 0.8 percent share of market. Coca-Cola, it appeared, attempted to market Mr. PiBB in any area where Dr Pepper achieved a 5 percent market share, and especially in the areas of the Southwest and South where the flavor was most widely accepted. One analyst believed that Coca-Cola considered Mr. PiBB only a regional flavor and had no intention of marketing the drink nationwide. If a Coke bottler was bottling Mr. PiBB, his franchise agreement would legally prevent him from bottling Dr Pepper.

Fortune magazine, commenting on Mr. PiBB, states:

> Clements maintains that he isn't terribly concerned about Mr. PiBB. He doesn't expect to lose bottlers who are doing well with Dr Pepper, he says. "Any bottler who has only had us for a short time, and whose Dr Pepper volume is so low that it's only a small percentage of his profits—those are the bottlers vulnerable to switching. There may be 20 of them all together, and if we lost them all, it wouldn't even mean $100,000 in gross volume." Clements adds, with some glee, that more than 50 Coca-Cola bottlers signed on with Dr Pepper even *after* Mr. PiBB was introduced.[5]

Mr. Clements reviewed the competitive situation in 1976 as follows:

> Coke's promotions on Mr. PiBB have broadened our market because it calls attention to the flavor, and we had no help in all those years. We were doing it by ourselves. Basically it stimulates our people to do a better job, and our market share and sales volume usually improve when Mr. PiBB comes into the market. Our main emphasis now to combat Mr. PiBB is to make sure that we are doing the right kind of fundamental job on Dr Pepper.
>
> Coke has tried to introduce Mr. PiBB in some international markets, and it has failed worse than it has here. I've said lots of times, half in jest, that if Coke had known how hard Dr Pepper was to sell, they would never have tried to imitate it. Coke and PepsiCo will be back pushing Coke and Pepsi-Cola, if they're smart, rather than these less important brands. Their problem is dilution—not at the national advertising level—they have plenty of dollars—but dilution at bottler "level of effort."

At the retailer level, Dr Pepper competed for shelf-space allocations, display opportunities, and cooperation on promotional events. In larger supermarkets Dr Pepper was judged by store managers on the basis of product sales performance in terms of gross margins and turnover and frequency and efficiency of delivery. Some retailers demand price-off promotions, all of which were not passed on to the consumer. In fountain and cup vending outlets, Dr. Pepper competed primarily against Coke and 7UP for one of the four lines which a typical dispensing machine could handle.

At the bottler level, Dr Pepper competed for the best available bottlers, and once the franchise had been signed, competed for his or her time and enthusiasm.

TARGET CONSUMERS

Sugar Free and regular Dr Pepper were targeted at two different consumer groups. Sugar Free's target was women 18–49 years of age who were

---

[5] A. M. Lewis, *Fortune*, December 1973, p. 124.

the largest consumers of diet soft drinks. Sugar Free, formulated with a saccharine sweetener, was the second fastest growing diet soft drink in the country. "Aggressive marketing has enabled many of our bottlers to capture over 20 percent of the diet business in their market and in some cases the share of market for Sugar Free is approaching 50 percent of the total diet market. In Seattle the Dr Pepper Company with the Portland bottler had developed and conducted a separate test marketing program for Sugar Free Dr Pepper with superior results."

Young people 8–18, Mr. Clements explained, were the primary target group for regular Dr Pepper, with secondary emphasis on the 19–34-year-old group.

> We feel the teens is the time to really concentrate on making the lifelong Dr Pepper drinker. When people get older, they're very hard to change, but the teens are looking for something unique to discover and make their own drink. After all, they are the biggest per capita consumers of soft drinks. Market studies now indicate the preference of this age group for Dr Pepper; and once a consumer acquires a taste for Dr Pepper, the loyalty for our product remains extremely strong.

In 1975 Dr Pepper gallonage was divided along product lines—85 percent regular and 14 percent Sugar Free; by channel, 59 percent bottler, 20 percent fountain, and 21 percent cans.

Advertising and promotion

Advertising was a key, direct link between Dr Pepper and its bottler and consumer markets. "One of our major challenges is to build consumer taste habits for a unique and indescribable drink. Milk tastes like milk, coffee like coffee, and Dr Pepper like Dr Pepper. You don't know what it is like until you taste it," Mr. Clements stated. "One of the first things I did as executive vice president was to bring in a new advertising agency." *Fortune* magazine described that event:

> Clements says he is delighted with Young and Rubicam. "They were quick to grasp the potential we had," he remarks. "They took our market research, and came up with a concept that they were able to translate into a clever sales message." As anyone who has watched television, listened to the radio, or glimpsed a billboard in recent years undoubtedly knows, Y&R produced the slogan "America's Most Misunderstood Soft Drink." Young and Rubicam felt that the notion of a "misunderstood" soft drink would appeal to young people—traditionally the biggest consumers of soft drinks—who like to think *they* are misunderstood. But the slogan also had some basis in fact; Dr Pepper, it appeared, *was* misunderstood.[6]

---

[6] Ibid., p. 121.

Dr Pepper engaged in three types of advertising and promotion: national and local media advertising, including television, radio, magazine, and outdoor advertising; sales promotion materials and campaigns; and a bottler equipment assistance program. Ten percent of advertising and promotion funds were used to help reduce the cost to the bottler of purchasing vending and dispensing equipment for the single-drink market. Dr Pepper management say increased advertising and promotional funds are crucial to achieving growth goals. These expenditures were programmed for a 20 percent annual increase for the next five years, and a special "ready-markets" program had been developed to invest extra advertising and promotional efforts in key market areas.

In 1975 one industry analyst estimated, Dr Pepper spent approximately $6.5 million for television and magazine programs, or an estimated 30 percent of its advertising and promotion budget. Another approximately $4.5 million, the analyst estimated, was matched by bottler funds in cooperative programs to buy local television and radio spots, outdoor and newspaper advertising. Although Dr Pepper advertising funds were higher per ounce than per ounce expenditures of the two leading cola companies, they were meager compared to the dollars Coke and PepsiCo spent on national advertising. Mr. Clements commented on this circumstance:

> We are providing more money for marketing support for Dr Pepper than at any time in our history, but it is small compared to some of our competition, inadequate to the objectives we would like to achieve, and too little compared to our needs and opportunities. We will provide some national advertising, still far too little and too thin to give us any significant impact, but it will help in creating and keeping alive awareness of Dr Pepper with the consumer.

The content of Dr Pepper media advertising was the same whether the commercials were used in a national, cooperative, or "ready-market" program. Dr Pepper followed a strategy different from the traditional patterns of the two major cola producers. Most Coke and Pepsi-Cola advertising featured upbeat music, music or jingles that frequently repeated the brand name and associated it with an attractive scene of young people enjoying themselves in a sports activity or a pleasant family situation. It was designed to keep a high level of "top of mind awareness" consistent with a soft drink's position as an impulse purchase item. Dr Pepper advertising, on the other hand, was designed to build both awareness of the brand and to position Dr Pepper as a unique and original flavor that was not a cola. Dr Pepper's current campaign focused on the theme of "the most original soft drink ever."

The placement of Dr Pepper television advertisements also deviated from Coke and PepsiCo's; the latter companies used a "scatter approach" which meant the regular placement of frequent 30- and 60-second "spots" on a variety of programs. Dr Pepper, with the objective of maximizing the impact of its budget, sponsored entire programs. In 1975 the program began with a New Year's Eve special over ABC starring Chicago, the Doobie Brothers, Olivia Newton-John, and the Beach Boys. Other programs included the "Grammy Awards" in March, the "Emmy Awards" in May, and the "Miss Teenage America Pageant" in November.

Company marketing staff also prepared tailor-made complete advertising programs for all franchise bottlers. In addition, Mr. Clements in 1976 reintroduced his ready-markets concept. In this program, additional funds were allocated to supplement cooperative advertising expenditures in key market areas where Dr Pepper's medium-term growth potential was high. It focused on already developed markets where current penetration was relatively high and areas with relatively high per capita soft drink consumption, such as the Southeast. Mr. Clements said the program resulted in more predictable growth for the company because it put resources against potential. It also rapidly increased sales volume which, in turn, provided funds for development of other markets.

Although only four bottlers, serving populations of 500,000 to 2 million each, were in the ready-markets program in 1976, and little money was being spent, close to 5 percent of 1977's advertising budget would go to ready-markets development. Mr. Clements said the company was phasing back into the program after having drifted away from it in 1974–75. The full program would eventually involve 18 markets on a rotating basis, with three markets added and three dropped each year.

In addition to media advertising, corporate funds sponsored "special marketing programs." F. F. Avery, executive vice president, reviewed these:

> For the past several years we have had prize-winning floats in the Orange Bowl parade, in the Annual Tournament of Roses parade in Pasadena, California, and in the Cotton Bowl parade in Dallas. Second, approximately two years ago the Dr Pepper Company purchased Miss Teenage America, and it is now operated as a separate division. Third, we have signed an exclusive sponsorship agreement with the North American Soccer League. Finally, I would like to make you aware of the fact that Dr Pepper has had for some time the marketing rights to a product called Hustle.

Dr Pepper sales promotion activities were designed to motivate the consumer at the point of purchase. Sales promotion expenditures included the costs of retail point-of-sale materials for packaged goods such as display racks, seasonal end-of-aisle display promotions, price-off deals to both the consumer and the retailer, coupons, giveaways, posters, and Dr Pepper–identified route sales force uniforms and delivery vehicles. In fountain outlets sales promotion funds were spent on signs, Dr Pepper–identified menu-boards, and decorative paper cups.

All Dr Pepper sales promotion funds (approximately 40 percent of the company's advertising and promotion budget) were spent in conjunction with the cooperative advertising program. Industry analysts estimated Dr Pepper's contribution was approximately $8 million in 1975 and was allocated to bottlers on the basis of concentrate purchases. This resulted in the better developed market receiving the most sales promotion dollars.

Sugar Free employed a related advertising campaign using the theme "It Tastes Too Good to Be True." In 1975 Sugar Free received about one fifth of company advertising funds—the first time significant resources had been allocated to the product. Some bottlers allocated as much as 50 percent of their cooperative advertising and promotion funds to Sugar Free, believing that it was a superior product and that diet drinkers had a propensity to experiment with new flavors.

THE FRANCHISE BOTTLER SYSTEM

Major company objectives between 1967 and 1973 had been to build a strong franchise bottler network and to achieve national distribution of Dr Pepper by upgrading the network in territories already served and franchising strong bottlers in areas where Dr Pepper was not yet available. In 1976 company management believed both of these objectives had been achieved, giving Dr Pepper a major advantage over its next largest competitor—7UP. National distribution had been achieved substantially through associations with Coke and PepsiCo bottlers (see Exhibit 3).

EXHIBIT 3
Dr Pepper franchises by national brands produced

Brand configuration	Number of plants
Dr Pepper only	45
Dr Pepper and Coke*	192
Dr Pepper and Pepsi†	164
Dr Pepper and minor brand(s)	96
Total	497

* Dr Pepper and Coke were the primary brands, but the bottler might also bottle secondary brands.
† Dr Pepper and Pepsi were the primary brands, but the bottler might also bottle secondary brands.
Source: Researcher's estimate on the basis of very limited and perhaps inaccurate data.

In 1976 Mr. Clements announced a new corporate target—"deeper market penetration." One aspect of deeper market penetration involved increased attention to expanding the single-drink business—a task assigned to the Fountain Division. The company ranked third nationwide in fountain syrup sales. In recent years fountain sales had been the fastest growing part of Dr Pepper's business and accounted for over 20 percent of concentrate volume in 1975.

Mr. Clements stated:

> And we want to continue to upgrade our existing franchise network. What we bring a prospective, strong bottler is an opportunity to increase total sales by broadening his market base. It brings new soft drink consumers to him, and we offer higher growth rates than the rest of the industry; Coke and PepsiCo have as high a share of market as they are going to get in cola products. These are easily substantiated claims in areas where Dr Pepper has some consumer franchise. Where an established franchise is switched to a different bottler, it's an immediate sales addition that's really golden because it is on top of an already profitable operation.

Historically, Mr. Clements's decision to obtain the best and strongest bottler for Dr Pepper was a major shift in company policy. Prior to 1967 the company emphasized the importance of Dr Pepper being the bottler's only, or at least primary, product. Management felt Dr Pepper would be neglected if the bottler held another brand franchise, especially a cola. Franchised bottlers were members of the Dr Pepper "family."

The national franchising program not only increased the number of franchisees but it impacted the personal approach and feeling of family which were an important part of Dr Pepper's bottler relationships. A number of new multibrand franchisees were substantial organizations run by professional managers who operated multiple-plant firms. J. K. Hughes, executive vice president, remarked:

> We try harder to build and maintain a close, personal relationship with each of our bottlers because this is important to the character of our operation; we do a superior job at it. But it does get increasingly difficult as we get larger and our bottlers get larger.

The 497 bottlers who made up the Dr Pepper network varied substantially by type of market area serviced, degree of market penetration, distribution methods, and management and financial capabilities. The franchisees' independent status and Dr Pepper's position as a secondary brand meant that the company did not have full accessibility to data on the franchisee's total sales, profits, and capital investment. Management was in agreement that a strong bottler had an aggressive route sales force that achieved substantial shelf space in supermarkets and extensive distribution in other outlets, ran frequent promotions, had good production facilities, was profitable and had a good capital base. The strongest bottler usually had the highest local market share—typically this was Coke or PepsiCo. Dr Pepper used per capita sales and percentage sales growth as the main measures of performance by a franchisee (see Exhibits 4 and 5).

All but 45 franchisees also bottled other brands; 53 did not actually produce Dr Pepper at all. One hundred six franchises were held by 25 com-

EXHIBIT 4

Per capita standing by franchise for representative states and franchises in representative states for period ending December 31, 1975*

Arkansas: 11

California:
1. Bakersfield
2. Brawley
3. Fullertown
4. Fresno
5. West Sacramento
6. Oxnard
7. San Diego
8. Chico
9. San Bernardino
10. Ukiah
11. Sunnyvale
12. Gardena
13. Eureka
14. Daly City
15. Mt. Shasta

Colorado: 7

Connecticut:
1. Meriden

Maryland: 4

Massachusetts:
1. Sagamore
2. Springfield
3. Newburyport
4. Needham

Michigan: 10

New Mexico: 7

New York:
1. Jamestown
2. Olean
3. Rochester
4. Batavia
5. Plattsburgh
6. N. Tonawanda
7. New York Metro
8. Endicott
9. Buffalo
10. Syracuse
11. Glens Falls
12. Massena

North Carolina: 21

Pennsylvania: 18

Rhode Island: 1

South Carolina:
1. Spartanburg
2. Abbeville
3. Greenwood
4. Columbia
5. Rock Hill
6. Florence

South Dakota:
1. Rapid City
2. Huron
3. Sioux Falls
4. Pierre
5. Aberdeen

Tennessee: 17

Texas: 55

Utah: 6

Vermont: 1

* Arranged with number 1 being highest per capita sales in state.
Source: Company records.

EXHIBIT 5
Per capita leader cities in consumption of Dr Pepper

1. Waco, Texas	11. Sherman, Texas
2. Fort Worth, Texas	12. Mangum, Oklahoma
3. San Marcos, Texas	13. Paragould, Arkansas
4. Lufkin, Texas	14. Paris, Texas
5. Nacogdoches, Texas	15. Childress, Texas
6. Dallas, Texas	16. Sulphur Springs, Texas
7. Elk City, Oklahoma	17. Lubbock, Texas
8. Longview, Texas	18. Dublin, Texas
9. Amarillo, Texas	19. Palestine, Texas
10. Mt. Pleasant, Texas	20. Plainview, Texas

Source: Company records. Cities arranged in order of consumption: Waco highest, Plainview lowest of the 20.

panies who operated multiple bottling plants and who sometimes engaged in other lines of business. The company referred to these firms as "conglomerates." One of the larger firms was General Cinema Corporation of Boston, with total soft drink sales of just under $200 million; it operated 16 Dr Pepper franchises. Other major firms holding multiple Dr Pepper franchises were RKO General, Universal Foods Corporation, Wometco, and M.E.I. Approximately 50 percent of the 25 conglomerate companies were independently owned Coke or Pepsi-Cola bottlers; for example, Coca-Cola Bottling–Los Angeles and Coca-Cola Bottling Company of Memphis. The latter firm, operating six Dr Pepper franchises, had joined the Dr Pepper Company in 1975 and immediately and substantially improved Dr Pepper's competitive position in this trading area.

The variety of bottler and territorial circumstances meant Dr Pepper had to design a wide number of marketing programs for its bottlers. Mr. Clements elaborated:

> You'll have one franchise that is almost totally rural with one town with 5,000 people where the soft drink business hasn't changed in three generations. Then you'll have a territory like New York City that's totally urban and very volatile. Franchisees vary, too, in their sophistication.

A New England bottler talked about his business and his new Dr Pepper franchise:

> I hold three of the four top national brands in this area, Coke, 7UP, and Dr Pepper. I also bottle Squirt and my own label flavor line. I took on Dr Pepper because it is a flavor leader. Coke offers Mr. PiBB, but PepsiCo has no entry in that flavor market. If I take on the Dr Pepper franchise, my Pepsi-Cola competitors can't have either Mr. PiBB or Dr Pepper. Introducing a new flavor is difficult. I'm not making any money on Dr Pepper right now, but I have it for its long-term growth potential over the next 10 or 15 years.

Bottler sales and relations

Industry trade sources gave Dr Pepper high marks for its bottler philosophy and organization. Mr. Clements outlined this philosophy:

> We don't go take orders for concentrate to make Dr Pepper. We sell ideas and marketing programs. In the franchise system the bottler is *independent*. He can live up to the franchise contract and still not do a maximum job in developing the market. Our job is one of persuasion. Right now our toughest challenge is to get the multibrand bottlers to do a good job on Dr Pepper.

The task of persuading 497 franchised bottlers to work harder for Dr Pepper fell to the 34 zone managers, 7 divisional managers, and 2 area managers who made up Dr Pepper's bottler field sales force. Zone managers called directly on the franchisees within their territory, working with the bottler to set sales and distribution goals and administering cooperative advertising funds and other bottler-oriented incentives. Zone managers also initiated Central Trading Area meetings involving several bottlers with contiguous territories. These meetings developed and coordinated special promotions with chains whose trading areas covered common territories.

Zone managers prided themselves on their capacity to build close Dr Pepper–bottler relationships. One commented:

> Dr Pepper has an enviable reputation. To bottlers Dr Pepper reps are "good old boys, one of us." They think Coke reps are pompous and stuffy, 7UP distant and cool, and PepsiCo a corporate machine. At the same time, Dr Pepper reps have the most professional approach to market planning and budgeting. Our annual specific marketing plans include monthly case sales forecasts by package type with coordinated advertising, promotion, distribution, and sales force incentive programs. Few of the small family-run bottling businesses would do any planning on their own. Nobody else offers anything like our special marketing plans.

A primary assignment, and one zone managers regarded as critical to the motivation of bottlers, was the management of cooperative advertising and promotion funds. In support of the local bottlers' Dr Pepper marketing program, the zone manager planned local television, radio, newspaper, and billboard advertising, as well as retail point-of-sale materials. The costs of coupon campaigns, merchandise, and price-off promotions also came out of these funds.

The base budget for Dr Pepper cooperative advertising was 25 cents per gallon of forecasted sales, with Dr Pepper and the bottler each contributing 12½ cents per gallon. Supplementary cooperative funds were available to newly franchised bottlers, ready-market areas, and special markets like New York City. Instead of the 50/50 contribution system in the base budget, Dr Pepper contributed 65 percent of supplementary funds while the bottler contributed 35 percent.

Dr Pepper zone managers could offer additional programs to bottlers in the form of packaging and equipment assistance. In the packaging program Dr Pepper made cash payments to the bottler to reduce the package costs outlay when introducing new package sizes. The equipment assistance program helped reduce the bottler's capital investment.

The company also used a variety of other incentives to motivate franchisees and their sales forces. On the national level there was the annual Dr Pepper Bottler Meeting, a three-day resort extravaganza where Dr Pepper executives introduced the coming year's marketing and distribution strategies to bottler top management and their spouses, amid swimming, golfing, dining, and sightseeing. An annual travel incentive contest for Dr Pepper bottlers with significant sales increases was also popular.

The Dr Pepper zone manager also worked with bottler management to set up periodic cooperative sales incentive programs for the bottlers' sales force, who could win prizes and premiums from a special catalog. The zone manager could also ask for help from the parent company staff: a consumer relations specialist would run sampling programs or appear on local television and radio interview shows, a promotion expert would consult on sales motivation programs, and a national chain store account contact person would help in calling on large accounts.

The franchise

The basic definition of the relationship between the company and its bottlers was the Dr Pepper bottler's license agreement, or franchise contract, and all such contracts were secured in a vault in Dr Pepper's Dallas headquarters. It granted the franchisee, without cost, the exclusive right to produce and distribute Dr Pepper soft drinks in a defined geographic area as long as the franchisee met the terms of the agreement. It required the Dr Pepper Company to provide adequate amounts of concentrate of good quality.

The franchisee had the right to terminate the contract on 90 days' notice, but as long as s/he was party to the contract the list of obligations and restrictions was substantial. Most important were maintaining high sanitary and product quality standards and not selling the product outside his or her territory, nor knowingly selling to a third party who subsequently resold outside the territory. Prior to a 1970 court ruling in a dispute between the Coca-Cola Company and one of its franchisees, franchise rights could be revoked relatively easily if a bottler failed to sell the product. Since that decision, however, franchise cancellation had required a three- to four-year-long process during which the franchise company built evidence of cause and gave the franchisee opportunities to correct the offenses or sell his or her franchise. The franchisee was free to sell the territory to whomever he or she chose, if the buyer met the company's qualifications.

The selection of appropriate franchise candidates, negotiation of a sale, and the enforcing of franchise agreements were the responsibility of the franchise department, directed by Don Antle. "My role in a franchise sale is to save taxes for both parties," said Mr. Antle. Due to industry overcapacity, Dr Pepper franchise sales were made to already established bottlers. Mr. Antle explained, "An outsider would have difficulty investing in the soft drink business today because of the low ROI. A franchise is only salable to a buyer for whom it is incremental volume." In 1976 franchises sold for between $1.50 and $2.00 per case of Dr Pepper business per year.

Packaging

Dr Pepper was packaged in 16 different sizes and types of containers in 1976, as shown in Exhibit 6, although not all packages were available in every market. Container sizes and materials were selected by individual franchised bottler, depending on their equipment capability, their desire to invest working capital in packaging materials, packaging offered by competitors in their territory, and consumer preferences. Many bottlers did not own their own canning lines, so approximately 50 percent of the Dr Pepper sold in cans was produced at corporate-owned canning lines in Dallas or by various contract canners around the country for resale to Dr Pepper who resold it to franchise bottlers.

EXHIBIT 6
Dr Pepper package assortment, 1976

	Ounces							
	6.5	10	12	16	24	32	48	64
Returnable bottles	x	x	x	x	x	x		x
Nonreturnable bottles	x	x	x	x	x	x	x	x
Cans			x					

Maintaining a competitive packaging position was a particular problem for Dr Pepper. Dr Pepper was not widely available in the large 16-, 32- and 64-ounce sizes until 1975, and industry analysis attributed the plateauing of regular Dr Pepper growth in 1973, 1974, and 1975, in part, to lack of larger package availability during a period when consumers were especially price conscious. Maintaining a competitive packaging position was complicated by Dr Pepper's being only one of several brands competing for a franchisee's attention. No one company was dominant in introducing new packages; successful introductions were usually accompanied by heavy advertising and promotion expenditures by the concentrate producing company and required substantial bottler working capital investment in packaging materials, advertising, and promotion.

Experimentation in all phases of packaging was a characteristic of the industry in 1976. Supplier firms were developing new forms of old containers—"thinner" cans and more effective plastic shielded bottles; new sizes of present packages—a gallon glass bottle; and new types of containers—a plastic bottle.

Pricing

The only prices directly controlled by Dr Pepper were the prices charged franchised bottlers for bottling concentrate and food service retailers for fountain syrup. Wholesale prices for the finished product were set by individual bottlers and varied from territory to territory depending on bottler-costs and market conditions. Each retailer also set his own price.

Dr Pepper price policy attempted to maintain a fixed contribution rate, as a percentage of sales, while at the same time keeping concentrate prices competitive. Contribution averaged between 50 percent and 40 percent of sales after deducting ingredient, packaging, and advertising costs. Dr Pepper increased syrup and concentrate prices only to recover increases in ingredient costs and believed similar policies were followed by Coca-Cola and PepsiCo. Although Dr Pepper concentrate prices were slightly higher than the other four major concentrate producers, it required less sugar so that finished product costs were competitive. Exhibit 7 presents estimated comparative cost data for the five major concentrate companies.

Dr Pepper attempted to price bottler concentrate so that bottlers could sell finished product at prices competitive with Coke and Pepsi-Cola, before special price promotions, although concentrate represented only a small portion of finished product cost. For example, a case of a dozen, 32-ounce bottles of Dr Pepper wholesaling at $3 contained less than 47 cents

EXHIBIT 7
Estimated cost information

Product	Bottler cost per unit/gallon concentrate	Bottler cost per 16-oz. case @ $20 sugar	Product	Bottler cost per 16-oz. case @ $20 sugar
Dr Pepper	$218.28	$0.9884	Pepsi-Cola	$0.9242
Sugar Free Dr Pepper	400.17	0.8630	Sugar Free Pepsi	0.8878
Coca-Cola			Mountain Dew	0.9900
(finished syrup)	2.08	0.9600	Teem	0.7900
Mr. PiBB	67.84	0.9049	Royal Crown (2 gals)	0.8611
Sprite	76.10	0.9435	Sugar Free RC/Diet	0.7917
Tab	194.00	0.8954	7UP	0.9915
Fresca	161.79	0.9190	Sugar Free 7UP	0.7197

Source: Company records.

worth of concentrate. Consequently, Dr Pepper's cooperative advertising expenditures, allowances for special price promotions, and cash contributions for equipment and packaging materials were more important than concentrate prices in influencing bottlers. Special retail price promotions played a small role in Dr Pepper's pricing policies as the company hoped to built a customer base loyal to the drink's unique flavor rather than attract less loyal, price-conscious consumers. Larger package sizes, however, such as 32, 48, and 64 ounces, were used to appeal to value-conscious consumers as packaging represented a smaller proportion of total costs than for smaller packages, thus reducing consumer costs per ounce of soft drink.

Analysts noted that the sale of fountain syrup was a price-competitive business, Dr Pepper usually met Coke's, the dominant factor in this market segment, fountain syrup prices. Retailer deposits on the steel tanks containing fountain syrup and point-of-sale promotion materials were also competitively priced. Like bottler concentrate, fountain syrup cost was only a small proportion of the price the consumer paid for the finished drink. Finished drinks from a $15 tank of syrup would yield $140 or more in finished drinks.

Fountain division

The Dr Pepper Fountain Division accounted for 21 percent of company dollar sales in 1976. Mr. Rautenberg, Fountain sales manager, defined the division's mission as selling the "idea" of Dr Pepper to a retail outlet, and then arranging for Dr Pepper's Manufacturing Division or for a franchised bottler to supply the syrup. Fountain or postmix syrup was different from bottling concentrate in that it was already partially mixed with water and contained 100 percent of the sugar necessary to make the finished drink. At the point of sale, dispensers, most of which could handle only four different flavors, mixed the syrup with carbonated water. Fountain syrup was sold in 5-gallon reusable steel tanks or in 1-gallon disposable plastic cartons.

Dr Pepper's Fountain Division was organized into six regional sales territories covering the Northeast, north central central states, Midwest, Southwest, Southeast, and the West. Mr. Rautenberg commented that his division's organization was very much like Coca-Cola's Fountain Sales Division. Exhibit 8 presents an estimate of fountain personnel and annual gallonage for the five major concentrate producers.

Dr Pepper Fountain Division served eight different types of accounts: fast-food chains, vendors, theaters, schools, concessionaires, bottlers, military installations, and jobbers. The 7,100 direct sales accounts purchased 84 percent of the division's total gallonage and had 8,000 delivery points serving 48,000–50,000 individual retail outlets. Indirect sales, through independent jobbers, who were free to set their own prices to retailers, accounted for 16 percent of total fountain syrup gallonage.

EXHIBIT 8

Comparative fountain division personnel and sales estimates, 1975

	Coca-Cola	PepsiCo	Seven-Up	Royal Crown	Dr Pepper
Personnel	490	12	7	n.a.	94
Percent of company gallonage	30	16–17	<5	<2	21
Annual sales, millions of syrup gallons	110%	<20%	2%	n.a.	10–20%

n.a. = not available.
Source: Researcher estimate.

Mr. Rautenberg noted that Fountain Division profitability was sensitive to small increases in sales volume, as most operating costs were fixed and only direct product costs increased with gallonage increases. He was proud that the division had the company's lowest operating costs, on a percentage of sales basis, and believed their costs to be lower than Coke's and PepsiCo's.

The division's goal was to double gallonage in the next five years and to double again by 1985. This was to be accomplished through wider availability, particularly through adding more fast-food chain accounts. Mr. Rautenberg remarked that, "one good McDonald's with $70,000 a year in sales will sell as much Dr Pepper in four months as a supermarket does in a year. This is because they sell a lot of drinks in large-size containers, frequently 14–20 ounces at a time."

In 1976 Dr Pepper was sold in 1,100 of the 3,400 McDonald's outlets in the United States, up from 50 stores in 1972 and 25 stores in 1971. In most fast-food installations, management believed Dr Pepper was the second most popular brand, selling between 12–35 percent of the outlet's soft drink sales. The average McDonald's sold 1,000 gallons of Dr Pepper syrup per year. Prior to the introduction of Dr Pepper, cola flavors might account for 85 percent of soft drink sales in a typical outlet, with the three other flavors accounting for the remaining 15 percent. Mr. Rautenberg commented that Seven-Up was aggressively pursuing fast-food accounts. He believed that they had not been as successful as Dr Pepper due to installation problems, as fountain dispensers in each store had to be carefully adjusted to mix the correct amount of syrup and carbonated water for each specific flavor. Dr Pepper management believed that their quick and efficient installation service gave them a competitive advantage.

MANUFACTURING

Dr Pepper engaged in three manufacturing activities: concentrate production, the production of finished product in cans, and the operation of five wholly owned subsidiary bottling and distribution businesses. The production of concentrate (the basic flavor-coloring liquid) for franchise bottlers and syrup (concentrate plus sugar) for the company's Fountain Division was Dr Pepper's central and most profitable business. The researcher estimated that it provided approximately 44 percent of company dollar sales, 64 percent of total gallonage, and 79 percent of company profits. The five Texas bottling and distribution subsidiaries accounted for 28 percent of company dollar sales and most of the remaining company profits. The canning of finished product, the researcher estimated, accounted for 23 percent of company dollar sales and approximately 21 percent of total gallonage.

Concentrate production

Concentrate was produced in a section of Dr Pepper's headquarters building in Dallas and in Birmingham, Alabama. The process required few employees and simple equipment, and output could be doubled from current facilities with minimum capital investment. Producing concentrate began with piping the flavoring ingredients from large stainless steel tanks to three sealed mixing vats in an adjacent room. From there the concentrate was piped to a filling line to be packaged in 1-gallon moulded plastic jugs for shipment.

Canning

The company operated a canning facility in Dallas. With a capacity of 6 to 7 million cases a year, this operation supplied the company's own subsidiaries as well as regional franchise bottlers. The remainder of needed canning capacity was obtained via a network of 52 canners located throughout the United States. Of that number, 34 were Dr Pepper bottlers who operated as contract canners as well as producing their own requirements; 18 were independent companies who did contract canning for a number of soft drink companies.

Under the contract system, Dr Pepper determined the production schedule, purchased all raw materials and packaging required, paid the canner a fee for mixing and packaging the drinks, and then sold the finished products to franchisees at a break-even price of 15 cents to 20 cents per case over cost. This system involved major working capital requirements for Dr Pepper and a higher per case cost for the franchisee than for franchises with their own canning line. But management stated that it did make canned Dr Pepper available to all territories and did minimize the company's capital investment in canning equipment.

Bottling and distribution subsidiaries

Dr Pepper's four subsidiary bottling plants in Dallas, Ft. Worth, Waco, and San Antonio, plus the company-owned Southwest Fountain Supply

Company, accounted for most of the company's capital investment and most of its labor force. Dr Pepper was in the bottling business, management said, in order to better control operations of its important home-market areas, to build a base of operating experience from whence to advise franchisees, and to experiment with new production and distribution techniques. Dick O'Connor, vice president, Corporate Bottling Plants, in charge of these operations, considered Dr Pepper Bottling to be an industry leader in devising new distribution methods in response to cost pressures and changing retailer needs.

The four plants produced regular and Sugar Free Dr Pepper and Salute flavors, in multiple-sized, returnable and nonreturnable bottles; canned product was obtained from the Dallas canning plant. All four plants usually achieved a 20 percent or better share of market; selling prices, production costs, and profitability varied according to competitive market conditions and plant efficiency. Management considered its newer Dallas facility to be about average in performance compared to other plants of its scale. An industry analyst commented, "They have a fine operation. As far as I know, Dr Pepper is the only major concentrate producer whose bottling operations are profitable. They must do as well as an average local bottler who probably takes down 10 percent, aftertax ROI."

The four plants employed approximately 700 production and delivery personnel, most of whom were unskilled. Dr Pepper plants were not unionized, but the Teamsters Union had conducted a vigorous and almost successful campaign in 1973.

Southwest Fountain's objectives were similar to those of the bottling plants. Its rate of sales growth was higher than for bottling operations, but profits tended to be minimal. Southwest sold Coca-Cola and other fountain syrups as well as Dr Pepper.

Mr. O'Connor identified increasing capital requirements, increasing distribution and production costs, and changing distribution methods as the three major trends affecting operations of bottling companies in recent years. New production equipment with greater efficiency, capacity, and better quality control capabilities, along with larger vans needed to carry the greater number of products and package sizes, had led to a minimum capacity of 5 million cases per year for an efficient bottling plant. This factor, as well as current capacity constraints, had led the company to embark on the construction of a single large bottling facility to serve Dallas, Ft. Worth, and Waco. It was to be completed by 1978. Projected cost of the facility, an industry analyst estimated, was approximately $15 million. It was to be completely financed from internal sources of funds.

Dr Pepper's experimentation with new distribution methods came about as a result of rapidly rising labor and transportation costs, combined with substantial retailer pressure for increased price flexibility and improved service. Currently Dr Pepper corporate bottling plants employed four distribution methods: direct sales of premix (ready to be dispensed) and post-mix syrup (soda fountain adds carbonated water) sales to fountain outlets (12 percent of total volume), traditional route sales of packaged goods to small outlets (50 percent), chain store delivery tandems (18 percent), and presold bulk delivery (20 percent).

Route sales were the traditional method of soft drink distribution; a driver/salesperson visited each account on a weekly schedule selling off the truck. Currently 50 percent of the soft drinks sold through the route system were made through vending machines or in coolers in small stores. Many high-volume, chain store accounts had been diverted from route selling to tandem or presold methods. The chain store delivery system used two route salespersons with two delivery trucks working side by side to provide adequate volume and selection for service to major chain store outlets.

Presold, bulk delivery, the most efficient distribution method, was only a few years old; and Mr. O'Connor expected it would soon expand to 50 percent sales of total sales volume. In 1976 only two bottlers in Texas, in addition to Dr Pepper, were successfully using presold bulk delivery. This method required advance salespersons who called on chain headquarters and store management to sell weekly orders for later delivery in specific quantities on a specific schedule. At the appointed time, large vans delivered the palletized and containerized soft drinks. Later the same day, Dr Pepper merchandisers stocked the shelves and arranged displays and point-of-sale advertising. Retailers liked this system because palletizing decreased receiving and handling costs in the store. Mr. O'Connor explained the system's benefits for Dr Pepper:

> Presold bulk delivery is cheaper by 10 cents per case, but that's only the tip of the iceberg. The real benefits come when we get top salespeople and top merchandisers on our staff into the large chain stores. We'll get better availability and better shelf space allocations and create a better relationship between store management and ourselves.

PURCHASING

Raw materials were the largest single expenditure category at Dr Pepper. Although the department dealt with over 1,000 suppliers of bottles, cans, crowns, cartons, chemicals, and flavors, two items—containers and sugar—accounted for the bulk of purchases.

Sugar presented special purchasing problems according to Mr. Hughes, executive vice president:

> While our franchise bottlers purchased their own sugar requirements to make Dr Pepper syrup from our concentrate, we buy considerable quanti-

ties of sugar for our own use for fountain syrup in our canning operations and in company-owned bottling plants. The average price of raw sugar duty-paid at New York was $9.14 in February 1973. By November 1974 it had reached $57.30, increasing more than six times within 22 months. The prices remained in the upper $20 to $40 during the first four months of 1975, but showed constant declines through the end of the year with raws averaging $14.80 in December.

Large sugar purchases near the 1975 high had adversely impacted the company's 1975 earnings. Dr Pepper did not employ "hedging" practices in its sugar operations.

Dr Pepper bought containers from large national packaging companies at competitive prices. It did not purchase supplies for its franchise bottlers, but it did help them with advice concerning equipment. Mr. Hughes commented:

> Having Dr Pepper in cans, available to all of our bottlers, is a high priority. We are now in the midst of a program to assist our canners to convert their can lines to two-piece aluminum cans as rapidly as possible. We want their lines to have the capabilities of producing two-piece steel cans as well.

RESEARCH AND QUALITY CONTROL

Frank Phillips, head of the research and quality control department, stated his group's primary task was "to keep quality Dr Pepper in the marketplace." Most research activity was centered on keeping abreast of new products, production processes, packages, and raw materials being developed by competitors and suppliers. Tests done on finished beverages ensured that Dr Pepper products met standards of appearance, were adequately filled and capped, and contained the proper levels of carbonation, acidity, concentrate, sugar, and coloring. Eight field quality control technicians visited each of the franchised bottling plants and contract canning facilities four times a year to collect samples and inspect production facilities and procedures.

Already developed, but not yet marketed, Dr Pepper products included individual servings of powdered hot Dr Pepper in an aluminum foil packet, as well as individual servings of cold Dr Pepper in plastic syrup packs to which the consumer would add carbonated water. In production process technology, attention was directed at spray and freeze-dry powdered Dr Pepper mixes and high-protein powdered beverage mixes.

Plastic bottles were being given considerable departmental attention. Industry proponents believed they would be safer and lighter weight than glass, when perfected, reducing consumer safety problems and cutting distribution costs. Critics pointed out that there were still technical problems; for example, bottles swelling under pressure and leaking carbonation and that high-speed equipment necessary for full utilization was not yet available. Until early in 1975, Du Pont and Monsanto led in the plastic bottle field, but Du Pont dropped out of the business, "selling its technology and patent processess to willing parties." Monsanto, in close cooperation with Coke, recently announced plans for two new production sites. Mr. Phillips estimated that industry costs to produce plastic bottles, on a scale large enough to compete with glass, would involve more than an $80 million to $100 million investment. He estimated that conversion to plastic bottles would be expensive for bottlers, too, requiring an investment of $50–$100,-000 to modify each bottling line for the new container.

FINANCE

"This has always been a great company, and I enjoy working here! I've been drinking Dr Pepper since I was a kid," enthused Alvin Lane, Jr., vice president of finance. "And it's a great industry to be in. Until recently raw material and supply prices have been remarkably stable. And when costs, particularly sugar, went up so dramatically in 1974, we were able to pass along most of these increases fairly rapidly. We can change our concentrate price to bottlers when required; Coke changes its price only once every three months."

Reviewing the statements (see Exhibits 1 and 2), "You will note that net profit margins increased to 8.6 percent in 1975 as compared to 7.7 percent in 1974. This improvement was due primarily to a combination of strong sales growth and good control of expenses. Let me admit that the lowering of sugar prices which began in the spring of 1975 was very important to our results. Looking ahead, we do not see sugar prices rising during 1976. Beyond 1976 the crystal ball becomes clouded, but we feel that the availability of corn and synthetic sweeteners together with an improved supply/demand relationship for sugar portends well for consumers. As you know we have approved for use in Dr Pepper high-fructose corn sweeteners on a 50 percent sucrose (sugar) replacement level and are testing even higher levels.

"An important key to the bottom line though is advertising and promotion (see Exhibit 9). It typically has run around 20 percent, but a 1 percent swing there can have a dramatic impact on results.

"Almost 50 percent of our total assets are invested in cash equivalents. Our receivables are almost all current—only 7 percent over 30 days and virtually nothing over 60 days—turnover every 19 days and our inventories turn over about every 20 days. Most of our fixed assets support our bottling business."

Dr Pepper had paid quarterly dividends for 184 consecutive quarters and had increased dividends every year for the past 14 years. It was company policy to pay out approximately 60 percent of its prior year earnings in divi-

EXHIBIT 9
Distribution of revenues as a percent of sales

	1970	1971	1972	1973	1974	1975
Retained in business	4¾	5	5½	5½	3½	4½
Dividends	5	5¾	5	4½	4½	4½
Other operating expenses	1¼	1½	1½	1½	1¾	2½
Depreciation and maintenance	3	2¾	2¾	3	2½	2½
Taxes on income	9½	9½	9¾	8¾	6¾	8¼
Payrolls	11	11	10	10¾	9½	9
Promotion, advertising, and expansion	21½	21½	21	19¼	17½	16½
Raw materials and packaging	44	43	44½	47	54¼	52¾

Source: Company records.

dends to its shareholders. It was also company policy not to incur long-term debt.

Dr Pepper had initiated three stock splits since 1967 with the objective of gaining wider share distributions; no public offering of common stock had been made in recent years. Increases in the number of shares outstanding were due to the issuance of new stock for an executive stock option plan and the issue of 146,000 shares in 1973 in a "pooling of interest" acquisition of Dr Pepper Bottling Company of Ft. Worth and three related companies. Officers and directors owned less than 5 percent of Dr Pepper's common stock, and no ownership group owned 10 percent or more of the stock. Dr Pepper's common stock, listed on the New York Stock Exchange, had ranged in price as follows: 1972, $23 to $27½; 1973, $18¾ to $30; 1974, $6½ to $22⅞; and 1975, from $7 to $15⅛.

GOVERNMENTAL INTERVENTION

Dr Pepper, along with other soft drink manufacturers, was subject to federal regulation by the Food and Drug Administration, the Consumer Product Safety Commission, and the Federal Trade Commission. The Food and Drug Administration established product purity requirements and labeling requirements for soft drinks. Dr Pepper's franchised and corporate-owned production facilities passed sanitation inspections conducted by the FDA. The company was also required to assure the FDA that the ingredients used in the secret Dr Pepper flavoring formula were FDA "permitted ingredients."

The Consumer Product Safety Commission monitored injuries caused by broken or exploding soft drink bottles through its representative hospital reporting system. Management was also concerned over the possibility of citizens' consumer groups making an issue of bottle safety. Changing packages to 100 percent canned product would be particularly time consuming and costly to the Dr Pepper Company. One executive explained:

It would take years to rebuild capacity. There are only two line manufacturers in the United States, each producing 25 can lines per year. Many smaller bottling companies would go out of business because the plant and working capital expenditures would be prohibitive. We will just have to sweat this out. Packaging legislation and franchise illegality would hurt the industry, but it would hurt us more than the big guys. Now, a small bottler can break even on a $500,000 minimum investment in a bottling line on 500,000 cases per year. With a $2 million minimum investment in a can line, he or she would need to sell 2 million or more cases per year to break even. We don't have the resources to buy canning lines for our bottlers, and our multibrand bottlers would look to their bigger selling products first if there is a capacity shortage.

The still unresolved Federal Trade Commission challenge to the legality of exclusive franchise territories was a matter of substantial concern to the Dr Pepper management. They believed that the elimination of the exclusive franchise system would pose a greater problem for Dr Pepper than for its two larger competitors. Both Coke and PepsiCo owned more bottling franchises, including a number in very large metropolitan areas, than did Dr Pepper. Dr Pepper still had a substantial proportion of its total volume moving through smaller, nonurban, independent franchised bottlers.

Consequently, they supported the National Soft Drink Association and the Dr Pepper Bottlers Association in supporting general legislation "to declare legal the current system of exclusive franchised soft drink territories." At the hearings in support of that legislation, Mr. Clements stressed that the system was particularly important to a small growing firm such as Dr Pepper first because it best supported a route delivery service operation which supplied hundreds of thousands of small outlets, and second because the franchise system enabled the company to conduct better sampling programs essential where a distinctive flavor/new product was being introduced. The legislation was still "in process" in the fall of 1976, with hearings scheduled for September. The Federal Trade Commission had announced its opposition to the legislation.

ORGANIZATION

Dr Pepper was organized along functional lines (see Exhibit 10). Mr. Clements (62) was chairman, president, and chief executive officer. He was assisted by two executive vice presidents—Mr. Hughes (49) and Mr. Avery (46), and a staff of eight vice presidents heading up major subunits. Since 1971 the company had undergone several reorganizations with the objective of obtaining effective functional groupings, to make the best use of existing managerial resources, and to facilitate the attraction and introduction of new management talent.

Mr. Clements discussed some of the reasons for these organizational changes with the researcher.

People are the key to carrying out our strategy of being number one; limited management resources can hold us back. I'm proud of our people. But lack of management depth is a challenge.

When we hit that flat period in 1974–75, operations didn't turn around as quickly as I wanted them to. Some of the policies and procedures I felt were important had eroded, and we'd kind of drifted away from our strategy and the importance of the bottler. Money wasn't being spent on prime-ready markets as it should have been.

We had kind of drifted away from our strategy, and I think strategy is something you don't change unless there is a major, basic need. You don't try to win every battle, you just try to win the war. If we changed our strategy to combat Mr. PiBB and abandoned our strategy of being number one—why we would have just weakened our position! We've gotten our discipline back.

The market isn't going to wait. We need even more organizational strength. We are going to see a dramatic difference in our future rate of growth. We have so many opportunities. We're not in a position to acquire anything because we don't have the depth of management to spare. But we are building some management strength in our four bottling plants, and we will soon be in a position to pick up some more bottling plants when and if we need them. We don't yet have the knowledge and expertise to do the international job we would like to do. Our computer system is not adequate for some of the things we want to do. We should use it to help exploit our fountain opportunities.

A key need is to build organizational strength into marketing. We are doing just that—we are adding 16 managers now and more down the line. Really we have never had product managers before, and that is the kind of people we are hiring.

INTERNATIONAL

Dr Pepper's major international operation was in Japan; other market areas included Canada, Puerto Rico, Guam, the Bahamas, and overseas U.S. military installations; distribution in these areas amounted to less than 1 percent of company sales. The Japanese venture had not yet shown a profit, and one industry analyst estimated 1975 losses at $2 million. But management remained confident of the soundness of the Japanese move. In March 1976 Mr. Hughes commented:

> During the past summer we conducted a consumer research program in Japan. The results were similar to results we have seen in new Dr Pepper markets in this country: (1) we achieved an above-average level of consumer awareness and consumer trial; (2) we had been most successful in gaining product support with teenagers; (3) our marketing direction needed a shot in the arm of a basic Dr Pepper sales program—sampling and more sampling—particularly among the youth.

EXHIBIT 10
The Dr Pepper organization, 1976

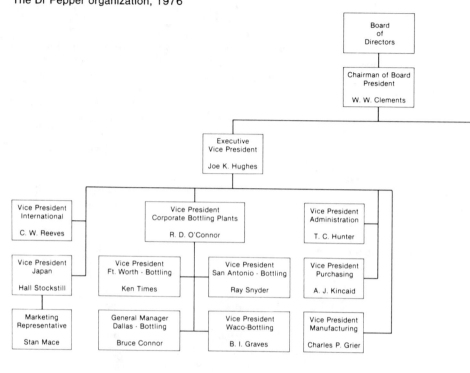

Dr Pepper had first become interested in international soft drink markets in the late 1960s. At that time, Japan was the most attractive soft drink market outside the United States, with per capita consumption approaching 100 bottles and growing in a sound economy. In 1972 Dr Pepper entered into a 50/50 joint venture with the world's largest soft drink bottler who held the Coca-Cola franchise for Tokyo and served two other large urban market areas. It offered good production facilities, well-established distribution, and a very favorable pricing structure. However, by the time Dr Pepper came on the market in July 1973, supported by a heavy advertising and promotion campaign, inflation and price increases had triggered a precipitous decline in the Japanese soft drink market. By mid-1976, company management described the Japanese market as improving and Dr Pepper as having "a little niche."

Beverage World's survey of the Japanese soft drink market predicted a rebound in 1976 and longer term growth settling down to about 10 percent a year. Per capita soft drink consumption in 1973 was 45.4 liters as opposed to 120 liters in the United States. Cola, lemon-lime, and grape were the

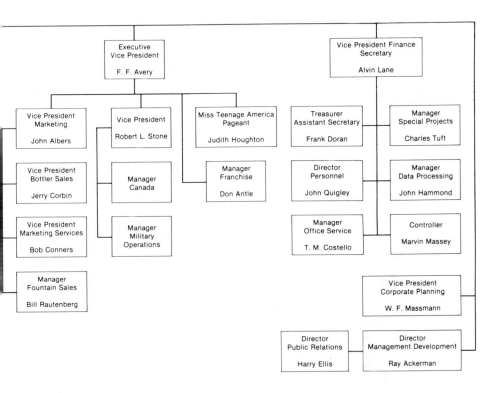

dominant flavors, enjoying 79 percent of the market. Vending machines accounted for 25 percent of all soft drink sales; soft drink sales in supermarkets accounted for less than 10 percent of total soft drink sales.

Mr. Hughes commented about the firm's international position:

> First of all, we don't want to bite off more than we can chew. We only have a two-person international staff. Second, we already have a commitment in Japan that's worth putting a lot of resources behind to ensure success. And, finally we don't want the glamour of international business to divert financial and management resources from achieving our full potential in the United States.

Despite the company's difficult entry into Japan, Dr Pepper management still considered international expansion the company's next challenge after establishing a strong domestic position. The attractive aspects of international expansion were that, generally, soft drink margins were higher overseas, bottlers had to provide fewer package and container types, and per capita consumption was substantially lower than in the United States, presenting room for potential growth. On the negative side, there was a high cost of market entry in terms of "up-front advertising" and promotion expenditures (management estimated in excess of $1 million per year for three to five years in each new market), and the already entrenched market positions of Coke and Pepsi.

Mr. Clements explained his company's international opportunities:

> When you talk about international opportunities, we're like a kid in a candy store with just one thin dime. He has to pick the best from lots of good opportunities. I'd like to move into all of the markets. But one thing I've always held onto was the importance of concentration—capitalizing on the opportunities we have here first. I haven't wanted us to dilute our time and our resources—you don't want to get diverted. This is one reason why we dropped Pomac and Schweppes. Schweppes is an excellent product, and we had the entire Southwest. But I dropped it and Coke of Dallas picked it up.
>
> International markets are profitable once they're established. It was easier and less expensive when Coke and PepsiCo got in. But you don't have to buy connections and influence any more. Prior to the payoff exposures, our guy would just pack his bag when we saw payoffs were needed, even when we were invited to go there. We may look at the Mideast and follow Seven-Up strategy there—that is lower the concentrate price and put all of the advertising and promotion burden on the franchisees plus making specific contracts for type and amount of advertising.
>
> We have had a three-year ban on acquisitions. We were lucky not to get caught up in the conglomerate craze. It's hard to find anything as profitable as concentrate production, and I don't want us to spend a lot of management time on evaluating deals.

A PERSONAL MANAGERIAL PHILOSOPHY

At the conclusion of a long interview and many Dr Peppers, the researchers asked a question about the box of inscribed marbles on Foots's desk.

> They have the Golden Rule on them. I've given thousands of them away to my own people, to my bottlers, and to the sales and marketing groups of which I am member. You can keep one on your desk or carry it in your pocket but what counts is in your heart. Maybe they will remind you to practice the Golden Rule in relationships with other people.
>
> I've had many people ask me, "Can you build a competitive business on the Golden Rule?" I feel you cannot build any business that will last unless

you practice the Golden Rule. That rule is our foundation, and we try to watch carefully that our people don't engage in anything that will damage the integrity of this company.

I write my bottlers a letter occasionally, especially during National Bible Week, and suggest a need for all of us to read the Bible, and I never make a speech without referring to my belief in God. I just couldn't do it any other way. A majority of my colleagues share this belief—Harry (Ellis) and Rick (Avery) do. We have that kind of people in our company.

I don't hesitate to profess my beliefs in God and in my business. He gave you whatever talents you have. You can't just take; you have to put something back.

The twinkle in Mr. Clements's eye disappeared; his countenance became solemn. The researcher was convinced that Foots believed—and followed—his words.

case 10

The Seven-Up Company (A)

You ought to go out to St. Louis and visit the Seven-Up people; they have a most impressive track record and bright prospects for the future. As the industry's "David," they won't liquidate our two "Goliaths," but they have clearly outperformed Coke and Pepsi in lemon-lime. They have done a first-rate management succession job too with a new top-management team in place. Bill Winter, the new CEO, has already made some very sensible moves, particularly bringing in John Kidwell to strengthen Seven-Up's marketing thrust. And Paul Young is a first-rate, experienced treasurer; Seven-Up doesn't try to manage its income flow reporting—they call it the way it is.

Specializing in a clear, carbonated, lemon-lime flavored soft drink, Seven-Up had approximately 60 percent of this flavor market in the United States, outselling Coke's competitive product Sprite by almost three to one. Pepsi's Teem had approximately 0.3 percent of the overall U.S. soft drink market, Coke's Sprite, 2.6 percent, while Seven-Up enjoyed a 7.6 percent market share. 7UP was sold in the United States, Canada, and 81 other nations.

The company's legal trademark, the Uncola, some industry reporters indicated, was symbolic of the company's efforts to portray 7UP to the consumer as competitive with, yet distinctive from, cola products which dominated the soft drink field. Bottled labels identified the product as 7UP beverage rather than a lemon-lime drink. Company advertisements featured product name rather than the specific flavor category.

The company reported consolidated sales of $213.6 million for 1975 with aftertax profit of $20.3 million. This was the first year that company sales had exceeded $200 million; it had been only six years earlier that Seven-Up had broken the $100 million mark. Since 1967 the company's average annual growth rate in sales and net income had been 12.1 percent and 18 percent, respectively, while recent return on market invested capital averaged 25 percent. In 1970 the company purchased a manufacturer of food colors, flavors, and perfumes; and in 1973 a producer of lemons, lemon concentrate, and oils. But in 1975 soft drink sales were still 80 percent of total sales and 89.5 percent of total profits (see Exhibit 1).

EXHIBIT 1
Net sales and income before taxes in percentages for major product categories

	1971	1972	1973	1974	1975
Net sales:					
Soft drinks	83.3	82.7	81.8	80.6	80.2
Lemon products	10.8	10.4	10.7	10.5	12.9
Flavors, colors, and fragrances	5.9	6.9	7.5	8.9	6.9
Income before taxes:					
Soft drinks	82.4	85.5	86.2	84.5	89.5
Lemon products	5.5	3.8	2.8	2.0	5.6
Flavors, colors, and fragrances	12.1	10.7	11.0	13.5	4.9

Source: Company records.

In commenting on Seven-Up's performance, one analyst commented:

> Seven-Up has benefited from two major marketing successes, whose momentum is still continuing. In repositioning itself away from older users toward teenagers, Seven-Up in 1968 bet upon the highly memorable "Uncola" theme. This not only strengthened the brand with all users, but also opened the door to improved distribution in the fountain market, an area the company had previously left to competitors. The second big success was Sugar Free 7UP introduced in 1974, which was far more popular than anticipated.[1]

Another analyst noted privately, "Seven-Up has its challenges, too! Their primary brand—regular 7UP—lost market share in 1974 and 1975; that is always a danger signal. They had a period in 1975 when bottler relationships were bad, although the new senior vice president in marketing has made major improvements there. He has his job cut out for him; competing against Coke—with all of their power—is rough, and Coke seems to be moving more aggressively with Sprite now. In addition, there is the ever-present problem of governmental action re saccharin and the unknown of changes in franchising.

"But I'm optimistic about their future. Their new advertising program 'UNdo it' is brilliant and well timed. Their move into the United Kingdom with Cadbury-Schweppes indicates they may become more aggressive in the international field. There are real opportunities for a lemon-lime drink

---

[1] Faulkner, Dawkins, and Sullivan, *Industry Review*, March 4, 1976, p. 15.

abroad since that flavor is preferred in many areas to a cola drink. And, trade rumors have it that they intend to move rapidly into the lemonade powder mix game. They could do some interesting things there."

COMPANY HISTORY

The history of Seven-Up mirrored many of the elements of a traditional American entrepreneurial success story. In a "rags-to-riches drama," the founder C. L. Grigg was born in a log cabin in Prices Branch, Missouri, population 25. Coming to St. Louis to seek his fortune, he worked first in dry goods and later in advertising, without great success. In 1920, joining with a coal merchant, E. G. Ridgway, he formed The Howdy Company to manufacture an orange drink. At a later date this partnership was joined by a lawyer, F. Y. Gladney, after the latter's unsuccessful personal efforts to sell stock in the infant firm. Descendants of these three families were part of the executive group in 1976, and the company still evidenced in its policies and practices the fundamental family values of its founding fathers.

Corporate executives espoused and practiced a leadership philosophy which emphasized the partnership of all parties, for example, company and franchised bottlers and the importance of concern for all individual needs. Management communications stressed accurate presentation of facts and circumstance, and company officers were willing to view corporate accomplishments as a combination of luck and skill. H. C. Grigg, the son of C. L. Grigg, commented on the company's historical record: "We sat on a horse backward, rode him in the wrong direction, and he ended up just where we wanted to go."

Grigg's son was referring to events surrounding the introduction of "Bib Label Lithiated Lemon-Lime Soda," as the new drink was first known. The drink was introduced in October 1929, just before the stock market crash. In 1937, renamed 7UP, the drink had to compete with over 600 other lemon-lime drinks in the marketplace. By 1976, 7UP was the third largest selling soft drink in the world. Because it utilized less sugar than cola drinks, World War II sugar rationing provided opportunities for sales expansion nationally and internationally.

During the mid-60s, however, company sales began to plateau. The owning families installed a new president, Ben H. Wells, son-in-law of founder Gladney, a former preparatory school teacher of English and for several decades the head of the company's marketing department. Under Mr. Wells's leadership, management made three strategic decisions which still were critical to the company operations in the mid-70s. One of Mr. Wells's early moves was to commission a consulting study of the current market position and product image of 7UP.

During prior years, 7UP had the dual reputation of a medicinal health drink and as a mixer for alcoholic beverages. Basic product quality, a green, medicinal-looking, small bottle plus an advertising campaign with slogans such as "Tunes Tiny Tummies" gave the drink its entry to the children's and adults' health market. Advertising slogans such as the "Cure for Seven Hangovers" were used. 7UP plus Seagrams Seven Crown Whiskey became a popular midwestern drink. "People were buying 7UP for a mixer or for indigestion," Mr. Wells commented. "Our problem was we weren't a soft drink."

With the decision made to identify with and compete as a soft drink, the company's advertising agency developed the "7UP The Uncola" trademark and an advertising program to support this slogan. Trade observers commented that the decision was critical and successful both in concept and execution. "What they did was to, in effect, bet they could dominate the lemon-lime sector, and also take sales away from the cola sector which has traditionally held over 50 percent of the soft drink market. It meant they were going to step up their competition against Coke and Pepsi. They have done it well!"

Second, in 1967 Seven-Up went public with a substantial but noncontrolling block of stock being sold to the general public. In 1974 William E. Winter, formerly marketing vice president, was made president and chief operating officer of the firm—the first nonfamily member to hold that position.

Finally, under Mr. Wells's direction the company purchased the Warner-Jenkinson Company in 1970. That firm had been the dominant source for 7UP extract for over 50 years. In 1973 the company acquired Ventura Coastal Corporation which supplied Warner-Jenkinson with some of its lemon oil requirements. In 1974 Ventura purchased the Golden Crown Corporation, a producer of reconstituted lemon, prune, and lime juice, as well as a manufacturer of lemonade powder mix. In 1972 the company purchased the Phoenix, Arizona, 7UP bottler, their only domestic, company-owned franchise territory. Exhibit 2 gives a statistical summary of the Seven-Up Company from 1969 to 1975.

A FIRST VISIT TO THE COMPANY

"That must be it," the taxi driver indicated pointing at an 11-story, boxy brick building with Seven-Up in green script letters over the main entrance. Entering the building, the researcher found a narrow lobby bounded by a curtained glass wall on one side, a bust of what appeared to a "founding" father at the far end, and a uniformed guard sitting at a desk on the other side.

"I'll call public relations for you," he said. "They are on the tenth floor; a secretary will meet you there." Stepping out of the elevator the researchers were reminded that they were, indeed, in the heartland of 7UP. In a scene common to all operational departments, there were clocks with 7UP faces,

EXHIBIT 2
Seven-year statistical summary, 1969–1975

	Year ended December 31						
	1975	1974	1973	1972	1971	1970	1969
Net sales	$213,622,918	$190,879,628	$146,748,362	$132,519,867	$124,379,262	$111,648,288	$103,007,833
Cost of products sold	112,421,231	110,046,723	75,783,214	69,722,488	66,247,562	60,047,748	55,044,699
Gross profit	$101,201,687	$ 80,832,905	$ 70,965,148	$ 62,797,379	$ 58,131,700	$ 51,600,540	$ 47,963,134
Selling, administrative, and general expense	61,263,716	51,212,637	45,164,104	40,153,791	36,550,453	32,461,502	30,014,561
Operating profit	$ 39,937,971	$ 29,620,268	$ 25,801,044	$ 22,643,588	$ 21,581,247	$ 19,139,038	$ 17,948,573
Net miscellaneous income (deductions)	(93,508)	2,456,835	1,304,302	606,197	661,145	457,011	228,885
Income before income taxes and extraordinary items	$ 39,844,463	$ 32,077,103	$ 27,105,346	$ 23,249,785	$ 22,242,392	$ 19,596,049	$ 18,177,458
Federal, state, and foreign income taxes	19,504,000	15,489,000	13,023,000	11,205,265	10,914,386	9,779,390	9,587,856
Income before extraordinary items	$ 20,340,463	$ 16,588,103	$ 14,082,346	$ 12,044,520	$ 11,328,006	$ 9,816,659	$ 8,589,602
Extraordinary items (net)	—	—	—	—	—	—	(198,159)
Net income	$ 20,340,463	$ 16,588,103	$ 14,082,346	$ 12,044,520	$ 11,328,006	$ 9,816,659	$ 8,391,443
Net income as a percent of sales	9.5	8.7	9.6	9.1	9.1	8.8	8.1
Per share of common stock:							
Net income*	$1.88	$1.54	$1.30	$1.10	$1.03	$0.89	$0.75
Dividends†	0.75	0.61	0.4325	0.416	0.40	0.325	0.24
Book value†	7.93	6.45	5.50	4.62	3.72	3.08	2.50
Market price range (OTC) Common (high-low bid prices)†	36–14¾	30¾–10½	37¼–21¾	50⅛–33⅜	36⅛–26¾	30¾–17¾	22¾–14¼
Depreciation and amortization	$ 2,899,639	$ 2,347,569	$ 1,750,273	$ 1,339,384	$ 1,129,534	$ 1,189,705	$ 1,134,413
Capital expenditures	6,839,430	6,819,836	7,506,958	3,086,443	2,565,297	1,902,143	2,892,668

Working capital:						
Current assets	$ 86,594,829	$ 67,331,096	$ 58,761,951	$ 52,329,788	$ 45,845,959	$ 40,674,266	$ 35,416,921
Current liabilities	34,815,728	24,933,460	20,054,165	17,711,046	15,944,106	15,164,446	14,681,230
Total working capital	$ 51,779,101	$ 42,397,636	$ 38,707,786	$ 34,618,742	$ 29,901,853	$ 25,509,820	$ 20,735,691
Current ratio	2.5 to 1	2.7 to 1	2.9 to 1	3.0 to 1	2.9 to 1	2.7 to 1	2.4 to 1
Other assets:							
Land, buildings, and equipment	$ 32,739,830	$ 29,101,568	$ 24,626,482	$ 19,310,765	$ 17,155,484	$ 15,976,359	$ 14,805,879
Miscellaneous investments	2,454,842	2,953,990	1,800,626	2,298,733	1,930,319	1,926,520	2,655,864
Intangibles	4,205,133	4,295,836	4,388,420	3,539,410	2,499,686	2,522,549	2,494,957
Total other assets	$ 39,399,805	$ 36,351,394	$ 30,815,528	$ 25,148,908	$ 21,585,489	$ 20,425,428	$ 19,956,700
Total	$ 91,178,906	$ 78,749,030	$ 69,523,314	$ 59,767,650	$ 51,487,342	$ 45,935,248	$ 40,692,391
Capitalization and reserves:							
Long-term debt	$ 2,129,352	$ 2,652,860	$ 3,140,984	$ 2,447,818	$ 1,735,063	$ 2,805,964	$ 3,249,580
Other liabilities	596,131	389,399	442,043	379,122	364,788	353,440	660,662
6% cumulative preferred stock	3,588,000	3,588,000	3,588,000	3,588,000	3,588,000	3,588,800	3,588,800
$5.71 convertible class A preferred stock	—	4,615,100	4,860,600	5,079,900	7,307,900	7,390,400	7,408,800
Common shareholders' equity	84,865,423	67,503,671	57,491,687	48,272,810	38,491,591	31,796,644	25,784,549
Total	$ 91,178,906	$ 78,749,030	$ 69,523,314	$ 59,767,650	$ 51,487,342	$ 45,935,248	$ 40,692,391
Return on common equity—at end of year	23.6%	23.9%	23.6%	23.7%	27.8%	28.9%	30.0%
Average shares of common stock outstanding†	10,636,841	10,467,739	10,457,812	10,378,538	10,345,034	10,335,038	10,326,961

* Based on weighted-average number of shares outstanding during each year adjusted to reflect shares issuable upon exercise of stock options and for stock splits in 1969 and 1972.

† Adjusted for 2-for-1 stock splits in 1969 and 1972.

All data have been restated on a pooling of interest basis to include the operations of Warner-Jenkinson Co. acquired in 1970 and Ventura Coastal Corporation acquired in 1973.

Source: Company report.

7UP wastebaskets, 7UP Uncola murals, and in the center of the room a festive Christmas tree constructed of red and green 7UP beverage cans. Each floor had its own large vending machine filled with 7UP, and the company cafeteria welcomed customers with the sign "Have a 7UP Today."

Later, escorted by the head of public relations, the researchers were taken to W. E. Winters's 11th floor office with its decor of plexiglas, abstract paintings, contrasting Mayan sculpture, and modern floor coverings. At one end was a large executive desk graced with a family picture; shelves, containing business books and AMA publications, provided the background. At the other end of the large office was a beautifully appointed, conversational grouping of chairs in front of a large picture window.

"Welcome to Seven-Up. I'm Bill Winter. We are pleased to have you here, and we want to cooperate with your research in every possible way. Let's sit over here where it is more comfortable and you can check the view."

In the next hour, Mr. Winter covered, in depth, a variety of topics including the history of the company, corporate strategic goals, the current situation and organization of 7UP bottlers, and the competitive situation confronting Seven-Up. At times, in answer to a researcher's question, he referred to tabulated volumes of reports to pin down a specific detail.

> There is no status quo in this industry; it's competitive and fast changing. You either go backward or forward—there's no middle ground. We are going to go forward! In terms of our corporate sales and profit objectives we look to an annual 9–11 percent growth in dollar sales and 10–15 percent growth in net income. We believe we are going to have to meet those objectives over an extended period of time; as an average, over a five- to seven-year period. We are going to have to do that to be consistent with industry standards. Now in order to achieve those goals we see growth taking place in three different ways and have developed an ongoing five-year plan for 1976 through 1980.
>
> Our strategy includes basically three things: one is developing increased volume and increased market share through existing businesses. A second is the development of new products in existing businesses, and the third is via the acquisition of new businesses. By the way, we have five criteria for evaluating acquisition prospects. First, the prospect must be in the food, or food-related industry; second, it must have continuing good management; third, it must have demonstrated growth in sales and earnings over the past three years; fourth, in terms of sales, it should be in the $15–$20 million range. Finally, we must be able to arrange a merger transaction that is mutually satisfactory and that will not dilute Seven-Up's earnings.
>
> Obviously to meet objective number one, we need the cooperation and sincere commitment of our *developers*—we don't call them *bottlers*. Personal relationships are so important. We have to compete not only for the housewife's dollar but for developer time and loyalty. Our developer organization is quite different now than it was when I joined the company in 1946. Then 75 percent of them bottled 7UP exclusively; now almost all

bottle and distribute other national brands. We have to make our interests and our developers' interests compatible.

Of course we are always on the lookout for new products for our existing organization. We have thought of beverage powder sales sold through our developers . . . particularly in the institutional trade. We have had opportunities to buy fast-food chains, but at least currently we have no interest. If the right kind of snack food opportunity comes along, we might take a good look at that.

We don't have immediate plans for further acquisitions of bottling plants. We were asked by the owners of the Phoenix, Arizona, franchise to buy them out and we own one Canadian bottling operation.

We have made two important acquisitions of new businesses—Warner-Jenkinson in 1970 and Ventura Coastal in 1973. Our annual report details the results (see Exhibit 2). We are now in three product areas, and all are profitable. In each of these areas, though, competition is intense and we have competitors who have greater sales and financial resources.

Mr. Winter also spoke about the nonsoft drink product areas of The Seven-Up Company. His comments, along with those of other executives, are combined with industry data in the section on nonsoft drink divisions. Following this section comes material on the soft drink division. The information in this section is organized by function. Because of the complexity of the marketplace, the marketing function is expanded by an investigation of Seven-Up's position in the various soft drink market segments.

NONSOFT DRINK DIVISIONS

In 1970 Seven-Up acquired the remaining 80 percent of the shares of Warner-Jenkinson, the company's longtime supplier of 7UP extract. The price paid was 74,095 shares of Seven-Up convertible preferred stock with a stated value of $100 per share and carrying a rate of 5.1 percent. These shares were converted into 316,172 shares of Seven-Up common stock over a five-year period at various prices. As of December 31, 1975, the market value at $32.50 would produce a total value of $10,275,590. Warner-Jenkinson sales (excluding intercompany transactions) and net income dropped from $22,328,000 and $2,554,000 in 1974 to $18,991,000 and $1,176,000 in 1975 because of recession and regulatory circumstances. But, by 1976, sales and earnings had returned to normal patterns and the company's St. Louis manufacturing facilities were being substantially expanded.

Warner-Jenkinson, in addition to producing 7UP extract, was a highly respected technical leader in the manufacture of flavors, colors, and fragrances for food, drug, and cosmetic companies. With the exception of one large and very profitable firm—International Flavors and Fragrances—the majority of companies in these industries were small with sales averaging about $1 million. Typically firms had a proprietary interest in a formula and a customer list. A frequent method of entering the highly fragmented industry was to buy a company for its brand names, formulas, and customers. In 1973 and 1974 Warner-Jenkinson made two cash acquisitions, a flavoring company for $1.2 million and a small manufacturer of fragrances for $100,000.

Warner-Jenkinson competed against several hundred other companies which manufactured over 1,000 different flavors. Some of the nation's best-known producers of food mixes, candies, and cereal were its customers. The subsidiary had been a technical leader in the production and synthesizing of flavors and had recently introduced spray dried flavors and imitation chicken and beef flavors. The subsidiary also manufactured 10 basic food colors and 400 derivative blends. Colors were subject to governmental regulations in the form of certification of each production batch by the Food and Drug Administration. That federal agency's banning of Red Dye #2, used in the United States since 1906, had been in some measure responsible for the 1975 decline in this subsidiary's profit. By 1976 Red Dye #40 was in active production and customer use.

In 1973 Seven-Up acquired Ventura Coastal Corporation for 133,590 shares of common stock; in 1974 Ventura purchased the assets of the Golden Crown Citrus Company of Evanston, Illinois. Seven-Up had purchased about 20 percent of its lemon oil needs from Ventura prior to acquisition; this was approximately 2–3 percent of Ventura's central overall sales volume. Benefiting from the best lemon crop in California's history and from an unusually hot summer throughout the United States, the Ventura subsidiary's 1975 sales were $26,906,000, an increase of 43.2 percent over 1974. Net income was $985,000, significantly higher than the $44,786 earned in 1974. Although 1976 results were not expected to reach these levels because of the January–July California drought, an expansion of fruit processing facilities was underway at Ventura which would double capacity by 1977. Lemon was one of the fastest growing flavors in the food industry, and management was optimistic with regard to its future.

Ventura was in the business of processing and packaging frozen concentrate for lemonade and the growing, processing, and selling of fresh lemons and lemon products. One analyst stated that Ventura was to the frozen lemonade market (1974 market, at retail, over $40 million) what Coca-Cola's Minute Maid was to the frozen orange juice market; it sold between 35 percent and 40 percent of the market. Ventura sold the principal portion of its concentrate production to large grocery chains under 56 brand names; its ten largest customers accounted for approximately 70 percent of its sales. Ventura's dominant competitor was a cooperative—Sunkist Growers, Inc.—which processed over 75 percent of the orange and lemon production in the western United States. Sunkist sold Warner-Jenkinson about 65 percent of the lemon oil required for 7UP extract production.

Paul Young, executive vice president and treasurer, commented:

We use California and Arizona lemon oil in our extract, and Ventura had the reputation of producing the highest quality lemon oil in the world. There are an estimated 75,000 acres of land suitable for lemons in those two states. With Ventura we acquired 2,300 acres plus an additional 2,800 under contract. In 1974 we planted 135,000 new lemon trees on some 750 acres of land; they will yield fruit in 1977. The record 1975 lemon crop increased by 30 percent the availability of lemons to Ventura and eliminated the traditional need to purchase lemon juice concentrate from outside sources. And it positions Ventura to meet the growing needs of Golden Crown.

Golden Crown's original products had been reconstituted lemon, lime, and prune juice. In 1975 its product mix was expanded to include diet frozen lemonade, lime, orange, and grape concentrates all of which were produced for Golden Crown by Ventura. In 1976 it was test marketing a lemonade flavored powdered drink mix. Expanding West Coast juice sales prompted planning for a bottling plant to be built in that area in 1977.

SOFT DRINK OPERATIONS

The product category which dominated all others in its share of corporate sales appeared in the company's annual report as "Soft Drink Extracts and Finished Products; Canned and Bottled Soft Drinks and Fountain Syrup." "Extracts," 37 percent of 1975 sales, were sold to Seven-Up bottlers who produced the final consumer products. Packaged 7UP and fountain 7UP syrup were available to consumers in the take-home and fountain markets, respectively, in regular and sugar-free form.

"Finished Products" accounted for 43.2 percent of corporate sales. These final products constituted the sales results of the company-owned franchised bottling plants (two in the United States and Canada) and of the Seven-Up enterprises division of Seven-Up, U.S.A., Inc. The latter organization was formed to supplement bottler production capacities to ensure that the required mix of 7UP packages was available in each territory. Primarily, the subsidiary produced and delivered 7UP in cans, though it had expanded recently to include production of fountain syrups and of bottled products in the economy sizes of 64 ounces and 2 liters.

Though the packaging of soft drink products had undergone multiple changes over time, the basic ingredients and formula for regular 7UP had not been altered substantially since the product's invention in 1929. However, the company had introduced fountain 7UP essentially as a new product when it entered the fountain segment in 1960. Other variations on the 7UP theme took place in the diet market. These began with a reduced calorie drink called "Like" which was replaced by "Diet 7UP" in 1970. Diet 7UP was taken off the market when the saccharin-sweetened Sugar Free 7UP was perfected and introduced in February 1974. In addition to these products in the 7UP line, the company marketed a line of Howdy flavor drinks which had accounted for about 1.5 percent of sales for the past several years.

Production and purchasing

Production facilities for the supply of extract sold to Seven-Up developers were concentrated in the Warner-Jenkinson subsidiary. This company manufactured all domestic and some international extract in its St. Louis facility. The production process required fewer than 20 people to produce the volume necessary for the 7UP consumed in the entire United States.

The Seven-Up Company did not purchase cans, sugar, or glass for its bottler network. The company did purchase sugar for its own use in producing finished products in the soft drink and nonsoft drink divisions. Seven-Up had recently begun to buy forward in the futures market in an attempt to deal with price changes in sugar. The supply of another key ingredient, lemon oils, was secured by purchasing roughly 20 percent of the amount from Ventura and contracting for much of the rest.

The distribution game

Mr. Winter commented:

> The soft drink business, and I don't think I'm being overdramatic about it, as a franchise business is extremely different than most other types of franchise businesses. The kind of personal rapport that is established between the franchiser and the franchised bottler impacts greatly on the performance of both parties. Our developers all see themselves as marketing and advertising professionals. We must convince them that their greatest asset is the 7UP trademark and that we have the marketing know-how to develop not just a national but an international brand. Regardless of where the consumers are, the brand must be presented in one consistent posture; if we didn't do that in the United States, for example, we would wind up with 469 different kinds of advertising and marketing strategy for 7UP.
>
> It's a very emotional, attitudinal kind of thing. We must position the brand . . . yet consider the individual developer's point of view. This is particularly important when you consider, say, a 7UP Coca-Cola bottler. That person has just so much time, effort, and money to put into selling each of those two products, so it's critical to have a developer's commitment. Over-all, it's pretty difficult; it's a real challenge.

The agreement

At Seven-Up, bottlers were called developers because, as one executive explained, "Almost anyone can handle the mechanical procedures involved with bottling a product, but the real test is how to go about developing the territory." The development aspect of a bottler's function was clearly implied in this title, though not specifically spelled out in sales terms in the domestic franchise agreement. Distribution targets were given, and bottlers had to maintain a minimum penetration of 65 percent of the beverage outlets in their territories. Developers were not allowed to sell 7UP outside of their particular territories, sell knowingly to a third party, allow a retailer to warehouse the drink for resale, or promote and distribute an imitative lemon-lime drink.

In exchange, a franchisee received the rights to produce both regular and Sugar Free 7UP in packaged and fountain form. A separate agreement was necessary to can 7UP products, since all plants did not have the volume to justify a canning line. If a developer did not take advantage of the franchise to produce any of the bottle products, the company reserved the right to step in on its own and do so, though such an action was not always practicable. Under all other circumstances, developers held the right to the sale of 7UP within their respective territories and expected The Seven-Up Company to maintain and promote the 7UP trademark nationwide.

The players: developers

The smallest Seven-Up developer marketed to a population of roughly 15,000 people and sold an estimated 50,000 to 75,000 cases annually. This was in stark contrast to the largest developers who were located in cities containing several million people with sales of several million cases per year. The researchers estimated that roughly 100 bottling operations accounted for nearly 70–75 percent of Seven-Up's volume. This left the remaining 350+ plants responsible for 25–30 percent of domestic sales.

This was a significant change from earlier days when most developers had been small-scale entrepreneurs. In 1975 some of these family-run, smaller developers remained, yet added to the team were those entrepreneurs who had started small and enlarged their base through acquisition of their neighbors. Moreover, an entirely new breed had entered the game: the corporate conglomerates. The largest developer in this category was the Leisure Division of Westinghouse which owned franchises in southern California, Indiana, and Puerto Rico. According to Mr. Winter, the conglomerates tended to have larger, more successful operations, though when sales were measured in terms of bottles per capita, the smaller developers outperformed them. Mr. Winter felt that there was a growing trend toward conglomerate franchise ownership which had slowed somewhat due to concern over the eventual outcome of the FTC ruling and of the convenience-packaging legislation.

Regardless of the size or success of the franchisee, however, there were no domestic developers who bottled 7UP to the exclusion of all other soft drinks. Within the network there were 13 so-called exclusive bottlers; the word "exclusive" here meant that 7UP was the only major brand of soft drink they distributed. In some cases these developers bottled another drink for private labels, or under their own label; in other cases they produced another franchised drink which was not considered a major brand, such as Hire's Root Beer.

The remainder of the 469 Seven-Up developers held franchises for other major branded products as shown in Exhibit 3.

EXHIBIT 3

	Bottlers
7UP (exclusive)	13
Coke and other	97
Pepsi and other	153
Dr Pepper and other...	36
Royal Crown Cola and other	104
7UP and other franchises	66

Source: Research estimates.

Several industry analysts believed that the developer network at Seven-Up was hampered competitively by the number of small bottlers it included and that, because of their size, these bottlers were not able to take advantage of the proliferation of large packages as promptly as the compeitition. In early 1976 one executive at Seven-Up explained, "We are behind Coke and Pepsi. They introduced the 64-ounce and got a big jump on that; now we are catching up. But as we're catching up, we've been losing share, and I think you can look at where they've introduced some of their larger sizes and you can see the impact it's had. The fact is, you have to get the bottler committed to saying, 'I need the big size.'"

Rapport between the developers and the company was given high priority by top management in 1976. Direct contact with developers was maintained through district sales managers. As part of this program, a group called the Association of Seven-Up Developers had been established in 1974. The group's objectives were to solidify company-developer relationships and to formalize developer input into marketing, legal, and public affairs decisions. Senior company officers met with committees of the Association both informally and formally several times a year. Mr. Kidwell noted, "For some of the strategic direction of the campaign . . . we discuss the programs with the group in advance, share the research, and get their concurrence before going into finished advertising."

The players: Seven-Up Bottling Company

The Seven-Up Company itself owned only two bottling plants in Phoenix, Arizona, and Toronto, Ontario. At Coke, company-owned bottlers were responsible for 10 percent of total volume. Some trade observers commented that Coke was encouraging bottler consolidation. This led to speculation regarding the continuation of Coke's policy of independent versus company-owned bottling operations. The Seven-Up Company stated that they were not actively encouraging developer consolidation, but when the opportunity presented itself, they recognized the marketing economies of scale to be gained from working with a single territory in place of several. Company management stated that they did not currently foresee additional company purchases of franchises, and explained that in the case of the Phoenix plant, the owner had come to the company and asked to be bought out as he wished to retire. Further, the franchise was located in a warm-weather, rapid-population-growth area. Management added that buying up franchises was a complicated issue when the majority of franchisees owned competitor's franchises as well; Seven-Up was not interested in purchasing a plant which also bottled and promoted a major competitor's beverage.

The players: Seven-Up Enterprises Division of Seven-Up, U.S.A., Inc.

As a service to developers, Seven-Up Enterprises provided canned and bottled 7UP products for those developers unable to produce them within their own facilities. Through the operation of Seven-Up Enterprises, the company stated "All 7UP developers are assured access to the wide range of 7UP packages required to serve their respective markets."

This division produced finished products in cans, bottles, and fountain syrup containers through nearly three dozen production centers nationwide. These centers were canners contracted on a 30-day basis, cancellable by either party. Since the early 1950s, when the division really got its start with the introduction of cans into the U.S. market, there had been relatively little turnover among these producers despite the 30-day terms. Contractors were of two types: independently owned firms and Seven-Up bottlers or canners. The latter were authorized by The Seven-Up Company to produce product requirements not only for their own territory but for other franchise areas as well, and thus bore full ownership responsibility. The independent contractor, on the other hand, relied upon The Seven-Up Company to bear all business risks revolving around inventories, and so forth, as s/he had no title to ingredients or finished product, which belong to Seven-Up.

Production centers were located in 34 cities in 25 states. In geographical terms, a partial breakdown was as follows: three centers in the Far West, four in the East, eight in the Midwest, and ten in the South. Arnold Larson, vice president and general manager of Seven-Up Enterprises, commented, "We can reasonably economically blanket the country with a new package.

While we retain our organizational autonomy, we maintain a close relationship with home office marketing because we can really help break in new products. For instance, after the cyclamate scare many of our franchises were gun shy of our reformulated diet product, and we were able to produce the product, demonstrate its appeal, and in this way help the marketing department sell its new product."

Seven-Up Enterprises was also expected to provide strong support to the introduction of the new 2-liter packages in several major markets, and in general to produce the over-32-ounce packages for those developers who could not yet invest in these popular sizes. As stated in the 1975 annual report, "Many 7UP bottlers now have facilities for producing the variety of package types and sizes they need in their local markets; however, many others still do not. For this latter segment, Seven-Up Enterprises provides a practical solution to their packaging needs."

Domestic marketing

In early 1976 John Kidwell was appointed senior vice president and director of marketing. He had been president of Seven-Up of Canada Limited from 1970 to 1976. An industry commentator noted, "When John took over as director of marketing, he inherited some major strengths as well as several problems, not the least of which was the sustained loss in market share for regular 7UP. He and his predecessor appeared to respond differently not only to this challenge but also to goals for the marketing area. I believe poor developer company relationships were a major factor in the decline of regular 7UP market share."

"I am much more of a strategist than a marketing and advertising creative man," Kidwell stated. He believed that the steps he had taken thus far reflected that strategic orientation citing his work with the developer network, his reorganization of the marketing department, and recruitment of new personnel as well as the development of the "UNdo it!" campaign. In the following sections, he and his team describe their opportunities and challenges.

Mr. Kidwell commented on developer relationships, "When I returned I met almost immediately with the executive committee of the Association of Seven-Up Developers. I was amazed at the deterioration that had occurred between the company and our developers just in regard to simple human relationships. When you had a bad franchisor-franchisee relationship, you have to understand that it has taken a long time to develop, and for that reason you can't solve the problem overnight. But progress has been made in these last months. Some of the credit should go to our reorganization. We wanted not only to achieve strategic goals but to bring about closer contact and clearer communication with the developers—specially in the develop-

EXHIBIT 4
Organization chart

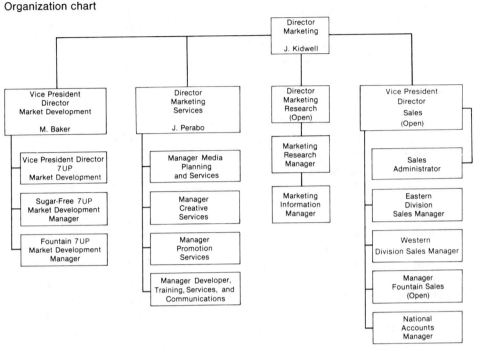

ment of their individual marketing plans." Later in that year he remarked, "I would say that the developers themselves are pleased with the direction we've taken. But it's true that we still have to live together for a while before the relationship is fully reestablished."

Departmental reorganization of domestic marketing

Mr. Winter, in a trade paper interview, explained some of the rationale behind John Kidwell's marketing restructuring. "Before, our marketing organization was action oriented. We were structured to prepare for action ... and, quite frankly, there was confusion in our marketing communication. Now we are building on top of that some organized planning and a base for credibility for our marketing actions."

Prefaced by a comprehensive analysis of the marketplace, taking place over a period of months, John Kidwell divided marketing into five subunits: market development, services, research, sales, and fountain syrup sales (see Exhibit 4). Each was given "clearly defined functions and responsibilities and was to be headed by experienced persons."

Michael Baker, formerly director of marketing for Canada, was brought in to head up the new market development group. Reporting to him were market development managers, whose responsibilities were similar to those of brand managers, for each of the three major market segments: packaged 7UP and packaged Sugar Free 7UP, Fountain 7UP, and Sugar Free 7UP. These managers were seen as "conceptualizers" who assisted the sales organization in analyzing and solving the marketing needs of Seven-Up developers.

While these managers had periodic contact with the developers to keep in touch with the marketplace, the day-to-day responsibilities of working with the developers fell to the sales function. This function was divided into two departments, the packaged sales department and a new fountain syrup sales department. Both departments were responsible for the execution of sales programs and the attainment of sales objectives for products in their respective markets. They were to sell home office marketing programs to the developer network and to be the direct communication link with developers for all marketing affairs.

The packaged sales department, by far the larger of the two, was organized geographically into an eastern and a western division. These division sales managers supervised regional and area sales managers. It was the area sales managers who worked most closely with developers to determine how the allotted marketing dollars could best be combined with the developers' own funds and spent within the developers' territory.

The third function, marketing research, supported the work of the first two functions, development and sales. The research function was divided into two departments, marketing research and marketing services. The former was a new addition to the marketing organization; formerly marketing research had been conducted on a less formal basis or by an outside organization. James Perabo had been hired as the director of marketing services. The work of this department included media planning (with the exception of local advertising which was the responsibility of the market development manager), promotion services, packaging, graphics merchandising racks, vending, and sales and management training—all services provided for developers.

As an example of how the new organization worked, John Kidwell explained the critical process of the development of the company's advertising program.

First, market development recommended to Kidwell a strategy based on supporting documentation provided by marketing research. Upon his approval, the suggestion went back to market development where a document was prepared for presentation to the advertising agency. Then followed a discussion of the campaign with the agency to see if the proposed objectives could be met. Once the agency had come up with its program, that effort was presented to the Creative Review Board of the company (Kidwell,

Baker, and Perabo). The strategy had next to be approved by Mr. Winter before being put into operation. The company sought to involve the developers in the process, principally through the marketing committee of the Developers Association.

A third critical marketing area, to which John Kidwell devoted substantial attention early in his new assignment, was a review and redirection of the company's advertising thrust. One result of this effort was the UNdo it campaign, launched in October 1976. "From a strategic point of view Seven-Up is where it should be at this point in time," he stated. "We think of UNdo it as a strategic positioning rather than an advertising execution." To understand better the current UNdo it campaign, the researcher reviewed the company's advertising history and talked with John Kidwell about the current situation.

Advertising and promotion

Seven-Up's 1975 soft drink dollar sales were roughly one third the size of those of Pepsi and one fifth the size of Coca-Cola sales. Total dollar sales volume for these companies was 11 and 13 times that of Seven-Up, respectively. These differences in scale naturally provided the two larger companies with certain advantages. In 1975 Seven-Up paid out approximately 17 percent of sales in marketing expenditures for a total of $36 million (see Exhibit 5). Seven-Up could expect to be outspent in marketing by the two leading colas alone at the rate of roughly eight or ten to one. In terms of advertising expenditures specifically, one industry analysis estimated that

EXHIBIT 5
Comparison of how the sales dollar was spent

	1970*	1971	1972	1973	1974	1975	1976
Cost of product sold	53.8¢	53.3¢	52.6¢	51.6¢	57.7¢	52.6¢	50.2¢
Marketing services	17.1	17.1	17.3	17.2	14.9	16.8	18.6
Employment costs	12.0	11.1	8.2	8.0	7.3	7.3	7.4
Payroll and fringe benefits							
All other expense (net)			4.4	4.7	3.3	4.7	3.6
Taxes	8.8	8.8	8.4	8.9	8.1	9.1	9.6
Paid to shareholders	3.5	4.2	3.7	3.4	3.6	3.9	5.3
Reinvested in the business	4.8	5.5	5.4	6.2	5.1	5.6	5.3
Total	100¢	100¢	100¢	100¢	100¢	100¢	100¢

* Restated to include Ventura Coastal Corporation.
Source: Company records.

for the years 1972 and 1975 Pepsi's outlays were $34 and $42 million; Coke, $35 and $42 million; Seven-Up, $14 and $14 million; Royal Crown, $8 and $14 million; and Dr Pepper, $4 and $4 million.

The Uncola campaign

In 1968 Seven-Up initiated an aggressive program to change the 7UP image from a mixer or stomach tonic to a soft drink, going head to head with the colas in the process. This was the birth of the "7UP The Uncola" campaign, developed by the J. Walter Thompson advertising agency. The Uncola strategy focused on 7UP as an alternative drink of equal quality and enjoyment to the colas if not, in fact, their superior in refreshment. Advertising began with a heavy reliance upon television, with particular emphasis on network TV and its 60-second appeals to the targeted youth audience of 16- to 24-year-olds. Later in the year, the full array of advertising media came into play with the usage of outdoor billboards, newspaper supplements, radio, and prime-time TV.

Graphics and delivery of the advertisements were progressive and designed to convey an impromptu contemporary feeling, just off-beat enough to appeal to the teens and 20s of the era. The campaign utilized the unique colors and drawings of pop art and "art nouveau" forms which broke sharply from the typical commercial art techniques. Print ads using lots of white space were strikingly simple, dominated by bold headlines proclaiming 7UP as "The Uncola." Advertising copy was littered with puns such as "Don't be left out in the Cola"; "Turn Un"; "Give Un to Others"; and "For Fast Relief from the Common Cola."

The campaign was not launched without reservation, however. For one thing, the slogan seemed to counter the traditional advertising caveat against the use of negatives; for another, the campaign itself was a far cry from the standard soft drink "life-style" advertisements depicting beach and party scenes of energetic young soda drinkers. Another type of resistance came from some Seven-Up developers who also bottled a cola product. However, it was difficult for anyone to maintain opposition in the face of the deluge of requests for Uncola posters, lamps, decals, and buttons that poured in from precisely the youth market Seven-Up intended to engage.

"See the light" campaign

In 1975, as unit sales of regular 7UP continued the decline begun in 1974, the company attempted to put a fresh face on The Uncola image with a new theme called "See the Light." This campaign was intended to portray 7UP as a clear, clean "uplifting" beverage highly compatible with food. Colors and design of packages were modified to resemble an illuminated marquee in which the brand name was set off "in lights." The campaign, however, did not achieve desired objectives.

"UNdo It!" campaign

Seven-Up management saw the new "UNdo it!" campaign as a logical extension of the company's eight-year investment in the Uncola trademark and believed that it reinforced regular 7UP as *the* alternative to colas. The "UNdo it!" slogan carried both a positive and a negative message: don't drink another cola and do drink the Uncola instead. The intent of the campaign was to make the cola drinker aware of her or his cola drinking "habit" and to provide a challenge to that habit with an Uncola. The "UNdo it!" advertising campaign had extension through promotion, display, and packaging contacts with consumers.

John Kidwell explained, "Cola consumption is a habit, but people who consume cola also drink 7UP, and they do see advantages in interrupting their 'cola habit.' If we marketed strictly to the 7UP drinker, there wouldn't be any growth."

Mr. Kidwell, on several occasions, talked about the target audience for UNdo it. "Our target group is concentrated among the 16–34 age group." In addition, citing the company's own research, he noted that approximately 55 percent of the 18+ age group are multibrand soft drink consumers and that this group also had high priority. "One thing about this industry is that it's not like the toothpaste, cigarette, or even beer industry where people tend to use one product or product category to the exclusion of another."

7UP consumer statistics, moreover, were unusual in the industry being skewed to the older population. Seven-Up marketers inferred from this fact that "older people" were using 7UP as a mixer. The company maintained certain cooperative programs with some liquor companies, although the overall marketing thrust did not stress the potential of 7UP as a mixer. "Our principal objective is to get . . . cola drinkers to drink more 7UP. At the same time we don't want to sacrifice that part of the market represented by heavy 7UP users."

According to Kidwell, the frequency of advertising exposure was a critical factor in breaking the "cola habit." This was one reason why "UNdo it!" would break with both industry norms and the historical pattern of 7UP by cutting back on both spot and network television while increasing the usage of network radio, print, and outdoor media in its mix. Kidwell commented, "The cost of television has gone up disproportionately high to what the industry can afford. . . . The Seven-Up strategy in the past had depended heavily on TV, but now we are using a balanced media mix and putting almost equal weight on television, radio, and outdoor. We're able to attain much increased frequency this way, and frequency is very important to us this year." A large part of the media purchases were planned during high cola-drinking time periods such as weekends, the summer months, and during high-consumption hours such as lunch and late afternoon. In the past, Seven-Up had established its budgets on a per capita basis, but now the company had set minimum reach levels for all markets with the developers in the more important areas receiving extra media dollars.

The Seven-Up Company, as the franchisor responsible for trademark control, made the final decisions on overall marketing programs but in cooperation with the Developers Association. Their cooperation was important because, for the most part, 7UP local advertising and promotion programs were done on a 50-50 cost basis. The franchisee elected to use or not use these programs, but it would have been highly unusual for a developer not to participate in them. Company marketing personnel helped each developer to tailor a specific promotional program for his territory.

The promotional arm of the "UNdo it!" campaign also stressed flexibility. "Flexibility" referred to the ability of the promotional program to adapt itself to the individual bottler's needs both in terms of timing and frequency. It was hoped that promotions at the local level would be responsive to the fact that while there was a minimum level below which a bottler should not go, some markets were more competitive than others and as a consequence required more promotional support. Frequent special "cents-off" activity was planned to facilitate the habit-changing decision of the consumer, for research had indicated consumers were price-aware.

Thus Seven-Up hoped to bolster frequency of purchase, gain competitive ground, and recover from the effects of the price-cutting activity of competitors in 1975 which Kidwell termed "almost predatory." He commented, "We couldn't keep up with either Coke or Pepsi. I think that price promotion is one of the things which had an impact on our share of market for regular 7UP. It's one of the things we've had to take into consideration in our marketing plans. It is extremely important in determining the particular brand that a person chooses at a particular time."

A National Promotion Fund, a Frequency Promotion Fund, and a National Merchandising Fund had been established to support developers.

The National Promotion Fund provided funds to encourage the participation of all Seven-Up developers at four different time periods when 7UP products would be promoted nationwide. As a promotion ran for two weeks, this encompassed only eight weeks out of the year. The Frequency Promotion Fund was established, therefore, to make available to developers a series of additional monies, up to a fixed amount, upon which they could draw for promotional campaigns other than the four nationally scheduled ones. The National Merchandising Fund supported developers' purchases of point-of-purchase materials, principally illuminated signage.

One analyst estimated that about 70 percent of the Seven-Up 1975 media expenditures in the United States were assigned to spot TV, 10 percent each to national TV and to spot radio, and 8 percent to outdoor billboards with minor amounts to newspapers and magazines.

Another analyst sensed a shift in the Seven-Up marketing budget from a preponderance toward media advertising to an increase by an estimated 50 percent in dollars spent on local promotional programs, for example, "cents-off," display, and packaging programs. He estimated the breakdown of marketing expenditures for 1977 at 40–45 percent of the pie for advertising, another 35–40 percent for promotions, 10–15 percent for packaging, and the remainder for market research.

Packaging

Seven-Up had been an innovator in packaging. In 1971 the company introduced the award-winning Plasti-Shield bottle; glass encased with plastic which kept the beverage cooler longer and decreased breakage. The new containers were lighter, easier to handle, and conserved shelf space as well.

In 1975 Seven-Up was the first soft drink producer to switch to metric packaging. Since the FDA had ordered all alcoholic beverages to be packed in metric sizes by 1979, Seven-Up may have anticipated similar legislation for its industry. They were well received by consumers in the 60 markets in which they were introduced by 1976. One reason cited for this reception was that the packages offered more product for the money; a liter holding 33.8 ounces generally sold for the same price as the conventional 32-ounce bottle. To announce the metric innovations the company had used Seven-Up humor in slogans such as "Follow the Liter" and "A Quart and Liter Bit More."

"We are still behind our major cola competition in the availability of 32- and 64-ounce bottles," Mr. Kidwell noted. "We have many incentive programs for developers to encourage usage of the larger sizes and metric packages." The company was also monitoring plastic bottle developments.

Pricing

Within the take-home market segment, price leadership was often taken by Pepsi. During the summer of 1975, Pepsi preempted Coke to become the leading firm in this market area. Pepsi's success was attributed to an aggressive marketing policy that took advantage of Pepsi's owned bottlers to squeeze margins in key urban markets and thereby underprice Coke. Coke's retaliation had led to increased "cents-off" promotional activity during 1975 and 1976.

By the middle of 1976, however, retail prices for the major soft drinks showed no significant differences from one to another, though Seven-Up obviously felt it had to increase its level of promotional support to bottlers to keep up with the pricing strategies of the leading colas. In October 1974,

Seven-Up had increased its extract price to developers by 11 percent. This was the first increase in three years. Prices were again raised by the company in June 1975 by 25 percent; these increases not only offset rising costs of sugar and inflation but were earmarked for added marketing support. Developers initially did not appear pleased with the 1975 concentrate price hike, but since the company had stated its intention to plough back much of its increased revenue into advertising and promotional programs, they seemed more accepting.

The only clear price differential which continued to exist at both the retail and wholesale level was that between Sugar Free 7UP and the diet drinks of the other major producers. The developer ingredient cost per case for Sugar Free 7UP was considerably below the cost of competitive diet brands.

In the fountain market, Coca-Cola was the dominant figure and price leader. As sales to this segment were extremely price sensitive, wholesale margins were significantly lower than in the take-home market; thus by maintaining a low price to jobbers Coke could make it difficult for competition to make any headway in this market. Seven-Up products, generally speaking, were comparable in price to Coke's. At the fountain retail level, prices to the consumer remained consistent for all of the major soft drinks and were rarely discounted.

Two key markets

The take-home market (primarily grocery stores) was the largest market segment of the soft drink industry and provided nearly 60 percent of Seven-Up soft drink sales. It was a competitive area in which one of the company's products, Sugar Free 7UP, had enjoyed substantial success and in which regular 7UP had experienced loss of share of market during the last several years. In 1975 the industry in the United States suffered an average decline of 0.2 percent for all brands; regular 7UP sales declined an average 3.6 percent. In the first quarter of 1976, industry average sales increased 13.9 percent and regular 7UP sales increased 8.7 percent.

Senior management stressed the importance of reestablishing the growth pattern of regular 7UP. Mr. Kidwell told the researchers that his immediate goals for regular 7UP were to reverse the decline in market share and to recapture the 7½ percent share of all markets previously held by the regular product; this called for an increase of one percentage point from the Seven-Up estimated 1976 share.

Kidwell believed Seven-Up had already taken important steps towards reaching this goal. The reorganization of the marketing department was expected to help regular 7UP get back to, and stay on, target. He anticipated that the market development function, which had not existed previously, would be of particular importance in this endeavor. In addition, the reorganization divided the fountain syrup and regular sales groups into two individual units so that different strategies could be worked out for each.

A further consequence of the new system was that Sugar Free 7UP was also treated as a separate entity from regular 7UP. Prior to Kidwell's tenure both products had been included in the same "integrated marketing plan." He suggested that this invited cannibalization of the regular sales by Sugar Free 7UP. "We can't prove that conclusively, but the fact is we have been marketing the two products together for the last two and a half years, and this might have contributed to the regular 7UP problems."

An industry analyst noted that one strategic unknown would be Coke's program for Sprite, its lemon-lime drink. "Their primary interest has been in promoting their cola drinks. Sprite right now is only available to about 50 percent of the U.S. consuming public. But, what if this should change?" Mr. Kidwell commented, "We have to be very concerned about Sprite. Coke is powerful, and where it is very strong—in the Southeast and Southwest—Sprite is very strong. But we have strength too. Many of our Coke bottling relationships go back before they had Sprite; I don't think those bottlers would give up 7UP for Sprite. Our reserve power would be to shift the brand to the local Pepsi bottler."

Sugar Free 7UP had been a major success story in both the take-home and fountain markets. Diet drinks comprised approximately 15 percent of soft drink volume, and Sugar Free was acknowledged to be the fastest growing diet drink in this field. It ranked third in market share with Diet-Pepsi first and Tab second.

Mr. Kidwell was optimistic about Sugar Free's future and had set a goal of 10 percent of the diet market segment to be achieved by the end of 1977. The product's critical characteristic was that most consumers could not distinguish between the taste of Sugar Free and regular 7UP whereas they noticed differences in taste between the regular and diet colas. On this premise Seven-Up had used "taste tests" to sell accounts in the fountain market. Champagne glasses filled with Tab were compared to those filled with Sugar Free 7UP. In 1975 these "taste tests" led to breakthrough fountain sales with McDonald's.

Company market research indicated that the diet soft drink consumer was, typically, female and somewhat older than the consumer of regular drinks. To reach these consumers, Seven-Up planned to capitalize on the perceived taste advantage of Sugar Free 7UP. "Through independent research studies we have established that we have the best tasting diet soft drink on the market." Sugar Free's 1977 advertising theme would be "Taste More Taste." This approach was innovative in that it emphasized taste as the principal quality of the diet drink; most competitors stressed their diet products' low calorie attributes. Seven-Up expressed the opinion that by virtue of the product's name, consumers already understood this fact and, therefore, it was not necessary to repeat the message in its advertisements. National consumer sampling would play a large role in the campaign, principally through retail outlets.

"Fountain is the other key market to keep your eye on," a seasoned industry executive commented, "not just because it's a high-growth area but because it is so critical strategically. That is why Pepsi, Dr Pepper, and Seven-Up are working so hard at 'cracking' Coca-Cola's dominance. Coca-Cola must have between 60–90 percent of that business. But, to understand 'fountain,' you have to keep three points in mind: first, it is extremely complex; second, it calls for sophisticated selling policies; and third, it is a rough competitive game."

That the fountain business was complex was readily apparent to the researchers. Part of the complexity resulted from the fact that it was not one but multiple markets—fast-food chains, vending companies, certain military and institutional accounts, and anywhere else that soft drinks could not be bought in a bottle or a can. In one sense, simply defining where a fountain market existed, what its segments, trends, and opportunities for growth were, was a major task. One result of this complexity was a paucity of reliable data on which to base company plans.

The process of selling to the fountain trade was a complicated maneuver. Using McDonald's as an illustration, the first step of the process meant gaining headquarter's approval. Once this was secured, the product could become automatically available in the 800 McDonald's *company-owned* franchise operations. However, like most franchise organizations, McDonald's was not legally allowed to dictate to its *independent* franchises which beverage they should purchase and it was under pressure from the FTC regarding such tie-in arrangements. Therefore, the independents could choose between the soft drink brands headquarters recommended. This meant that Seven-Up, after selling McDonald's, had yet to convince 2,800 franchised outlets across the country. At this stage, salespeople presented their case to the 12 or 13 regional McDonald's representatives, and if successful, were then able to approach individually the 83 cooperative groups of McDonald's franchises. Adding to this uncertainty was the fact that no legal contracts were made in the fountain market, leaving clients free to switch products at any given moment.

Coke, the key player in the fountain trade, determined the competitive ground rules. That company was both a manufacturer and the seller of fountain syrup. Historically, Coke had gotten its start in soft drinks as a fountain operation, and had retained the right to sell its syrup directly to beverage wholesalers without having to involve Coke franchises in the process. In this way Coke benefited not only from the economies of scale in producing the syrup in approximately a dozen centers (as compared to Seven-Up's approximately 400 fountain developers) but also could avoid some of the cost of an intermediary distribution network. Another critical advantage was that since the Coca-Cola Company did sell the product, Coke could control all pricing for the fountain market from its headquarters in Atlanta and could quote one national price to beverage buyers.

Most recently Coke had begun a new development in distribution called "cross-franchising." Regional distribution centers were set up, on a profit/loss basis, from which Coke itself would fill orders for clients within the fountain market of an entire region, without being restricted by any wholesalers or middle persons. Pepsi had just lost the Burger Chef account, and some trade analysts believed Coke's cross-franchising program was hurting Pepsi's position within the fountain market.

Pepsi, as opposed to Coca-Cola, did not manufacture or sell fountain syrup directly to wholesalers, except through its own bottling operations, and, therefore, could not set a single national price in the same way that Coke could. Pepsi, therefore, engaged in a complicated process of buying fountain syrup from its franchisees which PepsiCo then resold to beverage wholesalers. In this manner Pepsi could act as the seller of the product for its franchised bottlers and, in combination with the syrup produced in company-owned facilities, could manage to develop a national pricing policy without violating the legal ramifications of its franchise agreements.

According to Tony Rebello, manager of Seven-Up's fountain market development department, there were two key competitive characteristics in the fountain business. First, all involved parties were highly price sensitive and everybody is squeezed but the final account. Coke has certainly played a major role in keeping prices to wholesalers and accounts low, but the food service companies themselves are a dominant force in maintaining low margins for concentrate producers. Retail margins, on the other hand, did not suffer the same pressure. The average cost of a gallon of syrup to a fast-food chain was $2; after adding the ice, water, and cups, the chains resold the syrup to consumers for an average of $25 per gallon.

Seven-Up did not enter the fountain market until 1960. The company had had to overcome quality control problems with the filtration of city water supplies used at fountains and cup vending machines. By 1970 fountain sales represented a 7 percent share of 7UP unit sales. By 1974 the company could note that fountain sales were growing at a rate double that of overall company sales and had reached 12 percent of unit sales. In 1975 they dipped to 10.6 percent. One industry analyst believed this was due to the tremendous rise in sugar prices which left the bottlers unable to meet "national prices" suggested by Seven-Up for leading nationwide fountain customers.

In 1975 Seven-Up negotiated the distribution of Sugar Free to McDonald's, the first time a major chain had taken on a diet drink. In 1976 the 1,000-unit Burger King and 2,400-unit A&W Root Beer chains were sold. In some areas of the country such as Atlanta, Sugar Free had gained 0.8 per-

cent of the market versus a 0.5 percent share for Tab. While analysts estimated that marketing and promotional allowances made this a break-even
operation, Seven-Up management believed fountain had good long-term
possibilities (see Exhibit 6).

EXHIBIT 6
Seven-Up distribution in the fast-food area

Chain	Market share (sales $ percent of fast-food market)	Type of 7UP sold
McDonald's	20	Sugar Free
Kentucky Fried Chicken	11.7	Regular
International Dairy Queen	6	Regular
Burger King	4.8	Both
Burger Chef	2.8	Sugar Free
A&W International	2.7	Both
Hardy's	2.6	Sugar Free
Denny's	2.6	Regular
Jack-in-the-Box	2.5	Not sold
Pizza Hut	2.5	Regular

The 1976 reorganization of the marketing department had divided fountain sales into two subunits: one aimed at national fast-food accounts, and
the second aimed at key developers. Mr. Kidwell's target was an increase of
10 percent in fountain sales by the end of 1977. He commented about the
fountain market: "We are taking a very hard look at the whole economics
of this business as it affects our bottlers and as it affects our company. We
are attempting to determine just where the profitable end of the business is
and where the unprofitable end is. There are areas of cost accounting, for
instance, in fountain that need clarification. Often in cold drink sales accounting, a developer includes vending, fountain, and cold bottle. Yet all
the expenses are lumped against the fountain department only. So, until we
get our developers to differentiate their expenses, it's going to be difficult to
determine where we stand profitwise with fountain. We think there is the
strong possibility for some pretty significant gains, both in profits and
volume."

Mr. Kidwell sought guidance on the question of reinstituting a "suggested national pricing program" for large accounts and had hired a consulting firm to deal with this issue. In 1975 the demise of the national
pricing policy cost Seven-Up the accounts of several large vending
companies.

All concentrate producers considered price to be a major factor of their
marketing program; in some cases it seemed that determining a price was

the entire marketing program. Rebello, however, spoke of the necessity for Seven-Up to design a fully integrated marketing program which included components other than price alone. New marketing plans for fountain sales included pricing allowances to help developers in their distribution efforts but also involved advertising on menus and signs within accounts and point-of-purchase displays. Special ads were developed showing 7UP being consumed in athletic stadiums, and newspaper advertising was also to be used. Promotional items included Uncola glasses and free-drink coupons given with McDonald's sandwiches to increase both 7UP consumption and traffic through McDonald's outlets. Seven-Up stated it would reimburse developers for every free gallon given away in a promotional effort and would financially assist incentive programs for developers' fountain salespeople.

One industry analyst predicted Seven-Up had yet to face a major challenge to its expansion within the fountain market. "You look at Coke's power in the fountain business," she suggested, "and imagine to yourself what would happen to Seven-Up if Coke decided it wanted to create consumer demand for Sprite. The best place to start would be in the fountain area where Coke rules and sell Sprite to the food service people as a product of the Coca-Cola Company with the Coca-Cola quality guaranteed. To sweeten the deal, Coke could relate the distribution of Sprite to that of Coca-Cola with tie-in programs, that is, 'Buy a certain amount of Coke and get a gallon of Sprite free ... or buy Coke, Sprite, and Fanta flavors and we'll give you the equipment for it.' Once Sprite was reasonably well established here, Coke could move into the packaged segment with a product that had already been recognized and sampled by millions of Americans."

Canada

The first move of Seven-Up into non-U.S.A. markets began in 1935 when Canadian operations were initiated; in 1975 Seven-Up Canada Ltd. contributed 12 percent of corporate sales. 7UP market penetration exceeded that achieved in the United States; it was second only to Coke in share of market. Sugar Free 7UP, introduced in 1975, had captured 15 percent of the diet market, including sales to McDonald's. In 1976 competition had increased dramatically and the company announced the objective of "containing market share erosion in the face of extreme competitive pressure and legislative uncertainty. Over the long term, however, sales were expected to have a 10–15 percent growth rate."

The company's 1975 annual report noted that Canadian and other international sales amounted to about 20 percent of total consolidated sales with net income at a slightly lower percent to total. The net profit figure was achieved after an unusually high foreign exchange loss, primarily from Argentina and Mexico, which reduced net income by $1,146,574.

International

"Seven-Up has major opportunities in International," an industry observer noted, "just because the market is so large and growing and they are such a tiny factor at present. They have done a superb job in Canada, and they are strong in parts of South America." Mr. Charles Thies, president of Seven-Up International, was also optimistic. "True we missed the days when you could get into the market inexpensively, but our objective is still to color the world with green 7UP bottles—gradually."

In 1975 International was responsible for roughly 8 percent of company sales and coordinated a network of 186 franchised bottlers in 81 nations. Seven-Up International had but a few exclusive bottlers; it was in combination with Coke bottlers in 30–35 international markets and with Pepsi bottlers in a similar number of markets. 7UP was bottled in tandem with Orange Crush in 16 plants and with R. C. Cola in a dozen plants worldwide. The remaining hundred plants bottled 7UP in combination with local brands. Operations ranged in size from Amsterdam, where 9 million cases of 7UP were sold annually, to a small Australian "outback" station with sales of a few thousand cases.

Current goals were to again double sales volume within a five-year span, while continuing to contribute 10 percent of overall company profit. To achieve those goals, International's program was to concentrate increasing advertising and promotion efforts on markets in developed countries in an effort to reduce dependency on Mexico and Argentina. One analyst estimated the geographical breakdown of sales to be 80 percent in Latin America, 8 percent in Europe, and 12 percent in other areas.

Seven-Up International was organized into seven regions each headed by a regional director bearing profit responsibility. While in some cases marketing activities could be performed regionally (as in the case of the Andean or Benelux countries), more often it had to be done on a country-by-country basis. Moreover, it was not possible to transfer marketing themes directly from the domestic to international markets. Aside from language problems, colas were not necessarily the primary soft drink within foreign countries so that the Seven-Up Uncola and "UNdo it!" campaigns were not applicable. A small marketing staff in the United States provided services to the regional directors; this staff was comprised of a vice president of marketing to whom the two coordinators of market planning and of marketing services reported. Chuck Thies commented: "The whole structure is not entirely defined. We hope to grow to the point of having a regular market function within each region. For this reason, the regional director may have quite a bit of marketing autonomy."

Overseas franchise agreements varied from country to country, depending upon what Seven-Up could negotiate. However, they typically included quotas for a minimum percentage of sales growth and spending in support of the brand, a percentage figure regarding distribution penetration, and a time of agreement which ranged from five to ten years. In general these terms were similar to those employed by the two leading cola companies. Seven-Up International felt that some of the advantages of potential franchisee gained when working with Seven-Up were that the prices charged for extract were more reasonable and that the franchisee was allowed much more autonomy, in developing the local market.

Most industry analysts noted that the key to success in the international markets was a strong and committed local bottler. For this reason Seven-Up recently had been giving increasing attention to signing on very successful bottlers. This represented, however, one of International's greatest challenges. Chuck Thies explained: "In most developed markets, there are fewer and fewer available bottlers, so the opportunity to go with one of them is reduced. If you don't fit with their product portfolio, they are simply not interested. A bottler can't start out with 7UP alone anymore because it simply is not profitable to bottle only one drink and have only one brand riding in your trucks given the relatively small size of most of the markets. In Sao Paulo, for example, trucks carry rum along with 7UP; and in Holland, though this is dying out, 7UP is sold from milk trucks. Furthermore," he added, "Coke has the ability to use economic leverage to preserve fidelity among its bottlers abroad." He cited the case of a South African bottler who had owned franchises for Coke, Schweppes, Canada Dry, Pepsi, and 7UP. Coke bought out the franchise, retained the Coke, Schweppes, and Canada Dry franchises, and eliminated Pepsi and 7UP.

This type of situation sometimes left Seven-Up International in the position of having to deal with less-than-optimal franchisees. In cases where the bottlers were not strongly motivated or did not have the financial strength to properly develop the market, Seven-Up management staff worked with them to develop marketing plans and contributed sometimes as much as 80 percent of initial marketing expenditures. If all else failed the company tried to renegotiate the franchise. In the past Seven-Up had made a policy of not owning any franchises abroad in deference to the nationalism of various countries. In 1976, however, Thies felt they would consider investing in an enterprise in a country with a stable currency.

In 1977 International planned to "attack" seven or eight "threshold" markets similar to the programs unleashed in London and Sydney, Australia, in 1976. "Beachheads" would be established in the city's metropolitan area and then distribution would fan out from this established basis. In the United Kingdom the "beachhead" agreement was with the Schweppes organization in London. Initial efforts were quite successful, aided by a long, dry summer season. There were, however, still some problems to be worked out. Schweppes, being a mixer company, did not have production or "glass" capacity to produce larger bottle sizes and the range of packages consumers desired. Nor did Schweppes bring to the arrangement a particularly strong distribution system within food stores due to the nature of their own line of products.

Even in threshold markets like London, it was difficult for Seven-Up to conscientiously spend as much money as it felt it should for effective market entry. Mr. Thies explained that the amount of money the company spent to develop a market depended upon primarily two elements—reach and availability. "Reach" referred to the cost of reaching people through the media, promotions, and so forth; and "availability" referred to the availability of product or the percentage of outlets which offered 7UP. The reach figures varied dramatically from country to country depending upon general economic conditions. Availability of product most often depended upon the capacity of the bottler. While both favorable reach and availability figures had to coexist for Seven-Up to be able to justify marketing expenditures in an area, most frequently availability proved the critical factor.

Chuck Thies stressed two other key factors impacting international operation: investment considerations and local and international competition. With regard to investment, he was interested in the "break-even" period for the company and Seven-Up's ability to bring home profits. "In countries which are unstable, the break-even period acceptable to us is quite a bit shorter than say in Scandinavia where we are willing to wait three or four years."

Naturally, competition was also critical for 7UP's performance in a given market. Often when 7UP entered a foreign market, rapid expansion was inhibited by the presence of local, less expensive lemon-lime-flavored products. 7UP's primary advantage over these products was its high quality, though this necessitated higher costs as well. In terms of the colas, 7UP was at something of a disadvantage in that its taste was more fragile and could vary greatly according to the quality of the water and of the sugar used in its production. The major international competitors of 7UP were Pepsi and Coke.

PepsiCo International provided technical and marketing assistance to 534 franchised and 21 company-owned facilities in 134 countries around the world. Pepsi's strongest operations were in Central and South America and Eastern Europe. Pepsi was also active in the Middle East where Coca-Cola was under Arab boycott pressure.

It was estimated that 46 percent of Pepsi's 1975 gallonage came from overseas markets, with 22 percent sold in Latin America. Estimates of foreign unit growth approached 6½ percent, as compared with domestic growth rates of 3½ percent. By 1975 Diet Pepsi had been introduced in 28 areas in six different countries. Along with its Pepsi line, the company marketed abroad a Miranda line of flavor beverages as well as a pure juice product. Since 1965 Pepsi-Cola sales had increased 293 percent; this performance was greatly exceeded, however, by the Miranda flavor line which grew 563 percent in the same period.

Coca-Cola, the dominant international firm, sold its product in 134 countries around the world, through 750 bottlers, 16 of whom were company owned. An estimated 44 percent of Coke's sales dollars and 55 percent of its earnings came from international operations. Coke made it evident that the country intended to take a long-range view of market opportunities. Efforts were underway to imprint Coke as a brand name, even in some countries where the drink was not yet available. In 1976, for example, Coke launched a program promoting soccer clinics and games for children in Africa and the Middle East which was expected to cost the company about $5 million over the next few years.

Coca-Cola, it appeared, was trying to break into the Egyptian market. Two of its subsidiaries, some journalists noted, made the company increasingly interesting to Egypt: The Foods Division and Aqua-Chem, Inc., which manufactured water purification equipment. Both divisions could provide technology sought after by the Arab countries. In addition, because Coke was so diversified geographically, some maintained that it would not be so badly hurt as other soft drink companies by currency complications. Coke was the only major producer, for example, to be strong in both Latin America and in the more stable, developed markets of Europe.

Chuck Thies talked with the researcher about a decision which he believed highlighted the complexities of developing overseas markets.

> Should we enter the Cairo market? It has a population of approximately ten million and would be relatively inexpensive in terms of "reach" costs for Seven-Up—perhaps $50,000 the first year. But the Egyptian pound is a "soft" currency, and it is a major problem getting money out because of Egypt's balance of trade problems.
>
> One way to handle this difficulty would be for Seven-Up to plough back its share of whatever money the bottler made the first year into marketing expenditures to develop the brand. By the second year we might expect something in hard currency with more to come the third year—providing the Egyptian economy didn't turn down. The investment problem is exacerbated since initially the franchise would probably have to purchase bottling equipment outside of Egypt for hard currency. One possible device might be for the local investor to manufacture glass for export to bring in hard currency income with which to make the initial capital investment and to buy extract from us.
>
> There is a soft drink vacuum in Cairo. Currently, U.S. soft drinks are being black-marketed, which suggests a strong demand for quality soft drinks. Labor is relatively inexpensive; and, therefore, distribution costs would not be a problem. Coke is presently making every effort to enter the market, while Pepsi which had owned a plant in Egypt has been nationalized. All of these factors spell "opportunity." However, it's a gamble because the real opportunity lies ahead: Anyone reporting to shareholders

reports on the basis of what they can see, and in U.S. dollars. To enter Cairo you have to gamble on the Egyptian economy. Coke could afford to make a mistake here, or could even do it wrong the first time and come in and do it right a second time; Seven-Up could not. Should we try?

Finance

Paul H. Young, executive vice president and treasurer, spoke with the researchers about his association with the company and critical company financial policies.

> This is a fine company. One of the reasons it has been so successful is that everyone here lives and breathes 7UP; no one here has taken a bath in it, but they are dedicated. And that dedication to 7UP has kept us from going into other distant fields. We are not going to acquire just any type of company.

Since becoming a public company in 1967, Seven-Up had traded on the over-the-counter market. Approximately 55 percent of the equity was still owned by families of the co-founders. With a relatively small float and a trading volume that averaged between 150–250,000 shares per month, Seven-Up stock prices had been relatively volatile. Company objectives for its shareholders were to achieve share price appreciation and provide a fair dividend. A 40 percent dividend payout ratio had been typical at Seven-Up. Expansion had been financed almost entirely through internally generated funds, and Mr. Young noted that one of the company's major short-run concerns was "protection against unsound capital utilization." To guard against such an event, all capital decisions involving $100,000 or more are referred to the board of directors for financial justification. "We have the best rate of return on reinvestment of any company in the industry."

Capital expenditures for property, plant, and equipment, orchards development and acquisition investment amounted to approximately $9 million in 1973, $7 million in 1974, and $7 million in 1975. Approximately 45 percent of the total 1975 expenditures were allocated to the development of nonsoft drink product group facilities. Estimated 1976 capital expenditures were $8.5 million with 80 percent being allocated to soft drink product group facilities, primarily a new bottling and canning facility for the company-owned Phoenix operation.

Technical

Seven-Up maintained strict quality evaluations of all franchised bottling plants. The plants were monitored by the technical field service group, 11 people who worked directly with the bottlers. Said Dr. B. C. Cole, vice president and technical director, "It's our goal to see that all Seven-Up bottling plants are in such sanitary condition and operate with such sanitary controls that they need not fear, in fact, they may even look forward to visits by state and federal inspectors because of the control programs and plant evaluation program we have which outline what we consider good manufacturing practices." The company had set up a rigid system of quality specifications that culminated in an award for those sites which met the standards, and bottlers competed vigorously to achieve this symbol of high-quality maintenance. During the past 30 years the company had terminated few franchise agreements.

Pertinent to the subject of diet drinks, Cole explained that saccharin was approximately 300 times as sweet as sugar; cyclamates 30 times as sweet; and research was being done presently on the usage of high fructose sugars which were 140 times as sweet as ordinary table sugar. The high fructose sugars were produced from any starchy material, such as potatoes, wheat, barley, or corn. Their advantages lay in the facts that once fully developed, they would be readily obtainable from materials within this country, and that they could be used in place of ordinary sugars to lower the calorie level of soft drinks without lowering the sweetness level.

In light of the dynamic future predicted for another new form of product, powdered drinks, the researchers asked Dr. Cole about the possible development of a carbonated 7UP soft drink in powdered form. He responded:

> To the best of my knowledge you'd have to revise the nature of the laws of the solubility of gasses (CO_2) in water to do that. Unless you put the mixture under pressure, you can't stir in the carbonation, or get it in any way other than by packing it in under pressure as we do now. Not even adding dry ice pellets, which are pure CO_2, could you get the mixture carbonated beyond a level of one volume. 7UP is presently carbonated at a level of 3.7 volumes.
>
> Now people have been doing things with powdered drinks and they have not done them because they had an equal carbonation and an equal product, but because there are lots of people who will mix it up readily . . . it's a good product. It is not a carbonated soft drink; it is a drink of a different character.

The researcher learned from Dr. Cole that 7UP at a carbonation level of volume one tasted much the same as any soft drink that had lost most of its carbonation: flat, without sparkle, watered down. Cole added, "7UP is designed to be carbonated, and if we were going to make it to be used as a noncarbonated product, we'd have to change its flavor constituents quite a lot."

Another research subject broached with Dr. Cole was that of nutritive drinks such as Hustle (Dr Pepper). His response was:

> It is not the purpose of the carbonated soft drink industry to supply to the consumer a balanced diet. In fact, it is not the purpose of the soft drink industry to supply health foods.

Undoubtedly in the life of each person there should be some happiness and enjoyment. Carbonated beverages fit into this field. They are fun products and were never designed to supplement the diet or to replace foods commonly called "nutritious foods."

Soybean-based beverages constitute an excellent source of protein, but they are not carbonated soft drinks at all; they are now more like beef broth or something. We are now talking about a way to supply nutritious materials to people who are underfed.

Dr. Cole added that in his own personal opinion it would be much less costly to distribute a nutritive product in a dry, concentrated form rather than to package it in bottles which had to be washed, sterilized, and so forth, if one's goal were to provide economical, balanced diets to poverty-level consumers.

case 11

The Seven–Up Company (B)

"Powders are an exciting and expanding part of our industry, and they pose some key strategic and operating challenges for us," Clark Russell, staff director for new products, commented. Mr. Russell had returned recently to Seven-Up after an eight-year marketing assignment with a major consumer goods company. Prior to this assignment, he worked for Mr. Kidwell.

We have a great executive team here, willing to tackle the tough decisions. Bill and John are great strategists—and more important, great guys with high ethical standards.

Golden Crown did some experimenting last year with the powders field. They introduced Golden Crown Old-Fashioned Lemonade Flavor in an 8-quart setup in five test markets from Boston to Los Angeles, and the results were very encouraging.

Powdered soft drink mixes are the fastest growing segment of the beverage market and clearly are some of the fastest growth items for the grocery trade. Trade sources attribute their exploding sales to their relative per ounce economy, their convenience in packaging and storage, and the growing number of "improved" flavors. I would add some massive advertising; one leading firm plans to distribute 50 million coupons next year.

And, it is a field controlled by the big multiline companies—General Foods (Kool-Aid) and Borden (Wyler's) followed by RJR (Hawaiian Punch) and Pillsbury (Funny Face and Squoze). Squoze is an interesting new entry since it is a sugar plus an artificial sweetener; powder came either sugar presweetened or without sugar. Minor brands and private labels hold only ten percent of the market.

The question now is do we really move into this game? I came into this decision on the late side; Golden Crown is an entrepreneurial operation, and their management has submitted a proposed plan to us [see Exhibit 1 for summary of this plan]. Their market strategy is pretty straightforward. They plan to introduce a line of five flavors—orange, grape, lemonade, cherry, and fruit punch—in a 10-quart container for the home market. The powder would be priced under national brands and at the level of private brands. They would do a minimum of advertising and use traditional promotional tools of extended datings, free goods, and coupons.

They would plan on going national using ex-Wyler and ReaLemon food brokers, who would deal directly with the trade. These brokers are available since their previous manufacturers had switched to a direct sales program.

And they are good, too—Golden Crown used them successfully in the test market campaign. If they go ahead, I would still urge them to "beef up" their own field sales force. Manufacturing is no problem since, with the exception of General Foods, all powdered drink mixes are packed by specialist companies who do this for the trade. It is not unusual to go into a co-packer's plant and see several competitive brands being packed on various lines. And, the market just seems to go up and up. Should we push ahead? Is this the right track?

In another interview with the researchers, Mr. Kidwell commented, "I think it is an excellent idea to be in powders, but it does raise operating and strategic questions for us. Surely someday we will be able to get carbonation in a pill, or the problem will be licked another way. It just doesn't make economic sense to haul sweetened water and heavy cans and bottles around. And how much longer will the industry be able to hire driver-salespeople? Who will want to do the heavy, routine work of loading and unloading cases all day? Plastic containers must come, too."

EXHIBIT 1
Summary of soft drink mix proposal

Our objective would be to introduce a full line of Golden Crown Soft Drink Mixes into major markets with a minimal amount of investment spending. Below is a summary of projected operating results:

Net sales	$3,912,600	100.0%
Cost of sales	3,023,200	77.3
Gross profit	$ 889,400	22.7%
Operating expenses:		
Marketing	$ 804,100	20.6%
General and administrative	46,500	1.2
Total expenses	$ 850,600	21.8%
Operating profit	$ 38,800	0.9%
Interest expense	47,200	1.2
Profit before taxes	$ (8,400)	(0.3)%

Market objective

In order to develop a viable marketing plan, we have to determine our position in the marketplace. We have concluded that Golden Crown does not have sufficient brand identity to support a full-scale advertising campaign. On the other hand, our brand is not entirely without recognition. This year over 9 million units were sold under the Golden Crown label; and in many areas, it appears in over 80 percent of the retail outlets.

Consequently, we propose that in our next campaign Golden Crown should be

EXHIBIT 1 (continued)

positioned at the $1.49–$1.59 retail level, featuring a 10-quart can and allowing the seller to realize gross profits of 31–35 percent.

To accomplish this end, we would establish a list price of $16.44 per case, which converts to a retail price of $1.69 as compared to projected retails (based on list price) of $1.89 for Kool-Aid and $1.99 for Country Time.

Our guaranteed season-long (ending 8/31) promotional allowance would reduce our price to $12.33 per case as compared to $14.64 for Kool-Aid (net of promotions), and should convert to retails of $1.49 (31 percent) for Golden Crown as opposed to $1.69 (28 percent) for Kool-Aid.

By positioning Golden Crown against Kool-Aid (10-quart canister), we will avoid the price cutting that is certain to prevail among the remaining companies' 8-quart brands. Our final objective would be not to replace any of the high-flyers but to obtain sufficient sales to provide a base for expanded advertising and brand awareness in 1978 and 1979.

Introductory plans

Because the season is relatively short and opportunities for presentation to buyers limited, the first offer would provide a program that cannot be refused.

Golden Crown would present structured offers of "one case free with one case purchased" in controlled quantities. This half-price offer, coupled with the gross margin support indicated earlier, should assure us of distribution and follow-up support. As an alternate to this type of introductory offer, we would structure a second offering that would give the retailer a fixed reduced price throughout the introductory period and would be equitable to our other offers.

All introductory programs would be scheduled to expire on May 1. To encourage early placement, we would offer extended dating (standard trade practice) and an on-label 20 cents coupon for all products shipped before May 1. We would anticipate a 25–30 percent redemption of these coupons, and our budget would include a provision for $50,000 under promotional allowance to provide for these redemptions.

Follow-up sales

As indicated earlier, our follow-up deal would offer "one case free with three cases purchased" at the $16.44 per case price. This nets down to $12.33 per case. With late introductions last year, we experienced between two and three turns on our introductory sales. Our budget projects distribution of 80,000 cases with follow-up sales of 240,000 cases. At this level, we would be close to break-even.

To encourage additional purchasing and promotion by our customers, we would develop a plan that offered a rebate of 50 cents per case on all shipments once a predetermined level has been reached. The established quotas would be set at levels equivalent to five times the introductory order; and if they are attained, the quotas will provide Golden Crown with substantial profitability.

As an incentive to the brokers, a bonus would be offered for each account in their territory that meets its quota. In addition to the broker's incentive, a bonus plan would be offered to our regional sales managers related to the broker's performance.

EXHIBIT 1 (continued)

Included in the budgeted promotional expense is a provision of $105,000 to cover these additional promotional costs.

Advertising

We do not foresee any problems in securing the initial distribution as outlined above. With proper pricing by the retailer, together with our on-label coupon, we feel that we can expect meaningful consumer support. However, this response may not be sufficient enough to provide us with a successful season. In addition to trade promotions, we must have some advertising support. Following is an outline of advertising plans that are included in our budget:

```
Coupon ads:
    May ...................... $25,000
    June  ....................   30,000
    July  ....................   30,000
         Total ads  ........... $85,000
    Estimated
       redemptions ...........   40,000
         Total coupon ads  .................... $125,000
TV game shows ...........................   20,000
Miscellaneous..............................   10,000
Budgeted advertising expense...............  155,000
```

At the end of the introductory period, we plan to review our distribution and evaluate these advertising plans.

Financial requirements

Preestablished practices in this product category dictate that all early orders receive extended payment terms. Because we would be the new entrant into the field, we must offer a sufficient time period to allow the customer to establish movement of our product. Also, due to the fact that our product is being packed by co-packers, we must invest in large inventories. We estimate that we will be drawing funds during the early part of the season to cover inventory needs and extended sales terms. Following is a tentative schedule of our needs:

```
March ........................... $500,000
April .............................   700,000
May  .............................   500,000
June..............................   300,000
```

Repayment is projected for the period July through September.

Long-range plans

If we meet the unit sales objectives that are set forth in this plan, then we can look forward to appreciable growth in unit sales with a decreasing amount of promotional expense in future years.

Other new products

In past years, we have marketed Golden Crown frozen concentrate for lemonade. Primarily, this product was distributed to customers of Ventura Coastal Cor-

EXHIBIT 1 (concluded)

poration as a substitution for other labels. With the strengthening of the Sunkist label in this category and the entry of Country Time into a frozen product, we feel that consideration should be given to developing a new Golden Crown Old-Fashioned Lemonade Concentrate.

Another product that we have been looking into, is a powdered breakfast orange. We are monitoring the market and feel that this might be a possibility for introduction in 1978.

case 12

Polaroid-Kodak

INTRODUCTION

On April 20, 1976, Eastman Kodak Company announced that it would challenge Polaroid Corporation's 28-year-old monopoly of the instant photographic field. At a press conference held that day in the grand ballroom of the Pierre Hotel in New York City, Walter A. Fallon, president of Kodak, personally demonstrated two new cameras and an instant film which he spoke of as offering "remarkable color quality" to the consumer. Dr. Albert Sieg, leader of the company's seven-year-long development effort, stated that the chemistry of the new film was "fundamentally new."

The earliest responses from Polaroid Corporation were varied. Several days prior to the Kodak announcement one Polaroid employee was quoted in the press as saying, "I've seen it. It's primitive, but it works." Later, on the afternoon of the Kodak demonstration, Polaroid issued a formal statement:

> We have had a chance to make a brief comparison between the Polaroid instant picture system and the new Kodak system. The comparison renews our confidence that our leadership in the field of instant photography remains unchallenged.

At the Polaroid annual meeting, held one week after the Kodak announcement, Edwin Land, founder, director of research and chairman of the board of the company, informed his stockholders that their company had filed suit in Federal Court charging Kodak with the infringement of ten Polaroid patents. In an emotion-laden session, during which there were periods of prolonged applause from the crowd, Land commented on the situation:

> This is our very soul that we are involved with. This is our whole life. For them it's just just another field. . . . The only thing that keeps us alive is our brilliance, and the only thing protecting our brilliance is our patents. . . . We will stay in our lot and protect that lot . . . (it is) an overlap of

their way onto our way. How serious this is remains to be seen. That's for the courts to decide.[1]

Land continued, in a session that some reporters described as being a strange blend of ridicule and outrage, to comment that since the introduction of the Kodak system Polaroid had been "in a state of euphoria" and that their real fear had been that Kodak's product "might incorporate some of the really brilliant ideas we've had but never incorporated ourselves," and that "the new guys would like to confine its use to cocktail parties."[2]

Other events at the Polaroid annual meeting centered on several new products now in the late planning or preproduction stages; among these were instant color transparencies; instant color movies; an 8- by 10-inch instant camera and film; and, finally, a camera the size of a room for making full color, instant, life-size copies of museum paintings that, in Land's words, ". . . will change the whole world of Art . . . make great paintings available in every high school . . . (and) bring museums into the home."[3] Land also demonstrated an improved SX-70 film incorporating a coating to reduce surface reflections as well as the ability to develop properly over a wider temperature range.

POLAROID CORPORATION

Origins and growth

In 1949 the first full year of sales for the Polaroid camera (a 5-pound, $90, revolutionary product that produced brown-and-white pictures one minute after exposure), the firm's sales more than quadrupled (to $6.7 million) over those of the previous year. Twenty-seven years later the company's sales broke the $800 million mark, proving to all the skeptics that what they had considered a mere fad was, in fact, one of the most dramatic achievements in the history of photography. In the 28-year period, from 1947 to 1975, Polaroid's sales grew at an average annual compounded rate of over 25 percent (see Exhibit 1), while profits and common stock price advanced by more than 17 percent per year (see Exhibit 2). In an accomplishment matched by only a handful of companies, Polaroid's average price-earnings ratio during this entire period was 44. By 1969 each dollar invested in Polaroid common stock in 1948 had grown to more than $500. This consistent and clearly outstanding financial performance could be broken down into several distinct phases.

Although for most people the story of Polaroid began in Boston, Massa-

---

[1] *The New York Times*, April 24, 1976.
[2] *The Wall Street Journal*, April 28, 1976.
[3] *The Boston Globe*, April 28, 1976.

EXHIBIT 1

Polaroid Corporation, summary of sales, 1948–1975

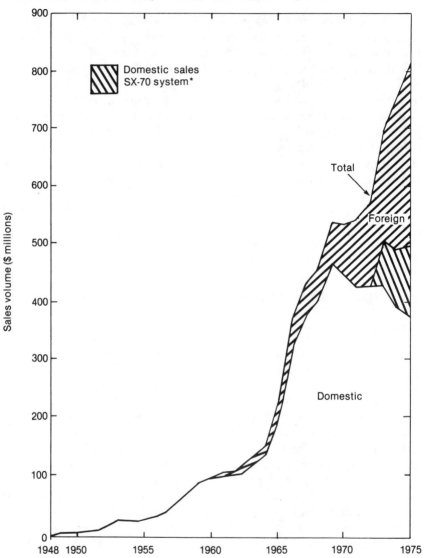

Casewriter's estimate.
Source: Company annual reports.

EXHIBIT 2

Polaroid, summary of EPS and stock price, 1948–1975

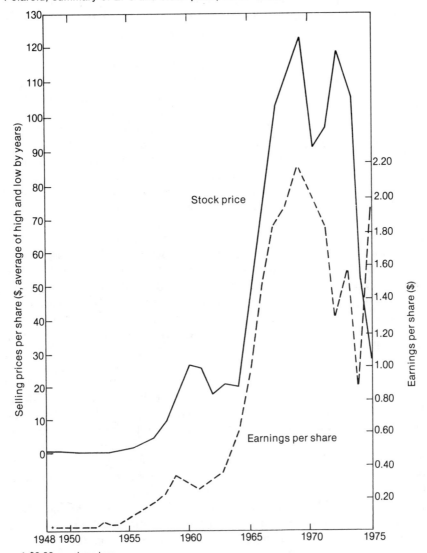

* $0.32 per share loss.
Sources: Company annual reports, Merrill Lynch, Inc., historical library.

chusetts, in November 1948 with the first retail sales of the now famous "picture-in-a-minute" Polaroid Land Camera, in reality Polaroid (or more accurately Edwin Land) had been in business for almost 20 years by that time. Land's initial research, begun when he was a freshman at Harvard University in 1926, was with means of polarizing light. In 1932 he and an associate created the Land-Wheelwright Laboratories, Inc., to develop, manufacture, and sell light polarizing filters. The company's first product was the "Polaroid" filter; the name Polaroid was derived from the fact that the filter was composed of cellul*oid* material which *pola*rized light.

The first two customers of any great size for Land and Wheelwright were Eastman Kodak Company, which signed a contract in 1934 for the purchase of "Polascreens," and American Optical Company, which signed a contract in 1935 for the purchase of filter material to be used in "Polaroid Day Glasses" (sunglasses). The money from these contracts provided the young company with funds to continue its development of Polaroid filter products. An additional $750,000 supplied by two investment banking firms in 1937 (in the form of a private placement) enabled the company to continue its search for profitable applications for the filter. At that time, the most promising applications appeared to be in 3-D movies (which required special polarized glasses to be worn by each viewer) and automobile headlights and windshields (where it was thought the product could reduce the glare from the headlights of oncoming vehicles at night).

Polaroid's sales grew from $142,000 in 1937 to $1.481 million in 1948, most of the increase represented by sales of Polaroid filter material for use in sunglasses.[4] The company was never successful with its plans to have polarizing filters used in movies, automobiles, and elsewhere to the extent originally evisioned. This resulted in a much smaller company than Edwin Land appeared to be comfortable with. Late in 1943 Land began working on the ideas that would form the basis for an "instant" photographic process and camera. His first patent application on the topic appears to have been made in June 1944, and by that time work on the Land Camera must have been underway at Polaroid. In 1945, by means of a rights offering to existing, stockholders, $2 million was raised by the company.

From 1947 to 1962 Polaroid's revolutionary instant photographic product was essentially a black-and-white print system for amateur use. While as first introduced the product was far from perfect by comparison with conventional materials, it did, however, offer the consumer a way of making pictures that was truly unique. Until 1950 the large bulky roll film camera could produce only sepia (brown-and-white) pictures of sometimes uneven quality from a film of comparatively low ASA speed. In May 1950, however, the company introduced a true black-and-white film with an ASA speed of

---

[4] The casewriter has excluded sales made to the government during World War II.

100. In 1955 panchromatic films with ASA speeds of 200 and 400 were introduced. In 1959 a black-and-white film with an ASA speed of 3000 was introduced. This last improvement in the company's film was three times as fast as any other black-and-white print film available to amateurs at the time. It allowed most pictures to be taken with existing light, even those taken indoors at night.

In 1960 the development time to obtain a finished print was reduced for all films from the original 60 seconds to 10 seconds. Also in 1960 the company introduced its first camera with automatic exposure control. By the end of 1962 the company had sold 4 million Polaroid cameras in its 15-year history as a photographic products company. See Appendix A for information on the market for amateur photographic products.

Major strategic policies

During its exploitation of the market for its black-and-white instant photographic system, Polaroid's financial strategy appeared to be to always preserve capital for investment in the aspects of its business that would yield the highest possible returns. Plants and equipment were usually rented or leased; camera manufacture was always subcontracted to others; and negative material, although developed by Polaroid itself, was always purchased under long-term contracts from Eastman Kodak. Capital investments were made only in the critical or truly proprietary aspects of manufacturing. The company never made any significant use of long-term debt.

In the marketplace, the company reached out directly to the consumer by advertising. Dealers and distributors were looked upon merely as means to deliver the product to the consumer—as passive rather than active participants in the sales cycle. Industry observers were always amazed by the company's willingness to have its products sold at nearly cost by outlets which used them to build retail traffic. The company shied away from distributors and concentrated on direct sales to large retailers. Moreover, the company never appeared to be concerned by the high turnover in its sales staff which, in the opinion of many observers, it treated more as order-takers than true salespeople. Rarely, if ever, did the company utilize sales incentives for dealers in the form of co-op advertising programs, mixed-case discounts, or introductory specials. In terms of the product itself, the company frequently surprised the market with sudden introductions of improvements in the product. Generally available on an allocated basis to dealers during the first few months following their introduction, these improvements quite often left dealers with merchandise which they had to dispose of as best they could, before they were able to replace it with the newer form.

With respect to the other companies in the industry, Polaroid remained apart. It never licensed others to manufacture cameras for its highly profitable films. Indeed, the company built an extensive wall of patent protection about its camera designs and diligently defended its position as the sole manufacturer of instant cameras and films in any form whatsoever.

Perhaps most important, the company never appeared to be interested in diversification at all. Every product introduced since 1948 related solely to the photographic process in its instant form. The company never gave any public indication of any interest in any other activity.

An important aspect of Polaroid was always Edwin Land's total involvement and identification with his company, of which he owned about 20 percent during the early 1960s. Land's management style seemed to some outsiders to be almost more a form of philosophy than anything else. Annual meetings at Polaroid were always a unique experience for stockholders; sales and earnings figures were hardly ever mentioned. At typical meetings Land would demonstrate one or more new products or processes he and his large research team had developed. Most often these demonstrations, which in many cases were much like seminars or lectures, were totally unrelated to the products the company intended to introduce in the future. From time to time Land would remind his stockholders why Polaroid existed: "Our function is to sense a deep human need . . . then satisfy it. . . . Our company has been dedicated throughout its life to making only those things which others cannot make. . . . We proceed from basic science to highly desirable products."

Results by 1962

By 1962 Polaroid's financial success over the last 15 years had been impressive. Since 1947 sales had grown by an average of 42 percent per year compounded, profits by 25 percent per year, and the common stock price had advanced at a rate of some 41 percent per year. By the end of 1962 Polaroid had become the second largest photographic products company in the United States. However, also by this time sales had remained almost level for the third year in a row, implying that Polaroid had perhaps saturated the market for its black-and-white product in all its forms (amateur roll films, professional sheet films, X-ray film, and transparencies) and that the total market was not growing very rapidly.

The introduction of instant color

On January 28, 1963, the stock market analysts' dreams were answered: Polaroid introduced a color print film with a development time of 60 seconds. First sold on a limited basis in the Miami, Florida, area, the film was compatible with all existing Polaroid cameras. As with the earlier black-and-white system, this product was another major technological achievement for the company. Prior to Polacolor, color film processing and printing required more than 20 steps and 93 minutes. The new Polacolor film not only offered color to the owners of Polaroid cameras but it also produced its own protective plastic coating as a part of the development process. At that time all of Polaroid's black-and-white films required the application of a protective coating by hand, a messy and often difficult procedure for many amateur photographers.

In June of 1963 the company introduced film in convenient packs in both the ASA 3000 speed black-and-white print and Polacolor types, designed to be used with a new automatic exposure Colorpack camera, the Automatic 100, priced at $100 retail. Following much of the same strategy it had used with black and white, the company gradually reduced the prices of its cameras. In 1964 a lower priced version of the Colorpack was introduced at a suggested list price of $75, followed a year later by a full line of cameras carrying suggested list prices ranging from $50 up to more than $150. In 1967 a second generation of Colorpack cameras was introduced with slightly lower prices overall. In April 1969 the company introduced its first truly low-priced camera, the $29.95 Colorpack. All of these cameras used Polacolor film, ASA speed 75, in the same easy-to-load pack size.

During this same period the company began to emphasize foreign sales of its products, where selling strategy closely followed that employed domestically (see Exhibit 1).

In an effort to gain distribution for its products in drugstores, supermarkets, and other unconventional photo outlets, in 1965 the company introduced its Swinger camera and film. Swinger was a $19.95 (list price) semiautomatic exposure, fixed-focus, plastic-bodied camera that used a low-cost black-and-white roll film which did not require coating after processing. Several million of these cameras were sold in just three years. In 1968 the company completely phased out the Swinger by introducing its Big Swinger at a suggested list price of $24.95. The Big Swinger was identical in every respect to the previous model, with the exception of price and the fact that it used ASA 3000 speed film in the same packs as Polaroid's other cameras. In 1969 the introduction of the Colorpack camera, which listed for only $5 more than the Big Swinger, virtually halted all sales of the latter. The Colorpack offered fully automatic exposure and the ability to use Polacolor film at a retail price differential of about $3 on the average. By 1970 all traces of the Swinger and Big Swinger had been removed from retailers' shelves. Even the roll film for the original Swinger became almost impossible to obtain.

Results by 1972

As with the previous success in black and white, color caused explosive growth at Polaroid. By 1969, however, the company was facing softness in the demand for its products once again as may be seen from Exhibit 1. Fortunately for the company, during this period foreign sales expanded rapidly as a result of the gradual introduction of the same products which had given the company its growth in the domestic market during the 1960s.

The SX-70 system is introduced

In November 1969 Polaroid, through a rights offering to existing stockholders, raised $99 million. The prospectus stated that the company was about to undertake another step in its search for the absolute form of one-step photography: the money was to be used to help finance the research, development, and manufacture of a totally new instant color film and camera system. Just a little more than three years later, in November of 1972, the first SX-70 cameras and film went on limited sale in the Miami, Florida, area. The camera, available in only one model, carried a suggested list price of $180, six times that of the company's Colorpack model, while the film was priced at $6.90 (list) for ten exposures, compared with $5.49 for Polacolor pack film's eight exposures.

Shrouded in the greatest of secrecy from the beginning of its design, the SX-70 system was another truly revolutionary product. The company had designed a product that was intended to alter the fundamentals of the industry and eventually make obsolete both earlier instant camera systems, that is, roll and pack film types. In Land's own words, "Photography will never be the same ... with the gargantuan effort of bringing SX-70 into being, the company has come fully of age." With a romantic flair that only he (Land) could fully have appreciated, the name SX-70 was chosen because it had been the code name of the original camera project in 1944.

From the consumer's point of view the SX-70 was indeed a different kind of Polaroid camera and film. What had previously generated large quantities of chemically coated waste paper, for example, used negative material and related paper goods, was now a totally litter-free system. Of perhaps equal importance, there was now no need to time the development of the picture. Other features included automatic ejection of the picture from the camera by a small electric motor (powered by a fresh battery present in each film pack), single-lens reflex viewing and focusing, a folding design that allowed the camera to be carried conveniently in a large pocket or purse, and less need for periodic cleaning of critical mechanical components inside the camera. See Appendix B for a more detailed explanation of the differences between the Colorpack and SX-70 systems.

The SX-70 program

As originally conceived, the SX-70 program was designed to accomplish two major changes at Polaroid. The first of these was the total integration of the company. All of the manufacturing for SX-70 would be carried out within Polaroid. Towards this end, a color negative manufacturing plant and camera assembly plant were designed and built. The program also required an expansion of the firm's existing chemical production facilities and film packaging operation. The total cost of these additions to plant and equipment were estimated, by most observers in 1969, to be about $150 million, including the cost of research and engineering for the SX-70 camera and film.

Although the company never formally disclosed the cost of the SX-70 program, Land once referred to it in an interview as "a half-billion-dollar investment." Some outside estimates have placed the actual figure at much more than that. Speculations as to the source of the $350 million additional investment requirement have centered on two items. First, the company admitted publicly that it was not until January of 1974 that the SX-70 product was breaking even on a variable manufacturing costs basis. It was not until early 1976 that most outside observers felt that the product was profitable in a conventional normal accounting sense. Several estimates of the total cost of these manufacturing-related expenses center on a figure of about $250 million over the entire period from 1969 to 1976. Second, some outside observers have concluded that the design and development costs of the film and, most notably, the camera were much higher than anticipated. Both of these factors were related to the second major change SX-70 was intended to bring to Polaroid—the perfection of photography.

For Edwin Land, SX-70 was the realization of a dream, not merely a new product. He often referred to it as "absolute one-step photography." As he stated in a booklet entitled *The SX-70 Experience* (included with the annual report for shareholders in 1974):

> A new kind of relationship between people in groups is brought into being by SX-70 when the members of the group are photographing and being photographed and sharing the photographs: it turns out that buried within us—God knows beneath how many pregenital and Freudian and Calvinistic strata—there is a latent interest in each other; there is tenderness, curiosity, excitement, affection, companionability, and humor; it turns out, in this cold world where man grows distant from man and even lovers can reach each other only briefly, that we have a yen for a primordial competence, for a quiet good-humored delight in each other; we have a prehistoric tribal competence for a non-physical, non-emotional, non-sexual satisfaction in being partners in the lonely exploration of a once empty planet.

Thus at age 63, Edwin Land brought into existence his highly personalized message to civilization in the form of the SX-70 system.

The design criteria for the SX-70 had been very straightforward: The photographer must have only to compose a picture and press a button—the photographic process was to be totally segregated from the creative act.

In real terms this philosophical task created a number of problems for designers. Rather than use the company's successful $30 Colorpack camera as a starting point, Land ordered his engineers to start from scratch on a totally new design. The parameters of the camera were startling: it must fold to a size appropriate for a pocket or purse; it must be a single-lens reflex viewing and focusing design; it must focus from less than a foot to infinity; and it must be totally automatic (exposure, processing, etc.) and litter-free.

The result, after more than three years of intense development work was a $180 masterpiece of design. The reflex viewing system alone cost millions; a single mirror, one of three in the camera, took over two and one-half years of full-time computer work to engineer. The eyepiece design alone cost $2 million to develop. Company sales projections of at least several million cameras (up to 5 million by some accounts) to be sold the first year alone were used as the basis for capacity decisions in the plants under construction during the design stage. Long before the camera design was finalized the company's color negative pilot plant began turning out finished packs of SX-70 film.

Marketing the SX-70

In 1973, the first full year of sales for the SX-70 system, 470,000 cameras and 4.5 million packs of film were sold. The company reported that the system had contributed $75 million to its sales that year. During the year the company grappled with several technical problems. The camera factory, still in its infancy, was turning out a disturbing number of defective cameras even though it was operating at only a fraction of its capacity. At one point the company began to open Polaroid service centers in major cities across the United States in an effort to help consumers with their problems.

A more troublesome technical problem was encountered when it was discovered that fumes from the battery present in each film pack (this had been done to eliminate the need for a yearly battery change on the part of users) were seriously degrading the color quality of the pictures. Related in part to this problem was the fact that the battery had a shelf life of only several months at best. After a considerable period of time during which the company worked with the company which manufactured the batteries, Polaroid made the decision to build a plant and produce its own batteries. Within a few months the shelf life of the film was extended to six months and color quality improved dramatically.

By far the greatest problem facing Polaroid by the end of 1973 was the fact that camera sales were nowhere near the projected level. Both camera and film manufacturing operations were running at only a small fraction of their rated capacity. Although the company sold about 4 million Colorpacks and an estimated 100 million packs of Polacolor film in 1973, both negative and camera manufacturing for this product line were subcontracted to others.

In 1974, in an attempt to stimulate SX-70 sales, the company introduced an SX-70 Model II camera. Identical to the original in every respect except for price ($140 suggested retail) and exterior finish (all plastic versus chrome-plated plastic and genuine leather for the original), it was estimated by trade sources that this model helped to boost SX-70 camera sales during 1974 to about 750,000 units. The casewriter's estimate for factory sales of the SX-70 system in 1974 was $100 million domestically.

Faced with continuing resistance to the product from consumers, in May 1975 the company introduced an SX-70 Model III camera which carried a suggested list price of $99. The Model III abandoned the reflex viewing arrangement of the other two models and replaced it with a conventional, and far simpler, viewfinder type. The company reported that it sold a total of about 1 million SX-70 cameras during 1975. The casewriter's estimate for the 1975 sales volume of the SX-70 system was $150 million, about 80 percent of this from domestic sales.

In 1975 the company reported that it had sold about 4 million Colorpack cameras for the third year in a row. In March 1975 the company introduced its Supershooter Colorpack camera at a suggested retail price of $24.95. Also in March the company introduced Polacolor II Colorpack film, which offered the consumer excellent color in an instant product for the first time. Prior to Polacolor II instant prints had tended to be somewhat subdued and lacked saturation as compared to conventional color prints and slides. Both Supershooter and Polacolor II were manufactured by Polaroid in its own plants.

In January 1976 Polaroid introduced a Model IV SX-70 called the Pronto!. Pronto! was a nonfolding, nonreflex, moulded-plastic-body camera with a suggested list price of $66. This model was widely discounted by retailers to $49 (only a few dollars over cost), and by late April 1976 sales and advance orders of Pronto! had exceeded 400,000 units. Industry observers began predicting that during 1976 as many as 2 million SX-70 cameras might be sold.

Polaroid in April 1976

As of April 1976 the suggested retail and common discount prices of the most popular models in each of Polaroid's instant systems were as follows:

	Camera prices		Film prices	
System	List	Discount	List	Discount
SX-70 (Pronto!)	$66	$49	$6.99	$5.50
Colorpack (Supershooter)	28	23	6.75	5.50

There were three major differences between these systems. First, in terms of pricing, while the Supershooter sold for less than half of the price for Pronto!, the cost per print was about 25 percent higher due to the fact that Colorpack film had eight exposures per pack versus ten for SX-70 film. Second, the color quality of the pictures made from Polacolor II film were far superior to those possible with SX-70 film.[5] Polacolor II prints rivaled conventional color prints in quality. Finally, in terms of camera operation, while all the Pronto! user did was to focus and press a button, after which the motor in the camera ejected the print which developed automatically in about 12 minutes with no litter, the Supershooter user had to pull each exposure from the camera, time the development for 60 seconds, and then find a place to dispose of the used negative (which was covered with a highly alkaline processing jelly).

In terms of manufacturing costs each system had contrasting patterns. While both SX-70 film and Polacolor II film were essentially identical in that they both required a negative processing reagent, and print material, each SX-70 pack also required a battery to power the camera's flash, exposure, and print ejection motor. From the perspective of cameras, however, the Pronto! was essentially a Supershooter with a mirror and an electric motor added. These facts led industry observers to speculate as to the actual source of profits from each system as well as to try and predict the degree to which prices could be changed if necessary.

By April 1976 Polaroid had about 25 million Colorpack cameras in use worldwide, as compared with an estimated 2 million SX-70s. Most industry observers agreed that the Colorpack system was the most profitable of the two, contributing at least 95 percent to the company's earnings. See Exhibit 3 for a five-year summary of Polaroid's financial statements, including full data for 1975.

EASTMAN KODAK COMPANY

Origins and growth

George Eastman had a bit of a jump on Edwin Land; he marketed his first camera in 1888. Kodak's motto, "You press the button, we do the rest," and the ubiquitous "yellow box" were revolutionary developments of their time, sweeping America and the world for 60 years before the first Land camera appeared. Kodak was the world's first integrated photographic firm, so fully integrated at one point that it owned its own stockyards so that it could control the quality of the source for its large needs of photographic grade gelatin.

---

[5] Or the new Kodak instant film (casewriter's personal judgment, and assessment of industry opinion).

EXHIBIT 3

POLAROID CORPORATION
Consolidated Financial Statements
Year Ending December 31, 1975
($ millions)

Income Statement

Net sales	$813
Less:	
Cost of goods sold	$468
Advertising expense	52
Research and development	64
Administrative expenses	121
Operating profit	$108
Less:	
Interest expense	$ 1
Plus:	
Interest income	9
Other income	7
Profit before tax	$123
Less:	
Income taxes	$ 61
Net profit	$ 62
Cash dividends paid	$ 10

Balance Sheet

Assets

Current assets:	
Cash	$ 22
Marketable securities, at cost	158
Receivables	181
Inventories	244
Prepaid expenses	26
Total current assets	$631
Fixed assets:	
Property, plant, and equipment, at cost	$435
Less: Accumulated depreciation	232
Net property, plant, and equipment	$203
Total assets	$834

Liabilities and Stockholders' Equity

Current liabilities:	
Notes payable to banks	$ 12
Payables and accruals	80
Taxes payable	53
Total current liabilities	$145
Stockholders' equity:	
Common stock at par value	$ 33
Additional paid-in capital	122
Retained earnings	534
Total stockholders' equity	$689
Total liabilities and stockholders' equity	$834

Source: Polaroid Corporation 1975 annual report.

EXHIBIT 3 (continued)

POLAROID CORPORATION
Five-Year Financial Review
($000, except per share and employee data)

Summary of Operations	1975	1974	1973	1972	1971
Net sales	$812,703	$757,296	$685,536	$559,288	$525,507
Cost of sales	$467,934	$485,158	$358,046	$260,075	$243,575
Selling, advertising, research, engineering, distribution, and administrative expenses	236,995	239,347	251,628	236,741	180,934
Total costs	$704,929	$724,505	$609,674	$496,816	$424,509
Profit from operations	$107,774	$ 32,791	$ 75,862	$ 62,472	$100,998
Other income	16,772	13,425	14,277	13,574	16,074
Interest expense	1,272	1,098	316	836	346
Earnings before income taxes	$123,274	$ 45,118	$ 89,823	$ 75,210	$116,726
Federal, state, and foreign income taxes	60,684	16,731	38,005	32,676	55,708
Net earnings	$ 62,590	$ 28,387	$ 51,818	$ 42,534	$ 61,018
Earnings per share*	$1.91	$0.86	$1.58	$1.30	$1.86
Cash dividends per share	$0.32	$0.32	$0.32	$0.32	$0.32
Average number of shares	32,855	32,855	32,853	32,844	32,837
Financial Position at Year-end					
Working capital	$485,666	$412,600	$390,734	$352,432	$330,908
Net property, plant), and equipment	203,351	224,341	228,334	224,535	213,272
Stockholders' equity	689,017	636,941	619,068	576,967	544,180
Other Statistical Information					
Additions to property, plant, and equipment	$ 21,829	$ 39,951	$ 40,265	$ 44,560	$ 60,167
Depreciation	39,151	39,614	35,326	32,018	22,329
Number of employees, end of year	13,387	13,019	14,277	11,998	11,654
Payroll and benefits	$225,896	$223,154	$191,315	$160,247	$136,741

* Per share earnings based on average number of shares outstanding during the year.
Source: Company annual report for 1975.

As any trip to the average corner drugstore in the United States would reveal, Kodak products, film and cameras, clearly dominated the market for conventional amateur products in 1976. Most estimates of Kodak's market shares were 90 percent for film and 85 percent for cameras at that time. The firm's share of the expenditures for processing and printing of amateur films was only about 15 percent, largely a result of a 1954 consent decree with the U.S. Justice Department which stipulated that Kodak would sell its films and processing separately. However, when the dollar value of the print paper, chemicals, and processing equipment the company sold to independent photofinishers was added in, the company's effective market share for processing was probably closer to 50 percent overall.

EXHIBIT 4

Eastman Kodak Company summary of sales and earnings, 1966–1975

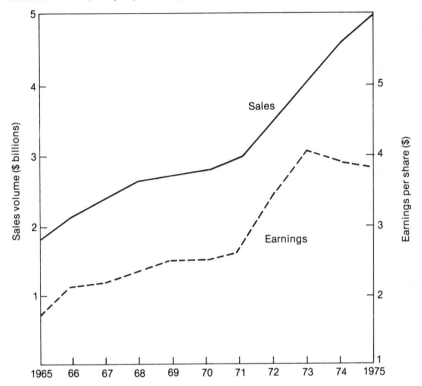

Source: Company annual reports.

Note: Approximate percentage of total sales contributed by divisions (including interdivisional sales) were as follows:

Division	1966	1975
U.S. and Canadian photographic	60%	50%
International photographic	21	31
Eastman chemicals	19	19

Source: Casewriter's estimates from data in company annual reports.

Kodak was active in many more markets than those for conventional amateur still films, cameras, and processing. For example, through its Eastman Chemicals Division (1975 sales $1 billion) it sold a wide variety of chemicals, fibers, and plastics to industrial customers. The company's domestic and foreign photographic divisions (1975 sales $4.5 billion combined) marketed a wide range of products including amateur movie films and equipment, professional still and motion-picture films and equipment, medical and industrial X-ray films and equipment, various graphic arts and audiovisual products and microfilm, and other business products. Kodak was, with rare exceptions, the leader in each market in which it competed.

Compared to Agfa-Gavaert of Belgium, the only other full-line photo-graphic products company in the world, Kodak was a giant; its photo-graphic sales alone were three times those of Agfa in 1975. See Exhibit 4 for a ten-year summary of Kodak's sales and earnings.

Major strategic policies

Kodak's dominance of the photographic industry seemed to most observ-ers to stem primarily from its leadership in film technology. To Kodak's competitors the firm's complete mastery of all aspects of the photographic art was a mighty barrier. Since the introduction of Kodachrome (ASA speed 10) in 1935, the first color film for amateur use, Kodak had managed to keep ahead of every other company in almost every aspect of photography. It was Kodak that foresaw and nurtured the color slide and color print for the amateur market. It was not until 1954, when the Justice Department forced Kodak to sell film and processing separately, that other companies were even allowed to participate in Kodak's lucrative color products. In the 20-year period in which it captured all of the profits from both film manufac-turing and processing (a situation *all* film manufacturers agree is the ideal), it also prevented the formation of independent photofinishing laboratories equipped to process color products sold by its competitors. The net effect of the tied-in sale of processing was thus to retard the dispersion of color film technology and to allow Kodak to become the dominant company in ama-teur color photography.

Even after 1954 Kodak was able to capitalize on its previous success by constantly forcing competitors to upgrade the quality of their color film products. Most firms simply did not have the expertise in the research labo-ratory to continue the fight. During the 1950s Kodak effectively displaced all foreign and domestic competitors from the U.S. market. In addition it successfully defended itself from inroads by formidable would-be competi-tors. In the early 1960s a joint venture between Bell & Howell and Du Pont, which had been formed in the late 1950s, failed completely.[6] Du Pont de-scribed its color film research program as an exasperating effort in which each time they were able to improve their film to meet Kodak's high qual-ity, Kodak film mysteriously became even better. In 1961 when Du Pont's film was finally ready for introduction at a total cost to both companies es-timated by some to be in the tens of millions of dollars, Kodak responded to the threat with Kodachrome II, a color slide film with an ASA speed of 25 and far better color quality than the original against which the Du Pont

---

[6] At the time Kodak's film and camera business alone was about ten times the size of Bell & Howell's total sales.

entry was targeted. The Du Pont product was withdrawn before it ever reached the market.

For a time some competitors attempted to increase their share of the market by lowering their prices slightly. The response from consumers was nil, indicating what was interpreted to be an unwillingness to accept less quality, or less assurance of quality, under almost any circumstance. In 1976 most competitive color film products were sold for a slight premium over Kodak's prices. What appeared to be responsible for the survival of most of Kodak's competitors was the existence of a small following, those who wished to avoid the supersaturated colors, extremely high resolution, or mass-market image of Kodak's color films. Although Kodak had always manufactured a full line of cameras for its films, the company's early success in dominating the amateur color film market was almost solely a direct result of the firm's expertise in color film technology.

1963: The first Kodak system

Since the introduction of the company's Instamatic camera and film products in 1963, however, Kodak's emphasis in the amateur photographic market had been on systems—unique film formats packaged in a cartridge or magazine usable only in cameras designed expressly for that configuration. On February 28, 1963, the Instamatic system was introduced with complete availability of the product on that day to 75,000 retailers in 147 countries supported by major advertising in eight languages. Prices for the camera, available in five models, ranged from $20 up to over $100 (list). Ten million Instamatic cameras were sold in the 26 months following their introduction.

In that same year Kodak also introduced Kodachrome-X (ASA speed 64) color slide film for 35mm and Instamatic cameras and the Super 8 film and camera system for the amateur movie market. The major feature of the Super 8 and Instamatic systems was that the films were cartridge loaded into cameras equipped, in most models, with automatic exposure. For the first time in conventional amateur photography consumers were relieved of two major obstacles to their picture taking: the manual dexterity which had been required for loading roll-film cameras, and the decision-making problem of setting proper exposure. The Instamatic cameras also featured a more convenient flashbulb device, the Flashcube, which provided four flash bulbs in an easy-to-insert configuration (including a disposable reflector for each bulb). Previous to the Flashcube, flashbulb devices tended to be rather bulky and unreliable.

As one might have predicted, both systems resulted not only in a dramatic increase in the sales of Kodak's cameras but also an equally impressive increase in the rate with which film was used in these by consumers.

1972: The second Kodak system

In May 1972 Kodak introduced its Pocket Instamatic system in a manner similar to that used in 1963 with the original system. The major improvement for consumers purchasing the Pocket Instamatics was the dramatic reduction in the size of the camera, which was about one third that of the original model. Prices for the camera, available in five models, ranged from $25 to more than $200 (list).

Also in May of 1972 Kodak introduced its XL Super 8 amateur movie system. The major feature of this product was that it allowed the user to film under most existing light conditions. For example, the light from a single candle on a birthday cake was, in most instances, adequate for proper exposure of subjects within several feet of the cake. In the fall of 1972 Kodak added a line of sound movie cameras to its XL Super 8 line, bringing the total number of Kodak Super 8 movie cameras to five, ranging in price from $35 to $200 (list).

In April 1975 Kodak introduced a new generation of Pocket Instamatics, the Trimlite series. The major improvement in this version of the Instamatic was the use of a small piezoelectric crystal to generate electricity to fire a new form of flashbulb, the Flipflash. One of the cameras in the line was also equipped with a telephoto lens which could be brought into position by moving a small slide at the top of the camera. Industry observers were quick to note that the name, as well as the fact that the most expensive camera in the line was equipped with a provision to use an ASA 400 color print film, was indicative of the fact that Kodak was close to bringing out its long-awaited XL still camera color film, which would dispense with the need for flashbulbs almost entirely.

Industry reactions

The effect of the two Instamatic waves on the conventional amateur market was significant. By the end of 1975 it was estimated that Kodak had sold more than 60 million Instamatic cameras in just a little more than a decade. During this same period all of Kodak's competitors combined had sold, by most estimates, no more than 10 million Instamatic-type cameras. By surprising the industry with radical changes in both camera structure and film requirements, the company was able to consolidate its position in the marketplace. Independent camera manufacturers were faced with a need to invest in increasingly complex production equipment to remain competitive in terms of price with Kodak. Kodak's expanding use of precision plastic optics, integrated circuits, and piezoelectric-type devices left many manufacturers dumbfounded. Film manufacturers were equally amazed by Kodak's ability to push film technology to new limits by the use of smaller negatives and higher ASA speeds in both color print and transparency films without significant reductions in quality. Independent processors were forced to buy new processing equipment and learn new techniques to stay in business. And always, all of Kodak's competitors had to face the fact that Kodak's product would be on sale for a year or more before they were able to react effectively.

To counteract some of the criticism it was receiving from other manufacturers, Kodak freely licensed its systems. For Kodak the benefits were twofold. First, of course, it probably lessened Kodak's vulnerability to antitrust suits. More important, perhaps, Kodak benefited from the fact that the major effect of licensing was really only that of increasing the number of cameras in use which could use its highly profitable films. In the still film amateur market, the Pocket Instamatic format, which used a negative only 25 percent of the size used until that time, had substantially eliminated all but one or two of Kodak's film sales competitors.

All of this success for Kodak in the marketplace made more than one company seek restitution elsewhere. In 1973 Bell & Howell filed a private antitrust suit against Kodak charging that the Pocket Instamatic and XL Super 8 systems were introduced in such a way that competing manufacturers were prevented from marketing their own products. The suit also charged that the practice of marketing systems was restricting competition in the amateur photographic products market. Kodak settled the suit by offering to give Bell & Howell 18 months advance notice prior to the introduction of any new conventional amateur systems.

Also in 1973 Berkey Photo, Inc., filed a private antitrust suit against Kodak charging the firm with restrictive marketing practices and asking for treble damages of $300 million, advance disclosure of new products, free patent licenses, free know-how and technical advice, and a general breakup of Kodak into separate companies. At the time of this case the suit was still pending.

In 1974 GAF Corporation filed a private antitrust suit charging Kodak with marketing systems, changing the components of systems to adversely affect competitors' products, disclosing new systems far in advance of the actual intended date of introduction to discourage sales of competing products, and the use of huge advertising budgets to ensure the dominance of Kodak in various markets. The GAF suit, in the pretrial stage at the time of this case, sought treble damages of proven losses, free know-how and technical advice, the breakup of Kodak into ten separate companies, and the dedication of the trademark "Kodak" to the public domain.

Also in 1974 Pavelle Corporation filed suit against Kodak charging that the company had test marketed, at the same time as Pavelle, a color print paper and related chemicals at prices below which Pavelle could profitably sell these, causing Pavelle to file for bankruptcy. In addition to most of the charges mentioned in the other suits against Kodak, Pavelle specifically sought the divestiture by Kodak of its color print and chemical businesses. At the time of this case this suit was still pending.

Kodak had not always been the defendant, however. Since 1972 the company had been challenging certain Polaroid patents in foreign countries (most notably Britain, Canada, Germany, Australia, and Japan) in an apparent attempt to clear a path for an instant camera and film of its own. While such challenges were not technically legal actions, they could become the basis for evidence to be submitted in the event of a U.S.-based patent infringement suit was ever filed against Kodak by Polaroid. Such a suit was in fact filed by Polaroid at 4:59 P.M. on April 26, 1976, the day before the annual meetings of both companies.[7]

Kodak's instant system

As stated previously, on April 20, 1976, Eastman Kodak publicly demonstrated its own instant photographic product for the amateur market. In February 1976 the company had announced that sometime in April it would make that demonstration; however, it was not until the day of the demonstration that the company revealed that its product would go on sale first in Canada, on May 1, 1976, and in the United States on July 5, 1976. While rumors of a Kodak instant product had been circulating in the industry for more than a decade (peaking at one point in 1969 when leaks of a Kodak-Polaroid agreement to allow the former to market a Colorpack compatible film of its own by sometime in 1975 were reported in various publications), it was not until early 1970 that Kodak formally announced that work on a Colorpack type film was under way.

In its 1973 annual report, however, Kodak indicated that it had altered its research goals somewhat:

> In the field of rapid-access photography, the basic *decisions* have ... made feasible a film that will yield dry prints of high quality without waste, to be used in equipment priced for a wide spectrum of consumers.

This announcement by Kodak left some industry observers puzzled as to whether Kodak's film was still intended for use in Colorpack-type cameras. In 1974's annual report the company clarified its statement further:

> During the year, Kodak completed the design of its own instant cameras and finalized the format and characteristics of a litter-free film for instant prints.

---

[7] Polaroid was also involved in other legal actions. In 1975 it sued Berkey Photo for the infringement of patents relating to the SX-70 camera. Berkey had introduced a camera which used SX-70 film. In a cross action Berkey was charging Polaroid with the monopolization of the instant photographic market, held that the patents in question were invalid, and was seeking a cancellation of the trademark "Polaroid." Also in 1975 Bell & Howell and Polaroid had become involved in a dispute relating to the production of instant movie camera equipment by B&H for Polaroid. As of the time of this case the Berkey suit was outstanding; the Bell & Howell conflict had been settled out of court.

EXHIBIT 5

Polaroid and Kodak instant cameras compared

Aspect	Polaroid Pronto!	Kodak EK6 instant camera
List price	$66	$69.50
Exposure system	Fully automatic	Fully automatic
Focusing range	3 feet to infinity	3½ feet to infinity
Focusing method	Estimation	Rangefinder, zone symbols
Film counter	Yes	Yes
Method of film ejection	Automatic	Automatic (manual in EK4)
Weight	15 ounces	29 ounces
Size	Small; irregular shape	Medium; rectangular solid shape
Carrying strap	For wrist	For neck
Flashbulb type	Flashbar, 10 shots per bar	Flipflash, 8 shots per bar
Lens	3-element plastic, 116mm	3-element plastic, 137mm
Shutter speeds	1 to 1/125th second	1/20th to 1/300th second
Warranty period	1 year	3 years
Flash distance	3 to 12 feet	4 to 10 feet
Full-flash capability	Yes	No
Flash warning light	No	Yes
Camera power source	Battery in film pack	Batteries in camera, change yearly
F-stop range	F/9.4 to F/22	F/11 or F/16

Source: Company publications and news articles.

Thus Kodak had, within a comparatively brief period, moved away from the idea of making a film for existing cameras. It now intended to market a system of its own design.

In its 1975 annual report the company devoted a total of four pages to a detailed explanation of its progress in instant photography, as well as two full pages describing its new Ektaprint 100 Xerox-type copier which had been on limited sale since October 1975.

Some observers, noting that most of Polaroid's basic patent protection had run out by 1969, were concerned with the seemingly ponderous method by which Kodak finally reached the market with an instant product of its own. But others, as they compared the Kodak system with its competition (see Exhibits 5, 6, and 7), were more impressed by Kodak's decision to bring out a completely new system, and the company's stated intention of freely licensing others to build cameras which could use the film. With respect to licensing the production of film cartridges and the film itself for its instant product, however, Kodak was silent. As one executive of a competing film manufacturing company commented, however, "It would take us three to five years and a lot of money to come up with a film for that camera."

Kodak's annual meeting

At the Kodak annual meeting held one week after the introduction of the Kodak Instant and, coincidentally, on the same day as Polaroid's annual

352

EXHIBIT 6
Polaroid and Kodak instant cameras and films compared

A. Cameras

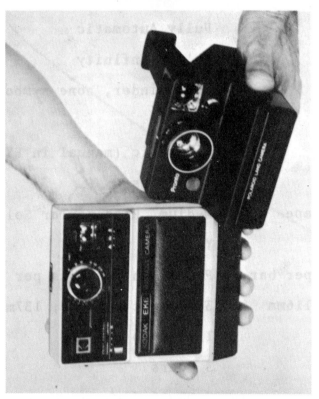

Photograph courtesy *Modern Photography*.

B. Films

Characteristic	Polaroid SX-70	Kodak PR-10
Type	Color print film	Color print film
Format	Square	Rectangular
ASA speed	100	150
Image size	3.13 by 3.13 inches	2.63 by 3.56 inches
Image area	9.77 square inches	9.35 square inches
Development time	About 12 minutes	About 10 minutes
Color quality*	Good	Good
Color stability*	Good	Good
Exposures per pack	10	10
List price per pack	$6.99	$7.45
Average retail price	$5.50	$5.50
Exposed through	Front	Rear

* Source: Published specifications and casewriter's personal judgment and assessment of industry opinion.

EXHIBIT 7
Price comparison of Polaroid and Kodak instant systems

	List price	Average retail price*
Polaroid:		
Camera: Pronto!	$66.00	$49.00
Film: SX-70	6.99	5.50
Flash: Flashbar	3.28	1.89
Cost per picture:		
Available light	0.70	0.55
Flash	1.03	0.74
Reprints (by mail from Polaroid; 88 cents handling charge per order):		
Wallet size	$ 0.39	Same
Same size	0.49	Same
5 by 5 inches	2.25	Same
8 by 8 inches	5.50	Same
11 by 11 inches	9.95	Same
Kodak:		
Camera:		
EK4	53.50	39.00
EK6	69.50	49.00
Film: PR-10	7.45	5.50
Flash: Flipflash	2.30	1.19
Cost per picture:		
Available light	0.75	0.55
Flash	1.04	0.70
Reprints (available from any Kodak dealer):		
Same size	0.85	0.68
3½ by 4½ inches	1.00	0.80
5 by 7 inches	2.25	1.80
8 by 10 inches	5.35	4.28
11 by 14 inches	10.75	8.60

* Based upon interviews with camera dealers in the greater Boston area in May 1976.
Source: Casewriter's fieldwork.

meeting, Walter A. Fallon, Kodak's president, responded as follows to several stockholder questions about the new product:

> There will be no time for resting on laurels, however. I can tell you that the curtain will rise on yet another member of the Kodak instant family within the coming year. This will be the Kodak EK8 Instant Camera, a folding model designed and built at the Kodak Camera Works in West Germany.

Fallon continued by saying that expressions of interest in the Kodak Instant from the trade were "at a high and very positive pitch." When asked if Kodak planned to introduce an under-$20 EK2 instant camera, Fallon declined to comment. At that point, however, he did confirm that the EK8 would "probably" be available by early fall 1976 and that it would carry a suggested retail price of about $140.

EXHIBIT 8

EASTMAN KODAK COMPANY
Consolidated Financial Statements
Year Ending December 31, 1975
($ millions)

Income Statement

Net sales	$4,959
Less:	
Cost of goods sold	$2,927
Advertising expense	*
Research and development	313
Administrative expenses	632
Operating profit	$1,087
Less:	
Interest expense	$ 15
Plus:	
Interest income	40
Other income (expense)	(6)
Profit before tax	$1,106
Less:	
Income taxes	$ 493
Net profit	$ 613
Cash dividends paid	$ 332

Balance Sheet

Assets

Current assets:	
Cash	$ 76
Marketable securities, at cost.................................	672
Receivables	804
Inventories	986
Prepaid expenses	82
Total current assets	$2,620
Fixed assets:	
Property, plant, and equipment, at cost.........................	$4,348
Less: Accumulated depreciation	1,970
Net property, plant, and equipment	$2,378
Total assets	5,056†

Liabilities and Stockholders' Equity

Current liabilities:	
Payables and accruals	$ 688
Taxes payable..	246
Dividends payable	143
Total current liabilities.......................................	$1,077
Other liabilities:	
4½% convertible debentures, due 1988	66
Other long-term liabilities	75
Deferred income taxes	129
Total liabilities	$1,347

EXHIBIT 8 (continued)

Stockholders' equity:

Common stock at par value	$ 404
Additional paid-in capital	268
Retained earnings	3,037
Total stockholders' equity	$3,709
Total liabilities and equity	$5,056

* Not reported separately; included with "Administrative expenses."
† Includes $58 of miscellaneous assets.
Source: Eastman Kodak Company 1975 annual report.

Later on the day of the annual meeting, at a luncheon held for security analysts, Fallon commented on the Polaroid patent suit by saying, "We believe that our patent position is sound. We don't knowingly infringe anybody else's valid patents."

See Exhibit 8 for Kodak's financial statements for 1975.

APPENDIX A

A brief note on the amateur photographic products market

Because of the highly concentrated nature of the photographic industry it was very difficult to come by precise data on the size and character of the segments that made up the total market for amateur photographic products. Most firms treated their market data with the same degree of secrecy as their film and camera designs. This note is a composite picture made from a wide variety of public sources.

The market in 1962

In 1962 the total U.S. domestic market for amateur photographic products was about $1.4 billion at the retail level. In that year about 2.2 billion snapshots were taken by amateur photographers.

The total U.S. domestic factory sales of Eastman Kodak for all its photographic products was estimated to be $600 million at that time. Polaroid Corporation's reported domestic sales were $100 million in 1962, about 40 percent of this volume related to film sales.

In terms of consumer patterns in 1962, about half the pictures taken were in color, half in black and white. The average consumer used about four rolls of film per year. Sixty percent of the pictures taken were taken by women.

The market in 1969

In 1969 the total U.S. domestic market for amateur photographic products was about $3.5 billion at the retail level. About 4.5 billion snapshots were taken by amateur photographers that year.

Kodak's domestic sales for all of its photographic products were about $1.5 billion that year. Polaroid reported domestic sales of $466 million that same year. Kodak's domestic sales of still camera films to the amateur market were about $265 million at the time, about $140 million of this from sales of Kodacolor film, about $100 million from Kodachrome and Ektachrome, and about $25 million from its black-and-white films. Polaroid's domestic sales of film to the same market were estimated to be $240 million, about $135 million of this from Polacolor and about $105 million from ASA 3000 speed film. The Kodak figure excluded the company's sales of processing services and its sales of equipment and supplies to the photofinishing industry.

Kodak, by doing all of its own manufacturing for film and camera products, enjoyed an estimated pretax profit margin on these items of about 70 percent. Polaroid, which subcontracted both negative and camera manufacturing, was thought to gross about 45 percent pretax on its cameras and films.

The market in 1975

In 1975 the total U.S. domestic market for amateur photographic products was about $6.6 billion at the retail level. In that year about 7 billion snapshots were taken by amateur photographers.

Kodak's domestic sales for all of its photographic products was estimated at $2.5 billion. Polaroid reported total domestic sales of $500 million. An analyst's estimate of Kodak's and Polaroid's film sales to the domestic amateur still film market was "about $500 million for each," which was obviously a bit high for Polaroid.

In terms of consumer patterns in 1975, about 90 percent of the pictures taken were in color, 10 percent in black and white. The average consumer used about eight rolls of film per year. Sixty percent of the pictures were taken by women. Market data suggested that 92 percent of America's homes owned at least one conventional camera and 49 percent owned at least one Polaroid camera. Surveys taken by Kodak suggested that as many as 24 million American homes would buy an instant camera with "improved features."

In 1975 the total world market for amateur photographic products was about $14 billion at the retail level. Worldwide sales of cameras and films were estimated at $2 billion for Kodak, $800 million for Polaroid, and $2 billion for all other companies combined. About $1 billion in retail sales was related to "sophisticated" equipment.[8] Of the remaining $8 billion or so, the majority was related to the photofinishing industry which was composed of the multitude of retail outlets and processing laboratories worldwide.

Retailing amateur products in 1975

Sales of sophisticated equipment excepted, the average photographic products dealership made its money primarily from processing services. The use of film and cameras of all types as traffic builders and loss leaders had consistently forced dealer margins on both of these items down to minimal levels, in many cases to no more than 5 or 10 percent above cost. Retailers, however, seemed to be holding the line on processing prices where margins of 25 percent or more were common.

APPENDIX B

Major differences between the Colorpack and SX-70 systems

Film configuration

The general form of all Polaroid instant photographic materials was as follows:

A. The negative.   Whether a color negative or black and white, it contained all of the basic components of what would become the image in the final print. However, the negative *itself,* never became the actual print.

B. Processing chemistry.   In both color and black-and-white processes a highly viscous, alkaline reagent was employed to extract the latent image from the negative and transfer it, by simple diffusion, across a very thin layer of the reagent to a receiving surface. In all cases the reagent was stored in airtight pods which were broken open by rollers in the camera.

C. The print.   In all cases the function of what was to become the print was identical. It was always a receiving surface which became the final print, that is, a surface which received the image migrating from the negative and retained it (at which time processing was complete). In the case of the Colorpack film, this surface was present on a paper-based card which was separated from the negative and reagent to halt processing. In the case of SX-70 film, the surface was present on the interior face of a transparent mylar sheet which was permanently bonded to the negative material at the edges to prevent reagent from leaking out.

---

[8] "Sophisticated" equipment included cameras, projectors, and various accessory items which were usually only available in stores where more than 50 percent of sales came from photographic products. Prices for this equipment were much higher than those for mass-market items.

Camera design

Several differences existed in the operation of the cameras and films of the two systems. First, because the SX-70 print was to be viewed from the same direction in which it was exposed, the image reaching the film needed to be reversed by the camera. In the case of the SX-70 camera a mirror was used to achieve this. Second, because the negative and chemistry were to become a permanent part of the print in SX-70 film, all of the products of the various chemical reactions needed to be inert with respect to the final image as it resided on the interior surface of the mylar sheet. Third, because the SX-70 print developed outside of the camera, it needed to be shielded from light from the moment it was ejected from the camera. This was accomplished by the use of an "opacifier," a chemical layer which prevented light from reaching the negative during processing but which allowed the color-forming dyes to migrate through it to reach the mylar-supported surface.

As to the operation of the two systems, except for the litter associated with the Colorpack and the need to clean the camera's rollers periodically, there were, in the casewriter's opinion, virtually no differences between the two systems.

APPENDIX C

Dates of significant strategic events

POLAROID

1934:
  Contract with Kodak for Polascreens
1944:
  Instant photographic research begun

1948:
  Contract with Kodak for negative
  First camera introduced at $90
1950:
  True B&W film introduced ASA 100
1955:
  ASA 200 & 400 B&W films introduced
1959:
  ASA 3000 B&W film introduced

KODAK

1934:
  Contract with Polaroid for Polascreens
1935:
  Kodachrome color film introduced ASA 10

1948:
  Contract with Polaroid for negative
1954:
  Film and processing sales split apart
1961:
  Kodachrome II introduced ASA 25

1960:

B&W film development time reduced from 60 seconds to 10 seconds

First auto-exposure camera introduced

1963:

Contract with Kodak for color negative

January, Polacolor film introduced

June, ASA 3000 and Polacolor films introduced in pack format for new auto-exposure pack camera at $100

1964:

Cheaper Colorpack camera at $75

1965:

Full line of Colorpacks $50 to $150

Swinger $20 B&W roll film camera

1967:

Second generation Colorpacks $45 and up

1968:

Big Swinger $25 uses ASA 3000 in packs

1969:

April, $30 Colorpack camera introduced

November, $99 million raised for R&D and total integration of company

1972:

November, SX-70 camera introduced at $180

1974:

SX-70 Model II introduced at $140

1975:

March, Supershooter introduced at $25

March, Polacolor II introduced

May, SX-70 Model III introduced at $99

1976:

January, Pronto! announced

March, Pronto! introduced at $66

1963:

Contract with Polaroid for color negative

February, Instamatic introduced, 5 models $20 to $100+

Super 8 introduced

Kodachrome-X introduced for 35 mm and Instamatic cameras

1969:

Polaroid's basic patents expiring

Rumors of Kodak ability to market Colorpack compatible film by 1975

1972:

February, Pocket Instamatic introduced 5 models from $25 to $200+

May, XL Super 8 system introduced

Fall, Sound XL system introduced giving company total of 5 movie cameras priced from $35 to $200

1975:

May, Trimlite series introduced; includes telephoto model

1976:

February, announces April demonstration

April, demonstrates and announces May sales in Canada, July sales in United States

April, announces folding model at $140 for possible fall 1976 introduction

case 13

Tensor Corporation

TENSOR HISTORY TO 1969

Jay Monroe, president, summed up the early history of Tensor Corporation as follows:

> I had a considerable amount of mechanical aptitude as a kid and always wanted to be an engineer. But in the 1930s engineering was still a closed field to Jews. Jewish kids just did not grow up to be engineers. Sperry Gyroscope was the largest hirer of engineers in New York City, and they did not hire Jews.
>
> Consequently I decided to be an inventor so that I could be an engineer. I attended Cornell and majored in electrical engineering. At the end of my senior year in 1945 I went to Western Electric to apply for a job. Even though I got a perfect score on the engineering employment qualification test, Western Electric could not figure out what to do with me.
>
> This inability to find a meaningful job at many of the large companies is one of the reasons for the existence of the large number of small companies in the New York City area. Of the ten members of my Cornell Jewish fraternity in my graduating class, all are now presidents of small companies.
>
> Shortly after I got out of school there was a marked change of attitude in the country in general, and anti-Semitism was no longer condoned or tolerated by most Americans. I took a variety of jobs for short periods to gain experience, and in 1949 I was a partner with Gerald Starr in the formation of Tensor Electric Development Company.
>
> Tensor Electric Development was solely a government contractor for the first ten years of the company's history. A number of consumer products were tried during that period, but none was successful enough to justify continued production. The idea remained, however, that the only way to be free to guide your own destiny was through developing and marketing a consumer product. It took ten years to invent that product, but finally in 1959, we thought we had developed the basis for a profitable company from a consumer product—the Tensor lamp.

The Tensor lamp

High-intensity lamps consisted basically of a step-down transformer built into the base of the lamp, an automobile headlight bulb, and a reflecting cone. Jay Monroe had designed the small transformer in order to power a lamp whose light would be bright enough to compensate for his poor vision and focused enough to keep from disturbing his wife's sleep while he read in bed. The first lamp, which used a tin measuring cup for a reflecting cone, was designed by Mr. Monroe in 1959. The *Lamp Journal* for August 1964 reviewed the physical characteristics of the high-intensity lamp:

> Its chief advantages are: white light, high intensity, and size, perhaps in that order. Each of these three features was available before the advent of high-intensity lamps, although not all at the same time from the same lamp.
>
> The advantages of white light, high intensity, and [small] size in the high-intensity lamps are achieved at the sacrifice of bulb life. The shortest bulb life of a 75-watt bulb in common use is 55 hours. At 25¢ retail per bulb this amounts to $\frac{1}{2}$¢ per hour bulb cost; power cost is $\frac{1}{4}$¢ per hour. The equivalent conventional lamp, using a 200-watt bulb, would cost approximately $\frac{1}{30}$¢ per hour for the bulb and 1¢ per hour for power. In general, short bulb lives notwithstanding, the miniatures are cheaper to operate than equivalent incandescents, but considerably more expensive than equivalent fluorescents.

When his friends began to ask him to make lamps for them also, Mr. Monroe decided that the new lamp had commercial possibilities. He set up a production line inside the Tensor factory to begin small-scale manufacture. The Tensor lamp encountered rapid success from the start of its commercial introduction in 1960. Exhibit 1 gives sales of Tensor lamps from 1960 through 1965. Exhibit 2 gives the 1970 corporation officers of the Tensor Corporation.

EXHIBIT 1
Tensor lamp sales, 1960–1965

Year	Sales
1960	$ 1,000
1961	50,000
1962	285,000
1963	850,000
1964	3,893,000
1965	6,863,000

During this period of expansion, Tensor was constantly pressed by the necessity for more management personnel and larger facilities. In 1964 Tensor sold off the government contract division to Gerald Starr and con-

EXHIBIT 2
Corporation officers, 1970

JAY MONROE
President
b. 1927. Graduated from Cornell in 1945. Majored in electrical engineering. Founded Tensor Electric Company in 1949.

GEORGE SAVITSKY
Vice President—Sales and Marketing
b. 1938. Graduated from Pace College in 1960. Worked as an accountant with a N.Y.C. accounting firm before joining Tensor in 1964.

STANLEY JARET
Treasurer
b. 1930 Graduated from City College of New York in 1953. Worked in public accounting with a N.Y.C. accounting firm until joining Tensor in 1964.

WALTER GLOUMAKOFF
Director of Manufacturing
b. 1934. Attended Rutgers University. Concentrated on engineering courses. Worked for Rotobroil. Joined Tensor in 1964.

EDMUND SOVATSKY
Vice President—Engineering
b. 1934. Attended Brooklyn Vocational High School. Joined Tensor in 1950.

centrated completely on the Tensor lamp. A December 1964 article in *Business Week* detailed some of the changes which had taken place at Tensor since the introduction of the high-intensity lamp:

Tensor is showing a growth pattern typical of rapidly growing small companies. Early in their growth they usually rely heavily on outsiders to beef up a slim executive staff. As they grow, they soon find they can afford larger administrative overhead to handle much of the farmed-out work.

Just six months ago Monroe ran Tensor with only four other executives—an executive vice president, two marketing executives, and a treasurer. Ten outsiders helped run the company. Two full-time consultants reshaped production lines to fit Tensor's hodgepodge plant that rambles through eight floors of three adjoining buildings in Brooklyn. Legal counsel handled most business dickering, such as adding new plant space, as well as legal problems. Two advertising agents handled last year's $300,000 advertising campaign and also acted as material purchasing agents. New equipment and design changes were recommended by other consultants.

While most of the outsiders still work with Tensor, many of their extra duties have been turned over to a beefed-up home office executive team. Tensor has recently added a comptroller, a production director, and a troubleshooting presidential assistant.

Still Tensor's shape, like its lamps, is something less than classic, but it seems to be paying off. A consultant-tailored incentive labor plan cut pre-lamp costs in half; bookkeeping and inventory controls are working smoothly; plant security is being tightened—losses so far have been cut in half; and this year Tensor lamps are expected to show a healthy profit.[1]

As sales of Tensor lamps continued to expand in 1965 and 1966, Tensor added to corporate overhead by (1) leasing new executive offices in Great Neck, Long Island; (2) leasing a new one-story manufacturing plant in Brooklyn, which replaced the old manufacturing facility; and (3) investing in new mass-production machinery, which for some operations could handle ten times the company's 1965 lamp volume. The new Great Neck office included a much expanded laboratory for Mr. Monroe, who believed he could turn his attention away from administration and back to inventing.

During the 1965–66 period the company was receiving letters from many of its customers praising the high-intensity lamp for its ability to give sufficient light to allow older persons and persons with poor vision to read and carry on other visually detailed operations.

The success of the Tensor lamp did not go unnoticed by other lighting manufacturers. A mid-1965 investment report by du Pasquier & Co., Inc., summarized the competition as follows:

There are now at least 15 manufacturers of high-intensity lamps, and this number is expected to increase. Tensor estimates that it had some 50 per-

---

[1] "The Little Lamp That Grew Up," *Business Week*, December 19, 1964, pp. 64–65.

cent of the market for high-intensity lamps in 1964 and that this percentage is currently being maintained (total industry sales of high-intensity lamps in 1964 are estimated to have been $8.0 million).

Tensor feels it is now over the critical period where a competitor could come out with a single design that would capture the bulk of the market. There is considerable speculation of the effect of a large manufacturer such as Westinghouse or GE would have entering the market with a major advertising campaign. It is doubtful, however, that a major company will enter the arena until the total market is larger, and in the meanwhile Tensor is continuing to achieve broader distribution and the name to provide effective competition. Of incalculable value is the fact that all, high-intensity lamps are increasingly becoming known as Tensor lamps regardless of their manufacturer.

Tensor's major competitor is the Lampette, which is manufactured in Japan and Germany for Soss Manufacturing. Some $2.5 million worth of Lampettes were sold in 1964. Lightolier, a leading manufacturer of lighting fixtures, and Rotobroil are shortly expected to introduce high-intensity lamps.

As Tensor faced the future of the high-intensity lamp market at the end of 1965, many uncertainties remained about the eventual size of the industry and Tensor's role in it. The Tensor lamp was the only high-intensity lamp manufactured in the United States. This gave competitors who used foreign suppliers a cost advantage which was reflected by being able to offer a lower price to the consumer or higher margins to the sales and distribution network.

Furthermore, although Tensor had advertised heavily and established a brand name with the consumer, that brand name had been built on the basis of product utility. Recent competition, however, seemed to emphasize styling. Mr. Monroe disdained this attempt to turn the high-intensity lamp into a "fad" item. He believed that the market would respond best to an appeal to utility rather than style. Mr. Monroe therefore continued to emphasize utility, and Tensor was the last major marketer of high-intensity lamps to introduce a telescoping lamp neck into their product line.

Tensor's goal in the high-intensity lamp market was to maintain the 50 percent share of market the company held in 1965. In order to assure the financial ability to support a higher forecasted sales level, Tensor sold 100,000 shares of stock at 11⅛ per share net to the company. This new stock, issued in the summer of 1966, gave Tensor a wide ownership and a listing on the American Stock Exchange. It also gave the company the necessary cash to finance the advertising budget ($100,000 in 1963; $300,000 in 1964; and $1 million in 1965 and 1966) and the new building and equipment expenditures.

But 1966 and 1967 did not produce the high level of sales the company had been forecasting. Sales increased slightly in 1966 to $7.4 million, but fell more than 30 percent in 1967. Net income plummeted from earnings of over $0.5 million in 1965 to a deficit of $0.5 million in 1966 and a similar loss in 1967.

Looking back on those two years, Mr. Monroe commented that the stupidest thing he had done was to "lose contact with the plant" and to allow overexpansion:

> It was extremely painful to me and to the company and its employees to undergo the major contractions of late 1966 to early 1967. We closed down the Great Neck offices and moved back to the plant in Brooklyn. Both salaried and hourly employees were cut back drastically in order to allow the company to survive.
>
> The major cause of our misjudging the market size was the erroneous belief that the high-intensity lamp was an all-purpose lamp which would replace many other forms of lighting. We interpreted the letters we were receiving as a sample of the reaction of the general public. Actually the bright light of the high-intensity lamp was not needed by younger people with good eyesight. It was no more useful to them than a good incandescent lamp, and it made their eyes tire more rapidly. One rumor which was current in 1966 and 1967 was that the more rapid tiring of the eyes caused by high-intensity lamps resulted in permanent eye damage. This rumor was subsequently proved to be completely false, but it did nothing to improve our declining sales.
>
> Another problem we had with our demand forecasts is a common problem with any new product area: the boundaries of our forecasts were so wide that the forecasts themselves became almost useless as a planning tool.
>
> Two demand factors contributed significantly to our inability to assess accurately future high-intensity lamp sales. The first factor was our lack of ability to predict sales to the consumer as opposed to factory sales to wholesale and retail outlets. In mid-1966 we ran a trade promotion. Shortly thereafter we received a significant number of reorders, and we concluded that consumer demand was remaining strong. The large number of retail and wholesale outlets that began to carry Tensor in 1964 and 1965 were all well stocked for the mid-1966 demand level. But in late 1966 consumer sales fell off sharply, and our distribution channels were stuck with an inventory appropriate for a much higher demand level. Consequently, factory orders did not recover for some time.
>
> The second factor which affected our forecasts was the extra consumer demand generated by the large amount of advertising and promotion. We "overadvertised" to try to build up our name while the market was still immature, and this contributed to a larger final demand than would have been experienced in a time of less aggressive promotion. In addition, a number of new competitors entered the market in 1964–65. Each new entrant needed a large promotional campaign in order to carve out an initial market share; promotional campaigns often increased the total market rather than resulting in "conquest" sales from other manufacturers. These campaigns stimulated some demand which was not sustainable when the promotion level became more normal.

EXHIBIT 3

Comparison of theoretical Tensor lamp sales under normal conditions versus actual experienced demand, 1960–1968

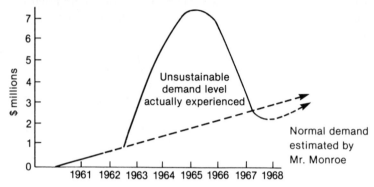

Exhibit 3 shows schematically the unsuitable demand on which Tensor based its 1966 and 1967 sales forecasts. Mr. Monroe estimated that the dotted line represented the sustainable demand for high-intensity lamps which Tensor would have experienced without unusual pipeline and promotional sales.

The Tensor tennis racket and disposable flashlight

Mr. Monroe commented on Tensor's expansion into a new product line:

> In late 1967 it was clear to me that the drop in high-intensity lamp sales was not just a temporary phenomenon. Tensor lamps, because of our strong brand name, retained a 50 percent market share. However, total high-intensity lamp sales were contracting to meet a stable level of demand which represented the share of market for high-intensity lamps in the total lamp market. From that point, I expected that high-intensity lamp sales would only increase as fast as population growth.
>
> I did not want to take the risk that stabilized Tensor lamp sales would not be sufficient to support the company's organization. I was also displeased that sales in the high-intensity lamp market were becoming more dependent on product styling than on product utility. This trend emphasized fad rather than lighting improvement. Consequently, I began to look around for other new product possibilities. The Tensor lamp had helped the company to build a valuable national name, and I believed that our reputation would be a big help in any new area we entered.
>
> My major source of recreation is playing tennis, and early in 1968 I noticed that the waiting list for metal rackets at pro shops was growing longer and longer. This was an indication to me that metal racket production capacity for the major producers of tennis rackets was lagging behind demand. Metal tennis rackets did not seem to represent any major manufac-

turing innovation, and by early 1968 the contraction in lamp sales had left us with plenty of spare production capacity.

In February we made the decision to go ahead with the design work on a metal tennis racket, and by May production had begun on a small-scale basis. We priced our racket with the premium models put out by the competition, and evidently our name made the price stick.

The Tensor steel tennis racket sold well from its inception, and by the end of 1968 tennis racket sales were contributing a substantial part of Tensor's sales. The only miscalculation apparent in the introduction of the Tensor tennis racket was the use of a soft gauge of steel in the very early rackets. This caused a large number of customer returns of rackets with snapped handles. Tensor quickly changed to a harder gauge of steel, and customer returns subsequently declined to less than 2 percent.

Largely because of the tennis racket, Tensor became profitable in 1968 and 1969—even though 1969 sales remained substantially below the 1964 level. Exhibits 4 and 5 detail Tensor's financial statements from 1962 to 1969.

Tensor had introduced one other new product in 1968—a disposable flashlight retailing for $1.98 and guaranteed to last for at least one year. Mr. Monroe had first seen the product as a French import, but when the French company would not issue Tensor a license to sell the flashlight under the Tensor name, he designed his own version.

Mr. Monroe had not been enthusiastic about the disposable flashlight, but at the time of its introduction in mid-1968, it had helped to fill some of Tensor's excess production capacity. Most of the disposable flashlight sales were "premium sales." Under this arrangement Tensor printed another company's name as well as its own on the product. The other company could then use large quantities of the product in consumer or trade promotions and as prizes in sales contests. Although Tensor continued to make minor design and packaging improvements in disposable flashlights, the specialty nature of the premium market made a stable sales level above $1 million annually extremely unlikely.

TENSOR IN 1969–1970

Competition

By 1969 Tensor's competition in the high-intensity lamp market had dwindled to only two other firms with national distribution and a number of smaller firms with regional distribution. The two nationwide competitors were Lightolier—a company with $40 million in annual lamp sales, of which 5–8 percent were high intensity—and Universal. Universal, a high-intensity lamp company with headquarters in Chicago, had an annual sales

EXHIBIT 4

Tensor Corporation and Subsidiaries:
Income Statements
Years Ending December 31, 1962–1969
($000 except for last three items)

	1962	1963	1964	1965	1966	1967	1968	1969
Net sales	$ 757	$1,415	$4,263	$6,863	$7,445	$5,135	$3,262	$3,825
Cost of goods sold........	518	765	2,454	4,137	5,649	4,040	2,259	2,393
Gross profit ...	$ 239	$ 650	$1,809	$2,726	$1,796	$1,095	$1,003	$1,432
Selling, general, and administrative expense	321	495	1,238	1,711	2,669	1,513	914	1,206
Operating profit (loss) .	$ (82)	$ 155	$ 571	$1,015	$ (873)	$ (418)	$ 89	$ 226
Interest expense	—	—	6	41	80	42	29	27
Other income (expense) ..	(31)	5	3	13	(8)	13	43	42
Income before taxes	$ (113)	$ 160	$ 568	$ 987	$ (961)	$ (447)	$ 103	$ 241
Taxes (refund)	(24)	74	270	450	(465)	(200)	45	125
Profit (loss) before extraordinary items	$ (89)	$ 86	$ 298	$ 537	$ (496)	$ (247)	$ 58	$ 116
Extraordinary income (loss)	—	—	—	—	—	(195)	45	60
Net income ...	$ (89)	$ 86	$ 298	$ 537	$ (496)	$ (442)	$ 103	$ 176
Shares outstanding ...	300,000	300,000	313,535	325,200	425,200	425,200	430,200	434,700
Earnings deficit per share*	$(0.30)	$ 0.29	$ 0.95	$ 1.65	$ (1.17)	$ (0.58)	$ 0.14	$ 0.27
Return on stockholders' equity*	(28.1)	21.3	40.2	40.8	(25.7)	(16.7)	3.6	6.4

* All returns based on profit (loss) before extraordinary items.
Source: Annual reports.

of $1 million. George Savitsky, Tensor's vice president of sales and marketing, estimated the high-intensity lamp market, including the regional firms, at about $7 million. Tensor's line of high-intensity lamps sold at retail for prices ranging from $8.95 to $50.00. A major portion of the volume was concentrated at two points in this range—$12.95 and $19.95. By comparison, some of the private-label brands imported from Japan sold for as little as $3.99. The Lightolier price range was $12.95 to $25.00.

EXHIBIT 5

Tensor Corporation and Subsidiaries
Balance Sheets,
Years Ending December 31, 1962–1969
($000 except for book value and price)

	1962	1963	1964	1965	1966	1967	1968	1969
Assets								
Current assets:								
Cash	$ 29	$108	$ 336	$ 79	$ 104	$ 124	$ 329	$ 90
U.S. government securities	—	25	—	—	—	344	325	350
Accounts receivable ..	127	302	777	1,382	1,177	501	700	743
Inventories	137	159	677	1,383	1,643	649	563	889
Claims for refund of income taxes	35	—	—	—	531	227	21	—
Prepaid expenses	2	13	110	19	30	18	43	40
Total current assets	$330	$607	$1,900	$2,863	$3,485	$1,863	$1,981	$2,112
Fixed assets:								
Machinery and other equipment	$ 78	$ 74	$ 123	$ 419	$ 669	$ 630	$ 529	$ 489
Leasehold improvements	5	10	45	128	177	111	112	112
Less: Accumulated depreciation	26	29	59	133	234	281	275	288
Total fixed assets	$ 57	$ 55	$ 109	$ 414	$ 612	$ 460	$ 366	$ 313
Other miscellaneous assets and deposits	4	3	64	205	163	118	104	159
Total assets	$391	$665	$2,073	$3,482	$4,260	$2,441	$2,451	$2,584
Liabilities and Stockholders' Equity								
Current liabilities:								
Accounts payable	$ 38	$102	$ 751	$ 614	$ 668	$ 385	$ 320	$ 226
Notes payable	—	—	—	550	1,000	—	—	—
Current portion of noncurrent liabilities	—	—	15	4	47	43	43	43
Accrued liabilities	21	72	151	146	138	126	124	127
Federal income taxes payable	15	88	280	350	—	-	-	65
Total current liabilities	$ 74	$262	$1,197	$1,664	$1,853	$ 554	$ 487	$ 461
Noncurrent liabilities:								
6½% promissory note payable	—	—	$ 135	$ 450	$ 412	$ 375	$ 338	$ 300
Due under contract for purchase of leasehold	—	—	—	33	28	23	17	12
Deferred federal income taxes	—	—	—	20	35	—	—	—
Total noncurrent liabilities	—	—	$ 135	$ 503	$ 475	$ 398	$ 355	$ 312

EXHIBIT 5 (continued)

	1962	1963	1964	1965	1966	1967	1968	1969
Stockholders' equity:								
Common stock: Par value 10¢ per share	$ 30	$ 30	$ 31	$ 33	$ 42	$ 42	$ 43	$ 43
Additional paid-in capital...............	253	253	292	327	1,431	1,431	1,447	1,473
Retained earnings	34	120	418	955	459	16	119	295
Total stockholders' equity	$317	$403	$ 741	$1,315	$1,932	$1,489	$1,609	$1,811
Total liabilities and stockholders' equity	$391	$665	$2,073	$3,482	$4,260	$2,441	$2,451	$2,584
Book value per share	$1.06	$1.34	$2.36	$4.04	$4.54	$3.50	$3.74	$4.17
Stock price range:*								
High	Not	Not	14	18.375	15.75	9.625	10.25	11.25
Low	traded	traded	3.375	10.5	3.75	4.25	4.125	6.0

*Price on March 2, 1970 = $6.875.
Source: Annual reports.

The metal tennis racket market was much more difficult to estimate. All manufacturers wished to withhold from competitors possibly helpful information on the size of the market and the unit volume that each manufacturer was selling.

The three brand names in the market were Wilson, Spalding, and Tensor. In 1969 Tensor had introduced a lower cost model of its metal racket under the brand name of Melbourne. This was an effort to broaden the appeal to new market segments without diluting the Tensor brand name. Tennis rackets which carried the Tensor brand name ranged in price from $34 to $60 at retail. The aluminum racket was the least expensive at $34; the steel racket sold for about $40; a new 24K gold-plated line sold for $50; and the new top-of-the-line stainless steel racket was priced at $60. Tensor's Melbourne brand was produced in both aluminum and steel with selling prices from $19.95 to $29.95. Although the Tensor steel racket at $40 was competitive with Wilson and Spalding, private-label rackets sold as low as $12. A 40–50 percent retail markup on factory price was considered normal in sporting goods distribution.

Although estimates were only approximate, Mr. Savitsky believed that Tensor in mid-1969 was selling 10–20 percent of the market in comparison to 45–70 percent for Wilson, 10–15 percent for Spalding, and 10–20 percent for the combined small private-label manufacturers. He also estimated that Wilson had 60 percent of the wooden racket market, while Spalding had 30 percent, and all others accounted for the remaining 10 percent.

Mr. Monroe had a different estimate for market share based on the metal rackets he observed at country clubs and on some information he had heard about the total market size. Mr. Monroe believed that 4 million tennis rackets were sold annually and that recently 35 percent of tennis racket sales were metal rackets. Combining these figures with his own observations, Mr. Monroe reasoned that Wilson metal rackets were outselling Tensor ten to one. Wilson Sporting Goods, Inc., was a $100 million subsidiary of a $3.5 billion conglomerate. Spalding had annual sales of $65 million and had recently been acquired by a $220 million conglomerate.

Marketing

Mr. Monroe saw marketing as the key area in Tensor's recent recovery. He believed that Tensor's quality image had allowed the company to market successfully a second and third consumer product. Exhibits 6 and 7 give same advertising and pictures of lamps and flashlights; Exhibits 8 and 9 do the same for tennis rackets. George Savitsky commented on Tensor's image:

> We established our image with the customer by advertising and with the dealer by not allowing price cutting. Our advertising was quite heavy as a percent of sales, but it helped us maintain our market share in periods of expansion and later contraction. Perhaps we even "overadvertised" on Tensor lamps, but the name we developed gave us an image which we could trade on to our advantage in 1969.
>
> As far as our channels of distribution were concerned, we initially avoided discount stores as much as possible. We didn't want to do business in areas of severe price cutting. Whenever that happens we'll leave the business to others. I believe Tensor was 98 percent effective in stopping price cutting on Tensor lamps. We brought suit under fair-trade laws, cut off distributors who were cutting their prices, coded our lamps so we could determine which distributors were selling to the retail price cutters, and even bought up some of the discounters' lamps to dry up their supply.
>
> We feel we are continuing to enhance our image with tennis rackets. Recently we refused a large order from a major retailer because they wanted us to put our name on the tag and cut the price. This willingness to turn away business that is not on our terms is what establishes a reputation. Perhaps we will soften our stance in tennis rackets after this reputation is firmly established.

Tensor's allocation of margin to the various aspects of its distribution network depended on the product involved. In the lamp business, where Tensor had a narrow margin, most of this margin was allocated to the channel of distribution. The manufacturers' representatives received only a 5 percent commission.

For tennis rackets, on the other hand, Tensor was able to allow more margin to the sales force. At present the tennis rackets were being sold on a 10 percent commission basis.

Tensor's two sales forces consisted solely of manufacturers' representatives. The first group, numbering about 25, sold high-intensity lamps to 30 department stores and chains and to 300–400 wholesalers. Retail outlets

EXHIBIT 6
Sample lamp advertising

A lot of people think they own a Tensor.

A lot of people think anything that's smaller than a breadbox and plugs in is a Tensor.

So whenever somebody's imitation Tensor disappoints him, we're the ones who end up getting the blame.

The truth is that an awful lot of the little lamps you see around aren't even high intensity, let alone Tensor high intensity.

It takes more than a cute shape and a tiny bulb to make a high intensity lamp. It takes a transformer that steps up the current on its way from the wall to the bulb. And the more powerful the transformer, the more efficiently the bulb burns.

Hidden away in its base, Tensor has the most powerful and sophisticated transformer of them all. So Tensor shines with the whitest, brightest, most natural light.

Our lamp costs a little more but it's worth hunting for. (There it is— up front, on the left.)

When you're actually in the store ready to plunk your money down, turn all the little lamps on. You'll find that, watt for watt, Tensor outshines them all.

Would you expect anything less from the people who invented the high intensity lamp in the first place?

Tensor Corporation, Brooklyn, N.Y.

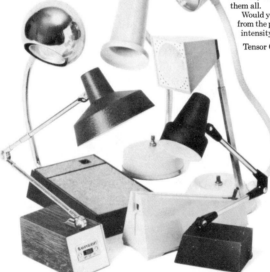

serviced by these wholesalers probably averaged 100 per wholesaler. The second sales force, also numbering about 25, sold tennis rackets to sporting goods stores, specialty stores, and pro shops. This sales force serviced about 2,000 accounts.

In addition, Tensor was in the process of developing a 25-man "premium" sales force to sell the disposable flashlight and other Tensor products to companies for use in sales contests and promotional campaigns.

EXHIBIT 7
Lamp and flashlight sample pictures

Tensor Model
6500

Tensor Model
7200

Tensor Model 100
Disposable Flashlight

As manufacturers' representatives, Tensor's salespeople served the same distribution outlets with non-Tensor products. Mr. Savitsky was uncertain of the extent of the increase in volume on present product lines that Tensor could obtain by raising sales commissions or by developing additional Tensor product lines appropriate for sale by the present sales force.

Finance

Stanley Jaret, the treasurer, outlined the company's 1969 financial position as follows:

> Now that we are back in the black again, our problem is not cash. We had almost $450,000 in cash and marketable securities at the end of 1969. Most of this cash resulted from our failure to expand sales—and therefore inventories and receivables—as fast as we had anticipated when we acquired new equity in the summer of 1966.
>
> Our real problem is to assure that we retain control of the company. Jay owns 26 percent of the stock, but none of the rest of the management owns more than a nominal amount of Tensor's equity. As far as we are able to determine now, the stock is widely distributed with no other party owning any significant percent. We could use our cash to repurchase some of the stock on the open market and virtually assure control, but our stock price doubled with our return to profitable operations, and any significant volume of buying seems to boost the price sharply.
>
> We have made some structural changes to keep Tensor from being taken over. For instance, at our next stockholder meeting we will propose cumu-

374

EXHIBIT 8
Sample metal tennis racket advertising

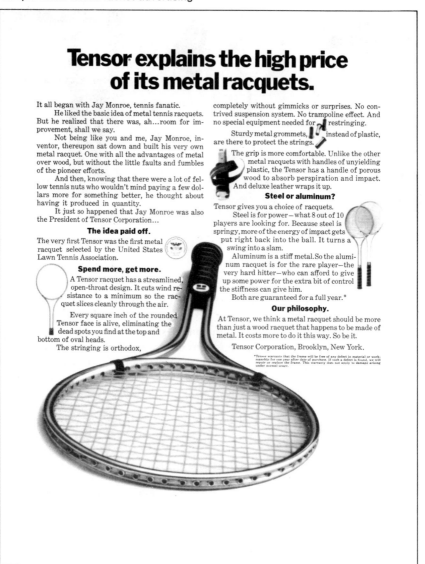

Tensor explains the high price of its metal racquets.

It all began with Jay Monroe, tennis fanatic.

He liked the basic idea of metal tennis racquets. But he realized that there was, ah...room for improvement, shall we say.

Not being like you and me, Jay Monroe, inventor, thereupon sat down and built his very own metal racquet. One with all the advantages of metal over wood, but without the little faults and fumbles of the pioneer efforts.

And then, knowing that there were a lot of fellow tennis nuts who wouldn't mind paying a few dollars more for something better, he thought about having it produced in quantity.

It just so happened that Jay Monroe was also the President of Tensor Corporation...

The idea paid off.

The very first Tensor was the first metal racquet selected by the United States Lawn Tennis Association.

Spend more, get more.

A Tensor racquet has a streamlined, open-throat design. It cuts wind resistance to a minimum so the racquet slices cleanly through the air.

Every square inch of the rounded Tensor face is alive, eliminating the dead spots you find at the top and bottom of oval heads.

The stringing is orthodox, completely without gimmicks or surprises. No contrived suspension system. No trampoline effect. And no special equipment needed for restringing.

Sturdy metal grommets, instead of plastic, are there to protect the strings.

The grip is more comfortable. Unlike the other metal racquets with handles of unyielding plastic, the Tensor has a handle of porous wood to absorb perspiration and impact. And deluxe leather wraps it up.

Steel or aluminum?

Tensor gives you a choice of racquets.

Steel is for power—what 8 out of 10 players are looking for. Because steel is springy, more of the energy of impact gets put right back into the ball. It turns a swing into a slam.

Aluminum is a stiff metal. So the aluminum racquet is for the rare player—the very hard hitter—who can afford to give up some power for the extra bit of control the stiffness can give him.

Both are guaranteed for a full year.*

Our philosophy.

At Tensor, we think a metal racquet should be more than just a wood racquet that happens to be made of metal. It costs more to do it this way. So be it.

Tensor Corporation, Brooklyn, New York.

*Tensor warrants that the frame will be free of any defect in material or workmanship for one year after date of purchase. If such a defect is found, we will repair or replace the frame. This warranty does not apply to damage arising under normal usage.

lative voting for positions on our expanded nine-man board of directors. Directors will have staggered three-year terms, allowing management to retain control for two years even in the eventuality of a raid. With our large cash position and our deficits for 1966 and 1967, a raid was a distinct possibility. Also, we recently voted an employee stock plan. The employee stock

EXHIBIT 9
Sample metal tennis racket pictures

Tensor Aluminum Tennis
Racket

Tensor Steel Tennis
Racket

fund buys shares on the open market. This should put more shares in
friendly hands. Finally, a management stock bonus plan has been started.
The four officers of the company received 5,000 shares of stock (restricted
for ten years as to sale) in 1968. Forty-five hundred additional restricted
shares were given to management in 1969.

I would say our biggest area for present improvement of financial management is internal control. We should be able to avoid the capital expenditure errors we made in the past, and also to remain more current in our
sales projections.

Production

In 1969 Tensor employed approximately 200 persons in its Brooklyn
headquarters and plant facility. Most of the production jobs required only
short training periods, and manual dexterity was the major requirement for
many of them.

The lamp section of the plant consisted of a couple of subassembly lines, a small amount of in-process inventory to smooth the work flow, and finished inventory at the shipping end of the plant.

Tennis racket production started with precut metal rods. These rods were bent, drilled, and finished. A handle and grip then were added at the end, and the racket was strung and stored on a long rack by size and type. As orders were received, they were filled by picking the rackets off the easily accessible storage rack and sending them to shipping.

Walter Gloumakoff, the plant manager, summarized the Tensor production operation as simple and flexible:

> Our strength is in keeping operating costs low and in not sinking resources into production tooling. We have quite experienced toolmakers who save us time by cooperating in the product design stage. As a product is being designed, they simultaneously create the tools to produce it. That way we don't create any new products we can't produce. Our toolmakers also save us money by designing more economical limited purpose tools instead of general-purpose tools which do more than is required. A good example is the $2,000 drill rig made up to drill the string holes for our rackets. A general-purpose tool to perform the same task might have cost as much as $10,000.
>
> We are essentially a design and assembly business with low fabrication content. We did bring some of the lamp fabrication in-house when sales dropped off, but that was mainly to fill idle production capacity.

One production decision which was a continuing possibility was the transference of some manufacturing to Japan. This was an alternative available not only for lamp production but also for any other electromechanical devices which Tensor developed in the future. Because of the original uncertain nature of the lamp market there was a need to make the large fixed-volume and design commitment necessary to secure Japanese production at a low cost. Recently, however, design maturation and cost competition had forced a reconsideration of the desirability of lamp importing.

In the area of new products, Mr. Monroe continued to believe that the best course to follow was to retain start-up and initial production in the Brooklyn plant until the design could be stabilized and some estimate of the demand was possible. Using this production strategy, original Tensor selling price would be based on eventual Japanese production costs rather than actual Brooklyn production costs. Tensor would make little or no profit on any new electromechanical product until production could be transferred to Japan.

Research and development

Tensor's research and development was concentrated entirely in the hands of Jay Monroe. He had ten other people working for him on development projects. Every couple of months Monroe made out a list of ideas that were of current interest to him. Then he and the development staff worked on that list until each item was either finished or discarded. The February 1969 list, shown in Exhibit 10 consisted solely of innovations concerned with tennis.

EXHIBIT 10
February 1969, R&D list

1. Improved tennis ball.
2. Nylon tennis string.
3. Deep groove in hardened frame.
4. Flanged eyelets.
5. Fiberglass racket.
6. Stainless steel racket.
7. "U" channel for aluminum racket.
8. Lithographed nameplate.
9. Box to hold string.

Source: Company document.

Mr. Monroe believed that Tensor's product development was less fruitful than would be possible if he could find a larger congenial staff to do development work. The general problem was that sophisticated research and development personnel often required the freedom to conceive and independently execute their own ideas, rather than execute engineering details under someone else's direction. Mr. Monroe had found only one tool and model maker (known throughout the company as "Mac") who was a major help to him in his development work. Mr. Monroe stated the personality problem this way:

> I know I don't have the easiest personality to work with, and many qualified applicants will not like development work at Tensor because of the way I run it. I do feel, however, that my talent is being underutilized, and that I could direct much more extensive development work.

By June 1969 Tensor had completed all the projects on the February list except the "U" channel, which had been dropped, the fiberglass racket, which was waiting for completion of final testing, and the improved tennis ball, which was still pending. The delay on the tennis ball was attributed to the inability to find a molding method which did not require a capital investment of $1 million or more. However, in April 1970, Tensor finally finished the design of a hairless rubber ball which had the characteristics on a cement or composition court that a regular tennis ball had on a clay court. Mr. Monroe had designed this ball in the belief that tennis had become too fast a game on nonclay courts and that his ball would allow a normal clay court speed on a nonclay court. The new ball could be mass produced with less than $100,000 in equipment investment.

Tensor was uncertain about the company's ability to market tennis balls with such radical characteristics. Consequently, Tensor planned first to gain experience by introducing under the Tensor name a conventional tennis ball manufactured in Ireland.

Telephone message recorder.   During early 1970 Tensor was also planning to announce the introduction of a $200–$250 (a firm price had not yet been decided) telephone message recorder. Jay Monroe had invented the recorder so that he would not have to take messages personally for his children when they were not at home. With his message recorder all he would have to do was turn on the recorder; it was designed so that it could be attached to his children's telephone, which had its own separate number.

The telephone message recorder consisted of a cassette recorder, a tape to give messages to the caller, a tape on which the caller can leave messages, and an automatic on/off mechanism. The breakthrough in the Tensor product was a low price achieved through simple design and the use of recent advances in the size and capability of cassette recorders. Tensor also

EXHIBIT 11
Photograph of Tensor telephone message recorder unit

planned to market a lower priced model which would not include its own cassette recorder. Any tape recorder could be attached to this model.

The present message recorder market had four brand entrants. Three of those four were priced far above the Tensor level, and the fourth was a very recent entry priced at $150–$200.[2] Mr. Monroe was hoping that his latest product would have wide acceptance by individual consumers. Previous message recorders were used mainly by businesses. Exhibit 11 shows a photograph of a Tensor message recorder unit.

Mr. Monroe estimated the present message recorder market at $10 to $15 million annually and growing extremely rapidly. One question being debated by Tensor management in late 1969 was how to finance the introduction of the message recorder. Management estimated the capital required at $1 million and was not anxious to jeopardize the existence of the company by risking internal operating capital. One possible solution was to form a majority-owned subsidiary and issue stock to the public. The subsidiary could then develop separate management and production facilities.

This strategy of public capitalization of the message recorder did not seem to Mr. Monroe likely to succeed, however, because of the lackluster state of the U.S. economy and the low level of the stock market in early 1970. An alternative to public capitalization was for Tensor to introduce the recorder over a period of time which would cause less financial risk. A slow product introduction would have less market impact but would allow Tensor to cut its losses earlier if the product was not accepted by the consumer. Under this alternative Tensor planned to manufacture the first recorders at the plant in Brookyln. If the product were successful, mass production could be shifted to Japan to keep costs down.

Paddle tennis racket.   In late 1969 Tensor began production on a paddle tennis racket. Tensor management predicted that this market, although only $50,000–$100,000 annually, would be highly profitable. Exhibit 12 is a photograph of the Tensor paddle tennis racket.

Sportsmen, Inc.   In order to expand into additional sporting goods areas, in February 1970 Tensor acquired Sportsmen, Inc., a small Long Island manufacturer of fiberglass billiard cues, archery sets, and fishing equipment. The Tensor 1969 annual report stated that Tensor planned "to utilize the sporting goods distribution channels we have established to increase the sales of Sportsmen's existing products while developing new products combining Tensor's technology and Sportsmen's manufacturing facilities." In particular Tensor hoped to employ the fiberglass manufacturing techniques which the president of Sportsmen had developed. Mr. Monroe believed that fiberglass usage in consumer products was expanding

---

[2] This recent entry was imported from Japan and was roughly competitive with Tensor in its product characteristics.

EXHIBIT 12
Photograph of the Tensor paddle tennis racket

and that these techniques might be useful in any number of future Tensor products.

Sportsmen, Inc., sales had previously been as high as $1 million, but lack of marketing expertise had resulted in a 90 percent sales decline and in unprofitable operation. Tensor purchased Sportsmen for approximately $15,-000 cash and 5,500 shares of stock. Valuing Tensor shares at the closing price of $6.75 recorded on the purchase date, Tensor paid about $30,000 below book value. Exhibit 13 shows the Sportsmen product line.

As opposed to the 1960–67 period, when Tensor seemed content to confine new products to new lamp models, the 1969 approach was spread out in a number of diverse product areas.

Organization

Tensor's organization at the end of 1969 was similar to its preexpansion organization in 1964. It consisted of Mr. Monroe and one executive each in marketing, finance, manufacturing, and development engineering. Exhibit 14 gives the 1970 Tensor organization chart. These five executives had a five-year contract for compensation totaling $147,000 annually.

The interrelations among the five executives were frequent and informal. The financial job consisted of a preliminary financial profit forecast for the company derived from marketing and production estimates and a monitoring of operations to assure that the company was not below forecast.

Production scheduling was a combined effort of marketing and production. Marketing supplied forecasts and production scheduled on that basis. Marketing forecasts were continually revised on the basis of orders being

EXHIBIT 13
Photograph of the Sportsmen, Inc., product line

PRODUCTS OF SPORTSMEN, INC.

EXHIBIT 14
1970 organization chart

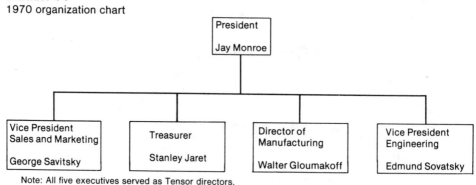

Note: All five executives served as Tensor directors.

received. Production, which was not set up to derive economies from long runs, was able to adjust rapidly to changes in demand.

The central coordinating device in the Tensor organization was the daily lunch meeting of the five top executives, which took place in the company conference room. Almost all corporate decisions were made at these meetings. Each executive, including Mr. Monroe, took an active part, and decisions were made by discussion until a consensus was reached. Exhibit 15 is a sample of the topics discussed at one luncheon meeting.

EXHIBIT 15
Topics of discussion at one lunch meeting in February 1970

A recent speech by economist Pierre Rinfret.
Tennis racket returns.
Logo and printing on Tensor-marketed tennis balls.
Sportsmen acquisition.
Financing the message recorder introduction.
Deciding where to invest development time.
Trading off risk and gain in development decisions.
What the executives want to sell regardless of the return.

THE FUTURE

Each of Tensor's five executives was asked to express his feelings about his job and his goals for the future of Tensor. Their answers were as follows:

Jay Monroe, president

I think of the whole company as a toy. My motive for establishing and operating Tensor is for the sheer fun of running it. I have no official duties of any kind and feel that management on a day-to-day basis is boring and not worth the time it takes.

I feel it is a tragedy that the present economic system has made my motivations unacceptable. Product decisions in the United States are being made more and more on the basis of return on investment. This means that industrial art and creative technical development suffer. The state of product development of consumer products would be higher if business were willing to make decisions on aesthetic rather than return on investment criteria. The creative guy wants to gamble, but the professional manager stifles him.

From my own point of view, I want to be able to produce a product I like even if it did not show any chance of an acceptable level of return. Above all, I don't want to have to take my ideas to a professional manager and have to convince him economically of the idea's worth. This may not be in the short-term best interest of the other stockholders, but I believe that the company will contribute better and more interesting products.

My goal for new products is to market only "classy" products which contribute to the image of the company. For instance, we could probably profitably expand into tennis clothes, but I am determined to avoid the bad image of the garment industry.

One element of management I don't like is the constant degradation of ethics necessary to restrain a competitive operation. It seems that no matter how low you sink, someone is always more unethical. This cycle is repulsive. For instance, kickbacks to marketing channels and questionable advertising claims may become increasingly necessary to continue to compete. I believe this practical necessity is unethical and very objectionable.

In terms of size, I am happy to have Tensor remain at its present volume. We have four other executives, all roughly the same age, who are content to spend their lives with this company. Perhaps we should grow enough to keep up with expanding wages and overhead, but I've experienced rapid expansion once, and I don't want to go through that again. In addition, any major expansion that required new equity would seriously endanger management control of Tensor's ownership.

Stanley Jaret, treasurer

My goals from the company are a responsible position, a good living, security, and a job I can enjoy. I would like to see Tensor stabilize at around $6–$7 million sales. Any further increase would probably necessitate a major organizational change. I am content with the present arrangement and do not feel that the company needs to try to cope with an expansion larger than $3–$4 million.

One of my personal goals for the company is to assure that Tensor remains above break-even. If we can stay profitable, we substantially reduce the threat of takeover or insolvency.

George Savitsky, vice president—sales and marketing

My job is to tear apart everything Jay wants to do and figure out what parts we can do and what parts we can't. The general pattern is his ideas and my exploitation.

As far as new products, I'd like to see more products which fit into our present channels of distribution. We have a fairly meager volume per store, and I would like to increase our worth to our distribution channels.

I would like to see steady growth for Tensor through product diversification. I don't believe I would enjoy the impersonality of a $50 million business, but I would like the excitement of a $20–$30 million company.

Edmund Sovatsky, vice president—engineering

My greatest pleasure is to finally put a product into production after fooling with the design for a few months. I like sporting goods as a product area because the time from idea to market is exceptionally short.

My sales goal for the company is $10 million per year or a little over. I dislike emergencies and feel that a company that size is still small enough to be controlled. Also, I like the freedom I have to make decisions, and I believe that freedom would be impaired if the company grew too large.

Walter Gloumakoff, director of manufacturing

My objective for Tensor is profitability with a reasonable growth curve which would include diversification in products and in manufacturing assets. I am particularly fond of electromechanical consumer products. They represent more of a challenge than strictly mechanical products.

I would like to see Tensor achieve a sales level of $30–$50 million. At that volume production would be a lot more complicated. Production is always a rat race, but I love it.

SUPPLEMENT: TENSOR CORPORATION

The following article appeared in the January 8, 1970, issue of the evening edition of the *Boston Globe*. Additional information relating to the controversy described is included in Exhibits A1 to A3.

Tensor's friend at Chase too friendly with Arabs[3]

New York—An advertisement bearing the headline "Tensor Corporation no longer 'has a friend at Chase Manhattan' " appears in today's edition of *The New York Times.*

Tensor's president, Jay Monroe, said in the quarter-page ad that the company would close out its account at the New York City bank whose slogan is, "You have a friend at Chase Manhattan."

---

[3] The *Boston Globe*, evening edition, January 8, 1970. Reproduced with permission.

Monroe, president of the company which manufactures high-intensity lamps and tennis rackets, said in the ad the action was being taken as a protest to reported efforts of Chase Manhattan's chairman of the board, David Rockefeller, and a former chairman, John J. McCloy, to induce President Nixon to reshape Middle East policies to mollify the Arab states because of what Monroe said was the bank's "considerable economic interests in the oil-rich region."

When informed of the ad's contents, Rockefeller issued a statement in which he said, "I believe, as I always have, that the United States must do everything it can to safeguard the security and sovereign existence of Israel.

"My sole interest," he added, "is in seeing that hostilities are ended and peace is achieved, a peace taking fully into account the legitimate aspirations of the parties involved."

Monroe, who is of Jewish origin, said in the advertisement: "Now Mr. Rockefeller has apparently decided it is best to put his mouth where his money is. I feel that turnabout is fair play. Accordingly, Tensor's account is being withdrawn from the Chase."

A source close to Tensor said the company maintained an account with the bank that was "in excess of $50,000." He said the cost of the ad was about $2,200.

Monroe said he based his statement about the Rockefeller's advocacy of a new Middle East policy on a story in the Dec. 22 issue of *The New York Times*.

The *Times* article had reported that a group including Rockefeller and McCloy had discussed the Middle East political situation at an unpublicized meeting with President Nixon at the White House Dec. 9.

The article said: "According to officials familiar with the discussion, the consensus in the group was that the United States must act immediately to improve its relations with oil-producing and other Arab states. The group was said to feel this was necessary to deflect what the group feared to be an imminent loss of United States standing in the Middle East that might be reflected politically as well as in terms of American petroleum interests in the area."

EXHIBIT A1
Article from *The New York Times*, December 22, 1969

U.S. policies in Mideast are under fire
Industrialists reported to warn Nixon on loss of influence with Arabs

Tad Szulc
Special to *The New York Times*

Washington, Dec. 21—President Nixon is reported to have received warnings from a group of top American industry leaders with oil and other interests in the Middle East that the United States is rapidly losing political and economic influence in the Arab states because of its present policies.

EXHIBIT A1 (continued)

The industrialists' concern over the deterioration of the United States position in the Middle East and over the proportional growth of the Soviet importance there—attributed by them in part to Washington's past support for Israel—was expressed at an unpublicized meeting at the White House on Dec. 9.

Bankers attended

A White House spokesman has confirmed that Mr. Nixon had asked the group to discuss with him the "political situation in the Middle East." The members included David Rockefeller, president of the Chase Manhattan Bank; John J. McCloy, former president of Chase Manhattan; and Robert B. Anderson, former Secretary of the Treasury and a director of Dresser Industries Company, which has oil interests in Kuwait and Libya.

Administration officials said that the President had invited them to hear their views on the eve of the Dec. 10 session of the National Security Council, which was dedicated to a review of the United States policy in the Middle East.

Attending the industrialists' meeting with Mr. Nixon was Henry A. Kissinger, the President's special assistant for national security affairs. White House officials emphasized that those conferring with the President were "people with a political knowledge of the Middle East situation and the oil situation in the Middle East."

Action was urged

Administration officials declined, however, to disclose what specific advice the industrialists had offered Mr. Nixon and none of the participants were available today for comment.

According to officials familiar with the discussion, the consensus in the group was that the United States must act immediately to improve its relations with oil-producing and other Arab states. The group was said to feel this was necessary to deflect what the group feared to be an imminent loss of United States standing in the Middle East that might be reflected politically as well as in terms of American petroleum interests in the area.

The group was said to feel that United States weapons deliveries to Israel, including the recent shipment of supersonic Phantom jets, and Washington's alleged support of Israeli policies in the Middle East conflict were turning moderate and conservative Arab leaders as well as radical Arabs against the United States.

That basic evaluation was presented to Mr. Nixon early this year by William W. Scranton, former Governor of Pennsylvania, who toured the Middle East on a presidential mission.

But the increase in Middle East hostilities in the intervening period and the aggravation of the over-all situation had led a group of United States oil executives to submit a private memorandum to Mr. Nixon last September urging the preservation of American interests as a basis for the United States policy in the region.

The September meeting of oil executives was reportedly held in Beirut, Leba-

EXHIBIT A1 (concluded)

non. Subsequent meetings were held in Beirut in October, informants said, and a session on Oct. 29 was attended by Mr. Rockefeller.

According to authoritative sources, Mr. Rockefeller then met with President Abdel Gamal Nasser of the United Arab Republic in Cairo on Oct. 31, to discuss the Middle East political situation along with some of the Chase Manhattan Bank's projects in Egypt.

Official quarters said that Mr. Rockefeller reported to the Administration at the time that President Nasser hoped the United States, through a change in its policies, could help him to become freer of the growing Soviet influence. The Soviet Union supplies most of the United Arab Republic's military equipment. The United States has had no diplomatic relations with Cairo since the 1967 Middle East war.

Others who conferred with Mr. Nixon on Dec. 9 have had direct communication with Arab leaders as well. Mr. Anderson, for example, talked with President Nasser and King Hussein of Jordan in Cairo last March.

It was this direct experience in the Middle East that, in the judgment of the White House, qualified these industrialists to present their views to Mr. Nixon.

However, officials said that the views expressed by the visiting group to the President were not mentioned directly when the National Security Council met Dec. 10 to debate the Middle East policy.

Authoritative informants said that the United States oil industry is concerned over the danger of Arab terrorist attacks on American petroleum installations and over the possibility that the greater British and French sympathies for the Arab policies may in time result in the erosion of the American oil presence in the Middle East.

EXHIBIT A2
Advertisement in *The New York Times*, January 8, 1970

Tensor Corporation no longer "has a friend at Chase Manhattan"

An Open Letter to the American Public:

It would appear that our neighborhood banker, who goes to great pains to tell us that he is our friend, has a rather narrow (mercenary) definition of the word friendship.

As reported in the December 22 issue of The New York Times, David Rockefeller, president of The Chase Manhattan Bank, and John McCloy, its former president, have warned President Nixon that U.S. policies in the Middle East are resulting in a loss of political and economic influence in the Arab world.

One must wonder how much Chase Manhattan's considerable economic interests in the oil-rich region figured in the decision to urge a new policy which would mollify the Arabs. Certainly world conditions do not indicate that such a change is in order. Israel is a truly democratic state, a modern oasis surrounded by feudal baronies. With the support of cynical Communists countries, the Arab chieftains

EXHIBIT A2 (continued)

have attempted to destroy Israel. With the moral support and material help of Americans, Israel has survived, so far.

Now Mr. Rockefeller has apparently decided it is best to put his mouth where his money is. I feel that turnabout is fair play. Accordingly, Tensor's account is being withdrawn from the Chase.

Ours is not one of the corporate giants, and no doubt Chase Manhattan will carry on very nicely without Tensor's business. But if others—small depositors and giant corporations alike—join in this protest againt a "dollar diplomacy" based on oil interests, our former friends at Chase may learn that free men do not live by oil alone.

Sincerely,

Jay Monroe
President
Tensor Corporation

EXHIBIT A3
Article from *The New York Times,* January 9, 1970

David Rockefeller says he supports security of Israel

David Rockefeller, chairman of the Chase Manhattan Bank, said yesterday that the United States "must do all it can to safeguard the security and sovereign existence of Israel."

Mr. Rockefeller said that his interest in Middle East issues was "in seeing that hostilities are ended and peace is achieved—a peace directly negotiated between the parties involved and taking fully into account their legitimate aspirations."

His statement followed the publication in The New York Times yesterday of an advertisement signed by Jay Monroe, president of the Tensor Corporation, manufacturer of high-intensity lamps, asserting that the corporation "no longer 'has a friend at Chase Manhattan.'" The advertisement cited a dispatch in The New York Times Dec. 22 reporting that Mr. Rockefeller had been among a group of business leaders who met with President Nixon and warned that the United States was losing influence in the Arab states because of policies the Arabs felt favored Israel.

A spokeman for the Chase Manhattan Bank said Mr. Rockefeller's statement was in answer to the dispatch and not to the advertisement.

Mr. Rockefeller said he had been convinced during a recent trip to the Middle East that more and more thoughtful Arabs "appear disposed to explore reasonable compromises."

He said that in the meeting with the President, he intended "merely to suggest that the United States encourage these more positive and conciliatory sentiments."

Reached by telephone, Mr. Monroe said he was not a Zionist but supported Israel's "democratic position in the Middle East." He said he had withdrawn an account with a $250,000 line of credit from the bank.

part two

POLICY
ADMINISTRATION

chapter
7

Designing and managing the overall organization

In Part II we ask you to shift your attention to the task the general manager faces in leading the organization in the accomplishment of the purposes identified and decided upon by the processes described in Part I. We are passing from the formulation of strategy to the implementation of that strategy via the people in the organization. We will no longer be concerned only with the overall purposes that the organization is trying to achieve but will now devote our attention as well to the broader tasks of designing the appropriate structure and processes and managing the overall organization. Except for the Zurn Industries case, Part II deals largely with single-business organizations, as did Part I. The general management task in diversified companies will be explored in more detail in Part III.

The first part of the book is analytical in the usual sense of that word because it deals primarily with the economic environment of the firm and with the functional areas of the business such as marketing, production, and finance in the development of the strategy for the firm. Quantitative analyses and techniques are of greater help with strategic issues than with the administrative tasks involved in leading the organization in the accomplishment of its strategy. What you have learned in Organizational Behavior, Accounting and Control, and from your own experience in organizations will be the most relevant inputs to the administrative challenges that face the general manager.

The concern of this chapter is one about which a great deal has been written. The challenges of motivating people to contribute their best efforts in the achievement of purposes for the most part established by others for the benefit of others have been the subject of thought, research, and writings for thousands of years. Academic disciplines, such as psychology and organizational behavior, have developed which have much to say about these problems. Specific courses dealing with the behavior of people in organizations and methods of measuring their peformance exist in every school of business, and any business library is likely to have hundreds of books and thousands of articles which deal with these problems.

OBJECTIVES

The preceding should lead any sensible reader to ask what we need to add at this point to the knowledge to which you already have been exposed in your courses and readings concerning the behavior of people in organizations. Our objectives are not to repeat what you have learned elsewhere but to emphasize three factors that should strongly influence the manner in which you apply what you have learned, as well as the lessons from your own experiences in working with people, to the problems of the cases:

1. We are dealing with specific companies with specific problems, administrative histories, and strategies which define purposes, key tasks, and constraints. It is highly desirable to attempt to generalize about how categories of problems similar to those in the case should be solved, but that should come after you address the problems at hand, not before. Your task is to suggest what steps Mr. Millman should take in The Adams Corporation (the first case in Part II) to bring about the changes he desires, and not to discuss the characteristics of the ideal management-control system, compensation system, or decentralized organization structure for geographically decentralized firms without ever addressing Mr. Millman's specific problems.

2. In dealing with the specific case situation, you will have to keep in mind that you are also dealing with real people, not idealized or typical people. You will frequently not know as much about the individuals in the case as you would like, and as you would know in real life, but at least do not ignore what information is available. You learned the importance of taking into account the values of Jay Monroe in understanding why he acted as he did in the Tensor case and how you could advise him so that there might be some chance he would act upon your advice. In a similar manner, you will have to take into account the people with whom you are dealing in this part of the book. Clark Kramer in the Midway case brings certain values to his role as a manager, and these influence his approach to the way in which he chooses to, and is able to, work with his organization.

3. Most importantly, your task will be the design of organization structure and processes and the management of its members as a means of achieving the overall purposes of the organization. We all desire a humane and satisfying work environment, but that environment must be effective in meeting organizational as well as individual goals. You will find in the Lincoln case an explicit and unusual attempt to address both of those goals. Organizations in which individual efforts do not contribute sufficiently to the attainment of organizational goals seldom prosper and sometimes fail, at

least in the private sector. If an organization depends upon the voluntary support of its customers, the feedback from the marketplace ultimately will have an impact.

What you have learned elsewhere about interpersonal relationships, human motivation, measurement and control systems, organizational design, and leadership should surely be applicable to the general manager's task of leading the organization in the achievement of its strategy. We will be interested in the application of this knowledge, however, and not in the knowledge itself. In that sense, your task in this part of the book will be somewhat different than what you are likely to have been exposed to in other courses dealing with the topics described above.

We also hope that in this section you will develop for yourself some of the skills essential to the manager and not just an understanding of the job and the intellectual ability to analyze problems and recommend action to someone else. The development of your personal skills can be facilitated by your classroom discussion of administrative situations. Listening to others, learning to understand what they mean as well as why they are saying it, and convincing them of the merits of your position are important skills to learn. Acting out, where appropriate, exactly what you would say or do in the specific situation is useful practice. Ample opportunities for such role-playing exist in the cases, and even a brief attempt to *be* the person involved and to talk as though you were that person, not simply to advise him what to say, will emphasize the difference between recommending to another and acting yourself in the situation. You will find that it is very much easier to tell Mr. Pierce of the Rose Company what he should say to his new subordinates than it is to say it yourself to one of your classmates who is playing the role of a subordinate.

FRAMEWORK

To assist you in the task of designing and managing the overall organization, we shall suggest a simple framework, or approach, just as we did for the problem of strategy formulation in Part I. We will emphasize again that these two tasks of formulation and implementation are split apart largely in the minds and writings of the observer; no manager can focus on one without considering the other. He will concentrate his attention on one aspect or the other as the occasion demands, but the overall achievement of purpose requires a blending of formulation and administration suitable to the company. A brilliant strategy without a means of accomplishment is of no greater value than a superb organization without a purpose.

We suggest you think of the problem of managing the overall organization in terms of the sources of influence available to the manager in working with the organization. The tasks to be accomplished will be, in large part, the result of the objectives chosen and the strategies developed. The sources of influence that the manager has in leading the organization in the accomplishment of these tasks can be grouped into five categories:

1. The organization structure: the definition of responsibilities and the establishment of reporting relationships among individuals and subunits.

2. The information systems: the collection, flow, and presentation of information concerning the operations of the organization.

3. The reward systems: the multiple forms of rewards which can be earned (or foregone) by the members of the organization, including pay, incentives of all kinds, praise and personal satisfaction, promotion, and so on.

4. The allocation of resources: the allocation of sufficient resources to units or projects, which not only is essential to the accomplishment of the objectives set out but also often becomes a source of personal satisfaction to the individuals involved.

5. The most intangible source of influence of all, but perhaps the most important, is what we commonly lump under the catch-all of *leadership:* the overall behavior of the manager as it affects the desires and the abilities of the members of the organization to work toward the accomplishment of the organization's goals.

The totality of the general manager's job, then, can be thought of as developing and maintaining a strategy that is a creative and productive fit of the various elements that affect the formulation and the implementation of that strategy:

Strategy formulation		*Strategy implementation*
Corporate environment		Organization structure
Corporate resources	STRATEGY	Information systems
Management values		Reward systems
Corporate responsibilities		Allocation of resources
		Leadership

Organization structure, information systems, reward systems and human motivation, resource-allocation procedures, and leadership are all familiar topics. With the exception of the nature of effective leadership, the sources of influence available are in themselves not overly complicated. Experts in various aspects such as organization structure, compensation schemes, or information systems are always ready to advise on the latest developments in their specialties. What is both complex and less common is the judgment required to combine the tools available to all in such a manner that they are effective over a long period of time. The test of effectiveness from the viewpoint of the general manager does not lie in the sophistication or even "correctness" of any one element but in the way that they fit together and reinforce each other to serve the broader purposes dictated by the strategy of the company. Rather than expand upon these topics individually, we would like to direct your attention instead to some of the challenges that arise in combining all of these elements into a coherent, consistent overall approach that is suitable for the organization and the purposes it seeks to achieve.

FORMAL AND INFORMAL ORGANIZATION

The familiar black lines on the organization chart, along with titles and job descriptions that describe what the inhabitants of the boxes are supposed to do, portray a far neater and more rational world than exists in real life. Actual activities, if not formal job descriptions, must accommodate to some degree the skills, interests, and power positions of those who inhabit the boxes as well as what needs to be done for the organization to perform effectively.

In most organizations there are far more relationships that need to be taken into account than those represented by connecting solid lines. Where alternate or dual reporting relationships are fairly clear, we tend to represent them by means of dotted lines. The term *dotted line relationship to* is often used, for example, with regard to division controllers who may have a solid line relationship to (be a direct subordinate of) the division general manager but who have a dotted line relationship to the group or corporate controller.

When the multiple relationships become so numerous that a chart showing all the appropriate dotted lines would resemble a drawing of a battle-scarred spiderweb, we sometimes drop the lines altogether and describe it as a matrix organization, in which responsibilities for results are far more explicit than lines of authority. Such organizational forms are common in industries where large projects exist which require many months or years to complete, as in the defense industry. The product manager form of organization, in which the person "responsible" for the success of a product line does not have much, if any, authority over the product development, manufacturing, or marketing functions that affect the success of his product line, can also be thought of as a matrix form of organization. In such organizations, results are expected to come less from reliance on formal lines of authority than on a common commitment to work together to do what needs to be done, with each party expected to resolve, in a constructive way, the conflicting demands often placed on him or on the resources under his control.

There is also a separate category of relationships brought about by the existence of staff personnel at various levels. The manager of facilities planning can be a subordinate of one of a number of executives, including the president. He is unlikely to have any direct authority over others reporting to those executives or to those who are below him in the organization. His opinions and advice do carry some weight with others in the organization who have no formal reporting relationship to him, however, and in a manner which is seldom spelled out explicitly. Perhaps the most striking example of the importance of the sometimes unclear but often important role a staff man can play is in the case of the executive assistant to a busy president. In the Larger Company (A) case you will have a chance to discuss the appropriate role of staff and the ways in which the staff can exert influence on people over whom they have no formal control.

Beyond the complexities we try to represent by terms such as *line, staff, solid lines, dotted lines,* and *matrix organization* lies what we commonly call *the informal organization.* That is a euphemism for "the way things really work," and it covers everything about which we cannot be more explicit. It consists of the pattern of relationships and ways of working with each other that build up in conjunction with any formal organization structure and process or that arise even in the absence of such prescribed patterns of interaction.

As you deal with the cases in this section, your challenge will be to go beyond the formalities of the organization structure to discern how the organization actually does work in the particular situation with which you are concerned. Your objective should be to develop the ability to work with and influence the organization in all its complexities and, at times, seeming inertia and apparent "irrationalities." Your goal is to elicit individual behavior that is in furtherance of, rather than in hindrance of, the corporate objectives. You will encounter frustration on the part of managers in the middle of the organization in the Northern Industries and the John Adams cases, which you can consider from the leader's as well as the subordinate's point of view. In Lincoln, you will find a leadership that appears to understand very well what makes the members of the organization work hard. And it is, after all, people that make organizations work effectively and not the reverse.

To consider formal reporting relationships and titles unimportant is of course a mistake; they constitute the starting point. Without some degree of formal structure and definition of tasks and reporting relationships, an organization, even if committed to a purpose, is little more than a crowd. To believe the formalities can be so well specified that the informal workings of any organization can be ignored, however, is unrealistic.

Authority and responsibility

If one person could actually perform all of the tasks necessary in the conduct of a business, the problems of management would be simplified considerably. The sole proprietor does not need organization charts, job descriptions, or formalized compensation systems. Most of the things we talk about in this chapter would have little relevance to the manager who works for himself.

As the demands of the business require the addition of people, however, problems of splitting up what needs to be done unavoidably arise. Our largest companies have thousands of people classified as managers, each responsible for the actions of units reporting to them. When the managerial tasks have expanded and then been subdivided, problems of coordination and reintegration follow. Information on what various units are doing is necessary not only to ensure that the efforts are complementary but to monitor progress, help in planning for the future, and evaluate the performance of the people involved so that they can be properly rewarded for their efforts.

It would of course be ideal if the overall needs of the company could be subdivided into tasks that were perfectly clear, with sufficient authority given to each subordinate manager so that he could control all of the key factors affecting the performance for which he will be held responsible. Under these conditions we could then evaluate and reward him on the basis of clear objectives related to performance over which he would have considerable control. Authority would be commensurate with responsibility, rewards would be based on explicit and controllable performance measures, and the principles of management would have been complied with.

The preceding is a better description of the goals of an organization structure, information system, and reward system than it is the result of such systems in practice. Because of the unavoidable complexities of most management jobs, such ideal conditions are seldom attained.

A more realistic set of observations about the relationships between authority, responsibility, and evaluation that exist in most organizations and that you are likely to encounter as you progress up through the management ranks might be the following:

1. Your responsibilities are likely to exceed your authority for a long time. You will be expected to work with the people and the organization to secure by means of persuasion and logic the cooperation and resources you cannot command.

2. The evaluation of your performance will seldom be completely explicit. Judgments and opinions not clarified either before or after the evaluation period will be important. Furthermore, the basis of evaluation is likely to become less clear and explicit the higher up in management you progress.

3. Your superiors will always talk about the importance of not sacrificing the long-range in order to achieve short-range goals. If your time perspective is longer than that of your superiors, however, you are likely to find yourself in trouble for failing to meet short-run goals important to them. You have the difficult job of achieving an acceptable balance between these conflicting objectives.

4. Decisions concerning evaluation and reward systems may often be influenced more by what will improve performance than matters of fairness or logic. Giving a person conflicting objectives or holding him responsible

for more than he can control may be neither fair nor logical, but it is used at times in most organizations because it is often both unavoidable and effective.

5. Your boss probably knows better than you do the conflicts, illogicalities, and possible unfairness of the system under which you have to work. Probably he is now operating under more pressures and conflicts than you are. He learned to perform well in your environment, perhaps by not becoming overly disturbed by the matters discussed above but by concentrating instead on doing what needed to be done, trusting that in the responsible and effective organization competent effort would be recognized and rewarded regardless of the formalities of the system.

As you move on to jobs of increasing responsibility, you may be able to use your increased power, wisdom, and experience to change some of the inconsistent or frustrating factors you experienced when you were in those positions. If so, your subordinates will surely thank you for it. On the other hand, you may also come to the conclusion that such conflicts and frustrations are not necessarily undesirable from the viewpoint of the organization as a whole, that they can in few cases be resolved completely, and that your most constructive role is to strive for a balance between rationality and practicality.

It might be useful to ask yourself periodically just what you think your boss really expects of you and not just what the formalities of the measurement system are. Most likely he is just as smart as you are, has more experience than you do in the organization, and probably understands your position and pressures better than you give him credit for. He knows as well as you do that there are actions you could take to look good on the formal measurement systems that would be unwise from a broader perspective, and he has some of the same pressures himself. It is easy to lose sight of the fact that good performance on your part very likely helps him with his problems; it is easy to forget how much you have in common.

Evaluation and rewards

Just as most of us want to have the authority to influence the results for which we will be held responsible, we also would like our rewards to be based on clear and explicit measures of our performance. Rewards, both monetary and nonmonetary, are of considerable importance to most people. Of the various sources of influence available to the manager, rewards are probably the most significant as well as the most studied and discussed.

The rewards one gains from employment are of course much broader and more complex than just the monetary benefits earned, and these other satisfactions may compensate for, or at least distract attention from, what are perceived as shortcomings in the financial arrangements. You will have been exposed to much in your organizational behavior courses concerning the many factors that make for satisfaction in a job environment, and we urge you to draw upon that knowledge. Not the least of these other factors will be the signals you give to your subordinates concerning your opinions of them and their work. When you become engaged full time in your career, it will be useful to reflect upon how much time you spend thinking about what your superior thinks of you and why he made this suggestion or that comment concerning your work. Your subordinates will be just as concerned with your opinions of them, no less inclined to read more meaning into your actions and comments than you intended them to convey, and no less inclined to feel better after receiving justified praise and to feel worse when ignored or criticized unfairly.

Just because financial rewards are but one aspect of the ways in which the manager can reward his subordinates for past performance and thereby provide incentives for the future, it does not follow that financial rewards are unimportant. Most people do, after all, depend on their jobs for their livelihood, no matter how much they might also enjoy their work and appreciate recognition for a job well done. Even when the money itself takes on less importance because of the effect of taxes or diminished personal needs or the high levels of compensation being earned, the compensation takes on importance as a way of "keeping score" and measuring success in the job itself as well as position and progress with regard to others in the organization. To think that all a manager has to worry about with regard to rewarding his subordinates is compensation is naive, but to think that the level of compensation is not important to most people is equally naive.

There are a number of issues related to compensation and incentives that continue to plague practitioners. How much should you take into account either the personal aggressiveness or the personal needs of individual managers? How often should you match the offer a manager has secured from the outside, perhaps as a way of improving his internal bargaining power? How much should you reward a manager for past contributions or excellent efforts, even if the results are not up to expectations, perhaps for factors over which he has little control? We all like to be measured only on matters that we can control, but the general manager is often held responsible for results, not effort. At what level do we expect managers to share in the risks of the enterprise and not just be measured and rewarded for performance with regard to matters they can control?

In any large organization there is of course the need for some rationality and comparability in job descriptions, compensation plans, and pay levels. Much effort has been expended both by companies and consulting firms to deal with these problems. Managers often are caught in a dilemma: they would like to make the rewards as objective as possible to avoid the unpleasantness of having to justify their own decisions to those who performed poorly as well as to remove the suspicion that personal feelings or biases may have entered into the judgment. On the other hand, totally formula-based and objective measures frequently are unable to capture the full measure of the job done by the specific individual, and most managers feel the need to have some discretionary bonus available as well.

Partly because of the different needs of various organizations and partly because of the common dilemmas all managers face, the variety of basic compensation schemes and incentive-pay packages that have been developed is huge and includes combinations of cash, deferred cash, stock, and fringe benefits. The term *cafeteria approach to compensation* has even come into common use to describe plans which enable employees to choose that combination which most suits their tastes.

The Adams Corporation and the Barclay Company will give you some opportunity to explore just what it is that should be rewarded in the behavior, performance, potential, or personal situation of subordinates. In the Lincoln Electric Company you will find a highly unusual as well as effective combination of great attention to the motivation of the work force with a strategy which takes advantage of the higher productivity that results from their incentive plan and the important aspects that accompany it. It will be useful to examine some of the statements of James Lincoln in that case concerning what makes people put forth their best efforts to see if there is some application to other situations you will encounter.

It is unfortunate, however, that the establishment of high rewards for narrowly defined performance, either in monetary terms or with regard to opportunities for promotion, can lead to behavior clearly not in the best interests of the corporation. The temptation to emphasize short-run profits at the expense of long-run development is but one familiar manifestation of this. Every once in a while there are articles in the press on more serious aberrant behavior that high pressure for performance can lead to. In a recent example, division personnel falsified records over a period of years to show increased profits of $8.5 million, which was sufficient to result in the involvement of the SEC, delay of the annual meeting, and much publicity and consequent embarrassment to the company. "When we didn't meet our growth targets, the top brass really came down on us," one former executive stated. "Everybody knew that if you missed the targets enough, you were out on your ear."

Similar pressures have led, for example, to instances of falsification of automobile exhaust emission tests, violation of pollution laws, and illegal payments of bribes in violation of corporate policy and (later) the law in efforts to secure business, all without the knowledge of higher levels of management. Many observers have attributed much of the reason for the extensive price-fixing that took place in the electrical equipment industry in the 1960s, as well as many later violations in other industries, to the desire on the part of managers to earn bonuses or promotions by performing well in the measures established or, in some cases, to avoid demotions or even loss of jobs.

As the rewards and punishments associated with performance increase, the temptation to do what is not in the best interests of the company or what is ethically or legally wrong increases. The challenge for you as a manager is to find that productive middle ground in which people will be motivated to expend their best efforts, but not in such a manner as to bring trouble to their companies or themselves. The means by which you can increase or decrease the pressures for performance are much simpler and better understood than the means by which you can determine and maintain the appropriate balance.

Cooperation versus competition

The responsible, effective general manager will want to keep track of the cooperative-competitive dimension of the working relationships within the organization. It is unavoidable that some will progress faster and further than others in all organizations; the traditional pyramidal form of organization ensures that. Since the positions higher on the organizational pyramid generally involve more money, prestige, power, and (hopefully) personal satisfaction, the matter of who is chosen for promotion is seldom a matter of indifference to the contenders. Even if promotion is not a factor, current pay and incentives are often structured to provide the maximum rewards to those performing the best on the measures used. That is the purpose of reward systems: to provide an incentive to continued good performance in the future by rewarding good performance in the present.

As in any field of competitive endeavor, however, it is necessary to establish limits as to what kind of behavior or degree of competition is acceptable. The question of what constitutes "acceptable competitive behavior" has surely arisen for each of you with regard to the various organizations and groups of which you have chosen to be a member. Parents learn to establish and enforce standards of behavior within the family; referees and umpires enforce the rules in sports; the manager, who unavoidably has such a strong influence on the "rules of the game," must do likewise. If he does not, he will soon find that rewards for individual performance can combine with personal ambitions to create an atmosphere which discourages cooperation and which is less than satisfying to many with valuable talents to contribute to the organization.

As an example of the power of simple techniques to affect both the competitive relationships and the working environment within an organization, consider the approach which was followed by a major consulting firm for a period of time in scheduling the work loads of their staff, deciding what new engagements they could accept, and planning their hiring requirements.

It was the practice to appoint project leaders for each of the engagements for clients, and these project leaders would then plan the amount and type of work that would have to be done and assemble the people they would need to finish the job on time and under budget. The assignment of consultants to jobs was therefore, in effect, done by the various project leaders, who had to decide which consultants to "employ," taking into account the rates they would be charged for different consultants as well as when and for how long the consultants would be available to work on that project. The work schedule for individual consultants would then consist of their backlog of commitments to various project leaders, with unallocated time charged to "personal development" or "new business development."

The project leaders did not bargain with the consultants available on the basis of rates; these were determined periodically by the company. The internal rate charged for each consultant was influenced by demand, however, as were the pay and promotion prospects. It was, in effect, an internal market system under which project leaders bid against one another for the use of resources already under the control of the firm.

As a means of helping the project leaders in their scheduling task as well as collecting information useful in coordinating the new commitments of the firm with the available resources and the planned hiring schedule, charts were kept showing the work load by consultant and by project. At one point it was decided to post these charts for all to see and to update them once a week. Who was in demand and who was not therefore became public knowledge within the firm. The weekly posting understandably became an item of considerable interest to all and embarrassment to some. What do you suppose the effects of this simple decision to post this information were? Did it encourage cooperation, or did it not matter in this case? Did it encourage greater effort by all? How would you like to work under such a visible control mechanism? It is questions such as these to which you will want to apply your judgment—not just the technical aspects of evaluation or reward systems.

We face the paradox that we want the organization to be highly competitive in its external relationships with other organizations, but we wish to limit the internal competition so that it does not affect the incentives for individuals to work cooperatively as they do battle with the external world. We want the marketing department to develop a team spirit and work together to gain sales from their competitors, much as we expect a football team to consider the opponent an enemy to be beaten. We do not, however, want this attitude to affect the ability of the marketing people to work with each other, even though we may offer individual sales commissions. Neither do we want our own manufacturing and marketing departments to overlook the corporate interest as one fights to keep manufacturing costs and inventories down while the other wants a variety of products available in the field.

Unavoidably we seek to measure and reward individual performance within the organization, which may sometimes be achieved at the cost of—

or at least without regard for—the performance of others and the overall objectives of the company. Balancing the cooperative-competitive dimension is a difficult judgmental task and one which requires continuing attention. The issues are raised clearly in the Adams case, where you will deal with how to convert the increasingly ineffective "old Adams" into a more competitive and effective "new Adams." The tools and techniques by which you can increase or reduce the amount of internal competition and affect the broader working environment are well known, and the challenge is to employ them wisely and responsibly.

SUMMARY

The accomplishment of purpose is achieved by means of people working together on a voluntary basis. As a manager you will have considerable opportunity to influence or guide that behavior, but only in rare instances can you direct it on a continuing basis. The challenge is to devise structures, procedures, rewards, and an overall working environment that make possible the enthusiastic support for what needs to be done and not just the compliance with what the boss dictates or what the policy manual says. The latter is a description of the least attractive aspects of a bureaucracy; the former describes an organization made up of individuals for whom the achievement of personal goals contributes significantly to the overall goals of the organization. If you can relate the needs of your people to the needs of the organization, success cannot be far behind.

We have said little about leadership as a separate topic. We know, however, that throughout history the personal skills of the leader have had a major impact on the willingness of people to commit themselves to his purposes and his plans. The study of the characteristics of effective leaders in politics, the church, the military, as well as business has long fascinated observers. The major observation we might offer at this point, as you try to apply what you already have learned about leadership, is that effective leadership depends upon a successful matching of the needs of the situation with the skills and personality of the leader. We urge you to examine both the cases to come and your own skills and development with that in mind. Individuals are limited in the extent to which they can modify their behavior or acquire new skills. Success as a leader is more likely to come from a steady development of skills and the matching of those skills to the requirements of the job than the blind pursuit of a style that happens to have been successful for others with different skills in different situations.

Technical abilities and skills are likely to be of relatively less importance as you rise through the managerial ranks. More important will be the ability to recognize and deal with issues beyond your own experience and specialized training. You will need to develop the ability to conceptualize and communicate the problems in such a way that others can understand and be convinced of their importance. Progress will come from organizing and motivitating those with specialized knowledge and skills to apply their efforts to the constructive solution of the problems. In addition to conceptual skills, effective leadership requires the ability to break down problems into manageable parts for which tasks can be assigned and progress measured. You will need to be good at gaining support and commitment for what you think needs to be done, in spite of the different interests and positions of some of those on whose help you rely.

In the cases that follow, we will generally be looking at the problems from the viewpoint of the general manager, seeking to understand how he can use the sources of influence available to him in order to motivate the members of the organization to work towards the achievement of the organization's goals. To understand this task better, however, we suggest that you form the habit of always putting yourself in the place of a subordinate as well. How would you respond to the incentives or changes you are considering as the superior? How long before you would see through changes that are presented in a less than honest fashion? Even if the changes and reasons for them are well understood, what other actions might those changes induce you to take? We do not need to feel that we are pandering to the needs of subordinates in order to give some thought to how their jobs and careers could be affected by changes stemming from the organization's needs.

As you work your way through the approach we have suggested for your analysis of the cases in Part II of the book, your objective should be to develop a set of recommendations for each specific situation which has the following characteristics:

1. Your recommendations flow from your analysis of the case facts.

2. Your recommendations include a program of action and specify, to the best of your ability, how the resources required—people and money—will be obtained.

3. Your recommendations recognize that you are most often dealing with an existing, ongoing business rather than a completely new situation, and that you do not often have the luxury of starting anew. Frequently your changes will of necessity be incremental to an existing pattern of doing business. The more drastic the changes you recommend, the stronger the argument will have to be to gain their acceptance by people on whose cooperation and support you depend.

section 3

Designing
the overall
organization

POLICY
ADMINISTRATION

The Adams Corporation (A)

In January 1972 the board of directors of The Adams Corporation simultaneously announced the highest sales in the company's history, the lowest aftertax profits (as a percentage of sales) of the World War II era, and the retirement (for personal reasons) of its long-tenure president and chief executive officer.

Founded in St. Louis in 1848 the Adams Brothers Company had long been identified as a family firm both in name and operating philosophy. Writing in a business history journal, a former family senior manager comments: "My grandfather wanted to lead a business organization with ethical standards. He wanted to produce a quality product and a quality working climate for both employees and managers. He thought the Holy Bible and the concept of family stewardship provided him with all the guidelines needed to lead his company. A belief in the fundamental goodness of mankind, in the power of fair play, and in the importance of personal and corporate integrity were his trademarks. Those traditions exist today in the 1960s."

In the early 1950s, two significant corporate events occurred. First, the name of the firm was changed to The Adams Corporation. Second, somewhat over 50 percent of the corporation shares were sold by various family groups to the wider public. In 1970 all branches of the family owned or influenced less than one fifth of the outstanding shares of Adams.

The Adams Corporation was widely known and respected as a manufacturer and distributor of quality, branded, and consumer products for the American, Canadian, and European (export) markets. Adams products were processed in four regional plants located near raw material sources, were stored and distributed in a series of recently constructed or renovated distribution centers located in key cities throughout North America, and were sold by a company sales force to thousands of retail outlets—primarily supermarkets.[1]

---

[1] No single plant processed the full line of Adams products, but each plant processed the main items in the line.

In explaining the original long-term financial success of the company, a former officer commented: "Adams led the industry in the development of unique production processes that produced a quality product at a very low cost. The company has always been production oriented and volume oriented, and it paid off for a long time. During those decades the Adams brand was all that was needed to sell our product; we didn't do anything but a little advertising. Competition was limited, and our production efficiency and raw material sources enabled us to outpace the industry in sales and profit. Our strategy was to make a quality product, distribute it, and sell it cheap.

"But that has all changed in the past 20 years," he continued. "Our three major competitors have outdistanced us in net profits and market aggressiveness. One of them—a first-class marketing group—has doubled sales and profits within the past five years. Our gross sales have increased to almost $250 million, but our net profits have dropped continuously during that same period. While a consumer action group just designated us as 'best value,' we have fallen behind in marketing techniques, for example, our packaging is just out of date."

Structurally, Adams was organized into eight major divisions (see Exhibit 1). Seven of these were regional sales divisions, with responsibility for distribution and sales of the company's consumer products to retail stores in their area. Each regional sales division was further divided into organizational units at the state and county and/or trading area level. Each sales division was governed by a corporate price list in the selling of company products but had some leeway to meet the local competitive price developments. Each sales division was also assigned (by the home office) a quota of salesmen it could hire and was given the salary ranges within which these men could be employed. All salesmen were on straight salary and expense reimbursement salary plan, which resulted in compensation under industry averages.

A small central accounting office accumulated sales and expense information for each of the several sales divisions on a quarterly basis and prepared the overall company financial statements. Each sales division received, without commentary, a quarterly statement showing the number of cases processed and sold for the overall division, sales revenue per case of the overall division, and local expenses per case for the overall division.

Somewhat similar information was obtained from the manufacturing division. Manufacturing division accounting was complicated by variations in the cost of obtaining and processing the basic materials used in Adams products. These variations—particularly in procurement—were largely beyond the control of that division. The accounting office did have, however, one rough external check on manufacturing division effectiveness. A crude market price for case lot goods, sold by smaller firms to some large national chains, did exist.

EXHIBIT 1

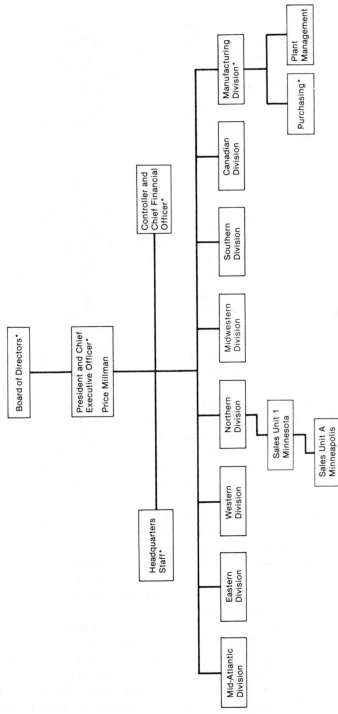

* Located in St. Louis.

Once a quarter, the seven senior sales vice presidents met with general management in St. Louis. Typically, management discussion focused on divisional sales results and expense control. The company's objective of being number one, the largest selling line in its field, directed group attention to sales versus budget. All knew that last year's sales targets had to be exceeded—"no matter what." The manufacturing division vice president sat in on these meetings to explain the product availability situation. Because of his St. Louis office location, he frequently talked with Jerome Adams about overall manufacturing operations and specifically about large procurement decisions.

The Adams Company, Mr. Millman knew, had a trade reputation for being very conservative with its compensation program. All officers were on a straight salary program. An officer might expect a modest salary increase every two or three years; these increases tended to be in the thousand-dollar range regardless of divisional performance or company profit position. Salaries among the seven sales divisional vice presidents ranged from $32,000 to $42,000, with the higher amounts going to more senior officers. Jerome Adams's salary of $48,000 was the highest in the company. There was no corporate bonus plan. A very limited stock option program was in operation, but the depressed price of Adams stock meant that few officers exercised their options.

Of considerable pride to Jerome Adams had been the corporate climate at Adams. "We take care of our family" was his oft-repeated phrase at company banquets honoring long-service employees. "We are a team, and it is a team spirit that has built Adams into its leading position in this industry." No member of first-line, middle, or senior management could be discharged (except in cases of moral crime or dishonesty) without a personal review of his case by Mr. Adams. In matter of fact, executive turnover at Adams was very low. Executives at all levels viewed their jobs as a lifetime career. There was no compulsory retirement plan, and some managers were still active in their mid-70s.

The operational extension of this organizational philosophy was quite evident to employees and managers. For over 75 years, a private family trust provided emergency assistance to all members of the Adams organization. Adams led its industry in the granting of educational scholarships, in medical insurance for employees and managers, and in the encouragement of its "members" to give corporate and personal time and effort to community problems and organizations.

Mr. Adams noted two positive aspects of this organizational philosophy. "We have a high percentage of long-term employees—Joe Girly, a guard at East St. Louis, completes 55 years with us this year, and every one of his brothers and sisters has worked here. And it is not uncommon for a vice president to retire with a blue pin—that means 40 years of service. We have led this industry in manufacturing process innovation, quality control, and value for low price for decades. I am proud of our accomplishments, and this pride is shown by everyone—from janitors to directors." Industry sources noted that there was no question that Adams was number one in terms of manufacturing and logistic efficiency.

In December of 1971 the annual Adams management conference gathered over 80 of Adams's senior management in St. Louis. Most expected the usual formal routines—the announcement of 1971 results and 1972 budgets, the award of the "Gold Flag" to the top processing plant and sales division for exceeding targets, and the award of service pins to executives. All expected the usual social good times. It was an opportunity to meet and drink with "old buddies."

After a series of task force meetings, the managers gathered in a banquet room—good naturedly referred to as the Rib Room since a local singer, Eve, was to provide entertainment. At the front of the room, in the usual fashion, was a dais with a long, elaborately decorated head table. Sitting at the center of that table was Jerome Adams. Following tradition, Mr. Adams's vice presidents, in order of seniority with the company, sat on his right. On his left, sat major family shareholders, corporate staff, and—a newcomer—soon to be introduced.

After awarding service pins and the Gold Flags of achievement, Mr. Adams announced formally what had been a corporate secret for several months. First, a new investing group had assumed a control position on the board of Adams. Second, that Price Millman would take over as president and chief executive officer of Adams.

Introducing Mr. Millman, Adams pointed out the outstanding record of the firm's new president. "Price got his MBA in 1958, spent four years in control and marketing, and then was named as the youngest divisional president in the history of the Tenny Corporation. In the past years, he has made his division the most profitable in Tenny and the industry leader in its field. We are fortunate to have him with us. Please give him your complete support."

In a later informal meeting with the divisional vice presidents, Mr. Millman spoke about his respect for past Adams's accomplishments and the pressing need to infuse Adams with "fighting spirit" and "competitiveness." "My personal and organizational philosophy are the same—the name of the game is to fight and win. I almost drowned, but I won my first swimming race at 11 years of age! That philosophy of always winning is what enabled me to build the Ajax Division into Tenny's most profitable operation. We are going to do this at Adams."

In conclusion, he commented, "The new owner group wants results. They have advised me to take some time to think through a new format for Adams's operations—to get a corporate design that will improve our effectiveness. Once we get that new format, gentlemen, I have but one goal— each month must be better than the past."

Barclay, Inc. (A)

In December 1973, Robert Cannon became the new president and chief operating executive of Barclay, Inc., a firm operating in the electrical equipment field. In 1973 it was estimated, Barclay's sales were $100 million and the enterprise employed over 2,600 people.

Barclay, Inc., had recently been purchased by a group of wealthy investors. In view of their other varied business interests, the investing group planned to operate Barclay as a separate, independent company. Mr. Cannon was given complete responsibility for the direction of Barclay's affairs. He had achieved an excellent reputation among industrialists as a manager capable of dealing with difficult business problems, and the investors had agreed that he was to have a free hand to make whatever changes he thought necessary to improve the company's lackluster profit performance.

Barclay manufactured and sold electrical equipment for industrial and consumer use. Its industrial products included a wide variety of standard and specialty motors. The company had achieved an excellent reputation for engineering design work. Over the years its legal staff had built up an imposing number of patents protecting improvements created by company engineers. In the consumer products line, the firm manufactured and sold a line of small "traffic" household appliances for American markets.

In recent years company sales had increased substantially, but profits had gradually declined to a point where only a very small profit was anticipated for 1973. While industrial products had been extremely profitable for many years, the competitive situation had changed substantially in the late 1960s. Consumer appliance operations varied from early losses to small profit contributions in 1970 through 1973. Barclay was encountering increasing competition for its appliances from full-line companies such as Sunbeam. Despite this, Mr. Cannon believed that in the long run the consumer traffic appliance area would become the most important and profitable part of the firm's business. He hoped to add new appliance items as rapidly as production and marketing facilities permitted.

EXHIBIT 1
Organization chart

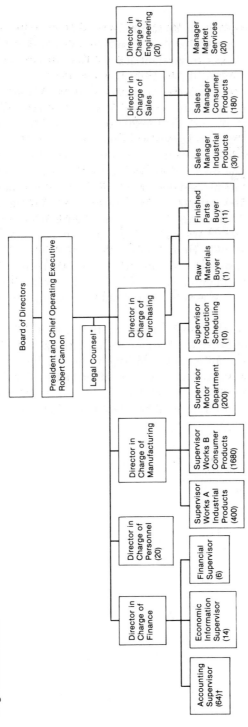

* Full-time legal counsel.
† Indicates number of staff or employees, or both.

In the manufacture of these products, Barclay purchased substantial quantities of two raw materials ($16 million, estimated in 1972). These raw materials were subject to substantial price fluctuations, and it was important for Barclay to buy at "the right time and price."

The new owners of Barclay requested that Mr. Cannon prepare salary recommendations for board consideration in December 1973. His recommendations were to cover the top 20 executives in the company including himself. Knowing the backgrounds of the new owners, Mr. Cannon knew he would have to be able to defend his assignments of salary to specific jobs. He also knew that the owners had been critical of the "haphazard way" in which salary payments had been made by the former general manager.

To carry out this assignment, Mr. Cannon asked the member of the personnel department in charge of the executive payroll for the amount paid in salaries to the top 20 managers of the firm in the year 1973. This sum amounted to $860,000. He excluded individual bonus payments and incidental privileges, such as company furnished cars. Bonus payments for the Barclay management group had declined steadily during the past years, and salary payments were now the important element in the firm's compensation program.

He then prepared to assign funds from this "common pool" to individual jobs in the organization. Mr. Cannon realized that after he had determined an ideal salary structure, he would have to modify his assignments on the basis of historical precedent as well as other factors. But he believed that the process of allocating the total salary fund to individual jobs, without prejudice of past history, would help him in thinking through his problem.

The Rose Company

James Pierce had recently received word of his appointment as plant manager of Plant X, one of the older established units of the Rose Company. As such, Mr. Pierce was to be responsible for the management and administration at Plant X of all functions and personnel except sales.

Both top management and Mr. Pierce realized that there were several unique factors about his new assignment. Mr. Pierce decided to assess his new situation and relationships before undertaking his assignment. He was personally acquainted with the home office executives, but had met few of the plant personnel. This case contains some of his reflections regarding the new assignment.

The Rose Company conducted marketing activities throughout the United States and in certain foreign countries. These activities were directed from the home office by a vice president in charge of sales.

Manufacturing operations and certain other departments were under the supervision and control of a senior vice president. These are shown in Exhibit 1. For many years the company had operated a highly centralized functional type of manufacturing organization. There was no general manager at any plant; each of the departments in a plant reported on a line basis to its functional counterpart at the home office. For instance, the industrial relations manager of a particular plant reported to the vice president in charge of industrial relations at the home office, the plant controller to the vice president and controller, and so on.

Mr. Pierce stated that in the opinion of the top management the record of Plant X had not been satisfactory for several years. The board had recently approved the erection of a new plant in a different part of the city and the use of new methods of production. Lower costs of processing and a reduced personnel requirement at the new plant were expected. Reduction of costs and improved quality of products were needed to maintain competitive leadership and gain some slight product advantage. The proposed combination of methods of manufacturing and mixing materials had not

415

416

EXHIBIT 1
Old organization

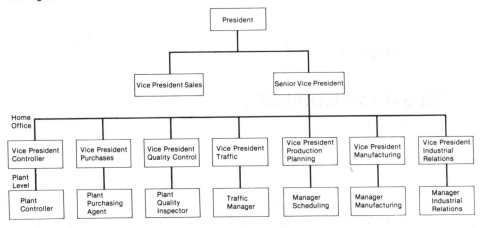

been tried elsewhere in the company. Some features would be entirely new to employees.

According to Mr. Pierce the top management of the Rose Company was beginning to question the advisability of the central control of manufacturing operations. The officers decided to test the value of a decentralized operation in connection with Plant X. They apparently believed that a general management representative in Plant X was needed if the new equipment in manufacturing methods and the required rebuilding of the organization were to succeed.

Prior to the new assignment Mr. Pierce had been an accounting executive in the controller's department of the company. From independent sources the casewriter learned that Mr. Pierce had demonstrated analytical ability and general administrative capacity. He was generally liked by people. From top management's point of view he had an essential toughness described as an ability to see anything important through. By some he was regarded as the company's efficiency expert. Others thought he was a perfectionist and aggressive in reaching the goals that had been set. Mr. Pierce was aware of these opinions about his personal behavior.

Mr. Pierce summarized his problem in part as follows:

> I am going into a situation involving a large number of changes. I will have a new plant—new methods and processes—but most of all I will be dealing with a set of changed relationships. Heretofore all the heads of departments in the plant reported to their functional counterparts in the home office. Now they will report to me. I am a complete stranger and in addition this is my first assignment in a major "line" job. The men will know this.

EXHIBIT 2
New organization

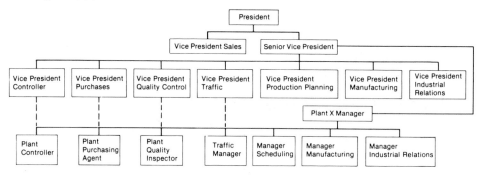

When I was called into the senior vice president's office to be informed of my new assignment, he asked me to talk with each of the functional members of his staff. The vice presidents in charge of production planning, manufacturing, and industrial relations said they were going to issue all headquarters instructions to me as plant manager and they were going to cut off their connections with their counterparts in my plant. The other home office executives admitted their functional counterparts would report to me in line capacity. They should obey my orders, and I would be responsible for their pay and promotion. But these executives proposed to follow the common practice of many companies of maintaining a dotted line or functional relationship with these men. I realize that these two different patterns of home office–plant relationships will create real administrative problems for me.

Exhibit 2 shows the organization relationships as defined in these conferences.

case 17

The Larger Company (A)

The phone rang, and highly indignant words blared: "Masters, what do you mean by submitting a report to all the executives without first talking it over with the division manager!"

Masters replied, "My men made every effort to see him. They never got past his secretary. He instructed her to have them talk to the works manager."

"I don't believe a word of it. Vining is up in arms. He says the report is vindictive. What are you trying to do—embarrass the division manager? I don't believe your men ever tried to see Vining and I question the veracity of their statements!" The phone on the other end was hung up with a bang.

Masters said to himself, "Gunn must be hot under the collar or he wouldn't have called me when I was away from my own office visiting another plant."

The next day Masters's office received Gunn's letter confirming this telephone conversation and demanding an explanation. A week later Masters received a letter from Gunn's superior, a Mr. Jordan, stating: "I have read the aforementioned report and discussed it with Mr. Gunn. He has advised me that the report is essentially untrue, inaccurate, and overstated. I am not satisfied to have such wide differences of opinion and have scheduled a meeting to be held in my office on _____. I would appreciate it if you would be present."

In light of the phone call and the two letters, Mr. Masters decided to reassess all events leading to this climax.

❋   ❋   ❋   ❋   ❋

The cast of characters is as shown in Exhibit 1. The Larger Company had an elaborate organizational structure as a result of its scale of operation. At the headquarters office of the corporation the president had a group of staff vice presidents in charge of functions. Mr. Masters was a staff department head reporting to the vice president, manufacturing. The headquarters staff

EXHIBIT 1
Organization chart

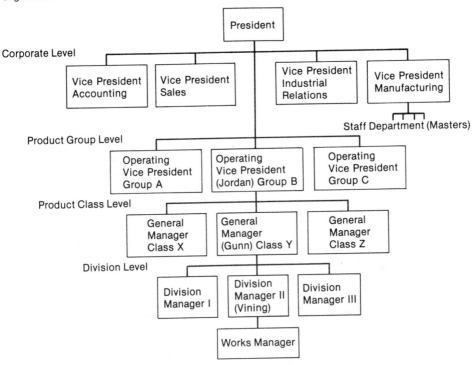

departments assisted in policy formulation and made staff studies for the operating organization when requested. Members of such departments were encouraged to offer ideas for the good of the company. Their proposals were considered by a management committee consisting of the vice presidents at the headquarters level and the operating vice presidents in charge of product groups. Mr. Jordan of this case was the operating vice president, Product Group B.

Under the product groups there were general managers of product classes. They supervised the division managers, who were in charge of the sales and manufacturing operations of one or more plants. Mr. Gunn was general manager of Product Class Y. One of the four division managers under him was Mr. Vining of Division II.

⁕ ⁕ ⁕ ⁕ ⁕

Two years before this incident occurred, Mr. Masters's staff department proposed to the management committee, with the approval of the vice president, manufacturing, that representatives of Mr. Masters's office join with representatives of the vice president, accounting, to make studies in each plant of the producers for and actual practices regarding expense control. The suggestion was approved and enthusiastically endorsed by the general managers. They sent a letter through channels to each division manager advising that periodically a team of two men would visit each plant to make a comprehensive analysis of expense-control practices and systems.

After a visit these field representatives of headquarters were to prepare a report giving findings and recommendations. They were to discuss it with the appropriate division manager and his staff. Thus they would be able to incorporate any specific plans of action set in motion by division managers. Next, a report was to be submitted to Mr. Masters. Both his department and the accounting office were to make comments. The final document was then to be submitted to the vice president, accounting; the vice president, manufacturing; the operating vice president, product group; the general manager, product class; and the division manager concerned.

This general procedure had worked smoothly within the company until general manager Gunn of Product Class Y exploded. In the first plant studied, the two team members spent approximately four weeks examining documents, interviewing line management, interrogating industrial engineers, observing operations, and so forth. The employees of this plant were very cooperative. Some of the facts revealed by them could have been embarrassing to the division manager. The team was enabled to make specific recommendations for improvement to the division manager. His reception of the report was good. According to him, the study had given him an opportunity to review his situation and get his house in order. He intended to implement the recommendations unless they were changed in the review process at the higher level. Sixteen other plants were visited with reasonably good acceptance of the work of the team.

◦　◦　◦　◦　◦

In his review of the Division II situation, Mr. Masters found that the team had observed all the required organization routines. Mr. Sawyer, representing Mr. Masters, had a master's degree in industrial engineering and had 12 years with the company. Mr. Peters, from the accounting office, had served that department for 30 years. Both men had shown ability to gain confidences and to use them discreetly. They were considered straightforward, conscientious, and unobtrusive in their work. In Division II the team obtained from plant personnel considerable information which pointed up a number of practices and procedures requiring improvement. In the opinion of the team members, the operating organization at the lower levels sincerely wanted to make these changes. The team thought that there was some resistance at some level within the division to these suggestions and, in fact, to any from headquarters.

While the study was in process, Mr. Sawyer advised Mr. Masters about the possible impact of the information which was being collected. Mr. Masters emphasized the necessity to report to the division manager, and Mr. Sawyer promised that he and Mr. Peters would do so.

The team made several efforts to see the division manager, but his secretary informed them that he was busy. They questioned the secretary closely to learn if the manager had knowledge of the procedural requirement that he and his staff go over the report with the team. She replied that he knew the requirements, but was too busy to discuss a headquarters program. He would ask his assistant, the works manager, and several staff members to go over it, and what they approved would be all right with him. Eventually this meeting was held.

The members of the local management staff took a very reasonable attitude; they admitted the bad situation portrayed in the analysis and offered their assurances that immediate steps would be taken towards improvement. The team members thought that the local management staff was glad to have their problem brought out in the open and were delighted to have the suggestions of the headquarters representatives.

    ❀   ❀   ❀   ❀   ❀

When Mr. Masters reviewed the report, both team members expressed their complete dissatisfaction with the brush-off they got from the division manager. Masters took this as a cue to question them extensively concerning their findings and recommendations. In view of the sensitive character of the situation and the possible controversy that it might create, he was reluctant to distribute the report. It was the consensus of the remainder of the staff and the representatives of the accounting office that the usual transmittal letter should be prepared and distribution made. Mr. Masters signed this letter and took no other action until the telephone call came from Mr. Gunn.

section 4

**Managing
the overall
organization**

**POLICY
ADMINISTRATION**

case 18

Robin Hood Archery Inc.

I like being in charge and I don't think I could ever work for anyone
again. Naturally, I've had a lot of problems but it's been fun.

Speaking, was Al Adams who, immediately upon graduating from an
MBA program in June 1976, took over as president of Robin Hood, a wholesaler and manufacturer of archery equipment.

One thing about running a company is that you carry it in your gut all
the time—you might be lying on the beach with your family on Sunday, but
you're still thinking about the company. And, in my situation, there's no
one I can talk to about even basic things, like cash flow; I'm really on my
own.

I'm overwhelmed by detail and really have little information. I think
business school makes you feel you need more information than you can
get—at least in a small company. But I like having a lot of problems to work
on rather than being tied to a desk concentrating on one problem.

With all these details and operating problems, it's difficult to find time to
make strategy. Sometimes you make what seems to be a simple operational
decision only to realize that it will have an impact on your strategy for a
long time. It's the old chicken-and-egg problem—you need a strategy so
you have a context for your operational decisions, but you have to make
your operational decisions while you're trying to find time to develop a
strategy. CML's criticism of my predecessor was that he wasn't a planner.[1] I
can sympathize with his problem—it's hard to find the time to plan.

When they took me on, CML told me to leave things alone for awhile
and just develop an understanding of the business. But you can't do that.
People knock at your door all day long. I feel that I've developed good
enough understanding now so that I can sit down and make some of the decisions that my predecessor never made and which, if I'm not careful, I'll be
making by default.

---

[1] The CML Group, Inc.

PERSONAL BACKGROUND

Before school, Adams had been a Navy pilot for six years. He eventually became an aircraft division officer, a key management job which involved responsibility for approximately 100 men.

> I had to get involved in everything. I felt that if I was going to lead men who are mechanics, I better understand their job from their point of view—so I'd pitch in with the ground crew on repair and maintenance. And I got involved with the men's personal problems as well as their Navy duties. Basically, I was in the middle of everything and that's the way I like it, rather than being on the fringe, like a consultant, for instance.

Adams left the Navy to avoid the frequent transfers which would disrupt his family, particularly since the oldest of his four children was getting ready to attend school. Being older than most of his contemporaries at school (33 when he graduated), he felt a sense of urgency to make up for starting late. At the same time, he found many of the cases and his company visits presenting situations which didn't appeal to him.

> In the large companies it seemed everyone had a little corner and that was all they were concerned about.

Between his first and second school years, Adams worked for the CML group, a Boston-based, diversified company, whose ten wholly owned subsidiaries' products were recreation oriented. Adams joined CML's lean staff of six people as an assistant to the vice president, finance. He got along well with the CML people who, he felt, liked him because he could go into a small business and not turn people off by posing as a business school expert. Adams also shared CML's enthusiasm for recreation and the feeling that business is an important part of life but not the only thing.

TAKING THE JOB

During his second school year, Adams conducted a job search which included interviewing with big companies as well as with small ones. His main criterion was that the position be one of operational responsibility. Although he received attractive offers from some large companies, he still harbored reservations about taking on a job which would have a narrow focus and which would leave him somewhere else than in the center of activity. Adams became interested in a position as vice president at CML's Ericson Yacht subsidiary. At the same time, CML became interested in having him take over as president of Robin Hood, CML's smallest holding and a profitable but no-growth company.

Initially, Adams would have preferred to work at Ericson Yacht because boating appealed to him whereas archery—"Well, I'd never thought much about it." However, he eventually decided that being the president of a company would provide much better experience than being the number two man at another, even if an apparently more glamorous company. He could later transfer his developed managerial skills to a product in which he had more interest. He felt the Robin Hood position offered him a chance to be in the middle of the action as he had been in the Navy.

In fact, after he finally made the decision to take the Robin Hood job, he felt a euphoria about the prospect of using his business and personal skills to run a company. However, when he visited the company before completing school, he found it was in chaos, and he became apprehensive, thinking that perhaps the company was too fragmented for him to handle.

Also giving rise to second thoughts were his reservations about his ability to get excited about selling archery equipment, and the tendency of the name and concept of Robin Hood to provoke mock hilarity among his friends.

> I was never concerned about prestige. I think some people from Harvard, particularly those who go to Wall Street, wear Harvard on their sleeve. I don't go along with that routine. Even so, I have to admit that people's reactions to Robin Hood concerned me. For a while, at school, I'd even say I was going to work for CML rather than mention Robin Hood. People would laugh and say all the ridiculous things like, "Where's Maid Marion," or "My name's Little John." (You won't believe this, but we actually have a guy on our sales force named Little John.)

THE COMPANY

Robin Hood comprised three main operations. The major one was wholesaling a full line of archery equipment and accessories; Adams's Montclair, New Jersey, office handled the storage and shipment of the equipment and what little paperwork accompanied the operation. Within three blocks, Robin Hood had its own pro shop which was small but profitable. And in Sailorsburg, Pennsylvania, 150 miles away, Robin Hood had seven people manufacturing arrows in a leased house. The company employed a sales force of six people which had been established in March 1974; before that, Robin Hood had sold only through a dealer catalog.

GOING TO WORK

After evaluating Robin Hood in light of his personal and professional goals, Adams decided to take the job. He went to New Jersey, found the homes in the towns immediately surrounding Montclair out of his price range, and finally settled on a home in western New Jersey, about an hour's ride from work. CML provided the down payment which Adams would pay back from his bonus, thus not reducing his regular personal cash flow.[2]

CML's only direction was that Adams, after learning the business, should

---

[2] Adams was paid a salary plus a percentage of pretax profits over a certain amount.

determine a strategy which would provide "quality earnings," that is, good steady margins and reliable customers. Because Robin Hood's historic return on assets was low, CML was not intent upon growth there, at least in the short run.

During his first two weeks, Adams worked under Robin Hood's then president, Herman Schmidt, whom CML chose not to inform that Adams would soon take over. Adams soon learned that Schmidt had established no goals or strategy, and was overwhelmed with detail because he was unable to delegate responsibility. Schmidt handled everything informally, keeping few records on purchases, sales, or inventory. He was also prone to defer to the assertive people in the company, thus allowing the formation of enclaves of informal leaders as well as groups of those who preferred to shirk responsibility. Although he was having the benefit of a two-week breaking-in period, Adams felt that he would have great difficulty presiding over this chaotic, yet functioning, company when he finally took over.

Becoming president

Schmidt was informed that Adams would take over as president and that he would have to return to international marketing which provided 25 percent of the company's sales and which, having developed himself, Schmidt liked very much. He had started in the company as a stock clerk and worked his way into marketing. He apparently knew he was weak in finance, felt overwhelmed by the top position, and suspected that he would eventually be replaced—he seemed merely surprised that CML had taken so long. He went on a two-week vacation as Adams took over.

Adams received expressions of support from the 13 people in his office, most of whom were middle-aged women performing clerical work. The difficulty of trying to impose some order on the company was aggravated by the staff's constantly asking him routine questions which would interrupt Adams's train of thought on more substantive matters. An example was the bookkeeper who had asserted herself into a position of power under Schmidt. She knocked on Adams's door "30 times a day to ask routine questions like in what ledger to enter a purchase or sale."

Within two hours of his first day as president, Adams learned that one salesman was blithely preparing two price lists; he couldn't understand why Adams said such a practice was illegal. Adams chose the price list to be used.

During the first week, the bookkeeper informed Adams that everyone in the company was due for a raise.

> I had no idea what to say; that was one problem I'd never had in the Navy. And business school had never specifically addressed how you determine how much you need to pay to keep people, especially clerical help.

Adams learned that Schmidt had given a blanket 8 percent raise each year, and Adams noted that the people whom he considered more aggressive had the highest salaries. He decided to give everyone a 6 percent cost-of-living increase, and, to those he thought deserved it, an extra 2 percent increase in pay plus an increase in the company's contributions to their life and medical insurance policies.

Another problem which came up soon after Adams became president concerned the United Parcel Service, which Robin Hood used to deliver its orders. The UPS workers went on strike, and the local post office said it couldn't accept any more than 20 parcels a day. Adams had warehouse personnel mail 20 parcels from each post office in the adjoining towns as well as from Montclair.

Authority

In terms of his authority, Adams's biggest problem was the sales manager, Merton, an imposing-looking 37-year-old man who wore his hair in a long ponytail and who seemed to have wrested considerable power from Schmidt. Merton immediately started to try to gain an upper hand over Adams by assuming authority which Adams was intent on keeping for himself. One example was Merton's reaction to an order from Vermont for $7,000, a large order in the archery business. Merton was set to accept the order and ship it immediately. Adams, however, insisted on making an informal credit check during which he learned that the order had come from an aggressive discounter who could threaten the sales of a nearby Robin Hood outlet of long standing. Feeling that the large archery equipment manufacturers could beat Robin Hood on price and, therefore, in appealing to discounters, and that Robin Hood's major sales strengths were service and delivery to dealers, Adams decided against accepting the order. His intention was to retain the loyalty of the company's Vermont dealer and to serve notice that Robin Hood would emphasize service to its network of small dealers. The sales manager and other personnel thought Adams was, as it were, a little green:

> It was a major decision, really. It set a course for the company. And I was worried that I might be being misled about the discounter's operation or that I was naive. That sort of decision comes up every day—you have to decide on a course of action with little information, sometimes with little confidence, and without having defined the company's strategy.

Adams found it difficult to evaluate the advice given him by company personnel because of his lack of familiarity with archery and the archery industry, and because he did not know what personal motives might be prompting a given line of reasoning. And he felt that if he appeared weak, people would take advantage of him; if he appeared weak and indecisive, people would make decisions for him.

> At first, it's easy to be defensive when someone strongly recommends something; it's easy to ask yourself what their real motives are. Don't get

me wrong—it's not a feeling that "they" are out to get you; I think it's feeling that when a new president comes on, people naturally want to have him make decisions they like. And, I found it too easy to react favorably to a, let's say, brownnoser, because he was supportive; he can make you feel comfortable in an uncertain situation. But, even if you react favorably to him, you know that you don't want yes-men helping you make decisions. You want someone who's willing to give you a good argument so you can look at a problem from all sides. Of course, to do that you have to know what you're talking about yourself. So I decided that before I asked for any advice or input, I'd research the problem myself. Research takes time, and it is a major reason for my hectic pace and long hours.

Control

In addition to asserting his authority, Adams's initial daily problems centered around imposing controls on the company's operations. Adams felt a lack of control was indicated by an inventory turnover of $1\frac{1}{2}$ times a year and by there being no perpetual inventory; in the past, inventory control had consisted only of a semiannual physical audit. Being unfamiliar with purchasing and wanting to get out from under it, Adams delegated responsibility for it to a young man who, with Schmidt's help, had recently immigrated to the United States. Adams felt that the man, who seemed to feel a sense of debt to Schmidt, had been somewhat self-effacing and had not had an opportunity to demonstrate his abilities. Adams felt he had considerable native ability and gave him responsibility for purchasing. Adams set up a perpetual inventory system which the young man quickly understood and implemented; Adams then gave him a raise and responsibility for an open-to-buy of $2,500.[3]

While at school, Adams had paid lip service to the importance of cash flow, but its importance became concrete during his second week as president when he was faced with a payroll to meet, $300,000 of accounts receivable due, and $0 cash. This situation was caused, in part, by the poor control systems at Robin Hood, but also by the nature of its business—most archery equipment was normally sold during the fall hunting season and dated 120 days, whereas Robin Hood had to purchase equipment in the spring. Financial statements for August 1975, January 1976, and August 1976 appear in Exhibit 1. Adams had to borrow money from CML.

Overall, however, Adams found lack of information to be his biggest problem in getting control over the company. There was no information on when and where the different products sold, on inventory levels, or on margins. Adams didn't have the time to get the information himself but hoped that the systems he had installed would provide it once they had been in operation for awhile.

---

[3] An authority to buy goods for resale to the amount of $2,500.

EXHIBIT 1

ROBIN HOOD
Consolidated Financial Statements
August 1975–1976
($000)

Balance Sheet

	August 1975	January 1976	August 1976
Assets			
Current assets:			
Cash	$ 54	$ 21	$ 37
Accounts receivable	213	101	370
Inventory	492	529	703
Other current assets	15	8	1
Total current assets	$774	$659	$1,111
Plant and equipment	$ 40	$ 52	$ 58
Less: Accumulated depreciation	(11)	(13)	(17)
Net plant and equipment	$ 29	$ 39	$ 41
Other	1	2	3
Goodwill	53	52	50
CML cash account	(54)	4	(349)
Total assets	$803	$756	$ 856
Liabilities and Stockholders' Equity			
Current liabilities:			
Accounts payable	$ 73	$ 74	$ 150
Accrued liabilities	41	9	22
Accrued taxes	24	3	7
Total current liabilities	$138	$ 86	$ 179
Capital stock	1	1	1
Paid-in surplus	548	548	548
Retained earnings	116	121	128
Total liabilities and stockholders' equity	$803	$756	$ 856

Income Statement
(for month)

	August 1975	January 1976	August 1976
Sales	$174	$ 70	$ 287
Less cost of goods sold	117	47	195
Gross margin	$ 57	$ 23	$ 92
Expenses:			
Selling and administrative	$ 12	$ 11	$ 19
Shipping and warehouse	7	7	9
General and administrative	11	17	18
Total expenses	$ 30	$ 35	$ 46
Operating income	$ 27	$ (12)	$ 46
Interest	0	0	0
Profit before taxes	$ 27	$ (12)	$ 46
Taxes (credit)	14	(6)	24
Net income	$ 13	$ (6)	$ 22

Source: Company records.

Marketing and sales

Within a week of taking over, Adams had to consider the installation of a WATS line. His competition had toll-free phone numbers which dealers could call, and some dealers had requested Robin Hood to provide the same service. Adams felt a WATS line afforded his competition an advantage insofar as it was an aspect of the service which he felt should be Robin Hood's main strength. However, a WATS line (incoming only) would cost $245 a month.

> I had to do an analysis, figuring what incremental sales would be necessary to justify the extra expense. So I divided the $245, no zeros omitted, by our estimated contribution figure. It seemed a bit silly after dealing with the big numbers you do at business school, but you can two hundred forty-five dollar yourself to death in a small company.

Again, Adams felt he was confronted with a strategic decision while solving an operational problem which had popped up. He decided to install the WATS line, informed his customers, and was pleased that after a month or two the WATS line seemed to be giving rise to the needed incremental sales, even net of Adams's estimate of cannibalization of sales which normally would have been made by mail or regular phone calls. Adams then learned that the company had reserved space in some archery magazines and that he would have to work with the women in charge of advertising to create copy before the deadline for copy submission—the next day. "I'd like to plan our advertising a little more than that," said Adams.

The sales force, the company's biggest single expense, was of major concern to Adams who felt it might even be unnecessary. Its six members, all friends of Merton, received $150 a week draw against a 6 percent commission on all sales in their assigned territories.

In the 2½ years of its existence, the sales force had increased sales a total of $400,000 over what they would otherwise have been, and had increased direct expenses by about $160,000. Adams determined that with the average margin being 32 percent, the increase in expenses (which did not include associated office overhead) wiped out any additional profit the extra sales may have provided. A problem was that Robin Hood had previously had steady sales of $1.3 million a year while selling to dealers only through its catalog. When the sales force came on board, it received commissions on these assured sales as well as on additional sales. Adams's calculations indicated that one salesperson's calls costs an average of $218 each; another's averaged $32.[4]

---

[4] The January 1976 issue of *Sales and Marketing Management* stated that the average cost per call of account representatives, including those in the wholesale industry, was $20 in urban areas and $39 in rural areas. A noted sales management authority estimated the average cost per call for industrial salespeople was $75.

Adams had considered placing the salespersons on commission only for those sales they personally wrote. However, he feared such a system might encourage the salespeople to push for orders, thereby antagonizing and straining Robin Hood's small but loyal customers. He also felt that because Robin Hood was known in the trade, any new dealer would want some of its products.

Another possibility was to disband the sales force and conduct an aggressive telephone campaign. His warehouse manager, Ken Prelopsky, had assumed responsibility for taking calls on the WATS line and had increased his already excellent rapport with the dealers. Prelopsky had found that not only had phone calls increased but that he was able to sell more over the phone than by mail:

> During hunting season, I've been getting a phone call every three or four minutes. And when dealers order something we don't have in stock, I suggest a substitute item which they more than likely will accept. I can also remind them to order other items; I might say, "By the way, you have enough Little John bows? The hunters will be looking for them." And they might say, "As a matter of fact, I only have one left; better send me a few." You can't do these sort of things by mail; you don't get the spontaneous reaction. And I know these guys; they trust me; and I know they often don't think ahead and I can help them. I also think that I could convince them to order things earlier and help our cash flow problem.

One of Adams's nagging concerns was the preparation of the company catalog which was scheduled to be ready within four months of the day he took over.

> The catalog is a major undertaking. It goes to press in September and comes out in February. It's what we send to all our dealers. It's what they buy from. Essentially, it *is* the company, and we're stuck with it for a year. So I have to make product decisions which will commit us to a certain line and to our manufacturers while I'm still trying to learn what archery is all about. The problem is aggravated by fads in the market. This year one type of arrowhead may be the big seller, only to give way to another type next year. Sales are affected by the large manufacturers.

He decided to delay publication of the catalog, feeling that, though a delay would lead to the catalog's being issued after the national archery trade show, its importance dictated that it be as productive as possible.

Simultaneously, Adams would have to decide when he would purchase his products because CML wanted a cash flow forecast. Whereas Schmidt had purchased large batches of items at one time, Adams wanted to purchase in a series of smaller lots to reduce his cash flow problems and his inventory carrying costs; therefore, he had to determine the flexibility of his vendors. Adams contemplated establishing a product committee of about five people to discuss each product category; he thought such a device

EXHIBIT 2

would help him make his decisions with more information and would give committee members a feeling of participating in making company policy.

At one time the catalog had been 250 pages; Adams felt that was much too long—it presented the small dealer with an overwhelming number of choices, and the company with a severe inventory problem. He initially considered cutting it down to 90 pages, then decided that in line with his full-service concept, its length should be somewhere in the middle to provide dealers with a sufficient assortment. A sample page of the 1976 catalog is provided in Exhibit 2.

Feeling that Robin Hood did not have the resources to advertise extensively, Adams felt there was probably little brand awareness of Robin Hood products among final consumers. He, therefore, decided to downplay Robin Hood branded products in the catalog in favor of products of those companies which, having greater resources, advertised more. As with many of his other decisions, he had to make this one with little moral support from the people in the company who did not understand his line of reasoning and who seemed to think that he was crazy to downplay the brand name of his own company. However, Adams decided to continue publishing the company's monthly newsletter, which was distributed as part of an effort to sustain the feeling of being part of a family among the dealers. Merton prepared the newsletter and wrote it in a style the dealers understood and liked. A sample newsletter appears in Exhibit 3.

EXHIBIT 3

ROBIN HOOD ARCHERY INC.

Dealer Newsletter—July 1976

1. It's July already, and we have some very significant announcements to make that will substantially reinforce our service program for your immediate benefit.
2. As of Monday, July 12, we will be installing a "toll-free" phone service for your convenience in placing orders.

   Robin Hood Fastcom—800-631-1252 (all states except New Jersey)

   a. We are installing this new dealer service on a three-month trial basis in an attempt to speed up our order service to you.
   b. The phone lines will be staffed during our normal working hours of 8 to 5 Eastern time. I would prefer to have a 24-hour service, but we couldn't possibly staff it with qualified people. So it will be 8 to 5 Eastern, 7 to 4 Central, 6 to 3 Mountain, and 5 to 2 Pacific time.
   c. This is something I have been thinking about for a long time, and I am very excited about finally being able to make this announcement.
3. My second announcement is to let you know that Al Adams has assumed the president's position at Robin Hood Archery. Al brings us a heavy management background that will give us the versatility that

---

EXHIBIT 3 (continued)

we have only thought about until now. He's an "outdoors" person, married, four kids, 34 years old, and the first day we worked together he gained my complete confidence in his ability to relate to what Robin Hood is all about. If you want to talk to the president, call and ask for Al. If you use the "toll free" line, I'll expect you to give him a big stock order.

Herman will be concentrating his efforts on our export business. This is a market area that has been growing each year, and one we have not had the time to devote our efforts to. With Al joining the company, Herman will be able to expand our foreign market as only he is qualified to do.

4. We are attempting to set up and use a mechanical addressing system. This new system will allow us more complete coverage in our newsletter mailings and make our overall postal communications more efficient. Before instituting this system I have one request: Please check your most recent invoice or statement from us, and if there are any corrections in your *business name or address,* please mail these in to me as soon as possible.

5. I am enclosing a new price list supplement with this issue of the newsletter. This is primarily an update and will pick up all of the new items that have been added since February.

6. I made the announcement of our new Economy Gamegetters and Economy Glass Hunting arrows last month, and you have responded very well indeed. We have very good raw material stocks on this arrow style, and our manufacturing capability is now in excess of 2,000 dozen per month. I don't anticipate any problems in being able to supply right up to the deadline. I requested that your orders be in 12 dozen lots. This has generally been followed, but where it isn't you will be charged extra for additional service. This is a necessity as my price workup is too low to offer any "no charge" frills.

    a. Less than 12 dozen quantities will result in a 40 cents per dozen boxing charge.

    b. Requests for cutting and installing SAP inserts will be 60 cents per dozen additional cost.

    c. Marking arrows with your store name at 50 cents per dozen.

7. Once again there are no XX75 Orange shafts available in hunting sizes. I now have 28,440 Orange shafts on back order with Easton and no scheduled delivery information.

8. We are tooling up at present to supply all arrows (except wood arrows) as "compound arrows" with nocks offset enough to provide optimum fletch clearance for right handed shooters. These arrows will still function out of conventional bows. I anticipate that our conversion will be complete by August 1, and all production after that time will be in the new style. Our current production is on a straight fletch basis and provides adequate vane clearance for most compound shooters.

9. In our last newsletter we provided a size chart on Easton shafts by grade. Please add 2213 in XX75 grade as one that I missed. Sorry about the omission.

EXHIBIT 3 (continued)

10. We are starting to utilize Marco vanes in arrow production to reduce costs. I cannot offer these for sale as I haven't yet been able to get enough for general stock and arrow production too. I mentioned these new vanes for two reasons, one to let you know what we are doing and to give you a little information on various vane weights on the market.

Item (based on 3 fletch)	Weight in grains
Pro Fletch (PF500)	43.2
Flex Fletch (FFP-500).......................	34.5
Bohning (5" vane)–New	36.0
Bear Weathers–New	39.8
Marco Fletch (MF500)–New	29.2
5" Trueshape Diecut Feathers	7.8

With everyone concerned about arrow speed, this might be an interesting comparison for feathers. Another note: Marco Fletch has the same cut or shape as a diecut feather.

11. Last month I mentioned how well my son Wally was doing with his "Little John" (detuned) peaked at 38 pounds. Some speed comparison data follows that is pretty graphic and should help you in your compound sales to kids and women that can't bow hunt now. One very interesting fact is that if my son could draw and hold a 42 pound recurve (which he can't), his arrow speed from the conventional stick would be 150 fps as opposed to 161 fps with the compound. I am also including some Carbonglas data comparisons against aluminum arrows.

	Bow and setup	Arrow data	Speed (fps)
Little John Compound	Peak 59 lb. Hold 27 lb.	2117 at 29" 3 fletch (PF400) 125 grain FP	178.8
Little John Compound	Peak 38.5 lb. Hold 20 lb.	1816 at 26" 3 fletch (PF400) 125 grain FP	161.0
Black Hunter Recurve	49 lb. at 29" 42 lb. at 26"	2117 at 29" 1816 at 26"	155.9 149.9

All shots of above were hand shot.

	Bow and setup	Arrow	Arrow weight	Speed (fps)
Little John Compound	Peak 59 lb. Hold 27 lb.	Carbonglas X17 at 29" 3 fletch (MF400) 150 grain FP	505 grain	192.2
		2117 at 29" 3 fletch (PF400) 125 grain FP	542 grain	181.4
		2020 at 29" 3 fletch (MF400) 150 grain FP	583 grain	175.5

Above test run with all arrows machine shot.

438

EXHIBIT 3 (concluded)

12. It is pretty obvious to me at this time that we are not going to get any delivery on Carbonglas this year. I am not going to continue to embarrass myself by making any further delivery promises.
13. Hidden Hunter Insulated Camo Suits: After a little supplier negotiation, I have a "fill-in" order to supplement our general stock on this item. In addition to our standard sizing I have been able to add two *new* sizes to the line. These are XXL (48-52) and XXXL (52-56) for the "bigger bowhunter" (like me). Since it takes more material to fold around the bigger guy, the new sizes will naturally cost more: HHS, $39.90—dealer, $66.50—retail; HHJ, $22.95—dealer, $38.25—retail; and HHP, $16.95—dealer, $28.25—retail. It's a shame that you can't get the Large Economy Size in clothes too!! We expect delivery by August 1.

Retailing and manufacturing

In addition to the problems arising in Robin Hood's main business of wholesaling, Adams had to deal with the pro shop and the arrow manufacturing operations. The pro shop had long been a sore point with CML's management who thought it was unprofitable. Adams's initial analysis indicated that it was profitable even if not a big money maker. However, he found it difficult to allocate the time and effort to day-to-day retail problems such as advertising, and was having difficulty devising a system for measuring and motivating Mr. Tucker who ran the shop. At the time, Tucker was receiving a base salary plus a percentage of the shop's profits.

Presenting even more difficult problems was the Arrow Division; its being so far away, Adams could exert little control over it. The division, newly created in November 1975, was run by Merton's wife, employed six of their female friends, and was located in a house leased from one of Merton's acquaintances.

The atmosphere at the division was not that of a conventional manufacturer's operation. The women often brought in their children and were sometimes absent for a few days. Adams's initial analysis indicated that the division was not getting the 32 percent margin Adams wanted it to. Although the division's capacity was constrained in its present location and although it needed a larger volume to make Robin Hood competitive in arrow manufacturing, Adams had turned down Merton's request to rent the house next door. (Adams did grant Merton a requested $1,000 for expanding the Arrow Division's storage space.) Adams did not want to increase his break-even, and he had doubts about keeping the division at all. He calculated that materials costs for the arrows totaled approximately $11 a dozen. Initially, overhead had been approximately $3.12; after start-up production had increased to what seemed to be a capacity of 2,000 dozen arrows a month. At that output, Adams figured his overhead was more like $2.25 a dozen. The price to retailers for the cheapest and most popular arrow was $15.95. Adams had received an offer from an arrow manufacturer to supply arrows for $15.50 a dozen. Although that amounted to an effective overhead rate of $4.50 a dozen, he figured his $3.12 figure did not include Merton's two days a week at the division, his travel expenses, inventory carrying costs, associated risks, and "grief." While analyzing the problem, Adams noted that Merton received a salary of about $15,000 a year and about $3,-000 in travel expenses.

> Although I've been thinking of disbanding the division, I gave him the $1,000 because maybe the extra space would save labor costs involved in moving the product around the present constrained facilities. I guess I also figured I should give the operation a chance to prove itself since I have to admit one of my biggest reservations about it is my not being able to control it because of its distance from Montclair. One risk of disbanding it is that arrows can be a faddish item—in coloring and different type heads—which can help us get in the door. However, I figured even if this $15.50 contract doesn't work out, I could reestablish an arrow division within three months, in a location under my control and with less overhead to deal with.

Making contacts

Soon after taking over the company, Adams contacted its founder, Mr. Jackson, who at 70 years of age had not been actively involved in the business for some time. However, Jackson was well known and respected throughout the industry. Through Jackson, Adams met some of the industry's better known personalities, including the principals of the larger manufacturing firms, the 1976 Olympic archery team coach, and a number of famous bow hunters. Jackson also introduced Adams to many of Robin Hood's dealers who, Adams learned, were often in the business first because they loved archery rather than to satisfy simple economic motives. For many, their archery dealerships were home- or garage-based businesses which they operated after hours and on weekends.

Personally and professionally satisfying were Adams's contacts with CML's other subsidiary presidents. At a company meeting, Adams was pleased that he was immediately treated as one of the family; he also discovered the other presidents had many of the same problems he did. Adams was gratified that he had defined the issues in much the same way the other presidents had, and that he was able to make positive contributions to defining and analyzing common problems.

> That first president's meeting was great. It was the first time I had someone to talk to face to face about my problems, and I liked them personally—we'd go jogging or swimming together. A big thing was that quite

often you can feel that you are forgetting something, that you aren't considering something you should be, but I came out of that meeting feeling that I had at least touched all the major bases.

THE ARCHERY MARKET

From what little published information was available and from his own contacts, Adams pieced together a view of the archery market. Manufacturing sales amounted to approximately $45 million. Although Bear Archery had 40 percent of the wholesale market and Martin Archery had about 11 percent, Robin Hood was still a major factor with its 4 percent market share because the industry was so fragmented—in many cases like a cottage industry. The U.S. market was growing at about 15 percent a year. In 1974 there were over 16 million licensed hunters of which about 1 million were bow hunters. Arrow dollar sales were almost equal to bow dollar sales. Adams determined that Robin Hood's sales were distributed as follows: Pennsylvania, 23.2 percent; Michigan, 16.4 percent; New York, 11.7 percent; Maine, 6.8 percent; and Ohio, 6.4 percent. The rest of Robin Hood's sales were spread nationally but with concentration in the eastern United States. Industry markups were approximately 25 percent for manufacturers; 33 percent for wholesalers; and 40 percent for dealers. Large companies like Bear Archery often sold to large sports specialists like the Hermann's sporting goods chain. Bear had an aggressive 18-man sales force, sold a large volume at discount prices, and had introduced into a rather sleepy industry modern marketing techniques such as the use of blister packs.

Robin Hood was constrained from expanding its sales because large accounts like Hermann's could get better prices by buying directly from large manufacturers like Bear. Feeling that Robin Hood could not compete on price with these larger companies, Adams felt it had best stay with its conventional, small outlets, and that it should emphasize being a full-service company, providing quick delivery, good credit terms, and liberal takeback policies for the small dealers.

Adams had determined that Robin Hood had a mailing list of about 1,400 dealers; approximately 1,200 were active accounts, and the average order size was $197. Ken Prelopsky, the warehouse manager, claimed that the small dealers did not mind paying a little extra to Robin Hood because they needed and appreciated its service. Robin Hood occasionally had seminars to inform dealers of the specifications and advantages of new equipment. The company also carried many parts which the manufacturers chose not to carry because they were slow movers. And Robin Hood repaired equipment for the price of parts and a small labor charge whereas many manufacturers granted no warranties or would take a long time to repair and return equipment. Prelopsky recalled several dealers telling him that even after having placed large orders with manufacturers, they were treated as strangers when they called the companies. On the other hand, Prelopsky knew the dealers personally, discussed their problems with them, and, equally important, treated them with respect. Although he had reservations about keeping the sales force, Adams felt that having one fit in with his full-service concept might make sense; perhaps rather than disbanding it, he could use it more effectively.

Adams noted that archery addressed two major markets, hunters and target shooters. Target shooting had suffered a serious decline in the United States to the point where it represented only about 15 percent of the market. But, several states had passed laws providing for two hunting seasons, one for firearms and one for archery, and these laws were encouraging many firearms hunters to take up archery so they could extend the time during which they were allowed to hunt. The politically powerful gun industry felt such laws cut into its sales and was lobbying to repeal them.

With recent innovation of compound bows,[5] archery could be a highly technical sport. Since most archers were enthusiasts and the equipment could be expensive ($75–$300 for a bow), Adams felt they would attach great importance to their purchase and, therefore, tend to be information seekers and want to handle the equipment before purchasing it. He felt such consumer behavior would bode well for the small pro shops and was surprised when mass merchandisers, who typically provided little information, were able to sell so much archery equipment, particularly since the industry advertised so little.

Adams felt Robin Hood was vulnerable as a small wholesaler because manufacturers could go around this middle link in the distribution chain and sell directly to small dealers just as the larger manufacturers were doing with their larger accounts. The power of the manufacturers was illustrated by Bear Archery's being able to insist on its approving dealers before allowing Robin Hood to sell its equipment to them. There was also the possibility of mass merchandisers taking sales away from the traditional pro shops. A more immediate threat was the current establishment of many archery shops in converted bowling alleys and warehouses where customers could shoot as well as purchase equipment. As yet, Robin Hood had no formal contact with such operations.

---

[5] A compound bow worked through a pulley mechanism which enabled an archer to pull back the bowstring at, say, a pressure of 45 pounds and hold it at 15 pounds; however, when the bowstring was released, during its last few inches of return to the straight position, it would assume a pressure of, say, 60 pounds. Such an innovation was particularly useful in hunting insofar as it enabled archers to shoot more accurately and with greater force than they could with conventional bows. An example of a compound bow appears in Exhibit 4.

442

Decision points

Adams felt he had done well in imposing at least a semblance of order on Robin Hood, but knew he had a long way to go. He still had not been able to set aside time for the sole purpose of creating a strategy. He was aware of some strategic alternatives and of some major operational problems which he was facing.

Adams wondered if it might be possible to expand the market for target archery by having salespeople encourage high schools to introduce it into their recreational curricula. Archery's having become an Olympic event only in 1972 after a 48-year absence, and the United States having won gold medals in the 1976 Olympics, he felt there could be a better chance of creating such interest than there had been before.

Adams also had to decide what to do about his sales force and about Merton. Adams felt Merton often tried to assume authority which should be Adams's alone, yet on a case-by-case basis, Merton always seemed to follow Adams's directions once it was established that Adams was the one making the decision. Adams felt that perhaps he had been too defensive about Merton, whose aggressiveness, though seeming threatening while Adams was getting established, merely showed a dedication to the job and a strong point of view which would serve as useful input to future decision making. Adams recalled an occasion on which he had inadvertently crossed Merton. Robin Hood had had a policy of charging a $5 service charge on orders under $20. But when Adams determined what the average order was, he decided to eliminate the charge. He had once taken a call from a dealer and told him he would not have to pay the extra $5 on a recent order. However, Merton had handled the original order and in line with the company policy then in effect had already charged the $5. Perhaps such situations had contributed to the conflicts Adams sensed.

If Adams fired Merton, his friends on the sales force, his friends at the Arrow Division, and his wife might all leave as well. Of course, all this might be desirable, but even if it were, Adams was unsure about the timing—should he wait until he had a more firm grasp on the company and its operations?

Schmidt had signed what Adams viewed as expensive leases for the Arrow Division, the main office, and for a malfunctioning copier. Adams said he would like to get out of some of these leases so that he could reduce his fixed costs and improve his cash flow. But he felt it was unlikely he could renegotiate the leases downward, and if he were able to get out of leases altogether, where would he move the company? He was considering moving to Pennsylvania where labor was plentiful and cheap and where welfare benefits were not as competitive with wages as they were in New Jersey. In New Jersey the minimum wage was $3.30; in Pennsylvania it was $2.35 per hour. If the whole operation were to be in Pennsylvania, he could assert more control over the arrow operation and use workers interchangeably between the arrow manufacturing and the warehouse season by season. One drawback might be difficulty in getting some of the present key employees to move with the company.

Adams also felt the company was overstaffed; at the same time, he wanted to delegate many of the routine decisions which Schmidt had made himself. Adams felt the clerical staff should take responsibility for the relatively minor decisions their jobs involved, but he was having difficulty in motivating them to do so. He had been successful at creating an urgency about filling orders which, in line with Adams's intent to provide excellent service, were now more promptly filled. He now had to develop the same sort of commitment to job responsibility and decision making.

Adams also wondered if he should refuse to see people about simple problems; for example, the bookkeeper with her questions about ledger accounts. A more closed-door policy would give him time to plan strategy but might, at the same time, isolate him from important information, especially when he was still new and needed it.

His surprise at mass merchandisers like Hermann's doing so well in the industry led Adams to question his analysis of the consumer behavior involved in buying archery equipment. Perhaps archers did not seek as much information as he thought they did. Or, perhaps they sought the information at pro shops, then bought the equipment at the less expensive outlets. Perhaps pro shops would become obsolete and Robin Hood would have to try to gain an entree to the mass merchandisers—but how could it do this when the manufacturers could go to these outlets themselves?

Given these possible trends, on which there was little or no published information, perhaps Robin Hood should integrate backward and get into manufacturing, perhaps through an acquisition. If he were to integrate backward, decisions like not selling to the Vermont discounter might have to be revised. Perhaps Robin Hood should integrate forward and get involved in converting buildings to pro shops and target ranges. Perhaps such an operation could even be franchised.

A major concern was the product decisions which had to be made for the catalog. Although Adams was developing an understanding of archery and archers, he knew he would have to rely to a great extent on company personnel for input. He wondered how best to structure the product committee's work and how to run the meetings.

And there was the nagging problem of cash flow. Buying in the spring and selling in the fall imposed severe problems on Robin Hood, especially since, in line with its dealer service concept, it allowed its small vulnerable dealers liberal credit. It dated small orders on a 2/10/30 basis and allowed 120 days on orders of over $1,000. One dealer had mentioned he would prefer a stepped dating schedule allowing for bigger discounts with earlier payments, for example, 5 percent off for payments within 30 days, 2 percent off for payments within 60 days, and no discount after 60 days. Perhaps such a schedule would encourage Robin Hood's dealers, who probably were not that concerned about the time value of money, to pay earlier and thus help alleviate the company's cash flow problems.

As he considered his many problems, Adams said:

> There is plenty to think about. Living an hour from work, I leave home at 7 in the morning and return between 8 and 9 in the evening. My family is almost in shock; they've never seen so little of me. It's particularly tough on the older kids because they had made friends in Cambridge and now have to adjust to a new home and to going to a new school. I bring in a sleeping bag and sleep in the office two nights a week so I can get my work done and return home at 4 the next afternoon to be with the kids. Fortunately, my wife is understanding; she's bothered only by my being a bit tense sometimes—I think it's because I have no peers at work I can talk to. She once said that she thought the sacrifices we both made to get me through school were temporary and would lead to much better things. Now she finds I'm still working long hours. And with our mortgage and school debts we really have little discretionary income. We hardly ever eat out, even though I'm being paid well. My description of the company may have been somewhat disjointed but that's the way it seems when you walk into something like that. I guess what I have to do now is continue wading through the daily problems, set some priorities, and establish a strategy. I feel up to it too; it's amazing how I've become so confident so fast.

case 19

Charles River Breeding Laboratories

Described by a competitor as the General Motors of the laboratory animal industry, the Charles River Breeding Laboratories of Wilmington, Massachusetts, had achieved major corporate success both in terms of financial results as well as in technical reputation. Company sales were $25,000 in 1950 with operating net profit of $1,400; comparable 1975 fiscal year data were $15,405,100 and $1,565,600. The company's technical publication, *The Charles River Digest*, unique to the industry, circulated quarterly to 13,000 members of the international research community.

Charles River specialized in the production of scientifically bred, high-quality laboratory animals for pharmaceutical and chemical companies, commercial testing laboratories, hospitals, and universities. Other firms in the industry manufactured cages and scientific equipment, feed and bedding supplies, animal by-products for use in research, and operated independent testing laboratories.

Charles River's first and still primary products were laboratory rats and mice; in 1976 sales of these animals comprised over 90 percent of the company's sales revenues. The company had been the leader in the breeding and introduction of disease-free rats and mice. Beginning in 1955, Charles River commercialized a process known as COBS® (cesarian-originated-barrier-sustained), allowing the company to produce disease-free animals which enabled researchers to conduct more effective experimental research. In 1976 this process had been adopted widely by breeders throughout the world.

The executive group of Charles River had been relatively stable over the past decade with company policy being to promote from within whenever possible. Executives described Charles River as a "family firm" and took pride in the Foster family's public generosity in giving Brandeis University a biomedical research laboratory building and the furnishing of a contemporary gallery at the Boston Museum of Fine Arts.

In reviewing his company's current situation, Henry L. Foster, DVM, president and chief executive, commented:

> So far it has been great. We just do what is necessary to produce the best and the results follow. When we went public, we announced a 15–20 percent per year growth goal in both sales and earnings, and we are sticking to that target. Once you become a public company, you enter a race and are always out of breath.
>
> Observers and investors are now asking—what next? We have to deal with that question *now* since the action lead time is a long one. Of course we will continue to grow in our basic animal product lines—but that is not enough. We are going to have to expand into new areas, and there are lots of opportunities.
>
> Where do we go now? How does a manager answer that question? And, how do I organize to get these decisions made? We want internal growth, new product additions, and acquisitions. But how do we do this without getting a case of corporate indigestion? We don't want to eat *too* much but we want a good meal.

LABORATORY ANIMAL USE

Laboratory animals, primarily rats and mice, were the basis for product safety testing, drug development and human health research, especially cancer treatment research. Most pharmaceuticals, cosmetics, toiletries, and food additives were tested on animals for toxic side effects before the FDA would approve their sale. Lab animals were used to measure side effects of environmental pollutants and industrial and agricultural chemicals. Medical research on the causes and treatment of cancer, heart disease, nutritional deficiencies, and birth defects also relied on experiments with laboratory animals. Studies using lab animals took place at drug companies, independent testing laboratories, universities, hospitals, and a variety of government agencies. The largest governmental users were the National Institutes of Health, the Food and Drug Administration, and the Environmental Protection Agency.

There were two important distinctions to be made about laboratory animals. One refers to the genetic makeup of the animals—whether they were inbred or outbred. The second concerns the method of raising the animals and their consequent state of health: "conventional" breeding methods versus various "pathogen-free" or "disease-free" methods.

Inbred versus outbred lab animals

Although any animal may be inbred or outbred, these terms usually referred to genetic and physical characteristics of the various rodent species which accounted for over 98 percent of all lab animals used in the United

States.[1] The most common rodents were mice, rats, guinea pigs, and hamsters.

Inbred animals were brother-sister mated for a minimum of 20 generations to produce specific heritable characteristics, such as susceptibility or immunity to a particular disease. For example, the C-3H inbred mouse strain carried a virus which can develop breast cancer in its young, while the SHR (spontaneous hypertensive) rat consistently exhibited blood pressure above 180°. These and hundreds of other inbred rodent strains were used to understand the effects of diseases and to develop drugs and other treatment methods. The largest user of inbred animals was the National Cancer Institute, but medical and drug researchers in universities, hospitals, pharmaceutical firms, and contract testing laboratories also required inbred animals. Inbred strains were more expensive than outbred because of the additional labor and record keeping required by brother-sister mating.

Breeders produced outbred animals by consistently avoiding brother-sister mating in order to produce a heterogeneous population. Heterogeneous populations were made up of animals with a variety of characteristics, much like the human population. These animals were used to test overall product safety and effectiveness. Many more outbred animals were used than inbred, and the largest consumer groups for outbreds were pharmaceutical companies and independent testing labs.

Conventional versus disease-free animals

Conventional methods of lab animal breeding involved putting animals in an enclosed pen or cage, and feeding, watering, and cleaning them. The breeder then waited for the animals to mate and sold the offspring as soon as they were weaned.

Until the mid-1950s, the conventional method was the principal way commercial breeders raised lab animals. It was a high-risk, labor-intensive business with many small-scale participants. Risk came from the frequent outbreaks of disease which could rapidly destroy a breeder's entire animal inventory. Commercial breeding businesses were small-scale operations because they were part-time endeavors and few breeders would risk the capital necessary to support larger scale breeding. Animals properly housed and cared for under small-scale conventional methods could sometimes perform

---

[1] Laboratory animals were distinguished by *species* and *strains*. As defined by the National Academy of Sciences in *Animals for Research*, a *species* is all animals of the same kind that can (actually or potentially) mate together and produce fertile offspring. Examples of common species names are cats, dogs, mice, hamsters, and so forth. A *strain* is a subset of a species comprised of a group of animals of known ancestry maintained by a deliberate mating system, generally with some distinguishing characteristics.

as well as animals reared under the more elaborate disease-free methods described below. All animal species and both inbred and outbred strains could be raised in a conventional manner.

In 1955 Charles River introduced the first of various disease-free animal breeding methods to commercial lab rodent breeding. Disease-free breeding techniques improved animal health, reduced the risk of losing animals from disease, but required special breeding facilities and processes. By the mid-1970s almost half of all lab rodents were raised using one or more of the following disease-free techniques.

Specific Pathogen-Free (SPF) animals were free of specific parasites and microorganisms which could impair their health, for example, salmonellosis.[2] The specific pathogens eliminated depended both on the species and on the breeder supplying the animal. The process required obtaining a healthy animal through selection or through chemotherapy to eliminate one or more specific pathogens and then following strict quarantine procedures to keep the animals from outside contamination.

Cesarian derivation was a technique which prevented diseases and parasites from being transferred from a mother to her young, and resulted in healthier, longer living, more vigorous animals. The process is termed a hysterectomy because the mother's entire uterus containing the pups is removed shortly before normal birth would occur. The uterus is then introduced, using sterile techniques, into a germfree plastic bubble where the pups are surgically removed and then nurtured by a germfree foster mother or hand-fed sterile milk. The animals could then remain in a germfree environment or be placed in a barrier system (see below).

Germfree animals were cesarian derived in a germfree environment, as described above, and were continuously maintained in a germfree isolator. They were completely free of all identifiable bacteria, viruses, fungi, protozoa, or other parasites (collectively called flora). The most common type of isolator was a 2- by 5-foot completely sealed clear plastic chamber. All water, feed, and bedding was sterilized, and researchers handled the animals through rubber-gloved sleeves which protruded into the isolator. Animals could die within 12 to 24 hours if removed from their germfree bubble. The advantage of using germfree animals was that a researcher could be more certain that any animal abnormalities were directly related to a research procedure rather than due to an environmentally induced disease.

Cesarian-Derived-Barrier-Sustained (or barrier-reared) animals began as

---

[2] Salmonellosis, in man, is a type of food poisoning which can cause severe dehydration.

germfree pups delivered by hysterectomy. Specific flora were then associated with the animals so that they developed normal digestive and immunological systems, enabling them to survive outside of the germfree isolators. The animals were housed in barrier buildings which were equipped with filtered air systems, temperature and humidity controls, autoclaves to sterilize feed and bedding, and controlled personnel access in order to prevent contamination.

Barrier facilities and germfree equipment required substantial capital investment. A plastic germfree bubble, for example, to house 50 mice cost $400 in 1976. (Prior to the development of plastic isolators in the mid-50s, a steel isolator cost $5–$10,000.) There were different degrees of barrier systems, and each company employed a unique combination of barrier styles. The simplest method provided a number of separate rooms for animals and controlled the direction of air flow and personnel from clean to dirty areas. The most sophisticated facilities involved the construction of many small breeding rooms and corridors with extensive air-conditioning and filtration systems, sterilizing facilities for equipment, feed and bedding, and elaborate personnel locks. One industry source estimated the minimum, initial investment for an acceptable small-scale barrier facility to be at least $500,000.

Scope of animal-based research and testing

The majority of laboratory animals were used in human health-related research, drug development, and drug testing. According to the National Institutes of Health (NIH), U.S. government expenditures for research and treatment development totaled $1.5 billion in 1975.[3] U.S. pharmaceutical firms spent $930 million on research and development in 1974, according to the Pharmaceutical Manufacturers Association. Pharmaceutical companies accounted for about 50 percent of the dollar volume of animals purchased, and government-funded research purchases accounted for over 20 percent.

The cost of the compound tested, physical facilities, and salary costs for Ph.Ds, MDs, and technicians were the major research budget expense items. One industry source estimated that of the $930 million pharmaceutical companies spent to screen 700,000 new compounds in 1974, lab animal purchases accounted for 5 percent of the total and lab animal maintenance accounted for an additional 5 percent of R&D expenditures.

---

[3] Of the total $1.5 billion NIH budget, $1.1 billion was allocated to research conducted by various agencies of the NIH itself (e.g., $30 million for the National Cancer Institute's Division of Cancer Treatment), or to researchers in universities, hospitals, and medical schools. Four hundred million dollars was allocated to contract research and testing by independent commercial testing laboratories such as Arthur D. Little or Hazelton, by universities, and by pharmaceutical firms. Much of this $400 million allocation supported animal-based research.

Animal usage by species

Rats and mice were the most widely used laboratory animals because they were small, readily available, and inexpensive. Hundreds of strains of mice and rats had been developed to be hosts for specific human cancer tumors or to exhibit signs of a specific disease such as arthritis. However, each species and strain had characteristics which were preferred for different types of research, and consequently there was limited substitutability among species and strains.

Dr. Joseph Mayo, director of the Animal Breeding Program at the National Cancer Institute (NCI) and a former researcher, explained why mice were widely used to evaluate cancer treatment drugs.

> First of all, through careful genetic control, mice can be bred to develop a susceptibility to a particular tumor. Secondly, mice are small and easy to handle, so the expense of housing and feeding the animals is minimized. More importantly, it means that the dosage level can be low. Vincristine, a compound we are testing now, interfered with cell division and costs $100,-000 a gram.

U.S. research used 41.7 million animals each year, and a comparable number, Dr. Foster estimated, were used annually in Europe. Rats and mice accounted for 96 percent of all laboratory animals used in the United States, with rabbits, guinea pigs, hamsters, dogs, cats, and monkeys also popular research subjects. Exhibit 1 shows the number of animals used yearly for U.S. research by species. "Wild animals," a heterogeneous category of animals collected from nature, includes amoebas, frogs, marine animals, cattle, poultry, lions, and elephants, most of which were used in agricultural and veterinary research.

EXHIBIT 1

U.S. laboratory animal usage by species, 1974

Mice	30,000,000
Rats	10,000,000
Hamsters	430,800
Guinea pigs	430,400
Rabbits	425,600
Dogs	199,200
Wild animals	81,021
Cats	74,000
Primates	51,300
Total	41,692,500

Source: Mice and rats estimates by Charles River Breeding Laboratories and the Institute for Laboratory Animal Resources. Other species data from U.S. Department of Agriculture, Report of the Secretary of Agriculture, *Animal Welfare Enforcement 1974*.

Lab animal performance requirements

Lab animal users considered animal performance and availability more important than price. One industry observer noted:

> Time pressures on researchers are great. Pharmaceutical companies are under pressure to meet market introduction dates, and academic research grants usually have a calendar-year limit. Therefore any delay in receiving the right number of animals at the right time, or receiving animals that die before the experiment is concluded, has cost the researcher both time and money far beyond the mere cost of the animals.

Lab animal performance during an experiment depended on the animal's state of health when it arrived at the researchers' facility. Breeding the animals in a healthy environment and minimizing transportation stress were the most important determinants of animal health. A breeder's ability to supply a healthy animal depended on obtaining a clean animal to start his breeding colony and then on maintaining production processes and facilities adequate to prevent disease introduction. The division leader of Arthur D. Little's Tumor Screening Program for the National Cancer Institute, Mr. Wodinsky, discussed the importance of familiarity with a breeder's operations in ascertaining animal quality.

> Most suppliers now offer cesarian-derived animals, so the basic animals do not differ much among breeders. The difference is facilities and production colony management that keeps the animals separate and healthy. It is the people working for them that are the critical factor in controlling contamination. I know the actual setup of all the breeders who supply us.

Dr. Henry Agersborg, associate director of research for Wyeth Laboratories, elaborated on the problem:

> A rat can lose 20 percent of its body weight in a day and will die of starvation in five to seven days. Loss of weight during transport is a shock to the animal's system. It may regain weight rapidly, but it might be permanently weakened and break down part way into an experiment. That is why transport stress can be a potential problem, and why we prefer a breeder who can guarantee same-day delivery. A local breeder only has an advantage if he does not use a public carrier. REA can take three days to transport animals 12 miles.

Almost half the animals used in laboratory research were transported by airfreight. Airborne, an airfreight forwarder specializing in lab animals, confirmed the problems of timely delivery and promoted its services which monitored the location and status of shipments.

Product availability and reliable delivery were important to researchers in three ways. First was obtaining the specific strain and species required among the several hundred varieties raised. Second was securing enough animals of the specific age, sex, and weight required to meet the needs of several hundred to several thousand animals per program per week. Finally, delivery reliability was very important because research procedures were frequently standardized on a particular breeder's animals.

INDUSTRY TRENDS

An industry observer identified four trends which were having a major impact on the laboratory animal breeding industry in the mid-1970s. These included slower market growth, more sophisticated uses of lab animals, rising quality standards for animals and facilities, and consolidation among breeders.

Slower market growth

Between the late 1940s and early 1970s, the demand for laboratory animals had grown from a few million mice and rats to approximately 42 million animals of many species. The most rapid growth in demand had occurred between 1965 and 1970 when volume doubled. The rapid growth in the mid-60s was spurred by a large influx of funds into government-sponsored research on cancer and viral diseases in combination with stricter Food and Drug Administration test data requirements on the efficacy and safety of new drugs. In the early 70s a cutback in federal funding for health research had slowed the growth of lab animal use for basic research, but pharmaceutical and chemical company use of lab animals for testing continued to expand at a rate of 7–12 percent per year. By 1974 government-sponsored research expenditures had resumed a growth rate of 5–10 percent per year. Exhibit 2 shows U.S. drug company research and development expenditures from 1950 to 1974.

EXHIBIT 2
U.S. drug industry research and development expenditures, 1950–1974 ($000)

Year	Expenditures	Year	Expenditures
1950	$ 39,000	1965	$351,000
1955	91,000	1970	619,000
1960	212,000	1974	930,000

Source: Pharmaceutical Manufacturers Association, *Annual Survey Report, 1973–74* and *1968–69.*

More sophisticated uses of lab animals

Continuing from the late 1960s was a long-term trend toward increased use of life-span studies of animals in both research and drug testing. In research, long-term studies were spurred by the desire for more information about the long-term effects of environmental and industrial pollutants and by intensified study of long-term health problems such as cancer and cardiovascular diseases. In drug testing long-term studies had become more common as a result of increasingly stringent requirements by the FDA to identify and disclose long-term effects of drugs. One pharmaceutical industry spokesperson stated that 1975 R&D budgets had risen to twice 1970 budgets in order to get the same number of new drugs approved by the FDA. In addition to increasingly longer studies, experiments using lab animals had become increasingly complex, frequently investigating the interactions of two or three drugs in a living organism. Both of these trends pointed to an increasing demand for well-defined, healthy animals which would survive the rigors of longer experiments.[4]

Rising quality standards

The increasing demand for healthier, well-defined animals was responsible for the growing proportion of cesarian-derived-barrier-reared (CDBR) and specific pathogen-free (SPF) animals sold by the larger commercial breeders since the mid-1960s. CDBR and SPF rodents lived longer and were more vigorous than the conventional animals breeders had traditionally raised. Although CDBR and SPF animal breeding required a substantial capital investment in facilities and equipment, the improved facilities allowed breeders to raise more animals per square foot and to better control infectious diseases within production colonies. The larger breeders' ability to supply SPF and CDBR animals in large volume at a cost only slightly above that of conventional animals was credited with further increasing demand for these improved lab animals.

Longer term and increasingly complex research and testing procedures continued to stimulate increasing demand for higher quality animals in the mid-1970s. Dr. Albert Jonas, director of Laboratory Animal Services at the Yale Medical School, was among a growing group of users imposing higher standards. Quality control screening procedures for animals brought in from the outside involved detailed pathology tests, bacteriology tests, and veterinary exams. Quality control standards were high both to screen out substandard animals and to ensure a stable and consistent data base for experiments.

Dr. Jonas commented:

> Quality in lab animals is becoming increasingly important because of the trend toward long-term studies, especially in carcinogenesis and in long-term effects of pharmaceuticals.

---

[4] The definition of a laboratory animal included, among other things, information about its normal heart rate, blood count, respiratory rate, blood chemistry, and intestinal flora.

Dr. Mayo agreed that users would be increasingly critical of animal quality, commenting:

> There will be big changes in animal breeding in the next five years. Users will demand more uniformity in terms of health and, for inbred animals, in genetic control. Researchers will be saying, "My results are different from yours. What animal did you use?" Few breeders will be able to supply the higher quality animals. Few are in a financial position to make the heavy investment in buildings and equipment.

Breeder consolidation

The decade between 1955 and 1965 had brought the transfer of most laboratory animal breeding from users' in-house facilities to commercial breeders. At the same time, many new breeders entered the industry and established breeders prospered. Even "backyard breeders" who raised animals in garages or sheds were successful in the early years. With the recent increase in quality demands and attendant capital investment requirements, few new companies entered into rat and mouse production after the late 60s. Smaller companies went out of business each year or were acquired by larger breeders, and by 1975 "backyard breeders" of rats and mice had largely disappeared.

In the new environment more than financial strength was needed to be a successful laboratory animal breeder. The failure of two large corporations who attempted to enter the industry in the 1960s, Ralston-Purina and Becton, Dickinson & Co., attested to the difficulties of breeding.

Ralston-Purina, which supplied over 50 percent of the lab animal diet market, attempted to establish a breeding facility in Puerto Rico. One industry observer commented that the original product had been good, but transportation to major market areas was difficult because of the remote location. In addition to its production and distribution problems, Ralston-Purina encountered marketing problems. Their animal diet sales force was not effective in selling animals since the purchasing agents who bought animal diets could not control a researcher's lab animal purchase patterns. Finally, minimum management attention was given to the endeavor because the $1.5 million facilities investment was such a small part of Ralston-Purina's overall capital budget. Dr. Foster commented that the purchase was like Ralston-Purina's buying another water cooler.

In 1964 Becton, Dickinson & Co., a large manufacturer of medical and laboratory supplies, acquired the Carworth Company, at that time the largest commercial breeder of mice in the industry. The company prospered for a few years after its acquisition, but began a downward spiral that continued until the division's sale in 1974 to Charles River. Between 1968 and 1973 Carworth fiscal year sales declined from $3.4 million to $2.9 million and gross margins declined from 38 percent of sales to 7 percent of sales. During the same period net income after tax went from a profit of $110,000 to a loss of $471,000.

THE MARKET FOR LABORATORY ANIMALS

The $78.5 million market for laboratory animals was fragmented and regionalized. In addition to government agencies, pharmaceutical companies and universities, food manufacturers, and cosmetic and toiletries firms were steady users of lab animals. The total number of lab animal purchasers was well over 2,000 with a multitude of departments and project groups purchasing animals at each company or institution. Most users of lab animals were located along the eastern seaboard between Washington, D.C., and Boston, or in the Great Lakes region between Chicago and Cleveland. California and Texas were the other sizable market areas.

Mice and rats were the most widely used species, accounting for 96 percent of the unit volume of sales and close to 50 percent of dollar volume. Most customers for laboratory animals used some hamsters, guinea pigs, and rabbits in addition to mice and rats. Markets for primates and animals from nature were significantly different from the market for smaller animals. Primates were used almost exclusively by the National Institutes of Health and by contract testing laboratories. Universities and government agencies were the primary users of animals from nature.

EXHIBIT 3
Estimated laboratory animal sales by species, 1975 ($000)

Mice	$25,000
Rats	20,000
Rabbits	3,000
Hamsters	1,000
Guinea pigs	3,500
Primates	10,300
Other species*	11,500
Total	$74,300

*Includes dogs, cats, gerbils, sheep, poultry, and a wide variety of animals from nature, such as fish and frogs.
Source: Researcher estimates.

Exhibit 4 shows the number of registered users and number of animals employed in research for the United States as a whole and for the ten largest user states. Exhibit 4 includes data only for species controlled under the

Animal Welfare Enforcement Act.[5] Mice and rats were uncontrolled species, so comparable data were not available.

EXHIBIT 4
Registered users and number of animals used by state, 1974

State	Number of users	Animals used
California	85	156,400
Illinois	63	122,800
Indiana......................	20	75,500
Massachusetts	46	69,500
Michigan	13	72,500
New Jersey	42	126,100
New York	102	227,100
Ohio	69	68,800
Pennsylvania	57	69,000
Texas	31	142,700
Total ten states........	528	1,130,400
Total United States	867	1,692,500

Source: U.S. Department of Agriculture, Report of the Secretary of Agriculture, *Animal Welfare Enforcement 1974.*

Laboratory animal markets outside the United States

Outside the United States, the majority of medical research and pharmaceutical testing using laboratory animals was conducted in Japan and western Europe. Most users maintained in-house breeding facilities, and commercial breeding activities were limited, although conditions varied widely among countries. Pharmaceutical and chemical companies comprised the largest user group as they did in the United States, and mice and rats were the most commonly used animals.

There was little data available on the dollar size of lab animal markets outside the United States or on the number of animals used, but Dr. Foster estimated the annual market at $60–$80 million, of which Europe accounted for $40–$60 million. The researcher estimated that of that total, $6 million was spent on laboratory animals by U.S. companies in their overseas facilities in 1974.[6] Exhibit 5 presents the researcher's estimates of the mar-

---

[5] "The Laboratory Animal Welfare Act of 1966, as amended by the Animal Welfare Act of 1970 (referred to as the Animal Welfare Act), empowers the Secretary of Agriculture to establish standards to regulate the transportation, purchase, sale, housing, care, handling and treatment of animals intended for use for research or experimental purposes or for exhibition purposes or for use as pets." U.S. Department of Agriculture, Report of the Secretary of Agriculture, *Animal Welfare Enforcement 1974.*

[6] Based on an allocation for lab animals of 5 percent of total overseas R&D expenditures of $124.5 million in 1974, as reported by the Pharmaceutical Manufacturers Association, *Annual Survey Report, 1973–74.*

ket available to commercial breeders in France, England, Italy, Japan, and Canada based on Charles River data.

EXHIBIT 5
Estimated lab animal sales

	$ million equivalents
France	$10.0
England	7.5
Italy	3.2
Japan	10.0
Canada	7.5

LABORATORY ANIMAL BREEDERS

The laboratory animal breeding industry was specialized and localized, with most breeders clustered around customer concentrations on the Atlantic seaboard and in the Midwest. Although the Institute of Laboratory Animal Resources cited 113 sources of laboratory animals in 1975, 27 firms produced over 98 percent of the animals used, and only 5 firms had annual sales of $2 million or more. Some firms participated in allied industries serving the health research community, such as lab animal cage, feed, and bedding supply, and the operation of commercial testing and research laboratories.

Within the laboratory animal breeding industry there were three major types of businesses, distinguished by the species of animals raised and by their production methods as follows: (1) large-scale breeding of cesarian-derived-barrier-maintained and germfree rodents, (2) small-scale breeding of conventional animals, and (3) primate importing and breeding.

Large-scale rodent breeding

The five large-scale breeding businesses with annual sales over $2 million were primarily producers of mice and rats and accounted for approximately 50 percent of total industry rodent sales (in dollars). Most of their sales were in cesarian-derived-barrier-maintained and germfree animals. Twenty-two small local breeders competed for the remaining 50 percent of the rodent market and raised animals in "conventional" or simple barrier facilities.

Charles River and the four other large-scale breeders carried a wide variety of rodent strains, and several of the firms raised additional species, such as hamsters, guinea pigs, or primates. Each company had a strong market position in its immediate geographic area as well as selling to major users across the United States. Charles River and ARS/Sprague-Dawley were the only public firms in the group, and the only firms to operate multisite facilities.

Jackson Laboratories, Bar Harbor, Maine. A nonprofit genetic research foundation, Jackson Laboratories had started the large-scale production of inbred mice in the United States in the 1930s. It raised over 75 strains of mice bred for specific research needs and had a quality reputation. The company commercially marketed 50 percent of its animals, the balance of which were internally for its own research. It offered animals raised by germfree and conventional methods.

ARS/Sprague-Dawley, Madison, Wisconsin. With approximately $3 million in annual sales, ARS/Sprague-Dawley was the second largest commercial breeder in the United States. It was a division of the Mogul Corporation (1972 sales, $32 million). Sprague-Dawley was a brand name so widely recognized that it had become a generic term for laboratory rats in the same way Kleenex had for facial tissues. A significant proportion of the company's business involved raising animals under government contract.

Harlan Industries, Indianapolis, Indiana. Harlan was the second largest breeder in the Midwest and had a substantial customer base among pharmaceutical companies. The firm was relatively young and was highly respected for the quality of its animals.

Simonsen Laboratories, Gilroy, California. Simonsen was the only significant supplier of animals on the West Coast. Company products included mice and rats, and guinea pigs. No information on company sales was available.

Small-scale commercial breeding

Traditionally, the laboratory animal breeding industry had been composed of small-scale, family-operated businesses which specialized in a single species delivered to a limited number of local customers. In 1975 these small-scale breeders still accounted for approximately 55 percent of lab animals sold and close to 30 percent of industry dollar volume. They produced about half the rats and mice available in the United States, as well as almost all hamsters, guinea pigs, rabbits, cats, and dogs. Small breeders raised animals by conventional methods or with simple barrier systems where the direction of airflow and personnel access were controlled from clean to dirty areas. Except for mice and rats, the animals were neither specific pathogen-free nor cesarian derived.

The operations of the Murphy Breeding Laboratory, Inc., were representative of a successful small-scale breeder. The company, founded in 1968, was the largest producer of quality guinea pigs in the United States and also raised mice for the National Cancer Institute. Company revenues were approximately $300,000 in 1975. As it was for many small breeders, the National Cancer Institute contract was crucial to the company's financial stability. It was one of the few companies to enter the lab animal breeding business successfully in recent years.

Jobber, satellite, or "backyard" breeding described the method used to raise most guinea pigs and rabbits. It differed from small-scale breeding businesses in that demand for these animals was erratic and few producers engaged in the business year-round. Under a satellite breeding system, the jobber or main breeder maintained a small conventional breeding colony at his own facility and subcontracted additional production demands to part-time breeders who kept under a hundred animals in a garage or backyard pen.

Primate importing and breeding

After mice and rats, primates accounted for the largest dollar volume of sales in the U.S. lab animal industry—approximately $10.3 million in 1975. This represented the sale of approximately 48,000 animals, including gorillas, baboons, and a wide variety of monkeys. Another 1,500 primates were raised each year by the National Institutes of Health in their Regional Primate Centers.

Most primates available commercially in the United States were trapped abroad. Primate importers purchased animals from trappers in the host country, arranged for transportation and quarantine, and treated any obvious diseases at their U.S. holding facilities before offering the animals for sale. Two major companies engaged in primate importing: Prime Labs and Primate Imports Corporation, which was 50 percent owned by Charles River Breeding.[7]

The market for primates was split equally between two user groups. Universities and government agencies comprised the first group and used a wide variety of primates in medical, psychological, and sociological studies. Commercial testing laboratories and pharmaceutical companies comprised the second group and used the smaller rhesus monkeys for drug screening and for testing cosmetics. About half of all primates used in research were rhesus monkeys.

The major sources of supply for primates were the Indian subcontinent (the only natural habitat of the rhesus), Africa, South America, and Indonesia. Rhesus prices had almost doubled since 1973, when the government of India had declared the monkeys an endangered species and reduced exports

---

[7] In August 1973 Charles River acquired 50 percent of the stock of Primate Imports Corporation for $268,400 and an option to acquire the remaining 50 percent prior to October 1976. In early 1976 Charles River indicated its intention to exercise that option at a price not to exceed $375,000.

from 50,000 to 20,000 per year. Further regulations were imposed in subsequent years. Both the export quotas and regulations were expected to be permanent.

The researcher estimated that commercial primate breeders in the United States produced fewer than 1,500 animals a year. In addition to Charles River, only three companies engaged in domestic primate breeding, and it represented a small part of their total annual sales. Litton Bionetics was primarily a supplier of biological and scientific equipment, while Gulf South was one of the largest commercial testing laboratories and used most of the primates it raised in its own research activities. Hazelton Laboratories, a company newly organized in 1969, was a rapidly growing diversified enterprise. (See the Appendix.)

CHARLES RIVER BREEDING LABORATORIES

Company history

From a warehouse loft with a $1,200 investment in used rat cages in 1947, Henry Foster built Charles River Breeding Laboratories into the industry's dominant producer of rats and mice with 1975 sales of $15.4 million, net assets of $16.9 million, and an OTC stock whose price-earnings ratio fluctuated between 20 and 60. (See Exhibits 6 and 7 for company financial information.)

Dr. Henry Foster commented:

> In 1947 I graduated from Middlesex Veterinary School in Waltham and wanted to establish a practice near Alexandria, Virginia. I couldn't find a location I could afford, but in my search I bumped into an abandoned rat farm in Clinton, Md. They sold me their old rat cages for $1,200 and showed me their records and customer lists.
> I had the cages shipped to Boston and started looking for a location. It was hard to find a landlord who would take a bunch of smelly rats, but I finally got the loft of an old warehouse on Leverett Street, behind Beacon Hill near the Charles River.
> I really didn't have a product to sell. No other veterinarian was in the field of animal breeding. Ventilation control in the loft consisted of opening and closing the window. I didn't really know what I was doing. There was no formal training in lab animals sciences available, but the one thing I had was my veterinary degree. I could create an image of professionalism, and "Dr. Foster" gave me access to researchers. I didn't get left in the waiting room with the other salesmen.

When Charles River first went public in 1968 the company was still regarded as specializing in rats and was the largest commercial breeder with sales close to $4 million. Between 1969 and 1975 Charles River sales grew 400 percent from both internal growth and acquisitions.

EXHIBIT 6

CHARLES RIVER BREEDING LABORATORIES
Consolidated Balance Sheets
October 31, 1968–1975
($000)

Assets	1968	1969	1970	1971	1972	1973	1974	1975
Current assets:								
Cash	$ 320	$ 203	$ 340	$ 202	$ 352	$ 284	$ 373	$ 316
Certificates of deposit	105	100	100	208	200	633	492	388
Marketable securities	949	712	150	646	—	1,009	577	452
Accounts receivable	585	761	808	1,284	1,357	1,775	2,495	2,635
Inventories and supplies	256	262	366	508	657	886	1,445	1,618
Other current assets	44	132	117	91	114	140	142	134
Total current assets	$2,259	$2,170	$1,881	$2,939	$2,680	$4,727	$ 5,524	$ 5,543
Property and equipment, at cost:								
Land	$ 173	$ 183	$ 262	$ 306	$ 626	$ 683	$ 1,139	$ 1,143
Buildings and improvements	1,643	2,277	2,707	3,135	4,284	5,462	7,078	7,519
Equipment	1,217	1,559	1,908	2,387	3,427	3,870	4,843	5,851
Motor vehicles	75	121	200	248	272	325	374	454
Construction in progress	187	47	571	1,579	1,491	1,120	520	1,390
	$3,295	$4,187	$5,648	$7,655	$10,100	$11,460	$13,954	$16,357
Less: Accumulated depreciation	(912)	(1,179)	(1,543)	(1,975)	(2,355)	(2,823)	(3,437)	(4,215)
Total property and equipment	$2,383	$3,008	$4,105	$5,680	$ 7,745	$ 8,637	$10,517	$12,142
Investments and other assets:								
Investment in Primate Imports Corporation	—	—	—	—	—	$ 284	$ 378	$ 535
Cost of purchased business in excess of net assets	—	—	—	$ 108	$ 104	102	97	91
Investment in Japanese joint venture, at cost	—	—	—	—	106	114	—	—
Cash surrender value of insurance on lives of officers and key employees	$ 25	$ 29	$ 37	44	51	140	208	645
Other assets	44	69	63	105	266	257	211	188
Total investments and other assets	$ 69	$ 98	$ 100	$ 257	$ 527	$ 897	$ 894	$ 1,459
Total assets	$4,711	$5,276	$6,086	$8,876	$10,952	$14,261	$16,935	$19,144

EXHIBIT 6 (continued)

Liabilities and Stockholders' Investment

Current liabilities:								
Loans payable	$ 268	$ —	$ —	$ 185	$ 322	$ 445	$ 365	$ 410
Current installments of long-term debt	203	298	163	113	121	13	154	388
Accounts payable	—	279	370	465	460	718	842	974
Accrued payroll	—	—	—	—	—	106	147	217
Accrued expenses and taxes	183	213	212	286	369	437	741	885
Accrued federal and foreign income taxes	254	255	228	340	147	338	321	360
Total current liabilities	$ 908	$1,045	$ 973	$1,389	$ 1,419	$ 2,057	$ 2,570	$ 3,234
Long-term debt:	$1,611	$1,573	$1,504	$1,978	$3,138	$ 723	$1,771	$1,893
Less: Current installments included above	(268)	(298)	(163)	(113)	(122)	(12)	(154)	(388)
Total long-term debt	$1,343	$1,275	$1,341	$1,865	$3,016	$ 711	$ 1,617	$ 1,505
Deferred income taxes	8	31	203	218	285	331	337	475
Stockholders' investment:								
Common stock outstanding, $1 par value	$ 686	$ 686	$ 690	$ 752	$ 1,414	$ 1,531	$ 1,531	$ 1,534
Capital in excess of par value	1,063	1,056	1,132	2,246	1,632	5,442	5,451	5,478
Retained earnings	703	1,183	1,747	2,406	3,186	4,189	5,429	6,918
Total stockholders' investment	$2,452	$2,925	$3,569	$5,404	$ 6,232	$11,162	$12,411	$13,930
Total liabilities and stockholders' investment	$4,711	$5,276	$6,086	$8,876	$10,952	$14,261	$16,935	$19,144

Source: Charles River Breeding Laboratories, Inc. annual reports, 1968–75.

Low and high bid prices for Charles River common stock, calendar year 1975

1975	Low bid	High bid
First quarter	19	24½
Second quarter	22	28
Third quarter	15	25½
Fourth quarter	17	24

Source: Adams, Harkness, and Hill.

EXHIBIT 7

CHARLES RIVER BREEDING LABORATORIES
Consolidated Statements of Income
For the Years Ended October 31, 1968–1975
($000)

	1968	1969	1970	1971	1972	1973	1974	1975
Net Sales	$4,243	$4,717	$5,505	$6,469	$7,993	$9,875	$12,574	$15,405
Cost and expenses:								
Cost of sales	$2,535	$2,678	$3,185	$3,791	$4,781	$6,091	$ 7,768	$ 9,921
Selling and administrative	925	1,042	1,213	1,350	1,683	1,824	2,406	2,595
Total cost and expenses	$3,460	$3,720	$4,398	$5,141	$6,464	$4,915	$10,174	$12,516
Income from operations	$ 783	$ 997	$1,107	$1,328	$1,529	$1,960	$ 2,400	$ 2,889
Other income (expenses):								
Equity in net income of affiliate, less amortization of goodwill	—	—	—	—	—	16	94	157
Interest income	—	—	—	—	—	94	88	87
Interest expense	(56)	(75)	(75)	(85)	(119)	(116)	(179)	(200)
Income before income taxes	$ 727	$ 922	$1,032	$1,243	$1,410	$1,954	$ 2,403	$ 2,933
Provision for income taxes:								
Current	$ 354	$ 441	$ 416	$ 547	$ 519	$ 951	$ 1,163	$ 1,367
Deferred	—	—	52	37	111	—	—	—
Total provision for income taxes	$ 354	$ 441	$ 468	$ 584	$ 630	$ 951	$ 1,163	$ 1,367
Net income	$ 373	$ 481	$ 564	$ 659	$ 780	$1,003	$ 1,240	$ 1,566
Earnings per share	$0.59	$0.70	$0.82	$0.48	$0.55	$0.67	$0.81	$1.02
Average number of shares of common stock outstanding (000)	631	686	689	1,376	1,412	1,493	1,531	1,534

Source: Charles River Breeding Laboratories, Inc., annual reports, 1968–75.

Still, in 1976 COBS rats and mice accounted for 90 percent of sales, and Henry Foster attributed much of the company's success to its pioneering commercialization of the COBS technique for breeding rats in 1955. Dr. Foster described the COBS introduction.

I was aware of a germfree derivation technique developed at Notre Dame. Building upon this technique we developed colonies of disease-free animals that could survive experiments without succumbing to an endemic disease and would not cloud results with the side effects of those diseases. Germfree animals were not in abundant supply because they were so expensive to maintain in a germfree state. What we did was to develop a technology that started with clean, germfree animals, then introduced flora which would allow them to live outside of isolators. The barrier facility we built kept them from being recontaminated by germs in the environment.

In order to build the new facility, I took out a $100,000 loan. With this we were able to construct a building with three separate units. We equipped it with the first steam and gas autoclave in New England for sterilizing feed, bedding, and cages. This was far in advance of the equipment anyone else had. We also installed a mechanized feed and bedding transport system.

All that investment and innovation appeared to be an unjustifiable capital expenditure, but it gave us some life insurance. With three separate areas we'd still have animals to sell even if an entire room were wiped out. Once you started to work with an institution and they developed baseline data on your animals, they wouldn't dump you unless you fell on your face and failed to supply them with quality animals on a continuing basis.

Not everyone could have gotten into the COBS business. Notre Dame was willing to give me three or four germfree animals to start only because I had a veterinary degree. I put myself completely in hock with the SBA loan. At the same time that our new facilities went up, I began to publish in scientific journals about developing techniques for large-scale animal breeding. This commitment to raise cesarian-derived animals was an indication of professionalism and gave us recognition. Harvard Medical School and Smith, Kline, and French discovered we could teach them something.

I started out with a handicap because the veterinary college I attended was not accredited. That made me work harder. It pushed me to do things I wouldn't have done otherwise.

Marketing efforts in 1955 heralded a major shift for Charles River Breeding Laboratories. From supplying mainly universities, medical schools, and hospitals, Dr. Foster set out to break into the large lab animal market at pharmaceutical and chemical companies. Not only did this provide a new outlet for CRBL's increased production but it smoothed demand for animals throughout the year.

Charles River Breeding Laboratories grew steadily and profitably between 1955 and 1965. At the urging of their now substantial pharmaceutical company customers, Charles River entered into the production of cesarian-derived *mice* in 1959. New breeding facilities went up in Wil-

466

mington, and new rat strains were added. In 1964 the company built its first overseas COBS facility in Elbeuf, France. By 1965 all facilities at Wilmington were upgraded to guarantee that Charles River was the only commercial breeder all of whose rodents were cesarian-originated, barrier-sustained [COBS]. Other breeders began to adopt similar techniques to remain competitive.

After going public in 1968, CRBL entered a period of rapid expansion. Between 1969 and 1971 Charles River acquired five companies, including facilities in Canada, England, and Italy. It entered into a joint venture with Ajinomoto to form Charles River Japan in October 1972,[8] a 50 percent interest in Primate Imports Corporation in October 1973. More strains of rats and mice were added to the Charles River product line, as well as four new species, including hamsters, rabbits, guinea pigs, and rhesus monkeys.

Product line

Fourteen strains of COBS and germfree mice and rats accounted for 90 percent of Charles River Breeding Laboratories' fiscal 1975 sales of $15.4 million, with COBS guinea pigs, COBS rabbits, and conventional hamsters rounding out the company's broad line of small lab animals. A 50 percent-owned Charles River subsidiary, Primate Imports Corporation, sold a wide variety of imported primates accounting for approximately a third of all U.S. primate sales. A new Florida production facility on company-owned Key Lois Island was to sell its first domestically bred rhesus monkeys in 1976. Exhibit 8 shows Charles River estimated sales by species for 1975.

EXHIBIT 8

Fiscal 1975 sales by species

Species	Sales ($000)
Rats	$ 8,500
Mice	3,500
Direct government business	2,500
Hamsters	500
Guinea pigs	200
Primate Imports (income share only)	160
Other (e.g., preserved specimens)	40
Rabbits	—
Key Lois primates	—
Total	$15,400

Source: Researcher estimates.

---

[8] During fiscal 1974 the joint venture was converted to a percentage of sales licensing agreement which provided for the use of the Charles River name and a continuing transfer of technical know-how.

Charles River production facilities

Almost half of Charles River's productive capacity was located at company headquarters in Wilmington, Massachusetts, 14 miles outside of Boston, where COBS mice, rats, guinea pigs, and rabbits were raised; all administrative and research and development facilities were also located there. Other Charles River Breeding Laboratories production facilities were located at four sites in the United States, as well as overseas. Exhibit 9 shows Charles River locations, products produced at each site, and production capacity.

The barrier system

The barrier rooms and their associated environmental control systems formed the core of the Wilmington production facilitites and accounted for the capital intensity of Charles River's business. A barrier room was a sealed room about 40 feet by 50 feet by 10 feet high. Animals were housed in metal or plastic cages stacked in tiers five to ten cages high and arranged in neat rows. Each separate breeding area had its own feed and bedding holding tanks. Sterilized feed and bedding were delivered to the breeding areas through an extensive pneumatic pipe system. A separate vacuum system removed waste to a central silo in the Charles River compound.

Personnel "entry locks" or cubicles prevented the people caring for the animals from bringing any contaminants into the barrier. In the first cubicle, the employee undressed and left all street clothes in a locker. Then in the second lock, the employee showered and shampooed. In the third lock, the employee put on a complete sterile surgical style uniform maintained in the unit. Even the employees' lunch containers were sterilized before being passed into the unit.

Charles River took extensive precautions to maintain contaminant-free breeding areas. All air entering the areas was filtered to exclude particles larger than 0.3 microns, and each area was kept at a higher pressure than the external atmosphere in order to prevent air leaks. Room controls were checked hourly to monitor room pressures and maintain temperatures between 72° and 74°F. An IBM System 7 computer automatically regulated energy use and monitored temperature, pressure, and energy alarm systems. The company also maintained six emergency generators.

Additionally, Charles River supported its own in-house maintenance team. Bill Keough, CRBL's treasurer and financial vice president, explained why.

> We have an environmental control-oriented facility that allows us to raise twice as many animals per square foot as any other breeder. Preventive maintenance on this system is high, and emergency repair is crucial. We can lose animals or a whole barrier facility if the system is down for

EXHIBIT 9

Charles River production capacity

Location	Products	24-hour-a-day capacity 000 animals per year*	General information
Wilmington, Mass.	Rats, mice, rabbits, guinea pigs	6,000	
Newfield, N.J.	Hamsters (not COBS)	400	
Stoneridge, N.Y.	Rats, mice	3,000	
Portage, Mich. (beginning 1976)†	Rats, mice	2,500	
Port Washington, N.Y.	Primate conditioning (imports)	24	
Key Lois, Fl.	Primate breeding	1.5	
Elbeuf, France	Rats	1,000	
	Mice	2,000	
St. Constant, Quebec	Mice	1,000	Also non-COBS rabbits, guinea pigs
	Rats	520	
Margate, England	Mice	600	Plus flexible space for 156,000 rats or 488,000 mice
	Rats	300	
	Guinea pigs	20	
Milan, Italy	Mice	900	
	Rats	300	
Atsugi, Japan	Rats, mice	1,000 (1976–77)	Licensing agreement only

*Except for Stoneridge, Portage, Margate, Atsugi, and Key Lois, all facilities operated at close to 100 percent of capacity.
†Acquired as part of 1974 Carworth purchase. In 1975, $1.7 million was invested in upgrading and expanding capacity to serve the Midwest market.

Source: 1972 annual report and 10–K.

long. Maintenance workers must be familiar with the system so that they can repair it rapidly, and their work must be perfect. Our own people know how to do it, will work overtime to get it done, and respond immediately. It's our insurance policy. These people are also a good technical resource when we build or renovate purchased facilities. We're better at building and equipping facilities than anyone else in the business.

Charles River labor force

Laboratory animal breeding was a labor-intensive as well as a capital-intensive enterprise. Production employees, called animal technicians, were needed to feed, water, and clean the animals; and weigh, select, and pack animals for shipment. Tasks were routine but exacting, and the work pace was fast. Two hundred of Charles River's Wilmington employees were directly involved in production. Their wages and fringe benefits accounted for close to 25 percent of total costs. Three shifts of technicians worked 24 hours a day, 7 days a week, operating the sterilization equipment while animal technicians worked one shift, 7 days a week, caring for the animals. Bud Otis, vice president of operations and officer of the corporation, described the work force and the difficulty of managing the production operation at Charles River.

It is crucial that the entire work force follows entry and exit procedures exactly in order to preserve the integrity of the barrier. People are the greatest source of potential contamination. Someone may have a sick cat at home.

It takes about 20 minutes for a technician to pass through the three-lock-barrier entry system, so employees do not leave the breeding rooms during their shift. People remain in a 40- by 50-foot room for eight or nine hours a day with only two or three other people. Personalities play a big part in maintaining morale.

This is an unskilled job. Most of the animal technicians are men and women between 18 and 24 who are just out of high school. Average tenure is about 18 months.

The real strength of our production areas is our supervisory personnel. We always promote from within, and we have a very good supervisory training program. Supervisors are mainly policing officials, although they are also responsible for setting the pace and meeting production deadlines.

Mr. Otis, who had begun working for Charles River 13 years ago as an animal technician, showed the researcher the Wilmington facility. They stood in the spotlessly clean shipping area outside one of the 46 breeding rooms, looking in through a plate glass window. Inside the breeding room three animal technicians and a group leader were working. They were all wearing one piece white and green jumpsuits with soft boots that overlapped the jumpsuits and tied above the ankle. White surgical caps covered their hair, and all wore surgical masks. Every hour a buzzer went off and

---

they replaced their masks and prepowdered disposable surgical gloves with fresh ones. A public address system piped in popular music. One technician was rapidly weighing animals and sorting them into weight groups. Two other technicians were moving back and forth along the banks of cages replacing water bottles. The group leader was checking the sex and weights marked on the exterior of cages of animals set aside for standing orders. Three animal technicians could pack 10,000 animals in a day but would have to handle 20,000 in order to achieve customer weight tolerances.

Marketing

Sumner Foster, CRBL's executive vice president, described to the researcher the marketing policies which he had designed and implemented. He attributed the company's 40 percent share of the East Coast rat and mouse markets to its ability to provide a reliable source of quality animals. CRBL's award-winning advertising program stressed quality and reliability, while extensive customer relations activity and efficient order processing supported the company's high-quality, high-service position. Charles River animals commanded a 10 percent price premium. Dr. Foster elaborated on the meaning of quality:

> We have credibility. Our animals perform well because our product is consistent and people know that our quality control is good. We bring our customers here to show them our innovative facilities and production processes. Our best sales tools are our animals and facilities wherever they are.

Sumner Foster emphasized the importance of a reputation for reliability when seeking new customers.

> We are a sure source of supply and guarantee delivery on standing orders. This is something few other breeders are able to do. When we go after a new customer who is standardized on another breeder's strain, we compete on the basis of superior quality and reliability of supply. Our size is important here because we can bring in animals from our subsidiaries to cover peak periods.

Animals were sold FOB at the production facility, and customers paid all freight charges. Charles River transported 60 percent of its animals in the company's climate-controlled delivery vans. The remaining animals were shipped air freight.

Advertising

Charles River's advertising activities included regular paid advertisements in scientific journals, plus the publication of a quarterly newsletter, *The Charles River Digest*, and a research bibliography. Sumner Foster explained that these activities were designed to project an image of quality, reliability, and scientific innovation. No other breeder engaged in such an extensive program.

Magazine advertisements were placed in a variety of specialty scientific journals, such as the *Journal of Toxicology* and the *Journal of Endocrinology*, in order to reach the researchers who were the primary decision makers for lab animal purchases. Other breeders advertised only in the *Journal of Laboratory Animal Science*, which targeted a less specific audience. Annual advertising expenditures were approximately $200,000.

The Charles River Digest was an informational quarterly with articles of general interest to the research community which reported all major projects using Charles River animals. It was received by over 13,000 researchers and scientific libraries. Every two years, the company also published an extensive bibliography of all scholarly articles and research reports mentioning Charles River animals. Sumner Foster stated that this extensive literature on Charles River animals was one of the major reasons for their wide acceptability.

Customer relations

Sumner Foster explained that the company's focus was on personal customer contact by top management at Charles River. "Top management has to be the visible part of the company. Users want to talk to someone responsible." Charles River engaged in three customer relations activities which he said emphasized CRBL's position as the only commercial breeder with in-house laboratory support, quality control, and research ability. These activities included management attendance at trade shows associated with national scientific conferences, participation in scholarly symposia, and consultation on lab animal health.

Gil Slater, director of marketing and operating head of Lakeview Hamster Colony, attended all regional and national scientific conferences and called directly on customers. Dr. Foster and Dr. George Pucak, director of veterinary services, attended and made presentations at symposia in the United States and abroad.

Since joining the company three years ago, Dr. Pucak had gradually assumed Dr. Foster's former role in consulting with customers and other researchers on lab animal health problems. Dr. Pucak spent close to 50 percent of his time with correspondence and user telephone calls in response to customer problems. He diagnosed and recommended treatments for diseases, as well as answering more general questions about research procedures and animal health problems.

Selling and order processing

Sumner Foster explained that most orders for small laboratory animals were placed over the phone for delivery in three to five days and were very

472

specific as to strain, age, sex, and weight within tolerances of a few grams. Consequently, up-to-date inventory systems and rapid order processing were important to Charles River in meeting the wide, short-term fluctuations in demand. All U.S. order processing was centralized in Wilmington. This allowed the company to maintain a computerized order processing system which provided a daily updated stock list of animal inventories in all U.S. and overseas facilities, with data supplied by remote access terminals in all subsidiary locations. Charles River sold a high percentage of animals raised and produced at close to 100 percent of capacity. Sumner Foster commented that the effective use of the computer for order processing, and customer sales analysis was one of the company's major advantages over the rest of the industry.

Pricing

According to Sumner Foster, the great volume of Charles River animals were outbred rats and mice sold in the lower price ranges, but there was steady demand for other species and for the more expensive inbred strains. Aged animals, pregnant and lactating females, and surgically altered animals also commanded higher prices. Exhibit 10 shows price ranges by species for Charles River animals.

EXHIBIT 10

Species	Price range (per animal)
Mice	$ 0.46–$ 3.30
Hamsters	1.20– 5.50
Rats	1.35– 8.75
Guinea pigs	3.90– 50.00
Rabbits	3.50– 60.00
Primates	50.00– 500.00

Bill Keough explained the company's position of price leadership in the industry.

> Charles River Breeding Laboratories is the industry price leader in every product. Our goal is to achieve an overall corporate margin of 10 percent after tax, and we are usually able to achieve price levels which cover costs and meet margin goals. Others in the industry follow our prices, at a level about 5–10 percent lower. However, our new COBS rabbits, which are more expensive to produce, sell at two to three times current prices for conventional rabbits, but we initially only want the premium quality segment of the market.

Dr. Foster explained his view of the company's pricing strategy.

We are lucky in our industry because it is price flexible, but sometimes I wonder how we operate so profitably when Charles River charges only $1.35 for a rat and competitors get as much as $1.28. Maybe a wise manager would say that you should get everything you can, but I don't want to lose credibility by being a pirate. I think there are ethics and morals, and we can practice them because we deal with ethical and moral people.

Charles River customers

Sumner Foster said that Charles River Breeding Laboratories now sold to over 2,000 customers in every segment of the laboratory animal market. Its preferred customers were the large East Coast pharmaceutical companies because they regularly purchased large quantities of animals. A good customer could place orders amounting to $167,000 per year. Exhibit 11 shows the percentage of 1974 dollar sales accounted for by each customer segment.

EXHIBIT 11

Customer type	Percentage of CRBL's 1974 dollar volume
Pharmaceutical and chemical companies	54
Governmental agencies	17
Universities	16
Commercial testing labs and hospitals	13
	100

Dr. Foster was pleased with this customer mix:

We have a broad market base and no single customer accounts for more than 5 percent of sales. No one customer could dramatically cripple us or chip away at our margins if they stopped buying animals for eight to ten weeks. Smaller breeders are very vulnerable to interrupted purchases, and something like that could put a small breeder out of business.

RESEARCH AND DEVELOPMENT

Charles River Breeding Laboratories was the only commercial breeder in the industry to maintain its own professional research staff and laboratory which was responsible for production quality control and for new product development. Sumner Foster commented that the research department gave Charles River a competitive advantage by providing a uniquely healthy product and an advantage in adding new species and strains.

The research staff at Charles River included Dr. George Pucak, a veterinarian who was a specialist in laboratory animal medicine; Dr. Roger Orcutt, a microbiologist specializing in intestinal flora; and a staff of ten full-time laboratory technicians. The research department operated from a fully equipped laboratory and animal quarantine facilities located at company headquarters in Wilmington.

Every eight weeks 25 animals were selected from each breeding colony. Tissue samples, cultures, and blood samples were taken from and tested for each animal. Technicians also inspected animals for parasites. Diagnostic technicians working in a separate necropsy, microbiological, and pathology lab examined all the animals which died in production colonies to determine cause of death. Also, randomly selected healthy animals were sacrificed for extensive testing to establish baseline data on bacteriology, serum chemistry, and tissue values which helped researchers to improve the efficiency of their experiments.

These extensive quality control procedures and in-house laboratory capability, management stated, were unique to Charles River. Dr. Foster explained the rationale behind these expenditures which amounted to $175,000 in 1974:

> We have imposed standards on ourselves by learning what kind of infections will cloud a researcher's results. We learned how to improve the environment and microbiologically define the animals. If you learn of something to give you a better product, you do it because you know it's right, and later the benefits will be there.

New product development

New product introductions had contributed 30 percent of Charles River's growth in sales between 1970 and 1975 and were expected to contribute to the company's growth over the next five years. There were three separate new product development activities at Charles River: (1) adding new mice and rat strains; (2) developing new COBS species, such as guinea pigs and rabbits; and (3) entering new lines of business, such as primate breeding.

The National Institutes of Health's genetic center supplied samples of newly developed strains of breeding animals to lab animal breeding companies. This had enabled Charles River to introduce two new rat strains and three mouse strains into commercial production in the last three years. Sumner Foster described the process.

> The whole process for introducing new rodent strains is rather routine because it's little different from starting foundation and breeding colonies for animals already in production. It takes about one year from the first cesarian to volume production of 10,000 to 20,000 animals per week. I can't even tell you how much it costs to start a new strain of small rodents because it is a normal part of our production activity. Any problems encountered are usually surgical and might take time, but are not expensive.

COBS development

The development of COBS animals in new species, such as guinea pigs and rabbits, was initiated as part of the company's growth plans after going public in 1968. Charles River saw the development of COBS rabbit and guinea pig products as a way to enter new markets with a domestic sales potential of $4 million a year. The company would introduce a unique product which no other commercial breeder had either the R&D expertise to develop or the production economies of scale to produce competitively. It would also enable Charles River to maintain its reputation for scientific innovation in commercial breeding techniques. The market risk inherent in the traditionally erratic demand patterns for these animals also made the necessary facilities investment very difficult for a less securely financed company.

Research efforts for COBS rabbits and guinea pigs focused on developing the correct feed formulas and the correct intestinal flora to introduce to the germfree animals so that they could be raised in barrier rooms on a large scale similar to the rat and mouse operations. Guinea pig development took six years, but by late 1975 Sumner Foster considered their 10 percent market share reasonable in light of their price level which was initially double that of conventional guinea pigs.[9] Rabbits had been a more difficult task and were just coming into production in early 1976. Sumner Foster related the problems encountered in developing the COBS rabbit that had cost the company close to $500,000 in expenses and committed facilities during its eight-year development period.

> We started to work on a COBS rabbit in 1968 and thought we could get it into production in a year as we did with new rodent strains. But, unlike rats and mice, nothing was known about the animal before we started, and it involved a much bigger R&D effort. We had no foster mother for the germfree young and had to hand feed them every hour, which is very expensive. We lost a lot of animals trying to develop the correct milk formula for hand feeding. Also the rabbit was a special problem in association from the germfree to a COBS state.

Primate breeding

Charles River began plans to engage in rhesus monkey breeding in 1971 with the goals of entering a growing new market and of continuing to develop its reputation for improved laboratory animals. By breeding animals under controlled conditions in the United States, the company hoped to eliminate major health problems that made rhesus difficult to use in research. Rhesus trapped in the wild had an unknown medical history and

---

[9] Due to a tight supply situation, breeders of conventional guinea pigs quickly followed with price increases of their own.

frequently carried tuberculosis, a Herpes B virus which was lethal to humans, and other diseases communicable to humans. The animals also frequently suffered from, Salmonella and Shigella, bacterial diseases which could weaken or kill the animals through severe dehydration.

Charles River's rhesus breeding program began with trapping the animals themselves in remote areas of northern India in order to select the healthiest animals and to by-pass the usual quarantine compounds in India and the United States. The company by 1976 had developed an expertise in testing, diagnosing, and curing rhesus diseases and designed innovative feeding, trapping, and quality control procedures for production colonies.

By early 1976 there were 1,500 healthy, thoroughly tested rhesus on Key Lois, which comprised a breeding stock expected to eventually produce 900 marketable animals annually. Rhesus dollar sales were expected to grow to $500,000 by 1978 from $50,000 in 1976. At the end of 1975 total development costs to date amounted to $700,000, of which the federal government had cost shared approximately $300,000 for noncapital expenditures.

Overseas operations

Charles River operations in Canada, England, France, and Italy accounted for a third of total company sales and net income in 1975 (see Exhibit 12). COBS rats and mice were each division's main product, but competitive situations, product lines, profitability, and growth potential varied substantially among the divisions. Lab animals bearing the Charles River name were first produced in Japan in 1976 under a licensing and royalty agreement with the Ajinomoto Company.

Dr. Foster stated that his overseas expansion strategy required establishing an independent operating division in each country where a large market share was desired. Each division was managed by a national of the country where the facilities were located, although the parent corporation supplied assistance in facilities construction, production management techniques, quality control, and pricing decisions. All of Charles River's overseas divisions, except for France, had been acquired between 1969 and 1971; and substantial investments had been made in upgrading facilities and training production personnel. Serving multinational markets from a single facility was difficult due to language barriers, currency exchange problems, customs clearance, tariffs, and tax structures. Charles River was currently investigating acquisition candidates in Germany.

Charles River France was constructed in 1965 with the aid of Rhone Poulenc, S.A., one of France's largest chemical and pharmaceutical firms. Their agreement included a 15-year contract for Charles River to supply Rhone Poulenc's lab animals at a reduced price, in return for their assistance in local financing, engineering, land acquisition, and zoning problems.

EXHIBIT 12

Division and Product lines	Approximate 1975 sales ($ millions equivalents)	Net profit after tax as percent of sales	Estimated market share*	Additional sales potential by 1980 ($ millions)
Canada:				
Rats, mice, rabbits, guinea pigs ...	$1.5	8	n.a.	n.a.
France:				
Rats, mice.....................	2.5	11–16	44+%	$1.5
England:				
Rats, mice, guinea pigs...........	1.0	10	25	2.0
Italy:				
Rats, mice.....................	1.0+	10	33+	1.0+

n.a. = Not available.
*Commercial breeders only.
Source: Researcher estimates.

One eighth of Charles River France's current production was sold under contract to Rhone Poulenc. CRBL's initial cash investment was low, and as a result the French division's ROI was substantially higher than the ROI for the company as a whole.

Financial policies

Charles River's vice president of finance, Bill Keough, characterized the company's capital structure as very conservative because of a heavy internal cash flow and a highly successful common stock issue in 1973. In that year Charles River had issued 110,000 common shares, raising close to $3.9 million, $2.3 million of which was used to retire long-term debt. Mr. Keough described the issue as an attempt to get a more widely held stock and to take advantage of an inexpensive source of capital. He commented:

> As a result, we have no problem getting money. I could pick up the phone and borrow $2 million within the next few hours. Our total unused debt capacity is between $5 and $6 million. Right now we're not more leveraged because we can't use it.

Since becoming public, the company had been gradually revising its performance goals. Mr. Keough explained the situation.

> We were previously getting a 10 percent ROI with a dollar of annual sales per dollar of facilities investment. Because we were willing to accept that 10 percent ROI, and because our operations were more efficient—no one else's sales margins are as good as ours—the marginal guy has gone out of business and we've discouraged others from entering. The financial com-

munity has been insisting that the return was too low, so now we're looking for 15 percent.[10]

Charles River declared its first dividend in 1975 in an attempt to broaden the company's base of stockholders and to stabilize its stock price which fluctuated between 20 and 60 times earnings.[11] The company was investigating the possibility of becoming listed on a major stock exchange during 1976, and Bill Keough described the type of investor he hoped these actions would attract:

> We don't want to become a speculative stock, we're just trying for steady growth. We want a loyal investor who believes in us and plans to be with us for the long haul.

Planning and management systems

Formal planning and reporting systems at Charles River were kept as simple as possible in order to minimize the company's administrative overhead. All company officers reported directly to Sumner Foster as executive vice president, who in turn reported to Dr. Foster. The primary management planning document was an annual business plan and budget, reviewed monthly in conjunction with computer-produced financial statements comparing budgeted to actual results. The only other regular financial reporting documents were weekly reports of the number of animals produced and shipped and a weekly payroll and overtime report. Mr. Keough commented:

> It's a conscious effort to keep things simple. The company is basically run by four people: the Fosters, Bud Otis, and myself. We all wear a lot of hats so that we're not burdened with staffing and can stay flexible, adapt quickly to change. We don't want the expense of having all the answers, so we just control the key areas, labor and sales. You can't run this business with a bureaucracy.

Although Mr. Otis, Mr. Keough, Sumner Foster, and Dr. Foster held a formal meeting every Friday morning and reviewed major management control documents weekly, the main communications channels in the company were personal and informal. Executives were in and out of each other's offices several times a day. Mr. Keough kept in his office closet a

---

[10] Part of that increase was expected to come from increased sales yield per square foot of plant and equipment costs achieved by changing male/female rodent production ratios to more closely approximate demand. This change had already contributed 1 percent to aftertax margins in fiscal 1975 and was expected to produce an additional 1 percent in fiscal 1976.

[11] In mid-1976 Charles River Breeding Laboratories had 1,007 shareholders. Dr. Foster held approximately 40 percent of the company's stock; and his brother, Sumner Foster, held approximately 2 percent.

large refrigerator well stocked with beer, affectionately referred to as "Duffy's." Everybody from delivery truck drivers to Dr. Foster dropped by after five o'clock.

Dr. Pucak described the atmosphere that contributed to such a high degree of internal cooperation at Charles River.

> Everybody is involved with everything around here. The atmosphere is open; and any idea you come up with, no matter how far out, is going to be discussed. We can all speak our minds. Dr. Foster creates a tremendous sense of pride. He works hard and sets the tone, yet we all feel we have contributed to the success of the company and share in its financial rewards.

Meeting strategic goals

In June of 1976, Dr. Foster spoke with the researcher about his company's future plans.

> Come on in. What do you think of our new conference table? We put it to good use every Friday when the four of us get together. Sometimes when we meet we have an agenda—specific questions; other times we just review our general situation.

Dr. Foster's office was a large, zebra-wood paneled room with a crisp, modern decor. A small marble conference table occupied one end of the room; at the other was a massive desk and chair. On the desk was an intercom system which allowed Dr. Foster to speak immediately with any of his officers or staff members. Behind the desk was a large digital clock and a hi-fi system capable of programmed output. The walls were decorated with abstract art, pictures of wife and family, replicas of the plaques honoring the Henry and Lois Foster gifts to Brandeis University and The Museum of Fine Arts, and a dozen or so framed organizational honorary awards and memberships in distinguished technical, industrial, and service (Rotary) institutions.

> We have a real challenge ahead of us in meeting our growth goals of 15 percent in both sales and earnings. Because of our current dominance in the industry, we cannot acquire additional laboratory animal breeding firms. We can, however, expect continued growth from our existing lines. But that won't be enough; we will never get to a hundred million that way! We are going to have to add some new products and do some acquisitions. In five years we must be in other areas.
>
> I'm only interested in ideas related to the general area of biomedical research. There is, for example, the whole area of potential uses of invertebrates for teaching rather than research purposes, and we should get involved. There is a San Diego business that collects marine specimens, but it is 3,000 miles away and too much of a management drain for sales of $200,000 a year.
>
> What Charles River can bring to an acquired company is capital and

management expertise. We need to get into a growing market with an already profitable company. We don't want any more businesses that need a dollar of facilities investment to produce a dollar of sales, and we can't absorb losses of $100,000 to $300,000 a year like our early Japanese joint venture experience.

We would want the principal to stay on for at least two or three years to provide operating expertise. We can't rebuild an organization or train a whole new team of people.

Biologicals

A natural area of interest would be the production of biologicals.[12] We could use our retired breeders and substandard animals; our entry would be essentially in the animal parts by-product business.[13] We already have generated $100,000 in preserved organ sales as a by-product of our monkey importing business with only a couple of people working on it. One of the problems though is that the market is so unorganized, and we don't have a marketing organization that sells to one of the key markets—schools and universities.

There is a possible, fine acquisition here—it's Quality Biologicals.[14] They are one of the largest in the business—I think about $20 million in sales, and a superior profit record. Let's look at their Dun & Bradstreet!

After studying it, Dr. Foster continued:

Guess they are only $5 million or $6 million in sales and about $2 million in assets. It's a private family firm, and their management is getting old. They sell things such as one-celled-animal slides, plastic models of specimens, and the general biologicals line to schools plus universities and wholesale suppliers in the United States and 30 different countries.

Contract testing and research

Another area we might consider is what some people call contract testing and research—I prefer to call that type of business an industrial toxicology laboratory. Its purpose would be to help get new products through the constantly changing testing regulations required by the Food and Drug Administration before human clinical trial tests can be done. Firms in this field

---

[12] The production of biologicals was a $30-million-a-year business in 1975, company officers estimated. The products included monkey kidney cell cultures which were used as a growing media for producing Salk polio vaccine, rodent liver powder used as a filter in separating portions of cells, and animal organs such as rodent lungs, brains, or eyes for special experiments. This estimate did not include school sales or related products, for example, slides, models, or laboratory specimens for dissecting purposes.

[13] Retired breeders were one year or older female rodents which had produced many litters of young in the production colonies.

[14] Disguised name.

are growing at 10 to 20 percent per year.[15] We were offered a $20 million diversified biomedical company, which had an industrial toxicology lab, several years ago, but we couldn't swallow it at the time. We would have to enter this field through an acquisition.

People like Revlon (cosmetics), Gillette (personal health care products), and Du Pont (paint)—all are customers, all are now doing industrial toxicology work. Some of their tests are long—two years or so—and they can't do everything themselves so they subcontract. We have a natural interest in this field.

At our March meeting of the Society of Toxicology, Dr. Russell Peterson, chairman of the Council on Environmental Quality, talked about the proposed Toxic Substances Act. If that is passed, every drug will have to be tested for long-term cancer-inducing possibilities. That will be good for our basic business. And, since they can't do all that long-term testing work themselves, they will have to use outside firms for some of this testing work.

To enter the field it takes good physical space and environmental controls (costing in total about $80–$100 a square foot), the technical competence to maintain large animal colonies over long time periods, good management, and superior toxicological competence. We would have to hire the latter, and it would have to be good. The risk would be that you have contamination when you are 18 months into a test or that your toxicologist misinterprets the data. That happened with a large midwestern drug company recently, and it really gave that company a black eye. In our case that "black eye" might damage our basic business reputation, and that would be serious. I worry about that.

A middle ground would be to subcontract the use of our facilities; we have some excess space in upstate New York. We could set up the colony, feed and care for the animals per their instructions, sacrifice animals per their schedule, and send the specimens to the main company.

On another occasion, Sumner Foster commented on some of the drawbacks of establishing a large-scale contract testing business. "With a general contract testing business, Charles River would be directly competing with some of our largest lab animal customers. Testing is very people dependent. The principals must be well known, respected in their field, and have personal contact at the FDA. It is very easy for a principal to go off and start his own testing business."

The director of product testing for a large cosmetic and personal care products company commented on contract testing noting that, beginning in 1974, many of the firms in his industry had brought this work back in-house. "There are few capable companies in the field. Many do tests, but they are not reliable enough to keep you out of the courts. The in-house testing trend may be because of this lack of reliability and short supply of competent firms. We went in-house out of necessity. We have 30,000 very expensive

---

[15] The Pharmaceutical Manufacturers Association estimated that U.S. pharmaceutical companies alone purchased $106 million worth of supplementary R&D services in 1974.

square feet of facilities; the best air-handling units in the country. We don't have as extensive facilities as CRBL, and we are not as automated as they are nor do we use COBS or pathogen-free animals for our work."

Clinical testing

Dr. Foster continued:

> You know we were once in the clinical testing field—that's different from contract testing. You analyze throat cultures, blood samples, or human tissue for your local doctor or hospital. We built up a half-million-dollar business and then quit. We were early in the game too and an innovator. But the little lab down the street would cut the price on a test a nickel or a dime and kill you. The only way to bring needed quality to this important field is to move away from human to instrumental analysis. You ought to talk with Bill on this.

Bill Keough in a later interview emphasized that much of the company's success had resulted from staying out of areas about which the company didn't know anything. He cited, as an example, Charles River's venture into the clinical testing business between 1968 and 1970. "Charles River was one of the first New England businesses in clinical testing, and now successful companies have sales of a $100 million a year. But we got out of it because it took too much management time for its profitability. The technology was changing so fast, each year you'd need a new machine, and price competition was more important than quality."

Cage manufacturing

"We were offered a chance again recently to buy a cage company in Maryland. It was a good company with a good record—there is money to be made there—but, we don't have expertise in that area," Dr. Foster said.

Charles River, the researcher learned later, had had an opportunity to enter the lab animal cage manufacturing business when the company purchased Carworth from the Becton, Dickinson & Co., but had chosen to sell Carworth's cage manufacturing division. The total market for both metal and plastic lab animal cages, company officers estimated, was between $7 million and $10 million a year. Hazelton Laboratories had recently acquired several leading metal cage-producing companies, and one New Jersey company accounted for nearly $4 million in annual sales of plastic cages. Plastic cage manufacturing was a simple technology and only required a $50,000 to $60,000 capital investment. Lab animal cages were a durable commodity product. Company officers believed there had been little recent design innovation and that patent protection was not available. The business was price competitive and relied on a substantial sales organization. Marketing costs alone were estimated to amount to 50 percent of sales.

Animal colony management and consulting services

Dr. Foster commented:

> We are now performing lab animal colony management services for our licensee in Japan. We have an administrator there who was trained here at Wilmington and who reports to us weekly by phone.
>
> But animal colony management for a drug firm or institution holding test animals is different from our production-oriented process at Charles River. I'm concerned about offering other expertise to our current customers. If anything went wrong, we could lose the total relationship. However, we could consult on facilities design. That's an area where we have expertise and most people are not qualified.

Making the strategic choice

Dr. Foster continued:

> How do I choose? It's terribly difficult to get started, and there is risk. What is my "vehicle" to get involved? There are so many possibilities open to us.
>
> How do we go about this choice? Do I set up a prestigious scientific biomedical committee, like the committees of the Academy of Science, to discuss where we should be going, where we should be looking? They should be paid a fine honorarium, and we could meet in Bermuda.
>
> I have to get staff assistance to give me the time to work on this. We missed a company in Canada, and I ought to go down and see the owners of Quality Biologicals. We need to start now. But I don't really know what buttons to push. What is the right button?

APPENDIX

Information on firms involved in the biomedical industry[16]

International Research and Development Company, 1972[17]

> Let me state that International Research and Development is an independent research laboratory engaged primarily in safety evaluation of

---

[16] Information abstracted from latest annual report available in Charles River Breeding's files on firms involved in the biomedical industry.

[17] The 1972 president's report by F. X. Wazeter, Ph.D. In 1972 company revenues were $2,134,377 with net earnings of $324,098, and 1971 revenues were $2,601,343 and net earnings of $384,391. Stockholders' equity in 1972 was $4,370,660.

484

chemical compounds. . . . Much of our business is in the areas of toxicology (the study of possible harmful effects of substances) and pharmacology (the science of drugs). Other major areas of involvement include environmental health studies, pathology, and chemistry; and more specific areas such as carcinogenesis, mutagenesis, and microbiology.

In addition to this research work, we provide all clients with computerized statistical analysis; preparation of all types of material to be filled with governmental regulatory agencies; and overall counsel on research needs. In short, IRDC serves as a totally self-contained, safety evaluation research arm for big business and small ... for private industries of all types, government and institutions . . . and for locations here and in other countries.

National Laboratories, Inc.[18]

The company's products
The company's products can be conveniently grouped as living cells, chemical media, animal sera, diagnostics, laboratory animals, and specialty laboratory equipment.

A changing market
Cancer research and treatment has been a high priority of the health industry over the past several years with the budget for the National Cancer Institute rising sharply each year. There are signs that the general budget tightening within the National Institutes of Health is now extending to the Cancer Institute, which is an important source of funding for the company's services and products. Spending in research appears to be shifting away from the large "goal-oriented problems" into more modest basic research programs. . . .

News release[19]
Cambridge, Mass.—National Laboratories, Inc., announced today that Dr. Arthur S. Sterling, senior vice president, has resigned effective March 1, 1976. Dr. Sterling has been with the company since 1965 and during that time has been instrumental in enabling the company to carry on a continuing cancer research program funded by contracts with the National Cancer Institute. His departure is likely to affect the company's ability to retain these contracts, the loss of which would have an adverse effect on the company's earnings.

---

[18] Disguised name. This material abstracted from the company's 1975 annual report. In 1975 National sales were $14,109,000 and net income was $576,000. Comparable results in 1974 were $11,763,000 and $432,000. Stockholders' equity in 1975 was $4,090,070; in 1974 it was $3,513,796.

[19] This material contained in a company news release published November 26, 1975.

Hazelton Laboratories Corporation[20]

As Hazelton Laboratories Corporation completes its sixth most successful year, it is appropriate at this time that we reflect on our past accomplishments, present growth, and future potential. Hazelton today is the result of a corporate growth program initiated in 1969. At that time it appeared that the life science industry offered unlimited growth potential. Subsequent analysis of this industry proved it to be in an embryonic state, highly fragmented in terms of specialized resources, and lacking a single company responsive to the increasingly integrated demands of the industry on a broad scale. Plans were formulated to amalgamate several of the leading companies of this industry into one large, well-financed company. This strategy was followed, and the company today is the culmination of 11 acquisitions.

The businesses of Hazelton all relate to the life science industry, and as originally projected in 1969, the industry continues to grow at a rate at least double that of the overall economy. The demand for safety and efficacy testing is increasing at an accelerating rate as industry and government develop new compounds and evaluate old ones. Demand is further increased by new government regulations requiring additional evaluation of well-established and widely used compounds and products.

Services provided: testing of products and chemical compounds; consultation on regulatory affairs; laboratory facilities design; and laboratory animal colony management. *Products evaluated:* agricultural, industrial and household chemicals; drugs; food and color additives; cosmetics; and medical devices. *Products manufactured:* animal housing systems; metabolism units; germfree environmental equipment; veterinarian surgical instruments and hospital equipment; intensive care oxygen units; and pathological waste disposal systems. *Laboratory animal breeding:* primate colony management; canine breeding; and primate breeding.

---

[20] Information abstracted from 1975 annual report. Hazelton revenues in 1974 were $11,306,892 with net earnings of $231,900, while revenues in 1975 were $15,961,946 with net earnings of $425,600. Contract revenue and costs were, respectively, $7,709,601 and $5,987,390 in 1974, and $11,152,951 and $8,421,459 in 1975. Net stockholders' equity was $3,832,232 in 1974 and $4,077,426 in 1975. Hazelton Laboratories Division and Hazelton Laboratories employed approximately 600 scientific and technical personnel. Company officers stated that Hazelton was the largest independent biological contract research organization in the world.

case 20

The Real Paper, Inc. (A)

The Real Paper (*TRP*) and its "giveaway" school edition counterpart, the *Free Paper*, were organized in July of 1972 by a group of former staff members of the *Cambridge Phoenix* for the purpose of publishing "metropolitan Boston's weekly journal of news, opinion, and arts."

All of *TRP*'s founders were former members of the Phoenix Employees Union. Their decision to form *The Real Paper* came after a bitter dispute with the ownership of the *Cambridge Phoenix*, which featured strikes, lockouts, picketing, fistfights, and legal action. Central to the organizing group's concept, *The Real Paper*'s operations and ownership were to be on a "community" basis. Staff members owned equal shares of TRP, Inc., and elected its board of directors. Paula Childs, a member of the editorial staff described *The Real Paper* as "a staff-owned, capitalistic enterprise. It's a group of people who came together so that they could have control—complete control—over their own business and at the same time make money doing it."

Starting without facilities, operating funds, or an established circulation organization, *TRP* achieved revenues of $462,000, profit before tax of $53,-000, and a circulation of approximately 30,000 paid and 40,000 free in its first eight months of operations. Comparable data for fiscal 1974 were $998,000, $73,000, and approximately 40,000 paid and 50,000 free circulation.

Substantial achievements, however, had not left the staff of *The Real Paper* without uncertainties. Bob Rotner, publisher of *TRP*, commented, "*The Real Paper* is making money, but we're still not out of the woods. We are subject to too many ups and downs." Jeff Albertson, associate publisher, noted "The personality of this paper is hard to talk about. It has been a problem, and we have had an identity crisis starting from day one. No one knows what 'it' is, and 'it' suffers from this lack of clearly defined purpose." And Paula Childs reflected:

> *The Real Paper* was founded on the theory that most cooperatives are formed on—you know—everyone shares equally and things are fair, just,

486

and good—and all that kind of stuff. But I, and a lot of people who came to the paper since its founding with those same thoughts about it, have since been disillusioned. Within *The Real Paper* there's a definite hierarchy, and there's a definite kind of bureaucracy. It's—it's a real—I mean it's in some ways just like any other business.

The milieu

Leaving the Harvard Business School with its carefully pruned plantings, manicured lawns, and freshly painted doorways, the researcher walked across the Larz Anderson bridge into Cambridge, past the Georgian-styled undergraduate living halls guarded by their high iron fences, and headed for the Lampoon Castle (home of Harvard's humor magazine). The Castle, itself a parody on Harvard's red brick and ivy style, served as a rough marker dividing University Cambridge from its more egalitarian neighborhood, Central Square.

Walking down Mount Auburn Street, the researcher dodged plastic bags of refuse awaiting collection as he passed a potpourri of small shops featuring services ranging from Chinese Laundry and Tim's Lunch to the Mules Mirage (a boutique) and Bowl and Board (an expensive furniture store). *The Real Paper* offices were located at 10-B Mount Auburn on two floors of a yellow, wood frame building nestled between the Cambridgeport Problem Center ("Free counseling, nonhassling assistance for legal, psychological, social, and family problems") and a row of triple-decker rooming houses. Ten-A housed a hairworks salon ("haircuts for men and women") and a school of dance whose students seemed to continue their lessons as they walked out of the building onto the sidewalk at the end of the class. Across the street other converted triple-deckers housed a number of research and professional offices.

The lamppost in front of *The Real Paper*'s office tolled a counterculture zeitgeist:

> Boycott Grapes: March! East–West Foundation Seminars in Spiritual Development. Meditations: Yin Meditations, Yang Meditations—Meditations of Light, Nectar, Inner Sound, Love, and Inner and Outer Infinity—Declaration of Godhood; Basic Techniques of Palm and Spiritual Healing; Stop Outrages in Psychiatry; Old Cambridge Common Pet Parade; Save the Cambridge Common Concerts; Filmmakers—Workshops; Boycott Lettuce; Our Rights We Will Defend with Our Lives if Need Be!

Mt. Auburn was a busy Cambridge street. Mixed with a heavy flow of commercial traffic were bicyclists, motorcyclists, and hordes of small foreign cars jousting with an infrequent standard size model as traffic inched its way forward to Central Square. Joggers were there, too, but in a minority position. And the pedestrian flow was heavy. Almost universally young, the passersby walked with a bounce that often sent long hair flying in the wind.

Legs and faces tended to be unshaven. Clothing was simple: smocks or T-shirts, army surplus rucksacks, colorful headbands or hats of Humphrey Bogart fame, blue jeans and sandals or hiking boots were the order of the day. The researcher was reminded that the metropolitan Boston area was a youth center heavily influenced by large numbers of young people who studied or worked there, or who merely drifted in and out.[1]

A loud exhaust backfire from a blue Porsche—a student with patched jeans of bright and varied hue—provided the last insight to the Mt. Auburn Street scene. "Porsche and Patches" mused the researcher as he turned and entered the door marked *The Real Paper*. Coming into the ground-floor area, his first impression was that the area was too small for the ten desks and numerous people working there. The main room was often a maelstrom of phone calls, shouts, advertising personnel walking back and forth, and a steady stream of visitors coming to place classified advertisements with Ellen Paul, the staff person in charge of that activity.

On one side of the main door a bicycle was stored; on the left wall a bulletin board hosted a series of announcements—a lost cat, flea market sales, advertisements for the City Dance Theater, numerous plays, and The 100 Flowers Bookstore. Ellen's dog, Martha, padded around the room seeking attention, occasionally barking but never committing any grave social errors. To the left was the receptionist Cyndi Robbins, wearing a flannel shirt, blue jeans, and sandals. Social pleasantries completed, she commented, "It is a hassling job with the phone and so many visitors, but I like it here—the people, the experience, and the atmosphere."

Looking to the back of the room, the researcher noticed a man (later identified as the comptroller, Howard Garsh) sweeping the floor and stacking telephone reminder slips in a cabinet. Cyndi's directions to the publisher's office sent the researcher to the back of the main room where the publisher and the advertising sales director shared a small office, furnished in the same spartan manner as the remainder of the office.

In a brief meeting the researcher explained his general interest in the alternative newspaper industry and his specific interest in *The Real Paper*. Both Rob Rotner and the researcher agreed there were opportunities for learning in the development of a case history on *The Real Paper*. Later, after consultation with other staff members, Bob welcomed the researcher to the group and agreed to collaborate on the project (see Exhibits 1, 2, and 3).

---

[1] At a later date, the researcher obtained some population data on two- and four-year colleges, degree-granting technical-trade institutes and universities located in the New England area. There were over 35 of these institutions in metropolitan Boston, with approximately 130,000 students; approximately 120 schools in Massachusetts, with approximately 320,000 students; and 250 in New England, with approximately 600,000 students (of which 2,262 were primarily students of religion). He was intrigued with the academic program for one of the schools: "The Institute of Anatomy, Sanitary Science and Embalming."

EXHIBIT 1

THE REAL PAPER, INC.
Statement of Income for Year
Ended April 26, 1974, and Eight Months
Ended April 27, 1973

	1974	*1973*
Net sales	$995,793	$462,557
Other income	2,675	269
	$998,468	$462,826
Costs and expenses:		
Cost of publication	$618,802	$273,468
Selling, general, and administrative	304,674	135,738
Interest	372	124
Total costs and expenses	$923,848	$409,330
Net income from operations before provision for federal income tax	$ 74,620	$ 53,496
Provision for federal income tax	1,092	2,100
Net income	$ 73,528	$ 51,396
Retained earnings, beginning of period	51,396	—
Retained earnings, end of period	$124,924	$ 51,396
Net income per common share, based on the weighted-average number of shares outstanding at the end of the year, which was 2,800 shares in 1974 and 3,300 shares in 1973	$26.26	$15.57

EXHIBIT 2

THE REAL PAPER, INC.
Balance Sheet
April 26, 1974, and April 27, 1973

Assets	*1974*	*1973*
Current assets	$161,812	$88,812
Fixed assets	6,220	2,223
Other assets	7,606	1,407
Total assets	$175,638	$92,442
Liabilities and Stockholders' Equity		
Current liabilities	$ 48,507	$37,320
Stockholders' equity	127,131	55,122
Total liabilities and stockholders' equity	$175,638	$92,442

HISTORY OF *THE REAL PAPER* AND ITS COMPETITION

Early interviews with staff members highlighted the need to study the intertwined history of *The Real Paper* and its primary local competitor, the *Boston Phoenix*.

The story seemed to begin in September 1965 when *Boston After Dark* (*BAD*) was born, in a spirit of entrepreneurialism, as a special centerfold

EXHIBIT 3
Cost breakdown (provided by Howard Garsh)

	Cost	Percent
Printing, composition, trucking, and circulation	$368,515	37
Salaries—editorial, circulation, art, free-lance editorial (including bonus)	217,147	22
Salaries—sales, accounting, and clerical	125,613	12
Selling, general, and administrative expenses	212,001	21
Net profit before tax (note: bonus totaled 4%)	74,620	8

supplement to the *Harbus*, the Harvard Business School student paper. *Boston After Dark* was meant to be a student's guide to Greater Boston's arts and entertainment world. As a "freebie" its distribution soon expanded to other Boston campus locations. In 1970 Stephen Mindich, a Boston University graduate and former art critic and advertising salesman for *BAD*, purchased the paper. His early and major innovation was to add politically oriented news to *BAD*'s coverage of arts and entertainment.

The second critical historical event was the founding, in October of 1969, of the *Cambridge Phoenix* by a 26-year-old Vietnam veteran as an "alternative" newspaper for the Boston area. The *Phoenix* statement of purpose indicated that it "was conceived with the discovery that Boston, the intellectual, artistic, and economic center of New England was a journalistic vacuum." Within a year, the undercapitalized *Phoenix* was bought by Richard Missner, a 26-year-old MBA. Throughout 1970 and 1971, brisk competition developed between the *Phoenix* and *BAD*.

Fusion magazine, commenting on the competitive situation noted:

> Local college students had a twin forum in which to see their revolutionary outrage expressed. . . . Horror stories of government murder and graft ran alongside reviews and advertisements for films and rock performances that created for viewers a fantasy world of glamorous sex and violence. . . . Needless to say, both writers and readers were college educated, white and middle class, reveling in selfrighteousness as they defended people they rarely met, attacking the economic system while enjoying some of the most extravagant luxuries it could provide. Boston's weeklies provided access to the many valuable varieties of this lifestyle, as well as the impression that it was profound.

The *Phoenix*, however, soon began to develop major operating and financial problems. Its financial backer withdrew, and the staff of the *Phoenix* became increasingly disgruntled with Missner, his leadership style, and his vision of what the paper should be. Once, holding up a copy of *The Wall Street Journal*, Missner indicated editorial changes he wanted made.

On May 2, 1972, the *Phoenix* staff agreed to form a union in support of a popular, just-fired editor-in-chief, whom Missner had planned to replace with a former advertising executive. A strike, a series of confrontations, and negotiations ensued. By the end of the month, compromises were effected and the union was officially recognized. Chuck Fager, one of the union leaders and a current member of *The Real Paper* staff, made the following comments on the strike and the effect it had:

> It was really a surprise that we unionized. Sort of WHAM! There it was. People in every department had gripes of their own. . . . So we went out. As a result of the strike, we went through a proletarianization. For instance, we noticed the mailman. Well, he saw our picket signs and he refused to cross the line. Management had to go down to the post office to get their mail. We hadn't seen things from this perspective. . . . But once we were out, our jobs were on the line; we stood to lose everything. . . . But it was fun too. We were working together in a way that we had not worked before—making signs, picketing, and cooking food.

TRP was "born" on July 31, 1972. The *Boston Globe* reported this event as follows:

> On July 27, in a 2:00 P.M. memo, he [Missner] informs all Phoenix staffers to get out by 5 o'clock. The paper, it seems, has been sold to none other than B.A.D.'s Stephen Mindich for a figure Mindich claims to be $320,000. Outraged at Missner's move, they met outside their locked offices and decided to publish their own newspaper by working without pay. It hits the streets on July 31, and it is called The Real Paper. On the same day, the new Boston Phoenix, with a second section called Boston After Dark, appears.[2]

Born into a field of competitive entrepreneurs, yet itself a creature of communal militance, *The Real Paper*'s trials were not yet over. For the first four weeks investors were sought, but to no avail. Chuck Fager said, "The most serious was the *New York Magazine,* but they weren't certain as to how willing we would be to respond to management policy. They were quite right to question that."

Walter Harrison[3] recalled some of the sacrifices of that period:

> We worked virtually 24 hours a day. The financial sacrifices were great. We all started collecting unemployment compensation. People donated phones and office space. We had meetings virtually every night. For the first two weeks with donations and sales we just broke even.

Then, by the fourth week, having found no backers but having established the viability of their new enterprise, Fager said, "A decision was reached. We had a meeting. Everyone wrote down on little cards what they had to have in order to keep going. Rotner presented a financial statement. And we found that we could cover salaries. Suddenly we had the option of independence, and almost everyone was willing to take it. Why have a backer if you don't need one?"

One hundred shares of stock were issued to each employee in lieu of back

---

[2] *Boston Globe–Globe Supplement,* June 9, 1974, p. 11.

[3] Assistant to the publisher.

pay. Corporate and administrative positions were filled by elections. According to Fager, "We had the equivalent of $50,000 to $100,000 of capital in our momentum, that is, free press coverage, willing advertisers, and hawker and reader willingness to buy."

The early months of the new association were rewarding, if not in a financial, certainly in a communal, sense.

The biggest change, some of the staff members say, has been the new atmosphere. Paul Solman, *The Real Paper*'s editor, says: "Having our paper shot out from under us may have been the best thing that ever happened. Coming over here and starting a new paper and running it ourselves, we've set a real precedent. Before this, 'democracy in the newsroom' has always had the clinker that one guy owns the paper, and you can't really tell the people what to do with their own money. But we've gotten rid of the clinker now."

Joe Klein, another writer, says that there is a greater feeling of participation at the paper by all of its staff. "I've never felt as close to the whole process of something I've worked on. I've never been so interested in the business side of the paper. . . . Everybody talks about how much like a family it is here."[4]

In the intervening year and one half, staff attention was turned to consolidating and expanding *TRP*'s position. Advertisers and readers gained confidence in *The Real Paper* as evidenced by its substantial growth in revenues and circulation. And, as would be expected, operational policies and practices were modified and personnel came and left. In 1974 *The Real Paper* was a well-recognized Cambridge phenomenon.

THE ALTERNATIVE NEWSPAPER INDUSTRY

Various members of its staff characterized *The Real Paper* as an alternative newspaper. Local newspaper columnists had, on occasion, described *The Real Paper* and the *Boston Phoenix* as "underground press" or "counterculture" papers. Some news distributors interviewed referred to them as "radical sheets" or "sex papers for freaks."

With circulation in the tens of thousands and distribution via hundreds of news outlets, the term "underground" seemed inappropriate to the researcher. If *The Real Paper* and the *Boston Phoenix* were alternative papers, alternative to what? What were the key, current developments? A survey of literature available in libraries and observations by industry members provided some limited information and insight.

Although the alternative weekly was often referred to as "a paper," the genre suited more a magazine than a newspaper model. It assumed a readership that obtained its basic news from other sources, such as daily newspa-

---

[4] *Nation*, April 23, 1973, p. 531.

pers, radio, or television. The alternative press typically serviced one or two specialized segments of a larger reader market, for example, a politically liberal or youth subcommunity. Most of the large and thriving alternative papers were located in large cities or near large college campuses.

In 1972 the Underground Press Syndicate estimated that there were 300 regularly published underground papers in the United States, with a combined readership of 20 million. The UPS also estimated that one in three persons in the 15–30 age bracket were regularly exposed to underground publications.

The model for the alternative newspaper was judged by many observers to be the *Los Angeles Free Press*. That paper, founded in 1964, was described by the Underground Press Syndicate as:

> . . . in basic ways demonstrably different from all predecessors. First, the Los Angeles Free Press was specifically designed for a mass, though specialized, audience; second, it was in a format inexpensive to produce, simple to learn, yet with high readability, creativity, general appeal and possibilities for development and refinement; third, it was economically self-supporting and self-spreading—it was successful; fourth, it was both hip and radical (the same thing, as we now know); and fifth, it was part of a people's movement and remained a part because it was, in general, operated in a communistic style.

Paul Solman, editor of *TRP*, commenting on the history of the industry and current trends noted:

> The rise of the underground press in the 1960s was concurrent with the rise of "The Movement" in this country. They were not so much businesses as they were political organizations. The relative inexpensiveness of offset printing enabled these organizations to turn to printed media. There was little stability and a great deal of manpower turnover within these organizations. Then as The Movement began to wane, these enterprises waned. The inheritor of these underground publications is the contemporary Alternative Press. It features the same format—offset tabloid—and many of the same people. But there was a dramatic transition in becoming a stable Alternative Press. This involved a commitment to becoming an ongoing business institution. It meant accepting responsibility, getting away from drug cartoons and sex stuff, avoiding the utter tripe we used to get, and making a transition from being purely political—and using language like "pig" and "Amerikka"—to doing something more than just indulging your political biases.

Change and evolution appeared to be very much a part not only of the alternative but also of the wider newspaper industry scene. That industry was the tenth largest American industry in terms of revenues ($5.5 billion in 1972) and the fifth largest employer (380,500 in 1972). Some 75 percent of that revenue came from advertising—local retail, classified, and national;

the latter category appeared to be diminishing somewhat in terms of importance.

Economically the industry had to bear the cost of high capital investment characteristic of many manufacturing operations, as well as the relatively high labor cost of many service organizations. Efforts to improve profits, described as marginal by some investment houses, depended on the newspapers' abilities to deal with distribution problems, antiquated production facilities, and a continuing rise in the cost of newsprint. The latter item has habitually made up 25–30 percent of the revenue dollar. Cost of Canadian newsprint had gone up 20 percent in 1973; and further major increases, as well as shortages, were expected to occur in 1974. Some papers had adopted a strategy of diversification into related communication areas as a "solution" to these problems.

THE REAL PAPER AND THE FREE PAPER

The Real Paper "book," as it was referred to by its staff, was an unstapled and folded collection of newsprint pages, typically 50 to 60 in number, in tabloid format. The front page usually featured *TRP*'s logo as well as a multicolored graphic design, which related to one of the feature articles in that issue. Titles or references to other stories were also highlighted on the front page.

In describing the paper's content, *TRP*'s editorial department distinguished between "the front of the book" and "the back of the book." The front of the book section accounted for the first 20 to 25 pages. It typically included several long feature articles, human-interest articles—for example, an attempt by girls to enter the all-male Boston Little League baseball competition—and a number of shorter news or political items. In addition, there were four regular features: Letters to the Editor; "Short Takes," a news column; a political cartoon; and Burt Solomon's "Cambridge Report," a column covering the political and cultural life of Cambridge.

Paul Solman, the editor, indicated that two to three "compelling" front of the book feature articles were the key to his editorial composition of the paper. A random sampling of some of these articles from the spring of 1974 issues follows: "The Great Commuter Race. Bikes Beat Cars and MBTA by a Wheel"; "TV Guide to Impeachment"; "The Behavior Mod Squad. Clockwork Prisons: Brainwashing Saga Continues"; "A Shopper's Guide to Confession. What You Have to Know to Get the Best Deal on Penance"; "Have You Been Swindled? Nuclear Disaster Strikes Plymouth: A Shocking Scenario for the Future"; "The Death and Resurrection of the Black Panthers"; "The Strange CIA Past of Deputy Mayor Robert Kiley"; and "Prostitutes in Boston." It was evident, from a review of the titles listed on the front cover of these same editions, that feature and news articles ranged from local and national to international topics and touched on a variety of cultural and political topics.

Letters to the Editor made interesting reading in their own right and often created a dialogue between readers and staff that gave continuity to the weekly issues of *TRP*. The letters printed were usually only a fraction of those received. A random survey indicated letters from a variety of well-known personalities (Daniel Ellsberg) to unknown readers—from Boston College and MIT professors to AWOL American soldiers living in Sweden. Most of the letters printed appeared to be from students, or the young in age or spirit living in the metropolitan Boston area. Correspondents' addresses, however, indicated readers in each of the New England states.

The second regular front of the book item, "Short Takes," in the words of its compiler Craig Unger, "tries to get six or seven news items which I think are most interesting, amusing, and politically significant that get the least media play. It has very broad limits ranging from local news to international news. About two thirds to three quarters are of a political nature, and the rest are amusing."

The back of the book section accounted for approximately 60 percent of *TRP*'s pages. It featured a number of regular departments, such as commentary and reviews on theater, cinema, music, and art; and "Local Color" by Henry Armetta, a column about the metropolitan Boston's entertainment field; plus a back page calendar for the upcoming week, which listed events of artistic interest in the Cambridge-Boston area. The staff of *TRP* believes that its coverage of arts and entertainment, particularly the music field, was excellent, and customers interviewed by the researchers tended to support that conclusion.

A substantial section of the back of the book was devoted to listings and classified advertisements. The researcher's random sample of approximately 100 purchasers of *TRP* indicated that the Listings and Classified sections were extremely popular. Listings provided an accurate and thorough calendar of well-known artistic events, as well as information on a host of lesser publicized activities, many of which were available at no or minimum cost. The film rating service gave staff evaluations of each film on a scale of worthless to masterpieces.

The classified pages' popularity was readily understandable to the researcher. They seemed to be an open-door communicating device among the many subgroup cultures in the community. This section had its own language system—the researcher was a WM–24–Stu (can you translate?). The advertisements or notices were a potpourri of every known youth interest or need. There were advertisements for jobs, apartments, and where to get advice about drugs, pregnancy, VD, and low-blood-sugar problems; Personals—"Sarah from Newton—why did you walk out on me?"; leads on where to buy a wide range of products, inquiries for pen pals—often from

496

EXHIBIT 4

Representative classified advertisements

WARM, sincere attractive WJM. Pisces, 29, dislikes dating bars and phony people, would like to meet warm, sincere, affectionate, cuddly slightly mesugah WJF 18-30, short and pretty, with long hair, for lasting relationship. Write CF, PO Box _____ Framingham, Mass. 01701

WHITE male 25 Walpole Prisoner wants letters and visits from young woman. I'm 6' tall weigh 160 blond hair blue eyes. *The Real Paper*, Box 749

TALL, dark, and sane. Are you still out there? Sorry didn't get in touch.

Please send phone number or suggest meetings. Let's get it together this time. Patricia, Box 750

I'M a young woman planning to bring former hillside farm in Western Mass. to long lost fullness. Educated, intelligent, willful, crazy, occasionally impossible, but often spontaneous, loving, energetic, able, funny, practical. Smoke insanely and visions a joy to me. Physically attractive, but so what? Want to feel the isness of things but that takes time and living. Want to make a home for friends to visit when in need

of love, slowness, wholeness, rest, healing. Box 728

WM 27 grad student, warm, aware, seeks female to enjoy the intoxication of spring with. I like tennis, books, nature, hiking, beautiful sex, politics, playing guitar. Let's get together. *The Real Paper*, Box 752

ONE well-adjusted woman wanted to share sunny spacious, furnished 2-bedroom apartment in North End for summer. $100/month rent. Please call Joan at _____.

prisoners; and a variety of travel and educational opportunities were presented (see Exhibit 4).

And if the reader wanted new relationships, they came offered in group packages from "encounter" to "philosophic" discussion meetings. If one wanted individual companionship it came in a variety of formats: male–female, male–male, and female–female.

Bob Williams, *TRP*'s advertising manager commented on the importance of the listing and classified sections in an interview with a *Nation* writer.

> The real reasons our paper or *BAD* are essential to the lives of the people who read them are the classified ads and the listings, Around here, people move around a lot, a couple of times a year at least. Things change hands all the time—apartments, stereos, TVs, cars, sex. There has to be a way for the things and the people to get together. Let's face it, Boston is one big party, with 350,000 kids looking for something to do. So the film listings, and the listings in general, are a big selling point. These things are the spine of the paper—the writers give it a competitive edge.[5]

The *Free Paper* edition of *TRP* was similar to *TRP* in most respects. In any given week there were some differences in editorial content because of a post office ruling that price preferences given one reader over another

---

[5] *Nation*, April 23, p. 533.

must be accompanied by a minimum 20 percent content difference. The post office also required that a certain percentage of a paper's circulation must be paid to obtain second-class mailing privileges. Circulation of the *Free Paper*, since it was distributed to school living and dining halls, varied with the local student population, dropping during vacation periods.

Supplements to *TRP* and the *Free Paper* were added to the regular editions about once each month. Jeff Albertson, newly assigned supplements editor, felt that the frequency of supplements would increase in the fall of 1974. Supplements were similar to the regular book in format and design. However, each was typically organized around one theme, such as buying guides to high-fidelity equipment, camping equipment, and so forth. Articles on the theme were prepared, and advertisers with a particular interest in that field were sought.

The metropolitan Boston competitive situation

In addition to several dozen weekly suburban newspapers covering their local scenes, three standard daily and two major weekly alternative newspapers were published in Boston. The daily newspapers included the *Christian Science Monitor*, whose masthead declared it to be "An International Daily Newspaper," and whose principal circulation was outside of metropolitan Boston.

The second paper, the *Boston Herald–American*, owned by the Hearst Corporation, was a recent merger of the *Herald-Traveler*, which had circulation strength in the suburbs, and the *Record-American* with "blue-collar" readership in Boston. An industry observer described it as an "independent, conservative, Republican paper. It's probably losing a lot of money. There is a rumor that Mr. Mindich is considering launching a major Boston daily, contingent upon future plans of the *Boston Herald–American*."

The *Boston Globe* was the largest of the three standard papers in circulation and was financially the most successful (net income of $3 million on $90 million in revenues in 1972). Local journalists conceded the *Globe*'s competitive aggressiveness, citing its use of specialists covering such topics as urban renewal, mental health, affairs of the elderly, and the women's movement. One observer described the *Globe* as a paper "which serves the liberal educational community well and the City of Boston with less enthusiasm. The *Globe* espouses its liberal causes stridently and rarely hesitates to show a bias in its reporting."

In attempting to gain information about the alternative newspaper competitive situation, the researcher visited a dozen newsstands in the Greater Boston area. Clearly the leaders in this race were *TRP* and the *Boston Phoenix*. But the customer had a variety of papers from which to make a selection, depending upon his or her particular mix of reading interests. Larger newsstands typically carried, at a minimum, three other nonlocal alternative papers: the *Village Voice,* the *Free Press,* and *Rolling Stone.* The *Village Voice* (weekly price 35 cents, 125 pages, over 150,000 circulation) was owned by *New York Magazine;* its masthead stated that it was "The Weekly Newspaper of New York." The *Voice* had an East Coast and national distribution pattern. Its content was focused on a wide range of local New York and national political issues and personalities; it had major, in-depth coverage of art, music, and the theater. As a member of the Audit Bureau of Circulation its advertisers included prominent local and national firms.

The *Los Angeles Free Press* (weekly, 35 cents, about 40 pages, circulation 150,000) also had achieved regional and national distribution. Its coverage included politics, the arts, and a 20-page classified "sex" insert—literally a cornucopia of erotica. In contrast to the more academic style of the *Voice* (an interview with three African female jurists and an analysis of Shakespearean theater), the *Freep*'s editorial style seemed to the researcher to be sensational and its word system and headlines were strident in character.

The *Rolling Stone*'s (biweekly, 75 cents, over 100 pages, circulation 300,-000) content was heavily built around popular music and the entertainment world, with some political coverage, for example, an interview with Jane Fonda on her latest visit to North Vietnam. While both the *Voice* and *Rolling Stone* carried classified advertisements, these tended to down play sex themes and products.

A Boston newsdealer mentioned the *Texas Monthly* as a prototype of recent entries in the field. *Newsweek* magazine reported that it sold for $1, "has taken provocative looks at the inner workings of the state's highway lobby, banks, law firms and daily newspapers, dismissing the latter 'as strikingly weak and ineffectual.' The *Texas Monthly* received the prestigious 1974 National Magazine Award for Specialized Journalism."[6] "*Ramparts,* of course," the newsdealer said, "has been around a long time, and there are a batch of others of the same cast."

In metropolitan Boston, *TRP*'s primary competitor was the *Boston Phoenix.* Both papers were similar in format and price, both were published weekly, both used the same distribution methods—although with different emphasis—and both had free school editions.

Differences were also apparent to the researcher. The *Phoenix* was a larger book—often over 80 pages compared with *TRP*'s 50- to 60-page editions. The larger *Phoenix* was divided into two distinct subparts: the *Phoenix* and its insert, *Boston After Dark*—the Arts and Entertainment section. The *Phoenix* enjoyed a larger circulation; industry estimates ranged from 80,000 to 110,000, with approximately 40,000 being the free edition. The *Phoenix* appeared to the researcher to enjoy a wider range of local and national advertisers than did *TRP*. In terms of visual appearance, the *Phoenix*

---

[6] *Newsweek,* June 17, 1974, p. 29.

appeared to be more crowded and less willing to use open space to lead the reader's eye around a page than did *TRP*.

The researcher wanted to obtain data on why a customer purchased *TRP* versus the *Phoenix* and what was the market for these two papers. A random survey of purchasers by the researcher obtained limited information. Most could not make explicit their preference for one paper over the other. *TRP* customers often mentioned "better Cambridge coverage," "more liberal," "easier to read," while *Phoenix* purchasers stressed "red hot classifieds" and "*BAD* is the best guide" (see Exhibit 5).

EXHIBIT 5

Comparison of article content of *The Real Paper* versus the *Boston Phoenix*

Category	The Real Paper		Boston Phoenix	
	Number of articles	Percent	Number of articles	Percent
International events or politics	2	1.7	5	2.8
Art, movies, books, TV, dance	32	26.7	59	33.0
Exposés	5	4.2	1	0.5
Rock music, other types of music, album review columns	15	12.5	32	17.9
Local events/politics.....................	21	17.5	34	19.0
Counterculture, e.g., communes, drugs	1	0.8	2	1.1
National events/politics	9	7.5	20	11.2
Movements, including prison reform, women's, gay	9	7.5	4	2.3
Sports	2	1.7	14	7.8
Miscellaneous, including food, "local color," travel, tax information	24	20.0	8	4.5
Totals	120	100.1	179	100.1

Source: These data were prepared by Kim Panushka of *TRP* staff. She surveyed eight issues of each paper for the months of March and April 1974. The total number of major feature articles for TRP was 120; for the *Boston Phoenix*, 179. Excluded were regular columns from staff writers.

In reviewing this competitive situation between *The Real Paper* and the *Phoenix*, a *Boston Globe* writer commented:

The two papers continue in the image of advocacy journalism planted firmly left of center and sprinkled with occasional muckraking. But while in days past they overlapped on stories, they almost never do today. In fact, except for arts coverage—particularly music—you can browse through two issues of the same week and not see two pieces about the same thing. What you will find is that the *Phoenix*, reflecting its publisher's little-subdued dream to become a force in the community, concerns itself more with the news of the day, dealing with many of the same subjects and events as the city's dailies. "We've made a shift to respond to news happenings," says Miller. "We want to be topical." *The Real Paper*, on the other hand, seems to be moving more and more towards becoming a weekly magazine, opting for stylized features and columns rather than news reporting. Part of the reason for this is undoubtedly *The Real Paper*'s constituency, which is more Cambridge-oriented than that of the *Phoenix.* . . .[7]

What was the market for the two publications? Bob Williams, advertising manager for *TRP*, gave one specific definition.

In Boston you have 350,000 young people, under 30, within 2.5 square miles of space. You don't find a concentration like that anywhere in the country except Boston. It's a unique market. These kids spend around $40 million or $50 million a year.[8]

Dennis Hale, staff writer for the *Nation* magazine, gave a more general comment.

So the New Journalism is not so much "new" as it is specific in its choice of audience. For the most part that audience consists of young, white, relatively affluent college students, graduates and dropouts. Like newspaper readers everywhere, these people have a set of opinions, of whose truth they are fairly certain, and they do not enjoy seeing these opinions challenged in print. At least, not too often. And the editors of "underground" and "alternative" papers are as sensitive as editors everywhere to the outer limits of their readers' tolerance.

Over a period of months, the researcher observed *TRP*'s operations and interviewed a substantial number of its staff. Early in his research, he studied the production process, the financial and accounting systems, the circulation department, and the advertising sales activity. As the research progressed he then worked with the editorial area. A summary of this information follows.

Production

Getting the "book" out each week was a central activity at *TRP*. As in any daily or weekly publishing operation, this activity was characterized by speed, deadlines, coordination of a host of detail and people, and the ever-present last-minute changes.

The production of *TRP* basically involved the laying out and printing of five types of copy within the time constraint of weekly publication and the size constraint of how large a paper could be profitably published. This process could be summarized around six stages of production.

First, the various "copy traffic controllers" accumulated the five kinds of copy: editorial, advertising, art, classified, and listings. Each controller determined the space required for his or her copy and relayed that information to the layout editor.

---

[7] *Boston Globe–Sunday Supplement,* June 9, 1974, p. 7.

[8] "Prospects for the Alternative Press," *Nation,* April 23, 1973, p. 533.

Second, on Thursday, as the accumulation of copy was drawing to a close, the comptroller, managing editor, and advertising sales director met to determine the number of pages in the book. The comptroller would project the week's profit and loss statement under varying assumptions about advertising, density, and number of pages in the book.

Third, the layout editor was informed as to the number of pages to be published as well as about additions or deletions to copy. He then proceeded to allocate sections of each page of the book to various kinds of copy. This involved the use of a "paste-up board," a full-scale representation of a page.

Fourth, the paste-up boards were transferred to the composition shop. Here copy, which had been typed in even columns, was physically pasted onto the paste-up boards, which were photographed and the resulting negatives developed. These negatives, along with the negatives of copy photographs—called "halftones"—were combined by taping them together.

Fifth, the final negatives were taken to the printing plant where printing plates were made and the paper was printed on a web offset press. It took about three hours to print an edition of 50,000 papers.

Sixth, on Saturday morning the newsstand distributors picked up papers from the printing plant for distribution to newsstands on Sunday. The hawker edition was distributed at 5:30 A.M. Monday mornings to hawkers. Subscription copies were addressed and mailed on Saturday for delivery to the post office on Monday.

Production of the *Free Paper* followed on Monday, when editorial people altered the layout boards and changed the front page design to conform to the required 20 percent content difference regulation. The paper was printed that same day and delivered to college campuses on Tuesday.

Neither composition nor printing facilities were owned by *TRP*, and that work was subcontracted to local, independent firms. "Both of those operations would require substantial capital investments in equipment," Howard Garsh explained.

Control

The comptroller's office consisted of two people, Howard Garsh, the comptroller, and Stanley Korytko, the bookkeeper.

One day, while walking into 10–B Mt. Auburn with the researcher, Howard said, "I don't see how you can do this study without some reference to the figures. Let's talk for a few minutes?" The researcher and Garsh walked upstairs, through a small office, and into a connecting closet that served as Garsh's "cubbyhole," as offices were referred to at *TRP*. Garsh proceeded to search for papers in his files and in the clutter on his desk.

A lot of what I do here deals with keeping track of the company's financial status, either projected or actual. Accordingly, there are several tools I use, the weekly P&L projection according to various book size assumptions, the monthly profit and loss statement, and the semiannual cash and operating budget projections. These budgets tend to be conservative, pessimistic, and possibly just a little extreme. That is, we overestimate expenses and underestimate income just so we don't get cocky and overextend ourselves.

Our auditor says he's never seen such beautiful papers. That's partly because we don't just make broad assumptions of percentage increases but instead get down to the real arithmetic of it. For instance, the budget is based on Bob Williams's projection of revenue from display advertising since that's the source of about 80 percent of our revenue.[9] We ask for the most reasonable, honest estimate that doesn't pull the figures out of the air. He talks to the salespeople, looks at the economy, and maybe talks to some advertisers. And his estimate is usually conservative. As you can see from this [see accompanying table]. Remember, his projections were made one year ago.

1974	Budgeted	Billed
April 5*	$12,000	$14,500
April 12	12,000	12,500
April 19*	12,000	14,000
April 26	12,000	15,000

*Including a $2,000 ad insert.

Our bread and butter is accounts receivable. We stay right on top of them. Our credit allowances are 30 days net. And we allocate 4 percent of revenue to bad debt, although experience shows that 1 percent is sufficient.

And we have virtually no accounts payable. Other than salaries, our major expenses are printing, composition, subscriber service, mailing, trucking, and editorial free-lance payments. We've never been in a position to keep any of them waiting. Certainly every account is paid within 30 days. There are reasons for this: first, we want a top Dun & Bradstreet rating, a reputation of being a good company to do business with, a company that pays its bills. Right now our D&B rating is two. D&B told us that all it would take to get a number one is for us to be in business a little longer. Second, we have the money so why not pay it; so we try to help them out by paying on the spot.

The main reason why you'll find differences between actual and projected is in the economics of each week's book, that is, the number of pages and ad density. In order to consider those very issues in our weekly business planning, I project the weekly P&L based on assumptions about number of pages and ad density. We like to see about a $2,000 profit and not more than 55 percent ad density. Within those parameters we come to a decision

---

[9] Regular advertisements from commercial customers, as opposed to classified advertising, for example, notices of apartments for rent.

about the number of pages in the book and transmit that decision to the layout editor who plans the book accordingly.

The economics of our operation greatly affect our performance. For instance, profitability increases very rapidly with an increase in ad density. As past weekly projections have shown, most of our costs are fixed, for example, mailing, trucking, sales expense, art expense. The only variable costs we have are composition, which really varies only slightly, and editorial freelance, which varies because nonstaff articles are used as editorial copy if we opt for a larger book. Printing costs, which increase by about $1,500 for every eight-page increase we make, and salespeople's commissions (10 percent of collections), which vary with billing but not by size of paper.

For instance, assuming a 56-page paper is average, we will probably spend a total of $20,000, most of which will be on fixed type costs. Typically we will get $2,800 from circulation revenue and $3,000 from classified advertising, and that means we'd need about $14,000 from display advertising to break even. Usually the salespeople can bring in some last-minute advertising if we think we're running low. But there's a danger in thinking you can cram a lot of advertising into a book, because too much doesn't look good. So it can cause a problem: At what ad density do you decide you have to increase the size of the paper? And is increasing the size of the paper economically profitable? Anything over that $14,000 is gravy until we have to increase the book size. And increases come only in jumps of eight pages. Because each jump costs about $1,500, only one full page of ads (worth about $640) never justifies a book increase of eight pages. But what is the cutoff? I don't know.

The special supplements are pure gravy. The profit margin varies between 20 percent and 50 percent because the regular kinds of expenses are charged against the regular edition, and so that supplement must only cover its incidental printing, composition, editorial free-lance, artwork, and mailing expenses.

Garsh's responsibilities also included relationships with the First National Bank of Boston. That bank, since *TRP*'s founding, had financed all major capital needs of the organization.

Circulation department

Kevin Dawkins, who had joined *TRP* in January of 1973, had just been put in charge of circulation activities.

TRP was distributed through four channels: newsstands, hawkers, subscription, and controlled circulation—that is, free distribution. The percentage breakdown of distribution channels in 1974 was newsstands 30 percent; hawkers, 14 percent; subscription, 4 percent; and controlled, 52 percent. In 1972, Kevin pointed out, the newsstand and hawker percentages had been reversed with hawkers selling over 30 percent and newsstands roughly 15 percent of *TRP* circulation.

Controlled circulation of the *Free Paper* goes to "every conceivable college from here to Worcester, Mass." A formula of one copy per four students was used, and never were more than 50,000 copies distributed. Dawkins commented, "It's gravy. It boosts our circulation which entitles us to boost our advertising rates. Besides, the audience is captive. This edition builds reading habits which can extend to higher newsstand sales. In college towns, though, if we miss delivery to the school for some reason, newsstand sales stay about the same. Sometimes I think the markets are separate."

As for newsstand circulation, two thirds occurred within Route 128 (metropolitan Boston) and one third beyond. *TRP* worked through one distributor, Greater Boston Distributors, Inc., within the Route 128 area. Greater Boston had over 800 outlets including the Union News outlets in subways, railroad stations, and Logan Airport.

TRP was sold at 75 percent of these newsstands. Money was paid only for copies sold. The price to the distributor was 12 cents; the distributor sold it to the independent newsstand operators for 19 cents, and the newsstand price was 25 cents. Greater Boston handled between 1,500 and 2,000 titles, among which were the most profitable in the country. Dawkins felt that *TRP* should be at more newsstands and be featured more prominently.

Newsstand relationships beyond Route 128 were handled through independent distributors. The newsstand circulation area extended as far to the west as Holyoke–Springfield, Massachusetts, as far east as Portland, Maine, and as far south as Providence, Rhode Island. The objective here was to penetrate outlying markets by first reaching college communities and communal areas.

Hawker relationships were one of Kevin's responsibilities. Hawkers were independent operators who bought a paper for 5 cents and sold it for 25 cents on busy street corners throughout Greater Boston.

In 1970, 200 hawkers used to sell almost 40,000 copies of the *Old Cambridge Phoenix;* now we have 100 hawkers selling 15,000 copies of *TRP.* We used to have 75 hawkers in Boston alone—now there are only 45. There is a very high turnover here, but we have a hard core of about 50 old-timers.

The papers are trucked to a number of distribution points in Boston and Cambridge. The hawkers buy the papers for cash, but if someone is in a rough way we will front him or her for 10 or 20 copies. They can turn unsold copies in the next week for new papers. All hawkers sell both our paper and the *Phoenix.*

The typical hawker is the kind of person you would see at a rock and roll concert—long hair, T-shirt, blue jeans, and sandals. They are street people, and they keep us anchored to that community.

They do pretty well. Richie on the Boston University Bridge must make $80 from *TRP* and the same from the *Phoenix* in a couple of days. Other hawkers can make $100 in two days, and some people living in a group setup can clear $25–$30 in two days, and they can live on that.

And they have their codes too: the oldest one in seniority gets to take the best corner, although the old-timers have the territory well staked out. We don't even know some of their real names. One of them calls himself King Kong. They don't want to have any tax records.

I'm trying to push hawker sales. We are advertising in *TRP*, and I'm preparing posters to put up around the city. Hawkers are great publicity for us, standing at each street corner and practically putting the paper through your car window. Everyone can see that front page, whereas on the newsstands we are buried. I'm trying to extend hawking to the suburbs by promoting hawking through guidance counselors.

They are street people—that community is important to us. And I don't think the *Phoenix* really wants to use them; they aren't sophisticated enough. The *Phoenix*, you know, has hired two former *Herald-American* pros for their circulation department.

Subscriptions had been an increasingly expensive channel of distribution to service. The paper was physically distributed by Hub Mail, Inc. The cost per paper per subscription was about 22 cents, making it the least economic of all channels. Since the mailing service refuses to operate on weekends, a mailed paper arrives at its earliest on Tuesday, whereas *TRP* was delivered to newsstands on Sundays. The one redeeming feature about subscription sales, Kevin noted, was that *TRP* gets "the money up front." Kevin intended to eliminate the discount that subscribers get by subscribing (raising the price from $10 to $13 per year) in an attempt to cover cost increases, and he hoped to negotiate a new mailing agreement which would have the paper in the mail on Saturday and delivered by Monday.

Kevin had growth in *TRP* circulation as one of his primary goals. He was assisted in this program by a "road man" who visited newsstand owners to "sell" them on the advantages of carrying *TRP*.

We are one of Greater Boston's top ten best selling accounts. They formerly had sort of a monopoly and weren't aggressive. Terrible things happen to people when they have power. But they are getting competition now and that helps us. We are considering selling papers via machines located in grocery stores.

Our toughest competition is the *Phoenix*. They are supposed to have 110,000 circulation, and their revenues are twice ours—they up their ad density and charge higher advertising rates than we do. But we will catch up with them! Within one year we will be bigger! I get excited about this! Walter Harrison (the former circulation director) has suggested to me that we experiment with a home delivery system.

In the spring of 1974 Bob Williams began to advocate broadcast media promotion as a means of building *TRP*'s visibility and consumer demand. Except for development costs, it was anticipated that the program would operate largely through reciprocal advertising, with commercial radio and television broadcasters.

Kevin concluded:

I want us to get recognition; we put out the best paper in the country, and I know because I am in touch with lots of them. Our problem is we just

506

aren't taken as seriously as we should be. We want to be an important part of the Cambridge–Boston community in the near future. We want people to use *TRP* as more than just reading material. We want to serve as "the reference" for what goes on here. We want it to be an important part of their lives.

Advertising sales department

The advertising sales department was concerned with selling display and classified advertising, and comprised five display salespeople, one classified salesperson, Linda Martin (the advertising traffic controller), and Bob Williams, the department director. Advertising sales accounted for approximately 80 percent of the revenue of *TRP*.

Talking about *TRP*'s advertising market, Williams said:

> There are basically two levels of advertisers we're concerned with. The first group is people who have clubs, restaurants, concert tours, Army-Navy stores, clothing, bookstores, record stores—all the people who sell mainly to college students. These people came in right away. They really had to. They need papers like ours as much as we need them. The second level is the larger companies—GM, stereo companies, Jordan Marsh, and the other big clothing stores, which don't have an immediate relation between advertising money spent and dollars earned. With these people, it's only a matter of time.[10]

There was no formal system of account assignment, since Williams believed that a strict delineation of "turf" was not healthy. Nevertheless, each salesperson seemed to have specialized in one way or another. For example, one salesman, Steve Cummings, concentrated in cameras, symphony, sex, and religion, for example, Boston Symphony Orchestra, adult bookstores, Indian Gurus, and meditation movements. The four most important industries for advertising revenue were stereo components, liquor, phonograph records, and cameras.

The approach each salesperson used was individualized. Price bargaining was allowed which "makes selling tougher," Bob commented. "Otherwise, it is just stating standard rates." A sense of flexibility, of tailoring to the advertiser's needs, seemed to the researcher to be a dominant theme in the advertising efforts of *TRP*. In two instances, the researcher observed that Williams was willing to bend contractual agreements or trade advertising for the specific products of the business. "It's those little guys we've got to help. They're where our future lies." *TRP*'s advertisers were primarily Boston firms, but about 15 percent of display advertisements were placed by national firms.

It seemed to Bob Williams that the *TRP* advertising staff sold access to a

---

[10] *Nation*, April 23, 1973, p. 533.

special kind of consumer—a youthful, liberal, student market. But "hard" and reliable data were limited. A 1974 company-financed survey of approximately 300 purchasers of *TRP* (*Free Paper* customers were not canvassed) provided the following profile: average age, 23.7; sex, 55 percent male and 45 percent female; 87 percent had some college education and 47 percent were college graduates; 24 percent were professional-technical personnel; 23 percent, full-time students; 12 percent, unemployed; 11 percent, clerical; 10 percent, blue collar; 5 percent, sales; 4 percent, managerial; 1 percent, housewives; and 10 percent, miscellaneous. Thirty-six percent of the papers were sold in Boston, 32 percent in Cambridge, 5 percent in Brookline, 3 percent in Newton, 3 percent in Somerville, and the remainder scattered in other Boston suburbs.

TRP's advertising charges were geared to its circulation rate base of 90,-000 copies per week. Rates for display advertisements were $14 per column inch, or $1,120 for a full page. Discounts were given for continuity of placement: 13 weeks, 10 percent; 26 weeks, 15 percent; and 52 weeks, 20 percent. Classified advertisements were $1.90 per line.

> In terms of rates we want to get between $11.00 and $11.50 per thousand readers and stay about 50 cents per thousand under the *Phoenix*. The more specialized your market is, the higher you can charge. Publications get $2 to $3 per thousand for a very general audience, to $5 to $6 for a somewhat specialized audience, up to $30 to $40 for a very specialized group.

> We don't cut our stated rates in the summer even though with school vacations, our free circulation drops, but we do make deals. Many of our advertisers are on yearly contract (a total of two thirds of *TRP* advertisers were on some kind of contractual basis)—they get more power in the fall and winter than in the summer, but it balances out. In this business, one half your customers don't even know what your circulation is; they are only interested in how much response the advertisement gets, and we have a very loyal readership.

> With free copies, we don't go above 52 percent at the top; Bob Rotner makes that decision. Free circulation is good, but it makes things a bit more fluffy—particularly for ABC[11] counts. It makes it harder for you to really prove your circulation.

Some of the problems Williams noted were the business community's lack of respect for *TRP* and the staff's prohibition of certain kinds of advertising. With regard to the former, Williams noted that some advertisers regularly abuse credit terms and said, "People don't respect us the first time around. They think we're just a weak underground paper. Meanwhile, the staff prohibits cigarette advertising because it felt that it was detrimental to the paper's image, but that means a loss of revenue."

---

[11] Audit Bureau of Circulation, an agency which attested to the circulation figures of newspapers and magazines.

As for the future, Williams doubted that *TRP* should follow the *Phoenix* to pursue suburban advertisers. He noted that the *Phoenix* was his roughest competition.

I don't think the future is necessarily there. There is a 50 percent bad-debt ratio on advertising beyond Route 128,[12] mostly motorcycle places, bars, and so on. The people who read *TRP* and shop are here in town. We sell our circulation and a kind of readership. It would be foolish not to exploit it here. The *Phoenix* is entering the suburbs and doesn't have the circulation to back it up. That will hurt alternative weeklies in general. Furthermore, we're still thrashing around editorially. It would have been unwise to move until we get that straightened out. Finally, we are best sold to small and medium-sized businesses, and they are most concentrated here in town.

The trick is to get local advertisers to transfer ad money from radio to print and more particularly, *TRP*. There are about 50 stations in this area, and ten of them program directly for the youth market. We do some reciprocal advertising with them now.

I love music and have a hi-fi set. The reality of Boston is that there is an important radio market here. If the company were interested, and it isn't, we could go into partnership with one of these stations. It would provide a great new combination for us. Bob Rotner once thought we should go into the newsstand distribution business.

By 1975–76, if my plans work out, we should be in a position to enter the suburbs. I am shooting for advertising sales this year of $1.5 million.

Editorial

Editorial offices were located on the second floor at 10–B Mt. Auburn Street. The physical layout consisted of a main room (about one fourth the size of the first floor) and two closet-size offices at the far end; one of the latter also served as a hallway to the back porch. Paul Solman (editor) and Tom Friedman (managing editor) were technically assigned this space, but all members of the department seemed to participate in its use. Jeff Albertson's (the associate publisher) desk was next to Tom's office.

The main room contained five desks, two tables, filing cabinets, and all of the usual paraphernalia of an editorial operation. A chair, with one of its casters off, occupied the center of the room. "We bought all of this equipment secondhand," Paula Childs noted. "We sure scrimp around here. Howard buys us discard, advertising promotion pencils but no pens. But we are getting more space in the basement here—that should help a lot."

The researcher agreed that space was needed. Even in a summer lull period, editorial personnel flowed in and out and often there were not enough

---

[12] A belt highway, approximately 12 miles west of the central city. Route 128 tended to be a dividing line between the more developed suburbs of Boston and the less developed, higher status suburbs of the city.

available desks and chairs. The room had a used and noncleaned look with papers on the floor and boxes of editorial supplies stacked in every conceivable place. A number of bulletin boards seemed to be a part of the communication system, telling Peter to get a photo at 10:30 and noting that a free-lance writer wanted his check right away—"He is flat broke." Office decor consisted of wall-sized pictures of Katherine Hepburn *et al.*, and advertisements for concerts and artistic events; a somewhat tired and dehydrated plant provided the final touch.

The researcher sought to capture the office tone. Clearly busyness was the order of the day, with editorial personnel constantly using the multiple phones and the limited desk space. Friendliness was another factor. Martha, the receptionist, seemed unflappable despite the constant barrage of questions and calls with which she was confronted. There was an air of informality. Standard dress seemed to be T-shirts, shorts, and sandals; it made the first floor look almost "Establishment."

Editorial proved to be a complex part of *TRP*'s scene to "paint" for the reader. After several abortive attempts the researcher finally decided to look first at "who was in the area and what did they do," next at the "organization and leadership of the work," and finally at *TRP*'s "editorial posture."

TRP's masthead (July) carried the names of 54 individuals, 32 of whom were listed under "Editorial." Of those names, Paul Solman commented, "14 are full-time personnel, 8 are part-time members who regularly contribute, and 10 are free-lance or irregular contributors to the book."

The editorial staff tended to specialize by function. On the "support" side, Paul and Tom were assisted by Jan Freeman (copy editor) and Paula Childs (listings and general editorial person), and general assistance to the entire group was given by Peter Southwick (photos) and recently "on board" Bruce Weinberg (production manager).

On the "creative" side the situation was more complicated since most staffers handled multiple assignments. The largest number worked primarily on "back of the book" material—the arts and entertainment section and, in addition, contributed regular columns used throughout the entire paper. The smallest number of full-time masthead personnel were involved with the development of feature stories. "When we came over from the *Phoenix* we had six full-time feature writers," Paul said. "Until recently we had four, but Joe Klein just left to go with *Rolling Stone* at twice what we could pay, and Ed Zuckerman is going back to journalism school. We need to hire another two writers; we're short-handed."

In addition to back of the book and feature writers there were a number of individuals (often part-timers) who specialized in writing a political or news column or, as in the case of Omar White, created a political cartoon. In addition to masthead personnel, there was a pool of free-lance writers who, on occasion, submitted articles to *TRP*. Boston seemed to attract a

EXHIBIT 6
Masthead, July 17, 1974

Real Paper

EDITORIAL
PAUL SOLMAN, EDITOR
TOM FRIEDMAN, MANAGING EDITOR
HENRY ARMETTA
HARPER BARNES
BO BURLINGHAM
STUART BYRON
PAULA CHILDS
STEPHEN DAVIS
CHUCK FAGER
JAN FREEMAN
ARTHUR FRIEDMAN
RUSSELL GERSTEN
ANITA HARRIS
JOE HUNT
JAMES ISAACS
JOE KLEIN, NEWS EDITOR
ANDREW KOPKIND
CHUCK KRAEMER
JON LANDAU
KAY LARSON
JON LIPSKY
DAVE MARSH
JIM MILLER
LILITH MOON
ARNIE REISMAN
LAURA SHAPIRO
BURT SOLOMON
PETER SOUTHWICK, PHOTOGRAPHER
CRAIG UNGER
BRUCE WEINBERG, PRODUCTION
DAVID OMAR WHITE
ED ZUCKERMAN

ADVERTISING
ROBERT WILLIAMS, DIRECTOR
JONATHAN BANNER
STEVE CUMMINGS
MIKE FORMAN
LINDA MARTIN
DONALD MONACK
ELLEN PAUL
RICHARD REITMAN
DICK YOUSOUFIAN

ART
RONN CAMPISI, DIRECTOR
DAVID BROWN
PAT MEARS
REBECCA WELZ

CIRCULATION
KEVIN DAWKINS, DIRECTOR
DON CUMMINGS
CYNDI ROBBINS
MIKE ZEGEL

BUSINESS
HOWARD GARSH, COMPTROLLER
STANLEY KORYTKO
WALTER HARRISON, ASST. TO THE
PUBLISHER
JEFF ALBERTSON, ASSOC. PUBLISHER
ROBERT ROTNER, PUBLISHER

Metropolitan Boston's Weekly Journal of News, Opinion and the
Arts. Address all correspondence to the Real Paper. 10B Mt
Auburn St. Cambridge, Mass. 02138 Telephones. Editorial and
Art. 492-8101. Advertising, Circulation and Business, 492-1650
Second-class postage paid at Boston, Mass Published weekly by
The Real Paper. 10B Mt. Auburn St. Cambridge, Mass. 02138
Copyright · 1974 by The Real Paper. All rights reserved
Reproduction by any method whatsoever without permission of
staff is prohibited
Unsolicited manuscripts should be addressed to Jan Freeman
and must be accompanied by stamped self-addressed envelope
Photographs should be submitted to Jeff Albertson. Photo Editor
Subscription rates 1 year. $10.00, 2 years. $18.00

Printing by Arlington Offset

large number of writers, many of whom could not find, or did not want, a regular organizational relationship.

The editorial group was responsible for the creation and processing of copy with copy coming from staff columnists, staff feature writers, solicited manuscripts from free-lancers, and unsolicited manuscripts. This editorial activity, Tom commented, was organized along the back and front of the book lines.

> Jim Miller is our music editor, and Stuart Byron is our film editor. They, along with Art Friedman, our regular theater columnist, and Kay Larson, our art columnist, hand me back of the book material each week. The back of the book tends to run itself, but Paul is looking for a back of the book editor. Both of us are front of the book oriented, and a good deal more of the budget goes into the front than the back of the book.

All staff members, with whom the researcher spoke, indicated that Paul was the central person in the process of generating or reviewing story concepts, interesting and assigning writers to develop those stories, and finally nurturing and reviewing the resultant manuscript as it evolved. It seemed to the researcher that this was an extremely personal and intuitive process, difficult for all involved to articulate and yet critical for *TRP*'s success.

At a regular Friday morning meeting the editorial staffers gathered with Paul in an informal session to review the copy program. Story ideas were reviewed, modified, or discarded in a free-flowing meeting with staffers sitting on the floor and Paul, his chair tilted against the wall, leading the discussion.

Paul's primary operating pattern, however, seemed to be on an individual-to-individual basis. He often began the process of copy creation by talking with a writer about an idea. "At any given time I expect I am working on 50 story ideas of which 5 may actually come to print. I work at home two days a week because I can concentrate better there and handle the writers more effectively by telephone."

The researcher appreciated the latter comment since Paul's office routine could be described as frenetic. He was constantly on the phone, answering questions, reviewing edit problems with Tom, or working with a writer. Paul's informal style and personal warmth made it easy for all to approach him; and he seemed always to be "in conference" outside the office building, on the stairs, or even walking through the office. "When do you get time to reflect?" the researcher asked. Paul smiled, "It's tough."

With full-time, front of the book personnel, Paul's primary function seemed to be reviewing story ideas that they brought to him. With part-time and free-lance writers, Paul seemed to play a more active role in initiating concepts, but he also reviewed their suggestions and manuscripts. He had a wide acquaintanceship in the Boston community and seemed to the researcher to have knowledge about and interest in a wide range of topics and institutions.

> I handle all of the free-lance work. It is a shifting group of people. Some work for other outfits, some are teachers, some have a cause, most need money—it's hard to make a living free-lancing. We pay them $75 for a short thousand-word story, $250 for a feature article or part thereof. Once in the judge and court system story, where a lot of research work was needed, we paid $600. But we negotiate with each; the budget puts on real limits.

Jan Freeman in commenting on copy development said:

> Paul's job is to think up ideas and then assign them to either regular or free-lance writers, although usually the regular staff generates their own ideas. It is a very difficult job, and I suspect the ratio of ideas to finished stories is about 15 to 1. The process depends a lot upon who is available and whether or not they are interested.
>
> A lot of what Paul wants to do this fall is to make the paper more useful. Tom would probably want more news stories of a political bent. Everyone's ideal would be to do more apartment rental agency stories. Did you read that? They are a real rip-off and take money under false circumstances. We did a lot of research on them. It was both an exposé and a news story.
>
> I want us to do more stories like that or the one in this week's issue on airline safety—more consumer-oriented pieces—but they take lots of time. We should do more local investigatives, like the article on the coroner's office in Boston's City Hall. We should do stories that make a real difference—a protest that demands a response.
>
> And we need more middle of the book material—material between the arts and listings and the political and news and feature stories at the front. We need think pieces, like the story in the *New York Times Magazine* section. A woman in an apartment house was robbed—bound and gagged. What was it like? What were her fears? Did she behave bravely enough? This was a special story, and a woman wrote it from a woman's point of view. We need more material on ideas and people. I suggested to Paul that we do an article on people living together—roommates or lovers—or whatever. It should be funny and yet factual. These aren't news stories—they are people and idea combinations. And we should do more on scientists and science articles—the article in the *New York Times* on "black holes" in space is a good example.

Tom, who had joined *TRP* in November of 1973, had as his prime objective introducing more organization into the editorial process. He felt progress had been made in this area, and by July, lead feature articles had been planned and were in process for the next five months.

> It was in my own self-interest to get some planning going—things were frantic here when I first came. I wish we had more full-time feature writers; we need at least three now. It would make my job easier. You get to know

the regulars and how to work with them; they have to produce. But it isn't as cost effective. People don't have story ideas regularly every week, and so there are bound to be slow times when we won't get stories.

Both Paul and Tom spoke highly of the caliber of *TRP*'s editorial staff, and conversations with other Boston journalists confirmed that evaluation. Some staffers had achieved awards, national publicity, and peer recognition from the wider journalistic field.

In trying to pin down *TRP*'s current editorial style and format, the researcher talked with various members of the staff. Tom Friedman reflected, "Partially it's form—longer paragraphs and in-depth analysis. Partially it's an emphasis on the human dimension. We just don't feed them information; we create an ambience whereby the reader can relate to the event. We give them more than historical background, we give them more than information—we get to the basic reasons."

Joe Klein, who had received several journalist awards, contrasted *TRP*'s and the *Phoenix*'s editorial style.

> Our style strives for both a sense of immediacy and perspective. Our copy is written more dramatically. We're also much more careful. We want to write the definitive story on the subject. Paul and I talk it out and decide what the story should be; it has to have a larger focus than just what happened last week; we take specific incidents and show how they reflect on institutions. I don't see that happening with any other publication in town.

Paul Solman commented:

> Our major articles, in contrast to the *Phoenix*, are long—we do in-depth reporting. Our feature article on selling the Encyclopaedia Britannica was a good example. The writer actually sold Britannicas. We want to be able to help people see why they behave as they do. Why does a blue collar making $14,000 spend 800 bucks on a set of encyclopaedias? Or our article on the hearing aid racket is another good example. We want to be at the cutting edge—what is really going on in that business. We want to answer questions. We want the truth. But the budget limits us; we are small, and they are larger. We can't compete with them in terms of coverage.
>
> The development of a pool of feature article ideas is fairly random. A lot depends on what I read or hear from friends. We get lots of suggestions from people outside the staff. And one of my critical inputs is to gather staff who can contribute ideas. I have a sense of balance for the makeup of the paper, but I don't have a specific formula for a certain amount of political, or human interest, or exposé material in any issue or any month.

Chuck Fager, one of the original staffers, reflected, "We have an ephemeral editorial policy now. Writers just stream in and out. The *Phoenix* does a better job of covering Boston and the State House than we do. But any differences between the *Phoenix* and us now is more individual writer style than editorial strategy."

An evolving editorial posture

In the summer of 1974 the researcher noted, the topic of future editorial direction was the object of considerable discussion, not only within the editorial staff but within the paper at large. Paula Childs commented:

> We're not covering events enough—issues that deal with people's daily lives. We're not covering what's happening with rent control, what's happening in the ecology movement, what's happening in the neighborhoods—that kind of stuff. Also, I think we're too Cambridge oriented. Our strongest following is Cambridge. We cover Cambridge things to a much greater extent than Boston. And I think that that's one of the reasons why people on the other side of the river continue to pick up the *Phoenix* instead of *TRP*.

Howard Garsh believed "more hard investigative reporting should be our first priority now." Walter Harrison wanted more emphasis on quality editorial work. Tom Friedman commented feelingly, "I want to have more impact on people's lives. My basic attitude is deep distrust of the people who run our country and our businesses. Some staffers want more emphasis on entertainment; some just want more people to buy it. I want the people to get the information they wouldn't get otherwise. I want more investigations. I want to work on an investigative paper, not just a successful operation. I'm trying to hold on to my sense of moral outrage."

Bob Rotner, from his perspective, saw two approaches to future editorial direction. "The edit people want witty headlines. The business people want headlines that sell. The edit people feel the paper ought to be political, serve the left. The business people see it as the ultimate guide to Boston, serving the consumer element. I want it to do more investigative reporting."

Paul Solman reflected not only on near-term and future editorial direction but plans to get there, noting:

> We are planning some minor modifications for the fall. We will have two long feature stories and a larger number of shorter stories that will provide more information in readable form. And we will expand the number of vignettes from New York City and Washington events. One of the latter might be an interview with the aide of a member of Congress.
>
> And we're trying to figure out what we want the paper to be. The paper is essentially a reflection of the people here, and they are not homogeneous. But in the longer run, we're working toward a personality for this paper that is intelligent, political, which I mean to say politically progressive, interesting to people, compelling, and well written.
>
> We're not real close now, but we're making progress. Our effort now is oriented to four activities. First, we simply want to get more copy available for our use. Copy can always be edited and rewritten. So getting the basic fund is important. This means asking more of our staff people, as well as really pursuing the free-lance sources. This also means we will have to pay

higher rates than competitors, pay for research, and make appeals to the really good people based on prestige, personal ties, and even convenience.

Second, we want to tie down regular contributors—good writers who may not be on the staff but can be relied on for quality stuff. We want to create a circle of regular free-lancers.

Third, we have to fight the tendency to diffuse our efforts. Accordingly, we created the position of managing editor which will free me from the day-to-day operational problems.

Fourth, we want to run two or three solid articles per week in the front page of the book that are smart and fascinating.

Success for most people is to be big and powerful. I don't have a specific vision of *TRP* and success, but I want it to be something that serves the people. I want us to be a wing of society—out there after the bad gals and guys. Yet I want it to be entertaining too, for literate people. And I want it to be instructive to the public.

LOOKING AHEAD

The former *Cambridge Phoenix* and *TRP* had been organized and had their early operating years during a period of major societal and youth unrest. Campus stories headlined strikes, riots, and "takeovers," while on the wider scene, the counterculture movement was in full bloom.

Reporters of the mid-70s youth movement indicated that much of the past turbulence seemed to have disappeared. While the president of Ohio University did resign in June of 1974, citing "the mindless destructive events of the past week," most college campuses seemed quiet and the counterculture movement had, in many observers judgments, "plateaued."

The transition from activism to a more restrained protest pattern was captured for the researcher in Sara Davidson's article on the Symbionese Liberation Army. She interviewed Dan Siegel, a well-known participant in the 1969 Berkeley disturbances about his changing career and life style.

> Siegel is 28, an attractive, modest-looking young man in a sports shirt and slacks. In 1969, when he was student-body president at Berkeley, he gave a speech that sent thousands surging down Telegraph Avenue to reclaim People's Park. Bob Dylan was singing from speaker vans: "You can have your cake and eat it, too."
>
> Siegel says he no longer had "the illusion that revolution will be easy or that a few gallant people can do it. Winning the hearts and minds of tens of thousands of people—that's what making revolution is about." He walks toward the courthouse where he is preparing a test case in which the community is suing the district attorney, and he says that it's funny but in some ways, he feels old.[13]

Given these changes, as well as major developments in the wider environment, the researcher wondered what, if any, impact these forces

---

[13] *New York Times Magazine,* June 2, 1974, p. 44.

would have on the future plans of *TRP*. He raised the question of future direction with Paula Childs. She commented:

> I'd like to see this paper eventually be able to own its own composition shop as well as its own printing company. I'd like to see this company own its own other media resources, like its own radio station. And I'd like to see the paper get to a large enough size that we can be covering the things we should be covering. You know. Right now we're in a tug-of-war between whether to be more like a magazine, or whether to be more like a newspaper. Right now, we're much more like a magazine than a newspaper.

Joe Klein, a former staff member, added:

> From here I'd like to see us grow in several ways. First, I want us to develop a broader base of readers and not be read by just street people and hippies. This would mean expanding into older neighborhoods and suburbs, as well as becoming more and more frequently read downtown. I want it to have impact. Furthermore, and I guess this is a second point, I want us to expand beyond Boston to a regional and even national scope. I want us to have as many readers outside of Boston as the *Village Voice* has outside New York. And third, I want us to become an alternative for top-notch daily journalists.

Bo Burlingham, another staff writer, asked:

> Have we reached the end of our growth with this format? It has worked so well. And the answer is so important because it affects so many things. Who do we hire? Young kids just out of college and ask them for a full-time commitment? Or, do we hire older more experienced part-timers who can work here—and write the book they always really wanted to create?
>
> It raises questions as to who our audience is—is it Cambridge, Boston, New England, or ————? How we work with that influences Howard's financing plans and Bob Williams's advertising programs. And questions, too, need to be asked editorially. Should we go on primarily with feature stories about current causes or events or institutions? There are lots of reasons why we should. They take less resources and time and are less risky. Or do we become an investigative journal? That's really rough. It takes lots of money and time to do well and it's risky.

Jan Freeman reminisced:

> So much of what we are, is what we were—a collection of people who grew up in the late 60s and who, by luck, got into an organization that we like and where we can do what we want.
>
> Our audience is like us—it's growing up! It's no longer the '60s. Our audience isn't clear any more—it is a mixture. Paul knows this. We know we can't just do what we do best. We never have been a doctrinaire leftist paper—we have sort of been, as I told you—a newspaper-magazine. But what's next?

A *Boston Globe* reporter, Nathan Cobb, raised the question of future direction with various members of *TRP* and the *Phoenix* staff. He commented:

Times change. *TRP*, having achieved financial success, wonders where to go. "It's much less clear now what we should be doing than it used to be," says Paul Solman. "It used to be automatic. You didn't have to think about what you did because there was a counterculture not being covered by anyone else. Now we're asking what kinds of things we can provide that no one else can."

∘ ∘ ∘ ∘ ∘

One suspects, though, that the two papers really are still viewed as a legitimate journalistic alternative by the fading remnants of the "youth culture." But out in the great beyond, out in those suburbs where folks are easing into their 30s and 40s, each may indeed be viewed as just another newspaper. "The dailies are getting more like us, and we're getting more like the dailies," says Joe Klein of *TRP*, an experienced and professional newsperson. "And that's all right with me. I'd like to see *TRP* on every doorstep."

Bob Rotner, publisher, in talking with the researcher about his job and responsibilities as publisher, noted:

But to plan the future of the paper, and to make sure that just because the paper is successful now, it doesn't mean that it's going to be successful in a year or two, and there are certain things happening in the city and the country which need to be understood. We're not making ourselves obsolete. . . . What I hope I can do now is to make the decisions about the future by going to the appropriate places and finding out what is going to happen in the future, and then to make sure that *TRP* is going in the direction it needs to go, so that it doesn't have to worry about the future.

Northern Industries, Inc.

Dale Morris had joined Northern Industries, Inc., only six months ago, and by mid-July was faced with a rather difficult task. He had just completed a three-month tour of Northern's Japanese operations and was now faced with the task of preparing a formal critique of those operations. Though his official report was to be sent to Mr. Allan Hill, vice president of personnel, Dale suspected that the report might have repercussions throughout the international organization.

Dale had three basic concerns about the potential impact of his report. His first concern related to the importance of this report to his own position. Dale knew that Mr. Hill was quite influential in Northern and that these reports were used in evaluating trainees for assignments and potential promotions. His second concern was for those managers in Japan who might be affected by his report. Dale was certain that he could seriously jeopardize the future of several people in Japan, depending upon the contents of his report. Third, Dale had a longer range concern about the potential repercussions of his report on members of the international organization with whom he would have future relationships. Since Dale was hoping to be assigned to the Far East operations, he did not wish to jeopardize his future relations with other Asian managers including Mr. Gilbert, vice president of the Far East. On the other hand, Dale felt a personal obligation to present a fair and objective view of what he had learned during his stay in Japan. However, this might also lead to his acquiring a reputation as a troublemaker in Northern Industries, thereby affecting his own future in the company, and have more immediate repercussions on his scheduled tours in the Philippine and Malaysian operations.

Background

Dale Morris had graduated with an MBA from a major West Coast university in December. Northern Industries had hired Dale in January for their international division to eventually work in their Far East region. Because of prior military experience in the Far East, particularly Japan, Hong Kong, and the Philippines, Dale had become interested in the Asian cultures and had returned to the university after his discharge to continue his education in business administration, emphasizing international business and marketing in Asia. In fact, Dale had returned to Japan the summer prior to his graduation and worked with Matsushita Electric Company—the largest consumer products company in Japan.

Dale had been interested in finding a job which would allow him to use his knowledge about the Far East. Fortunately, Northern Industries had been suggested to Dale by one of his professors, and after an interview with Mr. Allan Hill, the vice president of personnel, in New York, Dale was soon offered a position.

It was Northern Industries' policy that new graduates be placed on the payroll of the personnel department during their first year with the company. This was considered a training period in which the new employee would be given a broad exposure to the firm and the area in which he was to eventually work. In January Dale and his wife moved to New York to begin a one-year training program with Northern.

For Dale Morris it was to be a most interesting year. After an initial three months in New York, he was to spend three months in each of Northern Industries' major Far East operations—Japan, the Philippines, and Malaysia. At the end of his first year, he would be assigned to an International Division department which would lead to a foreign assignment. He anticipated his first assignment to be in the Far East, possibly at the regional headquarters in Hong Kong.

Northern Industries was an established worldwide corporation which sold durable consumer products throughout the world. Because of their narrow product line, they were basically organized with two divisions—the U.S. Domestic Division and the International Division. Within each division, there was a functional organization of marketing, manufacturing, and distribution, with staff functions of control and finance. In addition, there was a geographic organization of regional offices which were staffed with a vice president of the region and a small staff to monitor each of the operating functions.

While in New York, Dale Morris had met, briefly, Mr. Donald Gilbert, Jr., the vice president of the Far East region. Don Gilbert had been quite successful in the company, and a year earlier had been promoted from finance manager of Northern's Argentine operations to vice president of the Far East. It had been a surprise to everyone, but Don seemed to be doing a good job, and Dale had heard favorable comments.

With Don Gilbert's approval, Dave and his wife left for the Far East operations in April. His job description was not defined, except that he was expected to spend about three months in each operation getting to know the people and understand the nature of their operations. It was expected that he would also be able to carry out some special assignments for the local managements. The only specific task he had to perform was to write a report to Mr. Hill following his stay in each country.

NORTHERN INDUSTRIES—JAPAN

After World War II, Northern Industries had decided to open a sales office in Japan rather than to sell through the Japanese trading companies. Once in Japan, they had found the competition extremely intense and had eventually been forced to begin manufacturing in Japan as well. However, the relatively low volume of Japanese sales had forced Northern to export about 65 percent of their Japanese production to the United States. Though Northern's Japanese manufacturing costs were higher than their Japanese competition, they were able to charge a premium price for their product because it was perceived as a prestige American name, and consumers assumed it was being imported into Japan.

The Northern organization in Japan had approximately 1,200 employees, of which 300 were in the head office in Tokyo, performing a variety of tasks in the areas of accounting, finance, general administration, sales supervision, and so forth (see Exhibit 1). Non-Japanese managers had continually staffed the Japanese operations ever since the operation's establishment in 1955. In fact, all but two managers had been Americans.

When Dale Morris arrived in Japan, the managers included Mr. O'Connor, general manager; Mr. deCruz, marketing director; and Mr. Simon, finance director. Prior to joining Northern in Japan Mr. O'Connor, age 49, had worked in the U.K. and India with a consumer electronics firm. Mr. deCruz, age 36, had previously worked ten years with Northern Industries in South America. Mr. Simon, age 55, had worked with several firms and had been working in Central America before joining Northern in Japan (see Exhibit 1 for organization chart).

The situation

Mr. O'Connor had been informed of Dale's planned arrival and tour in Japan but had made no arrangements to meet Dale and his wife upon arrival. However, since both Dale and his wife had spent time in Japan, they had not had any difficulty in getting to a hotel or in finding Northern's office in downtown Tokyo.

On April 15 the Monday morning that Dale first visited Northern's Tokyo office, he had met Mr. Ito, the administrative manager responsible for all legal and administrative matters. Mr. Ito, at age 48, had been with Northern in Japan for about 12 years. Since Mr. O'Connor had not yet arrived, Dale had spent time talking with Mr. Ito and Mr. Simon about the

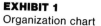

EXHIBIT 1
Organization chart

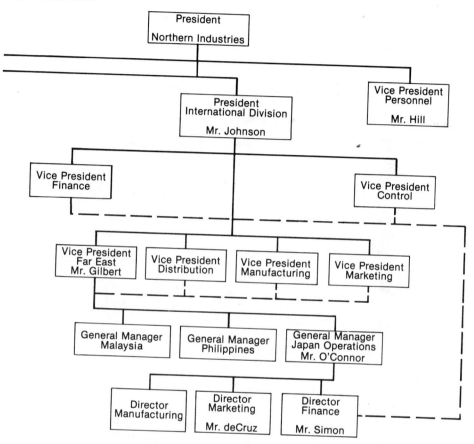

Japanese operations. Dale commented on his initial conversation with Mr. Simon:

> Mr. Simon was in his mid-50s and had been quite successful in some of his own business ventures prior to joining Northern in Japan. He had an air of competence and experience, and was very forceful. He opened the conversation by asking if we had furniture coming, which indicated that he didn't know much about the purpose or nature of my visit in Japan.
>
> After some small talk, he explained the situation in Japan. He mentioned that Northern had been losing money in Japan for the past four years and that when he and Mr. O'Connor came to Japan they decided that some drastic changes needed to be made in the operations.
>
> Mr. Simon had begun working to get the cash flow under control. To begin with, they disapproved virtually all cash requests until they could

522

understand the total cash needs. Second, he worked on the banks to get the cost of funds down to a reasonable level. When he arrived, Northern was being required to have a 67 percent compensating balance. He was now carrying about 35 percent. Because of the losses, he also had to bring in additional funds to maintain a minimum 10-to-1 debt to equity ratio on $25 million of debt.

The most drastic changes had been in the employment policy. In 14 months' time the number of employees had been reduced by 200. Since you can't fire people in Japan, these reductions were achieved by promoting selected employees into positions they couldn't handle so they would resign, or by telling them that their position wasn't needed but that since they needed money to support their families, they could keep their job without doing anything. He explained that the people he promoted would then be continually asked for information which they could not provide, and would thereby be forced to quit. He told those who "did nothing" that so long as they continued to come to work they would be paid, but he said that in order to "save face" they soon found other jobs. He stated that with this kind of elimination policy you couldn't help but lose some good men as well as poor ones, but it couldn't be helped.

During this 14-month period, Mr. Simon had personally interviewed all 80 employees in his department. He said he required his managers to "produce or get out." He was now happy with 80 percent of his second-level managers and was working to train them through job rotation and through biweekly training sessions.

Mr. Simon also commented that if his methods didn't work, it wouldn't be his worry since he planned to only be there for two more years before going back to his own business.

It was not until after lunch that Dale had met with Mr. O'Connor. Dale explained that first meeting:

After finally getting into Mr. O'Connor's office, there was some small talk about our trip and getting settled. Mr. O'Connor suggested that my wife and I might have some trouble getting along in Japan. When I assured him that we were both comfortable in Japan and spoke Japanese, he seemed not at all impressed.

He then explained Northern's situation in Japan. He began with the fact that Northern had been losing money for four years now, beginning with $1.5 million, then $3 million, then $4 million the year he took over. During the same period sales had been between $26 and $30 million. As a result of the losses, their bank debt had reached almost $20 million.

Mr. O'Connor explained that he had taken drastic actions over the past 14 months since he arrived, reducing overhead 40 percent by cutting employment by 31 percent. The losses had been reduced to $750,000. In addition, he had succeeded in getting the Japanese government to allow Northern to bring in an additional $10 million in equity to pay off part of the $20 million of local debt.

He commented that it seemed that all credit for his accomplishments went to the head office personnel who came to Japan for their two-week stints to buy cameras and pearls.

He also explained that he intended to be in Japan for four years. "It takes one year to find out what the problem is, another to solve it, and a third to watch and make sure everything is running smoothly." The final year he intended to enjoy Japan and find out what it had to offer.

He found it very difficult to accomplish anything in Japan and stated that it takes two weeks to do something in Japan which he could do in three days in India.

He also mentioned about several Japanese in Northern having nervous breakdowns. In one case, the newspapers had published some articles condemning foreign management techniques and referring to a "Mr. O" at Northern.

When we discussed the purpose of my stay, he simply suggested that it was easier for him to read than to listen and that I should outline what questions or areas were of interest to me and that he would see me the following week to discuss it. Well, it didn't take me long to feel uncomfortable and not particularly wanted.

After spending the week getting organized, talking with some of the managers at Northern, and putting together an outline of areas of interest, Dale went back to see Mr. O'Connor the following Monday, April 22.

When I gave him my outline, he read it over briefly and suggested that he could answer all the questions himself but said he would pass it on to his staff to prepare answers. He then suggested that I probably could be finished in Japan within several weeks. I walked out of his office not quite sure what to do but determined not to be put off so easily.

After that meeting, I talked with Mr. Ito and gave him a copy of my outline. He was quite enthusiastic and said he would begin arranging meetings with various staff and managers for me. He then encouraged me not to worry about Mr. O'Connor—that his bark was much louder than his bite.

Dale wasn't quite sure how to approach the situation after that initial reception. He didn't particularly like Mr. O'Connor nor did he feel that he would get much cooperation from him. His feelings were reinforced several days later when, while Dale was in Mr. Ito's office, O'Connor displayed his Irish temper. Dale explained:

While I was talking with Mr. Ito, I suddenly heard a loud roar and turned to see Mr. O'Connor charging out of his office and come crashing into Mr. Ito's office. He was furious. He had a crumpled letter which he threw down on Mr. Ito's desk and accused Mr. Ito of incompetence in getting good secretarial staff. "I don't have time, and I'm getting paid too much money to have to be correcting spelling errors!" he yelled. Then he stomped out of the office.

I could see that Mr. Ito was quite upset—as was I. Though he tried to treat it casually, Mr. Ito unwrinkled the letter and excused himself as he took the letter back to be retyped.

Dale spent the next several weeks interviewing key managers and working on marketing programs. Since Mr. deCruz, the marketing director, had left on home-leave several days after Dale's arrival, they had only a brief conversation prior to his departure. In Mr. deCruz's absence, Mr. O'Connor handled the marketing function. Dale commented:

> Though Mr. O'Connor held weekly "Marketing Coordination Meetings," I had not been invited to attend. I did sit in once, but felt that Mr. O'Connor was not pleased and thereafter stayed informed through the detailed memorandum which Mr. O'Connor issued after each meeting—summarizing the progress, problems, and responsibilities of each manager.

Mr. O'Connor's meetings ran about two hours—usually 2:00 P.M. to 4:00 P.M. Because of the efficiency with which he ran his meetings, and his harshness with managers who were unprepared, most managers would spend considerable time preparing for the meetings.

Dale's inability to gain Mr. O'Connor's support made it necessary for him to work more closely with the Japanese managers. However, it put Dale in an uncomfortable position:

> I was rather disturbed by Mr. O'Connor's attitude. I got the feeling he didn't really want me to find out what happens in the company, and was mainly interested in getting rid of me. This was also symptomatic of the biggest problem I saw in the company—a total lack of any human relations skills by the present management.
>
> With Mr. O'Connor's quick temper, you had to learn to accept his more or less constant rage. This attitude wasn't conducive to cooperation within the company and wasn't helping the poor morale in the company.

Dale soon followed a routine which developed at headquarters. He averaged two to three interviews per day, spending 1½ to 2½ hours talking to each manager.

On May 8, Mr. Don Gilbert, vice president of the Far East, stopped in Japan on the way to New York and Dale spent a few minutes with him. Dale commented:

> Mr. Gilbert told me he was glad to have me come to Japan and that if there was anything he could do to help, just let him know. He said he was interested in hearing my critique of the operations, since he was also interested in learning something from my study. He also mentioned that anything I said to him would be in confidence.

Dale hoped to spend more time with Mr. Gilbert on his return trip.

As Dale interviewed various employees, he began to hear repeatedly a problem raised with regard to communications. In talking with those managers who did not speak English, there was a feeling of frustration which could best be expressed from the following comments:

> Most foreign managers don't try to learn Japanese. Instead they use interpreters. However, because the other Japanese don't speak English, the foreign managers don't respect their abilities.

Even worse, those Japanese who can speak English think they are better than us. Most of the Japanese managers started as interpreters, but when new foreign managers were brought in, they would be promoted because they could speak English. Now they represent the major obstacle to communications. They want to protect their own positions, so they won't tell the foreigners when they have a problem. They know that if results are bad, New York will replace the American managers within two years.

By May 20, Dale had visited the factory and about a dozen dealers around Tokyo and felt he was beginning to understand some of the problems:

> Northern had made some policy decisions which now placed them at a competitive disadvantage. For instance, competitors began selling products without actual delivery about five years ago. It was really a savings program in which salespeople would collect monthly payments which were small, but over time allowed the consumer to buy the products. Since this was not Northern's normal sales procedure, New York had not allowed them to use this method. The result is that Northern is now unable to recruit good salespeople because commissions are only paid on product sales, not on advance payments as done by competitors.
>
> This also makes selling more difficult in Japan for Northern. As a result, the losses had increased and management had begun a cost-cutting survival program. With emphasis on breaking even, store supervisors and dealers were not able to obtain funds for repairs to store sign and displays, and so forth. The result had been a continuing decline in the looks of dealer shops.

Since New York had been involved in some of the decisions made in Japan, Dale was interested in talking with Mr. Gilbert to understand New York's position. However, Dale soon realized the delicate position this put him in after a discussion with Mr. Ito:

> In a meeting with Mr. Ito, he said that, after I talked with three or four more people, he would like to spend some time discussing what I had learned. I mentioned that I would like to talk with Mr. Gilbert, but he said I should first discuss things with Mr. O'Connor. However, when I pointed out that I was interested in getting the "big picture" from New York's point of view, he said that was all right. This was a good example of how delicate the situation was. Problems of hierarchy were a constant issue.

Mr. Gilbert returned on May 22 and spent about an hour talking with Dale that afternoon. He summarized their meeting:

> Mr. Gilbert was aware of the problems of recruiting and of employee morale. He was trying to get some help from an associated Japanese firm, but it was a slow process.
>
> During our conversation, I mentioned that I was having trouble communicating with Mr. O'Connor, and he said he wasn't surprised. He said that what was even worse was that the American management team wasn't getting along well. He was unhappy with this fact. When I said that Mr.

O'Connor had seemed more pleasant in the past several weeks, Mr. Gilbert replied that he had good reason to.

On June 6, Dale had inadvertently turned over a piece of paper on one of the marketing managers' desks on which the manager had taken a telephone message for Dale. On the back of the message was a diagram with the names—O'Connor and deCruz. Dale immediately inquired as to what it meant. Through persistence he finally learned that there was speculation that either O'Connor or deCruz might be doomed to depart the scene. Dale commented:

> It seemed that Mr. Gilbert and Mr. Johnson (president of International Division) were putting pressure on Mr. O'Connor. The speculation was that they were supporting Mr. deCruz in a quarrel between deCruz and O'Connor. Moreover, an unknown couple had come to Tokyo for a week and Mr. Gilbert's assistant had come to Tokyo with his wife to keep them company. There was speculation that if this person liked Tokyo, he would soon become a member of management. Nobody knew what was happening for sure, not even Mr. O'Connor. For the first time, I began to learn that there was some rift between Mr. deCruz and Mr. O'Connor. The Japanese knew that Mr. deCruz was a personal friend of Mr. Gilbert, and might be able to outstay Mr. O'Connor. On the other hand, Mr. O'Connor was antagonistic at Mr. deCruz's poor management of the marketing function.

By June 10 Dale learned from Mr. Ito that the new man was now looking at schools and was trying to locate an apartment. He was sure that one of the top managers was going to be replaced. Dale explained:

> Mr. Ito had seen Mr. Simon come out of Mr. O'Connor's office that morning looking quite sad. In addition, Mr. Ito had also seen the new man at the company on the past Saturday—looking through the accounting department. From this he inferred that Mr. Simon was the man to be doomed.

On June 11 Dale met two staff men working for Mr. Gilbert in marketing and distribution. They had come to Japan from Hong Kong to investigate a recent sales decline and inventory buildup. Dale worked with them during the week and became close friends with them.

On Friday, June 14, Dale entered into a conversation with Mr. deCruz, who had just returned, and the two staff men from Hong Kong. He stated:

> After discussing Japanese philosophy, we eventually began talking about the company's problems with Mr. deCruz. I told him that the Japanese perceived that Mr. Gilbert was undermining Mr. O'Connor's authority and that this was hurting the morale and operating ability of the company. He agreed.
>
> The men from Hong Kong confirmed that this was the actual case and that New York was aware of it. However, they said that top management didn't want to change management again, and they felt that Mr. O'Connor was to blame for letting this happen.

They felt he had alienated himself from the management team and had played politics rather than taking actions and setting definite policies.

As we began discussing more specific problems, Mr. O'Connor entered the room and took a seat. After about 20 minutes, he asked me when we were going to have lunch to find out what I had learned. We set lunch for Tuesday.

Later that day, Dale met with an industry news reporter who had followed Northern's operations in Japan since 1960. The reporter spoke freely of his own opinions about Northern's problems in Japan. Dale explained:

> He felt that part of Northern's problem in Japan came from the fact that they brought in managing directors who had been successful in underdeveloped countries. These men would then implement policies which had been successful before but were not appropriate in a developed market like Japan.
>
> He also saw the Japanese management as a problem. He said that Japanese who work in a foreign company and are able to speak the foreign language consider themselves better than other Japanese, and eventually become atypical of the majority of Japanese—becoming isolated from Japanese culture and social norms. He inferred that the Japanese managers were managers because they spoke English, not because they could manage. Because of this problem, their security would eventually become threatened from poor performance. The normal response would be to "cover up" poor results and to, in essence, interfere with communications to top management. This dysfunctional behavior would succeed because of the foreign manager's dependence on their English ability.

On Tuesday, June 18, Dale had lunch with O'Connor and Simon. As it turned out, O'Connor was listening and Dale was quite frank. Both men complained about Mr. deCruz as being incapable of handling the marketing job. O'Connor told Dale:

> Mr. deCruz is not a disciplined thinker. He has not been able to manage the marketing group, and I haven't been able to get rid of him. As you may know, Mr. Gilbert selected the managers and I had nothing to say about it. This is a real problem since we must work closely together if we want to succeed. I have told Don Gilbert that I just can't work with this man, but he refuses to do anything, and in this organization it is suicide to bypass the chain of command. As a result, I don't think we can come to grips with our real marketing problems.

Dale realized at lunch that Mr. O'Connor was taking his frustrations out by drinking. During lunch, O'Connor had three double martinis and two brandies. Near the end of lunch, O'Connor asked Dale to look at a specific marketing problem:

> One problem I don't understand is why we're losing so much money in our retail operations. Maybe you could look at it and see what you find.

Marketing management

Mr. deCruz, having returned from home-leave, immediately settled into working a 14- to 16-hour day. Dale soon learned that he normally came to the office about 6:00 A.M. and would go home after 8:00 P.M. Dale began to understand why the Japanese often commented that he was a "hardworking" man, though they seldom made any other value judgments about Mr. deCruz. During the week, Dale spent time looking at the retail sales problem. He spent most of his time collecting sales data by shop to determine where the problem areas might be. One problem he found, which was causing dealer frustration, was the slowness with which orders were being filled—some deliveries taking two weeks. When Dale questioned the order processing people, he found a slow, bureaucratic paperwork system which would delay shipments by seven to ten days. On Thursday, he questioned Mr. Simon, and found there was a conflict in policies. He observed:

> Mr. Simon expressed disagreement with Northern's marketing policy. He felt that controls should be tightened to "keep people from stealing us blind." He didn't seem to mind that it could be affecting sales since he was more concerned with eliminating shortages and cutting expenses.

Dale continued collecting sales data. That afternoon, before going home, Dale stopped by Mr. deCruz's office only to find himself involved in a conversation between Mr. Vano, the personnel section chief, and Mr. deCruz regarding employee bonuses. It turned out to be an enlightening experience for Dale, as he explained:

> I hadn't spent much time with Mr. deCruz so I couldn't form an opinion about his effectiveness as a manager. However, as he began discussing bonuses with Mr. Yano, I soon realized that Mr. Yano could not speak English very well and was, apparently, totally unable to follow the conversation. Mr. deCruz didn't seem to recognize the lack of communication and persisted in his questioning. As Mr. Yano became more nervous, I asked him in Japanese whether or not he understood the questions. Without replying, he finally excused himself and left the room. When he returned, he brought the secretary with him to translate. Later, Mr. deCruz asked me if I had realized that Mr. Yano was not understanding the discussion and was quite surprised when I said, "yes."

On June 20, during lunch with four Japanese marketing managers, Dale heard discussion concerning a misunderstanding as to who was in charge of the marketing organization. Dale explained:

> Mr. O'Connor had issued a memorandum, when Mr. deCruz went on leave, directing all marketing people to report directly to him. This had not been changed when Mr. deCruz returned. As a result, the marketing people were rather confused as to whom they should report.
>
> This led to a discussion of the political situation that had developed not only among the Americans but also within the Japanese management

group. It seemed people were spending half their time talking politics rather than working.

Mr. deCruz had invited Dale and his wife for dinner that evening. They were to meet at the office at 6:00 P.M., but Dale and his wife arrived about 5:30 only to find the 2:00 P.M. weekly marketing meeting still in progress. It continued until almost 6:30 during which time Dale, sitting near the open door, listened to the discussion. He explained his impression of the meeting.

> There seemed to be little discussion of the problems and little direction to the conversation. In fact, when one of the Japanese managers raised an issue for discussion, Mr. deCruz seemed to derail any positive discussion by telling anecdotes about his past experiences in South America. It was no wonder the meeting was dragging on so long, but it seemed a waste of time.
>
> When the meeting finally broke up, I talked with several of the Japanese managers. One commented that the pressure was off, now that Mr. O'Connor was no longer running the meetings. There was no memorandum sent out either.

During dinner, Dale questioned Mr. deCruz deeply to fully determine his strengths and weaknesses. He discovered that Mr. deCruz's total business experience had been in South America, where he had been born. Though he had been educated in Canada, he was fluent in Spanish and Portuguese. He had never been in a situation where he could not communicate directly with people, and seemed not to recognize the importance of this problem. He also seemed unable to empathize with people, which only made the problem worse. As a result, Dale believed that many issues which came up for discussion were never fully resolved.

> From our conversation and from observing Mr. deCruz, it seemed that if he discussed an issue once, he expected everyone to fully understand it and that it should "automatically" be taken care of. Earlier, he had expressed his distrust of the Japanese and as a result was doing much of the detail work himself—for promotions, sales data, and so forth. It was no wonder he was working 12 to 14 hours a day.
>
> He also seemed to be unaware of the political climate. He expressed awareness of Mr. O'Connor's dislike for him but couldn't understand why. He considered the job a challenge and refused to quit.
>
> He didn't understand the confusion within the marketing organization. Mr. O'Connor had even run the marketing meeting on the week Mr. deCruz returned. Mr. deCruz mentioned that one of the managers had asked if he should still report to Mr. deCruz.

On June 24, Dale discovered that he was unable to determine sales by product and channel. He then discussed the problem with the EDP manager, who agreed to develop a program and produce the data by Friday. The results looked quite useful, and showed a major weakness in Northern's sales. While competition was selling nearly 65 percent through department stores, Northern's sales were less than 2 percent. There were also many models which weren't selling and which Dale felt could be eliminated. He discussed this with Mr. deCruz.

> Mr. deCruz seemed unwilling to reduce models, or even to limit models by channel because of the complexity in doing so. He also recognized the weakness in department store sales but expected them to increase to 6 percent of total sales by year-end. I also suggested that he might think about hiring an outside man to start a management training program for shop managers. He admitted such a need but gave excuses why it couldn't be done. I found it very hard to discuss such needs because he kept giving excuses why it couldn't be done. He would also frequently change his position on an issue several times during the same conversation.

Mr. O'Connor then came into the office and sat down. In a rather frustrated tone he mentioned that he couldn't get any straight answers out of the distribution manager. The Tokyo warehouse lease had expired, and no one had yet found a new warehouse. This had been going on for six months. He suggested that Mr. deCruz look into the matter. Dale volunteered to help.

> As Mr. O'Connor began to leave, I replied, "I'm not of much value but I could go around with the Japanese to try and find a warehouse." He said he would appreciate it, so we had the distribution manager come in to discuss the matter. By the end of the next week we had found a new warehouse.

During lunch with several Japanese managers, Dale raised the issue of management development. The managers seemed willing to discuss the topic and expressed the feeling that they were not business executives, nor had they even received any training. Many of them had joined as interpreters, or even messengers, and had become managers because of their English ability, not their business ability. They expressed a desire for a good leader, whose ability they could respect, to teach them and lead them. They said they would "work like crazy" for such a man, one who would listen to and communicate with them.

On Monday, June 30, Dale arranged to have lunch with Mr. O'Connor to discuss his findings. He explained his observations:

> I told him that the basic problem was one that could be extended to the whole company. It was a problem of training. With a continuing turnover in foreign management, 12 general managers in 18 years, training had been ignored at all levels. None of the Japanese had been trained as managers.
> Mr. Simon, who had joined us, broke in and said, "How can you ever expect salesmen to be managers? That's just foolishness!" I ignored him, and he sort of faded out of the conversation.
> I expressed a need to begin training present managers in how to use management information to help them plan and make decisions. I explained that many of them felt they were only interpreters or errand boys

for the foreign managers. I said I wasn't sure that they knew what was involved in decision making. I felt that once the managers were involved in training, we could begin with the sales managers—many who had never even had sales experience.

I suggested that the most successful retail store could be used as a training ground for sales managers. The key to success is to develop shop managers who can recruit, train, and control their salespeople, and keep them in the company. This would also require greater flexibility on the part of sales managers in compensating their people—compensation varies widely from town to town.

I also expressed the need for an English training program within the company. I expressed my discontent at Mr. Simon's daughter charging $10 per hour to give English lessons to company employees. The money was even being deducted by the company from the employees' salaries.

After returning to the office, Mr. O'Connor had Dale come to his office and called in his secretary to take notes on the problems that had been discussed. Later Dale asked Mr. O'Connor some questions about the new replacement.

I asked Mr. O'Connor who the new replacement was. He asked me who I meant. I said that I had heard that Mr. Simon was being replaced. He asked me if that was true, and I said—so far as I had heard—it was.

He then told me that Mr. Gilbert had come to him about replacing Mr. Simon, but he had told Mr. Gilbert that if Mr. Simon went he had better look for another general manager. He said he couldn't believe how Northern operated. It was like one big social club.

I suggested that because he couldn't get rid of Mr. deCruz, he had actually lost much of his authority in the company. He looked at me and said, "I guess we all have to stand up and be counted some day, and maybe it's my time!" He continued, "I couldn't really believe that a company could operate like this and maybe its taken me this long to realize it's true!"

Dale and O'Connor finished their conversation at 5:30 P.M. The next day, Mr. Ito asked Dale what had happened.

Mr. Ito was curious as to our conversation. When I asked him why, Mr. Ito said that O'Connor had talked with him after I left, and Mr. Ito was surprised to find O'Connor in such good spirits and so friendly.

During the next two weeks, Dale completed a marketing survey in Japan. On July 15, Dale and his wife departed for the Philippines.

The report on Japan

After considering the implications of this report, Dale decided to send a draft of his report to Mr. O'Connor in Japan. (See Exhibit 2 for a copy of the letter and draft.) Though Dale had already received a short note from Mr. Hill reminding him of the expected report, Dale had decided to delay the report and sent a short note to Mr. Hill explaining the delay. He was now waiting for Mr. O'Connor's reply.

EXHIBIT 2
Copy of letter about Japanese operations

NORTHERN INDUSTRIES, INC. (PHILIPPINES)

Mr. J. O'Connor
Managing Director
Northern Industries (Japan)
Tokyo, Japan

Dear Mr. O'Connor:

After spending time in Japan's rather hectic environment, it's rather nice being in the more relaxed atmosphere of the Philippines. Northern doesn't have any really serious management problems here. The organization is about one third the size of Northern Japan which certainly makes for much easier control and problem solving. They have a good bunch of people who are willing to work seven days a week. The morale is also exceptionally high.

I have put together a few thoughts concerning Northern (Japan) and would be most interested in your comments and criticisms, and so forth. I have yet to report anything to Northern management, but would like to do as accurate a job as possible when the time comes.

I have appreciated your past comments about the Northern operation and would be interested in your comments on this letter. Thank you very much for your help and cooperation while I was in Japan.

Yours truly,

Dale Morris

To:	Mr. A. Hill, Vice President of Personnel	
From:	D. Morris	*Draft*
Re:	Report of Japanese Operations	

Over the past 18 years, Northern (Japan) has had ten general managers and numerous marketing and finance managers. With management turning over (on the average) every year and a half, it is virtually impossible for any single manager to have enough time to determine his problems, take appropriate action, and follow through to make sure that policies are properly implemented and adjusted as nec-

EXHIBIT 2 (continued)

essary. Each new manager introduces changes in operations and policies, some-times drastically different from the old methods of operations. Since no single management team stays long enough to follow through with his new programs, the Japanese managers have become extremely hesitant, and very slow, in imple-menting new policies or changing old ones. They seem rather certain that present foreign managers will soon be replaced by New York management, so they just sit back and wait. Since Northern (New York) has continued to follow this long-standing policy, the Japanese feel no urge to work in support of any specific for-eign management team. As a result, new management teams have the odds stacked against them since they can not obtain "real" cooperation from the Japa-nese management.

The above problem has also been intensified by foreign management's reliance on English-speaking Japanese. Employees who speak English or began as inter-preters have been most successful in becoming managers. With the rapid turn-over of foreign management, an interpreter may be promoted by succeeding management (since he can most easily communicate with the foreigners). How-ever, since these individuals have never been trained as managers, it would be more realistic to call them management interpreters. This leads to a lack of trust between both parties because the foreigners soon learn that these Japanese won't accept responsibility while the Japanese constantly fear for their jobs. This may be considered one situation where the Peter Principle is applied. Of course, the Japanese have been coping with this system for many years, and as a result are able to "act" as necessary to please or impress the foreign management. The writer is not sure that they even realize their own actions, but it seems quite clear to the lower level employees at Northern (Japan). The lower level employees have been directly affected by this "acting" since their own needs have been ignored, as they have no communication with top management.

The average company in Japan has a strong personnel department to handle the needs of the employees and the future personnel needs of the company. They are responsible for the hiring, training, establishing of wage systems, and even promotion of employees. This is an important function and must be handled properly in Japan, where lifetime employment is the custom. However, Northern has never had such a personnel department. Instead, each manager has the above-mentioned responsibilities: without company policy or control of recruit-ing, without equitable wage systems, and without training programs for training future managers. As a result, the problems of low morale and poor managers are not being dealt with in the long term. Long-run policies to improve morale and management ability became secondary to needs for immediate improvement of sales or profits.

The replacement of Mr. Simon is simply reinforcement of the historic policy of frequent management turnover. This will make it as difficult to work with the Japanese in the future as it has been to do in the past. The Japanese are also well aware of conflicts within top management, abilities of top managers, and interfer-ence by New York as top management tries to do its job. The Japanese are well aware of deCruz's inadequacies as marketing manager and have resigned them-selves to failure under his leadership. They are equally aware of the fact that Mr.

534

EXHIBIT 2 (concluded)

Gilbert has interfered in this matter, resulting in the undermining of Mr. O'Connor's authority. The above situations have simply sustained rumors of replacements and continued trouble for present management. This also leads to the Japanese spending much of their time and energy worrying about what the future holds for them, and many of them work only for their own benefits.

Many of the above problems were being effectively dealt with by Mr. Simon. His first year and a half was spent building a strong organization with people capable of handling their jobs. Unfortunately, this action has yet to be taken within the marketing organization.

A reporter for *The Times* told me that Northern's lack of success was caused by foreign managers who surrounded themselves with interpreters. He explained that Japanese have an inferiority complex to foreigners, but once a Japanese learns a foreign language, he feels superior to other Japanese. This eventually changes his attitude and principles so that he is no longer a "pure" Japanese in his thinking. As a result, the foreign managers never really learn the proper way to operate in Japan and never really understand the Japanese mentality. He further stated that most of the top management had experience in less-developed countries which has led them to implement policies which were not suitable for a highly developed and marketing-oriented country like Japan. He also pointed out that Northern's poor dealer sales in the past (when they established retail shops) were due to turnover in top management. The dealers lost their trust in Northern and felt that Northern was trying to cheat them when they continuously changed their marketing policies. As a result the dealers shifted their loyalty to competitive brands and Northern began to develop retail shops as sales dropped. I'm not sure that this isn't a bit too simplistic, but I'll leave this to your judgment.

case 22

Midway Foods Corporation (D$_2$) (revised)

In February 1958, Midway Foods Corporation produced three principal items: two packaged food products and its Midway brand of candy bar. In addition, it purchased from Sherwood & Co., Ltd., of England its Robin Hood brand of candy bar for resale in the American market. Since candy sales accounted for most of Midway's volume, the company was basically a competitor in the candy subdivision of the food industry. And since both bars utilized chocolate as a principal ingredient, in a more direct sense Midway was a competitor in the chocolate bar segment of the candy industry.

COMPANY HISTORY

During 1949 Midway Foods had gone into bankruptcy. When the present management purchased it, there had been no shipments for over eight months. At that time Midway occupied a decrepit factory building on Maxwell Street, a location immediately adjacent to Chicago's "flea market" where residents and peddlers sold or traded everything from fish and fur coats to buggy whips and rebuilt lawnmowers. Midway manufactured several food products under less than ideal conditions in a plant where it was extremely difficult to maintain even minimal sanitation standards. Its products were distributed in Cook County and surrounding areas through jobbers to a limited number of small retail accounts, and its Midway bar was known to local wholesalers for its poor quality, poor appearance, and a price fully equal to that of competing products. Because of the characteristics of its products, and also because the previous management had "robbed the trade" during the war when rationing made that possible, Midway enjoyed singularly bad relations with the trade.

In the 1956–57 season, sales had passed the $6 million mark and were expected to exceed $7 million in 1957–58. The brand had been successfully launched throughout the Midwest, and had achieved some distribution on a

535

nationwide basis. In the words of one industry source, "Midway not only has the goodwill of the trade, they have its respect." The company had moved to a five-story plant in Cicero, Illinois, increased employment to 100 people, and increased output of the Midway bar by more than 5,000 percent. The Midway bar was still below average in size, but had been considerably improved quality-wise so that it became average in the market. The product line had been reduced by the discontinuance of all but two of the packaged food items, and a second candy bar had been added—the Robin Hood bar.

Corporate characteristics

During his months of field exploration the researcher listed a number of factors that seemed to him to be dominant in Midway operations.

One characteristic appeared to be management's adherence to its explicitly formulated concept of corporate purpose. While the long-range target was "to become one of the major companies in the American candy industry," there were four shorter range purposes or missions. First, management wanted the company to achieve "scope," a size at which the Midway line would be an important one with its brokers, at which the company could support a certain minimum selling organization, and at which it could begin to achieve efficient use of television advertising. To implement this purpose, it was early company policy to aim for growth rather than profits and to plow all available funds into additional advertising to achieve increased sales. Second, Midway aimed to sell only nationally branded food, with "no one-shot deals, no subcontracting, and no unbranded items." Third, the company aimed to be a marketing company—a company that relied on its marketing skills for survival and growth, and one that would not take on any activities "for corollary reasons." People at all levels in the various departments seemed to understand and accept this concept of corporate purpose. Finally, the company wanted to accomplish these things without outside equity capital. Midway was privately held and intended to remain that way at least for the foreseeable future.

A second characteristic was management's readiness to take very sizable risks. Management stated that in order to go national as rapidly as possible the company had to spread its resources thin. "The risks in doing this are great, but so are the rewards," said Mr. Clark Kramer, president of Midway. To implement rapid expansion on limited resources, the marketing department prepared a budget which "has no fat in it for contingencies. If the marketing vice president[1] thinks we can get by on $4,000 for TV in Atlanta, that's all he asks for. If it rains, or the TV program is a flop, he has to come back for some more money," Mr. Kramer said. "I understand the risks in-

---

[1] Milt Lombard.

volved and concur 100 percent in doing it this way. Any other way we couldn't have grown the way we have."

A third characteristic was management's willingness and ability to make changes within the company and, in a more limited way, its initiative in influencing its competitive environment. This process of adaptation involved both destruction of existing systems and creation of new ones. Four examples, three internal and one external, were apparent to the researcher:

Internally, one example of this process was (1) the discarding of conventional record keeping in favor of punched card data processing. Each sales invoice coming to the company was represented on a punched card, and subsequent accounting and statistical reports were prepared from the cards. (2) The manufacturing department had become adept at tearing down and rebuilding old machines for higher speed and more automated operation. (3) Finally, the company's organization had undergone considerable change, and numerous "less adaptable" people had been let go in the process.

As part of its influence on its environment, Midway had been instrumental in destroying the conventional concept of a candy broker. Management had insisted that brokers employ detail men to call on retail outlets. In the first years, Midway paid part of the cost of these men. While not new in the food industry, permanent detail men were almost nonexistent in the candy industry prior to 1953. In the succeeding years Midway had "persuaded" its brokers to hire detail men and had replaced brokers who would not be persuaded. By 1957 other candy companies were beginning to follow suit, and brokers all across the country were beginning to recognize the need to hire detail men in order to remain competitive.

Fourth, and more difficult to define, was a group of characteristics descriptive of the people who made up the management of Midway. Youth (the average age of the four top executives was 39.8 years), drive, hard work and long hours, quick thinking and decisive actions, willingness to experiment, and, finally, esprit de corps seemed to characterize the personnel of Midway. One of the vice presidents said: "Even the clerks can tell this company is going places—one of them comes in at 4:00 A.M. during the rush season to see that things are ready to go out when the trucks arrive."

Finally, on a more technical level, corporate marketing strategy appeared to be clearly defined, and defined in terms which suited the company's position in the industry.

A visit to Midway

Leaving Chicago's Midway airport, the researcher took a bus north along Cicero Avenue, the heart of Cicero, a once notorious Chicago suburb situated on the "near west side." The bus passed several miles of combined residential and industrial buildings, including the Hawthorne plant of the

Western Electric company, "automobile row," and several partially completed urban clearance and renewal projects. The researcher got off the bus, walked west through a run-down semi-industrial neighborhood, which adjoined a slum area known as one of Cicero's toughest, turned a corner and saw the familiar picture of a Midway bar, freshly painted on a high wooden fence. The fence enclosed a yard at one side of the factory, an old five-story building with a sign painted high on one wall reading, "Home of MIDWAY Foods." The researcher walked into the yard, passed the parked cars, the loading dock, a shed used for storage of old machines and miscellaneous junk, and through the main entrance into the shipping room. On the far side of the shipping room he waited for the only elevator to come down and the freight to be unloaded, and then he and a messenger rode to the fifth floor.

The elevator opened upon a long, narrow hallway which was partially blocked by a receptionist's desk and which led into the general office area. The researcher said good morning to the president's secretary, an attractive brunette whose desk was at the end of the hall. To his right were desks, filing cabinets, and the partitioned offices of two of the vice presidents; on his left was the president's office. After a few minutes' conversation with the secretary, the researcher knocked on the president's door and went in. Mr. Kramer looked up from his work and said, "Good morning, come on in."

The researcher put his papers on Mr. Kramer's desk, took off his coat, and sat down to enjoy the comforts of the spacious, air-conditioned office that was in striking contrast with the remainder of the plant and its surrounding environment. In addition to the window air conditioner, the well-appointed office contained a sofa, rug, and several chairs; a TV set; and a long, ultramodern desk, behind which sat Mr. Kramer in his swivel chair.

"What would you like to talk about today?" Mr. Kramer asked.

"First I'd like a little background on some of the changes during the past seven years."

"OK. Let's go. Midway is an old company which prospered during the war and then went downhill into bankruptcy. It wasn't a going business when I bought it—a low-quality product, a small group of unskilled factory people, very poor trade relations, and a local distribution organization.

"We feel we have come quite a way since then. Sales have gone from about zero to over $6 million on Midway alone. We now have an adequate plant instead of the run-down one on Maxwell Street. And we have a second candy line, the Robin Hood brand which we market for Sherwood & Co. On that brand alone there has been considerable growth, over 150 percent since we became their marketing agents two years ago.

"A lot has changed. Milt Lombard has the factory in shape and running with reasonable efficiency. It's not like Maxwell Street where we used to have to set up the end of the production line in the street each day—and where Milt was sleeping in the factory when we went to operating a third shift. We now have national distribution on the Midway brand, and we are becoming one of the major television advertisers in our industry. Also, just this month we have added an administrative vice president to help us modernize our paper work and to increase our emphasis on profits. Hiring him was part of our plan to shift from 'phase one' to 'phase two.' "

"What do you mean, 'phase one' and 'phase two'?" the researcher asked.

"Phase one was growth. For the past seven years we have had one major objective, scope. We have been trying to expand sales, to achieve national scope. We weren't so interested in profits because profits on small volume don't mean very much. In fact, going for scope has tended to keep our profits small; we have invested most of our gross margin in additional advertising.

"But now we are large enough to begin aiming for profits. We are calling it phase two of our development, and it will be to expand more slowly and begin to reap the profits of our advertising investments. We need the profits for two reasons: (1) we have to add to our capital resources in order to continue our expansion and (2) we want to be sure we can run an \$8 million business at a profit before we become an \$80 million business."

"Does this shift mean you are going to be trying to operate at reduced risk from now on?"

"Exactly. Beginning with the 1958–59 season we will be aiming for a more conservative approach. Thus far we have gone all out to increase sales and have taken the risks because we had to in order to achieve the necessary scope. And if something went wrong, we were small enough so that I could make up for it by not drawing salary or some such thing. Now we have reached a size where that is no longer the case.

"One other thing; to achieve growth with real stability we must diversify both within the candy industry and out into the food field. We want to begin this when we have a good opportunity, and also when we have achieved more depth in our organization."

Executive personnel

As of mid–1959, Midway's executive organization was composed of the following personnel:

Clark Kramer	President
Hal Reiss	Marketing vice president
Andy Kallal	Sales vice president
Milt Lombard	Manufacturing vice president
Otto Lehman	Head of research and development
Ben Nagle	Administrative vice president

Management meeting

At a general management meeting held on February 14, 1959, the discussion turned to Item 2 of the agenda, "title and salary review." The first person to be considered was Sam Painter, a member of the administrative department.

EXHIBIT 1
Salary and bonuses for Sam Painter

Year	Month	Weekly pay	Bonuses
1956	July	$ 60	$ 30
	December		
1957	February	65	
	August	70	
	December		200
1958	January	75	
	March	80	
	April	90	
	August	100	100
	December		325
1959	February	120	

Midway management stated that Sam had been a controversial employee; some of his attitudes had been resented by fellow employees and by the executive group. Sam was 26 years old and had a high school diploma. Prior to employment at Midway he had been a dental technician. After six months with Midway, Sam had gone into the Army. Upon his release in 1956 he rejoined Midway at a salary of $60 a week. Changes in his salary since 1956 are shown in Exhibit 1.

C. Kramer: Now let's go on to Item 2.

B. Nagle: Well, this subject has been on a few agendas, but I think it now becomes more pointed. When Joe Rivers[2] left, Hal made a suggestion that Joe not be replaced, that the job be abandoned, and that the various people who had reported to Joe report to me. Some months ago, we decided not to have a controller for the time being. We also agreed that this group would review any promotions of people who report directly to a vice president. [With the departure of Joe Rivers, Sam Painter reported directly to Mr. Nagle.] We agreed we should all review these people because their positions must, of necessity, become bigger and broader. And I would like to have a sense of direction on the staff we now have. Now I've taken one of these jobs which seems to be a debatable one—that's Sam Painter's—and let me read to you a job description which I prepared for background. "Sam Painter reports to the administrative vice president and at present he supervises one accounts receivable clerk, one credit clerk, three customer service clerks, and one warehouse inventory clerk. His basic functions are responsibility for the

---

[2] Joe Rivers had been employed in the administrative department as Mr. Nagle's assistant. He had been encouraged to resign three months previously.

proper administration of accounts receivable, cash receipts, credit limits, customer order processing, customer claims, freight claims on customer-into-warehouse shipments, warehouse inventory control, and intrawarehouse shipments."

Basically, he delegates responsibility and commensurate authority within a section for the effective execution of the foregoing functions. He is supposed to train and develop personnel under his jurisdiction for the assumption of more responsible duties. His specific duties are as follows:

"(1) *Credit and collection.* Determines credit limits for new accounts, assumes responsibility for prompt collection of accounts receivable, and prepares monthly aging reports of overdue accounts receivable.

"(2) *Customer order processing.* He is responsible for seeing that the customers' orders and inquiries are promptly and efficiently processed. . . .'"

H. Reiss: Is this . . . do we have to go through this, Ben, with each one of these guys?

B. Nagle: Yes, yes!

H. Reiss: I don't think this is the function of this meeting.

B. Nagle: Well, people ought to know what he does.

H. Reiss: Fine. Whatever you want him to do, let him go ahead and do it, but I don't think we ought to be burdened with job descriptions in a meeting.

B. Nagle: I was asked to prepare job descriptions. I'm doing what I was asked to do.

H. Reiss: [to Mr. Kramer]: Do you feel that this is the proper function of a meeting?

C. Kramer: Did I ask you to prepare them?

B. Nagle: Yes, sir.

C. Kramer: Did I ask you to read them at the meeting?

B. Nagle: You said to bring them in.

C. Kramer: Yes, but I don't recall that I wanted them read, Ben. I don't know about the other fellows, but I can't digest it. I think it's not important, really.

B. Nagle: I don't think you can discuss the scope of a man without knowing what he does.

H. Reiss: What do you want to do with these people, Ben?

B. Nagle: I want to know what management wants me to do with them.

H. Reiss: Well, you're management. What do you want to do?

B. Nagle: Well, to be specific, in my opinion Sam Painter has been a controversial personality for some time. The job he now performs is a responsible job. He has neither title nor proper salary for the job. The job calls for a title.

H. Reiss: Of what?

B. Nagle: Of something.

H. Reiss: What?

B. Nagle: As a "customer service supervisor," for instance, and "credit manager."

H. Reiss: Why should the title be such a long one?

B. Nagle: Well, he had to start in as credit manager.

H. Reiss: Customer service supervisor would certainly cover credit.

C. Kramer: Well, that's easy, Ben. If you want him to sign as credit manager, he can sign as credit manager, but his title doesn't have to be a hyphenated eight-word spread.

H. Reiss: I understand customer service as covering all those areas.

C. Kramer: How does he sign letters now?

B. Nagle: Well, customer service, except. . . .

C. Kramer: Then it would be very simple to have him sign letters "Sam Painter, Customer Service Manager," wouldn't it?

B. Nagle: Except that with the salary he's getting. . . .

C. Kramer: But mechanically it would be very simple.

B. Nagle: Well, letters of collection would be more normal if they had credit manager.

H. Reiss: I kind of like the term "customer service manager," Ben, instead of credit manager. When you really think of it, credit is one of the customer services. It's much more inclusive, and I don't think it hits the customer quite so hard.

C. Kramer: Not so much stigma to it.

H. Reiss: That's right.

M. Lombard: How old is this Sam?

H. Reiss: I'd say about 26. Do you want to go into this, "When I was 26. . . ."

M. Lombard: No, I'm more concerned with the title in relation to what you think of his maturity. He may be doing the job. I have a fellow running Cicero now who is the acting plant manager.

B. Nagle: I think . . . do you want my opinion? I think on an objective basis he does a very competent job, gets his work done, and is capable of growth. The only objection to him is what I would call on a subjective basis. His social attitudes might not be what we'd like; he might not be a type of personality we'd like to live with intimately. But a fact is a fact. He does a good job, and the question is do we want to live only with people we love or sometimes must there be someone in the pile that we don't love?

H. Reiss: To add to what Ben says, I have found that among our outside people he is considered to be extremely valuable; he answers almost all their needs, does it promptly, and does it efficiently. And a lot of the correspondence that used to come into the sales department, well, about 90 percent of it, is now directed to Painter, which would certainly indicate the kind of confidence customers have in him.

C. Kramer: What is he getting paid?

B. Nagle: One other thing here. In the past two weeks I've had an opportunity to get down to the grass roots. I think he's done a very commendable job in the last six months in the area of human relations. The people who are subordinate to him, I think, are beginning to like him. He gets along with them. Six months ago the chronic complaint was that he was supercilious, was a wise little acre; but the people like him now, I've found.

C. Kramer: You mean in two weeks you've suddenly changed from one opinion to another?

B. Nagle: Me? No. I say I've had a chance to dig down and find out about this. People at his own level and at other department levels are not so antagonistic towards him as they were six months ago.

H. Reiss: More important, I think almost everyone in the place that works with him respects his ability. I have a great deal of respect for his ability. One of the reasons people who work with him may dislike him is that he's a perfectionist. He demands good work from people. He has a great many personality problems; the prime one is his basic insecurity. I don't think we want to get into this at this particular juncture. The problem up for discussion is: Does Sam Painter deserve the title of customer service manager and the salary increase that goes with it? Is it that much of a promotion?

C. Kramer: Milt, what's your opinion? Are you close enough to it to have any feeling?

M. Lombard: I don't have much to do with Sam. That's why I asked the question about his age and what you fellows think about his maturity. Is he mature enough to carry that title, whatever that title means? Will a promotion help him now, or will it hinder him? These are things you fellows can better. . . .

B. Nagle: Well, that's what we're here for. He's wearing the robe. Shall we give him the mantle now? This is the problem we're going to be faced with right along with the development of a corporation with comparatively young executives. You're not going to hire 40-year-old guys for those kinds of jobs, or 35-year-old guys. This is going to be our pattern in the future. They're going to be around 25 and 27. Because of our age, we're not going to hire mature people.

H. Reiss: Well, Sam's problem is a personality problem. He walks around as if he's the cock of the walk, and in the terminology of the street I think he could be classified as a wise guy, a punk.

B. Nagle: Right.

M. Lombard: This is the point.

H. Reiss: Wait a minute, Milt.

M. Lombard: I don't want to call him that because I don't have much to do with him.

H. Reiss: You call a spade a spade.

M. Lombard: All right.

H. Reiss: He tends to be arrogant, but when you pin it down it's his attitude rather than fact. Now I believe that you can change attitudes. I believe that people change with responsibility; they grow as they get additional responsibility. I believe that the guy should be rewarded for the work that he does. And if he can't overcome this, it isn't going to hurt him any more as customer service manager at a hundred and a quarter a week than it did as customer service department at a hundred a week. But if he can't overcome this, he's got to understand that this is as far as he goes.

C. Kramer: I think that's not too significant from my point of view. What I'm interested in doesn't concern his present title or the title he will get at this meeting or the salary he will be raised to. I'm much more concerned with what type of man he is. I agree that as far as I know Sam is a real "hot shot." We just stumbled onto a really good man. He's a real worker, he's intelligent, and he's interested. There are only two things I have against Sam. Number one, I think he's an arrogant young punk. Number two, I don't like his views on segregation. Now, I can live in perfect happiness with a customer service manager who believes in segregation, but I could not live in happiness or work in happiness with a department head that believed in segregation. I just don't think this conforms enough with my own personal philosophy about life. And in case you're concerned here, I don't want to make a big thing over this, but I want us to think about this. Now, Sam is relatively young, it's true. I agree with you, Hal, that I think he can be changed. He was brought up in a blighted area, and his background contains all the things that you would think would lead a guy to be just what Sam has become. So it's no surprise that he's become this. I think if we work with him we have a pretty good chance of getting him to understand some things, and to have a much healthier attitude towards life in general and business in particular. I'm in favor of taking the step, incidentally. But I would be very much against the next step unless Sam shows a distinct and specific change.

[Heated discussion.]

H. Reiss: I think we've blown this up out of all proportion.

C. Kramer: Well, perhaps it seems that way, but it's important to me, Hal, because the Midway organization is very near and dear to me, and I'm concerned about the type of people in it. I say that being a great worker, an intelligent man, is not sufficient to cover up all things.

H. Reiss: Clark, when you were 19—let's say your emotional development and maturation processes were at 19 what his will be at 27 or 28—when you were 19, did you ever get the urge to throw down to your seniors a provocative idea just to gain the center of attention?

C. Kramer: I'm sure I must have, but I don't believe this is the case with Sam. I don't think we should discuss Sam's views on segregation or the reasons therefor. I've said that I believe he has these views.

H. Reiss: But. . . .

C. Kramer: We can discuss it later. But I also said that if these are his true views and if he doesn't change them, I don't think I can live at peace with him in the company. And if he goes further, as he will expect to go, and as we will expect him to go, then he must change his views. I don't believe in everyone in the company conforming to my views on everything or even anything except a few things, such as Mother, God, Country, and Integration, for example, and a few others. These I believe in as being the basic principles under which our country has existed and will exist. And if I don't believe in these things, then what's the use of it all, you see? And I don't want anybody in our company who is an opponent of what I consider to be these basic truths.

o o o o o

H. Reiss: All I'm saying is that this is part of Sam, this attitude of challenging accepted ideas, challenging his superiors, challenging people with whom he works. We've either got to knock this attitude out of him or he's done in our company.

C. Kramer: Let's not question the worth of his being provocative and stimulating and so forth. I'm merely trying to peer into the man to find out what is really there, and I'm saying that as willing as I am to go along with this step, this is as far as I can go; and if it comes up again, as it surely will, and I feel that he has not changed basically and truly in this regard, you have my promise that he'll not go any further in our company.

B. Nagle: What shall we call him, customer service manager or supervisor? Makes a big difference if you're going to start handing out manager or supervisor titles.

H. Reiss: Well, which do you want?

B. Nagle: I think supervisor is. . . .

H. Reiss: Is supervisor higher or lower?

B. Nagle: Lower.

H. Reiss: Lower. OK.

C. Kramer: I personally prefer manager. I don't feel strongly about either one, but it's a better word, I think.

B. Nagle: You mean as manager, then we'll call him. . . . It doesn't make any difference, the title.

C. Kramer: Customer service manager is a title everybody understands, and so forth.

H. Reiss: One more thing, while we're at it. What sort of salary bracket is this job? I don't see the need of going through this routine any time a man wants to be promoted within grade. . . .

C. Kramer: Hal, we have agreed—at one of our first meetings we agreed—that any man that was being promoted in various departments into a position of being manager would be discussed at this meeting because all of us will have to live with him, and all of us have opinions about him; and in the absence of any formal job evaluation program the best way to evaluate these people would be just the four of us sitting around talking about them.

H. Reiss: Well, then, suppose Ben wants to give him $10 in two more months. Does he come back to the group again for this?

C. Kramer: No. That's not the point.

B. Nagle: I don't want to create another Joe Rivers situation.

C. Kramer: That's the thing I'm thinking about.

Mr. Nagle proposed a 25 percent pay increase for Sam, from $100 a week to $125. After discussion it was agreed that a $20 boost immediately, with another $5 in six months, would seem more appropriate.

case 23

Hawaii Best Company (A)

Gradually rising from his chair in his third-floor plush office overlooking Waikiki Beach in Honolulu, James Lind, president of Hawaii Best Company (HBC), greeted Charles Carson, vice president and general manager of the company's Islands Division, and invited him to take the seat across from his desk.

"Charlie, I am sure that something has gone wrong," he said as Carson remained standing. "You have many fine qualities—I was the one who recognized them when I promoted you to vice president—but I have been reviewing your progress these past few months and . . . and the results have not met our expectations."

Carson fidgeted at the window, watching the October morning across the harbor. His face reddened, his pulse quickened, and he waited for Lind to continue.

"The costs in your division are higher than budgeted, the morale is low, and your branch managers are unhappy with your stewardship," Lind said. "And your cooperation with Gil Harris has fallen short of satisfactory."

Carson grew angrier at the mention of Harris, a young aggressive man with a master's degree from a well-known eastern business school. Harris was a latecomer to HBC, but Carson knew that everyone was pleased with his performance.

"Charles, at the country club last week, I was speaking to one of our vendors. He intimated that your dealings with him had not been entirely clean. This is what hurts me the most.

"I know you are 49, that your son is only 8, that this is a difficult time for you and your family," Lind concluded as Carson stared out the window. "You have spent almost all your life in Hawaii; . . . it would be difficult for you to move to the mainland. It will be even harder for you to find a similar position in the Honolulu community. But I must ask for your resignation, and I will do my best to help you find a more suitable opportunity."

"Jim, I can't believe it," Carson finally replied. "It's just all wrong." He turned slowly from the window, his face blood red.

"I have been with this company for ten years. I built this division. Sure, this year's results are not quite what you expect, but my division is still the largest contributor to corporate profits. I'll bet your friend Gil has been telling you about the vendor deals. Well, it's a damned lie, and I won't stand for it! That boy will stop at nothing to grab power."

There was a long silence as Lind and Carson stared at opposite corners of the large office. "I will not resign," Carson suddenly declared, and he left the president's office coughing, his face flushed, and his heart pounding.

Lind stood motionless as he watched the door close. He was uncertain about what to do; it never had occurred to him that Carson might refuse to resign. He decided to proceed as he had planned, but with one modification.

"Janice, please take a memo," he said to his secretary, and he dictated a note to Charles Carson informing him that his employment with HBC was terminated as of that afternoon, October 10, 1972.

After sending out a general release memo informing all division heads that Carson had resigned and that Joseph Ward, a promising young executive, presently employed as the manager of planning in the Operations Division, would assume the position of acting general manager of the Islands Division, Lind hurriedly left the office. He had less than an hour to catch the 12:30 plane, intending to visit each of the seven branch heads on the outer islands, to tell them about the change and their new acting general manager.

While Lind was having his memos sent out, Carson was trying to contact his previous boss and old friend, Roy North, past president of HBC and presently an influential member of the company's board of directors and its powerful executive committee. Carson intended to have the matter taken to the board for deliberation.

BACKGROUND

Mr. North was one of five members of the board's executive committee, which customarily approved the appointments, promotions, stock options, and salary adjustments of personnel earning over $10,000. This included department heads, division managers, and vice presidents. The committee held at least one meeting a month, and these, like the regular monthly meetings of all 12 board members, were well attended. (Exhibit 1 shows selected data about the directors.)

Several of the directors were descendants or close friends of the founders of the Hawaii Best Company, but only James Lind and Thomas Johnson were HBC employees. Board members held 5 percent of outstanding stock; the rest was widely owned by the people and business concerns in Hawaii. No one outside the board represented more than 1 percent of the HBC stock.

EXHIBIT 1
Board of directors, 1972

Name	Age, place most of life spent	Background	Current activity	Previous association in years		Number of shares represented
				Industry	Company	
Choy, Eduardo	65, Hawaii	No academic degree; financial	Entrepreneur; corporate chairman; banker	0	15 as director	3,000
Donahue, John	70, Hawaii	Engineer; retired	Retired corporate executive of the company; vice president of property management company	40 with company	8 as director	500
Eichi, Ishi	40, Hawaii	Legal; attorney	Practicing attorney	0	2 as director	0
Fields, J. B. *	54, Hawaii	MBA (Harvard); finance	Executive vice president of very large multinational company headquartered in Honolulu	0	15 as director	2,500 plus 4% owned by his company
Fong, Charles	40, Hawaii	MBA (Harvard); finance	Executive vice president of a real estate development and investment firm	0	2 as director	500
Hanley, Don *	70, Hawaii	Secretary	Retired	19	19 as director	10,000
Johnson, T.†	48, Hawaii	Accounting	Corporate treasurer of the company	15	2 as director	1,000

Lind, James*†	53, Mainland U.S.A.	Engineer; alumnus of Columbia Business School	Corporate president	28	2 as president and director	4,000
North, Roy*	56, Mainland and 16 years in Hawaii	Engineer; financial analyst	Executive vice president of a conglomerate headquartered in Honolulu	16	10 as director	1,500
Rusk, Dean*	52, Hawaii	Accounting and finance insurance; alumnus of Harvard Business School	Executive vice president of a local large company operating in insurance, sugar, real estate, and merchandising business	0	5 as director	0
Simon, A. F.*	65, Hawaii	Contractor; entrepreneur	Corporate chairman and president; entrepreneur	0	20 as director	30,000
Vogel, Lawrence	63, Hawaii	Finance; fiduciary	Corporate president; fiduciary agent; represents a large local trust	0	10 as director	0

* Member of the board's executive committee.
† HBC employee.

In 1971, with $30 million in sales and an eps of $1, the Hawaii Best Company was a manufacturer and marketer of a special formula. The company was listed on the Pacific Coast stock exchange with 1 million shares outstanding which yielded a stable dividend of $1 per share over the last five years. It sold its line of special formula X to industrial, commercial, and residential customers in the state of Hawaii. Its manufacturing facilities and three sales branches were strategically located in Honolulu, and seven other sales branches were spread over the outer islands. The company usually negotiated hard for its basic raw material K, used in the manufacture of special formula X, from its only locally available long-term supplier. Imports of the raw material were deemed uneconomical for HBC, and a second source of local supply did not appear on the horizon.

The company also sold special formula Y, but only in the outer island branches and not in Honolulu. It was purchased in finished packaged form from several vendors within and outside the state of Hawaii, but the company was in no way involved in its manufacture.

Over the past years the company's sales grew at an average annual rate of 4 percent, but its market share remained constant. Relative to the competition, HBC's profit performance had declined and, according to one competitor, "it was only through some 'creative' accounting that the company barely made its dividend in 1971."

HBC had two rivals in its industry: the larger company had annual sales of $60 million, the smaller sales of $15 million a year. It was a fiercely competitive industry, and special favors or discounts, although illegal, were sometimes granted to woo customers from another company. And customers were precious; just ten clients accounted for one quarter of HBC sales.

HBC's ORGANIZATION STRUCTURE

Exhibit 2 shows HBC's skeletal organizational structure. The president, James Lind, was responsible to the board of directors. Thomas Johnson, vice president finance and secretary, and President James Lind regularly attended the monthly board meetings, and other vice presidents were also invited frequently to keep the board informed on matters of importance in the area of their specialty. According to Andrew Simon, chairman of the board of directors, "This practice gives us an opportunity to know what we have underneath the first layer."

In addition to managing five divisions and attending to the normal duties of the president, Lind took a special interest in the negotiations involving labor contracts and purchasing of raw material K and special formula Y. The specific responsibility for negotiating labor contracts rested with the vice president of industrial relations, John Wyle. Control of the purchase of raw material K lay with the senior vice president of operations. The vice president and general manager, Islands Division, was responsible for buying special formula Y.

EXHIBIT 2
Organization structure, 1972

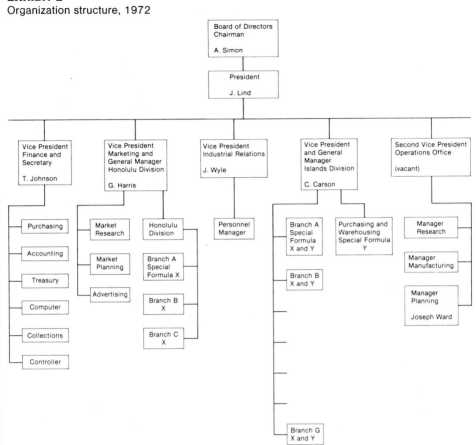

In all these negotiations, however, it was not uncommon for Johnson to get involved as well.

Among the corporate vice presidents in 1971, John Wyle, 51, had been the longest with the company. However, he had suffered two serious heart attacks since joining the company in 1945—one in 1959 and the other in 1968. According to the former HBC president North, "Wyle is the best industrial relations man we can find and he is a good personal friend of ours (their wives played cards together), but, frankly, his health concerns me and several of the directors."

Since joining the company in 1947 as a clerk, Thomas Johnson had risen to the position of vice president finance by 1968. In 1970, at the age of 46, he was elected to the company's board of directors at the suggestion of President Lind. Johnson had been actively under consideration for the presidency when Roy North vacated the position in December 1969. One member of the selection committee put it this way: "Johnson is quite happy in his present position. He is a little lazy. He never wanted the top job."

Gil Harris, 33, joined the company in March 1970 as vice president for marketing and general manager of the Honolulu Division, responsible for the conduct and performance of the three Honolulu branches and for the company-wide market research, market planning, and advertising campaigns.

As vice president and general manager of the Islands Division, Charles Carson had controlled the conduct and profit performance of all the branches in the state outside Honolulu. Carson also participated in the marketing decisions, such as advertising and promotions, and his division was charged a pro-rata share of expenses on the basis of divisional sales.

The Islands Division and the Honolulu Division were created by Lind in February 1970 after the sudden death of Vice President Sales Robert Gellerman, 46. Gellerman had been responsible for the company-wide sales and advertising throughout the state. Prior to the establishment of the two divisions, Lind consulted Chairman Simon, former HBC President North, and other members of the executive committee, and received their unanimous support. Also included in the restructuring were the functions of market planning and market research, which were consolidated under the new vice president for marketing and general manager, Honolulu Division.

The position of senior vice president operations had been vacant since May 1970, when Lind asked for the resignation of the man who had held that office. The three managers within the division—manufacturing, planning, and research—had since been reporting directly to Lind. They constantly vied for the attentions of the president and the corporate vice presidents in the hope that one of them could assume the vice presidency. Three key members of the board were acquainted with Donald May, the research manager, but the other two were virtually unknown to the board.

Arrival of James Lind

On January 1, 1970, James Lind replaced Roy North as president of Hawaii Best Company when the latter left the company to become an executive vice president of a multinational conglomerate headquartered in Honolulu. North, under whose control HBC had prospered for seven years, recommended Lind for the presidency after an unfruitful search for a candidate within the company and the Hawaiian community. The board of directors accepted Lind, then a top executive in a trade association in New York, and he soon proved to be a man of integrity, dedication, and charm.

Although the business community in Hawaii, according to some observers, was tight-knit and nearly impervious to outsiders, Lind was readily admitted and liked. The morale at HBC soared during the early months of his presidency because he was a man who was both extraordinarily hardworking—he put in up to 70 hours a week—and "human." He was one of the best fund raisers for community projects in Hawaii.

Financially, however, the company was not performing well under Lind's leadership. Rising labor and material costs, and the combination of the inflationary spiral and the fierce competition, put pressure on the profit margins. Lind began to make changes in key personnel in an effort to offset the problem.

In February he promoted Charles Carson, a man who had been with the company for over eight years, to vice president and general manager of the newly created Islands Division.

Three months later he asked for the resignation of Frank Adams, senior vice president for operations. Lind felt that Adams, after 27 years at HBC, was "utterly lacking in an ability to negotiate for key raw materials," and brought his grievance to the board of directors. Before Adams was asked to resign, a severance package was worked out and approved by the board. Adams, then 53, was utterly shaken. He became an estimator for a local construction firm at one quarter of his former salary. This was the first such severance in the history of the company, and as one director put it: "The event was extremely painful; it left deep scars on us and our families."

Lind's final major organizational change was to bring in an old friend of his whom he hoped could develop new marketing strategies for the entire company. Gil Harris, from the Global Chemical Company of New York, was made vice president for marketing and general manager of the newly formed Honolulu Division.

Lunch at the club

"Jason, thank you for meeting me here, and for canceling your other engagement to see me. I'm sorry, but I had to talk to you; something had happened that I think you should know about."

Charles Carson leaned heavily on the table in the restaurant of Honolulu's only country club. The man across from him curiously fingered the stem of his martini glass. Jason Fields, the executive vice president of the third largest international company based in Hawaii, was a busy and important man. An illustrious graduate of the Harvard Business School, Fields was one of the three most influential members of the company's board and its executive committee. Fields's employer controlled 4 percent of the HBC's outstanding stock. He did not have too much time to spend with Carson, his golf buddy and a VP of one of the two companies of which Fields was a director. (The other company was a major buyer from Carson's division at HBC.)

"I'll try to be brief," Carson said. "Jim called me to his office this morning and asked me to submit my resignation. I refused. But before he left for his bloodsucking trip, he terminated my association with the company as of this afternoon."

Fields raised his eyes briefly.

"I control the company's three largest customers, you know," Carson continued. "I can easily take them to the competition. But he still has the gall to accuse me of taking a kickback, with absolutely no proof! I think Harris has put him up to it. He's been charging a substantial proportion of his division's expenses to my division. I have been arguing with him about these expenses during the last several weeks, and he finally told me he'd have my head if I went to Lind about it.

"Not even a note of thanks. Not even a mention of it to the board," Carson murmured. "I wonder how long the board will allow Lind to destroy the very people who built this company.

"I don't know what to do."

"Neither do I, Charlie," Fields answered. "I'm truly sorry to hear about this. This is strange. I had no idea this was even being considered. The executive committee met this morning and Jim, of course, was there, but this was never mentioned. I'd like to help in any way I can, Charlie. . . . All I can say is wait and see what happens at the next board meeting. It's scheduled for October 17.

"Well," said Carson, "I just hope the board takes this chance to finally straighten up the organization. Its relationship to the company, the delegation of responsibility, the criteria for employee evaluation—there are a lot of things that have remained garbled and unclear ever since Frank Adams was asked to resign. The morale of the executive staff is low. Earnings are not improving. Everyone is concerned about his own skin. Who will be axed?"

Lind's turbulent ride

Lind was deeply shaken over Carson's refusal to resign, and on the plane to Maui he tried to analyze the situation. He realized that he had made a mistake in promoting Carson a year and a half ago, although the psychological tests that he had had administered to all executives at the time pointed strongly to Carson as the man for the job. Lind remembered, too, the annual physical checkup the company executives were required to undergo, and recalled sadly the high blood pressure and excessive cholesterol level that Carson's exams revealed.

"I must stick to my guns," Lind mused. "I refuse to be blackmailed by the three powerful customers Charlie has in his pocket. I cannot let my authority be challenged, especially by a man I believe has taken kickbacks."

After a sleepless night, Lind telephoned Andrew Simon to inform him of Carson's resignation.

"Yes, Jim, Jason Fields called me yesterday to tell me," Simon relayed.

"He was quite upset. And I saw Roy North at a cocktail party last night. He, too, knew about the event, and he appeared visibly disturbed. This is a sad situation. I am a little more than concerned, but you are the boss. We'll try to handle the matter appropriately at the board meeting next week."

Simon returned the receiver to the cradle thoughtfully. For the first time in his 20 years as chairman of the board, he felt that there was a conflict between the management of company affairs and the way he thought they ought to be managed.

Approaching 65, Simon was still active and healthy, and never missed a board meeting. He was once the caretaker president of HBC for one year in 1956. His deep concern for the company was reflected in the way he usually helped in its decision-making process—carefully—after long consideration and debate. He had discussed the matter of Adams's resignation privately first with Lind, then with the executive committee, and then with the entire board before Simon had been fully convinced that Adams should go. Similarly, he had spent long hours deciding on Lind's appointment, consulted extensively with several members of the board individually. Both Mr. and Mrs. Lind were interviewed thoroughly before the board selected him for the presidency.

case 24

Peter Olson

Peter Olson was 37 years old, and an assistant to the head of the Plastics Division of United Chemical Corporation. Peter had been with UCC for 14 years. UCC was a large chemical company with annual sales of approximately $1.25 billion; the Plastics Division, with sales of over $200 million, was one of UCC's fastest growing divisions.

Peter Olson graduated from Case University in 1956 and went to work for UCC immediately upon graduation as a research and engineering assistant. He held various positions in the fields of production and engineering, did well in all of them, and management let Pete know on many occasions that he was regarded as potential top-management material. In 1967 Pete was asked to move into the Plastics Division in charge of production planning. In 1968 he moved to the division's headquarters office, which was located in a small city about 30 miles from New York City, as head of long-range planning for the division. Early in 1970 he became assistant to the president of the Plastics Division. His salary was $27,000.

Peter Olson and his wife Toni had been married in 1959. Toni was a graduate of Wellesley and had lived on the East Coast all her life. Pete's career with UCC required the Olsons to make a number of moves, and although Toni made them without complaint, Pete knew that she had not been happy at the need for so many changes and did not enjoy their assignments in the South and Midwest. So far as the Olsons could tell, their two children made the adjustments to new surroundings very easily. Peter Jr., was 9, and Karen was 7.

When Pete took his job at divisional headquarters in 1968, both he and Toni were delighted to find an old salt-box colonial in the country 3 miles from the outskirts of Littleton. Littleton itself was a city of about 50,000 people and was a "bedroom" community for New York City. Both Toni and Pete found it easy to make friends in Littleton, and Toni was particularly happy to find so many women her age with interests similar to hers. Littleton's school system was excellent, and young Pete and Karen seemed completely happy in the Littleton environment.

Peter found that his new job as assistant to the president of the Plastics Division placed heavy demands on his time. Frequent trips to divisional plants were required, as were visits to large customers and branch sales offices. Pete believed that he was away from home on an average of 1½ weeks each month. During the remainder of his time, Peter Olson found that the demands of his office work were also heavy. His boss was a driver who expected a lot from his subordinates, and Pete spent many evenings at the division office and many others working at home. The work itself, however, was exciting, and Pete knew that he was doing a good job; he had been told that a nice raise would be forthcoming if his contribution continued high.

The Olsons had always been a close knit family, and Pete had realized for months that his absence from home and his long working hours created some strains on his relationship with Toni. Occasional minor frictions developed, and Toni said on several occasions that she was not sure whether "it's worth the rat race," but Peter's enthusiasm for his work, his evident love for his family, and Toni's own sense of balance succeeded in avoiding any serious problems. On two or three occasions Pete and Toni discussed how they might guide their activities to do more than simply offset the demands of Pete's job—they sought positive ways to build their own lives together. But the demands of Pete's job proved to be a more powerful force than the outcomes of these discussions.

In the late spring of 1970, UCC made some major organizational changes which were designed to create more authority at lower levels. Use of the profit-center concept was pushed further down in the organization. The Plastics Division itself was affected by the changes. Both UCC headquarters and the president of the division agreed that it should be split into four profit centers, though the structure and details of the changes had not yet been worked out.

On a pleasant spring evening in May, Peter Olson got home at about 9:45 to tell Toni that he had just been offered a position as head of one of the new profit centers. Annual sales would be in the neighborhood of $70 million, and the demand for the center's new lines of products was growing rapidly. Pete talked delightedly about the "million and a half" problems of sales, production, engineering, and organization that would be his responsibility, and the opportunity for advancement that the job represented. He was so excited that he talked without stopping for 40 minutes.

It dawned on Peter Olson that his wife had said nothing. Trying to find some way to wind down his oration, he said lamely, "Of course, we'll have to move out to Saint Louis. I've got to go out week after next, but you and the kids don't have to come until school finishes here."

Toni started fixedly at her husband. Finally she said "Peter dinner is cold. I'll have to warm it up." She rose and turned to go to the kitchen. As she got to the kitchen door she turned and said, "Peter, who the hell wants to live in Saint Louis?"

case 25

John Adams

> You know, if there is one topic I think we should spend more time talk-
> ing about somewhere in the Harvard Business School curriculum, it is
> "company atmosphere." It exists everywhere, obviously, but it certainly is
> hard to get a very good impression of what it will be like in a company you
> are considering going to work for. It turned out to be much more important
> to me than I had ever anticipated, and I really wish we had spent more time
> thinking about what it is, what influences it, how to recognize it early, and
> what the choices open to you are in learning to live with it. I sure ran into
> problems of this sort when I went to work for Accutronics right after I got
> my MBA in 1967.

John Adams, Harvard Business School graduate of 1967, was discussing
some of his experiences in his job of the preceding three years. Adams had
resigned his position a few weeks before and was stopping over briefly in
Boston to visit some old friends and classmates before proceeding to his new
job in Florida.

Spring 1967

Adams's first contact with Accutronics had been on a job interview trip
in the spring of 1967, shortly before his graduation from the Harvard Business School.

Accutronics was a Denver-based company that had started with the development and manufacture of specialized microwave and radar components and was trying to build up competence in highly sophisticated
electromechanical systems for military and space applications as well. The
company was strongly oriented toward research and technology. It had
grown very rapidly from sales of a few million dollars in the early 60s, when
it had been founded by a small group of business executives and university
scientists, to about $35 million per year in 1967.

In reviewing the impressions he had formed of Accutronics on this brief
1967 visit, Adams commented as follows:

I think what impressed me most about the company at that time was their strong commitment to growth and the emphasis they placed on individual ability and initiative in getting ahead. They really preached the virtues of competition. I must have been told a dozen times that they expected people to use their initiative and to take on responsibility for doing what needed to be done, and that as soon as you showed that you could handle the job, you would get more to do. They all said that there was simply too much opportunity for growth and too much to get done to worry about whether you would be infringing on someone else's private domain. In fact, the president had stated publicly that they were strongly committed to their policy of rapid growth, partly because this was necessary to provide enough career opportunities for the caliber of people they wanted in their organization.

I was to go to work in a headquarters staff group, which reported to the executive vice president, a fellow named Mike Butler. He was aggressive and forward and seemed to be a real go-getter. My first meeting with him was in his home, and he just about stood me up against a wall and fired questions at me. He wanted direct answers, too, not these "on the other hand" statements. He hit me with technical questions about radar sets, inertial guidance, what I expected to earn in five years, how many hours a week I would be willing to work, and so on. I don't think he expected me to know the answers to a lot of the technical questions; I think he was more interested in seeing how I responded to that sort of cross-examination. After awhile he called another vice president and told him—just as brusquely—that he had a good man at his house and arranged another interview for me.

Nobody was very specific as to exactly what I would be doing; they said they were much more interested in getting good men than fitting people in slots. Mike said the work at first would mostly be on special projects at headquarters and would also involve something he called "internal consulting," which meant working on problem areas in various parts of the company's operations. He said it would be an excellent chance to get around to various parts of the company and learn about their operations, and then after a few years to go out into one of the operating departments. He emphasized that they didn't want any career staff men, and that suited me fine.

The job met a number of the criteria that were important to me. It seemed like an environment in which I could get ahead, mostly on the basis of my own ability and level of effort and performance, rather than on seniority or politics; in fact, Mike told me that the main reason they were able to make such good headway against the big companies was that they didn't waste their time with very many rules or procedures or in internal jockeying for position and bickering. I must admit that appealed to me because I've been in organizations where it has been very different.

The company was also growing very fast, with no slowdown in sight. They all seemed to have a real drive to make Accutronics into a major industrial company, rather than just something which would provide them with security and a comfortable income. It looked like a good chance to make use of both my engineering and business training, too—a real challenge to try to deal with both the scientific and commercial worlds within the company.

The salary offer was pretty good—$13,000 which was above the offer most of the fellows seemed to be getting—but I did have a few higher offers elsewhere.[1] It sounded like the kind of work I would really like, though, and I was sure that if I did a good job the advancement in both position and money would be enough to keep me happy. I thought it might even give me some experience which could be useful if I ever saved enough money to be able to strike out on my own some day, which is still a dim goal I have tucked away in the back of my mind.

Adams had financed his business school education by a combination of savings and student loans and had graduated in the top third of his class. He was characterized by several of his professors as being unusually mature and well balanced; one of the slightly older students with some working experience whom they could rely on for constructive and commonsense comments. According to several of his classmates, he was the sort of person that people found it easy to talk to and had been well liked and respected. One friend characterized him as ambitious and a hard worker, but also a "strong family man," and said that he tried to spend as much time with his wife and child as is possible while attending the Business School. Another spoke of him as having a strong competitive spirit, but with equally strong ideas about fair play and consideration for others. He was remembered as being active in section activities, particularly the intramural sports program.

Previous to attending the Harvard Business School, Adams had obtained a degree in electrical engineering at a western college, had worked for a large steel company for about a year, and had served as an officer in the Navy for two years. He had been active in sports while in high school and college, and had won several wrestling championships. He and his wife were both from the same medium-sized northwestern city.

Fall 1967

In the fall of 1967, Adams wrote a few words to a classmate about his new job with Accutronics:

As far as the job is concerned, things are going just great. I have worked on a number of interesting projects already and have learned a lot both about how the company works and about some problems I never gave much thought to when I was at the B-School.

People certainly have a strong sense of identification with the company, as we used to call it so glibly, and I am beginning to see how it has come about. It does not come at all from what you could call a paternalistic atti-

---

[1] Average starting salary in 1967 for Harvard MBAs with an engineering degree was actually $12,000 (placement bureau records).

tude on the part of the company; it is completely different. I don't know what to call it; everyone is caught up in both the challenge and the reward of making the company grow. We have been doubling our sales every two or three years for a number of years, mostly through internal growth, and it looks like we will be able to keep that up for a while. There is no union out here, either; even the hourly employees seem to feel that they are a part of the team. The management tries to promote this feeling, of course, and they have done a good job of it.

They weren't fooling when they said the hours would be long! We don't get any overtime, of course, and I was amazed to find that people think nothing of working 60 hours a week regularly. I've worked over 80 hours a week for several weeks at a time, and if I had worked like that in the steel company I would have been carted off to the company headshrinker. Those hours are tough for the men with families, but I don't really mind it because this is such a dynamic and exciting place to be working. We have a congenial group in the department, and people seem willing to pitch in and get the job done. There are a number of us with MBAs in the department, and we all view this as a steppingstone for a better job out in the divisions.

One reason people work the way they do out here, I am sure, is that the officers themselves put in a fantastic workweek. They built up the organization from nothing and it took a lot of work, and their level of effort just filters down in the organization. If your boss works long hours, you do too. Besides, I think most people feel they are in on the ground floor now, and that the rapid growth will generate enough promotions to make the present long hours worthwhile. . . .

One thing that was both surprising and rewarding was to find that the level of education of most of the management out here is so high. Most people in my office have MBAs from somewhere, and of course we have a lot of Ph.D.s in the sciences around here. This makes the competition tougher, but it also makes it a much more rewarding place to work. I was also surprised at the number and quality of job applicants that we have. We seem to be getting the reputation of a growth company in a growth industry, and a surprising number of people from all over the country who want to change jobs for one reason or another seem to be attracted to our situation. Part of the reason for our popularity may also be the living conditions out here; we both have found them very pleasant.

Fall 1968

Adams wrote as follows about his first year at Accutronics:

Work is still exciting and worthwhile; the pace hasn't slowed down at all, and I feel I have learned a lot during the last year. I am still working on a variety of projects, just like when I started, but there are enough different things coming up constantly so that it by no means resembles a routine. I don't report directly to Walter Gorman (the department head) any more, though. We have expanded in this area a lot, and during the year two people with some previous experience were hired in above me. I must be the only member of the class of 1967 who has been "demoted" twice already and still likes his job! The company is still growing like a weed, though, so there are bound to be lots of opportunities opening up, even though people are brought in from the outside to fill some of them.

Nobody has left the department to go elsewhere in the company yet, either, although the department is now about two and one-half years old. That worries me a bit, because I didn't come out here to be a staff man all my life. I think part of the reason may be that some of the operating divisions and departments seem to regard us as spies from a competitor rather than as someone working for the same company, but maybe this is natural. They have been used to doing things their own way, and besides, I guess we often do regard them as enemies in our efforts to justify the importance of our department by ferreting out inefficiencies and showing how we can save money for the company. You inevitably get involved in politics and see people doing some things in order to protect themselves or "get" somebody else, but I guess that happens everywhere.

Just like with any job there are some drawbacks, of course. We do work long hours, and not all of it is necessary. Walter tries to establish an atmosphere whereby you come in on Saturdays unless you have something special going on at home, rather than coming in only if there is something special going on at work. I think one of the ways he tried to do this was pretty funny. On a few Saturdays when I was not in he left a little note on my desk saying "see me." Each time when I talked with him on Monday morning, he said he got someone else to do it and implied I missed out on something worthwhile without saying what it was. I came in about 11:00 A.M. one Saturday and found a note on my desk, and so I went right over to ask about it. He was completely at a loss about it because he had left it there only five minutes ago and there really was nothing that he wanted anyway! I still come in most Saturdays, though—it is simply expected, and most people do.

I now see that one of the reasons people work so hard is that there are a lot of what I would call "false crises," or deadlines which are shorter than they need to be just to get people to do more work. The president even stated at one of the regional management conferences that this was something he did deliberately in order to get more work out of his people, and I'm not so sure that I like that. But it does seem to accomplish his objective, even though people view it as something temporary.

I've gotten to understand the company a lot better during the past year, and I really give the management a great deal of credit for what they have been able to build up from virtually nothing. Lots of them are millionaires now, and the stock is still going up. I wish I had more money to put into it. And one of the most interesting things to me has been the insight you get into how the problems of a company change as it becomes larger, and how difficult it is for the management to change their behavior as the problems get too complicated to handle on the "personal" basis that worked so well during the earlier stages.

Summer 1970

Back in Boston briefly while en route to his new job in Florida, Adams commented as follows about his recent career at Accutronics and his reasons for leaving:

I've now taken another job; I left Accutronics a few months ago. I had my ups and downs out there, but when I left things were going very well for me.

After my first year I was shifted around a lot. Our department sort of fell apart, mostly, I think, because of opposition from the divisions. I went through a great number of "reorganizations," but for the year before I left I was working as one of the two assistants to the operations vice president. I had several divisions assigned to me, and I was supposed to know everything that was going on in those divisions. Our total sales, by the way, were over the $100 million rate when I left, which will put us in *Fortune*'s list of 500. Most of that was through internal growth, too, although we did buy several small companies.

I worked on all sorts of projects, and also sat in on a lot of top-management meetings, including the monthly operating meetings involving the officers of the company and the division managers. Usually when my boss visited any of the divisions I was responsible for, I went along with him too.

It was great experience to see how things work at that level in such a large and dynamic company, and I wouldn't trade it for anything. I was making good money, too, and was well liked, I think, by the people I worked with. Several said to get in touch with them if I ever wanted to come back. They were certainly nice to me when I left, and I have a lot of friends there that I will call up and chat with if I ever get to Denver again.

I guess the main reason I left is that I just didn't like the atmosphere in the company as well as when I started. It seemed to me that too many people were spending too much of their time on things which had nothing to do with making a contribution to the company, and I didn't see how I could avoid it myself, even if only in self-defense. I saw too many people lose out because they didn't pay enough attention to the politics involved, and I just didn't find playing politics very satisfying. Besides, I don't think I'm very good at it.

I certainly was naive when I graduated from the Business School. I had been in the service and worked some before that, and I thought I knew how the world worked. When I went out to Accutronics I really thought that getting ahead would depend mostly on solving problems for the company better than anyone else, and one of the main reasons I went with them was that they seemed to be looking for someone with exactly my viewpoint. I now doubt that more than 10 percent of the reasons for promotions in most companies depend on this. I'm convinced that the surest way to go down the drain in most organizations is to spend your time solving problems better, rather than impressing the people who make the promotions.

I have never made any list to see what happened to the people who were sort of in my department, but it would be interesting to see what became of

EXHIBIT 1
Department roster

Name	Age in 1967	Education and background	Brief job titles and comments for 1967–70 period
David Gordon*	27	MBA, Stanford	Staff assistant; left after one year
Andy Johnson*	27	MBA, Wharton	Staff assistant; left after 18 months
John Adams*	27	MBA, Harvard Business School (H.B.S.)	Staff assistant; various jobs; left after three years
Kirk Spencer*	28	MBA, H.B.S.	Staff assistant; left after 18 months
Frank Nolan	28	MBA, Stanford	Staff assistant; assistant to marketing vice president; left after four and one-half years
Gene Farrell	29	BA	Accounting staff; some supervisory (staff) positions
Bob Hartwell	31	BA	Systems and procedures work
Len Halstead	31	BA; CPA	Internal auditor
Ed Becker*	32	MBA, Columbia, formerly planning director for a division of a large company	Staff assistant; out for six months with nervous breakdown
Lou DiSantis*	33	MBA, H.B.S., accounting and data-processing experience	Accounting systems specialist
Leo Hoyt	34	MBA, Michigan, former consultant	Staff assistant and internal consultant; left after three years
Ray Nelson	35	MBA, H.B.S., former budget manager for a division of a large company	Budget analyst, financial analyst, left after three years

* Indicates personnel added during 1967–68.

that group. There were several in the 25- to 35-age category in my general area at headquarters when I arrived, and we hired several more during the year. After the first year there were so many reorganizations that it would be impossible to keep track. As I remember it, this [Exhibit 1] would be the list of people, with a little bit on their backgrounds and what happened to them.

Don't let the title "staff assistant" worry you; it really doesn't describe either your work or your relative position in the department very well. It was just a catchall title that was used a lot in our department.

It scares me to look at what has happened to the relatively few men in my group who have stayed—without exception, I think it is fair to say that they have given up. They have decent jobs, and they do whatever they are told, no matter how foolish it seems. Lou DiSantis is the example that I feel the worst about because he and I came to be good friends, and our wives also saw a lot of each other. He came to Accutronics because he hadn't liked the work atmosphere in the two large companies he had worked for and thought he would find something completely different out here. He enjoyed it for a while and really felt that he was contributing, but by now he has had to compromise so many times that he just doesn't have any spark any more.

The last time we talked about this he said he had concluded that the key is "to keep your nose clean, don't take a strong stand on anything, and just draw your check." He knows that much of what he is doing is wasted effort, but the only way to get along is to do it. I know he makes over $25,000, and he said if anyone ever found out what he *really* contributes to the company he would be fired for sure.

Mitchell, who was sort of in my department but whom I didn't put on the list because he is a lot older, is another example of the same thing. One time when I was talking to him about this and told him how dissatisfied I was because of the things we do which obviously bear no relation to the main task of the company, he said I was taking it much too seriously. "I don't give a damn what I do," he said, "I just do what they want me to and draw my paycheck. That's the only way to get along." Well, he is in a tough spot because of his age and lack of marketable experience, and he also has a large family. I don't really blame him, but I hope I never have to regard my job that way.

Maybe examples of some of the things that were going on will give you a better idea of why I left. The incident that stands out most vividly in my memory is something that happened about a year and a half ago. I was working for one of the corporate staff departments that reported to Walter Gorman, who in turn reported to Allen Lawson, one of the vice presidents at the time. Another department which also reported to Gorman did work which was related to ours, and I suppose these two departments could conceivably have been combined into one.

One day when George, our department head, was away on a trip, Fred, the head of the other department, called Andy[2] and me into his office. He closed the door, and then said that he was out to get George and wanted to know whether we were for or against him. If we were for him, he said we could help undermine George, and if we were against him, he would take care of us when he got control of George's department anyway.

Well, we never talked about *that* in school. We both said we didn't want to get involved in such power politics and got out of there as fast as possible. Andy and I discussed it, of course, but couldn't really decide what to do about it, aside from hoping the problem would go away. But when George came back from his trip, I decided that the best thing to do would be to tell him what Fred was up to so that he would at least be on his guard. I said I wanted to tell him something off the record, and he assured me that it would be completely personal and confidential between the two of us.

So, I told him what had happened. Before I had even finished, he stalked out of the office and left me standing there. He went straight to Allen Lawson without even bothering to look for Walter Gorman, and inside of two

---

[2] Andy Johnson, a co-worker. See department roster, Exhibit 1.

minutes I was in Al's office. A few minutes later a company lawyer came in also. I was ordered to tell them the story, Andy was brought in separately for his version; Walter was called in, Fred was called in, then we were all called in, and so on. This went on for days, and it soon became apparent that Al Lawson was trying to minimize the whole thing. Andy and I must have been asked a dozen times if perhaps Fred had been kidding. We were all asked what everyone else said, what they said someone else said, and so on. It was a first-class mess, and Andy and I came out of the worst. No action was taken against Fred, but Andy and I were clearly in Al's disfavor.

I had been at the company a little over a year at that time, and that was the first time I thought seriously about leaving. I'd be damned if I would quit under those circumstances, though; I never had been a quitter before and I didn't intend to quit then. What saved me was that I was picked up by Sam Merrill, who was the second in command in one of the divisions. I had worked with Sam on some projects previously, and we had gotten along fine. I worked for him about six months, and then his boss, the division manager, became the operations vice president, with responsibility for all of the company's operations. He took Sam along, and Sam took me along back to headquarters. This affair with Fred had blown over to some extent by then—Fred left the company a few months after it happened—but Al Lawson never did look me square in the eye again.

What really clinched it was when I found out, about a year after the incident, why Al had been so reluctant to have Fred placed in a bad light. I was told by a friend who left the company shortly after this had happened to Andy and me. It seems that Al had approached my friend with the suggestion that he act as an "informal source of information" for Al with respect to what was going on in Gorman's department, and my friend had turned it down. He suspected strongly that Fred had taken on the task because "all of a sudden Fred's wife just couldn't keep from talking about how closely Al and her husband worked together." This would all have occurred shortly before our fiasco.

Another thing that I must admit made me feel both furious and very sad was when I found out that at least three people had asked Al Lawson, who was my "big boss" for a couple of years, if they could offer me a job in their divisions. I found this out when I went around to say goodbye to several of these people as I was leaving the company, and they mentioned that they were sorry I had never come to work with them. I never heard about the offers, even though two of them would have been clear promotions at the time.

There were other incidents, of course, which seemed important at the time but which are easy to forget. There were so many things going on that were directed at promoting the interests of some individual or department rather than the company interests. The great quantities of viewgraphs and reports that we generated were one example of this; most of them were never used for any purpose at all, and we knew it. Walter Gorman wanted them to impress Al Lawson, I guess, and I'm not sure why Al wanted them. Nobody that had any line authority paid the least bit of attention to them, as became completely clear during my last year when I was sitting in on operating meetings.

We even had cases of our computer people simulating results from the computer by using it as a typewriter. At one point the management became enchanted with the idea of putting the entire operations of the company on a computer. The computer systems people had serious doubts about the feasibility of the project in relation to the resources and time available, but they were given the task and a completely unrealistic deadline anyway. Rather than say it couldn't be done, they pretended to meet the deadline by working out most of the figures on a desk calculator and printing the results on the computer. What do you suppose that does to your sense of "professional responsibility"?

It sounds amazing, but during one period even quitting became a real challenge. At one point the management came very suspicious about the possibility of persons taking confidential information from the company, either of a technical or commercial nature. There were some cases of individuals quitting and starting up competing companies in certain of the specialties they had been working in, but I guess that happens generally in a high-technology industry such as ours where the right idea or process is sufficient to attract all the financial backing you might need. Denver is full of such companies, and I guess Boston is too. As far as I know there were never any instances of people misusing commercial information, though, as opposed to the technical know-how they acquired.

Anyway, when Andy quit he left his letter of resignation, saying he was giving the customary 30 days' notice, on Gorman's desk one evening. The next morning he was met by Gorman, Al Lawson, and the company legal counsel as he came to work, and the four of them went to his desk and went through it, item by item. He was allowed to keep his personal papers, and was then asked to leave immediately. They said they preferred not to have anyone working there who was not happy with the company and that there was no point working any longer once he had given his notice.

This pattern was repeated with several people. They all got their pay for the next 30 days, of course, so that was not an issue. But it certainly is not a very nice atmosphere under which to leave a company, and it really made you wonder as to what sort of a reference you could expect from them in the future.

I don't think that sort of treatment of those who left the company was done with any ill intent or malice towards the people involved. It just seemed to be the natural outgrowth of the strong team spirit that the management tried to foster in the company and which they believed in themselves. They *really* believed there was an "Accutronics type," and the reaction was that if you didn't like it there you weren't an Accutronics type after all and didn't belong in the company. The fault was always seen as being in the individual rather than the system. There is some value to that kind of an approach, but I think they carried it too far. There were some periodic surveys made by teams of outside consultants to determine what people liked and didn't like about the company, but most of the results I ever saw looked like they pertained to some other company.

I don't want to give the impression that what happened in my group is normal at the company because I don't really know that much about the atmosphere in the other areas, although I know the politics were not confined to our area. I knew lots of people who were very strong in their support of the company, and it certainly had an excellent public image. There was a high turnover of professional personnel—around 2½ percent per month—during the last year I was there, but part of that may have come from the fact that it looked like the growth would be slowing down to a more normal rate because of the leveling off of defense spending, and the opportunities in relation to the costs involved just wouldn't be as great as several years ago. Four of us from the class of '67 went out there, though, mostly working in different areas, and I was the third to leave. I don't know if the fourth is still there or not.

Another thing that became obvious was that there was a big difference in the way people responded to what you might call the politics of the situation. I really think some people simply never realized what was going on. Of those who were aware of it, some "fought the system," some just accepted things the way they were, and some viewed it as a personal challenge and opportunity.

Frank Nolan was a wonderful example of the last type. He viewed it all as a big game and seemed to take genuine delight in finding out how things worked around the company so he could play the game better. He paid more attention to the informal things going on than anyone else that I knew of, and he also seemed to know more about what was going on in various parts of the company than anyone else. He always had a series of complicated explanations for what seemed like simple things, but in several cases I think he turned out to be right.

Just as an example of the kind of thing he paid attention to, I was told that when he first came with the company, which was a couple of years before I did, he made it a point to find out what colleges all of the top-management people had gone to, where they had first met, how they happened to join the company, what jobs they had had in the company, whom they seemed to be bringing along as proteges in the company, what social activities and clubs they were involved in, and so on. I guess information of that sort does help you to understand what is going on, but I have to admit that I don't like to think that those things are all that important, and I don't like to spend much of my time on them.

I became pretty good friends with Frank, and he was quite outspoken about a lot of things. We talked a lot about where the company was going and what the opportunities were likely to be for people like us within the company. He had been quite enthusiastic about the staff group that they were trying to build up, but after I had been there about six months he concluded that Walter Gorman, who was really his superior, was never going to make it into the top-management ranks. Frank attached a great deal of importance to working for someone on the way up in the company, and at that point he just about quit working for Walter. He didn't try to make any formal moves, he just managed to get started on some projects for Carl Lund, the marketing vice president, who he thought was going to move up. He took to working Lund's hours, which were a little different from ours, and simply told Walter that he was "on an important and confidential project for Lund" when Walter came to him with work. There were sparks for a while, but after a while Frank started working for Lund full time.

Frank based his conclusions about Walter on a whole lot of things—the progress the department was making and the reception we were getting out in the divisions, the apparent lack of strong backing of Walter by Lawson, Butler, and the rest of the officers, the fact that Walter and his wife had been at the company for over two years but were not on close social terms with anyone of consequence in the company, and a difference in dress and appearance. Gorman did look a bit like a gambling casino operator, and Frank felt there was a significant "All-American" bias in the management. He also felt that what our department was trying to do would not be seen as being as important to the company as either research, production, or marketing skills during the next several years.

Frank was right about Walter, by the way. About six months after this Walter was "reorganized" into a less important job, and a while later he left the company.

Frank also had a way of trying to trade information so that he always came out a little bit ahead in the exchange. He seemed to collect bits of information from all over that might make sense when put together. Whenever he would volunteer some information to you, you could be sure that the main reason was he thought you had something that he needed. In a way he was trying to place himself in the center of the wheel, with bits and pieces of information flowing back and forth along the spokes but with him in the center, putting things together.

Although Frank and I got along very well, I noticed that he always managed to cover up whatever he was working on whenever I came in his office. Nobody else did that, and we all used to joke about it a bit. Frank tried to maintain the impression that he was always working on something confidential and important.

It is easy to find fault with any company, I suppose, and I hope I am not being too critical of Accutronics. Many people seemed to like it, so maybe there is such a thing as an Accutronics type, and I'm not it.

I can't pass my experience off as "bad management" on the part of the company because it has been an enormous success story. I give a great deal of credit to the group of about six or eight who changed that company from an unknown with a few million dollars in sales in the early 60s to one of the outstanding growth companies of the past ten years, with a sales level which will bring it into the *Fortune* list of 500.

The growth may slow down, but they want to make it into a billion-dollar corporation in their lifetimes. They all started with nothing, they took big risks, and they still work extremely hard, and it has paid off. Individually, they are worth anywhere from several million to over 50 million dollars in terms of the market value of their stock by now.

I am sure my viewpoint of what was happening in the company would be different if I were in their position, but I still think they overrate the value of their "modern management approach," which they honestly believe is ten years ahead of the rest of industry, and underemphasize the part that several virtual monopolies which resulted from outstanding technical and production breakthroughs have played in their success. I think a lot of us were misled by this when we were evaluating the company as a place to work. I know I assumed for quite a while that any company with such an outstanding growth record *must* be "well managed," but the longer I was there the more convinced I became that the growth was due more to several critical technical breakthroughs than to exceptional management skills or approaches.

The management group is unquestionably smart and hard working, and they built up the company by competing fiercely against some of the giants of industry. I suppose this is probably why they seek aggressive and ambitious people and encourage competition within the company to the extent that they do. But you don't compete against Lockheed Electronics or General Dynamics or Litton when you come to work for Accutronics now; you compete against people within the company. It is people versus people, not companies versus companies, and I think that makes a big difference. I don't think that the kind of competitive behavior which paid off extremely well for the company is necessarily what you should encourage at lower levels within the company, because I really think it results in a lot of wasted effort. Also, some good people probably have left the company for just the reasons I did.

I think most of the things I didn't like were the results of our widespread pyramidal form of organization, and a basic management philosophy that the best man will be the one that climbs the pyramid, regardless of the environment or the nature of the competition. It is ironic that this was one of the things about the company that appealed to me in the first place. Their strong emphasis on competition and the "free enterprise" philosophy within the company made it seem like a place where I would have the greatest chance of getting ahead by my own abilities and work rather than by seniority or politics, and a place where I wouldn't be hemmed in by a lot of restrictions and formalized procedures.

I had lots of arguments about this with one of the personnel men that I knew quite well, and he was quite definite about the prevalence in top management of a strong belief that "the best man will get ahead, regardless of the environment." I kept asking him best man for *what,* and what about the need to cooperate within the company, to observe some kind of limits on the form of competition, and so on, but we never got anywhere. They oftentimes put several people or several departments on virtually the same tasks, for example, and made a practice of obscuring titles and responsibilities and then encouraging people to take on more responsibility if they could get away with it. They also did a great deal of reorganizing; the number of blue sheets that came around announcing changes in personnel or organizational structure was amazing.

I think that is just like offering a big prize to the winner of a boxing match and sending the referee home. You wouldn't have a boxing match following the Marquis of Queensberry rules for very long; you would have a street fight. Unless you restrict the grounds on which people are allowed to compete, I think that loose an approach to organization will lead to a lot of conflict and activities which are not good for the company and which may also be unpleasant for the people involved. I remember a quip of Harry Truman's with regard to the sometimes merciless criticism of public officials that "if you can't stand the heat get out of the kitchen." Maybe that is what I'm doing.

I have just accepted a job with a much smaller and highly technical company in the Cape Kennedy area. They sought me out and gave me a substantial salary increase, but the money is not the main reason I quit. I was making $20,000 a year at Accutronics, which was above most of the people who were roughly in my category out there and which I suppose is above what most of my classmates are making now. I just didn't like working there any longer because of some of the things I've mentioned to you.

I'm looking forward to the new job, both because of the challenges involved in the business as well as the financial opportunities for me. I also think that this management will be likely to keep things in check a little more within the company than was the case out at Accutronics. It's a tough balance to maintain, though—aggressive company behavior but a cooperative and satisfying working atmosphere. If I were just graduating and job hunting again, I sure would pay more attention to factors like this. Unless you fit in with the atmosphere you find in the company, you will either have to change yourself, quit, or be unhappy about it.

case 26

Albert Manufacturing Company

The Albert Manufacturing Company was founded in 1938 to produce various machined and fabricated components for industrial users. Shortly after the start of World War II the company began to make mechanical and hydraulic assemblies for aircraft. This part of the business grew, and in April 1947 it was set up as a separate division. To house operations the company leased a newly constructed plant in Wichita, Kansas, with 1.2 million square feet of floor space. By the end of 1954 sales of the Wichita Division were running at about $120 million annually. The division had approximately 1,200 employees.

Early in January 1955, Mr. Henderson, works manager of the Wichita Division and a vice president of the Albert Manufacturing Company, called Paul Bellows to his office. Bellows was purchasing agent for the division. Henderson told Bellows he had just received a telephone call from the manager of the local office of the Federal Bureau of Investigation. The manager informed him that an investigation then in progress by the FBI had brought to light information involving certain of the division's buyers. Henderson said he had arranged for the investigators to visit the division the following morning. He asked Bellows to receive them and to keep him informed as to developments.

The next day Arnold Rand and Peter Thomas, FBI agents, called on Bellows. Ralph Nance, assistant purchasing agent, was also at the meeting. After a brief exchange of pleasantries the following discussion took place:

Bellows: As you can well imagine Nance and I are very curious about this matter. We have not mentioned it to anyone, but we have speculated between ourselves as to the nature of the thing. What's the story?

Rand: Well, I guess I ought to go back to last fall. We were conducting an investigation on placement of government contracts at the P. B. Blake Company on the north side of town. After several weeks and rather by accident, Pete Thomas was interviewing a witness who was a buyer in Blake's purchasing department. The fellow confessed to having accepted a $4,500 bribe from a local tool supplier. Later we verified that he had received the money from the company he named. The supplier involved has gone on record that the money was a personal loan from their salesman and was to have been repaid. However, the buyer involved did not support this contention. The buyer turned state's witness and gave us several other instances of similar occurrences, but they were not as serious—at least there wasn't as much money involved.

Nance: Where is the tie-in with the Albert Manufacturing Company?

Rand: This buyer has made a sworn statement that he knows three of your buyers have also been accepting expensive gifts and perhaps being bought off as he was. . . .

Thomas: Bellows, this thing is nebulous as hell. We don't have much to go on, but there are enough basic implications that we think these three buyers of yours may well be tarred with the same brush.

Rand: I'd like to tell you about a fishing trip that our informant was on. He stated—and we have verified this—that he was one of 12 guests at an upstate fishing lodge, spent the weekend in substantial style, and returned. All expenses were paid by the supplier. Now get this—your three buyers were there along with the chief tool designer and two manufacturing engineers from Albert. It was at this occasion that our informant states he learned of the arrangements, shall we say, between the supplier and your buyers.

Bellows: What can we do to get this thing off the ground? What can we do to help clear this thing up?

Rand: We would like to examine your records to see who placed orders with the specific company mentioned in the charge and two other companies also implicated. Then we think that sworn statements will be taken. After that if there are any concrete leads we will conduct an investigation outside the company to ascertain if the individuals have increased bank balances, are living beyond their means, and stuff like that. . . .

Thomas: There is one thing that bothers us. We don't have jurisdiction.

Bellows: What do you mean jurisdiction?

Thomas: At the P. B. Blake Company we could investigate because they held prime contracts from the government. You don't, and therefore we can't come in and do the same kind of thing.

Bellows: Could you if we asked you to?

Thomas: That would take care of the matter completely.

Bellows: Well, that settles that. We are asking you now and will give you whatever you need in the way of an official request. Now then, when and how will you start the ball rolling?

Rand: In about three days if you can be ready for us. If possible, we would like to use a private office because of the secrecy necessary until we know where we are. We will also need personnel records, purchase order files, and a lot of other things.

Bellows: We will be ready for you. Let me say now I am more concerned than you are and want this cleaned up one way or the other as quickly as possible but with a minimum of disruption of the purchasing department. However, even if we have got to shake this department up hard, I will give you every support. Nance, get things organized to take care of this. Don't tell anyone what is going on until we decide the time is right . . . explain the presence of strangers by, well let them be headquarters auditors or something. Gentlemen, Ralph Nance will be your contact and will personally make all the necessary arrangements. Again, I want to assure you that you have our cooperation. Tell me, who are the vendors in question?

Rand: The Supreme Engineering Company is the firm specifically mentioned in the allegation. The other two are Superior Tool and Die, Inc., and Allied Tool Company.

Nance: Thanks; you can be assured that things will be set up for you.

Mr. Bellows was especially concerned about this investigation because he had given special emphasis to a strict code of ethical conduct with suppliers since he had assumed his current assignment. The departmental policy was that no employee was to accept any gift or courtesy that he was not in a position to reciprocate. In a variety of ways Bellows had tried to get this standard of conduct understood and accepted by all those in the department. The topic was frequently discussed at weekly meetings with purchasing supervisors. All male employees of the department had attended a company school where one of the subjects discussed was the company policy on bribery. The issue had been discussed at the monthly dinner meetings held for male employees of the purchasing department. Bellows had authorized his buyers to make a fairly liberal use of expense accounts so that they could reciprocate in buying lunches, and so on, for suppliers' representatives and not feel under any obligation to them. He knew that some of the production and engineering employees had accepted Christmas gifts and entertainment from suppliers, but he had believed that his buyers had been completely honest in dealings with suppliers.

The Wichita Division was highly specialized in that it made only a limited line of small gear trains, landing gear assemblies, hydraulic pumps and actuators, and certain fabricated assemblies. The vast bulk of the more or less common components needed were obtained from subcontractors. In 1954 the purchasing department had paid slightly over $55 million to subcontractors, or about half of the total sales of the division.

Buyers for the division were divided into groups, each headed by a senior buyer. These groups were organized along product lines, each being responsible for purchasing items that fell within a broad classification. A service group typed purchase orders, maintained the files, expedited orders that were overdue, and performed other functions of a clerical or routine nature. The entire purchasing department employed 128 people.

The flow of work into the department was in the form of requisitions that specified the items required and the date they should be available. A requisition was first processed by a member of the service group, who entered it in a master log and then routed it to the proper buying group. The assistant buyer for the group, upon receipt of a requisition, determined what previous suppliers had furnished the item. Any specifications that applied were pulled out together with the blueprint of the part. Then invitations to quote were sent out to approved sources or, if there was only one source, the supplier's representatives were contacted for negotiation. After a supplier had been selected, the assistant buyer filled in on the requisition the supplier's name and the price per unit. Certain other details also were added, such as the storeroom that was to receive the goods, discount terms, shipping point, and so forth. The requisition then was passed on to the appropriate buyer.

In most of the groups the effective control in selection of suppliers was in the hands of the buyers. However, in all groups every requisition had to be signed by a senior buyer. At this stage it went back to the service group. The necessary number of copies were typed, hecto masters for receiving and accounting were prepared, the facsimile signature of the purchasing agent was applied, and copies were mailed to the vendor. The requisition had been transformed from a request to purchase into a contract with a supplier.

About a week after the FBI agents started their investigation, Nance and Thomas discussed progress made during the preliminary stage. Thomas stated that he thought matters were progressing extremely slowly but that things should speed up in the near future. He and Rand had screened all the purchase orders placed by the division with the three suppliers in question during the past six months. All the orders had been for some type of tooling, primarily for tool repair work. All had been placed by the three buyers named in the original complaint.

Thomas gave Nance the following summary of the findings of the purchase order review:

1. All 1,976 purchase orders were initialed by the senior buyer for tools, Clinton Boles. The buyers that actually handled the orders and the distribution of orders among the suppliers in question were the following:

	Superior	Supreme	Allied	Total
Adolph Stimmer (assistant buyer).	622	257	48	927
John Lippen (buyer).............	73	159	0	232
John Ruppert (assistant buyer)....	280	531	6	817

2. While only 54 purchase orders were placed with Allied, the total dollar value of these orders was $86,409. The dollar value for Superior Tool and Die was $234,765, and for Supreme Engineering it was $303,040.

3. Among the orders were three, all placed with Supreme, which radically increased in price during the period of manufacture. The original quoted prices for these orders were $257.75, $1,166.00, and $2,500.00. The final

prices on the orders, as authorized by change notices to the purchase orders, were $1,186.50, $3,775.00, and $4,996.00.[1]

Nance had intimate knowledge of tool buying and of the tool buying group. He at one time had been responsible for buying tools at the home plant of the Albert company, and Stimmer then had been an assistant buyer reporting to him. Any tool supplier usually could build a new tool. Quotations of delivery and price could be readily obtained by furnishing the supplier with blueprints and specifications. Repair of tools was an entirely different matter. It was necessary for someone from the tool firm to inspect the tool requiring repair before submitting a quotation. Time was important because the tool generally was needed for production of a scheduled part. Therefore, repair jobs were often placed on an advise price basis; that is, the supplier would take the tool, and after inspection was completed at the supplier's plant, a price would be submitted. The buyer then would judge whether or not this price was fair. If the buyer decided it was too high, either a new price would be negotiated or the tool moved to another supplier.

The tool buying group, unlike the other buying groups, dealt in general with small firms. A relatively low capital investment was required to start a tool shop, and there were many local toolmakers that were highly specialized and extremely small, sometimes employing no more than four or five workers. Adequate credit and other information was difficult to obtain for these small firms.

About two weeks after they began their investigation, Thomas and Rand told Nance they were going to interview, under oath, Stimmer, Lippen, Ruppert, and Boles. They further stated that they wanted to discuss the progress made to date with Bellows and Nance as soon as they had had time to weigh the statements of the men. Nance suggested they meet the following afternoon. Rand and Thomas agreed.

The next afternoon Rand, Thomas, Nance, and Bellows gathered in Bellows's office. Rand opened the meeting.

Rand: Guess you will be surprised to learn that we are ending the investigation.

Bellows: You're all through already?

Rand: That's right. We have been unable to uncover any concrete evidence. We must have proof and, while there is no lack of suspicious circumstances, we just can't pin down anything definite.

Bellows: You can't come out here, tear into everything, arouse considerable doubt

---

[1] During the manufacture of tools, design changes often become necessary or desirable. Such changes sometimes cause revisions in the delivered prices. Change notices also may tempt the supplier, particularly one who deliberately quoted under cost to get an order, to demand an exorbitant price increase. This practice is frowned on by reputable tool vendors but is sometimes resorted to by marginal producers.

in our minds, and then pull out. We want these men either nailed to the cross or exonerated—is this too much to ask?

Nance: I thought you were making satisfactory progress.

Thomas: Paul, you must realize we work for a boss, too. He gave us almost five weeks to firm the investigation up. We just can't do it. There is a lot of smoke but no fire that we can find. So we want to give you everything we have, and if you come across some new evidence later on, we promise to give you all the help we can. That's all there is to it. We're sorry it turned out this way but. . . .

Nance: Tell us what the score is now before we discuss this aspect further.

Rand: OK. First, Lippen is clean. He was recently transferred out of the tool group and actually was in the group only three weeks during the period of time the alleged offense took place. Both Stimmer and Ruppert absolutely deny the charge. They admit close knowledge of the suppliers but were rather evasive on the question of entertainment. Stimmer stated he was at the fishing party I mentioned to you earlier. Ruppert says he doesn't associate with salesmen outside of the office.

Thomas: I handled the outside investigation. We went over every phase of Stimmer's and Ruppert's personal affairs—bank accounts, recent large purchases, standard of living, and so forth. Both are clean insofar as concrete evidence is concerned, but there is considerable doubt in my mind as to whether these guys are on the level. Stimmer lives well but not too far over the level he could support on his income. Ruppert took a very expensive vacation last year—two weeks in Florida at a fancy hotel. I believe a supplier paid a large part of the bills while he was there, but again I have no proof.

Rand: I think you should also know that we have checked the suppliers very carefully, too. I have tried to determine the expense account entries on the salesmen's reports turned into the companies. You realize that a company is in a box with the Internal Revenue if we catch it falsifying expenses. Again, nothing conclusive, but, Paul, you should know that these companies all have substantial entries listing entertaining your people. I believe your name was even listed a few times.

Bellows: If you could check all of the 2,200 suppliers we do business with, I bet you will find my name quite often. Needless to say, I don't even know many of the salesmen, but a purchasing agent's name on the sales report for a lunch impresses the sales manager—and who is going to check to find the salesman is doing a little padding?

Rand: That is undoubtedly true, but there were still many of Albert's personnel on the statements. I was surprised that people outside of the purchasing department were mentioned freely. However, there was nothing to implicate Stimmer or Ruppert.

Thomas: Well, what else can we say? We have a lot of suspicion that Stimmer and Ruppert are, at best, pretty close to these suppliers. Boles, of course, could be involved in this thing too. We didn't get around to checking his personal affairs as closely as the others, but I don't think he is completely out from under, from what little we have been able to determine.

Bellows: What do you say, Ralph?

Nance: Well, I don't believe we can do much more. We have the information and can be on the lookout for future indications. It is regrettable that we can't run this thing into the ground, but there isn't anything we can do about it.

Bellows: Then I want to thank you gentlemen for your help so far and, if we do uncover anything, we will contact you.

Thomas: Feel free to do that—even if we can't get out right away we can tell you what move you should make.

After Thomas and Rand had gone, Bellows and Nance talked over the situation. Nance expressed the following views.

Nance: Paul, I'm not sure what I should do, but I'll tell you one thing—I don't want these guys in the tool group any longer. I've got to have a senior buyer that I can trust completely and buyers that are above reproach.

This whole mess is like shadow boxing. Just last November I rated Boles as ready for advancement, and Stimmer and Ruppert certainly have always been considered as competent.

However, as I see it I have got to take action to make sure the situation is under control and guarantee this kind of thing doesn't happen again. Do you agree?

EXHIBIT 1
Wichita Division organization chart (purchasing department)

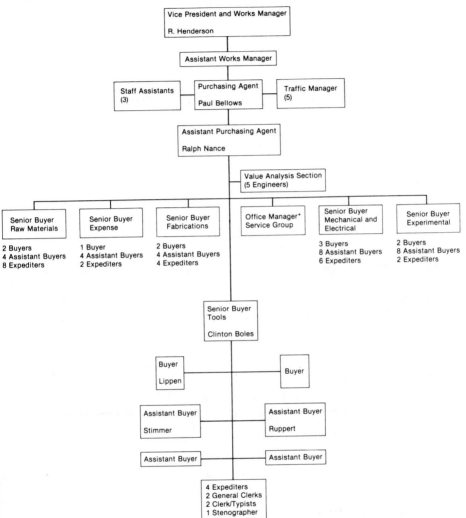

* Equal in classification to senior buyer. There were 18 clerks, typists, and stenographers in the service group out of a total of 43 for the entire purchasing department.

case 27

The Lincoln Electric Company

> We're not a marketing company, we're not an R&D company, and we're
> not a service company. We're a manufacturing company, and I believe that
> we are the best manufacturing company in the world.

With these words, George E. Willis, president of The Lincoln Electric
Company, described what he saw as his company's distinctive competence.
For more than 30 years, Lincoln had been the world's largest manufacturer
of arc welding products (see Exhibit 1). In 1974 Lincoln Electric was believed to have manufactured more than 40 percent of the arc welding
equipment and supplies sold in the United States. In addition to its welding
products, Lincoln produced a line of three-phase A.C. industrial electric
motors, but these accounted for less than 10 percent of sales and profits.

Lincoln's 1974 domestic net income was $17.5 million on sales of $236
million (see Exhibit 2). Perhaps more significant than a single year's results
was Lincoln's record of steady growth over the preceding four decades, as
shown by Exhibit 3.

During this period, aftertax return on equity had ranged between 10
percent and 15 percent. Lincoln's growth had been without benefit of acquisition and had been financed through internally generated funds.

COMPANY HISTORY

(Broadside)   Lincoln Electric was founded by John C. Lincoln in 1895 to
manufacture electric motors and generators. James F. Lincoln, John's younger brother, joined the company in 1907. The brothers' skills and interests
were complementary. John was a technical genius. During his lifetime he
was awarded more than 50 patents for inventions as diverse as an apparatus
for curing meat, an electric drill, a mine door activating mechanism, and an
electric arc lamp. James's skills were in management and administration.
He began as a salesman but soon took over as general manager. The Lincoln
Electric Company was undeniably built in his image.

EXHIBIT 1

THE LINCOLN ELECTRIC COMPANY

Arc welding is a group of joining processes that utilize an electric current produced by a transformer or motor generator (electric or engine powered) to fuse various metals. The temperature at the arc is approximately 10,000° F.

The welding circuit consists of a welding machine, ground clamp, and electrode holder. The electrode carries electricity to the metal being welded, and the heat from the arc causes the base metals to join together. The electrode may or may not act as a filler metal during the process; however, nearly 60 percent of all arc welding that is done in the United States utilizes a covered electrode that does act as a very high-quality filler metal.

The Lincoln Electric Company manufactures a wide variety of covered electrodes, submerged arc welding wires and fluxes, and a unique self-shielded, flux-cored electrode called "Innershield." The company also manufactures welding machines, wire feeders, and other supplies that are needed for arc welding.

Lincoln arc welding machines

In 1911 the company introduced its first arc welding machine. Both brothers were fascinated by welding, which was in its infancy at the time. They recognized it as an alternative use for the motor-generator sets they were already producing to recharge the batteries for electric automobiles. It was becoming apparent from the success of Ford, Buick, and others that the days of the electric auto might be numbered, and the brothers were anxious to find other markets for their skills and products.

John's mechanical talents gave the company a head start in welding machines which it never relinquished. He developed a portable welding machine (a significant improvement over existing stationary models) and incorporated a transformer to allow regulation of the current. As described by a biographer of John C. Lincoln:

> This functional industrial development gave Lincoln Electric a lead in the field that it has always maintained, although the two giants—Westinghouse and General Electric—soon entered the market.[1]

EXHIBIT 2

THE LINCOLN ELECTRIC COMPANY
Statement of Financial Condition
On December 31, 1974
(foreign subsidiaries not included)

Assets		*Liabilities and Shareholders' Equity*	
Current assets:		Current liabilities:	
Cash and certificates of deposit	$ 5,691,120	Accounts payable	$ 13,658,063
Government securities . . .	6,073,919	Accrued wages	1,554,225
Notes and accounts receivable	29,451,161	Taxes, including income taxes	13,262,178
Inventories (LIFO basis) .	29,995,694	Dividends payable	3,373,524
Deferred taxes and prepaid expenses	2,266,409	Total current liabilities	$ 31,847,990
Total current assets	$ 73,478,303		
		Shareholders' equity:	
Other assets:		Common capital stock, stated value	$ 281,127
Trustee—notes and interest receivable	$ 1,906,871	Additional paid-in capital	3,374,570
Miscellaneous	384,572	Retained earnings	66,615,762
Total other assets	$ 2,291,443	Total shareholders' equity	$ 70,271,459
Intercompany:			
Investment in foreign subsidiaries	$ 4,695,610	Total liabilities and shareholders' equity	$102,119,449
Notes receivable	–0–		
Total intercompany .	$ 4,695,610		
Property, plant, and equipment:			
Land	$ 825,376		
Buildings*	9,555,562		
Machinery, tools, and equipment	11,273,155		
Total property, plant, and equipment*	$ 21,654,093		
Total assets	$102,119,449		

* After depreciation.

---

[1] Raymond Moley, *The American Century of John C. Lincoln* (New York: Duell, Sloan & Pearce, 1962), p. 71.

EXHIBIT 2 (continued)

THE LINCOLN ELECTRIC COMPANY
Statements of Income and Retained Earnings
Year Ended December 31, 1974

Income:

Net sales	$232,771,475
Interest	1,048,561
Overhead and development charges to subsidiaries	1,452,877
Dividend income	843,533
Other income	515,034
Total income	$236,631,480

Costs and expenses:

Cost of products sold	$154,752,735
Selling, administrative, and general expenses and freight-out	20,791,301
Year-end incentive bonus	24,707,297
Pension expense	2,186,932
Total costs and expenses	$202,438,265
Income before income taxes	$ 34,193,215

Provision for income taxes:

Federal	$ 14,800,000
State and local	1,866,000
Total provision for income taxes	$ 16,666,000
Net income	$ 17,527,215

By World War II, Lincoln Electric was the leading American manufacturer of arc welding equipment. Because of the importance of welding to the war effort, the company stopped producing electric motors and devoted its full capacity to welding products. Demand continued to outpace production, and the government asked the welding equipment manufacturers to add capacity. As described by Lincoln President George Willis:

> Mr. Lincoln responded to the government's call by going to Washington and telling them that there was enough manufacturing capacity but it was being used inefficiently by everyone. He offered to share proprietary manufacturing methods and equipment designs with the rest of the industry. Washington took him up on it and that solved the problem. As a result of Mr. Lincoln's patriotic decision, our competitors had costs which were close to ours for a short period after the war, but we soon were outperforming them like before.

In 1955 Lincoln once again began manufacturing electric motors, and since then its position in the market had expanded steadily.

Through the years, Lincoln stock had been sold to employees and associ-

EXHIBIT 3

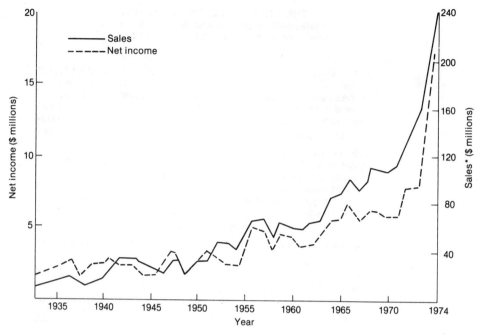

* Excludes foreign operations.

ates of Mr. Lincoln. In 1975 approximately 48 percent of employees were shareholders. About 80 percent of the outstanding stock was held by employees, the Lincoln family, and their foundations.

In its 80 years to 1975, Lincoln had had only three board chairmen: John C. Lincoln, James F. Lincoln, and William Irrgang, who became chairman in 1972.

Strategy

Lincoln Electric's strategy was simple and unwavering. The company's strength was in manufacturing. Management believed that Lincoln could build quality products at a lower cost than their competitors. Their strategy was to concentrate on reducing costs and passing the savings through to the customer by continuously lowering prices. Management had adhered to this policy even when products were on allocation due to shortage of productive capacity. This had brought an expansion of both market share and primary demand for arc welding equipment and supplies over the past half century. It had also encouraged the exit of several major companies from the industry (including General Electric) and had caused others to seek more specialized market niches.

Management believed its incentive system and the climate it fostered were responsible in large part for the continual increase in productivity upon which this strategy depended. Under the Lincoln incentive system, employees were handsomely rewarded for their productivity, high quality, cost reduction ideas, and individual contribution to the company. Year-end bonuses averaged close to 100 percent of regular compensation, and some workers on the factory floor had earned more than $45,000 in a single year.

Lincoln's strategy had remained virtually unchanged for decades. In a 1947 Harvard Business School case study on Lincoln Electric, James F. Lincoln described his company's strategy as follows:

> It is the job of The Lincoln Electric Company to give its customers more and more of a better product at a lower and lower price. This will also make it possible for the company to give to the worker and the stockholder a higher and higher return.

In 1975, Chairman William Irrgang's description was remarkably similar:

> The success of The Lincoln Electric Company has been built on two basic ideas. One is producing more and more of a progressively better product at a lower and lower price for a larger and larger group of customers. The other is that an employee's earnings and promotion are in direct proportion to his individual contribution toward the company's success.[2]

Management felt it had achieved an enviable record in following this strategy faithfully and saw no need to modify it in the future. Lincoln Electric's record of increasing productivity and declining costs and prices is shown in Exhibit 4.

Company philosophy

Lincoln Electric's corporate strategy was rooted in the management philosophy of James F. Lincoln. James F. Lincoln was a rugged individualist who believed that through competition and adequate incentives every person could develop to their fullest potential. In one of his numerous books and articles he wrote:

> Competition is the foundation of man's development. It has made the human race what it is. It is the spur that makes progress. Every nation that has eliminated it as the controlling force in its economy has disappeared, or will. We will do the same if we eliminate it by trying to give security, and for the same reason. Competition means that there will be losers as well as

---

[2] *Employee's Handbook*, The Lincoln Electric Co., 1974.

EXHIBIT 4
Lincoln Electric's record of pricing and productivity

A.   Indexes of annual selling prices of 3/16″ diameter electrode in No. 5 and No. 5p in 3,000 pound quantities, by The Lincoln Electric Company, in relation to indexes of wholesale prices of all commodities, intermediate materials, metal and metal products, and iron and steel, 1934–71.

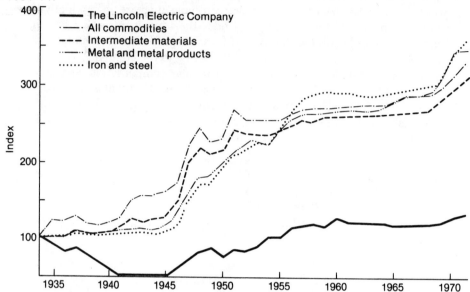

B.   Indexes of average annual prices of specific welders by The Lincoln Electric Company in relation to wholesale prices of machinery and equipment (including electrical) and of electrical machinery and equipment: United States, 1939–71 (1939 = 100).

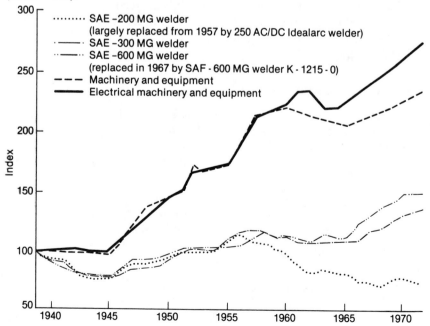

EXHIBIT 4 (continued)

C. Sales value* of products per employee for The Lincoln Electric Company and three prominent companies other than principally electrical; specified years in period 1934–71

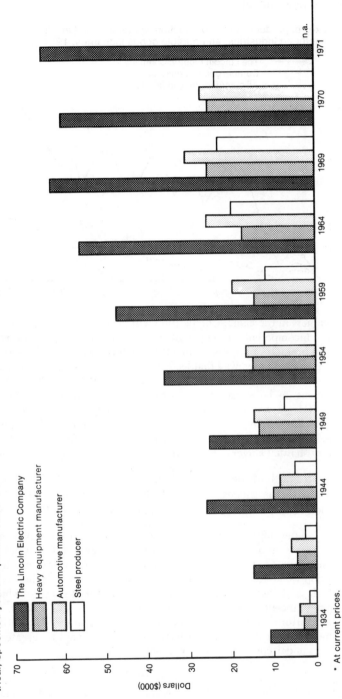

The Lincoln Electric Company

Heavy equipment manufacturer

Automotive manufacturer

Steel producer

Dollars ($000)

70   60   50   40   30   20   10   0

1934   1944   1949   1954   1959   1964   1969   1970   1971

n.a.

* At current prices.
n.a. = not available.

588

EXHIBIT 4 (concluded)

D.   Indexes of productivity per production worker for The Lincoln Electric Company, all manufacturing industries, and durable goods industries, 1934–71.

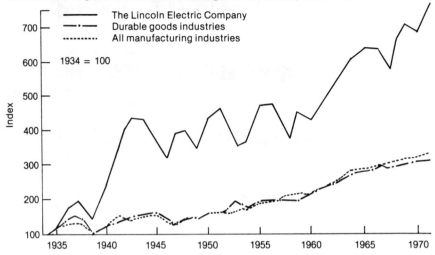

winners in the game. Competition will mean the disappearance of the lazy and incompetent, be they workers, industrialists, or distributors. Competition promotes progress. Competition determines who will be the leader. It is the only known way that leadership and progress can be developed if history means anything. It is a hard taskmaster. It is completely necessary for anyone, be he worker, user, distributor, or boss, if he is to grow.

If some way could be found so that competition could be eliminated from life, the result would be disastrous. Any nation and any people disappear if life becomes too easy. There is no danger from a hard life as all history shows. Danger is from a life that is made soft by lack of competition.[3]

Lincoln's faith in the individual was almost unbounded. His personal experience with the success of Lincoln Electric reinforced his faith in what could be accomplished given the proper conditions. In 1951 he wrote:

... development in many directions is latent in every person. The difficulty has been that few recognize that fact. Fewer still will put themselves under the pressure or by chance are put under the pressure that will develop them greatly. Their latent abilities remain latent, hence useless. . . .

It is of course obvious that the development of man, on which the success of incentive management depends, is a progressive process. Any results, no matter how good, that come from the application of incentive management cannot be considered final. There will always be greater growth of man under continued proper incentive. . . .

---

[3] James F. Lincoln, *Incentive Management* (Cleveland, Ohio: The Lincoln Electric Co., 1951), p. 33.

Such increase of efficiency poses a very real problem to management. The profit that will result from such efficiency obviously will be enormous. The output per dollar of investment will be many times that of the usual shop which practices output limitation. The labor cost per piece will be relatively small and the overhead will be still less.

The profits at competitive selling prices resulting from such efficiency will be far beyond any possible need for proper return and growth of any industry. . . .

How, then, should the enormous extra profit resulting from incentive management be split? The problems that are inherent in incentive dictate the answer. If the worker does not get a proper share, he does not desire to develop himself or his skill. Incentive, therefore, would not succeed. The worker must have a reward that he feels is commensurate with his contribution.

If the customer does not have a part of the saving in lower prices, he will not buy the increased output. The size of the market is a decisive factor in costs of products. Therefore, the consumer must get a proper share of the saving.

Management and ownership are usually considered as a unit. This is far from a fact, but in the problem here, they can be considered together. They must get a part of the saving in larger salaries and perhaps larger dividends.

There is no hard and fast rule to cover this division, other than the following. The worker (which includes management), the customer, the owner and all those involved must be satisfied that they are properly recognized or they will not cooperate, and cooperation is essential to any and all successful applications of incentives.[4]

Additional comments by James F. Lincoln are presented in Exhibit 5.

EXHIBIT 5
James F. Lincoln's observations on management

• Some think paying a man more money will produce cooperation. Not true. Many incentives are far more effective than money. Robert McNamara gave up millions to become Secretary of Defense. Status is a much greater incentive.

• If those crying loudest about the inefficiencies of labor were put in the position of the wage earner, they would react as he does. The worker is not a man apart. He has the same needs, aspirations, and reactions as the industrialist. A worker will not cooperate on any program that will penalize him. Does any manager?

• The industrial manager is very conscious of his company's need of uninterrupted income. He is completely oblivious, though, to the worker's same need. Management fails—i.e., profits fall off—and gets no punishment. The wage earner does not fail but is fired. Such injustice!

• Higher efficiency means fewer man hours to do a job. If the worker loses his job more quickly, he will oppose higher efficiency.

• There never will be enthusiasm for greater efficiency if the resulting profits

---

[4] *Incentive Management*, pp. 7–11.

EXHIBIT 5 (continued)

are not properly distributed. If we continue to give it to the average stockholder, the worker will not cooperate.

• Most companies are run by hired managers, under the control of stockholders. As a result, the goal of the company has shifted from service to the customer, to making larger dividends for stockholders.

• The public will not yet believe that our standard of living could be doubled immediately if labor and management would cooperate.

• The manager is dealing with expert workers far more skillful. While you can boss these experts around in the usual lofty way, their eager cooperation will not be won.

• A wage earner is no more interested than a manager in making money for other people. The worker's job doesn't depend on pleasing stockholders, so he has no interest in dividends. Neither is he interested in increasing efficiency if he may lose his job because management has failed to get more orders.

• If a manager received the same treatment in matters of income, security, advancement, and dignity as the hourly worker, he would soon understand the real problem of management.

• The first question management should ask is: What is the company trying to do? In the minds of the average worker the answer is: "The company is trying to make the largest possible profits by any method. Profits go to absentee stockholders and top management."

• There is all the difference imaginable between the grudging, distrustful, half-forced cooperation and the eager whole-hearted vigorous happy cooperation of men working together for a common purpose.

• Continuous employment of workers is essential to industrial efficiency. This is a management responsibility. Laying off workers during slack times is death to efficiency. The worker thrown out is a trained man. To replace him when business picks up will cost much more than the savings of wages during the layoff. Solution? The worker must have a guarantee that if he works properly his income will be continuous.

• Continuous employment is the first step to efficiency. But how? First, during slack periods, manufacture to build up inventory; costs will usually be less because of lower material costs. Second, develop new machines and methods of manufacturing; plans should be waiting on the shelf. Third, reduce prices by getting lower costs. When slack times come, workers are eager to help cut costs. Fourth, explore markets passed over when times are good. Fifth, hours of work can be reduced if the worker is agreeable. Sixth, develop new products. In sum, management should plan for slumps. They are useful.

• The incentives that are most potent when properly offered are:

> Money in proportion to production.
> Status as a reward for achievement.
> Publicity of the worker's contributions and skill.

EXHIBIT 5 (concluded)

• The calling of the minister, the doctor, the lawyer, as well as the manager, contains incentive to excel. Excellence bring rewards, self-esteem, respect. Only the hourly worker has no reason to excel.

• Resistance to efficiency is not normal. It is present only when we are hired workers.

• Do unto others as you would have them do unto you. This is not just a Sunday school ideal, but a proper labor-management policy.

• An incentive plan should reward a man not only for the number of pieces turned out, but also for the accuracy of his work, his cooperation in improving methods of production, his attendance.

• The progress in industry so far stems from the developed potentialities of managers. Wage earners, who because of their greater numbers have far greater potential, are overlooked. Here is where the manager must look for his greatest progress.

• There should be an overall bonus based on the contribution each person makes to efficiency. If each person is properly rated and paid, there will not only be a fair reward to each worker but friendly and exciting competition.

• The present policy of operating industry for stockholders is unreasonable. The rewards now given to him are far too much. He gets income that should really go to the worker and the management. The usual absentee stockholder contributes nothing to efficiency. He buys a stock today and sells it tomorrow. He often doesn't even know what the company makes. Why should he be rewarded by large dividends?

• There are many forms and degrees of cooperation between the worker and the management. The worker's attitude can vary all the way from passivity to higher imaginative contributions to efficiency and progress.

Source: *Civil Engineering-ASCE*, January 1973.

Compensation policies

Compensation policies were the key element of James F. Lincoln's philosophy of "incentive management." Lincoln Electric's compensation system had three components:

1. Wages based solely on piecework output for most factory jobs.
2. A year-end bonus which could equal or exceed an individual's full year regular pay.
3. Guaranteed employment for all workers.

The first component of this compensation system was that almost all production workers at Lincoln were paid on a straight piecework plan. They had no base salary or hourly wage but were paid a set "price" for each item they produced. William Irrgang explained:

Wherever practical, we use the piecework system. This system can be effective, and it can be destructive. The important part of the system is that it is completely fair to the worker. When we set a piecework price, that price cannot be changed just because, in management's opinion, the worker is making too much money. Whether he earns two times or three times his normal amount makes no difference. Piecework prices can only be changed when management has made a change in the method of doing that particular job and under no other conditions. If this is not carried out 100 percent, piecework cannot work.

Today piecework is confined to production operations, although at one time we also used it for work done in our stenographic pool. Each typewriter was equipped with a counter that registered the number of times the typewriter keys were operated. This seemed to work all right for a time until it was noticed that one girl was earning much more than any of the others. This was looked into, and it was found that this young lady ate her lunch at her desk, using one hand for eating purposes and the other for punching the most convenient key on the typewriter as fast as she could; which simply goes to show that no matter how good a program you may have, it still needs careful supervision.[5]

A time-study department established piecework prices which were guaranteed by the company, until there was a methods change or introduction of a new process. An employee could challenge the price if the employee felt it was unfair. The time-study department would then retime the job and set a new rate. This could be higher or lower but was still open to challenge if the employee remained dissatisfied. Employees were expected to guarantee their own quality. They were not paid for defective work until it had been repaired on their own time.

All of the jobs in the company were rated according to skill, required effort, responsibility, and so forth, and a base wage rate for the job was assigned. Wage rates were comparable to those in similar jobs in the Cleveland area, and were adjusted annually based on Department of Labor statistics and quarterly to reflect changes in the cost of living. This determined the salary or hourly wage. For piecework jobs the time-study department set piece prices so that an employee could earn the base rate for a job if the employee produced at a standard rate.

The second element of the compensation system was a year-end bonus. Each year since 1934, Lincoln had paid a year-end bonus to its employees. As explained in the *Employee's Handbook:* "The bonus, paid at the discretion of the company, is not a gift, but rather it is the sharing of the results of efficient operation on the basis of the contribution of each person to the success of the company for that year." In 1974 this totaled $26 million, an aver-

[5] William Irrgang, "The Lincoln Incentive Management Program," Lincoln Lecture Series, Arizona State University, 1972, p. 13.

age of approximately $10,700 per employee, or 90 percent of prebonus wages.

The total amount to be paid out in bonuses each year was determined by the board of directors. The concentration on cost reduction kept costs low enough so that, generally, prices could be set (and not upset by competition), based on costs at the beginning of the year to produce a target return for stockholders and to give employees a bonus of approximately 100 percent of wages. The variance from the planned profits was usually added to (or subtracted from) the bonus pool to be distributed at year-end. Since 1945 the average bonus had varied from 78 percent to 129 percent of wages. In the past few years, it had been between 40 percent and 55 percent of pretax, prebonus profit, or as high as twice the net income after taxes.

An individual's share of the bonus was determined by a semiannual merit rating, which measured individual performance, compared with other members of the department or work group. Ratings for all employees had to average out to 100 on this relative scale. However, if an individual had made an unusual contribution and deserved a rating above 110, there was a special corporate pool of bonus points that could be awarded so as not to penalize co-workers. Ratings above 110 were thus reviewed by a corporate committee of vice presidents who evaluated the individual's contribution. Merit ratings varied widely from as low as 45 to as high as 160.

In determining an employee's merit rating, four factors were evaluated separately:

Dependability
Quality.
Output.
Ideas and cooperation.

Foremen were responsible for the rating of all factory workers. They could request help from assistant foremen (dependability), the production control department (output), the inspection department (quality), and methods department (ideas and cooperation). In the office, supervisors rated their people on the same items. At least one executive reviewed all ratings. All employees were urged to discuss their ratings with their department heads if they were dissatisfied or unclear about them.

Lincoln complemented its rating and pay system with a guaranteed continuous employment plan. This plan provided security against layoffs and assured continuity of employment. The plan guaranteed employment for at least 75 percent of the standard 40-hour week to every full-time employee with the company two or more years. In fact, the company had not had any layoffs since 1951, when initial trials for the plan were put into effect. It was formally established in 1958.

This was seen by the company as an essential element in the incentive plan. Without it, it was believed that employees would be more likely to resist improved production and efficiency for fear of losing their jobs. In accepting the guaranteed continuous employment plan, employees agreed to perform any job that was assigned as conditions required, and to work overtime during periods of high activity.

The philosophy and procedures regarding the incentive plan were the same for management and workers, except that Mr. Irrgang and Mr. Willis did not share in the bonus.

Employee views

To the casewriter, it appeared that employees generally liked working at Lincoln. The employee turnover rate was far below that of most other companies, and once a new employee made it through the first month or so, he rarely left for another company (see Exhibit 6). One employee explained:

> It's like trying out for a high school football team. If you make it through the first few practices, you're usually going to stay the whole season, especially after the games start.

One long-time employee who liked working at Lincoln was John "Tiny" Carrillo, an armature bander on the welding machine line, who had been with the company for 24 years. Tiny explained why:

> The thing I like here is that you're pretty much your own boss as long as you do your job. You're responsible for your own work, and you even put your stencil on every machine you work on. That way if it breaks down in the field and they have to take it back, they know who's responsible.
>
> Before I came here, I worked at Cadillac as a welder. After two months there I had the top hourly rate. I wasn't allowed to tell anyone because there were guys who still had the starting rate after a year. But, I couldn't go any higher after two months.
>
> I've done well. My rating is usually around 110, but I work hard, right through the smoke breaks. The only time I stop is a half hour for lunch. I make good money. I have two houses, one which I rent out, and four cars. They're all paid for. When I get my bills, I pay them the next day. That's the main thing, I don't owe anyone.
>
> Sure, there are problems. There's sometimes a bind between the guys with low grades and the guys with high ones, like in school. And there are guys who sway everything their way so they'll get the points, but they [management] have good tabs on what's going on. . . .
>
> A lot of new guys come in and leave right away. Most of them are just "mamma's boys" and don't want to do the work. We had a new guy who was a produce manager at a supermarket. He worked a couple of weeks, then quit and went back to his old job.

EXHIBIT 6
Labor turnover rates and employee's years of service

A. Labor turnover rates (total separations) The Lincoln Electric Company, all manufacturing industries, and the electrical machinery industry, 1958–70 (monthly rate)

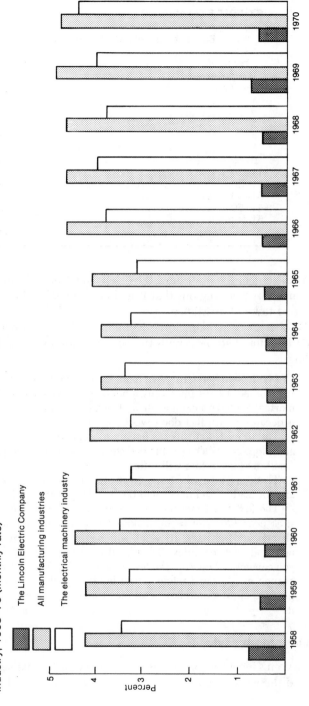

596

EXHIBIT 6 (continued)

B. Employee distribution by years of service

Years of service	Number of employees
Less than 1	153
1	311
2	201
3	93
4	34
5	90
6–10	545
11–20	439
21–30	274
31–40	197
41–50	27
51 or more	1
Total	2,365

At the end of the interview, the casewriter thanked Tiny for his time. He responded by pointing out that it had cost him $7 in lost time, but that he was glad to be of assistance.

Another piece worker, Jorge Espinoza, a fine-wire operator in the Electrode Division, had been with the company for six years. He explained his feelings:

> I believe in being my own man. I want to use my drive for my own gain. It's worked. I built my family a house and have an acre of land, with a low mortgage. I have a car and an old truck I play around with. The money I get is because I earn it. I don't want anything given to me.
>
> The thing I don't like is having to depend on other people on the line and suppliers. We're getting bad steel occasionally. Our output is down as a result, and my rating will suffer.
>
> There are men who have great drive here and can push for a job. They are not leaders and never will be, but they move up. That's a problem. . . .
>
> The first few times around, the ratings were painful for me. But now I stick near 100. You really make what you want. We just had a methods change, and our base rate went from 83 to 89 coils a day. The job is tougher now and more complex. But, it's all what you want. If you want 110 coils, you can get it. You just take less breaks. Today, I gambled and won. I didn't change my dies and made over a hundred coils. If I had lost, and the die plugged up, it would have cost me at least half an hour. But, today I made it.

Management style

Lincoln's incentive scheme was reinforced by top management's attitude toward the workers on the factory floor. In 1951 James Lincoln wrote:

It becomes perfectly true to anyone who will think this thing through that there is no such thing in an industrial activity as Management and Men having different functions or being two different kinds of people. Why can't we think and why don't we think that all people are Management? Can you imagine any president of any factory or machine shop who can go down and manage a turret lathe as well as the machinist can? Can you imagine any manager of any organization who can go down and manage a broom—let us get down to that—who can manage a broom as well as a sweeper can? Can you imagine any secretary of any company who can go down and fire a furnace and manage that boiler as well as the man who does the job? Obviously, all are Management.[6]

Lincoln's President George Willis stressed the equality in the company:

We try to avoid barriers between management and workers. We're treated equally as much as possible. When I got to work this morning at 7:30, the parking lot was three-quarters full. I parked way out there like anyone else would. I don't have a special reserved spot. The same principle holds true in our cafeteria. There's no executive dining room. We eat with everyone else.[7]

Mr. Willis felt that open and frank communication between management and workers had been a critical factor in Lincoln's success, and he believed that the company's advisory board had played a very important role in achieving this.

An advisory board of elected employee representatives had been established by James F. Lincoln in 1914. It had met twice a month ever since then. The advisory board provided a forum for employees to bring issues of concern to top management's attention, to question company policies, and to make suggestions for their improvement. As described in the *Employee's Handbook:*

Board service is a privilege and responsibility of importance to the entire organization. In discussions or in reaching decisions Board members must be guided by the best interests of the Company. These also serve the best interests of its workers. They should seek at all times to improve the cooperative attitude of all workers and see that all realize they have an important part in our final results.

---

[6] James F. Lincoln, *What Makes Workers Work?* (Cleveland, Ohio: The Lincoln Electric Co., 1951), pp. 3–4.

[7] The cafeteria had large rectangular and round tables. In general, factory workers gravitated toward the rectangular tables. There were no strict rules, however, and management personnel often sat with factory workers. Toward the center was a square table that seated only four. This was reserved for Mr. Irrgang, Mr. Willis, and their guests when they were having a working lunch.

All advisory board meetings were chaired by either the chairman or president of Lincoln. Usually, both were present. Issues brought up at board meetings were either resolved on the spot or assigned to an executive to be answered by the next meeting. After each meeting, Mr. Irrgang or Mr. Willis would send a memo to the responsible executive for each unanswered question, no matter how trivial, and he was expected to respond by the next meeting, if possible.

Minutes of all board meetings were posted on bulletin boards in each department, and members explained the board's actions to the other workers in their department.

The questions raised in the minutes of a given meeting were usually answered in the next set of minutes. This procedure had not changed significantly since the first meeting in 1914, nor had the types of issues raised changed significantly since then (see Exhibit 7).

EXHIBIT 7

A.   Management advisory board minutes, 1944
September 26, 1944

Absent: William Dillmuth

A discussion on piecework was again taken up. There was enough detail so it was thought best to appoint a committee to study it and bring a report into the meeting when that study is complete. That committee is composed of Messrs. Gilletly, Semko, Kneen, and Steingass. Messrs. Erickson and White will be called in consultation, and the group will meet next Wednesday, October 4.

The request was made that the members be permitted to bring guests to the meetings. The request was granted. Let's make sure we don't get too many at one time.

The point was made that materials are not being brought to the operation properly and promptly. There is no doubt of this difficulty. The matter was referred to Mr. Kneen for action. It is to be noted that conditions of deliveries from our suppliers have introduced a tremendous problem which has helped to increase this difficulty.

The request was made that overtime penalty be paid with the straight time. This will be done. There are some administrative difficulties which we will discuss at the next meeting, but the overtime payment will start with the first pay in October.

Beginning October 1, employee's badges will be discontinued. Please turn them in to the watchmen.

It was requested that piecework prices be put on repair work in Department J. This matter was referred to Mr. Kneen for action.

A request was made that a plaque showing the names of those who died in action, separate from the present plaques, be put in the lobby. This was referred to Mr. Davis for action.

EXHIBIT 7 (continued)

The question was asked as to what method for upgrading men is used. The ability of the individual is the sole reason for his progress. It was felt this is proper.

J. F. Lincoln
President

B.   Management advisory board minutes, 1974 (excerpts)
September 23, 1974

Absent: Tom Borkowski
       Albert Sinn

Mr. Kupetz had asked about the Christmas and Thanksgiving schedules. These are being reviewed, and we will have them available at the next meeting.

Mr. Howell had reported that the time clocks and the bells do not coincide. This is still being checked.

Mr. Sharpe had asked what the possibility would be to have a time clock installed in or near the Clean Room. This is being checked.

Mr. Joosten had raised the question of the pliability of the wrapping material used in the chemical department for wrapping slugs. The material we use at the present time is the best we can obtain at this time. . . .

Mr. Kostelac asked the question again whether the vacation arrangements could be changed, reducing the 15-year period to some shorter period. It was pointed out that at the present time, where we have radically changing conditions every day, it is not the time to go into this. We will review this matter at some later date. . . .

Mr. Martucci brought out the fact that there was considerable objection by the people involved to having to work on Saturday night to make up for holiday shutdowns. This was referred to Mr. Willis to be taken into consideration in schedule planning. . . .

Mr. Joosten reported that in the chemical department on the Saturday midnight shift they have a setup where individuals do not have sufficient work so that it is an uneconomical situation. This has been referred to Mr. Willis to be reviewed.

Mr. Joosten asked whether there would be some way to get chest X-rays for people who work in dusty areas. Mr. Loughridge was asked to check a schedule of where chest X-rays are available at various times. . . .

Mr. Robinson asked what the procedure is for merit raises. The procedure is that the foreman recommends the individual for a merit raise if by performance the individual has shown that the increase is merited. . . .

William Irrgang
Chairman

William Irrgang:MW
September 25, 1974

Workers felt that the advisory board provided a way of getting immediate attention for their problems. It was clear, however, that management still made the final decisions.[8] A former member of the advisory board commented:

> There are certain areas which are brought up in the meetings which Mr. Irrgang doesn't want to get into. He's adept at steering the conversation away from these. It's definitely not a negotiating meeting. But, generally, you really get action or an answer on why action isn't being taken.

In addition to the advisory board, there was a 12-member board of middle managers which met with Mr. Irrgang and Mr. Willis once a month. The topics of discussion were broader than those of the advisory board. The primary function of these meetings were for top management to get better acquainted with these individuals and to encourage cooperation between departments.

Lincoln's two top executives, Mr. Irrgang and Mr. Willis, continued the practice of James F. Lincoln in maintaining an open door to all employees. George Willis estimated that at least twice a week factory employees took advantage of this opportunity to talk with him.

Middle managers also felt that communication with Mr. Willis and Mr. Irrgang was open and direct. Often it bypassed intermediate levels of the organization. Most saw this as an advantage, but one commented:

> This company is run strictly by the two men at the top. Mr. Lincoln trained Mr. Irrgang in his image. It's very authoritarian, and decisions flow top down. It never became a big company. There is very little delegated, and top people are making too many small decisions. Mr. Irrgang and Mr. Willis work 80 hours a week, and no one I know in this company can say that his boss doesn't work harder than he does.

Mr. Willis saw management's concern for the worker as an essential ingredient in his company's formula for success. He knew at least 500 employees personally. In leading the casewriter through the plant, he greeted workers by name and paused several times to tell anecdotes about many of them.

At one point, an older man yelled to Mr. Willis, good-naturedly, "Where's my raise?" Mr. Willis explained that this man had worked for 40 years in a job requiring him to lift up to 20 tons of material a day. His earnings had been quite high because of his rapid work pace, but Mr. Willis had been afraid that as he was advancing in age he could injure himself working in that job. After months of Mr. Willis's urging, the man switched to an easier but lower paying job. He was disappointed in taking the earnings cut,

---

[8] In some cases, management allowed issues to be decided by a vote of employees. A recent example was when employees voted down a proposal to give them dental benefits paid by the company, recognizing that it would come directly out of their bonus.

and even after several years let the president know whenever he saw him.

Mr. Willis pointed to another employee and explained that this man's wife had recently died and for several weeks he had been drinking heavily and reporting to work late. Mr. Willis had earlier spent about half an hour discussing the situation with him to console him and see if the company could help in any way. He explained:

> I made a definite point of talking to him on the floor of the plant, near his work station. I wanted to make sure that other employees who knew the situation could see me with him. Speaking to him had symbolic value. It is important for employees to know that the president is interested in their welfare.

Management's philosophy was also reflected in the company's physical facilities. A no-nonsense atmosphere was firmly established at the gate to the parking lot where the only mention of the company name was in a sign reading:

$1,000 REWARD for information
leading to the arrest and conviction of persons stealing from the
Lincoln Electric parking lot.

There was a single entrance to the offices and plant for workers, management, and visitors. As one entered, the company motto in large stainless steel letters extending 30 feet across the wall was unavoidable:

THE ACTUAL IS LIMITED
THE POSSIBLE IS IMMENSE

A flight of stairs led down to a tunnel system for pedestrian traffic that ran under the single-story plant. At the base of the stairs was a large bronze plaque on which were permanently inscribed the names of the eight employees who had served more than 50 years, and the more than 350 active employees with 25 or more years of service who were in the "Quarter Century Club."

The long tunnel under the plant that led to the offices was clean and well lit. The executive offices were located in a windowless, two-story cement block office building, which sat like a box in the center of the plant. At the base of the staircase leading up to the offices, a Lincoln automatic welding machine and portraits of J. C. Lincoln and J. F. Lincoln welcomed visitors. The handrail on the staircase was welded into place, as were the ash trays in the tunnel.

In the center of the office building was a simple, undecorated reception room. A switchboard operator/receptionist greeted visitors, between filing and phone calls. The reception room reflected the spartan decor that was evident throughout the building. It was furnished with a metal coat rack, a wooden bookcase, and several plain wooden tables and chairs. All of the available reading material dealt with Lincoln Electric Company or welding.

One could leave the reception room through any of seven doors, which would lead almost directly to the desired office or department. Most of the departments were large open rooms with closely spaced desks. One manager explained that "Mr. Lincoln didn't believe in walls. He felt they interrupted the flow of communications and paperwork." Most of the desks and files were plain, old, and well worn, and there was a scarcity of modern office equipment. One reason for this was that the same criteria were applied for expenditures on equipment in the office as in the plant. The maintenance department had to certify that the equipment replaced could not be repaired. If acquired for cost reduction, the equipment had to have a one-year payback.[9]

The usually omnipresent Xerox machines were nowhere to be found. The explanation was that copying costs were tightly controlled and only certain individuals could use the Xerox copiers. Customer order forms, for example, which required eight copies, were run on a duplicating machine.

The private offices that existed were small, uncarpeted, and separated by green metal partitions. The president's office was slightly larger than the others, but still retained a spartan appearance. There was only one carpeted office. Mr. Willis explained:

> That office was occupied by Mr. Lincoln until he died in 1965. For the next five years it was left vacant, and now it is Mr. Irrgang's office and also the board of directors' and advisory board meeting room.

Personnel

Lincoln Electric had a strict policy of filling all but entry level positions by promoting from within the company. Whenever an opening occurred, a notice was posted on the 25 bulletin boards in the plant and offices. Any interested employee could apply for an open position. Because of the company's sustained growth and policy of hiring outsiders for entry level jobs only, employees had substantial opportunity for advancement.

An outsider generally could join the company in one of two ways: either taking a factory job working at an hourly or piece rate, or entering Lincoln's training programs in sales or engineering.[10] The company recruited

---

[9] Mr. Willis explained that capital projects with paybacks of up to two years were sometimes funded when they involved a product for which demand was growing.

[10] Lincoln's president and chairman both advanced through the ranks in manufacturing. Mr. Irrgang began as a pieceworker in the armature winding department, and Mr. Willis began in plant engineering. (See Exhibit 8 for employment history of Lincoln's top management.)

EXHIBIT 8
Employment history of top executives

William Irrgang, board chairman

1929: Hired, repair department
1930: Final inspection
1934: Inspection, wire department
1946: Director of factory engineering
1951: Executive vice president for manufacturing and engineering
1954: President and general manager
1972: Chairman of the board of directors

George E. Willis, president

1947: Hired, factory engineering
1951: Superintendent—Electrode Division
1959: Vice president
1969: Executive vice president of manufacturing and associated functions
1972: President

William Miskoe, vice president— international

1932: Hired, Chicago sales office
1941: President of Australian plant
1969: To Cleveland as vice president—international

Edwin M. Miller, vice president and assistant to the president

1923: Hired, factory worker
1925: Assistant foreman
1929: Production department
1940: Assistant department head— production department
1952: Superintendent—Machine Division
1959: Vice president
1973: Vice president and assistant to the president

D. Neal Manross, vice president— Machine and Motor Divisions

1941: Hired, factory worker
1942: Welding inspector
1952: General foreman, extruding department, and assistant plant superintendent
1953: Foreman—special products department, Machine Division
1956: Superintendent—Special Products Division
1959: Superintendent—motor manufacturing
1966: Vice president—Motor Division
1973: Vice president in charge of Motor and Machine Divisions

Albert S. Patnik, vice president— sales development

1940: Hired, sales student
1940: New London, Conn., as welder
1941: Los Angeles officer as junior salesman
1942: Seattle office as salesman
1945: To military service
1945: Reinstated to Seattle
1951: Cleveland sales office as rural dealer manager
1964: Assistant to the vice president of sales
1972: Vice president

Donald F. Hastings, vice president and general sales manager

1953: Hired, sales trainee
1954: Emeryville, Cal., as welding engineer
1959: District manager—Moline office
1970: To Cleveland as general sales manager
1972: Vice president and general sales manager

their trainees at colleges and graduate schools, including Harvard Business School. Starting salary in 1975 for a trainee with a bachelor's degree was $5.50 an hour, plus a year-end bonus, at an average of 40 percent of the normal rate. Wages for trainees with either a master's degree or several years of relevant experience was 5 percent higher.

Although Lincoln's president, vice president of sales, and personnel director were all Harvard Business School graduates, the company had not hired many recent graduates. Clyde Loughridge, the personnel director, explained:

> We don't offer them fancy staff positions, and we don't pretend to. Our starting pay is less than average, probably $17,000–$18,000 including bonus, and the work is harder than average. We start our trainees off by putting them in overalls, and they spend up to seven weeks in the welding school. In a lot of ways it's like boot camp. Rather than leading them along by the hand, we like to let the self-starters show themselves.

The policy of promoting from within had rarely been violated, and then only in cases where a specialized skill was required. Mr. Loughridge commented:

> In most cases we've been able to stick to it, even where the required skills are entirely new to the company. Our employees have a lot of varied skills, and usually someone can fit the job. For example, when we recently got our first computer, we needed a programmer and systems analyst. We had 20 employees apply who had experience or training in computers. We chose two, and it really helps that they know the company and understand our business.

The company did not send its employees to outside management development programs, and did not provide tuition grants for educational purposes.

Lincoln Electric had no formal organization chart, and management did not feel that one was necessary. (Exhibit 9 shows a chart drawn for the purpose of this case.)

As explained by one executive:

> People retire and their jobs are parceled out. We are very successful in overloading our overhead departments. We make sure this way that no unnecessary work is done and jobs which are not absolutely essential are eliminated. A disadvantage is that planning may suffer as may outside development to keep up with your field.

Lincoln's organizational hierarchy was flat, with few levels between the bottom and the top. For example, Don Hastings, the vice president of sales, had 37 regional sales managers reporting to him. He commented:

> I have to work hard, there's no question about that. There are only four of us in the home office plus two secretaries. I could easily use three more

EXHIBIT 9
Organization chart

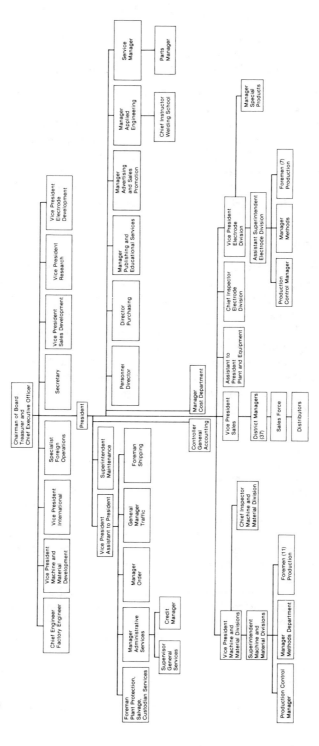

people. I work every Saturday, at least half a day. Most of our regional men do too, and they like me to know it. You should see the switchboard light up when 37 regional managers call in at five minutes to 12 on Saturday.

The president and chairman kept a tight rein over personnel matters. All changes in status of employees, even at the lowest level, had to be approved by Mr. Willis. Mr. Irrgang also had to give his approval if they involved salaried employees. Raises or promotions had to be approved in advance. An employee could be fired by his supervisor on the spot for cause, but if it was on questionable grounds it had to be approved afterward by either Mr. Willis or Mr. Irrgang. Usually the supervisor was supported, but there had been cases where a firing decision was reversed.

Marketing

Welding machines and electrodes were like "razors and razor blades." A Lincoln welding machine often had a useful life of 30 years or more, while electrodes (and fluxes) were consumed immediately in the welding process. The ratio of machine cost to annual consumables cost varied widely from perhaps 7:1 for a hand welder used in a small shop to 1:5 or more for an automatic welder used in a shipyard.

Although certain competitors might meet their costs and quality in selected products, management believed that no company could match Lincoln on their whole line. Another important competitive edge for Lincoln was its sales force. Al Patnik, vice president of sales development, explained:

> Most competitors operate through distributors. We have our own top field sales force.[11] We start out with engineering graduates and put them through our seven-month training program. They learn how to weld, and we teach them everything we can about equipment, metallurgy, and design. Then they spend time on the rebuild line [where machines brought in from the field are rebuilt] and even spend time in the office seeing how orders are processed. Finally, before the trainees go out into the field, they have to go into our plant and find a better way of making something. Then they make a presentation to Mr. Irrgang, just as if he were one of our customers.
>
> Our approach to the customer is to go in and learn what he is doing and show him how to do it better. For many companies our people become their experts in welding. They go in and talk to a foreman. They might say "Let me put on a headshield and show you what I'm talking about." That's how we sell them.

---

[11] The sales force was supplemented in some areas by distributors. Sales abroad were handled by wholly owned subsidiaries or Armco's International Division.

George Ward, a salesman in the San Francisco office, commented:

> The competition hires graduates with business degrees (without engi-
> neering background) and that's how they get hurt. This job is getting more
> technical every day. . . . A customer in California who is using our equip-
> ment to weld offshore oil rigs had a problem with one of our new products.
> I couldn't get the solution for them over the phone, so I flew in to the plant
> Monday morning and showed it to our engineers. Mr. Willis said to me,
> "Don't go back to California until this problem is solved. . . ." We use a
> "working together to solve your problem" approach. This, plus sticking to
> published prices, shows you're not interested in taking advantage of them.
>
> I had a boss who used to say: "Once we're in, Lincoln never loses a cus-
> tomer except on delivery." It's basically true. The orders I lost last year
> were because we couldn't deliver fast enough. Lincoln gets hurt when there
> are shortages because of our guaranteed employment. We don't hire short-
> term factory workers when sales take off, and other companies beat us on
> delivery.

The sales force was paid a salary plus bonus. Mr. Ward believed that
Lincoln's sales force was the best paid and hardest working in the industry:

> We're aggressive, and want to work and get paid for it. The sales force
> prides itself on working more hours than anyone else. . . . My wife wonders
> sometimes if you can work for Lincoln and have a family, too.

Manufacturing

Lincoln's plant was unusual in several respects. The casewriter was
struck by how crowded with materials and equipment it was, and how few
workers there were. It was obvious that employees worked very fast and efficiently with few breaks. Even during the ten-minute "smoke breaks" in
the morning and afternoon, employees often continued to work.

An innovative plant layout was partly responsible for the crowded appearance. Raw materials entered one side of the plant, and finished goods
came out the other side. There was no central stockroom for materials or
work in process. Instead, everything that entered the plant was transported
directly to the work station where it would be used. At a work station, a
single worker or group operated, in effect, as a "subcontractor." All required materials were piled around the station, allowing visual inventory
control, and they were paid a piece "price" for their production. Wherever
possible, the work flow followed a straight line through the plant from the
side where raw materials entered to the side where finished goods exited.
Because there was no union, the company had great flexibility with what
could be performed at a work station. For example, foundry work and metal
stamping could be carried out together by the same workers when necessary. Thus, work could flow almost directly along a line through the plant.

608

Intermediate material handling was avoided to a great extent. The major exception was where a large or expensive piece of machinery was used by multiple production lines, and the work had to be brought to the machines.

Many of the operations in the plant were automated. Much of the manufacturing equipment was proprietary,[12] designed and built by Lincoln. In some cases, the company had modified machines built by others to run two or three times as fast as when originally delivered.

Close coordination between product design engineers and the methods department from the time a product was originally conceptualized was seen as a key factor in reducing costs and rationalizing manufacturing. William Irrgang explained:

> After we have [an] idea . . . we start thinking about manufacturing costs, before anything leaves the design engineering department. At that point, there is a complete "getting together" of manufacturing and design engineers—and plant engineers, too, if new equipment is involved.
>
> Our tooling, for instance, is going to be looked at carefully while the design of a product is still in process. Obviously, we can increase or decrease the tooling very materially by certain considerations in the design of a product, and we go on the basis of total costs at all times. In fact, as far as total cost is concerned, we even think about such matters as shipping, warehousing, etc. All of these factors are taken into consideration when we're still at the design stage. It's very essential that this be done: otherwise, you can lock yourself out from a lot of potential economies.[13]

In 1974 Lincoln's plant had reached full capacity, operating nearly around the clock. Land bordering its present location was unavailable, and management was moving ahead with plans to build a second plant 15 miles away on the same freeway as the present plant.

Over the years, Lincoln had slowly back-integrated by "making" rather than "buying" a larger percentage of their components. For example, even though their unit volume of gasoline engines was only a fraction of their suppliers', Lincoln purchased engine blocks and components and assembled them, rather than purchasing completed engines. Management was continually evaluating opportunities to back integrate and had not arbitrarily ruled out manufacturing any of their components or raw materials.

Administrative productivity

Lincoln's high productivity was not limited to manufacturing. Clyde Loughridge pointed to the personnel department as an example:

---

[12] Visitors were barred from the Electrode Disivion unless they had a pass signed by Mr. Willis or Mr. Irrgang.

[13] "Incentive Management in Action," *Assembly Engineering*, March 1967.

Normally, for 2,300 employees you would need a personnel department of about 20, but we have only six, and that includes the nurse, and our responsibilities go beyond those of the typical personnel department.

Once a year, Mr. Loughridge had to outline his objectives for the upcoming year for Mr. Willis, but he did not operate on a budget.

I don't get a budget. There would be no point to it. I just spend as little as possible. I operate this just like my home. I don't spend on anything I don't need.

In the traffic department, workers also seemed very busy. There, a staff of 12 controlled the shipment of 2½ million pounds of material a day. Their task was complex. Delivery was included in the price of their products. They thus could reduce the overall cost to the customer by mixing products in most loads and shipping the most efficient way possible to the company's 39 warehouses. Jim Biek, general traffic manager, explained how they accomplished this:

For every order, we decide whether it would be cheaper by rail or truck. Then we consolidate orders so that over 90 percent of what goes out of here is full carload or full truckload, as compared to perhaps 50 percent for most companies. We also mix products so that we come in at the top of the weight brackets. For example, if a rate is for 20,000 to 40,000 pounds, we will mix orders to bring the weight right up to that 40,000 limit. All this is computed manually. In fact, my old boss used to say, "We run traffic like a ma and pa grocery store."

As in the rest of Lincoln, the employees in the traffic department worked their way up from entry level positions. Jim Biek had come into his position of general traffic manager after nine years as a purchasing engineer. He had received an MBA degree from Northwestern, after a BS in mechanical engineering from Purdue, started in the engineering training program, and then spend five years in product development and methods before going to purchasing and finally to traffic. Lack of experience in traffic was a disadvantage, but the policy of promoting from within also had its advantages. Mr. Biek explained:

One of my first tasks was to go to Washington and fight to get welders reclassified as motors to qualify for a lower freight rate. With my engineering experience and knowledge of welders, I was in a better position to argue this than a straight traffic man. . . .

Just about everybody in here was new to traffic. One of my assistant traffic managers had worked on the loading platform here for ten years before he came into the department. He had to go to night school to learn about rates, but his experience is invaluable. He knows how to load trucks and railcars backwards and forward. Who could do a better job of consolidating orders than he does? He can look at an order and think of it as rows of pallets.

Some day we'll outgrow this way of operating, but right now I can't imagine a computer juggling loads like some of our employees do.

Lincoln's order department had recently begun computerizing its operations. It was the first time a computer was used anywhere in Lincoln except in engineering and research, and according to Russell Stauffer, head of the order department, "It was a three-year job for me to sell this to top management."

The computer was expected to replace 12 or 13 employees who would gradually be moved into new jobs. There had been some resistance to the computer, according to Mr. Stauffer.

It's like anything new. People get scared. Not all the people affected have been here for the two years required to be eligible for guaranteed employment. And even though the others are assured a job, they don't know what it will be and will have to take what's offered.

The computer was expected to produce savings of $100,000 a year, plus allow a greater degree of control. Mr. Stauffer explained:

We're getting information out of this that we never knew before. The job here is very complex. We're sending out more than two million pounds of consumables a day. Each order might have 30 or 40 items, and each item has a bracket price arrangement based on total order size. A clerk has to remember or determine quickly whether we are out of stock on any items and calculate whether the stock-out brings the order down into another bracket. This means they have to "remember" the prices and items out of stock. This way of operating was okay up to about $200 million in sales, but now we've outgrown the human capability to handle the problem.

Although he had no previous experience in computers, Mr. Stauffer had full responsibility for the conversion.

I've been here for 35 years. The first day I started, I unloaded coal cars and painted fences. Then I went to the assembly line, first on small parts, then large ones. I've been running the order department for 12 years. Since I've been here, we've had studies on computers every year or two, and it always came out that we couldn't save money. Finally, when it looked like we'd make the switch, I took some courses at IBM. Over the past year and a half, they've totaled eight and a half weeks, which is supposed to equal a full semester of college.

To date, the conversion had gone well, but much slower than anticipated. Order pressure had been so high that many mistakes would have been catastrophic. Management pressure, therefore, had been to assure 100 percent quality operation rather than faster conversion.

Lincoln's future

The 1947 Harvard Business School case study of Lincoln Electric ended with a prediction by a union leader from the Cleveland area:

> The real test of Lincoln will come when the going gets tough. The thing Lincoln holds out to the men is high earnings. They work like dogs at Lincoln, but it pays off. . . .
>
> I think [Mr. Lincoln] puts too much store by monetary incentives—but then, there's no denying he has attracted people who respond to that type of incentive. But I think that very thing is a danger Lincoln faces. If the day comes when they can't offer those big bonuses, or his people decide there's more to life than killing yourself making money, I predict The Lincoln Electric Company is in for trouble.

Lincoln President George Willis joined the company the year that the above comment was made. Reflecting on his 28 years with the company Mr. Willis observed:

> The company hasn't changed very much since I've been here. It's still run pretty much like Mr. Lincoln ran it. But today's workers are different. They're more outspoken and interested in why things are being done, not just how. We have nothing to hide and never did, so we can give them the answers to their questions.

Looking forward, Mr. Willis saw no need to alter Lincoln's strategy or its policies:

> My job will continue to be to have everyone in the organization recognize that a common goal all of us can and must support is to give the customer the quality he needs, when he needs it, at the lowest cost. To do this, we have to have everyone's understanding of this goal and their effort to accomplish it. In one way or another, I have to motivate the organization to meet this goal. The basic forms of the motivation have evolved over the last 40 years. However, keeping the system honed so that everyone understands it, agrees with it, and brings out disagreements so improvements can be made or thinking changed becomes my major responsibility.
>
> If our employees did not believe that management was trustworthy, honest, and impartial, the system could not operate. We've worked out the mechanics. They are not secret. A good part of my responsibility is to make sure the mechanics are followed. This ties back to a trust and understanding between individuals at all levels of the organization.
>
> I don't see any real limits to our size. Look at a world with a present population of just under 4 billion now and 6.25 billion by the year 2000. Those people aren't going to tolerate a low standard of living. So there will be a lot of construction, cars, bridges, oil, and all these things that have got to be to support a population that large.
>
> My job will still be just the traditional things of assuring that we keep up with the technology and have sufficient profit to pay the suppliers of capi-

EXHIBIT 10

July 31, 1975

To: Mr. Norman Fast

Dear Mr. Fast:

I believe that you have summarized the Incentive Management System of The Lincoln Electric Company very well; however, readers may feel that the success of the Company is due only to the psychological principles included in your presentation.

Please consider adding the efforts of our executives who devote a great deal of time to the following items that are so important to the consistent profit and long-range growth of the Company.

   I. Management has limited research, development, and manufacturing to a standard product line designed to meet the major needs of the welding industry.
  II. New products must be reviewed by manufacturing, and all production costs verified before being approved by management.
 III. Purchasing is challenged to not only procure materials at the lowest cost but also to work closely with engineering and manufacturing to assure that the latest innovations are implemented.
  IV. Manufacturing supervision and all personnel are held accountable for reduction of scrap, energy conservation, and maintenance of product quality.
   V. Production control, material handling, and methods engineering are closely supervised by top management.
  VI. Material and finished goods inventory control, accurate cost accounting and attention to sales costs, credit, and other financial areas have constantly reduced overhead and led to excellent profitability.
 VII. Management has made cost reduction a way of life at Lincoln and definite programs are established in many areas, including traffic and shipping, where tremendous savings can result.
VIII. Management has established a sales department that is technically trained to reduce customer welding cost. This sales technique and other real customer services have eliminated nonessential frills and resulted in long term benefits to all concerned.
  IX. Managements has encouraged education, technical publishing and long-range programs that have resulted in industry growth, thereby assuring market potential for The Lincoln Electric Company.

Richard S. Sabo

bjs

tal. Then, I have to make sure communication can be maintained adequately. That last task may be the biggest and most important part of my job in the years ahead as we grow larger and still more complex.

After reading the completed case study, Mr. Richard S. Sabo, manager of publicity and educational services, sent the letter given in Exhibit 10 to the casewriter.

case 28

Zurn Industries, Inc.

In 1965 Zurn Industries was a 65-year-old company with sales of $12 million. Now, two quarters into fiscal 1979, annual sales were expected to surpass $300 million, making the company one of the country's 600 largest industrials. Net profits over that period grew from $580,000 to $10.6 million, and the market value of the company went up from $11.9 million on December 30, 1965, to $77.7 million on December 29, 1978. An overview of Zurn Industries' performance history is portrayed in Exhibits 1 and 2. Recent financial statements are given in Exhibit 3 and 4.

Just as dramatic in a symbolic sense had been the recent move of the corporate offices to a striking modern building on a large wooded tract overlooking Lake Erie's Presque Isle Bay in Erie, Pennsylvania. In commenting on the new corporate headquarters, Everett F. Zurn, chairman of the company's executive committee, noted that for many years preceding this move the company had had the facetious distinction of being the only New York Stock Exchange–listed company with its corporate offices in leased quarters located above a retail meat market.

Satisfaction with past performance, however, would not dissuade Zurn management, which by now was directed by a third generation of Zurn family members (see Exhibit 5), from considering how they would deliver the 15 percent annual earnings growth which they stated as a goal, and whether this strategy would necessitate changes in the way Zurn businesses were operated, or in the businesses they were in.

This case describes the growth and evolution of Zurn Industries through three phases. The first period, from 1900 to 1965, includes the origins and gradual buildup of the company. The second period, from 1966 to 1973, covers the rapid acquisitive expansion which transformed Zurn Industries into a leading integrated company in environmental control. The third period, from 1974 to 1978, shows the company shifting focus from growth to profitability. Finally the case discusses the problems and options seen by management as they face the years to come. Historic growth and future

EXHIBIT 1
Zurn Industries' operating performance

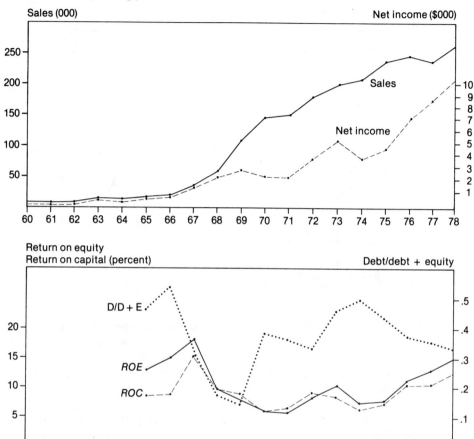

growth potential of the pollution control industry as a whole are discussed in the Appendix.

1900–1965: ORIGINS

Company origins

Zurn Industries, Inc., was founded in 1900 by John A. Zurn and Milton Rowley, who purchased from the Erie City Iron Works, where John A. Zurn was then employed, the patent and tooling for certain discontinued product lines. Among these was a patented backwater valve for preventing the flow

616

EXHIBIT 2
Zurn Industries' stock market performance

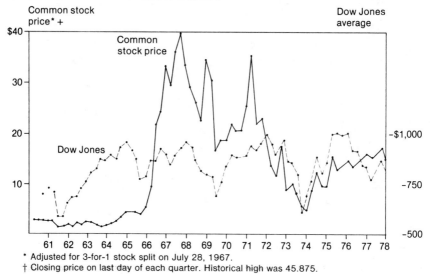

* Adjusted for 3-for-1 stock split on July 28, 1967.
† Closing price on last day of each quarter. Historical high was 45.875.

of storm and wastewaters back into a building's drainage system. In 1906 John A. Zurn bought out his partner and purchased a frame building at 14th and German Streets in Erie, Pennsylvania. By 1913 the company had outgrown the frame structure and constructed a two-story brick building on the same site.

The early 20s ushered in the era of the "Zurn Brothers." In 1920 J. A.'s son Melvin joined his father in the business, followed in 1931 by his brother Everett. The brother team directed the Zurn enterprise until the 1960s, with Melvin concentrating on sales and marketing, and Everett developing the company's manufacturing, engineering, and research program.

Broadening the capabilities

In 1928 the company had diversified into other product lines by purchasing the American Flexible Coupling Company, which manufactured a series of patented mechanical drive flexible couplings used to connect rotating shafts. The 1930s and 1940s saw a continued expansion of existing product lines and applications.

In 1954 the company established corporate headquarters separated geographically from its manufacturing facilities and reorganized its corporate structure into four operating divisions: Fluid Control, Hydromechanics, Mechanical Power Transmission, and Research and Development. Its name was changed in 1956 from J. A. Zurn Mfg. Company to Zurn Industries, Inc.

Going over-the-counter

On December 1, 1959, John Henry Zurn, eldest son of Melvin, and first active member of the third generation of Zurns, lost his life in an airline accident at the age of 34. His untimely death brought Zurn management to the realization that launching a program to achieve public ownership needed to be a priority objective.

In 1961 Zurn Industries, Inc., "went public" on the over-the-counter market. The stock offering at $8.00 per share (for a net of $7.20) represented a P/E of 16.6. Chairman Frank W. Zurn commented on the initial stock offering:

> The Mechanical Power Transmission Division's "Synchrogear" and "Amerigear" assemblies were used in the main propulsion system of practically every nuclear submarine launched by the United States. So we went public largely on the appeal that we were in the nuclear powered submarine program. We were viewed as a company having a strong potential in the future growth of atomic energy.

By the fiscal year ending March 31, 1965, Zurn Industries was earning a net income of $580,000 on sales of $12.4 million. Mechanical Power Transmission, Hydromechanics, and Fluid Control accounted, respectively, for 40 percent, 50 percent, and 10 percent of sales.

1966–1973: AN INTEGRATED COMPANY IN ENERGY AND ENVIRONMENT

Fiscal 1966 marked a milestone in the company's development. Under the leadership of Frank W. Zurn, who became president in 1965, Zurn Industries, Inc., embarked on an acquisition program to establish itself in the market for environmental pollution control equipment. Eight years later the company passed the $200 million mark in sales, with an organization capable of providing products, systems, and services in all four major environmental pollution areas—air, land, water, and noise.

Commenting on the factors which brought about this change in orientation, Frank W. Zurn explained:

> After we went public in 1961 our common stock price started to decline. It dropped more in 1962 and 1963. In 1964 the nuclear powered submarine Thresher sank with a loss of lives, and all nuclear submarine programs were halted. Admiral Rickover sent us a long cable advising us to roll back all shipments. The estimation was it would be at least six months until the cause of the disaster could be pinpointed and corrected. This was a shocking thing to us because at the time about 25 percent of our sales and 50 percent of our earnings were coming from the nuclear submarine program. As it turned out, the program was halted for about a year and a half. By 1965 we were really scratching and wondering what the future direction of the company would be.

EXHIBIT 3

ZURN INDUSTRIES, INC.
Five-Year Consolidated Financial Summary
($000 except for per share amounts)

Year ended March 31

Operating data	1978	1977	1976	1975	1974	1973
Net sales	$259,631	$232,559	$242,836	$235,244	$205,641	$162,635
Cost of products sold	190,975	169,521	178,188	181,989	155,024	121,227
Interest expense	2,743	2,600	3,116	3,229	2,795	2,673
Income from continuing operations before income taxes and extraordinary items	20,347	16,774	14,605	9,492	15,257	11,095
Provision for income taxes	9,700	7,925	7,600	4,700	7,800	5,609
Income from continuing operations	10,647	8,849	7,005	4,792	7,457	5,486
(Loss) from discontinued operations, net of income taxes	—	—	—	(175)	(3,873)	(158)
Extraordinary credit, net of income taxes	—	—	—	—	312	192
Net income	10,647	8,849	7,005	4,617	3,896	5,520
Dividend requirements on preferred stock	202	205	217	220	220	221
Net income applicable to common stock	10,445	8,644	6,788	4,397	3,676	5,299
Earnings (loss) per share of common stock:						
Primary:						
From continuing operations	1.93	1.61	1.28	0.86	1.37	0.99
From discontinued operations	—	—	—	(0.03)	(0.73)	(0.03)
Extraordinary items	—	—	—	—	0.06	0.04
Net	1.93	1.61	1.28	0.83	0.70	1.00
Fully diluted:						
From continuing operations	1.79	1.51	1.22	0.86	1.30	0.98
From discontinued operations	—	—	—	(0.03)	(0.63)	(0.03)
Extraordinary items	—	—	—	—	0.05	0.03
Net	1.79	1.51	1.22	0.83	0.72	0.98
Dividends paid per common share	0.60	0.44	0.34	0.28	0.28	0.28

Financial position at year-end

Working capital	56,658	60,076	61,281	65,681	70,821	57,640
Net property, plant, and equipment	47,231	37,169	33,499	28,799	28,425	29,900
Total assets	178,710	165,406	146,388	151,556	151,033	136,271
Long-term debt	36,582	37,094	36,608	47,153	53,335	44,459
Stockholders' equity	77,148	69,600	63,198	58,179	55,261	53,064
Per share of common stock	13.20	11.87	10.68	9.72	9.17	8.75
General statistics						
Expenditures for property, plant, and equipment	10,161	9,683	7,829	5,144	4,948	3,409
Depreciation and amortization	4,120	3,515	3,358	3,479	3,281	2,949
Number of stockholders of record	13,151	13,513	13,654	13,816	13,290	12,877
Weighted-average shares outstanding	5,398,428	5,364,877	5,321,325	5,287,848	5,285,417	5,293,085
Price range of common stock	17¾–13½	15⅞–11⅜	14–7¾	10–3⅞	17⅜–8½	36–13¼

Note: For comparative purposes, 1974 has been restated for "discontinued operations."
Source: 1977 and 1978 annual reports.

EXHIBIT 4

ZURN INDUSTRIES, INC.
Consolidated Balance Sheets

	March 31	
Assets	1978	1977
Current assets:		
Cash	$ 3,325,023	$ 3,197,921
Short-term marketable securities, at cost (approximates market)	550,000	22,512,888
Notes and accounts receivable:		
Trade accounts less allowances (1978—$1,190,000; 1977—$1,160,000)	$ 45,769,374	$ 39,387,658
Other notes and accounts	2,132,067	2,021,796
Total notes and accounts receivable	$ 47,901,441	$ 41,409,454
Contracts in progress	8,831,005	2,862,655
Inventories:		
Finished goods	$ 11,434,800	$ 10,197,989
Work in process	22,702,118	17,371,723
Raw materials and supplies	17,845,887	13,144,552
Total inventories	$ 51,982,805	$ 40,714,264
Prepaid expenses and deferred income taxes	6,011,953	5,535,143
Total current assets	$118,602,227	$116,232,325

	March 31	
Liabilities	1978	1977
Current liabilities:		
Notes payable—banks	$ 4,562,500	$ -0-
Trade accounts payable	21,023,656	$ 16,795,820
Salaries and wages and related payroll items	7,641,300	7,345,767
Advance billings on contracts in progress	2,730,779	1,422,756
Customer deposits	6,419,167	8,062,204
Accrued warranty and other expenses	14,623,465	11,730,510
Dividends payable	854,399	689,001
Federal and state income taxes	3,819,946	9,818,205
Current portion of long-term debt	268,353	292,399
Total current liabilities	$ 61,943,565	$ 56,156,662
Long-term debt:		
Notes payable	$ 18,576,872	$ 18,964,639
5¾% convertible subordinated debentures	17,737,000	17,837,000
Total long-term debt	$ 36,313,872	$ 36,801,639
Deferred income taxes	3,304,815	2,847,451

Other assets:		
Long-term notes receivable	$ 6,882,210	$ 7,586,515
Unamortized cost of patents and drawings	2,099,551	1,623,079
Goodwill	1,524,512	653,739
Miscellaneous	2,370,538	2,141,430
Total other assets	$ 12,876,811	$ 12,004,763
Property, plant, and equipment:		
Land and land improvements ..	$ 3,838,734	$ 3,036,365
Buildings and leasehold improvements	25,920,706	22,097,209
Machinery and equipment	37,705,467	32,269,701
Autos and aircraft	4,692,246	4,318,759
Construction in progress	4,001,738	1,583,890
	$ 76,158,891	$ 63,305,924
Less: Allowances for depreciation and amortization	28,927,429	26,137,131
Total property, plant, and equipment	$ 47,231,462	$ 37,168,793
Total assets	$178,710,500	$165,405,881

Stockholders' Equity		
Preferred stock, par value $1 a share:		
Series of $1.80 cumulative convertible (aggregate involuntary liquidation preference $2,037,240—1978) ..	$ 50,931	$ 51,964
Series of $1 cumulative convertible (aggregate involuntary liquidation preference $4,327,240—1978)	108,181	109,614
Common stock, par value $0.50 a share	2,681,949	2,659,222
Capital in excess of par value of stock	18,176,115	17,893,828
Retained earnings	56,129,072	48,885,501
Total stockholders' equity	$ 77,148,248	$ 69,600,129
Contingent liabilities		
Total liabilities and stockholders' equity	$178,710,500	$165,405,881

Source: 1978 annual report.

EXHIBIT 5
Zurn management

	Age	Position	Family relationship
Everett F. Zurn	70	Chairman, executive committee	
Frank W. Zurn	51	Chairman	Nephew of chairman, executive committee
David M. Zurn	40	President and chief executive officer	Nephew of chairman, executive committee
Albert A. Baker	55	Executive vice president	
Max O. Funk	61	Executive vice president	
Russell F. Lindsay	52	Executive vice president	
Edward J. Donn	53	Senior vice president—corporate relations	
Robert E. Lugenbeal ...	49	Senior vice president—finance and controller	
David H. Lund	50	Senior vice president—general counsel and secretary	
James A. Zurn	36	Vice president—treasurer	Son of chairman, executive committee

Source: 10-K.

In the spring of 1965 I was elected president and became a member of YPO (Young Presidents' Organization). During the next year I attended two YPO one-week seminars on the subject of mergers and acquisitions. As I listened to the Tex Thorntons and the Roy Ashes (Litton Industries), I got quite inspired by what they were saying. At the same time Zurn was courted by quite a few companies to join them, including an English company with whom we negotiated quite seriously. And so we learned a little reverse selling.

At about the same time the Clean Water Restoration Act was signed in 1966, Melvin and Everett Zurn went to a very inspiring week at the NAM (National Association of Manufacturers) on the subject of environment. They came back convinced that we ought to get into the environmental business, and that we ought to go into it in a big way. So we first tried on our own. We were already into water pollution to a limited degree. We hired some people with experience in electrostatic precipitators and spent about $400,000 trying to get into that market. We made many proposals, but never sold a job. From then on we started actively seeking acquisitions.

The first acquisition

The first acquisition was that of Erie City Iron Works in 1966—the same company where John A. Zurn once had been a foreman in the final inspection department—for $3.3 million in cash. Erie City's 1965 sales were $12.4

million with earnings of $525,000, both about equal to Zurn Industries' sales and earnings. David M. Zurn, president, commented on the circumstances and risks involved:

> At that time we were negotiating to sell some equity to a British group, David Brown. The John Hancock Life Insurance Company, which knew about those negotiations, gave us an initial commitment to lend the full purchase price. When the negotiations with the British group broke off, however, John Hancock reduced its commitment to $2.0 million if we agreed to come up with additional equity within a reasonable amount of time, without specifying how many weeks or months that was. Both Melvin and Everett then pledged their shares to borrow $750,000 each, short term, and we immediately started to work on getting a public offering out. Fortunately, the Erie City acquisition had a good earnings per share impact, which facilitated the offering.

Zurn Industries' business concept

After the Erie City Iron Works acquisition, the strategy guiding further acquisition was frequently stated. The first element of this strategy consisted of the "total approach" as formulated in the March 31, 1966, annual report:

> Stated simply, this concept implies the optimal utilization of a greater share of our skills and products for the purpose of engineering major projects from start to finish. Thus in helping to clean up municipalities' water pollution problems, for example, we are now able to incorporate into the overall design a variety of water pollution control systems, energy recovery units, and waste controls to effect total solution to that problem.

In the 1967 annual report Frank W. Zurn noted:

> Of equal importance [to this turnkey capability] is the further broadening of our product base as it relates to our work in controlling pollution, waste, and water supply.

In 1968 this broadening of capabilities was further formalized; Zurn was to be

> a total environmental control company, offering an integrated approach in land, water, air, and noise pollution control. In those fields, Zurn would offer products, systems, and services from initial study and design to final monitoring and management of the completed facility.

At the time this strategy was formulated, environmental concerns were just coming to the foreground. The federal government was laying the groundwork for establishing criteria and standards through such laws as the Clean Air Act of 1963, the Solid Waste Disposal Act of 1965, the Clean Water Restoration Act of 1966, the Air Quality Act of 1967, the Aircraft

Noise Abatement Act of 1968, and the National Environmental Policy Act of 1970.

Turning the concept into reality

Between 1967 and 1973, when the focus of Zurn Industries shifted from acquisitive growth to consolidation, 24 acquisitions were made (see Exhibit 6). Together with the company's original businesses, these acquisions resulted in 1973 reported sales of $196.6 million. They were placed in the following groups:

1. Environmental Management and Systems Group
   a. Environmental management
   b. Water pollution control systems
   c. Air pollution control systems
   d. Noise pollution control systems
   e. Environmental protection systems
2. Energy Group
   a. Energy systems
   b. Mechanical systems
3. Leisure Products Group

Environmental Management and Systems Group

The Environmental Management and Systems Group represented 65 percent of total sales in 1973.

Environmental management. Environmental management, which represented integrated "total project capability" and accounted for 20 percent of 1973 sales, originated with the acquisition in late 1968 of the Ludwig Engineering and Science Company of Los Angeles. Besides a staff of 200 experienced environmental engineers, offering total turnkey capability in water pollution control (Engineering-Science, Inc.), the company also had an engineering construction division engaged in building large water resources projects (Pascal & Ludwig, Inc.). A light construction division (Greynald Construction Co.) built "environmental communities," which were primarily waterfront housing developments.

Environmental systems. Within environmental systems, *water pollution control systems,* an original Zurn business, accounted for 17 percent of total sales by 1973. Several acquisitions were made to complement Zurn capability in this area, the main one being the 1967 acquisition of the Hays Manufacturing Company of Erie, which produced water supply controls; the acquisition of Wilkins Regulator Company (Los Angeles), manufacturer of automatic water pressure regulating valves; and the 1973 acquisition of

EXHIBIT 6
Acquisitions 1956–1973

	Date of acquisition	Consideration*	Market value†	Types of products and services	Year prior to acquisition		Organizational affiliation
					Sales	Profits	
Erie City Iron Works	January 3, 1966	$3,418,651	$ 3,418,651	Steam generating systems	$12.4M	$ 525K	Energy systems
Standard Fire Hose Company	June 9, 1967	83,600 shares common stock	1,954,150	Interior fire protection equipment	1.8M	63K	Environmental protection systems
Presque Isle Plastics, Inc.‡	June 12, 1967	184,000 shares common stock	4,485,000	Pressure injection molded plastics	6.3M	371K	Leisure Products Group
Hays' Manufacturing Company‡	August 9, 1967	125,000 shares $1.80 cumulative convertible preferred stock	6,627,903§	Water supply controls	8.5M	362K	Water pollution control systems
Fly Ash Arrestor Corporation	November 27, 1967	80,000 shares common stock	2,220,000	Particulate arrestors for air pollution control	1.9M	88K	Air pollution control systems
General-Erie Corporation	April 1, 1968	76,090 shares common stock	2,330,256	Air cleaners and dryers	1.4M	153K	Air pollution control systems
Metal Bellows Corporation	June 11, 1968	138,294 shares common stock	6,033,076	Welded diaphragm metal bellows	4.5M	207K	Mechanical systems
Ludwig Engineering and Science‡	September 12, 1968	206,901 shares common stock	7,293,260	Environmental engineering and construction	13.1M	199K	Environmental management
Erie Engine and Manufacturing Co.‡	September 20, 1968	70,000 shares common stock	2,905,000	Hydraulic machinery and equipment for the plastics and rubber industries	3.5M	101K	Mechanical systems

EXHIBIT 6 (continued)

	Date of acquisition	Consideration*	Market value†	Types of products and services	Year prior to acquisition		Organizational affiliation
					Sales	Profits	
Swartwout, Inc.‡	October 31, 1968	79,872 shares common stock	2,855,424	Air moving and ventilation systems	3.9M	(96K)	Air pollution control systems
Lamar Pipe Co.‡	December 3, 1968	176,150 shares common stock	6,363,419	Precast concrete pipeline systems	5M	354K	Water pollution control systems
Bay City Forge Company, Inc.	December 23, 1968	45,000 shares common stock	1,530,000	Specialty steel forgings	1.1M	81K	Mechanical systems
Sargent, Inc.‡	December 27, 1968	38,462 shares common stock	1,293,669	Incineration systems	2.4M	43K	Land pollution control systems
Clarage Fan Company	March 7, 1969	$1,864,453 150,000 shares $1 cumulative and convertible preferred stock	5,895,703§	Industrial fans and air handling systems	11.2M	556K	Air pollution control systems
Tri-Ex, Inc.‡	April 15, 1969	56,000 shares common stock	1,561,000	Heat exchangers	2.4M	90K	Energy systems
Goodfriend-Oster-gaard Associates‡	June 16, 1969	10,005 shares common stock	272,636	Acoustical engineering and testing	0.2M	4K	Noise pollution control systems
Cosco Fire Protection, Inc.	February 10, 1970	355,000 shares common stock	12,291,875	Design and installation of interior fire protection sprinkling systems	4M	126K	Environmental protection systems
The Robert Irsay Company	June 23, 1971	400,000 shares common stock	8,000,000	Design and installation of air conditioning, air cleaning, and heating systems	15M	1,246K	Air pollution control systems

Company	Date	Consideration	Business				Group
Vulcan Manufacturing Company	October 19, 1971	120,000 shares common stock	Thermal exchange systems and fractionating towers	2,325,000	7.0M	57K	Energy systems
Crowell Designs, Inc.	October 29, 1971	50,000 shares common stock	Recreational vehicle and water pressure systems	987,500	1.3M	24K	Leisure Products Group
Wilkins Regulator Co.	December 14, 1971	$2,000,000	Water pressure regulators	2,000,000	1.2M	102K	Water pollution control systems
Vinylplex Inc.‡	January 15, 1973	169,600 shares common stock	PVC water pressure pipe		2M	(20K)	Water pollution control systems
Golf Lynx, Inc.	March 22, 1973	450,000 shares common stock	Golf equipment		5.1M	823K	Leisure Products Group
Cypra Inc. ‖	June 22, 1973	21,000 shares common stock	Engineering of air control systems		1.3M	50K	Air pollution control systems
Marland One-Way Clutch Co.	January 31, 1976	$3,600,000	Mechanical energy conversion systems	3,600,000	3.5M	669K	Energy systems
Permutit Co. Inc.	July 31, 1977	$12,000,000	Wastewater treatment systems	12,000,000	32.4M	2,278K	Water pollution control systems

* Reflects retroactively on 2-for-1 stock split of the common stock in July 1967.
† Prior to March 20, 1968, at last bid on the over-the-counter market at dates of acquisition. On and after March 20, 1968, at closing price of the common stock on the New York Stock Exchange at dates of acquisition.
‡ Including one or more affiliated companies or subsidiaries.
§ Computed on basis of common stock into which the preferred stock is convertible (plus cash consideration on Clarage Fan Company acquisition).
‖ Transaction in fiscal 1974.

Vinylplex Inc. (Pittsburg, Kansas), manufacturers of PVC water pressure pipe. Several licensee arrangements were also consummated such as with Attisholz of Switzerland for a biological treatment system and with Balcke Machinenbau of West Germany for natural draft cooling towers.

The capability of the *air pollution control systems*, which together with pollution control provided 23 percent of overall sales in 1973, originated with the 1966 acquisition of the Erie City Iron Works, which in addition to its steam generator business presented some capabilities in waste heat energy recovery and the cleaning and cooling of hot noxious gases. Some of the main acquisitions in this field were the 1967 acquisition of the Fly Ash Arrestor Corporation of Birmingham, Alabama, which added a broad capability in wet scrubbers, mechanical collectors, and air instrumentation, and the 1971 acquisition of the Robert Irsay Corporation of Skokie, Illinois, which manufactured and installed air contamination control systems.

Land pollution control systems capability was obtained with the 1966 Erie City Iron Works acquisition (incinerators), and the 1968 purchase of Sargent, Inc., Kearny, New Jersey, to form the Zurn Incinerator Division. In 1969 a license was obtained from Deutsche B&W of West Germany to manufacture and market the "Dusseldorf System," an advanced line of municipal and industrial refuse incineration systems with steam generating capabilities.

Noise pollution control systems capability was developed with the 1967 acquisition of Goodfriend-Ostergaard Associates of Cedar Knolls, New Jersey, acoustical engineers.

Environmental protection systems (5 percent of Zurn total sales in 1973) consisted of the Standard Fire Hose Company of Santa Monica, California (fire-fighting equipment), acquired in 1967 and the Cosco Fire Protection Company of Gardena, California (automated sprinklers), acquired in 1970.

Energy Group

Energy, the second major Zurn field, represented 25 percent of total 1973 sales.

Energy systems mainly consisted of the steam generation and heat exchange activities of the Erie City Iron Works, the 1969 acquisition of Tri-Ex Thermal of Tulsa, Oklahoma (heat exchangers), and the 1971 acquisition of Vulcan Manufacturing Company of Cincinnati, Ohio (thermal exchange systems).

Mechanical systems consisted of the original Zurn Mechanical Power Transmission Division, the Metal Bellows Corporation of Sharon, Massachusetts (metal bellows modules), and the Erie Engine and Manufacturing Company of Erie (hydraulic machinery for rubber and plastics industries), both acquired in 1968.

Leisure Products Group

The Leisure Products Group, which represented 10 percent of total 1973 sales, consisted of the Presque Isle Plastics Company of Erie, acquired in 1967, and Crowell Design Incorporated of Point Pleasant, New Jersey (manufacturer of bilge pumping systems for boats), acquired in 1971. In 1973 Golf Lynx of Paramount, California, a pioneer in stainless steel investment cast golf clubs, was added to the group.

Financing the growth

In March 1968 the company became listed on the New York Stock Exchange. All subsequent acquisitions were made for either common stock or convertible preferred or cash (see Exhibit 7).

Since going public in 1961 the company went to the stock market four more times for either a primary or secondary offering (see Exhibit 7). The last such offering on July 26, 1972, had been scaled down from 572,000 shares to 141,000 shares due to unfavorable market conditions.

Immediately after this last public offering, members of the Zurn family and the Zurn Foundation owned 672,322 shares of common stock, or 12.8 percent of the total equity.

1974–1977: CONSOLIDATION AND OPERATIONAL FOCUS

The overall record of the acquisitive years had been excellent, with an average growth of sales, net income, and earnings per share between 1966 and 1973 of 41.3 percent, 31.8 percent, and 13.6 percent, respectively. Nevertheless, as of 1973 the following factors increasingly led Zurn management to shift their attention from acquisitive growth to margin improvement:

The stock market in general had cooled down on environmental companies, and Zurn Industries saw its P/E slide from a high of 54.7 at the end of 1970 to 22.0 at the end of 1973, making acquisitions for stock harder and less attractive.

The product lines required to implement the company's broad strategic plan were largely in place, reducing the need for further acquisitions from this point of view.

The overall profit picture did not eliminate concerns over the earnings dip experienced in 1970–71, and the somewhat more erratic profit picture per product line (see Exhibit 8).

Finally, some of the broader diversification moves were proving to be less successful.

As a result, no major acquisitions were made between 1974 and fiscal 1978, and some pruning of activities took place, with seven businesses sold

EXHIBIT 7
Primary and secondary offerings

Units	Price to public	P/E	Proceeds to seller
June 20, 1961	103,470 shares common from shareholders	$ 8.0*	16.6	$ 7.20
	71,530 shares common from company			
April 13, 1966	50,000 shares common from shareholders	12.0*	16.6	12.10
	200,000 shares common from company			
August 29, 1967	300,000 shares common from shareholders	24.0	25.3	22.60
	300,000 shares common from company			
November 12, 1969	$18M 5¾% debentures convertible	18M	38.5	17.73M
	at $28.50 (common selling at 26)			
June 28, 1972	322,000 shares common from shareholders			Canceled
	250,000 shares common from company			
July 26, 1972	141,000 shares common from shareholders	21.625	26.4	20.545

* Not adjusted for 3-for-1 stock split on July 28, 1967.

EXHIBIT 8A

Zurn performance by line of business, year ended March 31 ($000)

Net sales

	1978	1977	1976	1975	1974	1973	1972	1971
Environmental pollution control systems and services	$169,954	$135,816	$135,418	$138,737	$127,818	$99,274	$91,801	$82,626
Energy systems	63,580	77,941	83,896	74,705	56,377	50,283	45,524	47,662
Leisure products	27,180	19,771	24,486	22,947	22,594	14,299	6,999	7,545
	$260,714	$233,528	$243,800	$236,389	$206,789	$163,856	$144,324	$137,833
Intergroup sales	(1,083)	(969)	(964)	(1,145)	(1,148)	(1,221)	(990)	(1,914)
Totals	$259,631	$232,559	$242,836	$235,244	$205,641	$162,635	$143,334	$135,919

Operating income before income taxes

	1978	1977	1976	1975	1974	1973	1972	1971
Environmental pollution control systems and services	$ 6,911	$ 7,877	$ 6,517	$ 1,705	$ 5,786	$ 5,819	$ 6,268	$ 3,916
Energy systems	9,504	11,820	10,138	7,153	4,448	3,014	2,553	2,449
Leisure products	7,735	4,972	5,020	2,246	5,210	2,979	(195)	(418)
	$ 24,150	$ 24,669	$ 21,675	$ 11,104	$ 15,444	$ 11,812	$ 8,626	$ 5,947
Unallocated interest and other expenses	(3,803)	(7,895)	(7,070)	(1,612)	(187)	(717)	(648)	(575)
Totals	$ 20,347	$ 16,774	$ 14,605	$ 9,492	$ 15,257	$ 11,095	$ 7,978	$ 5,372

Source: 10-K and 1978 annual report.

EXHIBIT 8B

Zurn performance by line of business

Lines of business accounting for 10 percent or more of sales and related pretax income for the five-years ended March 31, 1971, are presented in the following summary:

	Year ended March 31				
	1971	1970	1969	1968	1967
Net sales ($000):					
Operating group:					
Environmental management:					
Environmental engineering, construction and resources development	$ 42,283	$ 33,804	$ 16,599	$ 14,050	$ 14,796
Environmental systems:					
Air and land pollution control systems	25,240	27,750	25,822	20,392	17,800
Water pollution control systems	26,348	25,944	25,245	23,842	24,397
Environmental safety and protection systems	14,690	10,355	6,113	9,223	9,375
Energy and heat exchange systems	23,348	19,508	17,148	16,542	15,383
Mechanical systems and leisure products	19,720	25,526	23,105	22,659	22,505
	$151,627	$142,887	$114,032	$106,708	$104,256
Intergroup sales	(5,342)	(1,783)	(552)	(1,851)	(2,967)
Totals	$146,285	$141,104	$113,480	$104,857	$101,289
Pretax income ($000):					
Operating group:					
Environmental management:					
Environmental engineering, construction, and resources development	$ 798	$ 160	$ 132	$ 153	$ (237)
Environmental systems:					
Air and land pollution control systems	(569)	(163)	1,711	1,758	960
Water pollution control systems	1,997	1,604	2,784	2,531	1,560
Environmental safety and protection systems	1,230	2,029	183	158	442
Energy and heat exchange systems	1,413	593	739	218	1,693
Mechanical systems and leisure products	267	1,198	812	1,759	1,992
	$5,136	$5,421	$6,361	$6,577	$6,410
Unallocated interest and other expenses	(611)	(530)	(373)	(173)	(38)
Totals	$4,525	$4,891	$5,988	$6,404	$6,372

or terminated over the period. Profit improvement was sought through increased financial control rather than centralization of functional activities.

Divestitures

On February 6, 1973, Zurn disposed of its interest in the Greynald Construction Company, a developer of planned communities, for a net loss of $3.8 million or 73 cents per share.

As of October 31, 1973 Zurn sold its heavy construction division, Zurn Engineers (formerly Pascal & Ludwig, Inc.), to its employees and decided to discontinue further participation in the future development of its last environmental community, Mandalay Bay. Net sales of those operations in the previous year were, respectively, $27.4 million and $2.5 million. The combined net loss of this discontinuance for 1974 was $3.9 million or 73 cents per share.

During fiscal 1974 Zurn also terminated the Leisure Products Group's injection molding activities and ended the program under which specialty molded plastic components were sold to a broad range of outside customers, and the machinery and equipment related to these activities were sold. As Edward J. Donn, senior vice president—corporate relations, commented:

> Our original entry into plastics was guided by the expectation that plastic components would be utilized in air and water pollution control equipment in greater quantities and at a more rapid rate of application than actually materialized. When this expectation failed to materialize, we decided to develop a line of proprietary products for the pleasure boating market. This judgment was somewhat motivated by the growing concern, at that time, over the degree of water pollution being caused by waste discharges from marine vessels. Applying our water pollution control technology to this problem, we were able to create a rather comprehensive line of plastic accessories for the pleasure boating as well as the recreational vehicle field. It soon became apparent that a decision would have to be reached determining the extent of our participation in this industry, which was primarily consumer oriented, had a broad marketing distribution base, required large amounts of up-front capital, and had the potential of producing a lower rate of return on investment and lower profit margins than spelled out in corporate guidelines. We decided to dispose of this business segment to a company engaged in this area. Henceforth, our remaining engagement in the leisure-time industry would be through our Golf Lynx operation.

Over the years, the Zurn Noise Pollution Control Group (Goodfriend-Ostergaard Associates) faded away together with active involvement in the noise pollution control area in general, largely because it became evident that the thrust of this area would come from original equipment manufacturers through the design and manufacture of products which would operate at lower decibel levels, and that future potential in this area was too small.

During fiscal 1977 Zurn Industries sold two divisions: Engineering Science of Arcadia, California (formerly a part of the Ludwig Engineering and Science Company), and the Metal Bellows Division, which had combined sales and net income in 1976 of $17.7 million and $348,000. The sales of Engineering Science completed the company's withdrawal from the "software" engineering end of the business. David M. Zurn explained:

> Though the original idea was to offer a total service, it soon became clear that a consulting engineering firm would not progress as part of Zurn Industries. They were mainly engineering for municipalities, and because they were a part of Zurn Industries, consulting engineering ethics dictated they could not specify our product. With industrial clients it wouldn't have made much difference, but in the public sector area such practice is viewed as a conflict of interest.

James A. Zurn, vice president–treasurer, commented:

> Metal Bellows was sold because they got involved in a medical product with high liability risk for which we could not adequately cover ourselves—a drug reservoir to be implanted in the body which would serve as a time-release mechanism for medical drugs.

Profit improvement in operations

Besides the trimming of subsidiaries which are not compatible with the company's long-range growth objective, major emphasis was laid on improving ongoing operations.

In 1972–73 the company had experimented briefly with building up a central staff in engineering, purchasing, and sales, but quickly abandoned the concept. "It was only a small nucleus, but it did not come through," commented Albert A. Baker, executive vice president. "I thought it was a good thing, but on the other hand, psychologically it wouldn't go in this company." Robert E. Lugenbeal, the senior vice president—finance and controller, added, "We are too diversified, and it is difficult for a staff to be useful to everybody. Since then we have concentrated on improvements by the use of data processing such as inventory procedures, collection procedures, and so forth. By now about half the diversions have the same procedures." "We cannot go very far, however, even in developing uniform control systems," stated David M. Zurn, "because the nature of our businesses varies so much. Some have standard costing systems, others are on a pure job cost system, and a third category is hybrid in nature."

Profit improvement at Zurn Industries was very much seen as a divisional responsibility, to be realized through line management. Commenting on the organization, James A. Zurn stated:

We have no large central staff. The first floor of our corporate headquarters contains about 50 people, data processing, accounting, and internal auditing. The second floor has about 12 people, communications and marketing, international, research and engineering, special projects, financial, legal and administrative, personnel, and community relations, and the third floor has the 6 members of top management. The group vice presidents are located at the divisions, not at the headquarters.

See Exhibit 9 for an organization chart.

An incentive compensation program for the group, divisional, and corporate staff levels included about 150 people, who could earn up to 50 percent of their base salary, based upon their return-on-capital performance plus several other factors including sales and profitability. Usually three to four people in the divisions participated besides the division manager, though it was left entirely up to the division manager to decide who would participate.

Planning and control

James A. Zurn commented:

> We have review sessions with our divisions and corporate staff on a formalized, scheduled basis at least two times a year. In the fall Frank, David, Edward Donn, Bob Lugenbeal, an executive vice president, and a group vice president travel to each division to review performance and capital budgets. In May the processs is reversed, and divisional personnel meet at corporate headquarters in Erie.

Growth

Despite an excellent reported earnings per share growth record over the 1974–77 period (32 percent, Zurn Industries' price-earnings multiple had remained at around 8 for the last three years. This was putting pressure on Zurn management to improve the sales growth rate, which had only been 4.2 percent annually from 1974 to 1977. Commenting on annual growth objectives Bob Lugenbeal stated, "Our goal is about 15 percent total, of which about 7½ percent is internal growth." "In terms of growth objectives, our corporate goal is to achieve a minimum 15 percent annual growth rate in sales and earnings," added Edward Donn. "Over the past five years we have exceeded that goal in annual earnings growth, but sales growth has been retarded as a result of self-imposed factors designed to increase earnings and return on investment, that is, (a) a determined marketing effort to be selective in bidding procedures, thereby enhancing our potential for increased profit margins; and (b) a program of divesting operating units which proved incompatible with long-range growth objectives. Concentration in these two areas continues to produce the desired operating results. Unfortu-

EXHIBIT 9
Organization chart

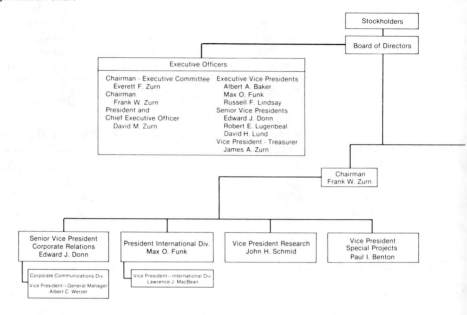

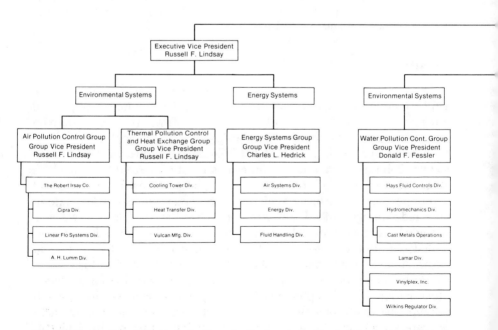

Note: Relative location on chart indicates lines of authority only; position not intended to reflect importance of organizational responsibility.

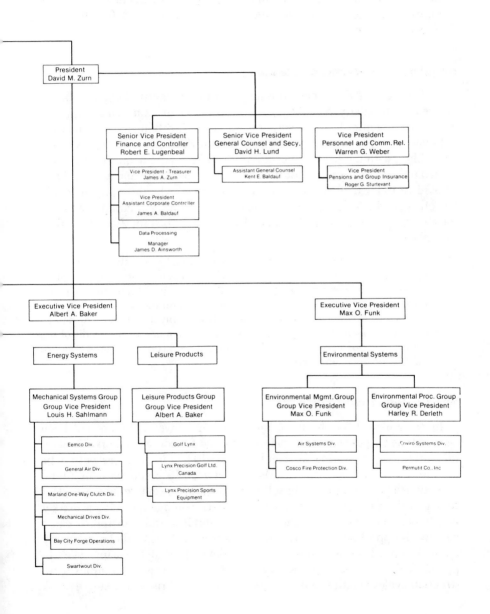

President
David M. Zurn

Senior Vice President
Finance and Controller
Robert E. Lugenbeal

Senior Vice President
General Counsel and Secy.
David H. Lund

Vice President
Personnel and Comm. Rel.
Warren G. Weber

Vice President - Treasurer
James A. Zurn

Assistant General Counsel
Kent E. Baldauf

Vice President
Pensions and Group Insurance
Roger G. Sturtevant

Vice President
Assistant Corporate Controller
James A. Baldauf

Data Processing
Manager
James D. Ainsworth

Executive Vice President
Albert A. Baker

Executive Vice President
Max O. Funk

Energy Systems

Leisure Products

Environmental Systems

Mechanical Systems Group
Group Vice President
Louis H. Sahlmann

Leisure Products Group
Group Vice President
Albert A. Baker

Environmental Mgmt. Group
Group Vice President
Max O. Funk

Environmental Proc. Group
Group Vice President
Harley R. Derleth

Eemco Div.

Golf Lynx

Air Systems Div.

Enviro Systems Div.

General Air Div.

Lynx Precision Golf Ltd.
Canada

Cosco Fire Protection Div.

Permutit Co., Inc

Marland One-Way Clutch Div.

Lynx Precision Sports
Equipment

Mechanical Drives Div.

Bay City Forge Operations

Swartwout Div.

nately, these good operating results have been recorded during a period of time when the securities market has undergone a series of gyrations which saw the price-earnings ratios of most companies drop to lows or near-lows. At the current time our securities are trading near the median or near the upper range of the price-earnings ratios calculated for other companies listed in the pollution control industry classification."

In the short run, however, the impetus for growth was enhanced by the acquisition of Permutit, and a large contract, surpassing $70 million, for Zurn cooling towers.

Acquisition of Permutit Corporation

In August 1977 Zurn Industries acquired the Permutit Company, Incorporated, a subsidiary of Sybron, for $12 million in cash. This company, which manufactured equipment for water purification and desalination with very few products that overlapped with Zurn products, had sales of $32 million with net profits in excess of $2 million. The acquisition was expected to add 16 percent to fiscal 1978 earnings per share and an additional 10 percent to fiscal 1979 earnings per share. Asked why the company could be both a good sale for Sybron, a conglomerate with a similar long-standing stake in the pollution control field, and an excellent buy for Zurn, Robert E. Lugenbeal responded:

> That's the main question we faced. We thoroughly investigated the company. The decision to sell Permutit goes back to before the recent excellent growth and margins which are due to Permutit's membrane program and reverse osmosis applications. Permutit had been on the block for 3½ years, originally at a price of 12 times earnings. It was fully investigated by 6 to 12 companies before we bought it. In fact it is very much to the credit of the management of Permutit that they were able to keep the organization intact under such conditions.

The Cooling Tower contract

In November 1977 the company's Cooling Tower Division had been awarded the largest single contract ever placed for cooling towers. Six natural draft towers measuring 535 feet high and 410 feet in diameter were to be built for the Tennessee Valley Authority between 1978 and 1982 for a total price of nearly $72 million. Russell F. Lindsay, an executive vice president to whom the Cooling Tower Division reports, commented: "It's a market which used to be the sole domain of Marley and Research-Cottrell. Because we saw an opportunity six years ago to capture a share of that market, we entered into a licensing contract with Balcke of West Germany. We approached the market cautiously because the technology is complex, construction cycles lengthy, and therefore the potential risks imposing. It took us three to four years to get our first contract because we wanted to gain experience in bidding and started out high. Last year we sold our first two units which were now still under construction." Dipping into his office drawer to show some pictures of the still uncompleted tower constructions, he added, "I always have them send some pictures along with the completion progress reports: It allows you to see very well how they are doing."

A growth and operating strategy for the 1980s

Forecasts of the long-run growth of the business areas Zurn Industries was involved in generally differed, and were subject to great uncertainty (see the Appendix and Exhibit 8). Zurn management sided with those observers who predicted considerable growth potential, and had decided to concentrate internal and external growth opportunities primarily in fields related to environmental control and energy.

As a member of management commented:

> The pollution control market is extremely fragmented and therefore difficult to forecast with any close degree of accuracy. From our company's standpoint, we make one initial breakdown, that is, the municipal market and the industrial, or private, sector. Traditionally, approximately 80–85 percent of our sales revenues are derived from the private sector, and the remaining 15–20 percent are municipally oriented. Over the past ten years, the industrial market has shown steady growth. The municipal market, however, which is primarily centered about water pollution control activities, has not shown growth as rapidly in the near term as forecasted. This slower rate of growth is basically attributable to the federal government's policy and ongoing program of gathering substantially more data regarding treatability standards prior to approving appropriations for specific projects and locales. It is our belief that for the longer term this market will reach the higher growth levels predicted because the subject of water and water use and reuse is a growing crisis not only in our country but worldwide.

Asked whether he agreed with the slowdown scenarios with respect to air pollution control, James A. Zurn commented:

> A lot depends on the national energy policy. If we are really going to burn more coal in this country, there is going to be a tremendous demand to at least hold the line on air standards as they are now.

Though the environmental area had so far not been as profitable as the other areas the company was involved in (see Exhibit 8), Zurn management felt confident this would improve. As Frank W. Zurn noted:

> The pollution control area will become more profitable because it will be more a replacement market and there will be less competitors. There were literally thousands of companies that entered this business in the late

1960s and early 1970s. Now there are already a lot less, so profit pressures should decline.

Commenting on how Zurn would achieve its overall growth objective, Frank W. Zurn stated:

> If we want to become a $500 million- or billion-dollar company, a substantial amount of growth will still have to come externally through acquisitions. The companies will be in our basic business areas, and there will probably be fewer but larger acquisitions.

The way Zurn management had approached the challenge of getting the internal growth from the divisions, or the profit margins with which to buy external growth, had always been to run a very decentralized operation with minimal involvement from corporate management. Time and again, however, the issue had come up as to whether the company should take more advantage of the potential for cooperation among its divisions. Current examples of such moves were the possible creation of a customer-oriented systems sales force and the consolidation of two fan-making divisions.

Systems sales

Some members and management felt that Zurn Industries ultimately should take more advantage of its broad product line position to approach major customers such as utilities, steel plants, and so forth, through a single sales force. In a typical utility construction project, for instance, they pointed out, the Robert Irsay Company could provide heating, ventilating, and air conditioning; the Cooling Tower Division could construct the cooling system; Permutit, the water purification system; the Energy Division, the small reserve boilers; the Mechanical Drives Division, the turbine connection; Clarage Fan, the air moving system; Hydromechanics, the wastewater drains; and Fluid Control, the various mechanical strainers. The Robert Irsay Company and the Cooling Tower Division in particular offered important pieces of any nuclear power plant project.

Others, however, pointed out that no "supersalesman" could do the job without the assistance of people knowing each product line, that product lines often sold on their own brand strength, and that clients might not always want to give too much of a project to Zurn Industries. In addition, it was felt there might have to be some changes in Zurn's traditional decentralized operating procedures if more emphasis were to be given to systems sales.

Consolidating operations

Typical of the problem of seeking consolidation of divisions was whether to integrate the Air Systems Division, Kalamazoo (formerly the Clarage Fan

Co.), and the Air Systems Division, Birmingham (formerly the Fly Ash Arrestor Company), which were both mainly producing large industrial fans. In addition, the Birmingham operation produced air pollution control systems for controlling particulate and gaseous emissions, including sulfur dioxide (SO_2) control equipment. These divisions had sales of around $19 million and $11 million, respectively.

As one member of management commented:

> After these two divisions were acquired (in 1967 and 1969), an attempt was made to amalgamate the resources of both operating units by combining various marketing, engineering, and manufacturing operations. What appeared functionally efficient on paper at that time did not prove out in reality in the marketplace. For example, consolidating two field sales offices into one had the effect of placing in one sales agent's hands two distinctly different types of fans (one Kalamazoo, one Birmingham), each capable of meeting the specification of the project being bid. Human nature being what it is, the natural tendency on the part of the sales agent would be to promote the brand name fan he was most familiar with, to the detriment of the other line. Similar conflicts of interest in related operating areas proved difficult to overcome at the time and the consolidation plan was abandoned.

As of now both divisions were operating totally independently and even reported to different executive vice presidents (see Exhibit 9). Some kind of cooperation still seemed to make a lot of sense, however, and as a first step management had decided to commission an engineering study to see what the cost and quality position was of both divisions in the various product lines.

On these and other similar issues Zurn management remained reluctant to change their current way of operating. As both Frank and David Zurn put it:

> We think the entrepreneurial aspect resulting from our companies being decentralized is far more important. The key to getting profits for us is people, and if you don't motivate people properly, or don't have the right people, you're going to strike out no matter how systems oriented you may be. If you have the right entrepreneurial team, we think you will be ahead.

APPENDIX

The market for pollution control

Perhaps the single most important aspect of the market for pollution control equipment was the fact that it basically was created by regulation and hence subject to substantial external uncertainties.

Water or land pollution clients were both industrial firms and governmental bodies, but air pollution clients were mostly private firms. Because pollution control investments were generally expensive and nonprofitable, both industrial clients and municipalities were often reluctant to comply and eager to seek delays, taking advantage of the often-prolonged uncertainty about definitive standards and compliance deadlines. Uncertainty about standards further complicated the choice among alternative technologies involved.

Though the industry had been generally looked upon as offering solid long-term growth potential, opinions had diverged through the years as to the order of magnitude of growth to be expected.

On one side of the spectrum were those forecasts which were based upon calculations of the expenditures which would be required for the different industrial sectors and local bodies to comply with all regulations and deadlines. One example was the President's Council on Environmental Quality, which in 1972 had estimated that "domestic expenditures on pollution control will approach $287 billion over the ten-year period ending in 1980. Some $93 billion of this will be spent on new capital equipment, and $194 billion on operating costs. $106 billion is needed for air pollution alone."

Other observers focused on the actual growth in equipment manufacturers' shipments, which was less spectacular, though still high.

The Industrial Gas Cleaning Institute, whose members were fairly representative of the air pollution control industry, reported a tenfold increase in sales bookings during the ten-year period 1963–73, equivalent to an average annual growth of approximately 26 percent. How some of the major competitors had performed over the period is shown in case Exhibit 10.

In 1974 studies of both the air and water pollution control markets, Frost and Sullivan made the following growth forecasts:

Air pollution control[1]

Continued growth in the total markets for air pollution control equipment and related goods and services is anticipated during the next few years as industries and utilities continue to increase their capital expenditures for these facilities. It is estimated that capital expenditures for these goods and services will increase from a level of about $1 billion in 1974 to over $1.7 billion by 1979, at an average annual rate of 10.5 percent. But after 1979, capital expenditures will level off and then fluctuate in the range of from $1.56 to $1.75 billion from 1980 to 1985 as the substantial backlog of needed air pollution control facilities is eliminated.

The anticipated capital expenditure pattern for facilities to control particulates should be of extreme concern to companies participating in this sector. It is estimated that this sector will only experience additional growth during the three-year period, from 1976 to 1979, after which the capital expenditures will continue to decline until 1981. The decline after

---

[1] Excerpts from "Air Pollution Abatement Market—November 1974," reproduced by permission of Frost and Sullivan.

EXHIBIT 10

Performance of some leading companies in pollution control

	Area of pollution control	1977 sales ($000)	10-year sales growth (per share)	5-year sales growth (per share)	1977 net profit ($000)	10-year earnings growth (per share)	5-year earnings growth (per share)	1977 average P/E	1972 average P/E	Value Line sales growth estimate 1974–76 to 1980–82	Restated pretax margins by business line, 1977
American Air Filter	Air	62.7	13.0%	16.5%	9.2	9.0%	12.0%	8.8	39.5	5.5%	Air, 7.2%
Combustion Equipment	Air, water, land	155.0*	43.5	35.5	12.5*	51.0	36.0	8.9†	30.5	11.0	Air, water, land, 9.3%
Envirotech	Water, air	115.2*	—	23.0	17.5	—	20.5	8.4†	33.4	11.5	Air, 9.6%*; water, 7.0%
Marley	Water	242.6	15.5	18.0	18.7	14.0	23.5	7.2	34.3	14.5	Water, 14%
Peabody International	Air, water, land	391.2	17.0	23.5	15.7	23.5	22	10.2	32.9	12	Air, 9.0%*; water, 8.2%*; land, 6.5%*
Research-Cottrell	Air	250*	25.0	17.5	8.2*	5	−12	9.9	52.3	10	Air, 5.1%*
U.S. Filter	Air, water	415*	2.0	4.0	14.3*	—	18.0	6.5†	27.8	16.0	Air and water, 6.2%*
Wheelabrator-Frye	Air	490* (270 in env)	—	25.0	23.5*	—	38.0	9.7†	24.5	13.0	Air, 13.5%*
Zurn Industries	Air, water, land	268	14.0	4.0	11.0*	9.0	14.5	8.2†	22.0	6.5	Air, water, land, 8.5%*; energy, 15.0%; leisure, 25%

* Value Line estimates.
† 1976 value.
Source: Value Line.

the peak year of 1976 is substantial considering that only five years after reaching a peak, the anticipated expenditures for particulate control will be at 25 percent of the peak value.

Whereas the capital expenditures for particulate control will exhibit an unfavorable growth pattern over the long term, the expenditures for gaseous control, especially sulfur oxides, will continue to grow until 1981, at a substantial average annual rate of about 35 percent. After 1981, it is anticipated that these capital expenditures will remain fairly constant.

In projecting these capital expenditures for particulate and gaseous control, one of the most important considerations was the type of technology that will be used by the utilities to remove particulates and sulfur oxides. The utilities have been and will continue to be the major purchaser of gas cleaning equipment and therefore the type of technology for air pollution control selected by the utilities has a substantial influence on the market sectors.

In making the projections for capital expenditures and related equipment, it was assumed that the utilities would select gas cleaning processes that will remove both particulates and sulfur oxides and that these processes would be based on the use of scrubbers and therefore, in most cases, will not require the use of electrostatic precipitators. Although considerable arguments can be given for or against this technology and the use of it by utilities, it is strongly felt that this technology is available and that pressure from the Environmental Protection Agency will result in the utilities adopting it.

part three

POLICY
FORMULATION
AND
ADMINISTRATION
IN DIVERSIFIED
FIRMS

chapter
8

The diversified firm: An overview

In these final chapter we would like to direct your attention to the general management problems of the diversified firm. The preceding text and cases, with but a few exceptions, have been primarily concerned with the strategic problems of essentially single-business firms such as Polaroid, Lincoln, or the soft drink companies; or with general management problems within more diversified firms which are essentially at a subunit level, rather than the much more complex multibusiness environment at the corporate level. The Rose Company, Northern Industries, and The Albert Company would be examples of this.

An understanding of the general management task at the corporate level of the diversified firm, the most important form of large-scale industrial organizations, is clearly helpful to those who aspire to, and the even fewer who will eventually reach, that position themselves. An understanding of these companies and the tasks their managers face is also important to the far greater number who will serve in specialist capacities in such organizations; act as management consultants to them; deal with them as suppliers, investment bankers, financial analysts, or loan officers; or even to seek to influence the behavior of such large companies via public policy. And to understand the job, there is no substitute for placing yourself in the position of the involved general manager to as great an extent as you can.

This chapter will provide some background on the development and the extent of diversification in American industry.[1] The next chapter will describe the additional complexities that strategies of diversification have brought to the general management task in such organizations. The last chapter will show how the framework of analysis you have developed and

---

[1] Portions of this chapter have been adapted from a working paper by Philippe C. Haspeslagh and Norman Berg entitled "Diversification and Mergers: Some Trends and Results." (Boston: Harvard Business School, January 1978).

applied to the general management problems of the single-business firm can be expanded and supplemented to be useful in dealing with general management problems at the corporate level in the diversified firm as well.

MEASURES OF DIVERSIFICATION

Various measures of diversification have been devised by different researchers, each selecting measures that best fit their interests and the data available to them. Economists interested in the degree of competition in markets and in market structure have tended to relate diversity to the number of different markets in which the firm competes. Economists more interested in issues of firm productivity and specialization have tended to look at diversification in terms of the number of products produced. In both cases, they have tended to use simple and standard measures of product count based on the Standard Industrial Classification (SIC) definitions of product class.

These measures have the great advantage of being easily obtainable from government-required reports, and also represent "hard" data in that they are both quantifiable and objective. They have a serious drawback from the perspective of one interested in the management problems of diversification, however, since they assume an equal "dissimilarity" between various product classes. There are also substantial problems arising from the variety of products sometimes included within the same classification as well as the similarity of products sometimes classified separately.

A less precise but more managerially relevant measure of diversification has been developed by Rumelt.[2] He has developed a set of categories defined largely in terms of "relatedness" designed to capture both important differences in the extent of diversity of a company as well as in the nature of the managerial relationships among the various businesses of a company. His classification system consists of four mutually exclusive major categories (and eight subcategories) as follows:

Single business: 95 percent of revenues from largest single-business unit.

Dominant business: Between 70 percent and 95 percent of revenues from largest single-business unit.

Related business: Less than 70 percent of revenues from largest single business, but different from (see below).

Unrelated business: Also less than 70 percent of revenues from largest single-business unit, but the remainder of the business activities judged to be less related to each other than for the related business category, above.

---

[2] Richard P. Rumelt, *Strategy, Structure and Economic Performance* (Boston: Division of Research, Harvard Business School, 1974).

DEGREE OF DIVERSITY

Although uniformly accepted measures of diversification do not exist, the evidence is clear that the extent of diversification, in American industry is both high and increasing. Recent estimates place the proportion of the *Fortune* 500 that are still "single-business" companies, according to Rumelt's definitions, at about 15–20 percent, and continuing to decline, as shown in Exhibit 8-1.

Since the *Fortune* 500 firms characteristically account for about two thirds of the industrial output, investment, and employment, and three quarters of the industrial profits in the American economy, the diversified firm is clearly the major and most important form of industrial organization in this country. The same trends are occurring in other industrialized economies as well. If you wish to understand the practice of business from the viewpoint of the general manager of the important firms in the industrialized economies, it is essential to include the general management problems of the diversified firm.

The trend to diversification began long before the 1949 starting point of the preceding diagram, of course. Economists have documented a trend of increasing diversification throughout the history of American industry. The most managerially relevant study is the classic *Strategy and Structure* by Alfred Chandler, a leading business historian. Chandler studied in impressive detail the pressures for diversification and accompanying structural

EXHIBIT 8-1

Estimated percentage of *Fortune* 500 in each category

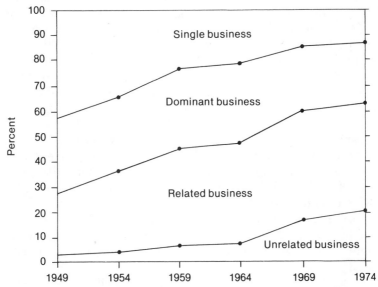

Source: Richard Rumelt, "Diversity and Profitability" (Los Angeles: University of California at Los Angeles Working Paper, 1977), p. 21.

change in General Motors, Du Pont, Standard Oil of New Jersey, and Sears, Roebuck; four companies which in the 1920s were in the forefront of companies developing new administrative structure to cope with the new complexities brought about by their increasing diversification.

By means of these detailed clinical studies as well as supporting research in another 70 large enterprises, Chandler explained convincingly both the pressures that led to diversification as well as the accompanying changes in organizational structure from the traditional functional form best suited to the single business to the now commonplace product division form as companies diversified. The addition of new activities invariably resulted in the creation of separate divisions to administer them. This in turn created multiple levels of general management and the questions of the "best" split of responsibilities among these various levels, questions which continue to be central to the management of our large companies today.

The substantial diversification present in American industry that has been taking place for well over 50 years did not occur smoothly during that period, however; neither did it occur in the same manner for all companies, or for any single company over time.

MAJOR MERGER WAVES

Diversification occurs as a result of some combination of internal development and acquisitions.[3] Information on acquisitions is more readily available to the public than information on internal development, and as a result much more analysis has been done on acquisitions than on internal development. Acquisitions have been of unending interest to many managers as well as students of business and of public policy, and we will explain briefly some of the major trends that have occurred with regard to merger activity.

Perhaps the least debatable characteristic of mergers is that they seem to come in waves. There is no satisfactory theory to explain or predict these waves of merger activity. (Although "merger" and "acquisition" have different technical meanings, we will use the terms interchangeably here.) In terms of numbers of manufacturing and mining firms acquired, there were distinct peaks around the turn of the century, in the 1920s, in the 1967–70 period, and again in the late 1970s. The first two merger waves are of relatively less interest in terms of contributing significantly to the diversification of American industry since they have been characterized as primarily "merging for monopoly" during the 1887–1904 era and "merging for oligopoly" during the 1919–30 era.

The third merger wave, however, which began in about 1955 but reached its peak in 1968–69, was characterized by a much larger number of conglomerate (neither horizontal nor vertical) mergers. It was estimated by

---

[3] See Malcolm S. Salter and Wolf A. Weinhold, *Diversification Through Acquisition* (New York: The Free Press, 1979), for extensive discussion of diversification objectives, guidelines, screening systems, and acquisition analysis.

the Federal Trade Commission that about 80 percent of the mergers that occurred during 1948–75 were of the conglomerate type, up very sharply from earlier periods. The peak reached in 1968–69 was high indeed by historical standards. Including firms in manufacturing and mining with assets (acquired) of $10 million or more, the yearly average jumped to almost $13 billion for 1968 and 1969, up from an average of about $3 billion for the preceding ten years. Almost 10 percent of the total mining and manufacturing assets changed hands during the 1965 to 1970 period, a trend which gave much concern to economists, lawyers, and government agencies interested in concentration and competition in the American economy. In terms of numbers of acquisitions reported, that peaked at about 2,400 in 1970.

In contrast to the earlier merger waves, however, the acquiring firms were no longer the largest companies. In addition, the volume of assets acquired by the larger firms was smaller relative to their size than for medium-sized companies. The contribution to the growth made by merger was therefore more significant to small and medium-sized firms than to the large, and the effects on overall concentration were generally modest.

It was during this period that a number of companies that came to be known as conglomerates expanded rapidly, with growth rates in sales and earnings and stock price that sometimes far outstripped industrial averages. Indeed, several of the diversified companies described in this book—Zurn Industries, Sybron, CML Group, and The Leisure Group—had their origins in the 1960s. Each started from a very different base, and each took advantage of the opportunities they encountered in a different way. As you study these companies, you will want to explore what it was about the environment at the time and their strategies that enabled these companies to expand as they did, and to compare their strategies with what you may know about other acquisition-minded companies such as Textron, Litton, or LTV.

The conglomerate boom of the late 1960s brought about an extensive investigation of growth via acquisition, since some economists, government agencies, and congressional committees feared that the changes occurring could have permanent and harmful effects on our industrial structure. Critics were concerned about the increased potential for a number of traditional anticompetitive practices such as reciprocity, cross-subsidization, and lessened price competition, as well as the social and political implications of the concentration of assets of dissimilar businesses under the control of single corporate managements without any obvious accompanying economic efficiencies. Indeed, at the growth rates experienced by Litton and LTV in the late 1960s, simple projection would have made each one of them approaching the total projected GNP by 1990. In addition, there was concern that misleading accounting practices were leading investors to overvalue some of these firms, with resulting risk of losses when the inevitable adjustments in valuation occurred.

The frantic merger activity collapsed of its own weight in late 1969, however, well before the extensive FTC investigation came to any conclusions about the matter. During this period the investment community assigned increasingly high price-earnings multiples to companies showing superior growth via acquisition, which in turn made this same continued growth possible. When it became apparent that such growth could not go on forever, and that in some cases much of the gain in reported earnings came from the accounting consequences of the acquisitions rather than any continuing improvements in operations, the price-earnings multiples declined drastically, and acquisitions based on an exchange of stock no longer were attractive. The operating troubles and highly leveraged capital structures of some of the companies compounded the problems of the conglomerates as a group. The average price-earnings ratio for one sample of ten large conglomerates fell from 35 at the high point in 1967–68 to well into the single digits in 1970, and the average stock price of the same sample declined by 86 percent in the same short period.

Still a fourth wave of merger activity started in about the middle 1970s, however. Just as other merger waves had differed from each other, in many respects this one as well had some of its own unique characteristics.

Unlike previous merger waves, which had coincided with periods of high stock market prices, this fourth wave developed during a period of depressed prices. There tended to be relatively more large transactions, often involving large, old, and often single-business companies doing the buying. More of the acquisitions involved companies in the service sector than previously. Although in 1974 and 1975 there were respectively 15 and 14 mergers involving offers of over $100 million, comparable mergers for 1976, 1977, and 1978 were 39, 41, and (estimated) 80. The total dollar volume of mergers was also up drastically in terms of reported amounts paid, from $11.8 billion in 1975 to $34.2 billion in 1978.

Large foreign buyers were increasingly active in the acquisition of American companies, paying a total of $6.3 billion in 1978 compared to $2.4 billion in 1976 for transactions in which a price was reported. The attraction for the foreign companies was largely the depressed state of the American stock market in relation to earnings and book values, the declining value of the American dollar in terms of foreign currencies, and the judgment that the American economy and political environment provided an attractive long-term investment opportunity. The Swiss-based CIBA-GEIGY Corporation, which you will encounter in a case later in this book, is an example of such a buyer.

In addition, more of the mergers involved cash rather than exchanges of stock, even though the premiums over the premerger market price averaged about 50 percent, or about double that of the preceding period. The payment of cash tended to impose a discipline on the merger activity that had been lacking in the earlier conglomerate boom, when a higher proportion of mergers involved the exchange of stock. The willingness of managements to pay such high cash premiums over the market prices established by individual investors for the same securities raised many questions as to the rationale for such acquisitions, however.

Hostile tender offers or takeovers (generally offers to purchase shares made directly to stockholders, without the support of the management of the company to be acquired) also became more common during this period, and were engaged in not only by "raiders" but by even the most respectable of companies. There was also a considerable increase in the divestiture of divisions or subsidiaries during the mid-1970s, although by 1978 this had dropped to about 37 percent of the total acquisition activity, from a high point of 50–60 percent in 1975 and 1976. The comparable figure for 1969 was only 15 percent; it appeared that a number of acquisitions made during the conglomerate boom were sold off in the middle 1970s.

INTERNAL DEVELOPMENT

Accompanying all of this acquisition activity, but receiving less attention because the efforts are not subject to public reporting in the same manner as acquisitions, has been the historic pattern of growth through internal development mentioned earlier.

Diversification via internal development is obviously a much slower process than by acquisition, and one which is likely to lead the company into areas much more closely related to its present businesses than diversification via acquisition. It is not necessarily a preferred route, and that it has not been an easy or profitable one for many companies has been well documented by Biggadike.[4] He found that it takes an average of eight years for internal ventures to become profitable. Fast,[5] looking at the success and longevity of new venture divisions in large corporations rather than at individual ventures, found similar difficulties and frustrations for managers charged with the task of developing new ventures internally.

Although precise comparisons are impossible because of the lack of data, diversification via internal development appears to have had an effect on our industrial economy comparable to that resulting from mergers. A number of our older highly diversified companies such as General Electric and Westinghouse, although they were active in the early merger waves, expanded into new product areas largely through the commercialization of developments from their research laboratories and the internal expansion of existing product or market capabilities. The dynamics of the diversification efforts were quite different and much slower, but the end result of both acquisition and internal development has been a population of large com-

---

[4] E. Ralph Biggadike, *Corporate Diversification: Entry, Strategy, and Performance* (Boston: Division of Research, Harvard Business School, 1979).

[5] Norman D. Fast, *The Rise and Fall of Corporate New Venture Divisions* (Ann Arbor, Mich.: UMI Research Press, 1978).

panies in which the company concentrating its resources on a single line or even a few lines of business is clearly the exception.

ECONOMIC EFFECTS

An important question, of course, is what the economic effects of all of this acquisition and diversification have been with regard to the performance of the firm and returns to investors. If certain strategies of diversification seem to lead to better economic performance than others, that would certainly be useful for managers to know.

This is an area in which academic researchers have been much interested, and a great amount of research has been done over the last decade or so. Extensive work has been done trying to find correlations between the extent of diversification and/or acquisition activity and performance measures such as return on capital or equity or total return to investors in the common stock. A number of these studies are summarized in the references below.[6]

Mergers obviously contribute to the growth in sales of the acquiring firm in the year of the merger. The degree to which mergers contribute to either the growth or the profitability of the acquiring firms over a longer period of time is much less clear, however; the evidence is somewhat contradictory and on balance inconclusive. It is clear that the stockholders of the acquired firm benefit in the short run from being acquired, simply because of the premium over market price invariably paid. Studies which have attempted to relate either specific mergers or overall measures of diversity to the profitability of the parent company, however, have generally found no significant impact. Similar studies concentrating on total return to investors rather than company-based measures of performance also have found no significant relationships between diversity or acquisitions and total return to the common shareholder. Indeed, about the only issue on which most of the witnesses at the recent Senate Hearings referred to in footnote 6 agreed upon is that the evidence with regard to the economic effect of mergers is inconclusive.

Rumelt's study, referred to earlier, did find significant variations in profitability when firms were grouped into his categories rather than by degree of diversification based on product counts or by the amount of acquisition activity. Working with a random sample of 273 companies from the *Fortune* 500 list, he showed, among other things, that strategies of related diversification in general resulted in superior economic performance, and that the worst category was the "passive-unrelated" one. It is far less clear that the

---

[6] Haspeslagh and Berg, "Diversification and Mergers"; Copeland and Weston, *Financial Theory and Corporate Policy* (Boston: Addison-Wesley Publishing Co., Inc., 1979), chaps. 17 and 18; and U.S. Senate, *Mergers and Economic Concentration—Parts I and II.* Hearings Before the Subcommittee on Antitrust, Monopoly and Business Rights of the Committee of the Judiciary, March–April 1979.

different strategies were in themselves the *cause* of the ensuing performance, however, as the industries the companies were in, or were able to
enter, play an important role in profitability, as he showed in later research.
A strategy of related diversification is fine for a company in a high-profit industry with perhaps considerable technology and capital investment required, with the opportunity to enter related industries with similar characteristics. This is what many companies in that fortunate position apparently
have quite properly chosen to do. As a result, that diversification strategy
ends up in Rumelt's high performance classification. It does not follow that
a strategy of related diversification is preferable for a shoe company or a
tire company, however, faced with low profits for whatever reason in their
own—and presumably closely related—industries.

An excellent example of the attempts to follow a strategy of related diversification can be seen in the origins of the Sybron Company, which you
will encounter later in this book. The original Pfaudler Company had a
dominant worldwide share of a slowly growing, cyclical, and technically
vulnerable market—glass-lined steel tanks—and was faced with the choices
of being acquired, continuing its slow and cyclical (although profitable)
growth, or striking out in new areas on their own. Closely related activities
had been explored and either rejected or tried without success. As a result,
the company ended up diversifying into less related fields. Unfortunately,
related diversification, about which a company may know the most and for
which it has the most relevant skills, may not solve their basic problems.

The conclusion to be drawn from the aggregate financial research that
has been done to date is that is provides little, if any, direct guidance to the
general manager concerned with developing a strategy of diversification for
his specific company. There are few clear and broad trends in overall performance by category that would provide a basis for useful prescription in
the individual situation. What is apparent, however, is that there is considerable variation over long periods of time in the performance of diversified
companies; some consistently perform significantly better than others. In
addition, there is evidence that some single-business companies have been
able to improve their returns from below average to average by means of
diversification.

MERGER MOTIVES

Much has been written about the motives of management which have
led to such a clear and pronounced trend away from concentration on a
single line of business. The search for such motives has been heightened by
the fact that neither traditional arguments favoring the economies of scale,
financial theory, nor empirical financial research provide satisfactory explanations for the observed trends of diversification and acquisition activity.

Underlying motives for any action are always difficult to prove; it is only the resulting actions which are directly observable. It seems apparent, however, that the underlying reasons for diversification have been the desires of management for some combination of increased growth, profits, and stability for the firm. Chandler found that diversification occurred historically when companies had accumulated resources in excess of what was needed to fully exploit their historic lines of business, and then applied these resources to new fields of endeavor in order to continue their growth. He noted that organizations, just as individuals, develop goals of their own, and in healthy organizations these goals include continued growth.

Paul Davies, then chairman of FMC Corporation, a large company which diversified aggressively in the late 1940s, stated his reasons very simply: "To make sure everything doesn't go to hell at once." Royal Little, the founder of Textron, frequently justified his wide-ranging diversification efforts in terms of the constant redeployment of assets from areas of lower return to higher return in order to earn the highest possible profits for the stockholders. Litton executives often justified their ambitious acquisition program in terms of the benefits to be gained from combining new technologies with existing businesses to achieve dramatic rather than incremental commercial advantages. Many firms have cited the advantages of size and increased stability of earnings as justification for acquisitions.

The trend to diversification can be thought of in even broader terms. It is another manifestation of the increasing professionalization of management which has occurred since World War II, at first in the United States, and now elsewhere. Just as the corporate form of management provides a means to efficiently extend the life cycle of the single business beyond the lifetime of the individual owners, the strategy of diversification represents a means to extend the life cycle of the corporation beyond the hazards and limitations of the single industry. The development of management skills which transcend specific industries has made diversification feasible.

Just because countless business executives have repeated these themes in one variation or another in explaining their actions does not mean that personal ambitions are not also involved, that the actions will always turn out to have been in the stockholder's interest, or that the manager's and the stockholder's interests are always congruent. As in all fields of human endeavor, motives are mixed and not always clear, and results are not always as hoped for. To consider the motives we have suggested as being important, however, is a useful starting point.

Growth in sales and profits and reasonable stability are often commented on by managers as being essential to the building of a successful organization. One can observe that nonbusiness organizations as well often seem to be guided by similar goals. It is not unheard of for government agencies and congressional staffs to aggressively seek larger and larger budgets and mandates. Even the highly respected March of Dimes charity, first started when Franklin Delano Roosevelt was President, changed its goals from the prevention and treatment of polio to research on and the treatment of congenital birth defects when the development of the Salk vaccine effectively put the original March of Dimes out of business.

You can usefully think of the great trend to diversification, then, as arising largely from the natural and widespread desire to make use of excess—or obtainable—resources in order to take advantage of an opportunity or solve a problem. Although this may describe the motives in broad terms, you will surely want to look carefully at each situation you encounter to discern just what that particular management was trying to accomplish, and how they went about it. Zurn Industries and The Leisure Group both started small and acquired many companies over a short period of time, but that is where the important similarities end. In the CIBA-GEIGY case you will find careful articulation of the reasons for seeking an acquisition, as well as extensive guidelines designed to assist in the search and evaluation process. That the motives that lead various managements to diversify may have much in common at the general level of a desire for some combination of increased stability, growth, and profits, in no way lessens the need to look carefully at the reasons for diversifying in the individual situation.

SUMMARY

The key issue for the general manager is not whether certain generic diversification strategies seem to be associated with high or low returns on average, but whether certain actions are likely to present a solution to the problems, opportunities, and aspirations of that particular company. To increase the stability of earnings or to improve from below average to average in growth or profitability over time by means of the shifting of assets from declining businesses to areas of more promise may not meet the tests of financial theory for ideal use of the shareholder's resources, although the assumptions behind that conclusion merit careful examination. It does represent a substantial accomplishment to most business executives, and an objective which explains much diversification activity.

chapter
9

New tasks and complexities

In the last chapter we noted the long-term major trend to diversification in American industry. In this chapter we will make these new tasks and added complexities that arise for the general manager as a result of diversification more explicit in order to provide you with a better understanding of the problems facing the general manager of the diversified firm. This will facilitate the development of a useful framework of analysis of the diversified corporation from the corporate general manager's point of view, a task to which we will turn in the last chapter.

LEVELS OF GENERAL MANAGEMENT

Historically, we have tended to think of the general manager as the executive to whom the functional managers report. The job evolved in this manner, and much of the literature, research, and teaching on management historically has made the implicit, if not explicit, assumption that general managers are responsible for a single business in an identifiable market and have the assistance of a number of functional managers in marketing, production, finance, and so on, to help them do what they cannot do all by themselves. Indeed, one of the essential tasks of general managers is often described as coordinating the activities of their functional managers in the achievement of the product/market strategy of the firm, an activity for which they are principally but not solely responsible. Most of the cases in this book have been about single-business organizations, or else on essentially single-business issues in "the middle" of larger organizations.

This conception of the job of the general manager has quite properly had an extensive influence on both research and teaching in the field of General Management or Business Policy. In addition to focusing our attention on a particular set of tasks, it has also resulted in the tendency to think of general management as taking place at a single organizational level. It is a natural outgrowth of thinking of the job of the general manager in terms of the

658

single business for which he or she does—or should—have considerable knowledge of both the industry, major competitors, his or her own company and people.

Such a conception of the general manager's position is inaccurate for virtually all of our larger corporations. The trend to diversification and therefore divisionalization and decentralization has created several new layers of general management above the traditional manager of the single business. General managers in diversified firms may have subordinates who are themselves general managers of businesses with hundreds of millions of dollars in sales volume.

There is a clear relationship between this increasing managerial complexity, brought on by strategies of product diversification, and the movement to the product division form of organization, brought on by the attempts to deal with this increasing complexity. The new organizational positions and levels created by the movement to product divisions present different challenges than the old positions and structure, which best served the needs of the single-business organization.

Scott[1] has developed a conceptual scheme and a set of terms which describe this evolution in a useful way. He characterizes the small, entrepreneurially managed firm without clear functional departments as a "Stage 1" firm, the traditional functional organization as a "Stage 2" firm, and the firm organized along product division lines as a "Stage 3" firm. It is a developmental model of organizations in that firms tend to move from one identifiable stage to another as they diversify, which tends to occur over time. The model is useful in that it emphasizes that the differences in the management tasks and the increases in complexity are more associated with the "stage" and therefore product diversity of the firm than they are with its size at any given stage. Finally, it provides a framework for discussing how the characteristics of organization change from one stage to another.

What Chandler described so well are the difficulties that companies encountered in trying to administer a number of different products by means of the single functional organization. The natural tendency as products were added was first to assign responsibility for the various functions of the new and different business to the well-established functional departments that already existed. The difficulties for the manager of comprehension of the overall business and of coordination of the functional activities increased rapidly as new activities were added. The eventual solution of having separate businesses report to a new and higher level of general management evolved from the traditional structure of functional units reporting to the top management of the company.

An intermediate step is often followed as companies add new activities

---

[1] Bruce R. Scott, "The Industrial State: Old Myths and New Realities," *Harvard Business Review*, March–April 1973 (No. 73212).

to an existing predominantly single-business operation. Instead of moving directly to the product division form of organization, a more gradual transition can be made by retaining the functional organization for the historic bulk of the business, but to have the new activities report as separate business units to the existing corporate management. For a variety of reasons such a structure generally evolves into the product division form of organization. The addition of more new activities would obviously push the organization in that direction, but even if no new activities are added, it leaves the president in the somewhat ambiguous position of having functional managers as well as business managers report to him or her.

As a result of this addition of new businesses and organizational levels, the task of the general manager of a division in the diversified company is in many ways most like that of his or her counterpart in the single-business independent company. In the typical large diversified company there will be one or more levels of management above the division manager, as well as varying amounts of staff personnel at the different levels. As one proceeds up through the levels to a group vice president (commonly responsible for a number of divisions) and to the president or chief executive officer of the entire organization, new tasks and complexities arise.

The demands placed on the top managers of diversified companies are not only complex but also different. As diversity increases, these demands would at some point seem to exceed the capacities of both people and organizations to deal with them effectively. Responsibility and power become increasingly removed from the reality of the business operations and the people running them. The connecting links between the two increasingly become quantitative reports, written summaries, conferences, staff assistants, and more abstract models of the various businesses and their environments. Economists and social scientists discuss the problem in terms of the managerial inefficiencies which unavoidably accompany increased size and diversity and which ultimately negate whatever other economic advantages growth via diversification might bring to the organization. Lammot Copeland, when he was president of Du Pont, stated his opinion in a more direct way: "Running a conglomerate is a job for management geniuses, not ordinary mortals such as we at Du Pont."

INCREASED STRATEGIC OPTIONS

The most dramatic new task which ordinary mortals must nevertheless master arises from the fact that both the present and potential strategic options of the firm have by definition been broadened considerably. The manager of the diversified firm (or the firm considering diversification) is no longer concerned only with the problems and prospects of a single business, with the attendant opportunity for involvement in the development of the strategy for that business and the allocation of resources to various functional areas and programs in support of that strategy. The manager must now make, or at least assume responsibility for, decisions with regard to which products and markets in which to compete, and not just how to compete in given product markets.

The fundamental notion of "our industry" obviously loses its meaning as the company diversifies. For the highly diversified company it becomes almost meaningless in the traditional product/market sense. The more a company diversifies, the less attention the manager can pay to any one industry, and the more the manager will be forced to rely on the judgments of others or on abstractions which try to capture the important characteristics of an industry for someone who is not intimately familiar with it. This may be useful in that it can provide a broader look across a number of industries than might otherwise be possible. An unavoidable shortcoming, however, is the loss of the ability to be as close to the trends and people and happenings of a specific industry as any good operating manager should be.

The new and critical strategic choice that faces the general manager at the corporate level, then, becomes the selection of products and markets in which to engage, and the development of both a rationale for that particular choice as well as a means of making that choice effective. General managers of diversified firms can no longer be primarily concerned with the development of strategy for a single business, but neither can they ignore the strategic position and performance of their existing units as they consider the broader issues of the product-market portfolio. Therein lies a substantial dilemma, to which we shall return later.

This enlarged strategic horizon for the firm complicates the job of the general manager in the search and evaluation of new activities. Without a managerially oriented rationale for what businesses to consider, the manager would be faced with the prospect of investigating the whole world of business activity. The development of such guidelines is not easy for the individual company, however; and if they are to permit one to go beyond the present businesses, as is their purpose, they will still require an understanding on the part of someone of the opportunities that exist for that company in new products and markets. In the CIBA-GEIGY case you will find one approach to the narrowing of this search for opportunity.

Questions of the divestment of existing operations—a necessary option to consider if one is to view the products and divisions of a company as elements of a portfolio—may not be as difficult analytically because of the greater familiarity with any operation which has been a part of the company. The analytical benefits the manager gains because of greater familiarity are no doubt more than offset by the administrative difficulties of selling an existing operation, however, as well as the unavoidable need to consider the effects of the divestment of an ailing division on the reported earnings of the company.

ALLOCATION OF RESOURCES TO OPERATIONS

Additions to and deletions from the portfolio of a corporation are dramatic but (for most companies) periodic and perhaps infrequent major resource allocation decisions. The allocation of resources to the various subunits of the corporation is another new and continuing task, however, influenced by every budget, capital appropriation request, incentive plan, and profit goal. The question is no longer the allocation of resources among the functional departments of a single business, with some requirements of balance among the departments in order to achieve the overall goals of the business. Instead, the president now has the option of channeling financial resources from one division to another, in accordance with that executive's perception of the best opportunities for spending the corporation's limited resources. The old challenge of allocating resources to their most productive use is raised to the level of choosing among separate and often dissimilar businesses. In broad terms this can be described as substituting an internal capital market for the traditional external capital markets.

Allocating resources is a task the corporate level can in no way avoid, since even "objective" decision rules, profit goals, or capital hurdle rates will influence the pattern of cash flows into or out of divisions. From the corporate point of view, there is no reason to assume that the divisions with the highest cash flow or profits are also those which should have the most money to spend on their own futures. Neither is there any reason to believe that the establishment of uniform profit goals for all divisions, or the establishment of incentive plans which are based on division profits, will result in the best allocation of resources to divisions in view of the long-run opportunities facing the corporation.

The objective is not just to evaluate each division's plans on its own merits but to evaluate each relative to the others. This poses very considerable analytical and administrative problems. A thorough review of a division is not something that can be done either quickly or frequently. If the goal is to evaluate the opportunities facing any one division in relation to the opportunities in all of the divisions, however, it is necessary to have the reviews close enough together so that comparisons can be made and remembered before the decisions are final. Analogies which compare the virtually instantaneous analysis of a large sample of common stocks to construct the most efficient investment portfolio, based as they are on the processing by computer of large amounts of readily available quantified data, are of little help for this substantial managerial task.

The more the corporate level seeks to actively influence the allocation of funds among the divisions, or what is even more difficult, to also influence the content of the strategy at the division level, the more someone must make trade-offs among unlike and little-known alternatives. It may be that no one of these problems is different in principle than the traditional single-business problems more familiar to all of us. Adding greatly to the number of problems, however, as well as attempting to evaluate the alternatives in relation to each other, creates a formidable intellectual and administrative task. It is complicated by the fact that the various levels and units in the organization have different interests, perspectives, and biases, and obtaining objective data—whether historical data or forecasts and judgments—is not easy. The past can be as difficult to interpret as the future is uncertain.

In addition, just because a company adopts the product division form of organization it does not follow that the strategy and operations of each division are necessarily independent of all of the other divisions except for the allocation of financial resources. Depending on the nature of the businesses of the various divisions and the approach of the corporate level to the relationships among the divisions, there may be numerous opportunities or even requirements for the coordination of research and development, manufacturing, or marketing activities of divisions with each other. Some companies prefer to let the self-interests of the individual divisions govern such matters; others prefer to play a more active role. In either event, interrelationships complicate the strategic evaluations and the allocation of resources.

MANAGING MANAGERS

A third task that arises for the chief executive in the diversified corporation is the training, selection, evaluation, motivation, and reward of general managers (division presidents) rather than functional specialists (vice presidents of manufacturing, etc.). The job of the general manager of the single business is more complex in many ways than that of his or her functional subordinates in that it involves both more variables and more complex variables than most functional responsibilities entail. In addition, the impact of many of the general manager's most important decisions can best be measured in terms of several years, or even decades; functional decisions and managers can usually be evaluated over a shorter period of time. One can of course evaluate a division manager very largely on "the numbers," but that can incur many long-run risks and costs. The general manager at the corporate level has to understand the performance and the potential of six division managers of businesses different from each other and located physically away from headquarters. This is a more difficult job than a division president faces in evaluating the six or so functional managers that report to him or her, where they are all in the same industry, organization, and (probably) location.

CORPORATE LEVEL STRATEGY

The fourth new task is an outgrowth of all that has been mentioned: the need to conceptualize a strategy for the corporation as a whole which is something more than the sum of the division strategies. The president of the diversified company has the task of defining and communicating just what the "central theme," "core skills," or "concept of the corporation" is in operational terms that go beyond the ones that can describe the single-product firm competing in the single industry, but not as abstract as purely financial goals. Financial goals unaccompanied by some notion of how and why they can be achieved are never very useful. Business level strategies, as we may call those at the division level, both influence and are influenced by the corporate level strategy. The president bears the ultimate responsibility for the content of each as well as the relationships between them.

An essential part of the concept of strategy in the diversified firm is the role played by the corporate level and the specific structure and processes they adopt in managing the overall organization. We tend to think of strategy as encompassing primarily product-market choices and strategies. You need only recall the case of Lincoln Electric to appreciate the impressive results that can come from combining an approach to organization and motivation which supports strongly the basic product-market strategy of that firm. The role and contribution of the corporate management in the implementation of strategy, an issue we shall return to in the next chapter, is an equally important element of the overall strategy for the diversified firm.

Developing a statement of strategy for the diversified firm that is a useful guide to action for those within the firm, and not just an attractive statement for outside consumption, is a most challenging intellectual exercise. We will develop a framework of analysis that will assist you in this in the next chapter. You will also have a chance to identify and evaluate the concept of strategy for the diversified firm as you study some of the cases in this book. Do the statements in the Zurn case concerning the environmental focus of the firm make sense, for example, in terms of what the company actually consists of? Are there any key differences in the strategies proclaimed by the CML Group, Inc., and The Leisure Group, both of which had much interest in small companies in the "leisure-time" industry? And in the Sybron (E) case, you will be exposed to some of the strategic issues still remaining for a president who led his company through 15 years of growth via diversification.

SUMMARY

New problems always prompt the development of new tools, techniques, conceptual schemes, and organizational arrangements to deal with them. So it is with diversification. Divisionalization and decentralization were the solutions to the managerial problems created by product diversity, which was in itself a response to other problems and opportunities. The creation of additional levels of general management above the product divisions resulted in new jobs at the corporate and group levels as well as the redefinition of the general manager's job at the division level. Many years ago the development of the teaching area of Business Policy represented a jump in the level of abstraction from that of the specialist and the functional manager to the generalist responsible for the enterprise as a whole. In some ways we now have similar adjustments to make in our thinking about these new levels of general management created in the diversified company.

It is unfortunate but unavoidable that as the territory becomes more complex and the problems to be dealt with more numerous, as is the case as a company diversifies, the president is forced to view the territory from increasingly higher levels of abstraction. At the same time that we are proudly adding layers to the beehive and constructing all kinds of elaborate tunnels within it, the Queen Bee is becoming more and more removed from the workers and their daily forays for pollen. But it is at the operating level that continuing contributions must be made in the ongoing industrial concern. As an experienced division manager in one highly diversified company remarked:

> We have got to keep in mind what makes the corporation go. It isn't headquarters; I never have seen a headquarters that generated income by itself. The foundation for the whole operation is in the divisions; it is in the divisions that the money is spent and the money is earned. That is mainly where we have to worry about selling things for more than they cost to make. Headquarters, of course, has an important role to play, but it is too easy for them to get preoccupied with their own needs.

We will turn in the next chapter to suggestions as to how you might build on the analytical and administrative skills you have already learned in order to deal with the general management problems of the diversified company.

10

A framework for analysis

The purpose of this chapter is to describe an analytical approach to the corporate-level general management problems of diversified companies that will be useful to you as you study the cases in the final section of the book. As has been explained in the preceding two chapters, diversified companies are the most important form of business institution in this country, and product diversity and the consequent development of divisional structures have created some significant additional complexities in the general manager's job at the corporate level in diversified companies.

In your role of manager, or advisor to the manager, your task is to *identify* the strategic position, problems, and opportunities of the company; to *evaluate* these in terms of the aspirations of the management and the seriousness of the problems or the attractiveness of the opportunities; and to *recommend* to the general manager a strategy, including the approach to organization, which will facilitate over time the achievement of a set of objectives.

STRATEGIC AND ORGANIZATIONAL ISSUES

You will find that the cases in this section will, to a greater degree than most of the other cases in this book, include considerable data on both the strategic and organizational issues facing each company. The approach to organization in diversified firms is even more intertwined with the corporate strategy than in the single-business firm. The cases developed for examining the general management problems of diversified firms have therefore not followed the more traditional approach of many Business Policy courses of considering problems of strategy formulation and implementation largely in a sequential order. This admittedly complicates your tasks of identification, evaluation, and recommendation—a complexity brought on by the nature of the problems with which you are dealing.

You will need to be concerned with the overall strategy and the approach to organization of the multibusiness firm over time and not just specific acquisition decisions or other large resource allocations to a specific business. Such decisions are obviously important, and the larger the commitment in relation to the resources of the company, the more important they become. The single acquisition or major resource-allocation decision is to the corporate strategy of the diversified company what the single capital expenditure project in a functional area is to the strategy of the single-business company, however. Both are important to do well, but both need to be part of a much larger mosaic for long-run success. A strategy of making individual acquisition or investment decisions without a concept of how the resulting business units will be managed, how they will relate to each other, and how they will contribute to the overall goals of the corporation is not any more likely to be successful than a capital budgeting program in the single-business company that is unrelated to the strategy of the company. In matters of corporate strategy, it is often what cannot be reflected accurately in the numbers that becomes important, and not just the careful analysis of the numbers. Individual acquisition or investment decisions often become the specific issues by which the overall strategies are tested for both their utility and relevance. They should be made in the context of a strategy and a plan for how they will be managed, however, and not be the determinants of a strategy.

ANALYTICAL APPROACH

The most fruitful way for you to extend to diversified firms your understanding of the job of the general manager derived from your study of the single-business company is to build on the approach and models that you have already developed. To do so we will need to examine some of the ways in which the main elements of that policy model, as we may call it, need to be modified or thought of differently in order to make them useful for this purpose. We will also look briefly at some of the analytical techniques such as portfolio planning models which have been developed to deal with the management problems of the diversified firm; these can provide useful inputs to the basic policy model.

The basic policy model, most easily applied to the general management problems of the single-business firm, was developed in Parts I and II and portrayed graphically on page 394. In applying that basic approach, we will make use of the concepts already developed but will emphasize the importance of the concept of *fit* or *consistency* of the various elements of the policy model with each other in a manner suited to the problems and needs of the multibusiness firm. In addition, we shall extend this same concept of fit to the relationships of the divisions with each other, with the corporate level, and with their individual external environments.

We shall also introduce a new concept, that of the *corporate role* in diversified companies. General management tasks are performed at multiple levels in the diversified company, and the role that the corporate level decides to play in the overall management of the corporation is important to each individual company. It is the means by which the corporate level can seek as well as maintain a *fit* or pattern of relationships between the business units, the corporate level, and the external environment that contributes most effectively to the corporate objectives.

FINANCIAL PERFORMANCE AND POSITION

Just as with a single-business company, one of the first elements in your analysis should be the financial performance and position of the company. You will want to look at the trend of sales, earnings, and margins, as well as the traditional balance-sheet measures that apply to all companies. You should be forewarned, however, that intelligent financial analysis of the diversified company is considerably more complex than for the single-business company.

One reason is simply the result of the number of different businesses in which the firm is engaged. If four different businesses each are important with respect to their contribution to sales and earnings and use of assets, you will feel compelled to investigate the performance and prospects for each of them. If the company consists of 40 such units, you cannot investigate them all, but neither can you ignore them all on the basis that no one of them is very important. The usual approach is to aggregate the businesses in some way for analytical purposes, but then important factors or details in individual businesses may be lost.

A second reason that your task is more difficult is that often the kind of information you would like to have is not broken out separately for public reporting purposes. There is considerably more information on business segments now than was available in the past, but for the larger and more diversified companies, the reporting breakdowns seldom get to the level of divisions. As you look at the breakdowns for some of our large companies, you will note that sales, profit, and asset figures are seldom listed for more than about six major reporting units, which may not even correspond to organizational units.

If you then concentrate your attention on overall corporate figures rather than product-market breakdowns, you will need to be careful that still a third difficulty does not lead you astray. For companies that have been engaged in acquisitions, it is often difficult to ascertain just what portion of the performance can be attributed to internal growth and what portion was simply due to the arithmetic of the acquisitions. Financial data and the prices paid for acquisitions are not always reported publicly, and even if they were, to pull this data together can be a major task. The sources of the sales and earnings growth therefore can be hard to trace, and balance-sheet items can be affected by the methods as well as the terms of acquisitions.

None of this is intended to dissuade you from attempting a financial analysis of the diversified company as a part of your overall evaluation. If anything, this is more important to do carefully with the diversified company, because the basic split of performance due to internal growth, as opposed to acquisition, and the health and prospects for major business segments are very useful to know. You will want to draw upon your knowledge of financial accounting and reporting practices, including how they have changed at times, to do the best job possible.[1] The difficulty of doing a careful job of financial analysis explains in part why financial analysts do not like dealing with highly diversified companies; obtaining and analyzing the information necessary to truly understand their operations is considerably more burdensome than for a single-business company.

We are specifically *not* viewing the management problems of the diversified company solely, or even primarily, from the standpoint of the investor or of financial theory. We hope that good theory and responsible practice would not be in significant conflict. The reason for continuing with the managerial viewpoint that was introduced at the beginning of the book is simply that it is the most useful one to adopt if you wish to understand actual managerial behavior and thereby develop your own managerial skills.

CONCEPT OF STRATEGY

Let us look at how we can apply the concept of strategy from the basic policy framework to the corporate level in the diversified company, as portrayed in Exhibit 10–1.

In Exhibit 10–1, we will use the term *corporate level* to refer to those units and people above the level of the specific business units. Product groups—organizational units made up of several divisions—are in fact an intermediate level between the business and true corporate levels, but this distinction need not concern us at this point. The main distinction to be made is that product-market strategies exist at the business level, as do general managers and functional organizations responsible for a traditional business. The corporate level has responsibility for a portfolio of businesses, as well as the traditional financial, legal, and administrative tasks common to all corporations. In Chapter 1 we suggested that a statement of strategy

> . . . should convey both what a company is trying to achieve and how it
> hopes to achieve it. The plan for achievement should include attention to
> the important factors influencing that achievement, as mentioned, and it
> should specify what major steps are to be taken, in what rough time frame,
> by whom, what resources will be required, and how the resources will be

---

[1] See, for example, Chapter 22 in *Managerial Finance* by Weston and Brigham for some discussion of accounting policies in mergers.

EXHIBIT 10–1

Typical corporate organization chart for a multidivision company

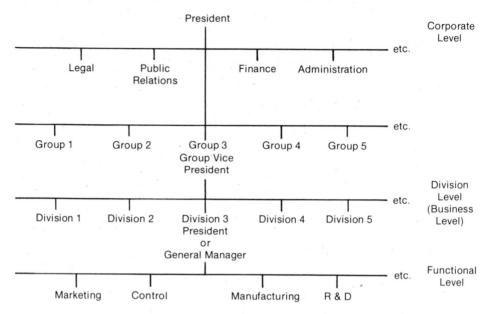

obtained. It should communicate, in as tangible a way as possible, just how this particular company has chosen to compete in the marketplace.

That general prescription applies to the corporate level as well as the business level. The main adjustment that has to be made is in the level of detail concerning specific businesses with which the corporate-level strategy concerns itself. For the single business, it is important for the manager to be familiar with, and the strategy to deal with, specific products, markets, competitors, functional policies, and so on, as we emphasized in the earlier cases and text. At the corporate level in the diversified company, comparable detail is not possible. The corporation, however, still needs to have its own longer-term objectives and plans for achieving them. These objectives and plans unavoidably depend upon and in turn influence the strategies of the individual divisions. A corporate-level strategy that is no more than a compilation of the strategies of the various divisions, however, is neither useful nor interesting.

A key change is that instead of devoting attention to how the corporation will compete in its many specific businesses, more attention now must be paid to what the resources, skills, and the underlying strategic thinking are that led to that particular set of activities. Just as a business-level strategy can be thought of as an organizing concept that helps relate the activities of the functional departments to the opportunities in the external environment, the corporate strategy in the multibusiness corporation can be thought of as the organizing concept which both explains and guides the activities of the many separate businesses within the corporation. The corporate strategy in the diversified company is more concerned with where the corporation is going to spend its money, and why; business-level strategies deal with the plans for spending it. Neither can be arrived at independently of the other.

There is a view that the overall corporate strategy can be largely the sum of the product-market opportunities and strategic plans at that business unit level, and that therefore there is not much need for a broader, corporate-level strategy that should be communicated to the divisions and be of use to them in devising their plans. In this view, the role of the corporate level is largely to assign priorities for claims on the limited corporate resources, allocating money to the divisions according to their promise.

A more commonly held view, and one which we support, is that even the most diversified company needs a broader conception of itself than as an allocator of resources to the most promising opportunities that arise. If there is little effort to influence what arises or attention paid to why that particular corporation should be better than anyone else in pursuing a particular market opportunity, superior performance is unlikely to result. A strategy for the overall corporation is just as important as a strategy for the individual division, and they need to be formulated and revised in relation to each other.

If we must forsake most of the product-market components of strategy familiar at the business level when we move to the corporate level, what is changed, what remains, and what new is added?

The concept of strategy at the corporate level in the diversified company should address long-term growth and profitability goals, just as in the single-business company. The derivation of these may range from somewhat arbitrarily selected goals arrived at by a "top-down" process to a consolidation of the plans submitted by the existing units, adjusted downward through conservatism or nudged upward as a form of encouragement or pressure. The overall financial objectives are not as readily derived from conditions in the existing businesses as in the single-business company, however, since the limitations of any single industry do not apply. Indeed, it is the desire to avoid the constraints arising from the conditions in a single industry that often causes companies to seek profits and growth elsewhere. It should be apparent, however, that just because the pharmaceutical industry has for decades ranked at or near the top of all industries in return on equity, or because Xerox or IBM or McDonald's have been highly profitable and growing companies, neither their financial achievements nor their lines of business are necessarily appropriate goals for any other company. In the Sybron (E) case you will have the opportunity to discuss the situation of a president much concerned with the problem of devising long-term goals for his company and observing carefully the performance and prospects of numerous other companies and industries that might provide a model for his company.

Corporate goals stated purely in financial terms do not, it should be noted, provide much operational guidance for the corporation with regard to the lines of business to engage in, nor for the divisions with regard to how to compete in the businesses they are already in. Such goals have more of an effect on the degree of risk that managers feel compelled to undertake in both product decisions and financing decisions. They also affect the pressure felt within the organization to achieve current goals, which may influence behavior in many ways, some of them to the detriment of the long-run health and reputation of the company.

The Sybron cases will also provide you with an excellent opportunity to discuss, in the context of one particular company, whether certain specific elements are appropriate in a corporate-level statement of strategy and how these should be communicated to—and, perhaps, enforced upon—the divisions. The president states as a fundamental strategic guideline for the divisions—of which there are almost 50, in various fields—that " . . . we propose to be the 'Cadillacs' of our industries. . . . We propose to do this by rather arbitrarily *always* pricing our products above our competition, never below." Is such a guideline a useful element of corporate strategy? If so, you will have to decide how it should be enforced in a specific case in which a division has announced a decision to reduce prices, in apparent contradiction to the above guideline.

Or, to take another example from the same company, how useful and enforceable are guidelines concerning cooperation between divisions, especially in a case in which one of the divisions does not see it as being in their interest to undertake a joint venture with another? And if you do not find these kinds of guidelines useful for the corporate level in this case, what would you suggest in their place?

The degree of risk that a company management is willing to undertake is an element of its strategy and becomes evident in the actions of the company. Historically, as Chandler points out, companies tended to diversify when they had an excess of resources over what they felt they could profitably apply to their traditional businesses, even though those base businesses might not have been in trouble. When faced with trouble and declining prospects in the basic business, companies have often sought to reduce their overall risk by diversifying, with whatever resources they could spare, into areas that seemed more attractive. In the 1960s, however, a new category of risk taking appeared, in which companies were very aggressive in obtaining resources for expansion and were willing to subject themselves to both highly leveraged capital structures as well as unknown and possibly risky new businesses in their pursuit of growth. The Leisure Group, which you will encounter later, is an example of highly ambitious but risky financial as well as operating strategies, with consequent high risk to investors and managers alike. In the Zurn case, the company followed a more conservative pattern of taking advantage of market opportunity to grow via acquisition, one which entailed less risk in both financial and operating terms. The point is not that one approach or the other is always the preferred one but that management's choice of the level of financial and operating risk that is acceptable—or, what is more important, the combination of the two—is an essential factor influencing other aspects of both corporate and business-level strategies. You need to be sensitive to what the preferences are for any given company, to examine whether the level of risk assumed seems reasonable in view of both the problems and opportunities facing the company, and most of all, to insure that the risks actually taken do not unknowingly exceed the comfort level of either management or stockholders.

A difficult component of the concept of strategy at the corporate level of the diversified company is that which addresses the kinds of businesses the company will engage in, and why. The allocation of funds to competing businesses presently within the corporation is an aspect of this problem, but it is much more amenable to analysis by means of various portfolio planning models that have been developed and will be discussed later than is the rationale for the product range of the company as a whole.

The range of product diversification can be viewed in primarily financial terms such as profitability, growth, cash-flow patterns, degree of risk in the operations of the business, and so on. These measures can be applied to existing as well as potential businesses. In the case of possible acquisitions, the immediate impact of the acquisition on the earnings, earnings per share, and balance sheet of the acquirer are also of interest to managers and investors.

Although financial measures invariably need to be considered, they do not themselves constitute a sufficient basis for deciding upon the degree and type of diversification that should be pursued, as the CIBA-GEIGY case illustrates. If only financial criteria are applied, there would be little difference between the range of products within the company and the variety of stocks in a nonspecialized common stock mutual fund and would likely present little more management contribution to the operations. Such a corporation could more accurately be thought of as a financial holding company than an operating company.

Related versus unrelated diversification

The way in which a particular acquisition or a diversification strategy can be justified in terms of research and development, manufacturing, marketing, or management skills that are related or complementary is important to examine and sometimes seems to be limited only by the ingenuity of those describing it. One type of relatedness can be viewed as what the corporation can contribute because of a general management ability that will be useful as an addition to, not a substitute for, the management of certain kinds of product divisions. Perhaps more frequently, relatedness is defined in terms of useful and more tangible skills in functional areas, an excess of physical resources, or technology that can be applied to an acquisition. In any event, the degree of relatedness of both present and prospective businesses is an element of the corporate strategy that you will want to examine.

In considering diversification alternatives, it is natural to look first at those areas most closely related to the existing businesses. Indeed, management would be remiss not to do so, since there is every reason to believe that familiarity is an advantage in evaluating and managing new opportunities and that it is easier to apply existing resources and skills to new opportunities if they are related in some manner. In addition, Rumelt's findings indicate that firms that engage in related diversification tend to have better performance than others, and those that engage in "passive-unrelated" have the worst records.

It does not follow that a strategy of related diversification is preferable, however. Part of the difficulty stems from the problems of classification, especially for an outside observer. What is *related* in a meaningful sense, and what is not? The concept is surely more than a pair of boxes, one marked *related* and one marked *unrelated;* it is more like a continuum or a spectrum. In addition, new businesses can be related in some aspects—a common manufacturing process, for example, such as familiarity with precision plastic injection molding techniques—and totally unrelated in other important aspects of the business such as product design or marketing. One has to judge both the degree of relatedness and the overall importance of the areas in which relatedness exists.

Apart from the difficulties of classification, another problem exists for the manager in applying the related-unrelated dimension to diversification strategies. The profitability of expansion into any field depends in part on the skills and resources of the parent and the acquisition and the extent to which each can contribute to the other. It also depends to a significant extent on the profitability of the field entered, however. If the base industry is profitable, related fields may also be. This tends to be true especially for companies with a significant core technology which provides the basis for related diversification. Other types of barriers to entry may have similar effects. One needs to look to the base industry and company to determine whether the admitted risks of moving to less-familiar territories outweigh the disadvantages of remaining close to the original business, continuing to apply skills and resources to related and familiar areas that may unfortunately have many of the very problems from which the company is trying to escape. The arguments favoring a strategy of related diversification are surely less applicable to a textile company than to companies like Xerox or Polaroid, both of which have very substantial technical skills and (historically) extremely successful core businesses.

In spite of the difficulties we have with both classification and cause-and-effect as far as the related-unrelated dimension is concerned, it is important to think about present as well as future activities in terms of how they are, or can be, related to each other. The main benefits of doing so lie in three areas:

1. The degree of relatedness is some evidence of how good the judgment and the knowledge of the parent is likely to be with regard to the requirements for success in the new industry and its ability to evaluate the positions and potential of the new acquisition. Indeed, the most important aspects of relatedness may be whether the parent has a strategic understanding of the needs of the new business which is insightful enough to enable it to see opportunities to improve the strategy or operations that others may have overlooked—not primarily whether one activity is related to another in a functional or market or technological sense. A corporate management that is thoroughly familiar with consumer packaged goods, for example, may have much to contribute to a venture in that field, even though there are no specific activities in any of the existing divisions that would be of value or could supply resources to the new company. Similarly, basic technical skills and experience in dealing with the problems of small, high-technology companies may represent a highly useful resource, even though there are no specific technical skills or facilities or patents that are directly applicable.

2. In addition, the more related the functional aspects of the possible diversification effort are, the more likely it is that the functional skills and resources of the parent will be of value to the acquisition. If one activity is to make a contribution to the other, the skills or resources have to be both applicable and available.

3. The more related the various businesses of the corporation are, the easier it is likely to be for the corporate level to understand the basic characteristics of each of their businesses. In addition, it will simplify the task of developing an appropriate role for the corporate level with respect to the management of these businesses, an issue which we shall discuss later.

It is important to look beyond the popular concept of synergy to investigate just what the advantages will be that stem from relatedness. Perhaps the most important thing is to avoid the illusion of relatedness, which has been used to justify almost any kind of diversification. An extreme but perhaps apocryphal example is that of the manufacturer of fork lift trucks that decided its real business and basic skill was in providing vertical transportation and therefore diversified into escalators, with disastrous results.

Although the related-unrelated dimension does not provide us with an explicit guideline for selecting the best diversification strategy in the individual situation, it is a very useful way to begin investigating alternatives. We all find it more comfortable, although perhaps less interesting, to remain with familiar activities. We have to remember that the very reason companies diversify, however, is that the present activities no longer meet the longer-term objectives. The more closely related the new activities are to the existing operations, the greater the chance that they will evidence similar problems. Carried to its logical extreme, the most "related" diversification is no diversification at all.

STRATEGY FORMULATION AND CORPORATE RESOURCES

In Chapter 4 we discussed the need to base a strategy for a company not only on the opportunities for and aspirations of that company but also upon its distinctive strengths as well. Successful strategies build upon the strengths and avoid the weaknesses of the specific company. The need to explicitly consider just what the resources are of the company and what the distinctive strengths are, or can be, is just as important when considering corporate-level strategies as business-level strategies. The corporate-level problem is more complex because the distinctive strengths, just as the strategy, generally have to be stated at a higher level of abstraction to be useful at the corporate level. It may be that a company wishes to define its basic competitive advantage in terms of a distinctive competence in supplying and selling mass-produced consumer packaged goods, for example, or working with high-technology firms, or specific kinds of technologies, or even strengths in the traditional functional areas. The challenge is not only to articulate such an approach in the annual report and to financial analysts but also to develop and transmit these skills within the corporation in a way that results in a competitive advantage for the corporation.

Financial resources and skills

One must not, of course, minimize the importance of financial resources as an important strength. They are the most readily applied resource of all. Such resources can come from many sources in a diversified company: a predictable cash flow in excess of current division needs, additional borrowing capacity, cash that could be freed up by better asset management or the sale of some businesses, and so on. An important (but temporary) financial resource in the development of some of the conglomerates in the 1960s was a reception in the capital markets that bestowed upon them a price/earning ratio high enough to make the issuance of stock for cash or for other companies unusually attractive. The Leisure Group is an example of a company that was able to obtain the financial resources necessary to support their rapid growth in part because of a very favorable market reaction to their strategy and performance. The integrated petroleum industry in the late 1970s and early 1980s is a prime example of an industry in which predictable large cash flows could provide resources for diversification on a scale far beyond that available to other industries and companies. The steel industry would be an example of an industry suffering not from a cash surplus, but a cash shortage; just as existing or obtainable resources are an advantage, a shortage is a clear liability.

As you study the cases in the book as well as think about the diversification opportunities of other companies and industries, the financial resources available to support diversification strategy are essential to examine. A strategy of diversification which does not take into account the amount and source of the financial resources required is just as deficient as a strategy for a single business which identifies great opportunity but neglects to put a price tag on the effort and to identify the source of the funds.

Allocating financial resources

The diversified corporation cannot avoid playing a continuing role in the allocation of funds within the existing businesses, and this can constitute a significant competitive advantage if done well. Whether allocations of capital or, more broadly, cash flow are based on judgment, formula, or a combination of the two, the procedure chosen will have an effect on current profits as well as which business units receive resources for future growth and which units supply these resources. Encouraging and rewarding high current profits from all may encourage divisions which have good opportunity to invest in research and development or gain-share market strategies at the expense of reduced profits to neglect such long-run development in favor of good current returns. Formulas or approaches which in effect permit each division to spend whatever cash flow they develop may well result in more capital investment than is warranted from a corporate viewpoint in declining areas and less than is warranted in areas of higher promise. It is only natural for divisions and companies to want to spend themselves whatever resources they develop, but there is no reason to believe all areas are, from the corporate viewpoint, equally worthy of support. Neither is there any reason to believe that any single factor such as current profits or profitability, market size or growth, capital project hurdle rates, or level of technology will result in an "optimum" strategic allocation. No matter what the formula chosen, some unintended adverse consequences are likely to ensue.

This opportunity to influence the allocation of funds to the divisions by means of an internal capital market, by-passing the traditional private capital markets and avoiding the loss of both taxes and transaction costs, is a significant potential advantage for the diversified company. The ability to do this well is an important skill and one which companies have spent much time and effort trying to improve. The more diverse the company and the more numerous the units, the more difficult the task becomes, and the more necessary it becomes to develop a more abstract framework or method of analysis to make up for the lack of first-hand knowledge of the divisions and industries themselves. The analytical methods which have been developed in the last decade or so to deal with problems of this kind are referred to as portfolio planning models, and we will discuss these in more detail later.

Undervalued situations

It is tempting to believe that the corporate level can develop a distinctive competence at finding and buying undervalued situations, companies that are available at a price that makes them attractive candidates without changes in their operations. It is the modern-day version of the "buy low and sell high" recipe for success in the stock market, with the additional handicap that premiums of from 25 percent to 100 percent over the market price will almost surely have to be offered to gain control and ultimately ownership.

The results of numerous empirical studies should make you careful about believing too strongly in the ability of managements to develop and exploit this skill on a consistent basis over a period of time, however. There is very little evidence that *any* particular investment strategy (other than buy and hold a diversified portfolio) is superior, after adjustment for risk, to any other for the passive investor buying securities in the public market. There is no reason to believe companies should be better at this than individuals or financial institutions. Just as with investing in the stock market, there are many examples of specific acquisitions which did, in fact, turn out to be undervalued at the time. Such individual examples should not obscure the low probability that such a skill can provide a competitive advantage over time for an operating company.

General management skills

One important advantage of the diversified company, claimed by many but difficult to verify, is the ability of the corporate level to provide both strategic and operational guidance to disparate business units because of the general management abilities of the group and corporate officers and staff, as well as the ability to design the appropriate organizational structure and processes so that these skills may be brought to bear in the individual situation. In both the CML Group, Inc., and The Leisure Group, you will find explicit statements as well as unstated assumptions concerning the impact of these general management skills on the operations of the acquired businesses.

The contribution made by such general management skills has been much debated in the investigations of diversified companies, with little evidence developed concerning its value that is convincing to those who hold opposing views. Most of us, perhaps, would subscribe to the notion that there are a number of general management skills that can usefully be applied without deep knowledge on the manager's part of the specific business, as is evidenced by the success with which some managers are able to oversee or even move into new businesses and be successful. At a more personal level, are you not investing time and money in learning management skills that transcend industry boundaries in the hopes that they can be usefully applied to whatever industry in which you end up working?

There are also strong arguments that can be made that the substitution of a knowledgeable and experienced group executive who will take the time to learn a reasonable amount about his specific divisions can play a more useful role, with regard both to advice and direction, than does the typical board of directors for the independent company. The group vice president has the advantage of broad experience, has access to funds from the corporate office, and has considerably more power to enforce more planning, reward good performance, and penalize poor performance than most outside directors or any outside consultant. As you study the cases in this last section, you should reflect upon just what the contributions—and limits to the contributions—of the group vice president or the corporate office can be to the operations of the divisions.

Strategic and operational improvements

Quite apart from the ability to find undervalued companies in the marketplace, when viewed as passive investments, is the ability to find companies which, as a result of whatever changes or additions the acquiring company seeks to accomplish, will be worth more as a result. This strength or ability is largely the consequence of the general management skills discussed above. This is the true creation of value and not just the recognition of undervalued situations. The changes can be of considerable variety—new strategies not contemplated, or at least not likely to be pursued, by the present owners or other potential acquirers; the pooling of resources or skills already existing within the corporation with the acquired company; the more effective management of existing operations; and so on. The flow need not be all one way; acquisitions are often sought for what they can do for the acquiring corporation and not just what the acquiring corporation can do to improve the operations of the acquisition. This is the creative skill that can result in significant and continuing value creation, but it is not an easy skill to develop or replicate. It is the one on which you will wish to concentrate the most in the cases that follow.

Summary of resources and skills

The purpose of this discussion of company resources and possible distinctive skills has not been to develop an exhaustive listing of these items but rather to suggest the ways in which the basic concept of corporate resources as they influence the selection of a strategy needs to be modified in its application to the corporate level of the diversified company. You will need to think carefully about each individual situation that you encounter to determine what the resources are that might be applied to new opportunities and what the distinctive strengths are that enable the company to exploit most fully its present opportunities.

The Zurn company, for example, believed its expertise was in equipment and systems to control pollution, and it acquired a large number of companies to build competence around this general area. The CML Group, Inc., and The Leisure Group, both interested in the leisure industry, defined their product interests quite differently, as well as the way in which they would work with the companies once they were acquired. Other examples of the rationale that companies have developed to guide them in the selection of products and markets in which to engage exist everywhere. Heublein, a very successful marketer of distilled spirits (and especially Smirnoff vodka), entered the beer business and the California wine business by acquisition largely because of the marketing skills they had which had formed the basis for their success in a closely related business. The acquisition of United Vintners was very successful; the acquisition of Hamm's Brewery was a disaster. Hamm's was sold at a substantial loss after a decade of unsuccessful attempts to apply their skills to the marketing of beer in the same way they had done with liquor and wine.

The challenge for the corporate level is to develop the distinctive strengths and acquire the resources needed to enable it to capitalize on the opportunities in the environment, not just uncover them or note that others have been able to exploit them successfully. If all a steel company management had to do was note that pharmaceutical companies are more profitable than steel companies in order to secure those higher returns for their own shareholders, there would not for long be either low-margin steel companies or high-margin pharmaceutical companies. In the diversified company, just as in the single-business company, successful results come not just from finding opportunity or developing competences but from the fit which follows from the creative and successful matching of the two. Such matching can only stem from a concept of what the distinctive resources or skills are of that particular company that will enable it to take advantage of specific opportunities that exist.

The point is not that certain definitions are inherently better than others but rather that it is important to think through very carefully just what the rationale will be for choosing activities in which to engage and for managing those activities most effectively. In the absence of guidelines based on product, market, or technology characteristics, selection is likely to stem largely from financial criteria, which can result in a very strange collection of businesses indeed. Such financial guidelines and stock market opportunity can combine to create companies no industrial logic can justify.

MANAGEMENT VALUES AND CORPORATE RESPONSIBILITY

The concepts of *Management Values* and *Corporate Responsibility* as we developed them in the earlier sections need little further elaboration or modification here. They are just as important in the diversified corporation as in the single-business corporation. With regard to management values, the major complicating factor is that more levels of management, with different perspectives and personal interests, have been added. As far as corporate responsibility is concerned, several new issues arise because of the nature of the diversified corporation.

One new issue is the responsibility the corporation has to local employees and communities. Whether or not divisions or multiunit companies are in fact better or worse citizens of their local communities than local companies is, at our present state of knowledge, a matter of debate. Also important from a public policy point of view is whether society is better served by a shutdown or phasing out of the less-promising operations in the portfolio of the parent's activities, as must sometimes happen, as opposed to letting those businesses continue to struggle along with marginal results until bankruptcy overtakes them. It is clear, however, that local communities have often been against the acquisition of local businesses by distant conglomerates, and a number of states have enacted antitakeover laws designed to make such acquisitions much more difficult. As a result of recent court cases, it appears that federal laws will override state laws restricting takeovers, and this avenue of local defense is likely to be ineffective.

At a broader level, the concentration of ownership of widespread and often seemingly disparate operating units that formerly were, and perhaps could again be, independent business units has concerned many observers. Large and distant corporations are understandably viewed as more remote from local needs and control as well as more powerful on the national level because of their size. The lack of clear empirical data as yet that such concentration results in improved economic performance for investors or for society eliminates one important counterargument to those who would restrict or break up such concentrations of power for social and political reasons.

PORTFOLIO PLANNING MODELS

As we mentioned earlier, one of the significant advantages a diversified company has relative to the single-business company is the greater variety of opportunities it has to invest its financial resources. The diversified company can contribute to the cash needs of some divisions with the resources obtained from other divisions, whereas the single-business company must obtain any net cash inflow that its operations require by acquiring the funds—equity or debt—on whatever terms the capital markets will provide it. The diversified company has internalized the traditional capital market function with regard to the allocation of funds among its own businesses, and the invisible hand of the market becomes the visible hand of the corporate management.

The objective of earning a maximum return on the resources available or on the effort expended is neither new nor revolutionary; credit for the first attempts to do so must go to our ancestors who sought out more fertile gamelands or gaming areas. Neither is the idea of using the resources of an older and established business to support the expansion of a more promising newer one within the same corporation a new one. The accounts of early diversification attempts describe clearly the pattern of applying resources earned in existing businesses to more promising areas elsewhere.

Several developments have occurred in the last 15 years or so which provide considerable assistance to the manager in thinking about the nature of the resource-allocation problem at the corporate level as well as in providing guidelines for the actual allocations themselves. These developments consist of a basic conceptual scheme, a simple language system, and the collection of empirical data that can lend quantitative support to efforts to identify preferred mixes of business within the product portfolio and to allocations to those businesses on a continuing basis.

The basic concept with which you should be familiar is the portfolio planning model, or PPM, as it has come to be called.[2] The habit of thinking about the resource-allocation problem in this manner is far more important than mastering the details of its application in the specific situation, which requires considerable experience as well as more detailed market and cost information than companies themselves normally possess at the time they initiate such planning efforts.

Portfolio planning models combine measures of industry attractiveness with measures of a division's position in that industry to provide help to the manager who needs to make a judgment concerning the attractiveness of investment in that division relative to other divisions. The widest popularization of this approach has been by the Boston Consulting Group. Their 2x2 matrix, as well as the logic supporting it and the implications of the model, have been explained extensively in their own literature and elsewhere. The essential elements of their matrix, and the terms they have applied to the various quadrants, are shown in Exhibit 10–2.

---

[2] For a more detailed explanation of portfolio planning models, see Malcolm S. Salter and Wolf A. Weinhold, *Diversification through Acquisition* (New York: The Free Press, 1979), Chap. 4; or Gerald B. Allan, "A Note on the BCG Concept of Competitive Analysis and Corporate Strategy" (Boston: Intercollegiate Case Clearing House, Harvard Business School, No. 9-175-175).

EXHIBIT 10–2

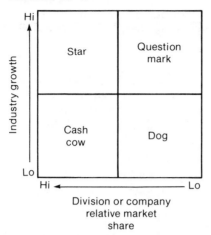

The matrix seeks to establish measures of relative industry attractiveness along the left-hand vertical scale and of the division's competitive position within the industry along the horizontal scale. In this simple format, the principal determinants of industry attractiveness are assumed to be the rate of growth of the industry. For the company position, the relative market share of the particular company or division is considered the single most important variable. The objective is to portray businesses in terms of their potential for generating cash flow; no substantive information about the nature of the industry influences or appears on the matrix.

With regard to the level of abstraction, then, this particular matrix is just as much removed from the details of the individual business as is the experience curve and the PIMS study of determinants of market profitability discussed in Part I. They all seek to build models and derive hypotheses concerning the profit potential of businesses and business strategies that can apply to any business and that can therefore be used to compare businesses otherwise quite dissimilar. The advantages of being able to do so are great, especially when many diverse businesses must be considered. The hazards of making judgments on the basis of such abstract data should also be apparent.

McKinsey & Company and Arthur D. Little, Inc., both leading management consultants, employ similar graphic models to assist the manager in conceptualizing and analyzing problems. Their models are more detailed and qualitative in that they include more factors than just market growth and market share in arriving at judgments about industry attractiveness and company competence to succeed in that industry; in those respects, the models are more like the policy model to which you were exposed in the earlier parts of this book.

There are many elaborations that are made in the models, and their representation in graphic form is limited only by the ingenuity and budget of the graphic arts department. One refinement is to portray the various divisions of the company on the chart in terms of circles, with the area of the circles representing the relative size of the units in terms of sales or profits or assets. Another is to construct such a chart for several points in time, so that trends in the development of businesses can be observed. Market-share measures and industry growth rates can of course both be quantified. To assist in assessing what countermoves important competitors are likely to make, charts can be prepared on competitors in order to assess what their options and likely responses will be.

The usefulness of this type of matrix is based on the assumption that specific patterns of cash flows are associated with each of the various quadrants and that the primary measure of the attractiveness of a business is the pattern of cash flows over time. For example, a dominant position in a growing industry (a *star*) will probably have both high cash needs and high cash generation but will provide the basis for rapid growth, the high profits presumed to accompany high market share and the potential of high cash flow as the growth declines but the market position remains strong (a *cash cow*). Companies with a small market share in slowly growing industries are considered to be *cash traps* or *dogs,* where the potential is unlikely to merit the investment required. The *question marks* are those that are uncertain, either because of the industry or the company position or both. They may require much cash to bring them into the star category; they may also end up in the dog category if events do not turn out well. The objective is to build a portfolio which is balanced in the sense that there are sufficient cash cows to provide the cash flow to support the question marks and possibly the stars, if they need it, and to ensure the continued emergence of stars as companies and industries decline and become less attractive for all participants over time.

A very substantial management problem that the portfolio planning models do not address, and which the facile terminology does little to ease, is that of the administrative difficulties of implementing whatever allocation decisions are made. It is all well and good to decide as a result of portfolio analysis that a given division is a dog, but how would you like to be the division manager of an operation so categorized? How would you explain the corporation's view of your division to your management team, understandably concerned with their own careers? It is for reasons such as this that companies are often not as explicit in the communication of their decisions, and the reasons for them, as the analytical framework would permit them to be. Even without labels or reasons, the resulting allocations can cause unproductive anxiety and opposition which require both skill and tact to overcome. Publicly identifying winners and losers has high costs, and companies look for ways to make the judgments and resulting allocations less threatening to everyone.

Another important assumption of such models is that the businesses plotted can be considered as separate units for the purposes of such analysis. In practice, this makes the consideration of interdependencies among divisions, if there are any, difficult to handle. It may also require the specification of business units for strategic planning purposes that differ from present organizational structure and reporting relationships and which therefore also are likely to be different than established patterns of accounting data and spending responsibility. A term that has come into use to describe groupings of businesses that are useful for portfolio planning purposes is *Strategic Business Units* or SBUs.[3] Companies that have seriously pursued portfolio planning methods have first had to study carefully their existing businesses in order to regroup them, if necessary, into a manageable number of SBUs and collect market and cost data to fit these new definitions. Interestingly enough, this number seems to seldom exceed 30 even in the large and diverse companies with a far greater number of divisions and profit centers. It appears that if the number of units to be considered at the top level becomes too large, the task once again becomes unmanageable, even with the assistance of these more abstract analytical approaches.

It should be apparent that the same cautions and reservations that apply to the application of experience curve data and PIMS analyses for the individual business apply to the application of a product portfolio approach built on these concepts. Unforeseen and uncontrollable external changes or disruptions can have a major strategic impact. In addition, the experience curve in particular is most relevant in cases where manufacturing costs are important and products are well defined. Seemingly minor changes in product characteristics or in marketing policies can sometimes counter the overall trend of the industry as well as the history of that specific product.

Portfolio planning models, then, represent a way to estimate what the cash flows into or out of divisions could be under various assumptions. A portfolio model is therefore also useful in helping to identify the cash flow characteristics of businesses that possibly should be added to the product portfolio. This does not differ conceptually from the objective of basic strategic planning for the single-business company, which is also to provide a means for estimating potential cash flows under a variety of possible strategies. The advantage of the portfolio model for the diversified company is that it facilitates the comparison of many alternatives and highlights the advantages of moving resources from one activity to another as well as the need to have a portfolio in which there are adequate sources to supply the essential needs. For the corporation as a whole, simple arithmetic indicates that cash needs which cannot be met from the divisions themselves can only come from corporate resources or external capital markets.

The data necessary to do a thorough job of applying a portfolio planning model to the problems of a specific company in cases for classroom use exist

---

[3] See, for example, William K. Hall, "SBUs: Hot, New Topic in the Management of Diversification," *Business Horizons*, February 1978.

in only a few specialized cases, designed for that purpose. As you study the diversified companies in this book, however, you should find it useful to keep in mind the concepts underlying the portfolio planning model, using whatever data available to you and making assumptions where necessary. Questions of relative promise, cash resources, and cash needs are important elements for all of those companies. The Leisure Group is perhaps the best example of demands exceeding resources and of the catastrophic consequences that can follow.

THE CORPORATE ROLE IN IMPLEMENTATION

In this final section we will address the important issue of the corporate role in both the formulation and the implementation of strategy in the diversified company.

For the diversified company, a major element of the corporate strategy is what the role of the corporate office will be in contributing to the operations of the divisions and to the overall performance of the corporation. It affects the formulation of strategy at the corporate and division levels as well as the organization structure and processes by which the strategies—corporate and divisional—are implemented. Even more so than in the single-business company, corporate strategy and the approach to the implementation of that strategy via organization structure and management processes are highly interdependent, and are influenced by the role that the corporate office chooses to define for itself.

The job of the general manager in the single-business organization arose when the burden of managing each of the functional activities, in addition to performing the necessary corporate-level tasks, became too much for one person. In a similar manner, the corporate role and positions in diversified companies evolved in response to the added managerial complexities brought on by strategies of product diversification. As you study cases such as Sybron and The Leisure Group and CML Group, Inc., you will find that the issue of what role the corporate or group levels should play in division matters is one of continuing concern. The problems are not just what is the best solution to issues of division investments of strategy or pricing or interdivisional cooperation, but who decides what the best solution is, using what criteria, and how such problems should be decided on a continuing basis.

The degree of involvement of the corporate level in the affairs of the divisions can be thought of in terms of a spectrum, with "laissez-faire" or "hands-off" at one end, and "managed" at the other:

"Laissez-faire	"Managed"
←	→
Conglomerates	Diversified industrials
Small headquarters	Large headquarters
staff	staff

Companies commonly referred to as conglomerates tend to be at the left end of this spectrum. Such companies tend to have diversified primarily by acquisition, often of seemingly unrelated activities, and usually within the past 20 years or so. Textron and Gulf & Western are two well-known examples in this category. Companies that tend to fall into the right-hand category of "managed" are more likely to be older industrial companies whose acquisitions took place long ago, if at all, and which have diversified primarily through building upon existing and often technically based skills into related areas. General Electric and Westinghouse are excellent examples of this category of "diversified industrials."

The important point is not that companies can be distinguished from each other in terms of the way in which they became diversified but that ways of managing the divisions and their approach to tasks and staffing at the corporate level are often associated with the history of diversification. Conglomerates tend to have much smaller corporate staffs in all areas than the older diversified companies. The disparity is especially true with regard to functions such as research and development, marketing, and production, which are frequently not present at all at the corporate level in conglomerates but widely prevalent in the diversified industrials.

These two categories are presented not because all companies fall into one category or the other or indeed remain where they presently are. Companies inhabit the spectrum with the majority somewhere in the middle. The issue of just what the role of the corporate level should be is a recurring question for many companies, however, since the evils of the present system and the advantages of an alternative approach often seem most apparent.

Is it not too difficult to draw up a list of functions that can be performed both more cheaply and with greater expertise at the corporate level than at the division level. Items such as dealings with the SEC, stockholder and investor relations, awareness of and reporting on government regulations affecting the conduct of business, and so on, are generally performed at the corporate level. When it comes to matters more closely related to the strategy and operations of the divisions and the relations between them, however, the approaches diverge. If there is much commonality in the manufacturing or marketing activities of the various divisions, for example, even though they may be in completely separate businesses, it becomes difficult for the corporate level to resist offering its expertise and advice to the operating units and to actively encourage, if not require, interdivisional cooperation. In addition, there may simply be the temptation to want to oversee and advise on all important decisions made in the divisions in the interests of hopefully improving the quality in addition to ensuring that the decisions made are best from the corporate point of view. As you may remember from the discussion of the problems of rationally allocating resources among competing divisions and the unavoidable fact that division self-interests will not always coincide with corporate interests, there is ample incentive to centralize and build staff.

Even the most casual observation of organizations indicates that the pressures for centralization and the establishment of staff units are widespread. Top managers are under severe time pressures, and one solution to these time pressures as well as the complexity and the remoteness caused by the number and variety of divisions to be dealt with is to create more staff at the corporate level so that they may take the time that the president is unable to spare to become familiar with the divisions. They can then brief him, or analyze and recommend action to him, or act in his stead. In addition, whenever trouble arises, the temptation is to centralize, even if lack of centralization is not what caused the trouble in the first place. It is also far easier to demonstrate the sharp-pencil economies that can be achieved by coordinating purchasing or transportation or computer services or dozens of other activities than to demonstrate the adverse effects of more central staff and direction on the initiative, flexibility, and accountability of the divisions.

The question is not only what the *best* answer is to the immediate problem but also what the best way is for problems of that nature to be solved, recognizing the severe time constraints on corporate top management. Immersing oneself in the affairs of any single division, either directly or vicariously through the mechanism of a staff, is no permanent solution to the problem. There *is* a general manager in the division. The reason the product-division form of organization developed was to separate the management of the product division from the management of the overall corporation, not to combine them. The lack of separation is what led to a new form of organization in the first place.

Corporate management in the diversified company can influence the organization by means of the same variables as the manager of the single-business company. As we discussed in Chapter 7, the organization structure, the information systems, the policies on the measurement and reward of managers, the allocation of resources, and the intangible but vitally important matter of personal leadership are all important in leading and guiding the organization in the accomplishment of its strategic goals.

The appropriate fit of these influences available to the general manager is more complex but not different in kind in the diversified company. Just as for the earlier cases, you will want to concentrate on what is most appropriate for the given situation. Organization structures inevitably reflect a compromise between the desire to have as few levels of management as possible in the chain of command while not letting the number of units reporting to any one individual exceed six or so. Information systems need to balance the amount and type of information given to higher levels not only with the cost of assembling it but with questions of whose responsibility it should be to monitor and take action on such information, on what matters various levels of management should be spending their time, and how much information higher levels of management need and can assimilate. It is quite possible to provide the chairman of General Electric with a video console on which he can call up the number of toasters sold in Seattle the day before, but it does not follow that looking at such information is a good use of the chairman's time, nor a useful influence on the eight or so levels of management between the chairman and the regional sales manager.

With regard to the system of incentives and rewards, it is clear that the greater the degree to which individual incentives reward performance that clearly is in the corporate benefit, the less the amount of involvement required by the corporate level to ensure that decisions made throughout the corporation are in the corporate interest and not just the subunit or the individual manager's self-interest. The problem, of course, is that it is difficult to structure reward systems so that little oversight is needed, and the more such systems attempt to be congruent with the corporate interests in all respects, the more cumbersome and detailed they become. Once again it is a trade-off, with the balance appropriate to the businesses and the culture of the company that is to be sought, and not the one right answer. It is clear that the opportunity for first-hand observation of managers by the corporate president decreases as the company grows and diversifies, which makes more reliance either on the judgments of intermediate managers or staff or on formal performance measures inevitable.

With regard to the role of the corporate level in the innumerable decisions and issues in which it could become involved, the dilemma is clear. The more the corporate level wishes to become involved in the substance of decisions in the divisions, the more information they will need if they are not to act capriciously and "shoot from the hip." As more information is gathered, however, the more the temptation is to assemble staff to check, analyze, and interpret it for the corporate manager. More people then are also needed at the division level, not only to assemble the reports, but to deal with the questions of the corporate staff so that the division manager can remain free to spend his time on the demanding job of running the division. Before long there will be staffs talking largely to staffs, hardly a happy arrangement. But with no staff and scanty information at the corporate level, the company is little more than a financial holding company, hardly a happy arrangement either.

Your challenge is not to settle upon one approach as better than the others for all situations but to try to think through what the most useful role of the corporate office is in the particular situation. An essential element of the strategy of The Leisure Group was a concept of what a professional and powerful corporate staff could do to improve the operations of the divisions that it purchased; the CML Group had much more modest goals. In the Sybron cases, the role of the corporate office is a major issue. Zurn Industries went through an experiment of building up its corporate staff, only to discontinue the effort after a relatively short time. The choices made are not just a matter of style or personal preference but depend upon the kinds of businesses the corporation is in and their strategy for competing in them.

SUMMARY

> If a company doesn't continue to do new and exciting things, its management dies. So does the company. You just have to keep growing. Stagnation in management makes you just as vulnerable as stagnation in the market.[4]

The above statement was made by Stuart Watson, then president of Heublein, a company which experienced decades of far above-average growth. It would be supported by hundreds of other presidents. Sentiments similar to his are the driving force behind most of the companies we regard as successful, and the diversification strategies to which we have introduced you in this last part of the book are one major way in which companies have sought to continue to do "new and exciting things." The challenge for you is to perceive the ways in which the firm, whether diversified or not, can manage its affairs so that managements, investors, and the public are all rewarded. In so doing, you will not have the benefit of a rigorous or comprehensive general theory. You will have to rely on the application of the basic but imprecise general approach we have developed, plus a generous application of common sense, judgment, and whatever experience you can bring to bear, commodities which companies reward far more handsomely than theories and concepts useful in the disciplines but limited in their application to practice.

As you deal with the problems of the manager at the corporate level in the diversified company, it is essential for you to keep in mind that the way any one problem can be solved is not necessarily the way such problems can or should be solved on a continuing basis. It is the diversity of the operations and the number of decisions that need to be made that led to the creation of more levels of management to compensate for the impossibility of the top management becoming as involved in operating affairs on a continuing basis as is possible in the single-business company. New roles had to be worked out, partly to handle the large number of familiar types of problems and partly to deal with entirely new problems. The role played by the corporate level in their contribution to the overall operations of the company influences the strategy formulation process at all levels as well as the effectiveness of the everyday operations of the firm.

The nature of the corporate role in the overall management of the diversified firm is but one of the elements which need to be consistent with each other. We have discussed the main elements involved in the strategy formulation process and in the challenge of leading the organization in the implementation of that strategy. Your concern should be the degree to

---

[4] *Forbes*, November 1, 1968, p. 51.

which these elements are supportive of each other—the degree of fit or consistency among them. There are no strategies or organizational approaches that are "best" in isolation. Your challenge is to find the creative fit among these elements that best reconciles the goals management is seeking with the opportunities in the environment and the administrative history and the resources of the company. Just as with each of us as individual persons, goals, resources, opportunities, and strategies will differ.

This book has presented an approach to managerial problem solving that you can apply to new situations; we have not tried to give you a handbook of correctly solved problems. Our objective has been to help you develop your own skills at analyzing the problems of the general manager, advising him on courses of action, and ultimately acting effectively yourself in that role.

case 29

CIBA-GEIGY Corporation (A)

In the spring of 1974 the top management of CIBA-GEIGY Corporation, the principal U.S. subsidiary of CIBA-GEIGY Limited (a publicly owned Swiss corporation), was impressed with the opportunities that a major acquisition program in the United States could bring the corporation as a whole. With the U.S. dollar undervalued relative to the Swiss franc and with prices on the New York Stock Exchange at a ten-year low, it appeared an opportune time to acquire U.S. companies at favorable prices. Officers of both the U.S. subsidiary and the Swiss parent hoped that reinvesting the U.S. cash flow in the United States would allow the U.S. subsidiary to repatriate dollars to the parent under more favorable conditions in the future.

Diversifying acquisitions were of particular interest to Mr. Don MacKinnon, a vice president of CIBA-GEIGY Corporation, who was pressing the case for corporate diversification in the United States. In his view, diversifying acquisitions could help open up new paths of growth for the U.S. subsidiary while providing a hedge against increasing R&D costs, which were limiting the company's traditional specialty chemicals business. In 1973 the parent company reported that the group's U.S. sales had increased only 4 percent in contrast to the worldwide average increase of 14 percent (measured in local currencies).

Mr. MacKinnon was interested in household products as one area of possible opportunity for CIBA-GEIGY. A recently formed Acquisitions Task Force under his direction had already identified Airwick Industries, Inc., as a possible acquisition candidate which could serve as an entree to the household market. However, since the task force had also identified attractive acquisition candidates in nonhousehold areas, Mr. MacKinnon was not sure whether CIBA-GEIGY should, in general, attempt to move into household products. He also had some questions and reservations about Airwick Industries in particular.

The following cases describe both the choices facing Mr. MacKinnon and his colleagues in making their recommendations to the board of directors of

CIBA-GEIGY Corporation and to the Swiss parent, and the context in which these choices had to be made. The (A) case will describe CIBA-GEIGY's historical background, present operations, organizational setting, corporate objectives, and diversification philosophy, for the purpose of gaining an understanding of the company's overall corporate strategy. The (B) case will describe Airwick Industries and the issues that CIBA-GEIGY's management faced as they tried to decide whether or not to acquire this company.

COMPANY BACKGROUND

The creation of CIBA-GEIGY Corporation paralleled the merger of the two parent Swiss companies, CIBA AG and J. R. Geigy AG, in October 1970. In contrast with competitors in Germany, England, the United States, or Japan, which could bank on their home markets for between 40 percent and 70 percent of their business, CIBA and Geigy had practically no home market. Approximately 98 percent of their sales were outside Switzerland, and both firms had significant holdings in the United States. The merger of the parent companies inevitably brought the two U.S. subsidiaries together into one organization.

By 1973 the newly structured U.S. subsidiaries accounted for almost one fourth of the merged companies' total sales. U.S. sales were distributed among principal markets as shown in Exhibit 1.

EXHIBIT 1
Breakdown of U.S. sales, 1973

Line of business	Percent of total
Agrochemicals	41
Pharmaceuticals	28
Dyestuffs and chemicals	16
Plastics and additives	13
Madison Laboratories*	2

* Madison Laboratories sold such consumer specialties as breath spray, dental cream, and skin care products.

CIBA-GEIGY's products were almost entirely specialty chemicals—patent-protected, high-technology products that had a specific purpose or filled a particular need. The company did not sell commodity chemicals like sulfuric acid or caustic soda or benzene.

Although CIBA-GEIGY Corporation did not issue public financial statements, 1973 sales were described as being in excess of $550 million. The worldwide CIBA-GEIGY group, consisting of the Swiss parent and its 60 af-

EXHIBIT 2
Worldwide group sales, 1973

Division	SFr. m	Percent of total sales
Dyestuffs and Chemicals	SFr. 2,047	24.5
Pharmaceuticals..........................	2,338	29.0
Agrochemicals	1,673	20.5
Plastics and Additives	1,433	17.8
Consumer Products	246	3.0
Photographic Group	417	5.2
Total	SFr. 8,154	100.0

EXHIBIT 3
Geographical distribution of group sales, 1973 (percent)

Region	Percent of total sales
Europe...	51
E.E.C.	35
EFTA	7
North America	26
Latin America	9
Asia	9
Africa, Australia, and Oceania	5

filiated companies, had total sales of approximately $2.6 billion. This placed the group about number 14 among the world's chemical companies. Exhibits 2 and 3 give a breakdown of sales by product area and geographic area for the CIBA-GEIGY group of companies. Exhibit 4 presents the group's published financial statements for 1973. Exhibit 5 summarizes the top-management structure of the CIBA-GEIGY group of companies.

CURRENT OPERATIONS

Headquartered in Ardsley, New York, CIBA-GEIGY Corporation had about 8,000 employees throughout the United States, most of whom were located at its principal facilities in New York, New Jersey, Alabama, Louisiana, Rhode Island, and North Carolina. The company's business was organized into four principal operating divisions:

The Agricultural Division sold mainly pesticides, used by commercial farmers to improve crop yields by controlling weeds and insects. This was the company's largest division. Its particular strength was in the sales of herbicides used to control weeds in cornfields. CIBA-GEIGY's pesticides business was in a solid number one position with 20 percent of the U.S. market.

EXHIBIT 4

CIBA-GEIGY CORPORATION (A)
Consolidated Summary of Group Financial Status
At December 31, 1973
(In millions of Swiss francs)

		December 31, 1973
Current assets:		
Liquid funds	1,493	
Receivables and other current assets	2,234	
Stocks	1,925	5,652
Less current liabilities:		
Suppliers	432	
Banks	945	
Other current liabilities, including provisions	1,281	2,658
Net current assets		2,994
Long-term assets:		
Interests in associated companies, and loans	244	
Fixed assets	6,326*	6,570
Total net current assets and long-term assets .		9,564
Less long-term liabilities:		
Debenture loans	375	
Other loans and long-term liabilities	958	1,332
Group equity (of which minority interests represent SFr. 138m, at December 31, 1973		8,232
Total equity and liabilities		12,222

* Current value. Use of acquisition value less appropriate depreciation would give a
valuation of SFr. 3997m.
     Source: 1973 annual report of CIBA-GEIGY Limited.

The Pharmaceuticals Division sold ethical pharmaceutical products through separate CIBA and GEIGY marketing organizations. Almost all of the division's products were prescription items; and they were advertised and promoted only to physicians, hospitals, and pharmacists, not to the general public. The division's most important group of products were those used to treat hypertension, arthritis, depression, and diabetes. In pharmaceuticals, CIBA-GEIGY was among the seven largest companies in the United States.

The Plastics and Additives Division sold a wide range of products, including epoxy resins, polymer additives, pigments, and fiberglass reinforced epoxy pipe. It was estimated that the company was number two or three in epoxy resins and number one or two in reinforced plastic pipe in the United States.

The Dyestuffs and Chemicals Division sold synthetic dyestuffs used in the textile, paper, and leather industries. It also sold a number of chemicals used to assist in dyeing and in textile finishing processes. In addition, the division did a large business in florescent whiteners, which soap and detergent companies used in their products to improve the appearance of the wash. In

EXHIBIT 5
Top management structure of CIBA-GEIGY Limited organization

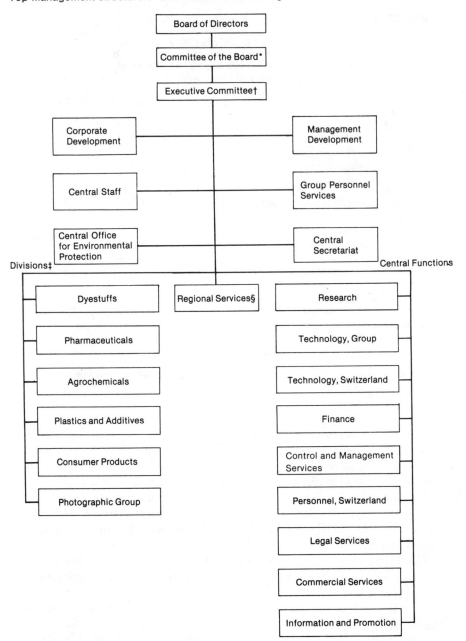

* Prepares the fundamental principles of business policy for consideration by the board, supervises business activity, sanctions investment projects in excess of 10 million Swiss francs, and deals with fundamental questions of personnel, investment, and financial policy.

† Responsible for the implementation of business policies approved by the board.

‡ Responsible for worldwide strategy in specific market sectors. Reviews specific product-market strategies of operating companies.

§ Monitors the group's investment in its 60 international affiliates. Reviews overall business plans of subsidiaries and parcels out sector strategies to group-level divisions for review.

dyestuffs, the company was number three in the U.S. market after Du Pont and Sandoz, and in florescent whiteners the company was number one.

In addition to these principal operating divisions, a small consumer specialties business was run through Madison Laboratories. It was not considered to be a successful operation by the top management of CIBA-GEIGY.

CIBA-GEIGY Corporation was managed by the corporate managing committee, consisting of the chairman of the board, the president, and the five corporate vice presidents. Each of the operating divisions had a division president who reported to one of the corporate vice presidents. Each division president was backed up by a team of divisional vice presidents who were responsible for such areas as marketing, production, research, and administration. The divisions were responsible for their own activities in all of these areas, but they were free to call upon the corporate staff for necessary services. Once their budgets had been submitted to the corporate managing committee and approved, the divisions had considerable freedom to operate within their budgets. In capital expenditures, however, all projects over $100,000 required the specific approval of the corporate managing committee.

Two of CIBA-GEIGY's larger plants, in Cranston, Rhode Island, and McIntosh, Alabama, served more than one division. In those plants the production activities were directed by the production vice presidents of the various divisions, but all the support services were managed by a corporate plant manager. The heads of all the corporate staff departments and corporate plants and facilities reported to one or another of the corporate vice presidents. Exhibit 6 presents the organization of CIBA-GEIGY in chart form.

RELATIONSHIPS WITH THE SWISS PARENT COMPANY

In the area of research there was considerable dialogue and exchange of information between the parent company and its U.S. subsidiary. Since both the subsidiary and the parent company invested large amounts of money in research, it was critical that these efforts be carefully coordinated. Similarly, capital expenditures were closely coordinated with the parent company to assure that the worldwide production capacity remained in balance.

Cash flows to the parent company from CIBA-GEIGY Corporation was an important link between the two entities and took four forms. First, dividends were paid to the parent company on an annual basis. Second, the U.S. subsidiary paid a significant amount of money to the parent company as part of its share of the group research budget. Third, cash flowed to the parent company in connection with royalty agreements. Finally, a minimal amount of cash flowed to Switzerland in payment for purchases of intermediate and finished products.

A regional services department in Switzerland was responsible for monitoring the group's investment in its 60 international affiliates. In addition, product line or division managers in each of the affiliates maintained close

698

EXHIBIT 6
Organizational chart*

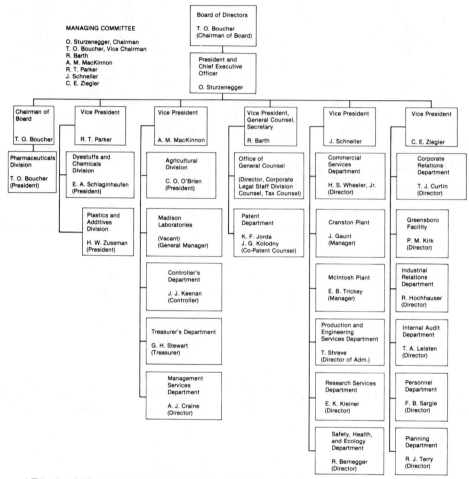

* This chart indicates lines of authority and is not indicative of position status.

contact with corresponding divisions at group headquarters. The influence of the headquarters divisions was reflected mainly through the planning system. The three-year plans of each subsidiary's divisions were reviewed with the corresponding division in Basle.

CORPORATE OBJECTIVES

CIBA-GEIGY Corporation's objectives were to continue to improve its long-term profits through new products derived from research and from acquisitions in related fields. As explained by Mr. MacKinnon:

We wish to remain a very research-oriented organization with vigorous and ongoing internal growth. However, we also look to our acquisition program as a means of complementing this growth. I should emphasize that we have no interest in becoming a vast conglomerate. We are not making acquisitions merely to become bigger. We are interested only in those companies which would complement our current business or put us into related new business areas.

Mr. MacKinnon added that acquisitions would be financed primarily with CIBA-GEIGY Corporation's own cash flows. The company was willing to invest up to $250 million in new acquisitions. Of this amount $150 million was expected to come from U.S. sources.

CIBA-GEIGY's ACQUISITION PROGRAM

A first step in implementing the acquisition program was the creation of an Acquisitions Task Force in September 1973. This group was chaired by Mr. MacKinnon and included CIBA-GEIGY's general counsel, corporate secretary, director of corporate planning, and three staff executives from the corporate planning and treasury functions. These three staff executives functioned as full-time members of the task force, reporting to Mr. Robert Terry, the director of corporate planning.

The group initially had two major responsibilities: first, to establish basic criteria for any acquisitions CIBA-GEIGY might make, and second, to determine areas of acquisition interest.

A memorandum, spelling out acquisition criteria and areas of interest, was prepared by the task force and approved by the corporate management committee. This set the overall guidelines for the acquisition search, and was distributed to leading investment banking firms and large commercial banks so that these organizations could refer potential acquisition candidates to CIBA-GEIGY. Exhibit 7 presents a copy of this memorandum.

EXHIBIT 7
Areas of acquisition interest and consent decree provisions

CIBA-GEIGY is at present entering into a major acquisition program, and this memorandum sets forth our acquisition interests and also discusses those provisions of the consent decree which affect our interests.

Acquisition criteria

In general, we are looking for acquisition candidates which meet the criteria listed below, and which might be available for cash. It is possible that in the case of a particularly attractive situation, we might be willing to take a major stock position offering the probability for a control position or full ownership at a later date.

1. The candidate should participate in growing markets.
2. The candidate should have a proprietary position in its markets.
3. The candidate's operations should be likely to be favorably affected by CIBA-GEIGY's know-how in the fields of research, development, manufacture, and marketing of complex synthetic organic chemicals.

EXHIBIT 7 (continued)

4. The candidate's business should be product rather than service oriented.
5. The candidate should have sales of $50 million or more.
6. The candidate should earn a good gross profit margin on sales.
7. The candidate should have the potential to yield a return on investment of 10 percent or more.
8. The probable purchase price should not exceed $250 million.

Since CIBA-GEIGY's business in the United States approximates 25 percent of the worldwide sales, we are particulary interested in companies that would offer potential for substantial growth outside the U.S. through the efforts of our worldwide resources.

Consent decree provisions

Under the terms of the consent decree into which CIBA and Geigy entered at the time of their merger in 1970, CIBA-GEIGY Corporation and its parent company, for a period ending in September 1975, may not acquire "any other person engaged in the United States in any of the same lines of commerce" as CIBA-GEIGY Corporation, except upon 15 days prior notice to the Department of Justice. If within such 15 days prior the Justice Department requests information relating to the proposed transaction as authorized by the Antitrust Civil Process Act, then the transaction cannot be consummated until an additional period of 60 days after the company furnishes the information so requested to the Department of Justice.

Areas of acquisition interest

We are not interested at the present time in exploring totally new business areas. We have, however, been able to identify the following areas of growth which we wish to pursue:

1. The whole area of specialty chemicals is of interest to us. A definition of specialty chemicals would include among others, certain of the following characteristics:
    They are sold in moderate volumes, but at high per unit selling prices, at least two times raw material costs.
    They are usually sold under brand names and are promoted to the end user based on performance specifications for what they do.
    They require a relatively high level of research and development, based on a knowledge of the customer's technology.
    Although gross profit margins typically run at least 50 percent of sales, heavy expenditures for marketing and research may yield only an average after tax margin on sales, but a high return on investment.
    The types of specialty chemicals we currently produce are listed in the previous section. Other types which could be of interest to us include such items as specialty adhesives; biocides; moulding compounds; coatings; specialty cleaning products; flame retardants; intermediates for cosmetics, detergents, and so forth; chemicals for pretreating and finishing textiles; and so forth.
2. Proprietary pharmaceuticals and cosmetic and toiletry products.
3. Animal health products, including feed additives and veterinary products.
4. Proprietary household and garden products such as those marketed by S. C. Johnson.

EXHIBIT 7 (concluded)

5. Suppliers of products to the health care industry, including disposable hospital and medical products, diagnostic aids, dental, and optical supplies.
6. Products, processes and related services for the environmental industry, that is, air, liquid, and solid waste treatment. It should be noted that our interest in these areas is not in the equipment side but our orientation is toward the chemicals and related services side.
7. Photo chemicals and related products.

We have not included such items as seed breeding and food additives (principally flavors and fragrances) on the above list as our Agriculture Division has already conducted extensive studies in these areas using outside consultants, and has identified most of the candidates which might be of interest to us.

In addition to contacting investment banking firms and commercial banks, CIBA-GEIGY also screened 15,000 to 20,000 companies. Working with Standard & Poor's and Moody's industrial directories, the task force first reviewed approximately 10,000 publicly owned companies, evaluating them in terms of their criteria for industry and growth. This manual screening was complemented by a computer review by industry, conducted for CIBA-GEIGY by a leading investment banking firm. The company also purchased the Dun & Bradstreet computer tapes, which allowed the task force to review another 8,000 additional companies, most of them privately owned.

At the same time as this massive screening was going on, the task force worked with all of the company's divisions to identify any companies or divisions of other companies in which they might have had an interest.

After several months of screening, about a hundred companies emerged as meeting CIBA-GEIGY's general criteria. The task force then prepared for review by the corporate management committee a two-page summary covering each of these organizations. It was from this group of a hundred companies that a final selection of six acquisition candidates was made.

case 30

CIBA-GEIGY Corporation (B)

In June 1974 the top management of CIBA-GEIGY Corporation was presented with a detailed task force report on Airwick Industries, Inc. CIBA-GEIGY had decided to concentrate its acquisition activities on six companies, and Airwick Industries was one of the six. While detailed reports were prepared from public sources on each of the six companies, a special Airwick Task Force from CIBA-GEIGY had actually interviewed key vice presidents at Airwick Industries. This unusual procedure reflected both CIBA-GEIGY's understanding that Airwick Industries might be looking for a merger partner and Airwick Industries' friendly disposition toward CIBA-GEIGY. For five years a French subsidiary of CIBA-GEIGY Limited had distributed Airwick products in France.

Based on this report and on publicly available information, Mr. Don MacKinnon and the Acquisitions Task Force had to decide whether or not to give their support to this potential acquisition. Since Mr. MacKinnon was the only executive at CIBA-GEIGY Corporation with extensive mergers and acquisitions experience, his opinion would be a highly respected input to the final decision. If it were decided to seek the acquisition of Airwick Industries, an overall plan had to be prepared, including a starting position and desired end position for negotiations with Airwick Industries' board of directors.

This case summarizes the basic substance of the Airwick Task Force report, along with the publicly available information on Airwick Industries. In addition, it presents the issues and questions raised by Mr. MacKinnon and the task force as they considered whether or not to proceed with this diversifying acquisition.

AIRWICK INDUSTRIES, INC.

Company background

In the late 1930s, an independent researcher worked with a blind subject for four years in an attempt to discover the natural odor opposites of the most common indoor malodors. On the basis of this work, he was able to develop an odor counteractant formula made up of 125 components, including among other things, a group of green plant extracts. It was this combination product, called Airwick Liquid, which eventually formed the business base of Airwick Industries' predecessor company.

Until Airwick Liquid was developed, most odor control products simply masked or overpowered unpleasant odors with a strong and supposedly more pleasant aroma. Airwick Liquid was, therefore, unquestionably a salable product, but substantial resources were required to penetrate the postwar, home-centered market. To overcome the lack of financial resources, the responsibility for developing a sales force and distribution system was assigned to a national distributor, while the company, then known as Airkem, Inc., limited its marketing efforts to products for industrial, commercial, and institutional applications, and to exploring foreign markets.

By the mid-1950s domestic retail sales of Airwick began to sag under intense competitive pressure. Even a transfer of marketing rights to Lever Brothers could not reverse the sales deterioration. In 1963 the company purchased the Airwick name from Lever and began to market Airwick Liquid itself. The company spent a good deal of money promoting the product that year, which resulted in a net loss in 1963, but the sales stopped declining. The company was profitable through 1974, although development costs and promotion for new products penalized earnings growth in the late 1960s.

As of June 1974 the company's principal products consisted of odor counteracting air fresheners, together with a full line of sanitary maintenance items, such as disinfectants, cleaners, and insecticides containing odor counteraction features, and certain swimming pool products. These products were marketed through four operating segments.

1. Consumer—household products distributed through food brokers in the United States and Canada.
2. Institutional—commercial, institutional, industrial products distributed through franchised distributors and 14 company branch offices in the United States and Canada.
3. International—household, commercial, institutional, and industrial products marketed through distributors in more than 50 foreign countries.
4. Aquatic—swimming pool treatment chemicals and dispensers sold through distributors and dealers in the United States and Canada.

Exhibit 1 shows the revenues and pretax income for each of the segments from 1969 through 1973.

The relative profitability of the principal segments of the company's business significantly changed beginning in 1971 due to three major factors: Consumer segment sales and margins increased sharply after 1970, reflect-

EXHIBIT 1

Revenues and pretax income for major operating segments: 1969–1973 ($000)

	Consumer				Institutional				International				Aquatic			
	Revenues		Pretax		Revenues		Pretax		Revenues		Pretax		Revenues		Pretax	
1973	$17,500	52%	$2,475	49%	$9,100	27%	$ 800	16%	$4,050	12%	$1,500	30%	$2,950	9%	$250	5%
1972	14,251	51	2,090	55	8,117	29	429	11	2,920	11	1,047	28	2,485	9	221	6
1971	11,066	50	1,222	47	7,048	32	615	23	1,895	8	590	22	2,158	10	203	8
1970	6,785	43	(23)	—	6,380	40	931	69	1,294	8	386	29	1,468	9	58	4
1969	4,606	37	(304)	—	5,835	46	1,210	86	1,022	8	310	22	1,118	9	193	14

ing (*a*) the completion of national distribution and the market acceptance of a new product, Airwick Solid, in U.S. retail markets, and (*b*) manufacturing efficiencies resulting from integrated, higher volume production of this product within the company's plants; earnings of the institutional segment declined, reflecting higher marketing expenses and increased costs of goods, warehousing, and transportation not offset by increases in selling prices; and international sales and margins increased, reflecting the broadening distribution and market acceptance of Airwick Solid in European retail markets.

Exhibits 2 and 3 present Airwick Industries' consolidated statement of earnings for the period 1969–73, and a balance sheet as of December 31, 1973.

Consumer segment

The Airwick Consumer Brands Division marketed six products, three of them in the air-freshener category. The three air fresheners—Airwick Solid, Airwick Liquid, and Airwick Spray—accounted for 97 percent of the division's net sales. The remaining 3 percent included On Guard, an automatically dispensed toilet bowl cleaner; Airwick Cat Litter Deodorant Spray; and a disinfectant spray. In 1973 all of Consumer division's profits were derived from Airwick Solid and Airwick Liquid.

The air-freshener market had shown substantial growth in recent years with the bulk of the growth in the solid type of product. Exhibit 4 summarizes the key sales trends for the 1970–73 period.

In addition to having experienced rapid growth, the air-freshener market was highly competitive. Many manufacturers and distributors were trying to stake out a position in the market for room deodorants. A number of competitors were larger, better known, and financially stronger than Airwick Industries and were capable of expending large sums in advertising and promoting their products.

Airwick's major competitors included Bristol-Myers with its Renuzit brand, American Home Products with its Wizard brand, Home Products Corporation with Days-Ease, and S. C. Johnson & Company with Glade. Intense competition developed in 1973 in the solid segment of the household air-freshener market. While the market was expanding significantly, competitive products proliferated. American Home Products was a new entrant, and it was believed that Gillette was preparing to enter the market. Exhibit 5 shows the share of market for the most recent four-week period ending March 15, 1974, in comparison with data for the comparable period in 1973. The averages for the past few years are also summarized.

As can be seen from Exhibit 5, Renuzit had recently eclipsed Airwick as the number one brand (all forms combined). However, consumer research in the solid segment showed that Airwick had maintained strength with an

EXHIBIT 2

CIBA-GEIGY CORPORATION (B)
Airwick Industries, Inc., and Subsidiaries
Consolidated Statement of Earnings

Year Ended December 31

	1969	1970	1971	1972	1973
Sales and other revenue:					
Net sales	$12,376,000	$15,724,000	$21,855,000	$27,307,000	$33,024,000
Other revenue	205,000	203,000	312,000	466,000	772,000
Total sales and other revenue	$12,581,000	$15,927,000	$22,167,000	$27,773,000	$33,796,000
Costs and other charges:					
Cost of sales	$ 5,120,000	$ 6,755,000	$ 9,495,000	$11,236,000	$13,778,000
Selling and administrative expenses	5,934,000	7,674,000	9,937,000	12,600,000	14,860,000
Interest expense:					
Long-term debt	53,000	45,000	46,000	47,000	59,000
Other	23,000	61,000	24,000	4,000	45,000
Miscellaneous charges	42,000	40,000	35,000	98,000	71,000
Total costs and other charges	$11,172,000	$14,575,000	$19,537,000	$23,985,000	$28,813,000
Earnings before income taxes	$ 1,409,000	$ 1,352,000	$ 2,630,000	$ 3,788,000	$ 4,983,000
Income taxes	702,000	610,000	1,195,000	1,677,000	2,300,000
Net earnings	$ 707,000	$ 742,000	$ 1,435,000	$ 2,111,000	$ 2,683,000
Average number of common shares outstanding (Note 1)	3,062,344	3,070,512	3,204,658	3,399,252	3,457,290
Earnings per share of common stock (Note 1)	$0.23	$0.24	$0.45	$0.62	$0.78
Cash dividends declared on common stock (Note 2)	$0.08	$0.08	$0.09	$0.11	$0.15

Notes:
1. Earnings per share of common stock have been computed on the weighted-average number of common shares outstanding in each year, after giving retroactive effect to the 3-for-2 stock split in 1972 and the 2-for-1 stock split and the reclassification on a share-for-share basis of class A and class B common stock for a single class of common stock in 1973 and retroactive adjustment for shares issued in 1972 in connection with the acquisition of King-Kratz Corporation in a pooling of interests (Note A–3 to Notes to Consolidated Financial Statements). Shares issuable under employee stock options and warrants are excluded from the weighted-average number of shares in determining earnings per share on the basis that the dilutive effect is less than 3 percent.
2. Dividends per share of common stock have been computed on the number of shares outstanding at time of declaration, after giving retroactive effect to the changes described in Note 1. The pooled company paid no dividends.

EXHIBIT 3

CIBA-GEIGY CORPORATION (B)
Airwick Industries, Inc., and Subsidiaries
Consolidated Balance Sheet
Year Ended December 31

	1973	1972
Assets		
Current assets:		
Cash	$ 1,770,000	$ 1,683,000
Short-term investments—at cost which approximates market value		993,000
Customers' receivables	3,747,000	3,101,000
Other receivables	137,000	61,000
Inventories (Note A–4):		
Finished goods	$ 2,379,000	$ 1,313,000
Work in process	393,000	180,000
Raw materials	1,980,000	1,185,000
Total inventories	$ 4,752,000	$ 2,678,000
Prepayments, advances, and other items	$ 515,000	$ 477,000
Total current assets	$10,921,000	$ 8,993,000
Property, plant, and equipment—at cost, less accumulated depreciation and amortization (Notes A–5 and D)	$ 5,187,000	$ 3,038,000
Other assets:		
Prepayments of obligations to former distributor, less amortization of $652,000 in 1973 and $569,000 in 1972 (Note A–6)	$ 351,000	$ 433,000
Patents, trademarks, and other, less amortization of $371,000 in 1973 and $334,000 in 1972 (Note A–6)	188,000	182,000
Prepaid pension costs (Note A–7)	470,000	500,000
Deferred charges and other	519,000	320,000
Total other assets	$ 1,528,000	$ 1,435,000
Total assets	$17,636,000	$13,466,000
Liabilities and Stockholders' Equity		
Current liabilities:		
Notes payable—bank (Note G)	$ 870,000	
Current maturities of long-term debt (Note E)	69,000	$ 92,000
Accounts payable	2,363,000	1,777,000
Accrued compensation and other expenses	759,000	538,000
Income taxes (Notes A–10 and F)	1,238,000	1,033,000
Total current liabilities	$ 5,299,000	$ 3,440,000
Long-term debt (Note E)	$ 511,000	$ 609,000
Deferred income taxes (Notes A–9 and F)	189,000	11,000
Commitments (Note G)		
Stockholders' equity (Notes H and I):		
Capital stock:		
Preferred—authorized, 100,000 shares of $1 par value, none issued	—	—
Common stock, par value $0.05—authorized, 6,000,000 shares; issued and outstanding, 3,464,942 shares in 1973 and 3,447,482 shares in 1972	$ 173,000	$ 172,000
Additional contributed capital	3,510,000	3,444,000
Retained earnings	7,954,000	5,790,000
Total stockholders' equity	$11,637,000	$ 9,406,000
Total liabilities and stockholders' equity	$17,636,000	$13,466,000

The accompanying notes are an integral part of this statement:

EXHIBIT 3 (continued)

Airwick Industries, Inc., and Subsidiaries
Notes to Consolidated Financial Statements
December 31, 1973, and 1972

Note A—Summary of accounting policies

A summary of the significant accounting policies consistently applied in the preparation of the accompanying consolidated financial statements follows:

1. Principles of consolidation. The consolidated financial statements include the accounts of the wholly owned domestic and foreign subsidiaries and the accounts of King-Kratz Corporation acquired in 1972 in a pooling of interests transaction. Material intercompany amounts and transactions were eliminated in consolidation.

2. Foreign currency translation. Current assets and current liabilities are translated at the rate of exchange in effect at the close of the period. Long-term assets are translated at the rates in effect at the dates those assets were acquired, and long-term liabilities are translated at the rates in effect at the dates these obligations were incurred. Exchange adjustments are charged or credited to income. The exchange adjustments resulted in an exchange gain of $36,000 for 1973 and an exchange loss of $52,000 for 1972. Revenue and expense accounts are translated at the average of exchange rates which were in effect during the year, except for depreciation and amortization which are translated at the rates of exchange which were in effect when the respective assets were acquired.

3. Pooling of interests. On October 31, 1972, the Company acquired all of the issued and outstanding shares of King-Kratz Corporation by issuing 81,586 shares of its common stock.

4. Inventories. Inventories are stated at the lower of cost or market; cost is determined using the first-in, first-out method.

5. Property, plant, and equipment. Depreciation and amortization are provided for in amounts sufficient to relate the cost of depreciable assets to operations over their estimated service lives. The buildings are being depreciated on the double-declining balance and straight-line methods over a 45-year period. Other depreciable assets are depreciated generally on the straight-line method over periods ranging from 2 to 20 years. Leasehold improvements are amortized over the lives of the leases or the service lives of the improvements, whichever is shorter, on the straight-line basis.

   The Company capitalizes, for both financial reporting and tax purposes, leased equipment where the terms of the lease result in the creation of a material equity in the property accruing to the Company. The consolidated balance sheet reflects all such leased manufacturing equipment as assets and long-term obligations.

6. Amortization policies. Payments to a former distributor are being amortized on the straight-line basis to the expiration date of the agreement.

   The cost of marketing rights to a line of products is being amortized on the straight-line basis over the terms of the underlying agreements.

   The cost of patents and trademarks are capitalized and amortized to operations over their statutory lives. Amortization is computed on the straight-line method.

   Goodwill is amortized on a straight-line basis over a period of five years.

7. Pension plans. The Company has a pension plan covering substantially all of its full-time employees. It is the Company's policy to fund normal pension cost. A United Kingdom subsidiary also has a pension plan for its employees. As of January 1, 1972, the Company amended its pension plan which resulted in increased benefits to its employees. As a result of the amended plan, the Company has incurred past service cost which it has funded and is amortizing over a ten-year period. The changes in the pension plan had no significant effect on net earnings for 1972. The pension charges to income amounted to $152,000 each in 1973 and 1972.

8. Research and development. Costs incurred in the development of new products are charged to income as incurred.

9. Deferred income taxes. Deferred income tax expense results from timing differences in the recognition of revenue and expense for tax and financial statement purposes.

10. Investment tax credits. Investment tax credits are accounted for by the "flow-through" method. Under this method, credits are recognized as a reduction of income tax expense in the year the assets giving rise to the credit are placed in service.

Note B—Acquisition

On January 31, 1974, the Company acquired approximately 90 percent of the issued and outstanding common stock of Seablue Corporation, a corporation engaged in the manufacture, distribution, and sale of swimming pool supplies and equipment for approximately $3,600,000 in cash in a transaction to be accounted for as a purchase. Further, the Company will offer to purchase the remaining 10 percent of the issued and outstanding common stock from the minority stockholders at the same terms offered the principal stockholders. If all of the remaining stockholders accept the offer, the Company's total purchase price will amount to approximately $4 million.

EXHIBIT 3 (continued)

Airwick Industries, Inc., and Subsidiaries
Notes to Consolidated Financial Statements (continued)
December 31, 1973, and 1972

Note C—Foreign operations

The following is a summary of the accounts of the foreign subsidiaries at December 31, 1973, and 1972:

	1973	1972
Current assets	$3,698,000	$3,021,000
Current liabilities	1,862,000	1,294,000
	$1,836,000	$1,727,000
Fixed assets, less accumulated depreciation and amortization	109,000	86,000
Other assets	9,000	9,000
	$1,954,000	$1,822,000
Less:		
Amounts due to parent company—net	$ 221,000	$ 160,000
Long-term debt	195,000	226,000
Deferred income taxes ..	3,000	
	$ 419,000	$ 386,000
Net assets	$1,535,000	$1,436,000

The cumulative amount of undistributed earnings of foreign subsidiaries on which the parent company has not recognized U.S. income taxes amounted to approximately $1,500,000 and $1,400,000 at December 31, 1973, and 1972, respectively. During the year, the Company received dividends amounting to $1,297,000 from foreign subsidiaries.

It is the Company's practice to provide currently for taxes which will be payable upon remittance of foreign earnings to the parent company, based upon estimates of the amounts to be received in dividends.

Note D—Property, plant, and equipment

These assets are summarized as follows:

	1973	1972
Land	$ 400,000	$ 221,000
Buildings and improvements	2,365,000	1,537,000
Machinery and equipment ..	3,705,000	2,238,000
Machinery under lease option agreement	202,000	202,000
Leasehold improvements ...	211,000	217,000
Construction in progress ...	68,000	
	$6,951,000	$4,415,000
Less accumulated depreciation and amortization	1,764,000	1,377,000
	$5,187,000	$3,038,000

Note E—Long-term debt

This item comprises the following obligations:

	1973	1972
Mortgage loan—5⅞% payable in monthly installments of $2,125 to 1985	$306,000	$332,000
Note payable—bank (interest rate ½ of 1% over minimum lending rate) repayable in installments of $50,000 in 1975 and $145,000 in 1976	195,000	246,000
Other	117,000	182,000
	$618,000	$760,000
Less: Unamortized discount	(38,000)	(59,000)
	$580,000	$701,000
Less: Current maturities	69,000	92,000
	$511,000	$609,000

The aggregate maturities of long-term debt are summarized as follows:

	1973	1972
1973........................		$121,000
1974........................	$105,000	128,000
1975........................	107,000	61,000
1976........................	177,000	221,000
1977........................	25,000	25,000
1978........................	25,000	
Subsequent	179,000	204,000
	$618,000	$760,000

Note F—Income taxes

The federal income tax returns of the parent company subsequent to 1969 are subject to review by the Internal Revenue Service. Income tax expense for the year ended December 31, 1973, is made up of the following components:

		Foreign		
	U.S. Federal	Income tax	Taxes withheld at source	Total
Current tax expense ...	$1,125,000	$829,000	$168,000	$2,122,000
Deferred tax expense ...	175,000	3,000		178,000
	$1,300,000	$832,000	$168,000	$2,300,000

EXHIBIT 3 (continued)

Airwick Industries, Inc., and Subsidiaries
Notes to Consolidated Financial Statements (continued)
December 31, 1973, and 1972

Income tax expense for the year ended December 31, 1972, is made up of the following components:

	U.S. federal	Foreign	Total
Current tax expense	$1,081,000	$596,000	$1,677,000

Deferred tax expense results from timing differences in the recognition of revenue and expense for tax and financial statement purposes. The sources of these differences in 1973 and the tax effect of each were as follows:

Excess of tax over book depreciation	$ 66,000
Computer development costs expensed on tax return and deferred on books	59,000
Convention expenses expensed on tax return and deferred on books	41,000
Other timing differences	12,000
	$178,000

Note G—Commitments

The minimum rental commitments under all noncancellable leases are as follows:

	1974	1975	1976
Plant facilities	$111,000	$107,000	$ 99,000
Equipment	88,000	87,000	87,000
Office facilities	142,000	119,000	112,000
	$341,000	$313,000	$298,000

	1977	1978	1979 and beyond
Plant facilities	$ 88,000	$ 82,000	$303,000
Equipment	53,000		
Office facilities	102,000	94,000	77,000
	$243,000	$176,000	$380,000

Some of the leases require the Company to pay for maintenance, taxes, and insurance. Total rental expense amounted to $454,000 and $308,000 for 1973 and 1972, respectively.

At December 31, 1973, the Company had a credit line with a bank amounting to $2 million. The related short-term debt outstanding was $870,000 at an interest rate of 9¾ percent per annum. During January 1974, the credit line was increased to $6 million. The credit line can be withdrawn at the bank's option. There were no compensating balance arrangements at December 31, 1973, under the line of credit. However, there is an informal understanding that the Company maintain a principal operating account with the bank.

Note H—Stock options and warrants

Under qualified stock option plans as approved by the stockholders on May 25, 1966, and April 24, 1968, options may be granted officers and key employees of the parent company within ten years to purchase an aggregate of 120,000 shares of common stock under the 1966 plan and 90,000 shares of common stock under the 1968 plan. The option price must be not less than the fair market value of the stock on the date of grant. Options are exercisable after two years from the date of grant but not later than five years from such date.

Under a nonqualified stock option plan as approved by the stockholders on April 26, 1972, options may be granted to employees of the Company within ten years to purchase an aggregate of 198,000 shares of common stock. The option price must not be less than the fair market value of the stock on the date of the grant. Options are exercisable two years from the date of the grant but not later than ten years from such date.

Changes during 1973 under the plans were as follows:

	Shares		
	Reserved	Granted	Available
Balance—January 1, 1973	263,600	88,500	175,100
Granted		61,800	(61,800)
Canceled		(5,500)	5,500
Exercised	(17,460)	(17,460)	
Balance—December 31,1973	246,140	127,340	118,800
Option price range	$4.813–$21.25		
Exercisable at December 31, 1973	30,540		

Changes during 1972 under the plans were as follows:

	Shares		
	Reserved	Granted	Available
Balance—January 1, 1972	131,100	115,500	15,600
1972 plan	198,000		198,000
Granted		40,500	(40,500)
Canceled		(6,000)	6,000
Exercised	(61,500)	(61,500)	
Balance—December 31, 1972	267,600	88,500	179,100
Option price range	$4.813–$19.50		
Exercisable at December 31, 1973	45,000		

EXHIBIT 3 (concluded)

Airwick Industries, Inc., and Subsidiaries
Notes to Consolidated Financial Statements (continued)
December 31, 1973, and 1972

Note 1—Capital stock

On April 26, 1972, the stockholders authorized the following changes in the capital structure:

a. An increase in the authorized Class A common stock from 400,000 shares ($0.05 par value) to 600,000 shares ($0.05 par value).
b. An increase in the authorized Class B common stock from 1,600,000 shares ($0.05 par value) to 2,400,-000 shares ($0.05 par value).
c. Both the Class A and Class B common stock outstanding were split on a 3-for-2 basis.

On January 24, 1973, the stockholders authorized the following changes in the capital structure:

a. An increase in the authorized Class A common stock from 600,000 shares ($0.05 par value) to 1,200,000 shares ($0.05 par value).
b. An increase in the authorized Class B common stock from 2,400,000 shares ($0.05 par value) to 4,800,-000 shares ($0.05 par value).
c. Both the Class A and Class B common stock outstanding were split on a 2-for-1 basis.
d. Class A and Class B common stock were reclassified on a share-for-share basis for a single class of common stock.

Accordingly, retroactive effect has been given to the financial statements for the Company's 2-for-1 split in 1973 and for the reclassification on a share-for-share basis of Class A and Class B common stock into a single class of common stock.

To the Stockholders
Airwick Industries, Inc.

We have examined the consolidated balance sheet of Airwick Industries, Inc., and Subsidiaries as of December 31, 1973, and 1972, and the related consolidated statements of earnings, retained earnings, additional contributed capital, and changes in financial position for the years then ended. Our examination was made in accordance with generally accepted auditing standards, and accordingly included such tests of the accounting records and such other auditing procedures as we considered necessary in the circumstances. We have received reports of other auditors with respect to their examination of certain of the consolidated foreign subsidiaries whose assets and revenue constitute 19.9 percent and 14.9 percent, respectively, in 1973 and 20.8 percent and 13.8 percent, respectively, in 1972 of the corresponding consolidated totals. Insofar as our opinion expressed herein relates to amounts for certain of the foreign subsidiaries, it is based solely on the aforementioned reports of the other auditors.

In our opinion, based upon our examination and the aforementioned reports of other auditors, the consolidated financial statements referred to above present fairly the consolidated financial position of Airwick Industries, Inc., and Subsidiaries at December 31, 1973, and 1972, and the consolidated results of their operations and changes in financial position for the years then ended, in conformity with generally accepted accounting principles applied on a consistent basis.

Alexander Grant & Company
New York, New York
January 31, 1974

extremely high 92 percent consumer intent to repurchase after trying the product.

In early 1974, Airwick was prepared to produce private label solid air fresheners for chain stores. The company has already signed production contracts with Grand Union, Purity, and Finast. A contract with A&P was about to be signed. Airwick managers predicted that the private label business would be as profitable as the existing Airwick Solid business on a per unit basis.

The idea behind Airwick's entrance into private labeling was to eliminate competition while gaining more factory volume for Airwick. In areas of the country where Airwick Solid had excellent distribution and was number one or a close number two, it was believed that when the chain added the Airwick private brand to the shelf, the marginal number three or four brands would be taken off the shelf. In areas where Airwick Solid did not do

EXHIBIT 4

Air-freshener market retail ($000)

	Total market		Solids		Aerosols		Liquids	
	Sales	Percent change prev. yr.	Share of total	Percent change prev. yr.	Share of total	Percent change prev. yr.	Share of total	Percent change prev. yr.
1973	$91,400	+34	43%	+110	34%	± 0	23%	+9
1972	68,000	+16	27	+ 73	45	+ 9	28	+1
1971	58,400	+13	19	+ 90	49	+22	32	+8
1970	51,700	n.a.	11	n.a.	55	n.a.	34	n.a.

n.a. = not available.

as well, private branding was thought to be a way of getting in the store and protecting Airwick from competitors that also may be interested in doing private label work.

Despite Airwick's planned entrance into private labeling, the company had been notably unsuccessful in developing and introducing new products. In the past all new product introductions (Airwick Solid, Cat Litter Spray, On Guard, and the disinfectant spray) were formulas taken directly from products sold by the Institutional Division. With the exception of Airwick Solid, they were all unsuccessful.

Airwick consumer products were sold through a system of 63 food bro-

EXHIBIT 5

Air-freshener market shares food stores (dollar basis)

	Four-week shares		Average—52-week shares	
	Ending 3/16/73	Ending 3/15/74	Last 12 mos.	Year ago 12 mos.
Airwick Liquid	4.5%	4.9%	4.4%	4.7%
Airwick Solid	19.1	17.0	16.1	18.7
Total Airwick	23.6%	21.9%	20.5%	23.4%
Renuzit Aerosol	6.7%	6.5%	6.8%	7.0%
Renuzit Solid	11.8	21.6	17.0	10.3
Total Renuzit	18.5%	28.1%	23.8%	17.3%
Wizard Aerosol.............	10.7%	8.8%	10.3%	12.8%
Wizard Solid	—	5.7	3.3	—
Wizard Wick	2.3	1.9	2.3	2.6
Total Wizard	13.0%	16.4%	15.9%	15.4%
Days-Ease Solid	5.5%	6.2%	7.5%	1.3%
Glade Aerosol..............	20.1	9.8	15.0	17.6
All other brands	19.3	17.6	17.3	25.0

kers across the United States. These brokers were under the supervision of seven Airwick-employed regional managers who reported to the sales manager.

Due to the desperate situation in 1963 when the existing broker network was established, Airwick started and continued paying commissions at the rate of 7.5 percent. While there were many exceptions, the standard industry commission over the years was 5 percent.

Heavy advertising was an important part of Airwick's marketing program. Given the increased competition, it appeared that advertising expenditures would have to increase in order to maintain position against competing products.

Institutional segment

The Airkem Institutional Division was responsible for two classes of products: commercial products and emergency odor removal products. Commercial products contributed substantially all of the division's sales and profits.

Commercial products included a semisolid odor counteractant trademarked "Solidaire," liquid and spray odor counteractants, odor-controlled insecticides, and sanitary maintenance items, such as disinfectants and detergents. The division also designed, manufactured, and sold equipment to dispense a number of these products and, in Canada, marketed a line of floor and carpet care equipment manufactured by another firm. Commercial products were used by institutions, such as hospitals, nursing homes, schools, and motels. Specialized odor-controlled formulations were sold for spray-system application in atmospheric control of odors emanating from factories and other industrial establishments.

Emergency odor removal products included counteractant formulations designed to remove or reduce certain odors, such as the odor of smoke from fire in residences, automobiles, and commercial and industrial establishments.

The division sold its products principally through about 55 franchised distributors that were responsible for sales in specified geographic areas in the United States and Canada. These distributors resold the products to the ultimate users, or in some cases used them in rendering services to their customers. The franchised distributors in the United States normally used the name Airkem in their trade styles.

The division also acted as its own distributor of Airkem products, and performed all the functions of a franchised distributor, through branch offices in 14 geographical areas, four of which were added in 1974. As compared to sales to distributors at the wholesale level, branch office sales direct to consumers produced higher revenues, but the start-up and staffing costs of the branches created higher operating expenses, which adversely affected the earnings of the Institutional Division since 1971. In total, the branch offices accounted for 31 percent of the Institutional Division's sales in 1973.

The division advertised the products trademarked Airkem nationally, principally through print media, and supplied distributors with merchandising aids and promotional literature. In institutional markets, Airwick competed with many large and small firms. No one firm dominated the market.

The Institutional Division competed in a growing market, which was estimated to be $500 million at the consumer dollar level or about $250 million in terms of factory dollars. There was very little data on the size and breakdown of the market since, unlike the consumer segment of the business, there was no auditing information service like SAMI.

International segment

Airwick's household products and some of its institutional products were also marketed abroad. Marketing in Europe and other international markets was managed by Airkem (Export) Limited, a British subsidiary. This subsidiary accounted for about 97 percent of the sales and substantially all of the profits of the international segment. Its principal plant, located in Hitchin, England, manufactured Airwick concentrates. Marketing in Latin America, the Caribbean, and Taiwan was managed from the home office of the company.

In building up its European-based business, Airwick had adopted the policies of not participating in advertising expenditures (except for the U.K.), not interfering in local marketing issues (all major marketing decisions were left to the distributors), and not signing long-term contracts with distributors.

Pretax margins overseas were higher than at home because more expenses were assumed by the overseas distributors than by U.S. distributors. The plant at Hitchin produced the compounds and concentrates sold by the international segment, while the distributors did the finishing and packaging.

Competition in foreign markets was generally less intense than in the United States since odor counteractants and related products were relatively new. The potential for growth in Europe was considered particularly good. While past growth in the international segment was almost entirely due to Airwick Solid, further exploitation of the Airwick Solid concept and the systematic development of the institutional markets provided a possible source of continued growth in the major EEC countries.

Aquatic segment

The aquatic segment of the company was comprised of King-Kratz Corporation and Seablue Corporation. The King-Kratz Corporation, acquired by Airwick in October 1972, produced and marketed a line of chemicals and dispensers for water treatment in swimming pools. King-Kratz and its competitors purchased their basic ingredient, iso-cyanarate, from Monsanto and FMC, and then tableted and/or packaged the various products for sale. King-Kratz products were sold to companies engaged in distributing swimming pool supplies and equipment. These distributors sold to dealers who, in turn, sold or used the products in providing services to pool owners.

Seablue Corporation, acquired by Airwick in January 1974 for $4 million in cash, was a distributor of swimming pool equipment and supplies sold under the trademark Seablue. It also manufactured and sold high-rate sand filters and diving stands. Seablue Corporation had sales and distribution centers in Atlanta, Baltimore, Charlotte, Cincinnati, Dallas, Houston, Kansas City, Memphis, Miami, and New Orleans, and sold to swimming pool builders swimming pool maintenance and service companies, and specialty stores. Prior to its acquisition by Airwick, Seablue Corporation was the largest customer of King-Kratz Corporation.

Swimming pool chemical needs were predicted to grow at 11 percent during the 1971–75 period. Approximately one half of these requirements were expected to be in "in- and on-ground pools," with the remaining amount in above-ground pools. (Above-ground pools were the round ones usually found in backyards.)

King-Kratz had a strong position in the in-ground market. They were also strong in nonresidential pools. Growth in these segments was expected by management to continue, provided raw materials were available. However, to get a foothold in the above-ground segment, King-Kratz would have to develop a homeowner-oriented product line and get it into mass merchandisers. This, it was thought by management, would require additional financial and marketing resources.

In 1974 King-Kratz was attempting to "get closer to the dealer" and to prepare for "going direct" in the near future. This modification in distribution policy was expected to result substantially in increased marketing expenses since the division would (1) pick up new customers to service, (2) be shipping more orders to more customers in smaller lots, and (3) have to spend more contact time with individual dealers.

Seablue's plans included adding products to their line of chemicals, which it purchased from outside suppliers, and diving boards, stands, and filters, which it manufactured. The company also envisioned backward integration by having King-Kratz manufacture more of their products, making more plastic parts themselves, and moving products back from Seablue

EXHIBIT 6

SEABLUE CORPORATION
Consolidated Statement of Earnings

	Year ended October 31			Two months ended December 31, 1973 (unaudited)
	1971	*1972*	*1973*	
Sales	$5,431,475	$7,571,283	$9,575,479	$797,508
Less: Cost of goods sold	4,081,843	5,702,997	7,155,008	651,030
Gross profit	$1,349,632	$1,868,286	$2,420,471	$146,478
Less: Selling expenses	264,288	360,806	446,611	52,919
Selling profit	$1,085,344	$1,507,480	$1,973,860	$ 93,559
Less: General and administrative expenses	777,843	929,759	1,238,289	163,749
Operating profit (loss)	$ 307,501	$ 577,721	$ 735,571	$ (70,190)
Add other income:				
Discounts earned	$ 48,077	$ 67,368	$ 83,799	$ 6,844
Interest income	—	4,283	124	89
Rental income	—	917	200	—
Currency exchange	—	—	14,148	—
Miscellaneous income	596	2,037	12,959	2,438
Total other income	$ 48,673	$ 74,605	$ 111,230	$ 9,371
Net profit (loss) before other deductions	$ 356,174	$ 652,326	$ 846,801	$ (60,819)
Less other deductions:				
Discounts allowed	$ 52,717	$ 71,701	$ 105,206	$ 10,013
Interest expense	45,185	63,349	129,531	19,866
State income taxes	5,210	6,764	12,209	—
Rent expense	—	64	295	—
Currency exchange	—	(50)	—	(83)
Miscellaneous expense	—	—	(1,795)	2,048
Total other deductions ...	$ 103,112	$ 141,828	$ 245,446	$ 31,844
Net profit (loss) before federal income taxes and extraordinary charges	$ 253,062	$ 510,498	$ 601,355	$ (92,663)
Less:				
Federal income taxes—current	$ 110,921	$ 236,246	$ 237,937	$ (44,989)
Federal income taxes—deferred	—	—	15,688	1,039
	$ 110,921	$ 236,246	$ 253,625	$ 43,950)
Net profit (loss) before extraordinary charges	$ 142,141	$ 274,252	$ 347,730	$ (48,713)
Less extraordinary charges (write-off of worthless investment)	6,000	—	—	—
Net income (loss)	$ 136,141	$ 274,252	$ 347,730	$ (48,713)
Net income (loss) per share:				
Before extraordinary charges ..	$2.41	$4.65	$5.89	$(0.83)
Less extraordinary charges	0.10	—	—	—
	$2.31	$4.65	$5.89	$(0.83)

to King-Kratz for national distribution. In 1974 Seablue was among the lowest performing profit centers in the company. Exhibit 6 shows Seablue's earnings statement for 1971–73.

Advertising

In 1974 Airwick advertised Airwick Solid and Airwick Liquid on a national basis. It advertised On Guard and the Cat Litter Spray in certain selected markets. It also advertised the products trademarked Airkem nationally, and supplied distributors with merchandising aids and promotional literature.

Though Airwick was a leading advertiser in the air-freshener market, the company could not spend as heavily on advertising as some of the companies with which it competed.

Exhibit 7 shows the total advertising expenditures for the leading marketers of deodorizers and air fresheners during the first six months of 1974.

EXHIBIT 7
Top five advertisers in deodorizer and air-freshener market:
January–June 1974

Brand	Advertising dollars ($000)
Renuzit	$1,883.1
Airwick	1,615.2
Wizard	1,594.7
Days-Ease	917.3
Glade	708.9

Source: LNA Multi-Media Report Service, vol. 2, no. 2.

Manufacturing

In the United States, Airwick manufactured its formulas at its Carlstadt, New Jersey, plant by compounding essential oils, aromatic chemicals, and emulsifying agents. The formulas were then blended with other ingredients and packaged into finished products at Carlstadt and at a second manufacturing facility at St. Peters, Missouri. The company also manufactured plastic packaging components. The King-Kratz products were processed at the company's Missouri plant. Swimming pool filters and diving stands were manufactured at the Seablue Corporation plant in Richardson, Texas.

In Canada, Airwick had in the past subcontracted the manufacture and packaging of most products. In June 1974 the company commenced direct production of some products at a newly leased Canadian facility, and anticipated that most products would be in production at that facility by the end of 1974. The company's British subsidiary manufactured the formulas at its plant in Hitchin, England, which were then transferred to independent distributors to be packaged as finished products and sold under Airwick's trademarks. In Latin America and the Caribbean most of the products were imported in finished form from the United States.

Most of the raw materials used by Airwick were regular articles of commerce and had been historically available in sufficient quantities for its manufacturing operations. However, since the latter part of 1973, the company experienced industry-wide shortages of some basic chemical components, including chlorine and disinfectant chemicals. These shortages limited the company's ability to expand sales and production in its institutional and aquatic marketing segments.

Research and development

Airwick's research and development program was primarily directed toward the development of new products and the improvement of present products. Theoretical studies were conducted relative to release mechanisms for odor control products and odor perception, counteraction, and measurement. Company engineers designed and developed dispensing units and designed and maintained molds used for forming containers for the company's products. The research and development department was responsible for quality control and package design for the company's products, and also furnished technical assistance to the field sales organization.

There were 38 employees in this department in 1974, of whom 26 held degrees in chemistry, biology, or engineering. Expenditures for company-sponsored research and development were approximately $418,000, $488,-000, and $629,000 during 1971, 1972, and 1973, respectively; and $671,000 was budgeted for 1974.

ASSESSMENT OF AIRWICK ACQUISITION

Conclusions and recommendations of the Airwick Task Force

After two weeks of interviewing and analysis, the Airwick Task Force concluded that if CIBA-GEIGY had a strategic interest in entering the household products business, Airwick could be an attractive way of doing it—assuming the price was not excessive.

The detailed findings of the Airwick Task Force included the following points:

1. Airwick is a profitable company whose earnings may have temporarily plateaued due to severe competition in the consumer segment of their business.

2. Competition in the consumer segment of the business will definitely restrict growth and reduce profitability of this segment in the immediate years ahead. Indeed, without a more carefully prepared marketing plan, a well-conceived new products program, and additional advertising expenditures, it will be difficult to achieve an increase in sales of much more than 5–6 percent annually.

3. The institutional segment of Airwick (Airkem Institutional Division) is in excellent shape. They have good management, good products, and a good marketing program. They participate in a large, fractured market where the leading competitor is estimated to have only 8 percent share of the market as compared to an estimated 5 percent for Airwick. There is good potential for this division.

4. The international segment appears to be a profitable part of Airwick in terms of contribution as a percent of revenues. Current growth rates can most likely be maintained.

5. While the aquatic segment appears to be healthy, it does not appear to be the kind of business that would normally be attractive for CIBA-GEIGY.

6. Airwick's present financial position is difficult because of a need for cash. At year-end of 1973 the company had only a minimum of debt outstanding, but as of May 7, 1974, it had $8 million in short-term loans outstanding paying prime interest rates. The cash shortage seems to have been caused by the recent acquisition of the Seablue Corporation for $4 million in cash; the necessity of building inventories for the aquatic segment of the business, which is seasonal; and the turndown in Airwick's consumer business over the last nine months.

7. Production is relatively simple and efficient. While the new St. Peters plant is impressive, the Carlstadt, New Jersey, plant is overcrowded and needs immediate relief.

8. The research and development activity appears to be suffering from underfunding and a lack of direction.

9. Airwick appears to be highly people oriented. The president addresses a substantial number of employees by their first name and seems to know a great deal about them. This personal attention is reflected in their benefit programs which appear to compare favorably with those of CIBA-GEIGY.

10. Potential synergisms:
    a. Madison Laboratories has personnel with marketing skills which may help Airwick; Airwick has the sales organization which Madison Laboratories lacks.
    b. CIBA-GEIGY has money which Airwick needs to grow.
    c. CIBA-GEIGY has available space and equipment which may be useful to Airwick.

  d. CIBA-GEIGY's chemical ability and research facilities could improve Airwick's products and provide Airwick with a better research and development effort with little increase in incremental costs.

  e. CIBA-GEIGY's Agricultural Division has products which could be marketed by Airwick.

11. A savings of $1 million in Airwick's overhead could be achieved which would add to the return of any contemplated investment in Airwick.

Questions raised by Mr. MacKinnon and the Acquisitions Task Force

Despite the conclusions of the Airwick Task Force, Mr. MacKinnon and the Acquisitions Task Force were concerned with several unresolved questions. For a start, it had not yet been firmly decided whether or not CIBA-GEIGY Corporation should be in the household products business. Neither was it clear that Airwick Industries was the best vehicle for developing a position in this business if, indeed, it was decided that household products was an appropriate field for CIBA-GEIGY Corporation. In addition, there was concern as to how to go about valuing a company whose major division was in a deteriorating competitive position. Linked to this concern was uncertainty over the appropriate negotiating strategy for a company like Airwick. Finally, assuming that Airwick could be acquired for the "right" price, it was not clear how this multinational business would fit into the geographic-based management structure of the CIBA-GEIGY group of companies.

These questions had special importance in the spring of 1974 since CIBA-GEIGY was just completing a tender offer for a majority of the shares of a hybrid seed company and was holding discussions with two other acquisition candidates complementing other areas of CIBA-GEIGY's business. While these diversifying acquisitions, if consummated, would not eliminate the possibility of further acquisitions, there was concern that postmerger problems would consume more top-management time and corporate funds than currently expected.

Household products. Prior to the merger of CIBA and Geigy, policy in both companies vacillated with respect to consumer products. After the merger, the group decided that consumer product markets should be considered an appropriate area for growth. Household products, lawn and garden products, and toiletries were targeted as prime opportunity areas. However, each local subsidiary had the freedom to decide for itself whether or not it was worthwhile entering any of these consumer market segments.

The potential acquisition of Airwick posed a "fish or cut bait" decision for CIBA-GEIGY with respect to consumer products in general, and household products specifically. In fact, CIBA-GEIGY was seriously considering divesting the small Madison Laboratories Division which was having a great deal of difficulty selling toiletries, developed for the most part in Switzerland, in the U.S. market. Madison had annual sales in the $8–$9 million range, and was only breaking even at the contribution to corporate overhead level. By the time the Airwick acquisition study was presented, CIBA-GEIGY had already held three sets of discussions with companies interested in acquiring Madison.

In analyzing both Madison and Airwick, an important question was whether research, product quality, and strong patents—CIBA-GEIGY's special strengths—were relevant to their long-run success. Superficial features often played an important role in such products, and this could offend the Swiss business philosophy. Consideration had to be given to the fact that advertising budgets could reduce profits for several years, and that this, too, might not be satisfactory. Finally, there was only limited management experience in the consumer products area.

At the same time, the Swiss parent had a small research program going in the household odor area, and several European subsidiaries were participants in the institutional cleaning market.

Assessment of Airwick.   Mr. MacKinnon and the Acquisitions Task Force agreed with the Airwick Task Force that the institutional segment of Airwick had good potential and might be able to provide an outlet for some CIBA-GEIGY products handled by the Agricultural Division. On the other hand, the domestic consumer segment was an area of concern. Airwick's sales projections seemed unrealistically optimistic, but there was no way of revising these estimates on any scientific basis under the current press of events. Furthermore, it was suspected that Airwick might have to develop a catch-up advertising program since the company had fallen behind the competition in this area. Finally, the softening U.S. economy was not an encouraging environment for nonessential consumer goods.

Even the attractive European market for Airwick's consumer products posed a troublesome dilemma. What would Airwick gain if it built the market abroad, only to see the big consumer products companies in Europe buying into the new market with "me-too" products at a lower price?

Airwick's aquatic operations were another concern. While they represented one third of Airwick Industries' total sales, CIBA-GEIGY had already decided on its own against going into this business. Both the president and chairman of Airwick had indicated to Mr. MacKinnon that neither a spin-off of this business to Airwick shareholders nor a straight sale of the division would be acceptable to them. Since they controlled over 30 percent of the outstanding shares between them, their wishes in the matter had to be considered carefully.

Valuation and negotiating strategy.   The valuation issue was complicated not only by the deteriorating competitive position of Airwick's Consumer Brands Division but also by the difficulty in establishing a value for discrete parts of Airwick's business. Joint use of assets by the several divisions made asset-based analysis highly tenuous.

Recent movement in Airwick's stock price complicated both the valuation and negotiating tasks. As a practical fact, Mr. MacKinnon knew that CIBA-GEIGY Corporation would have to pay Airwick shareholders a premium over market value. But on what basis should this premium be figured? During the first quarter of 1974 the price of Airwick's shares held steady around the $8 level. However, as both parties were preparing to enter final negotiations, the price of Airwick's shares ran up to about $10 per share. Since Airwick was being actively courted by other potential acquirers, Mr. MacKinnon suspected that news of potential merger negotiations had somehow leaked to the financial community. The resulting problem was what price would be required for the Airwick shareholders to feel they were receiving a substantial enough premium to support the acquisition. Exhibit 8 shows the price range of Airwick's common stock through the second quarter of 1974. It also shows the number of unexercised options held by Airwick's officers and directors.

EXHIBIT 8

Price range of Airwick's common stock*

	High	Low
1972:		
First quarter	$14.28	$ 9.12
Second quarter	21.88	13.78
Third quarter	24.81	17.50
Fourth quarter	23.38	18.68
1973:		
First quarter	23.63	14.13
Second quarter	19.38	13.38
Third quarter	24.38	15.88
Fourth quarter	23.88	8.50
1974:		
First quarter	11.00	6.50
Second quarter	13.00	6.00

*Adjusted to reflect a 3-for-2 stock split in May 1972 and a 2-for-1 stock split in February 1973.

Unexercised options, all directors and officers, April 4, 1974

Number of shares 97,300
Average option price $6.89

While CIBA-GEIGY had decided that a tender offer would be the most appropriate acquisition vehicle in this case, several management issues had to be resolved before such an offer could be made to the public. Airwick Industries had a stock option and bonus program for its management employees, while CIBA-GEIGY Corporation did not have stock options. There was thus a question about how to handle the stock options and whether or not to continue the Airwick bonus program if Airwick were merged with CIBA-GEIGY. In addition, since CIBA-GEIGY Corporation had never written management contracts with its key employees, a decision was needed as to what to do if such contracts were requested during the negotiations.

Organizational issues.   A final question of concern was how to integrate Airwick Industries into the CIBA-GEIGY management structure, if it were acquired. Under current arrangements, consumer product companies normally reported to country-based subsidiaries of CIBA-GEIGY Limited. Thus, consumer product companies in France reported to CIBA-GEIGY (France). This arrangement presented problems in the Airwick case, since the company had a major international segment operated from England. If current patterns were followed, Airkem (Export) Limited would have to be separated to some extent from the U.S. operations. This arrangement, it was feared, might lead to a decreased commitment on the part of Airwick's domestic managers to international development.

An alternate arrangement would be for the CIBA-GEIGY Corporation to assume direct responsibility for Airwick's worldwide operations. This posed difficult questions, too. How could you take direct business responsibility away from France for Airwick's French business when they have done such a good job for Airwick on a distributor basis in the past? What kind of commitment to Airwick products could you expect from French managers if everything were to be directed from New York?

A final alternative was to have Airwick report directly to Switzerland. This however, would involve a major break in CIBA-GEIGY's worldwide operating philosophy.

case 31

CML Group, Inc.

In early January 1971, John Morgan, general manager of Hood Sailmakers, Inc., the world's largest and most prestigious manufacturer of sails for big ocean racing yachts, was trying to make a final decision on whether to recommend to Hood's board of directors that $314,000 be requested for the establishment of a sailcloth weaving mill in Ireland. Hood had been a wholly owned subsidiary of the CML Group since February of 1970 but still operated with its own board of directors.[1] The project, even if recommended, would require approval by CML Group management, however, because of its size and nature. Hood was but one of the four recent acquisitions in the "leisure time" field that made up the CML Group, a company which had attained an annual sales volume of over $11 million in its first year and a half of operations.

In Mr. Morgan's opinion, several factors favored the investment. It represented a 13 percent aftertax return (based on cash flow) for the division, substantially better than Hood was making on its present asset base. Perhaps more important, both Ted Hood, founder and current president of the division, and his father, R. S. Hood, an influential Hood board member and general manager of the Hood cloth manufacturing operation, were in favor of the project, as they both felt that it would significantly enhance the long-run competitive position of the company and was therefore an important strategic move.

Mr. Morgan recognized that going ahead with the investment presented certain difficulties, however, and that several of these were of particular concern to CML corporate management. Most significant was Hood's sales and profits slump during fiscal 1970, when earnings had dropped about 30 percent from their peak year level. Though profitability was considerably better in the current year, sales had not risen appreciably above the prior year. As Hood had doubled its weaving capacity in 1968, only about 50

---

[1] Hood's board included five members, three chosen by the Hood family and two by CML.

percent of existing weaving capacity was currently being utilized. Under such circumstances, corporate management's reluctance to invest in substantially increased capacity for Hood was understandable, especially in view of opportunities to invest in other divisions. Corporate management also questioned Hood's ability to take on a major new commitment in light of the many pressing issues already demanding management time and energy. Secrecy surrounding Hood's unique weaving process presented a further problem. All Hood sailcloth was currently woven in the very closely guarded Marblehead facility. A second mill naturally increased Hood's risk of exposure. Finally, uncertainties such as future tariff levels, fluctuation in domestic demand, and possible competitive moves and reactions complicated the economic analysis.

Since Mr. Morgan had joined Hood as general manager only nine months earlier and had no prior experience in the industry, he recognized that he was still in a transition period with regard to learning an entirely new business and establishing his own position within the company. Several factors made it important to come to some decision on the Irish project fairly soon, however. Although the Industrial Development Authority (IDA) of the Irish government had agreed to supply as a nonrepayable grant $266,000 of the $580,000 total funds required, Hood had already requested several extensions of the original deadline for purchasing land and commencing construction. While Mr. Morgan felt that a further extension could probably be obtained, he sensed that an increasingly wide credibility gap was developing on the part of IDA over Hood's real intentions in Ireland. In addition, preliminary planning for the Irish facility, which had already cost Hood about $20,000 since early 1969, was currently being funded by Hood at the rate of $1,000 per month in retainer fees and travel expenses. Further delay was therefore both risky and expensive.

CML GROUP DEVELOPMENT

In May 1969 Charles Leighton, Robert Tod, and Sam Frederick[2] resigned from the Willard Corporation, a large diversified manufacturing company which had grown largely by acquisition, in order to establish their own company in the leisure time field.

Mr. Leighton had joined Willard in 1965 as group officer in charge of

---

[2] *Charles Leighton* (36 in 1971); MBA, Harvard Business School, 1960; product line manager, Mine Safety Appliances Corporation, 1963–64; instructor in management of new enterprises at the Harvard Business School, 1964–65; Group vice president, Willard Corporation Leisure Time Group, 1965–69.

Robert Tod (32); MBA, Harvard Business School, 1967; project engineer, Hooker Chemical, January–September 1967; Group operations manager, Willard Corporation Leisure Time Group, 1967–69.

Sam Frederick (36); MBA, Columbia, 1962; accounting with Arthur Andersen & Co., 1962–68; Group controller, Willard Corporation Leisure Time Group, 1968–69.

three divisions (a jewelry manufacturer and two boat manufacturers) with total sales of $7 million per year. Throughout the next four years internal growth and six acquisitions had raised the sales of the renamed "Leisure Time Group" to about $70 million; profits grew at about 25 percent per year during this period. By the time Mr. Leighton and his colleagues left the Willard Corporation in 1969 their group was one of the largest, most profitable, and most rapidly growing groups in the company, which then had sales of several hundred million dollars.

In the spring of 1969, Mr. Leighton described the original objectives of CML in a short pamphlet prepared for prospective investors:[3]

> We want to build an organization devoted to self-expression and individual creativity for profit. Basically, we intend to use the skills demonstrated by our success at Willard to build our own diversified company in the leisure time field. Our plan is to acquire companies and to operate them on a decentralized basis so that chief executives of acquired companies retain full authority for management of their business, with us at the corporate level providing supplementary assistance in the form of long-range planning help, marketing and manufacturing consultation, accounting, and most importantly, strong financial control and support. We are looking for companies with top-quality product lines and excellent trade names in businesses where management experience and creativity are more important to success than bricks and mortar. Companies we'll be interested in will generally have been founded by men with great creativity from a product standpoint, but who basically dislike the administrative burdens of running a growing business. A key element of our strategy is therefore to provide administrative assistance to these companies, thereby freeing up more of an owner-manager's time for the really creative things he's most interested in. Another key aspect is motivation. We plan to acquire companies only on an earn-out basis so that the owner-manager is fully motivated to realize the growth and profit potential which we feel are in the business when we buy it.
>
> From a financial standpoint our objectives are the following: growth in corporate earnings per share of at least 20 percent per year, a pretax return on CML's investment in acquired companies of at least 20 percent, and a 12½ percent annual profit growth of acquired companies.

With these objectives in mind CML's co-founders established the new company in early June 1969. Two million dollars of outside equity funds were raised in just ten days by selling 50 percent of the company to 18 large investors.[4] The best known of these was a major national foundation which invested $400,000 in the company, choosing CML Group for one of its first

---

[3] See Exhibit 1 for further discussion of objectives appearing in CML's first annual report.

[4] A total of 800 shares of convertible preference stock (convertible on a 1-for-1 basis) and 3,200 shares of common stock were sold to outside investors for $500 per share. As no investment banking fees were paid, total cost of the issue was only $364.

attempts to invest in new ventures. The four co-founders paid a total of $40,000 for the remaining 50 percent of the equity.[5] Mr. Leighton described as follows the relative ease with which outside equity funds were obtained despite the unfavorable economic climate prevailing at the time:

> At that time, we hadn't made any attempt yet to negotiate with prospective acquisitions, so we couldn't talk specific companies to financial backers. Despite this, we felt we had several things to offer. First, we represented a team whose combined skills balanced out any individual weaknesses. I've always maintained that covering yourself on weaknesses is far more important than having outstanding but spotty strengths. Second, we had a very good four-year track record at Willard. Third, we had a concept of management which we had spelled out in detail in a recent *Harvard Business Review* article and which had already proved itself at Willard. Finally, we had two very influential men behind us. One was my father-in-law, Dan Smith,[6] who provided invaluable advice and experience. Homer Luther was the other. At 29 he was already an extremely successful and influential investment manager. I had met him in 1964 while he was an MBA student at Harvard. We got to know each other as a result of a creative marketing study he made of the product line I handled at Mine Safety Appliances. We had kept in touch off and on since then, and after we decided to leave Willard we called him, since he had told me that if we ever needed money we should come to him. His introductions to potential investors and his assistance in general were invaluable. Dan Smith and Homer also became substantial investors in CML, and both are very active directors of the company.

EXHIBIT 1
Excerpt from a letter to the stockholders, July 30, 1970

To our stockholders:

A little over a year ago, the CML Group, Inc., was founded on the premise that a variety of new skills will be needed for business success in the 1970s. The ability to provide an environment which would encourage creative product development and innovative marketing will become a key success factor. Our previous business experience led us to believe that the orientation of business toward individual creativity could attract imaginative entrepreneurs and result in a high rate of profitable growth. Of course, financial control, production, and the other customary management skills will remain critical to the success of any business.

The leisure time industry is the best candidate for the implementation of this theory because it contains a number of very creative people who founded companies with interesting products. As a result of increasing discretionary income in all levels of society, this industry also has a high growth rate. It was decided to

---

[5] A total of 4,000 shares of common stock were sold to the four co-founders at $10 per share.

[6] Dan T. Smith, professor emeritus of finance, Harvard Business School.

EXHIBIT 1 (continued)

group several of these companies into one corporation emphasizing performance and quality.

Widespread equity ownership among the managers of the companies would provide strong motivation for capital growth and act as a measure of their common success. The creative leaders could become even more productive by delegating their administrative burdens and financial problems to qualified persons. An active corporate management team would be able to introduce modern control systems and other management tools to support long-term growth. The diversity of experience and skills of the CML management team would be an advantage in this effort. Accordingly, the CML Group was incorporated in June of 1969.

The principal objectives of the Group were established at the outset as follows:

First of all, the Group would seek several outstanding leisure time companies to provide a base for business operations. At the same time, the Group would keep itself in a strong financial position. Bank relationships would be developed and lines of credit established. A pattern would be established for the integration of new members into the Group; this would include the strengthening of autonomous management whenever necessary and the introduction of an extensive, but easily administered, control system.

Second, the Group would begin immediately to prepare itself for a public offering of its stock at the most favorable opportunity in the next few years. Improved marketability of the Group's common stock would provide a better tool for use in attracting additional companies and employees and would improve the original subscribers' return on their capital investment. The Group determined that a high rate growth in sales and profits of each company after joining the Group would be the most important factor in valuing the Group's stock at the time of public sale. Also important would be a record of making prudent acquisitions.

Ultimately and most importantly, the Group would begin to build for the long term. The desired environment would be developed slowly to ensure that creativity and innovation became permanent characteristics of the Group. The best management teams take time to form, particularly when business practices are considered a complement to innovation and art rather than the dominant force. The control systems would have to be structured so that the effect of changes within and without the business could easily be assessed and recognized.

Source: A letter to the stockholders appearing in CML Group, Inc.'s, July 31, 1970, annual report.

Acquired businesses

Exhibit 2 shows CML's balance sheet as of July 31, 1969, shortly after registration of the new company and before any acquisitions had been made, and as of July 31, 1970, following one year of operations. During its first year CML acquired four companies and reported fiscal 1970 sales of

EXHIBIT 2

CML GROUP, INC.
Consolidated Balance Sheet as of July 31, 1969 and 1970
($000)

	1969	1970
Assets		
Current assets:		
Cash	$ 242	$ 731
Short-term commercial paper......................	1,787	—
Net receivables	—	1,217
Inventories......................................	—	2,433
Prepaid expenses	14	109
Total current assets	$2,042	$4,490
Property, plant and equipment (net)	3	2,143
Investments and other assets:		
Investments......................................	—	876
Excess of cost over net book value of acquisitions ..	—	1,959
Other assets	7	137
Total assets	$2,052	$9,604
Liabilities and Stockholders' Equity		
Total current liabilities.............................	$ 14	$2,545
Long-term debt	—	3,424
Subordinated convertible debenture	—	498
Stockholders' equity:*		
Preference stock (par value $0.10)	$ 1	$ 1
Common stock (par value $0.10)	1	1
Capital in excess of par	2,038	2,771
Retained earnings	(2)	364
Total equity	$2,038	$3,137
Total liabilities and stockholders' equity ..	$2,052	$9,604

*Stockholders' equity information:

	Number of shares outstanding		
	Convertible preference	Common	
		Non-	
Source of equity	Nonfounders	founders	Founders
Sold during June 1969	800 (Series A)	3,200	4,000
Exchanged to acquire Boston Whaler	1,000 (Series B)		
Exchanged to acquire Hood Sailmakers	4,600 (Series C)		
Sold during summer of 1970		920	
Total outstanding as of 7/31/70	6,400	4,120	4,000

Series A ranks on a parity with common stock with respect to voting and dividend privileges. May be converted by holder into common stock at any time on a share-for-share basis. May be redeemed by CML any time after September 30, 1971, at the original selling price ($500 per share).

Series B ranks on a parity with common stock with respect to voting privileges. Receives a preferential annual dividend of $10 per share. See footnote in Exhibit 4 for conversion privileges.

Series C ranks on a parity with common shares with respect to voting and dividend privileges. See footnote in Exhibit 4 for conversion privileges.

Source: Company records for 1969; annual report for 1970. Errors are due to rounding.

EXHIBIT 3

CML GROUP, INC.
Consolidated Statement of Income and Retained Earnings
For the Year Ended July 31, 1970
($000)

Net sales		$11,109
Less costs and expenses:		
Cost of goods sold	$7,943	
General, selling, and administrative	2,553	10,496
Income from operations		$ 613
Interest expense (net)		190
Income before income taxes		$ 423
Provision for income taxes*		217
Net income ($21.25 per share)†		$ 206
Deficit, beginning of year		(2)
Retained earnings of pooled companies		161
Retained earnings, end of year		$ 365

* Represents a reserve against future income tax payments. No income taxes were paid in 1970. Income for tax purposes had been reduced to zero as a result of—

a. A tax loss carry-forward in connection with a relatively minor portion of one subsidiary's business spun off at the time of acquisition.
b. Amortization charges in connection with certain assets revalued for tax purposes at the time of acquisition.

† The annual report comments as follows upon earnings per share: Net income per common share and common equivalent share is based on the 9,675 weighted-average number of shares outstanding. For purposes of computing net income per share, the convertible preference shares—Series A, B, and C—are considered to be common stock equivalents. The weighted-average number of common and common equivalent shares assume conversion of the Series A on a share-for-share basis and the Series B and C on the basis of the number of shares issuable at the last sales price of common stock and the current level of income affecting the conversion rate of these securities.
    The 7 percent subordinated convertible debentures and stock options are not included in the net income per share computations, as their effect is not dilutive.
    Source: 1970 annual report.

approximately $11 million (see Exhibit 3 for the first year's operating results). Terms of purchase for acquired companies appear in Exhibit 4. A brief account of each acquired company follows.

Boston Whaler, Inc. Boston Whaler, CML's largest division, was estimated to be the tenth largest U.S. manufacturer of outboard boats. CML's 1970 annual report described this division as follows:

The first company to join the CML Group was Boston Whaler, Inc., of Rockland, Massachusetts, in September 1969. Their principal product is the Boston Whaler outboard motor boat. A 30 percent interest in Boston Whaler Bearcat, Inc., manufacturer of nonpolluting four-cycle outboard engines, was acquired at the same time. Dick Fisher, the chairman of Boston Whaler, has been instrumental in the founding of several companies requiring a high level of technical skill. The creativity and innovative talents of Mr. Fisher made this company particularly attractive as the first member of the Group.

EXHIBIT 4

Terms of payment for companies acquired

Accounting treatment	Name of company	Acquisition date	Original payment in shares of CML stock		Original payment in cash and notes ($000)		Additional earn-out ($000)	
			Common	Convertible preference	Cash	Notes	Minimum	Maximum
Pooling	Boston Whaler	9/30/69	250	1,000			$ 500*	$2,975*
Pooling	Hood Sailmakers	2/25/70	400	4,600			1,600†	5,000†
Purchase	Carroll Reed	10/1/70			$700	$ 600		400‡
Purchase	Mason & Sullivan	5/1/70			450	1,050		1,100‡

*Represents conversion value of 1,000 shares of convertible preference stock. Conversion value is contingent upon the earnings of Boston Whaler, Inc., for the period beginning 8/1/69 and ending 7/31/74, and on the market price of CML's common stock at the time of conversion.

†Represents conversion value of 4,600 shares of convertible preference stock. Conversion value is contingent upon the earnings of Hood Sailmakers, Inc., for the period beginning 8/1/70 and ending 7/31/75, and on the market price of CML's common stock at the time of conversion.

‡Additional cash amount payable through 1974 contingent upon achievement of certain earnings by the purchased company.

Source: 1970 annual report.

The Boston Whaler meets the high quality criteria of the Group. [A well-known consumer report] has rated Boston Whaler as the most outstanding outboard boat produced in the United States. The boats are easily identified by their distinctive and functional shape and a well-regarded trademark. Boston Whalers are made of a monolithic casting of plastic foam with a smooth molded fiberglass "crust" on both sides. This construction causes the Boston Whaler to be extremely durable and unsinkable. No other boat manufacturing company has developed the technical skills needed to build a comparable product.

An asset with long-term growth implications is the Boston Whaler marketing organization. There are eight sales representatives whose principal products are the Boston Whaler and Bearcat engines. More than 700 dealers are located throughout the world. The dealers are known to be the most reputable in the industry. Obviously, other products can be sold through this system as they are developed or acquired by Boston Whaler.

During the current fiscal year, Boston Whaler has introduced a new product, the "Outrage," a larger outboard boat with a new and distinctive hull configuration. A patent application is pending to cover the boat design. It is expected that the boat will have a pronounced effect on the design of larger outboard boats.

Major programs now under way in cost savings, manufacturing efficiency, and overhead reductions are expected to improve profitability to a level in excess of all previous years.

Despite modest volume and profit declines during 1970, Boston Whaler's long-term sales growth was expected to run somewhat above the 8 percent average for the industry. In addition, significant profit increases at current sales levels were expected reasonably quickly through improving margins. These had consistently run well under half the level of Willard's outboard runabout divisions of equivalent size, which CML management knew well from their previous experience.

Carroll Reed Ski Shops. This division was described as follows in CML's 1970 annual report:

The [Carroll Reed] Ski Shops, which joined the Group in October 1969, are a series of retail stores and a national mail-order business headquartered in North Conway, New Hampshire.

The business was founded by Carroll Reed in 1936 to service the burgeoning ski areas in northern New England. Mr. Reed's creative merchandising skills are the principal reason for the store's development into one of the country's best-known ski shops. The company has become known for its extremely high-quality merchandise, excellent service, and unique "country store" style that appeals to both men and women.

In the early spring, an executive vice president [and general manager] was employed by Mr. Reed. The new individual has had significant merchandising experience and will be of value in the day-to-day management of the business. This new management depth will better allow Mr. Reed to concentrate on the future expansion of the business. The Group believes that the company employees are a major asset who provide an excellent foundation for future growth.

During the fiscal year, the mail-order handling systems were substantially improved by the construction of a 6,000-square-foot addition in North Conway for order processing and additional storage space. The order processing was improved by introducing computerized equipment on a limited basis. A new ski shop of approximately 4,000 square feet is about to open in Simsbury, Connecticut, as the first in a planned program of store expansion.

Three residents of the northern New England area have been elected to the board of directors of Carroll Reed Ski Shops, Inc., and participate actively in the long-term planning for the business. They are Tom Corcoran [MBA, Harvard Business School, 1959], a former Olympic skier and president of Waterville Valley ski area; Malcolm McNair, professor emeritus of retailing at Harvard Business School; and Leon Gorman, president of L. L. Bean, Inc., in Freeport, Maine.

Growth opportunities exist for Carroll Reed Ski Shops in the gradual expansion of the retail store business. The mail-order business can be further expanded without significant addition of facilities or personnel. Carroll Reed Ski Shops also provides a vantage point to study several fast-growing sectors of the leisure time industry.

Mr. Reed had played a leading role as one of the early pioneers in recreational skiing in this country and had opened the first U.S. ski lift and school, headed by the world-famous Hans Schneider, in Jackson, New Hampshire, in the early 1930s. Several years later he sold his interest in the ski area and founded Carroll Reed Ski Shops (CRSS) in nearby North Conway. Not long after joining CML, Mr. Reed described CRSS's success over the years to the casewriter, as follows:

> When my wife and I began this business in 1936, we had no idea it would ever grow to what it has become. We simply did not want to go back to Boston, liked the Conway area very much, and felt we could make a living here in this kind of business by treating customers well so that they would stop in and buy something from us the next time they passed through the area. I feel that many of our customers have come to feel a personal closeness to Kay and me and like the way we do business, and that this is what has brought them back over the years. It's this personal touch, a certain integrity in what we stand for in each transaction, that gives us something special to offer. This is the main basis on which we are able to compete with large city stores selling much the same type of merchandise as we do.

During the summer of 1970, Mr. Tod made the following observations about CRSS:

> Carroll Reed has a number of important strengths. Most important are its reputation, based upon the quality and style of the items sold; its interesting, well-laid-out store in North Conway, which accounts for nearly half of total sales; its masculine image, despite the fact that 70 percent of all merchandise sold is for women; and the courteous, service-oriented manner

of its retail people. They have unusually capable people with exceptionally high employee morale compared to others in their industry.

Carroll Reed's mailing list for catalog sales, which account for about half of total sales, is another valuable asset. Average order size is nearly four times that of the mail-order industry as a whole, and about double that for small specialty houses like Carroll Reed. Another strength is Carroll's wide delegation of buying responsibility to six buyers. In most operations of their size, the top person tries to do all the buying personally.

The division's primary weakness, however, is its geographical dependence on one region—North Conway. This is alleviated somewhat by a couple of factors. Catalog sales reach a customer group scattered across the country. Even retail sales are not confined to North Conway residents. Because of its location as both a winter and summer resort, North Conway draws large numbers throughout the year from all over New England and Middle Atlantic states. Partly as a result of these factors their product line has shifted significantly from almost 100 percent ski equipment in the early years to an increasing percentage of primarily women's fashion sportswear, and now less than one third of their volume is ski related.

Another weakness is their dependence on one retail outlet for selling marked-down merchandise from the catalog business. This problem is particularly pressing because of the current push to expand catalog sales. Retail outlets are needed to dispose of unsold merchandise at the end of the catalog season. The current procedure is to turn much of this over to the discount basement of a large downtown Boston department store at about 17 percent of Carroll Reed's retail price.[7]

Mr. Tod felt there were several additional areas of CRSS's operation in need of some strengthening, including internal controls (such as inventory and catalog order processing) and market knowledge in the mail-order area. He thought that an expansion of mail-order sales was CRSS's greatest opportunity for profit growth. The second major retail store, which was being planned for Simsbury, Connecticut, would provide both a non–New Hampshire retail outlet and an additional retail outlet for the resulting increase in markdowns.

Mason & Sullivan Company. CML's 1970 annual report described this division as follows:

> The projected growth rate for the hobby sector is among the highest of the leisure time market because of early retirement and a renewed interest in hand work. The Group entered one of the fastest growing segments of the industry when Mason & Sullivan of Osterville, Massachusetts, joined in June. This business sells clocks, barometers, and music boxes in kit form and by mail.
>
> The founder, Ed Lebo, purchases the working parts of the various items in Europe. Wood, metal trim, and other parts are purchased from numerous

---

[7] Approximately 10 percent (at retail valuation) of total sales were made at markdown prices.

suppliers in the New England area. Because the designs are largely antique reproductions with handcrafted movements, there is virtually no model obsolescence.

The company has two unique aspects. It has a high-quality reputation among woodworking hobbyists throughout the United States and Canada; it also has established relationships with craftsmen-suppliers in Austria, Germany, Switzerland, and England.

Shortly after Mason & Sullivan joined the Group, the former chief executive of a large mail-order house was employed as vice president and general manager to assist in the day-to-day operations of the business. Efforts are being made to introduce control and information systems to support future profitable growth.

Mr. Lebo plans to expand the product line to include other related items.

Hood Sailmakers, Inc.   By any index, Hood was clearly the leading supplier of sails for large ocean yachts (over 40 feet in length), commanding over 50 percent of the U.S. market. Exhibit 5 shows the text of a *Yachting* magazine article describing the company and its products.

EXHIBIT 5

Ted Hood: Sailmaker to the Twelves
by B. D. Burrill

"They are the ultimate teaching and testing ground as far as we're concerned. A Twelve is under sail as much in three months as the average cruising boat in five years." Speaking was Frederick E. "Ted" Hood, the 43-year-old Marblehead, Mass., sailmaker who has made more sails for 12-Meter yachts than any man alive. And perhaps no man in the years since 1958, with the possible exception of Olin Stephens, has contributed more to keeping the America's Cup firmly bolted in the New York YC's trophy room than this genius of boat speed. During these years a small sailmaking operation that started in 1950 has grown into one of the world's largest, to a great extent as a result of the success his 12-Meter sails have enjoyed.

Ted Hood's involvement with the America's Cup and 12-Meter boats began in 1958 when he served in the cockpit of *Vim* during her brilliant bid to become the Cup defender. He served as an advisor to skipper Bus Mosbacher on sail trim and tactics, and generally made himself useful where help was needed. One day, when working on a coffee grinder, he somehow managed to loosen the bolted-down winch—Ted would be a good man aboard any boat on the basis of his physical strength alone.

Hood got his chance to make sails for *Vim* after her owner, the late Capt. Jack Matthews, had seen the sails he produced for the 5.5-Meter *Quixotic*, a Ray Hunt design built and sailed by Ted, which narrowly missed becoming the 1956 U.S. Olympic representative. In spite of a DSQ in the next to last race, *Quixotic* had only to beat one boat in the final race to win the trials. Well up in the fleet on the final leg, the main halyard shackle unaccountably opened, the sail came down, and she finished last. So Ted's first experience with Meter boats wasn't very happy. But he also made sails for *Easterner* and *Weatherly* in 1958 and two fa-

EXHIBIT 5 (continued)

mous red-top spinnakers borrowed from *Vim*, "Big Harry" and "Little Harry," were used by *Columbia* in her successful defense of the Cup.

In 1962 Ted designed and made just about everything except the hull and winches for *Nefertiti* which was the last boat eliminated in the trials by *Weatherly*, which had Bus Mosbacher at the helm. All of the Twelves, including the Australian challenger *Gretel*, used Hood sails that summer. *Gretel*, in fact, used a mainsail made in 1957 for *Vim* in the race she won over *Weatherly* in '62. This would seem ultimate proof of a theory which Ted still believes strongly, particularly with respect to mainsails, that good sails get better with age if they receive proper care. A Dacron sail develops a certain "set" much like the old cotton sails. After a few years the fabric has settled down and the stretch is gone.

One anecdote of the '62 campaign bears repeating. Just before the final trial races between *Weatherly* and *Nefertiti*, Ted Hood spent a whole day, at Mosbacher's request, on the rival Twelve making sure her sails were the best possible. Some sails even went off to Marblehead for recutting and were rushed back in time to be used against him. Some of *Nefy*'s crew felt this hurt their chances, but it's a mark of the man that he only wanted to win over the best possible boat, and he'd rather have been beaten by *Weatherly* than the Aussies. Hood now doubts that he'd ever again have the time to get involved in designing and campaigning a Twelve, business being what it is.

Not long after the '62 defense, the New York YC's Trustees passed a resolution interpreting the Cup's Deed of Gift to mean that challengers not only had to be designed and built in the challenging country but that gear and sails should come from there too. This has effectively cut off the challenging nations from Hood sails but they continue to order them from Marblehead as yardsticks. Many of the early pictures of the French trial horse *Chancegger* showed a lovely Hood main with one lower panel of a distinctly different color. Obviously the section had been removed for testing the Hood-woven cloth which continues to be one of the secrets of any Hood sail.

Hood sailmakers now have lofts in Canada, England, France, Australia, and New Zealand. And while a challenging Twelve from any one of these countries would be allowed to have sails made at the local Hood loft, they cannot use the fabric produced in Marblehead. Largely due to the great success of the English loft, there is a plan afoot to weave Hood cloth in Ireland. If this ever reaches fulfillment, the sail gap will almost certainly be narrowed.

Back in 1964, with future challenges in mind, the Australians sent their top sailmaker, the late Joe Pearce, to spend a year with Hood, and he became a top assistant. With Ted preoccupied by a second unsuccessful attempt with *Nefertiti*, Pearce became the man who dealt with the sails for the defender, *Constellation*, during the trials. Pearce may have learned quite a bit about the cut, but said his boss, "we didn't tell him much about the cloth."

Following this, and until his untimely death, Joe Pearce became the Hood sailmaker in Australia. He made *Dame Pattie*'s sails in 1967 but by mutual agreement there was no communication with Marblehead on the subject of 12-Meter sails. The same arrangement applies with Peter Cole, the present Aussie Hood sailmaker, who has supplied the motive power for *Gretel II*. The Hood loft in

EXHIBIT 5 (continued)

France, newest of the foreign operations, has not been involved in Baron Bich's undertaking.

Although nearly all of the technical improvements and lessons learned are applicable to Hood's normal business of making sails for cruising/racing yachts, there are some special problems and differences in making sails for the Twelves. To begin with, a 12-Meter has a ¾ foretriangle rig (the maximum allowable under the rule) while most boats today have masthead rigs. Mainsails must be fitted to masts and booms that are designed to bend to a far greater degree than on any cruising boat. Spinnakers are not made to the maximum size the 12-Meter rule permits—experience has shown time and again that shape is more important than sheer size when it comes to making a Twelve go downwind. Nevertheless, a maximum 'chute is made every Cup summer just to be sure that the theory still holds.

In preparing for a Cup summer, the Hood loft is looking for ways to make their sails lighter, smoother and stronger. The Twelves put tremendous strains on their sails and it is essential that they be strong and durable. But still, to save weight, less provision is made to prevent chafing than in a normal sail. As to the weight of sailcloth, there is continuous research into ways of making it lighter but still strong enough to retain its shape-holding ability. This work comes under the supervision of Ted's father, Steadman, known to everybody as "The Professor," who has done much over the years to insure the success of his son's business. The Professor's research is continuous and he says that progress is slow. But the following table on mainsail cloth weights used by the Twelves would seem to belie this claim:

Year	Weight
1958	14 oz.
1962	12 oz.
1964	10 oz.
1967	7.5 oz.
1970	6.9 oz. (or slightly less)

One characteristic of every U.S. defender since 1958 has been a tendency to hobby-horse less than her rival in the seas off Newport. While hull design is all important in this respect, there is little doubt that lightweight sails—weight saved up high where it really counts—have also contributed significantly to this advantage.

One recent development of Hood research that has reached a sufficiently advanced stage to be used on 12-Meter sails this summer is the Hood Ring, a replacement for the large hand-worked grommets in the corners of sails. Hood Rings have proved to be almost twice as strong as the best hand-sewn equivalent even though they are considerably lighter in weight. Hood Rings are inserted by special high-pressure hydraulic tooling and now there is virtually no handwork in a typical Hood clew since roping has also been eliminated.

Other new wrinkles in 12-Meter sails this season include Cunningham holes for

EXHIBIT 5 (concluded)

draft control in both genoas and mainsails. The latter have Cunninghams along the foot as well as the luff. When this was written, experimental zippers (two of them, side-by-side) seemed to have proved their worth as a further means of draft control along the luffs of mainsails. Hood and others have been using foot zippers on mainsails for many years. This year's lightest polypropylene spinnaker cloth is even lighter than *Intrepid*'s much talked-about Floater of '67, but The Professor won't say by how much. Mainsail headboards are now made of titanium for the ultimate in strength without weight.

Valiant and *Heritage* have the recently developed Hood Sea Stay, a hollow grooved rod in which the genoa luff is hoisted. This item eliminates hanks as well as the space between headstay and sail, thereby significantly reducing turbulence at the leading edge.

In perfecting 12-Meter sails, spinnakers and jibs are recut often. There has been a definite trend among U.S. Cup sailors toward working for perfection with the sails at hand rather than ordering one after another and trying to decide which of the lot is best, as was popular until 1964. *Intrepid*, for example, went through the entire '67 campaign with only two mainsails in her inventory. Hood has had great luck in making mainsails right the first time and thus virtually eliminating recutting. The 7.5-oz. main *Intrepid* used most only had one seam let out near the head. *Valiant*'s first Hood main had not been touched, at least through the Preliminary Trials. Ted points out that owners often will get him out to look at sails believing they need to be recut when what is really needed may be a proper knowledge of how to adjust luff and sheet tension or how tight to carry a leech line. Hood personnel spend long hours discussing and demonstrating adjustment techniques to 12-Meter crews.

The problem is trying to find enough time to satisfy everybody. There can be little doubt that over the long haul Ted Hood's success in making 12-Meter sails has meant much to his business, even though it is now quite a small part of the total. But one of the ironies of a Cup summer for Hood is that much less other work comes in. Many owners apparently feel that the loft will be too busy with the Twelves to pay much attention to them. This is not true—a 12-Meter sail goes through the same manufacturing process as any other. But what is certainly true is that what started as a bedroom sail repair business during college years would never have grown to be the international enterprise it is today had Ted Hood not become sailmaker to the Twelves.

Source: Article appearing in the September 1970 issue of *Yachting* magazine.

Some of the reasons behind the company's success were discussed in CML's 1970 annual report:

> In every major ocean race of recent years, the winning boats (including *Intrepid* in the recent America's Cup Race) have consistently used Hood Sails. When Hood Sailmakers of Marblehead, Massachusetts, joined the Group in February [1970], the Group became a very important factor in the marine accessories segment of the leisure time industry.

The business was started by Ted Hood as a hobby when he was a boy. Now there are sail lofts in Massachusetts, California, Canada, England, France, New Zealand, and Australia. The company weaves and finishes its own cloth in mills in Massachusetts, and, as such, it is the only fully integrated sailmaker in the world. Hood Yacht Systems, a division of Hood Sailmakers, manufactures masts, rigging, and specialty marine hardware.

The principal asset of the company is its technological and inventive skill. No other sailcloth maker has the technical ability to make such light yet strong cloth without the use of plastic resins. These innovative skills have also been applied in the design of sails and the manufacture of specialty marine hardware.

During the year, an entirely new style of sailcloth was introduced for use in the America's Cup. The company also began to extrude its own fibers for use in its "Floater" spinnaker cloths. The "Sea Stay" style of rod rigging became commercially available. Sail lofts were opened in France and California. A new [executive] vice president and general manager was employed to give additional depth in administration and production management.

Additional lofts are planned in the United States, and substantial sales growth is expected in the foreign markets. New marine accessory products are being developed for Hood Yacht Systems.

Competition for Hood came mainly from dozens of small local manufacturers, which generally had strong market coverage in particular regions of the country only. Hood in fact had itself been established in the late 1930s as a strictly local loft supplying the Marblehead market. Over the years it had grown both nationally and internationally to its current position of preeminence. Mr. Morgan, the new division general manager, described the company's success as follows:

Hood's success can be attributed to a couple of factors. The most important of course is Ted Hood himself. Ted is a soft-spoken, modest kind of guy with an amazing knowledge of sailing and racing. He exudes confidence. What an ocean racer wants most from a sailmaker Ted Hood can supply in abundance . . . expert consultation in sail design and individual help in getting the best out of sails once they're made. Since the CML merger much of Ted's administrative load has been reduced and he now spends much more of his time testing new designs and out working with customers. Not only is this the kind of thing he enjoys most but it's where Ted's time is most valuable to the company.

Hood Sailcloth is also a key competitive factor. Hood has a real product edge as the only U.S. sailmaker with its own weaving capability. In a very closely guarded process here in Marblehead we produce a tight-weave cloth of unusual lightness and strength. In fact, many in racing circles attribute *Intrepid*'s victory over Australia's *Gretel* in the 1970 America's Cup Race at least in part to the fact that *Intrepid*'s sails [using Hood cloth] weighed about half those of *Gretel*.

Hood sails were sold by five salaried salesmen and Mr. Hood himself through a variety of channels: direct to sailors (about half) and to dealers, naval architects, yacht builders, and the federal government. Hood competed only slightly in areas other than the large yacht market.

CML'S OPERATING PHILOSOPHY AND POLICIES

Hood's Irish investment was being considered in the context of an intricate set of relationships between CML and its divisions. According to Mr. Leighton, these relationships typically began taking shape even prior to acquisition itself and were strongly affected by personal factors:

> It would have been very difficult to have acquired any of our companies without our personal interest in their products. Bob Tod, for instance, is a great hydroplane enthusiast and for a time even held the U.S. Class B hydroplane speed record. This, together with our outboard boat experience at Willard, made it much easier to approach Dick Fisher about joining us. My own sailing background gave us some immediate rapport with Ted Hood. Ted and I had even competed once in the 1956 New England Men's Sailing Championships. I had come in second behind Ted, who went on to win the U.S. Men's Championships that year. All of us in the group are skiers, so Carroll Reed's business was not completely foreign to us. Learning Carroll Reed's mail-order business in turn provided a background for rapport with Ed Lebo when we first approached him about selling Mason & Sullivan.

Mr. Leighton considered preacquisition discussions to be extremely important because they provided an opportunity for both parties to get to know each other. This involved both discovering the owner-manager's underlying needs and aspirations and outlining clearly what joining CML would mean in terms of policies, procedures, authority and responsibility relationships, management changes, and so forth. This "foundation building" period was considered of prime importance because it paved the way for changes to be made after acquisition. According to Mr. Leighton, only by letting an owner-manager know beforehand what changes to expect could a transition be made smoothly. He commented:

> Most companies in our industry can benefit substantially from association with a larger, more sophisticated firm such as CML. We can provide capital and management know-how usually not available to a small company. We provide a vehicle for taking a small company public at favorable values and minimum expense. We can also provide a valuable environment for the top man in these companies. The independent businessman typically feels alone and would like someone to recognize his achievements and exchange ideas. His board of directors (if he has one) usually is not made up of professional managers who can give real guidance. He has no one to turn to for advice on a continuing basis. Therefore, he is typically a very lonely man under extreme pressure from long hours, and surrounded by subordinates he may not wish to confide in. About the only persons around to motivate and console him are his wife, banker, and accountant, and they may not be close enough to the business to do this effectively.

> Countering this strong need for association is, of course, an equally

strong need for autonomy. This creates an antagonism of forces which inevitably causes an owner anxiety during early stages of discussion with us. He has normally spent years building up his business and wants to make sure he will remain in control after acquisition. Our big initial job is to subdue these anxieties. For this reason we deliberately don't talk price or even ask for financial statements during early contacts. Instead, we try to get to know the owner's business, problems, and personality. We explain to him in detail what life will be like with us and exactly what changes in his operation he can expect. The whole emphasis is one of building up trust and understanding. At some point along the way he inevitably brings out his financial statements to show us. As a result of our emphasis on mutual understanding, we are less apt to get involved in a bidding match than if we were to negotiate mainly on a price basis.

According to Mr. Leighton, the acquisition process itself had varied considerably among companies acquired so far:

One of our companies first came to us about joining CML. Another I had heard might be available. I simply phoned the president and set up a meeting to talk. For a third company we had to make overtures over a number of months before we finally got anywhere. Another acquisition came to us in an interesting way. Last spring an acquaintance of mine and the former president of a medium-sized mail-order company phoned to say that he had a company he wanted to buy personally, but that the purchase price was above his financial means, and he wondered whether CML might like to buy it in partnership with him. We liked the company so much we bought it outright and put him in as general manager, with the former owner's concurrence, of course. This route is one we may use more frequently both for hiring new managers and acquiring new companies. I had a very qualified fellow in here not long ago who said he wanted to work for us. I told him we simply didn't have an opening at present, but that if he could bring us an attractive company we might acquire it and with the owner's approval put him in as general manager with attractive financial alternatives. He's working on one right now.

The corporate office

In January 1971 CML's corporate office consisted of four officers. Mr. Leighton, chairman of the board, focused mainly on relationships external to operations, concentrating primarily on new acquisitions, investor relations, and the raising of new capital. Mr. Tod, president, spent an estimated 90 percent of his time working directly with divisions and was the corporate officer immediately responsible for operations. Mr. Chaffee,[8] treasurer,

---

[8] Philip Chaffee (32): BS, University of Vermont, 1962; Financial Management Program, 1962–65, and then traveling audit staff, 1965–67, of the General Electric Company; manager of corporate auditing, ITEK Corporation, 1968–70. Mr. Chaffee had joined CML as controller in June 1970, and had assumed Mr. Frederick's duties as treasurer upon the latter's resignation in December 1970.

worked closely with divisional controllers in preparing accounting statements and various management studies, such as cost-volume relationships, product mix contribution analyses, and so forth. He also handled company-wide cash control, auditor relations, tax form preparation, and corporate office accounting. Management felt that the existing corporate staff was sufficient to handle expected growth for the next three or four years, with perhaps the addition of a financial controller to share some of Mr. Chaffee's current responsibilities.

Since July 1970, borrowing and cash receipts for the entire corporation had been consolidated at the corporate level. Divisions could therefore no longer borrow on their own or build up their own cash balances; all funds passed through central CML accounts. Each division paid (or received) interest on funds received from (or advanced to) CML. Apart from interest payments there were no corporate charges.

Financial control

Mr. Tod commented as follows on the company's philosophy regarding divisional autonomy:

> We want to give divisions their heads and let them make their own decisions within the broad policy constraints set at the corporate level. This much autonomy is workable only in the presence of complete, accurate, timely information on operations. Such data come in several forms. Prior to the beginning of our fiscal year each division submits three forecasts: monthly profit and loss for each of the following 12 months, end-of-month balance sheets for each of the following 12 months, and an annual capital budget showing forecasted expenditures by month. As the year proceeds, forecasts are compared on a monthly basis with actual operating figures.
>
> In addition to strictly accounting data we receive a number of key indicators from divisions on a monthly basis. These are vital measures of each division's performance. For instance, from one division I get catalog and retail sales and open-to-buy figures. For another I get bookings (orders), shipments, and discount levels for both dealer and direct sales, while another supplies order backlog, production, and inventory figures in addition to about six or eight others. For one division I look hardest at advertising response figures. Any variances are discussed in detail at regular meetings with division managements. Meetings are summarized in memo form and then sent back to divisions. If divisions don't agree with opinions or decisions stated in these memos, they are supposed to let me know right away. With this system I feel we have about as tight a control system as we could get without our actually making the decisions ourselves.

Part of the reason for the emphasis on close control, Mr. Tod explained, stemmed from a desire to avoid an experience CML management had had at Willard. One of their divisions that had been reporting adequate profits for several years had suddenly shown considerable red ink following an examination of inventories which had precipitated large writedowns. This situation had come as a complete surprise to both group and division management, and in management's opinion was simply the result of inadequate controls.

Mr. Leighton offered the following comments on operating control:

> We have two main operating policies: "No closets to hide in" and "No surprises." Together they spell full decentralization of operations *except for* financial information flows. If things go wrong in a division, division management has nowhere to hide because we've given them complete authority and responsibility for their operations. On the other hand, if things go well they take the bows. We don't want surprises either good or bad from divisions, and we try to ensure this by getting complete and frequent information on operations.

Division controllers were considered an important link in providing information flow from divisions to the corporate level, and CML had inherited what corporate management considered to be experienced men within three of the acquired companies. (The fourth required only a part-time bookkeeper.) Two of these men were CPAs, while the third was an MBA from the Tuck School at Dartmouth. All had extensive backgrounds in either public or corporate accounting.

Divisional general managers

Another important ingredient in CML's operating strategy was the division general manager. Professionally trained, experienced general managers had been hired to complement all four division presidents, partially relieving them of administrative duties and thereby giving them more time to do what they were best at. While several of the general managers hired so far were still quite new to the company, Mr. Tod felt that they were already proving to be valuable additions to the divisions.[9] He stated that one of the

---

[9] *Fred Snow* (35), executive vice president and general manager of Carroll Reed Ski Shops since March 1970; AB, Babson College, 1958; salesman, sales manager, promotions manager, and marketing vice president of Fieldcrest Company, 1959–70.

John Morgan (33), executive vice president and general manager of Hood Sailmakers, Inc., since April 1970; Princeton, electrical engineering, 1959; MBA, Harvard, 1966; prior to joining Hood, had had a number of technical and management positions at General Electric Company over a ten-year period.

Bob Lavery (49), vice president and general manager of Mason & Sullivan Company since July 1970; BS, Kansas State College, 1940; 25 years' experience in catalog sales, first with Montgomery Ward and more recently with a successful medium-sized mail-order firm where he had been president since 1961.

Dave Wilson (33), vice president and general manager of Boston Whaler, Inc., since January 1971; Cambridge, England, chemical engineering, 1961; MBA, Harvard, 1968; had worked for six years as a process engineer with a major U.S. chemical company, and since 1968 as president of a Canadian manufacturing concern where he had achieved profitable operations of the company for the first time since 1960.

most significant ways in which CML could benefit an acquired company was by recruiting for it people who would not normally be attracted to small companies, which often offered little opportunity for equity participation and promotion. Compensation of general managers was tied to earnings growth formulas similar to those of owner-managers, and involved liberal cash bonus and stock option possibilities based on performance. The relationship of a division general manager to an owner-manager was determined partly by this congruence of compensation interests, partly by the fact that each general manager had been selected by the owner-manager of the division involved from among several candidates prescreened by CML management, and partly by the understanding that the owner-manager ultimately had final say on all decisions affecting a division and in fact could fire the general manager if it became apparent that the two could not work together. All these arrangements had, of course, been discussed at length with owner-managers during the "foundation setting" stage preceding acquisition. All four general managers hired so far were still with the company in January 1971.

Financial controls and other influences ushered in by CML appeared to have caused some changes within acquired companies. Middle management personnel from various divisions described some of these as follows:

> It's not at all like it used to be around here. [The owner-manager] had always been an easygoing guy running the business pretty much on a day-to-day basis. I liked this myself. It suited my style. Unfortunately, all this is changing now. Things are becoming much more systematic and "big business" around here. We're feeling this most in cost reduction and in sales promotion, but every one is feeling it to a certain extent. I don't think this will cause people to quit, though. Most of the workers are very unskilled and easy to train, so they aren't likely to do much better elsewhere. Most of the management people are like me. They've come here because they love [boating, sailing, skiing] and will stick it out because they love the sport.

* * * * *

> [The new general manager] is a good man. We had about nine different men around here doing his job before he came. He made a tenth, but because he has just a little more finesse plus the authority of the job behind him things have been running much more smoothly around here since he came. I'm not sure, though, that any of the other nine couldn't have done just as well if they had been given the position.

* * * * *

> I think people are happier and things are running more smoothly since we joined CML. Previously, it was hard to get big decisions made. Problems would frequently just float along without ever being resolved. This was frustrating. [The new general manager] is the kind of guy who looks at the facts and comes to a decision on them. This has made life easier for all of us.

Mr. Tod's role

An additional important corporate link with divisions was provided by Mr. Tod himself. Mr. Tod tried to visit each division at least once every two weeks, and to spend not less than 50 percent of his time physically on site with division personnel. These visits enabled him to participate on an ongoing basis in divisional developments. According to Mr. Tod, discussion during these visits ranged over every aspect of a division's business: pricing policy, marketing strategy, expansion requirements, personnel problems, production scheduling, and so on. He stated:

> It's hard to generalize about this relationship because it's so different in each specific instance. How I deal with a division depends upon the division involved, its key man, its employees, its particular problems, and so forth. One division president, for instance, is constantly after me to spend more time with him and his people. Until recently another division has been quite reluctant to seek any help.
>
> There do seem to be certain patterns, however. When a new division first comes on board, Charlie and I try to schedule a luncheon for all its employees at which we introduce ourselves and discuss CML and our plans for the division. We deliberately wait two or three weeks after original announcement of the acquisition before having this luncheon in order to let division personnel get used to the idea prior to meeting us. During this period, we intentionally stay away from the division; this helps convey the impression that we don't intend to meddle too much in divisional operations. Before the luncheon meeting, Charlie and I try to learn as much as we can about the 12 or 15 key people in the division. We feel this is useful for getting to know a new division better and for establishing relationships with its key people.

While the above described the usual procedure, not every acquisition had had an initiation luncheon. One division president had objected to the custom so no luncheon had been held for that division.

Because, in principle, divisions operated relatively autonomously, Mr. Tod felt his influence upon operations was based less on exerting direct authority than on the confidence and respect he inspired as a manager. He commented on this situation to the casewriter as follows:

> The influence I can exert comes in preparation, really. I must have intimate knowledge of the business of each division, and must have the numbers involved in any particular situation at my fingertips. This means doing my homework. Otherwise, division people won't listen. They may pay lip service, but they'll make their own decisions in the final analysis. Of course, if they do, they'll have to live with them.
>
> I have to be able to understand our divisions' businesses as well as division presidents themselves in order to do my job. I think I will be able to continue to do this as we expand the number of divisions. Keep in mind that all our divisions are in the leisure time industry and in many ways aren't

really that different from one another. Our two mail-order businesses have a number of similarities, for example. The same is true, though to a lesser extent, of our two marine divisions.

I realize I have to walk a fine line most of the time between supervisor and boss, consultant, and advisor. The key to this role of course is working with people, and the key to that is flexibility . . . listening to people, getting to know their capabilities, and correctly evaluating their judgments. All this of course requires intimate knowledge of the facts of specific situations. Again, doing your homework is essential!

When asked to comment upon the kinds of divisional situations he became involved in apart from those involving routine financial control, Mr. Tod replied that these could be best classified according to the role he played in the development or solution of each. He saw himself playing several roles, but primarily those of—

1. Management consultant.
2. Management recruiter.
3. Participant in key decisions.

Mr. Tod described several situations as examples of each.

1. Management consultant.   This role typically involved the collection and analysis of information in such a way that it shed light on some important aspect of a division's operation. Mr. Tod described several instances in which he had played this role.

Consumer analysis.   Dick Fisher, himself an avid fisherman, had deliberately designed the Boston Whaler for the fisherman's every need. As a result, the product combined the general advantages of stability, maneuverability, unsinkability, safety, and performance with specific fishing-oriented features, such as a built-in bait box and a rack for fishing rods. Given this background and orientation, the company naturally directed advertising toward fishermen. Soon after acquisition Mr. Tod began to question whether such an orientation was really justified, however. He commented on this situation as follows:

> Working closely with the Boston Whaler sales organizaiton during the months following acquisition, I came increasingly to feel that a significant percentage of Whaler owners were using the boat for family and recreational in addition to strictly fishing purposes. If this were true, I felt that Boston Whaler advertising copy should reflect the fact. One problem was that there wasn't really much product-in-use data available within the division. During my visits there I had plenty of opportunity to discuss my feelings, though, and suggested from time to time that a customer survey might be made to get a better feel for who bought Whalers and just how the boats were used. It took a while before anything happened, but gradually people began to get interested. During this period I spent quite a lot of time with the division advertising manager talking about what information might be helpful and how it might be obtained. After a while he began putting to-

gether a questionnaire, and we discussed this and revised it several times. Finally, by September [1970] a completed questionnaire was mailed out to about 400 customers. Responses have shown a significant family recreational clientele, and recent ad copy is already beginning to reflect this.

Winter catalog program.   Mail-order catalogs of one division had traditionally been published and mailed twice a year. The winter catalog consisted of 32 pages; the spring catalog, typically a less ambitious project, contained 24 pages. Each had a total mailing of several hundred thousand copies.

A review of catalog sales in past years had convinced Mr. Tod that an expansion of the spring catalog, in terms of pages, items, or mailings, or any combination of the three, could add to profits substantially. To demonstrate this he reconstructed from divisional accounting data a detailed analysis of the company's catalog experience to date, showing how past changes in pages, items, and mailings had affected volume, tying in enough cost data to provide estimates of profitability. This analysis indicated an optimum mix consisting of a 10 percent increase in total items offered, an increase in the number of pages from 24 to 32, and a continuance of mailings at their former level.

Getting the division to implement this increase was another matter, however. Mr. Tod stated:

> Division personnel just didn't feel there was enough time to produce the eight additional pages before the deadline for mailings. It took a little pushing on our part to get this through, but eventually the division made it. I was able to help a little on a bottleneck situation involving page layout. By setting up a very simple PERT chart with deadlines for the various activities involved, I was able to persuade division personnel to farm out certain layout functions. As it turned out, by following the PERT chart, the catalog was completed three days before the mailing deadline. Partly as a result of the page increase, profits from the 1970 spring catalog were about $50,000 higher than the previous year.

The division president had the following to say about this situation:

> I didn't feel we were geared up at the time to handle the increased volume. One reason I sold to CML was to get their professional help in solving some of our internal systems problems like order processing and inventory control. We haven't had too much help on this so far, however. The increase in catalog volume before straightening out these problems inevitably caused some foul-ups with customers. I'm a little afraid that this kind of thing may undercut some of the goodwill and close personal contact with customers we've worked so hard to build over the years.

2. Management recruiter.   A second corporate role vis-à-vis divisions in which Mr. Leighton and Mr. Tod appeared to be equally active was that of management recruiter. Mr. Leighton described this role as follows:

> In talking with prospective acquisitions we typically find that the presidents really don't enjoy what they're doing. They have to be concerned with banking relations, accounting, marketing, production, and sales, but what they really want to do is develop more and better products.

To reduce the administrative load on division presidents, CML had helped recruit general managers for all four divisions, leaving the final hiring decision in the hands of division presidents themselves.

Mr. Leighton added:

> We try to get division presidents to hire a man who will complement them. Generally, we try to get an MBA who's been out and gotten six or seven years' experience. We would rather go out and pay someone in his early 30s a lot of money because he has tremendous potential and good background than to get someone with less experience more cheaply or someone with more experience but with less potential.
>
> We want the man that every company wants. We spend as much time trying to meet and recruit a man as we do a company. For example, we went night and day after John Morgan.

Mr. Morgan had graduated from Princeton in 1959 with a degree in electrical engineering and had joined the General Electric Company shortly afterwards. He worked there until 1964 in a number of technical and supervisory positions, including foreman of shop operations and project supervisor for the transfer of products from U.S. to European factories. Mr. Morgan then entered the Harvard Business School, graduating as a Baker Scholar with High Distinction in 1966. Following graduation Mr. Morgan returned to GE, where he subsequently held positions as manager of business planning, manager of marketing administration (both at the division level), and finally as manager of resource planning for a $600 million product group. He resigned in the spring of 1970 to become general manager of Hood Sailmakers.

Mr. Leighton commented as follows on the process of recruiting a Hood general manager:

> We had heard some very good things about John from his professors at Harvard. The feedback we got about his work at GE was also excellent. We heard that he was considered one of their most able young men. We decided that if he was that good, we would like him to join our team, so we went after him.

Mr. Morgan offered the following remarks on this situation:

> I really hadn't been thinking of leaving GE when Bob and Charlie approached me. I had recently been promoted for the third time since leaving the Business School in 1966. I was getting all the right signals from higher management, and I felt I was on the way up.
>
> I think what really appealed to me in CML's offer was the opportunity to build something on my own. Financially, I'm at about the same level as

at GE. Of course there's a possibility of building some equity here, but the risks are great also. Over the long run GE probably offered about as good an opportunity for building a personal estate. What I couldn't resist about the Hood offer was the excitement of working in a small operation where I could really influence the future of the company.

3. Participant in key decisions.   A third important role played by corporate management was that of participant in key decisions facing divisions. Mr. Tod offered the following as an example of the kind of decision he typically became involved in.

Production cutback.   During the third quarter of fiscal 1970, Mr. Tod and one division president had held quite different opinions over what constituted a wise production level for the division. Each side claimed a good case for its position. Division management argued that sales for January and February had been well ahead of forecast, indicating that another good year was in the making. Corporate management feared that trends in the general economy might significantly reduce fourth-quarter shipments and was urging sizable production cutbacks. Mr. Tod was unsuccessful in getting division management to accept his view, however, and production continued at high levels throughout the first three quarters.

Mr. Tod noted:

> I made my voice heard, but I couldn't convince anyone to follow me. In fact, I'm not sure whether if I'd been in the division's shoes I would have cut production myself, given the demoralizing impact this has on a division if high sales eventually materialize. From our standpoint, however, the risk of overproduction seemed sizable, and we were advocating a path of prudence.
>
> As it turned out, an unexpected stock market slide caused May and June sales to drop well below forecast. Inventories rose substantially as a result, requiring much more CML financing than originally budgeted. The division became dependent on us because it had to ask for additional financing to carry inventory. This puts us in a good position to exert our influence. At our urging, the division is reducing next year's forecast well below the level originally planned. In addition, it is making contingency plans to cover a further sales drop next year, and is cutting overhead substantially.

Hood's Irish project

Corporate management's involvement in Hood's Irish weaving mill project constituted yet a further example of its role as participant in key decisions facing divisions.

Hood's organization had grown rapidly in recent years. As recently as early 1967, production facilities had been limited to one weaving and one sail-making facility, both located at Marblehead, and all sales (already 30 percent foreign in 1967) had been made by Mr. Hood and three sales consultants working out of Marblehead. To reduce tariff expenses on sails shipped abroad and to give better service to foreign customers, Hood had begun setting up foreign lofts, first in England (1967) and later in France, New Zealand, Australia, and Canada. In the United States a West Coast loft had been opened during this period, and the Marblehead weaving capacity had been nearly doubled. This expansion had naturally been accompanied by an increase in the number of Hood employees, from a total of about 165 in 1967, all located in Marblehead, to approximately 300 by 1971, 175 in the United States and 125 abroad. The organization had also become increasingly complex, as evidenced by Mr. Morgan's sketch appearing as Exhibit 6.

The concept of a European-based weaving mill had originated in 1968 with the manager of the newly established English loft, which paid a 20 percent tariff on all sailcloth imported from Marblehead. Hood's interest in a European mill naturally increased with the opening of additional foreign lofts in 1968 and 1969, since duties on the sailcloth they imported ranged as high as 35 percent in France and 31 percent in Australia. The ad valorem value of cloth represented approximately 25 percent of the final selling

EXHIBIT 6

Organization chart of Hood Sailmakers, Inc.

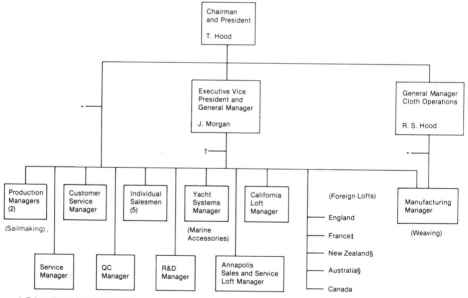

* Primarily technical direction and control.
† Primarily administrative direction and control.
‡ Owned 80 percent by Hood Sailmakers, 20 percent by the loft general manager.
§ Owned 50 percent by Hood Sailmakers, 50 percent by the loft general manager.
Source: Sketch prepared by John Morgan, general manager of Hood Sailmakers, in early January 1971.

price of Hood sails; import tariffs therefore constituted a significant percentage of each foreign sales dollar—from 5 percent in England to more than 8 percent in Australia and France.

Because of increasing pressure from the managers of foreign lofts, Mr. Hood in early 1969 hired a brother-in-law of the English loft manager to begin site studies for a European mill. The desirability of an Irish site soon became evident because the Republic of Ireland's inclusion in the British Commonwealth permitted tariff-free export to all Commonwealth countries, because the Irish government offered to underwrite 50 percent of capital costs for the new facility and to waive all tax on profits earned in Ireland, and because of low labor rates in Ireland. By August 1970 the Irish Development Authority (IDA) had agreed to fund $266,000 of the total $554,000 fixed capital required by the project, and quotes for the necessary equipment were already being solicited.

As shown in detail in Exhibit 7, the project called for a total investment of $580,000. Mr. Morgan calculated that the cash flow savings resulting

EXHIBIT 7

A. Capital requirements for Irish weaving mill ($000)

	Total cost	Sources of funds	
		IDA grant	CML
Land	$ 8.4	$ 4.2	$ 4.2
Building	216.0	108.0	108.0
Equipment	329.6	154.1	175.5
Working capital (net)*	26.0	0.0	26.0
Total funds required	$580.0	$266.3	$313.7

B. Aftertax cash flow savings resulting from transferring to Ireland all weaving of cloth sold outside the United States ($000)

	1971	1972	1973	1974	1975
Cash flow increase resulting from decreases in—					
Tariffs	$ 16	$ 18	$ 20	$ 23	$ 27
Variable costs of manufacture	56	63	65	83	96
U.S. corporation profit taxes	74	85	87	110	128
Subtotal	$146	$166	$172	$216	$251
Cash flow decrease resulting from an increase in—					
Fixed cost of manufacture†	98	97	96	96	96
Net cash flow increase (net cash flow savings)	$ 48	$ 69	$ 76	$120	$155

Note: Discounted cash flow return on $314,000 investment = 13 percent.
*Net of working capital freed in the United States as a result of moving a portion of the weaving operation to Ireland.
†Excludes depreciation.
Source: Company records.

from the new mill (shown in part B of Exhibit 7) represented a 13 percent aftertax return on CML's $314,000 investment in the project. Cash flow savings were expected in three areas:

1. Elimination of tariffs on cloth currently woven in Marblehead and shipped to lofts in Commonwealth countries.
2. A reduction in variable cost of manufacture arising mainly from lower labor rates in Ireland.
3. A reduction in U.S. corporate profits tax arising because the Marblehead mill would suffer a significant loss of contribution margin (approximately 40 percent) as a result of moving production to Ireland. The resulting reduction in profits reported in the United States would reduce U.S. taxes on corporate profits.

The only recurring cash outflow resulting from the investment arose from an increase in fixed manufacturing expenses. While no reduction in Marblehead's fixed expenses was expected despite the 40 percent reduction in throughput, Ireland would itself incur $98,000 of additional fixed costs (after depreciation).

Mr. Morgan offered the following comments on the Irish project:

> From my standpoint, the big advantage of the project is strictly financial ... the 13 percent aftertax return it represents for us. There are minor strategic advantages, of course. The investment will protect our positions in England and France, where duties have pushed prices about as high as they can go. If duties should go even higher, which we feel could happen, we might be pushed out of these markets if we are still shipping cloth from Marblehead.

Hood's board of directors was scheduled to meet on January 15 to decide on a recommendation with regard to the Irish investment. Mr. Tod saw three alternatives open to the board: (1) dropping the project outright, (2) going ahead with it full speed, or (3) delaying it until Hood's domestic market improved. The more he considered the many factors involved, the more he came to favor the third alternative. First, cash inflows were relatively small during early years of the project. They would therefore not significantly contribute to the earnings track record CML hoped to establish prior to going public in 1972. Second, the tax status of profits earned in Ireland raised a complex set of questions including (1) whether or not future investors would be evaluating CML's earnings on a before-tax or an aftertax basis, (2) future cash needs in Europe providing a use for profits earned abroad, (3) difficulties and costs associated with eventual repatriation of profits earned abroad, and (4) possible legal complications arising from the fact that earn-out for former Hood owners was based on before-tax rather than aftertax profits. Third, Hood was showing a somewhat lower return on the funds currently being advanced by CML[10] than some of the other divisions of the company. Therefore, while Hood profits had improved somewhat in recent months, the division had not yet entirely demonstrated an ability to achieve its full profit potential. Fourth, the continued slump in domestic sales had reduced Hood's Marblehead operation to 50 percent of capacity. This made a sizable investment in additional capacity difficult to justify. Fifth, and most important, Hood management was already spread extremely thin over a great number of activities and did not appear to have the time and energy at present to take on a major new commitment.

There were, of course, disadvantages to delay. The IDA grant might be lost. Hood funds and management energy would be expended just maintaining status quo on the project. The Hoods themselves, concerned with the long-run competitive advantages of the investment and eager to get under way, might be disappointed.

Mr. Tod commented on his position as follows:

> I just feel we can get a quicker payout by putting our money in other areas . . . expanding one company's product line, for instance, or improving another company's sales organization.

Mr. Leighton offered the following comments:

> I think over the long run it makes sense for Hood to begin weaving abroad. It's a question of timing, really. With sales down, plus an overcapacity situation, I'm afraid of what the Irish investment will do to Hood's current profit picture. In addition, I wonder whether at this point in time Hood has enough management time and energy to take on something like this. A start-up situation is never easy.

ACHIEVEMENTS TO DATE: FUTURE PROBLEMS AND OPPORTUNITIES

Hood's Irish investment was under consideration just 18 months after the formation of CML and 15 months since its first acquisition in September 1969. Mr. Leighton had the following to say about CML's achievements to date and the problems and opportunities facing the company in the months to come:

> Progress so far has been excellent. Three out of four companies will show significant profit increases this year over last—20 percent or more. In the case of one division profits will fall somewhat, but mainly because we are deliberately scheduling manufacturing below break-even in order to work off excess inventory built up last year. Fiscal 1972 should bring a big profit increase for this division.

---

[10] Totaling $800,000 in early January 1971.

As for further acquisitions, the biggest constraint at this point is pressure on Bob Tod. Right now, for instance, we are looking at three companies as possible acquisitions this spring. All are out of state and only one is in New England. This is quite different from our existing divisions, which are all easily accessible from Boston. The big question on further acquisitions becomes how many companies one man can handle at once. This depends, of course, on how spread out they are geographically, and on the quality of division management. If our divisions can more or less run themselves, we can spread Bob a lot thinner. The real key to further growth then becomes the development of good management teams within divisions, and this in turn depends heavily on the quality of people we can bring into CML Group companies. As a matter of fact, after acquiring our fourth company last July we completely stopped all acquisition search and spent six months just looking for people. Now that general managers have been installed in all divisions and we've got four really good division management teams, we're back looking at acquisitions again.

There are other ways of easing the pressure on Bob, of course. One would be to limit acquisitions to businesses very similar to existing divisions. This would reduce the learning effort required at our level. Another would be to eventually develop several Bob Tods as Group vice presidents for our three main areas: marine, sporting equipment and related accessories, and hobby crafts. An advantage of this would be the increased promotion opportunities it would open to new employees now being brought into the company. A disadvantage is that it would necessarily reduce the tremendous fun and personal involvement we are now having with our companies. How we go on this is a personal decision we'll have to make at some point. A third possibility would be to bring new companies in under existing divisions.

A long-term objective is to take CML public sometime after the fall of 1972. This would provide the three full years of audited operations required by the SEC. We'd like a major "quality" brokerage firm to handle the public offering, and want a large enough offering in our shares to provide for after-market trading. To achieve this we feel we will need from $750,000 to $1 million in aftertax profits.

As far as we're concerned, the current economic downturn couldn't have been timed better. It has pushed us to trim dead weight in divisions to a point where they are now lean and hungry. When the economy finally turns around, we should be in a position to show attractive internal earnings increases. This of course is the real key to the long-run success of CML Group: Our ability to show earnings per share increases through internal growth rather than through newly acquired earnings. Stated another way, we believe that our future success will depend far more on our ability to successfully manage than on our ability to successfully acquire.

case 32

Sybron Corporation (A) (condensed)

Current and historical financial data for Sybron are shown in Exhibit 1. An organization chart depicting the company in early 1971 appears as Exhibit 2.

The company's various operations in early 1971 consisted of approximately 25 domestic and 25 foreign divisions grouped around one international and five domestic groups. The basis for product grouping varied among groups. The Dental Products and Hospital Products Groups, for instance, each consisted of divisions grouped rather closely around a specific market, while divisions in the Instrumentation and Specialty Chemical Groups appeared to be related more by technology than by product or market. Within the Process Equipment Group, where neither a strong market nor a strong technology link appeared to exist, divisions operated in four quite distinct areas: glass-lined tanks for the chemical industry (Pfaudler), water treatment equipment design mainly for industrial customers (Permutit), laboratory equipment (Nalge, Thermolyne, and Erie Scientific), and contract basic research (Aero Chem). Worldwide sales and pretax profits by product type appear as Exhibit 3.

Product groups

Product groups as they existed in early 1971 are described briefly below:

Instrument Group. As the third largest U.S. manufacturer of process instrumentation, the two domestic and four foreign divisions comprising this group were engaged in what was described by group management as "a life-and-death competitive struggle" with two larger competitors for a rapidly growing world market.

A major corporate objective was to increase Sybron's overall commitment to instrumentation through acquisitions in Western Europe, or Japan, or both.

Dental Products Group. The companies making up this group constituted a major factor in the dental equipment and supplies industry, manu-

EXHIBIT 1

A. Sybron Corporation: Stock price history

Sybron Corporation: Historical financial data	54	55	56	57	58	59	60	61	62	63	64	65	66	67	68	69	70
Net sales	16	14	18	39	33	38	51	50	51	54	59	134	165	187	265	300	333
Net income (after taxes)	0.7	0.6	0.9	1.5	1.4	1.7	2.0	2.1	2.2	2.3	2.9	8.0	10.5	12.4	14.8	16.7	16.1
Income per share (after taxes)	0.34	0.30	0.44	0.48	0.44	0.52	0.59	0.61	0.64	0.66	0.84	1.15	1.30	1.44	1.35	1.45	1.38
Long-term debt	1	1	1	1	2	3	3	3	8	6	6	12	10	17	28	54	60
Common equity	8	8	9	14	15	17	18	20	21	23	25	59	72	87	124	134	140

* Annual high and low.

† $32 on 3/31/71.

Source: Financial data for Sybron are as reported in annual reports of Sybron Corporation and its successor companies, without retroactive restatement for pooling of interest of acquired companies. Per share amounts have been adjusted to reflect all subsequent stock dividends and splits. All dollar figures are in millions except for per share figures which are in dollars.

B. Stock price growth comparisons*

	Sybron "score sheet"†	
	Growth of stock price during decade (in %)	
	Decade of the 1950s	*Decade of the 1960s*
Sybron	9.7%	4.9%
Dow Jones Industrial	3.1	1.6
General Dynamics	9.8	0.6

* A memorandum written in early 1970 by Mr. Donald A. Gaudin, president, commented as follows on these comparisons: "With the ending of the 60s, our 'score sheet' records a full decade of Sybron performance. During this decade Sybron increased its stock value almost fivefold, which is better than three times the corresponding figures for the Dow Jones Industrial Average. Of the 30 companies we have been comparing ourselves with only five—Xerox, American Hospital Supply, Culligan, Nalco and Becton, Dickinson—outperformed us. In fact, we had a stock increase more than double that of 18 of the companies. For the benefit of some of our newcomers let me say that we have been issuing this report quarterly, comparing ourselves with essentially this same list of companies, for almost two decades."

† These figures are taken from a list updated regularly at Sybron and used to compare the stock performance of about 30 industrial companies.

EXHIBIT 2
Corporate organization chart

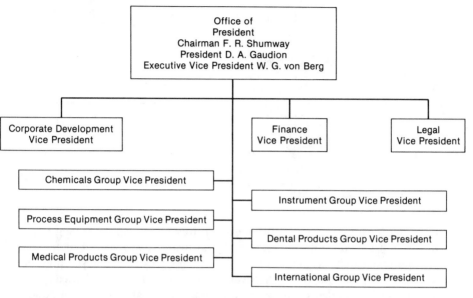

Size and composition of corporate staff

Corporate staff activity	Number of salaried personnel involved
Corporate development:	
Compensation	9
Manpower plannning	6
Industrial relations	4
Communications	3
Vice president	1
Total	23
Finance:	
Planning (and acquisitions)	5
Controller	12
Budget analysis	5
Treasurer	5
Vice president and assistant	2
Total	29
Legal:	
Patent	7
General legal	4
Vice president	1
Total	12
Grand total	64

Source: Corporate records.

EXHIBIT 3
1970 worldwide sales and pretax profits by product type

Product type	Percent of total corporate sales	Percent of total corporate pretax profits
Instrument	24	19
Health	41*	37
Process/water/waste equipment	23†	27
Chemicals	12	17
Total	100	100

* Consisting of:	Dental equipment and supplies	21%
	Medical and hospital equipment	16
	Laboratory products	4
	Total	41%

† Consisting of:	Industrial process equipment	18%
	Water and waste treatment equipment	5
	Total	23%

facturing the entire gamut of products required by the dentist. The group's Ritter Division concentrated on dental "hardware" consisting of such capital equipment items as dental chairs, lights, and X-ray machines; while the Kerr Division manufactured "software" items including dental waxes, filling materials, and drills. The Pattern Division acted as a retailer of dental products, selling both Sybron and non-Sybron equipment and supplies directly to dentists.

Hospital Products Group. This group's long-range plan defined its business as "providing the equipment, supplies, and service to meet the needs of the medical health market." Each of the four major divisions in this group had previously been an independent company selling a well-known line of established products through dealers, mainly to hospital and nursing home customers.

Process Equipment Group. This group consisted of four quite unrelated segments. The old Pfaudler Division, the original nucleus of the company, continued to manufacture mainly glass-lined steel tanks for the chemical process, pharmaceutical, and brewing industries. The Permutit Division represented a second segment within the group. It had suffered in recent years as a result of entry into the water and waste treatment field by a host of large, well-financed competitors apparently willing to sustain short-term losses in order to gain a foothold in what many considered a potentially huge market.

The Process Equipment Group's three laboratory products divisions, representing yet a third segment, were concentrating on (1) joint selling efforts, and (2) profiting from their solid marketing position with laboratory supply houses by developing and acquiring additional products to sell through existing distribution channels.

A fourth segment was the Aero Chem Division, a small high-technology research firm providing basic research mainly to the U.S. government. While originally acquired with the notion that it might supply technology to other divisions throughout the company, no significant successes to date in Aero Chem technology transfer could be reported.

Chemicals Group. The Chemicals Group, currently the most profitable and considered by many at Sybron to be the most promising growth area of the company, consisted of four divisions: two selling auxiliary chemicals to the textile industry (the Tanatex and Jersey State Divisions), and two others selling cleaning chemicals to marine and industrial customers (the Gamlin and Ionac Divisions). The fundamental emphasis in this group, according to its long-range plan, was "to take advantage of the many unique interdivisional relationships existing among our four divisions."

International Group. In 1970 operations outside the United States accounted for 35 percent of Sybron's total worldwide sales of $378 million. Of this total, 11.5 percent, or $44 million, came from sales of nonconsolidated foreign affiliates. The remaining 23.5 percent, or $89 million, came from consolidated foreign operations. Profits from foreign sales represented an even larger percentage of corporate earnings in 1970. A recent International Group long-range plan was forecasting a ten-year growth rate in sales from existing operations at approximately the average level forecast by domestic divisions. Because of corporate management's stated objective to increase foreign sales to 50 percent of total corporate sales by 1980, a major long-term corporate objective was to accelerate international growth through acquisition.

CORPORATE STRATEGY

The overall strategy of the company had changed markedly over the past 15 years. The basic strategic orientation beginning in the mid-1950s had been diversification and growth in order to overcome inherent liabilities of a low-growth, highly cyclical business threatened by technological obsolescence. In the opinion of top management the extended diversification drive over a 15-year period had by 1969 largely overcome these liabilities. With the achievement of size and greater earnings stability by 1969, top management did not appear to be anxious to diversify further.

Objectives

The following specific long-range objectives were put forth by Mr. Gaudion in a recent corporate long-range plan:

Qualitative
1.   To exploit the most profitable facets of selected markets whose inherent growth is at least twice that of the average U.S. industry.

2. To achieve active leadership positions in these markets through innovative marketing and superior products.
3. To gain a balance between cyclical and noncyclical products. Quantitatively, our objective is to have less than one quarter of our profits tied to the U.S. capital equipment cycle. Our objective is also to eventually have chemical production represent at least one third of total corporate profits.
4. To build earnings from overseas markets to at least 50 percent of the total.
5. To build the management depth necessary for a minimal $500 million size within five years.

Quantitative

1. To achieve a *minimum* 15 percent compounded earnings per share growth rate. This objective is the crux of the entire plan. As you have heard me state repeatedly, our price earnings multiple, our stock options, and our dynamic organization are all hinged to this level of growth.
2. To earn a minimum of 12 percent aftertax return on assets employed.
3. To attract a price earnings multiple substantially above the average of Dow Jones Industrial companies.

Policies

While generally unwritten, a number of policies apparently designed to meet these objectives were in evidence at Sybron in early 1971.

Operational policies. Frequent mention at all levels was made of Sybron's fundamental organizational policy of "minimum disruption," whereby each division was to conduct its own affairs with the least disruption and interference from other organizational elements. This policy was supported by several subpolicies regarding size and location of staff functions. As a general rule, staff functions were located at the division level rather than at higher levels in the organization. The typical division therefore did its own accounting, industrial relations, engineering, and research and development work. "Minimum disruption" was also supported by a general prohibition against staff at the group level, and by a deliberate policy of limiting the size and scope of the corporate staff. As shown in Exhibit 2, the corporate staff, consisting of just 64 salaried employees in early 1971, was confined to three areas: finance, corporate development (personnel), and legal. Virtually no corporate services were provided in purchasing, manufacturing, marketing, or research and development.

Despite its frequently mentioned importance, the "minimum disruption" principle appeared to be under considerable debate at Sybron in early 1971. The argument for less divisional autonomy was put as follows in the company's 1971 corporate long-range plan:

Real emphasis (prior to 1971) was on maintaining the operational momentum of our 50 operating units. This meant a concentration on virtual autonomy, so that responsibility could be clearly defined, performance measured, and compensation equitably administered.

It is now becoming clear, however, that the risks and costs of such extreme fragmentation are excessive at our present size. Even more importantly, we have negated many of the benefits we had anticipated from our "coalition strategy." It seems evident that the opportunity to use our cumulative strengths in a given business represents our soundest basis for building a true growth company.

Mr. Gaudion had defined Sybron's "coalition strategy" to security analysts in mid-1969 as "carefully interweaving solid coalitions of companies in growth markets." While intragroup coalitions did appear to be developing quite successfully among divisions within certain groups, largely through efforts of several group vice presidents to coordinate and consolidate the resources directly under their management, no significant instances of successful coordination between divisions in different groups had occurred by early 1971.

Marketing policies.   Distinct yet complementary marketing policies appeared to exist at various levels in the company.

Divisional level.   The major competitive thrust for the typical Sybron division appeared to be the achievement of "marketing momentum" sufficient to enable it to dominate its industry. This policy called for doing a better job than competition in the areas of market development and customer service, for concentrating on proprietary products, and for gaining sufficient share of each market to become a market leader.

Group and corporate levels: Group and corporate policies affecting marketing focused one way or another upon opportunities for joint marketing efforts. Because of respect for "division autonomy," full-scale "consolidated" marketing approaches were not being pushed upon groups or divisions. Instead, impetus for joint marketing programs had to come directly from the divisions involved.

Research and development policies.   Complementary policies regarding research and development also appeared to exist at various organizational levels.

Divisional level.   At the divisional levels, R&D expenditures were generally maintained at a level somewhat below competition. A corporate staff executive gave several reasons for this policy:

> Sybron just hasn't been very successful so far with funds spent for R&D. By almost any yardstick, R&D investments simply have not paid off for us. Furthermore, there's the feeling that in most of Sybron's markets incremental changes in existing products will be more important over the coming years than major product breakthroughs. In addition, Sybron's size makes it fairly easy to buy innovation from outside the company when a particular technology is really needed by a division.

Corporate level. To compensate for the relatively low levels of R&D expenditure by divisions, the major corporate R&D policy appeared to be outside acquisition of technology. As one corporate staff executive explained:

> Major internal R&D efforts are not advisable because of the fragmented structure of our corporation which presently consists of over 50 divisions. None is large enough to mount a sustained long-range development effort. Such an effort would seriously drain any division's resources. On the other hand, divisions are too diverse to justify centralizing development at the corporate level. For these reasons, we have frequently relied on acquisitions for significant new developments.

Pricing policy. Sybron's pricing policy was an integral part of its overall strategy of obtaining a leadership position with proprietary products in each of its markets. Mr. Gaudion stated this policy in a top-management memorandum as follows:

> We propose to be the "Cadillacs" of our industries. We propose to do this by rather arbitrarily *always* pricing our products above our competition, *never* below. If we arbitrarily raise prices and lose a substantial share of the market, this indicates loud and clear that we do *not* lead our industries and we must then either correct the weakness or, if it is uncorrectable, we must go out of that particular product line because we do not as a policy want to be in product areas that we cannot lead!

This policy also appeared to be under considerable debate in early 1971, however, as price leadership was becoming increasingly difficult to maintain in face of recent "softness" in a number of Sybron's markets.

STRENGTHS AND WEAKNESSES

These policies had apparently been designed in recognition of the following characteristic strengths and weaknesses of the company.

Corporate level

Several overall strengths were felt to be important. The most significant of these, large size, was felt to offer several advantages including (1) some reduction of wide cyclical swings in earnings, (2) a broad distribution of the company's common shares, and (3) some limited economies of integration, particularly in the financial and personnel areas.

While sheer size was considered one of Sybron's major strengths, it was also increasingly felt to be a potential weakness. Considerable attention at top levels of the company was being paid to the question of whether or not Sybron, at the $333 million sales level, had reached the point of diminishing returns in size, that is, whether the advantages of large size (financial stability, specialization in management, complementarity of skills, etc.) were beginning to be overshadowed by what Mr. Gaudion called "problems of giganticism," which manifested themselves in "the diminishing rate of return brought on due to the management problems of size alone." Mr. Gaudion singled out increasing difficulties of motivation and communication accompanying corporate growth as the fundamental cause of these problems:

> The percentage contribution of the single unit to the total becomes automatically smaller as a company grows. Therefore, division management gets an increasing feeling that they have little to do with overall performance. Yet their stock options, bonus, and so on are tied strongly to corporate performance.

Mr. Gaudion felt that the communication problem accompanying corporate growth stemmed from problems of effective "span of control." He felt that many decisions requiring sensitive short-term versus long-term trade-offs by divisional and group managers evolved ultimately upon the chief executive. Yet he was beginning to wonder whether he, as chief executive officer, could still evaluate such matters intelligently in an organization as complex as Sybron.

Division level

Divisional strengths and weaknesses in the various functional areas were perceived more or less as follows:

Marketing strength: Industrial and other nonconsumer marketing, particularly in markets where product design and customer training and service were important.

Weakness: Consumer marketing, wholesaling, and retailing. Emphasis on marketing was based on the experience of most divisions that engineering breakthroughs had generally not been a key ingredient to success in its markets, and that by developing and maintaining "marketing momentum" (through customer training and service, custom manufacture, sales training, intensive sales coverage, institutional advertising, etc.), divisions could withstand technological assaults

Research and development strength: In accordance with its policy of acquiring innovation, most Sybron divisions maintained close surveillance of technological developments within their markets. This ability to perceive and monitor developments critical to their markets and to harness such developments to a division's benefit when the time seemed ripe to do so, was considered by many in the company to be a valuable divisional strength.

Weakness: A low R&D budget relative to competition. Of the funds spent for R&D, the bulk went toward "refinement and improvement" of exisiting products, with the remainder used for new product development.

Manufacturing strength: Sybron divisions were generally best at custom-engineered, high-quality, specialty manufacture. The typical division was an old established company portraying an image of craftsmanship and possessing a high level of technical manufacturing skill developed over a period of many years.

Weakness: With its craftsman orientation, Sybron was naturally rarely low cost. The company had little experience at mass manufacture. In addition, it had no experience in extremely high-technology manufacture.

Role of the corporate president

Mr. Gaudion described as follows his role as president of the company:

I exert influence in a number of ways, I suppose. First, I help set overall corporate policy, such as our pricing and research and development policies. Second, I inevitably play an important role in rewarding our people, particularly our division presidents. They all know that I have a great deal to say about their promotion and salary increases, so they are naturaly trying to convince me that they are doing a good job and are working to meet the standards we've laid down for them at the corporate level. The big problem, of course, is that influencing these men effectively requires that I understand the problems of each division in considerable detail. For instance, I've got to understand why it's worthwhile for one division not to meet our 15 percent corporate earnings growth target in order to let it build for the future. Making such qualitative judgments is essential in order to avoid milking some operations. If a division begins to feel that I don't really understand the details of its operations, a credibility gap inevitably develops over my ability to evaluate its performance fairly. This can have a disastrous effect on motivation. Unfortunately, these judgments cannot be turned over entirely or even mainly to group vice presidents, because comparisons must inevitably be made between divisions in different groups. Some of my corporate staff people wonder whether in a company of Sybron's size and complexity the president can continue to make such judgments about the specifics of divisional activities.

case 33

Sybron Corporation (B)

In the late afternoon of April 19, 1971, Mr. Gaudion, president of Sybron Corporation, a diversified company with about 50 divisions organized into six product groups, received a telephone call from Mr. Fraser, vice president of the Instrument Group.[1] Following the usual civilities, Mr. Fraser launched into the substance of his communication:

> After a great deal of discussion and careful evaluation, the Process Control Division's management committee voted this afternoon to roll back on the price of the AL-4,[2] putting it more in line with competition. Because of the close interest you have shown right along in the AL-4 and in our pricing practices in general, I wanted to let you know about this right away. The division voted to announce to the trade tomorrow that effective immediately prices on the majority of AL-4 models will be reduced by about 8 percent. For the middle of the line standard model, this will mean a decrease from $358 to $330, leaving us still $10 above Anchor,[3] which as you may recall is our strongest competitor in this as well as many other of our major product lines.

Following these comments, Mr. Fraser paused, apparently waiting for some sort of response from Mr. Gaudion.

PROCESS CONTROL DIVISION

The Taylor Instrument Company, acquired by Sybron in early 1968 and set up as a separate Instrument Group, was the third largest worldwide manufacturer of process control instrumentation, outranked only by Anchor and one other competitor. Its Process Control Division (see Exhibit 1 for organization chart) manufactured and sold direct, mainly to industrial customers, a complete instrumentation line consisting primarily of recorders, controllers, and devices to sense process parameters such as flow,

---

[1] See Sybron (A) for details.

[2] Product name, function, cost, and price have been disguised.

[3] Disguised name.

766

EXHIBIT 1
Partial organization chart

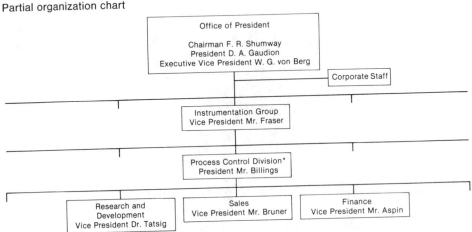

* The Process Control Division management committee included managers of all major functional departments within the division.
Source: Company records.

pressure, level, temperature, and humidity. This division was the largest division in the corporation with sales in excess of $40 million.

According to division management, the entire instrument industry had been under considerable competitive pressure recently on a number of fronts. To push ahead in several fast-growing segments of the market, particularly analytical instruments and digital computer control systems, several competitors had been making R&D outlays in recent years considerably larger than the Process Control Division (PCD). Another threat came from a smaller, marginally profitable, but rapidly growing competitor who had been "buying his way into the market" by cutting prices. This situation had created a price-cutting mentality throughout the industry and in management's opinion had been a prime cause for the severely depressed profit margins experienced by all major firms in the industry in recent years. PCD management pointed out, for instance, that the Anchor Company, one of their larger competitors, had shown such a sharp reduction in profitability during the past year that they had been forced to pass a quarterly dividend for the first time in more than a decade. This poor profit performance was thought to be a result of both general industry conditions and Anchor's own unusually large R&D outlays.

PCD provided instrumentation mainly to the food, chemical, paper, rubber, textile, and mining industries, commanding market shares in these industries ranging from 20 percent to 50 percent. Management estimated that PCD's share of the total industrial instrumentation market had declined slightly in recent years from about 12 percent during the mid-1960s to approximately 10 percent by 1971. The total instrumentation market was thought to be growing at the rate of 8–9 percent per year, with electronic instruments growing somewhat above and the more traditional pneumatic instruments considerably below this average level. While competing in both areas, PCD generally held larger market shares in pneumatic than in the electronic market segments.

PCD products were sold direct through a 135-person field sales force, with each salesman reporting to one of five regional sales managers. A salesman's annual compensation was based upon two factors: base salary, which had averaged approximately $12,800 in 1970, and sales bonus varying in 1970 from zero to $7,000, with an average of about $1,800 per salesman. Bonus for a particular salesman was calculated as a percent of actual sales volume attained during the year. The percentage figure used varied from ¾ percent to 2 percent, increasing in production to the ratio of a salesman's realized sales volume to a sales quota set at the beginning of the year.

While cost data were not kept by individual product line, Mr. Aspin, treasurer of PCD, estimated that variable manufacturing cost for the AL–4 was about $60 per unit. Total fixed costs associated with the AL–4 were not known. However, the relation between fixed and variable manufacturing cost for the AL–4 was not felt to be appreciably different from that of other PCD products which averaged about one-third variable, two-thirds fixed. Mr. Aspin was reluctant to rely very much on a fixed-variable distinction for product costing, however, since he felt that "over the long run most fixed costs are really variable." Even after taking account of the standard division GS&A overhead charge,[4] the AL–4 was felt to be clearly a profitable product at any of the prices charged for it so far.

Of the equipment used to manufacture the AL–4 line, approximately 50 percent consisted of special-purpose equipment not adaptable to manufacture of other PCD products. The remaining 50 percent represented general machine shop facilities utilized rather broadly in the manufacture of many PCD products. The special-purpose equipment representing an original cost of about $300,000 was capable of producing about 750 AL–4s per month. The machine shop had been running at 60 percent to 80 percent of capacity in recent months.

THE PNEUMATIC TEMPERATURE TRANSDUCER MARKET HISTORY

The AL–4 pneumatic temperature transducer, developed by PCD's R&D group over a three-year period at an expense in excess of $1 million[5],

---

[4] Exact percentage not revealed.

[5] These expenditures were accounted for as a general division overhead expense rather than charged directly to the AL–4.

had been introduced to the trade in January 1969 to supersede an earlier PCD design which had been steadily losing market share to Anchor. By 1969 the AL-4's predecessor held only about 11 percent of the total estimated 30,000-unit annual market, compared to 40 percent for Anchor. Davis,[6] a rapidly growing but marginally profitable competitor and widely considered to be the chief price-cutter in the industry, held about 8 percent of the market.

Dr. Tatsig, director of R&D for PCD, described a transducer as "a device for converting one form of energy to another." In the case of the AL-4 a mechanical signal generated by a mercury column in a capillary tube was converted into a pneumatic signal which was then relayed to a remote recording or controlling station. By means of this energy conversion process, the temperature of a fluid in a vessel or pipe could be accurately measured and transmitted. Temperature transducers were used in large quantities by many PCD customers, and constituted one of PCD's major volume items, with sales split about equally between pneumatic (represented by the AL-4) and electronic devices. While the electronic transducer market was growing faster than the pneumatic market (10 percent versus 2 percent or 3 percent), the latter nevertheless represented a large and potentially lucrative total market of about $10 million at 1971 prices. If PCD could succeed in substantially increasing its market share with the newly designed lower cost AL-4, management felt that the division stood to make significant profit gains in this market.

Dr. Tatsig described the history of pneumatic temperature measuring devices as one of alternative competitive seesawing between Taylor and Anchor. Prior to the early 1960s Anchor had held a lion's share of the market. A major drawback to their early transducer, however, was its inability to accurately amplify and transmit signals to remote locations. As a result, operators were obliged to read and control temperature to meter locations attached to the process itself rather than more conveniently to remote stations.

To remedy this situation, Taylor had introduced in the early 1950s the first transducer which permitted accurate measurement at locations removed from the process. By 1958 Anchor had itself come out with a competitive product, adding several product advantages including an improved corrosion-resistant mercury bulb material, the major component directly in contact with the fluid being measured. By 1960 Taylor had more or less followed Anchor's improvements, superseding its own earlier design with a predecessor design to the AL-4. Throughout the 1960s Anchor had continually updated its design while Taylor, despite considerable development effort, had not succeeded in improving its own to any significant degree

---

[6] Disguised name.

until the introduction of the AL–4. As a result, Taylor's market share by 1969 had fallen to 11 percent, or about 3,300 per year, compared with about 12,000 units for Anchor.

THE AL–4

There appeared to be some difference of opinion within PCD concerning the extent of the AL–4's product superiority over the 10–Q, Anchor's counterpart product. Dr. Tatsig claimed several distinct product advantages of the AL–4, including (1) greater variety of bulb materials allowing a broader range of application; (2) significantly less weight; (3) fewer critical elements in direct contact with the fluid (often corrosive) being measured; (4) a wider temperature range; and (5) considerably fewer parts, thereby increasing reliability and reducing maintenance costs.

Despite these advantages, the AL–4 appeared to have faced several initial obstacles when first introduced to the trade. Dr. Tatsig commented on these as follows:

> One advantage of the 10–Q over the AL–4 is that a damaged 10–Q bulb can be replaced at a cost of about $60, while changing an AL–4 bulb requires replacing an entire welded unit at a cost of $120. As bulbs are rarely broken, this factor is probably not a major consideration for our customers, however.
>
> Perhaps a more significant hurdle for the AL–4 has been the fact that its predecessor had not been a successful product. Because of this, it has been difficult to convince either customers or even our own marketing people of the real advantages of the AL–4.

Mr. Bruner, PCD's marketing vice president, described the relative product strengths of the AL–4 and 10–Q as follows:

> In 1969 we were in the position of coming out with a new product to compete with a highly entrenched competitor whose product from the standpoint of accuracy, repeatability, and ranges was about equal to our new design. To add to this, our design was not able to pass the specs using a stainless bulb which had become pretty much the standard in the industry. To get around this we developed a new bulb material, and as it's turned out this has proved to be superior even to stainless in a number of respects. However, there was no way to have foreseen this in 1969.

In light of all these factors, the AL–4 line had initially been priced to sell $10 below equivalent 10–Q models, with the medium-range model priced at $305 compared to Anchor's $315 midrange price. An across-the-board $5 price increase by Anchor several weeks prior to the January 1, 1969, AL–4 introduction date, but after publication of new AL–4 price lists put the AL–4 $15 under the equivalent 10–Q model on the date of introduction.

SYBRON'S PRICE LEADERSHIP PHILOSOPHY

These decisions had taken place at PCD less than one year following the Sybron-Taylor merger in early 1968. The pricing philosophy they implied appeared to be quite different, however, from that long espoused by Sybron management and repeatedly voiced with almost crusading vehemence by Mr. Gaudion himself. As far back as 1965 Mr. Gaudion had expressed this philosophy in a company-wide memorandum entitled "Pricing—an Oft-Neglected Element of Financial Control" (see Exhibit 2 for complete text):

> We will never knowingly undersell a competitor. In other words, we will undertake the responsibility to establish and lead the pricing structures of the industries we serve.
>
> o   o   o   o   o
>
> Instead of contributing to, or even participating in such industry price deterioration, we propose to be the Cadillacs of our industries. We propose to do this by rather arbitrarily *always* pricing our products above our competition, *never* below.

EXHIBIT 2

Pricing—an Oft-Neglected Element of Financial Control

Donald A Gaudion
August 11, 1965

The purpose of this report is to focus attention on the importance of pricing in financial control, to propose a Ritter Pfaudler Corporation statement of policy on this subject and an organization to introduce and police this policy.

We have already established the corporate policy that we intend to produce and market products that lead in their specialized fields. It is proposed, somewhat as a corollary to this that we also have a stated policy that we never knowingly undersell a competitor. In other words, we will undertake the responsibility to establish and lead the pricing structures of the industries we serve.

Lags, leads and balance in corporate growth

The businesses we are in can be segmented into the five functional areas of—

1. Marketing.
2. Manufacturing.
3. Research and Product Development.
4. Finance.
5. Industrial and Public Relations.

Each of these can be further broken down, of course, such as field sales, home office sales, advertising, product promotion, market research, and so forth, under the marketing function.

We have often stated that one of the most important assignments of manage-

EXHIBIT 2 (continued)

ment is to sense imbalance between any of these elements and take action to correct the imbalance. For example, if the company has the finest distribution in its industry but its product development or its manufacturing lags, then the company will fail. Or if it leads with the lowest cost manufacturing but has poor financial control or lags in distribution, it will fail.

Interestingly enough, however, progress is made as one function tends to move out ahead of the others. Then the laggards have to be beefed up as management tries to balance out the organization to prevent failure.

Pricing discussions

Much has been written in the management literature about pricing—discussions of the elasticity of demand for the product, how much new demand is created by a lower price, the wage-cost push on prices in the postwar period, the dangers of price inflation, and so forth. Furthermore, competitive pricing, the narrowing of gross margins, and so forth, are constantly talked about in business with pressures to cut costs to hold margins. What increments can be added to factory costs to establish prices? More valid arguments state that the price is always made in the marketplace without regard to costs.

But as a practical matter most industrial and capital goods pricing is a haggle between a salesman and a purchasing agent. Inaccurate estimating, overcapacity in suppliers' plants, pressure for greater sales volumes without regard for profits, direct costing, marginal pricing, and so forth, give the purchasing agent a field day as he works one salesman against another. This, of course, is the heart of the free enterprise system and is supposed to eliminate the high-cost producer. But it can also lead to expediency and so deteriorate an industry that no money is available for the product development, organization development, product promotion, and so forth, needed for its long-term growth. How can we beat the system to ensure us *above-average* growth?

Price leadership

Instead of contributing to, or even participating in, such industry price deterioration, we propose to be the "Cadillacs" of our industries. We propose to do this by rather arbitrarily *always* pricing our products above our competition, *never* below. What are the likely consequences?

In our products, merchandising, direct sales forces, field service, advertising and product promotion, organization stability, and so forth, are at least as good as, and hopefully in total *better than* our competition, we will continue to at least hold our share of our markets. And since we are in control of industry pricing, our margins and profits should increase. Why "in control?"

If we commit ourselves to selling even one dollar above the competition, we can control the industry because as we raise a price, say 5 percent, the competition which has been X percent below us *will not* then be $X + 5$ percent below us. They will raise their prices to where they are the same X percent below. They will always need the margin improvement as much as we. They are not likely to get a larger share of the market by pricing $X + 5$ percent below us. If they were likely to do so profitably, they would already have been pricing at $X + 5$ percent

EXHIBIT 2 (continued)

below us in order to increase their market share. So the chances are they will continue the traditional price relationship by increasing their prices as we do.

If we arbitrarily raise prices and lose substantial share of the market, it indicates loud and clear that we do *not* lead our industries and we must then correct the weakness pulling us down out of industry leadership. If it is uncorrectable, we must go out of that particular product line because we do *not* as a policy want to be in product areas that we cannot lead!

As a practical matter, however, it is our contention that we *won't* be going out of most of our businesses with this policy. The cost-price product and organizational leadership relationships in our industries are *not* that precise that a change of price means immediate loss of position. If we do not have *positive* industry leadership, we are close enough to it in our lines that we have time to maneuver.

This proposed policy suggests that price is the element that can be changed fastest. Every dollar of price increase goes *in total* into profit before taxes! Improving our position in the other areas is a more sluggish process and involves "spending money to make money." But by increasing prices and then feeding the money into constantly upgrading our organizations, our R&D, our sales, service, advertising, investor image, and so forth, we can underpin our industry leadership.

This does *not* mean we should stop trying to develop a more efficient organization through cost cutting. It *does* mean that we will benefit *more quickly* from price increases which *can then* be put to work developing the most efficient organization but also one that will continue to lead. Any adverse reactions to a price increase will not take effect fast enough but what we can offset them with improvements developed with the extra margins available.

The dire consequences of "going out of business" are *not* likely to happen. Our businesses have enough momentum that even if we do *not* have clear-cut industry leadership we will not immediately find orders going to zero even if we have the highest prices. We will get enough business at the higher prices to enable us to build industry leadership. It might be claimed that a more sound approach for industry leadership is to develop a more efficient organization first. Not only is this slow but also it takes money. Therefore, higher prices *immediately* is the only way to rapidly develop the full circle of strength.

If prices are allowed to deteriorate, the flat circle becomes a spiral corkscrew *and* the spiral is downward! Conversely, if prices are increased it becomes a spiral but the spiral is *upward* and leads all of the other elements of the circle *up* the spiral to leadership.

Current examples of price leadership

There are many current examples of Cadillac price treatment in industry. Magnavox is an example of a company that refuses to cut price on its line of hi-fi and television equipment. Whether its products are truly superior to their competitors' is hotly debated. Competition is fierce with such giants as GE, Westinghouse, and Philco. Perhaps its refusal to cut price contributes to the idea that it is a superior product? Or is it superior?

Xerox set a high per copy price on its reproductions even though its basic pro-

EXHIBIT 2 (continued)

cess of heating a resin on any piece of paper is undoubtedly the *lowest cost* process! It is much cheaper than silver-coated paper used in wet process reproduction. Is the quality of the final reproduction really better on the average than the average Verifax or Photostat? Is it really better than SCM? Many would question this. But by establishing an initial high price, rather than "buying its way into the industry," it has now built a formidable marketing organization and product development that will make it tough to unseat.

Many other examples of high price–quality images in industry could be cited, and they are not all based on a strong patent-based proprietary product position. Many are more like the Magnavox example.

And there are many examples, such as retailing of gasoline, where all of the brands are essentially the same and once a price war gets started the situation quickly deteriorates to a loss. An industry leader then has to restabilize the business and work the structure back up into a profitable area.

Organization

To effect this policy, one or more pricing czars will have to be established. Raising prices seems to be no one's responsibility. On the other hand, forces are constantly at work eroding margins. Purchasing agents are in business to hammer away at salesmen. Who in our organizations are set up to counter purchasing agent pressure? Salesmen, feeling they have no control over manufacturing costs, are primarily interested in getting the order. If they are told their prices are high, they feel their company is inefficient. Manufacturing people are interested in volume to "spread the overhead." The financial and industrial engineering departments are interested in improved efficiency through reduced costs. Inflation constantly raises the cost of purchased materials and labor going into our products.

Who in the organization is applying a small fraction of the time spent on cost reduction on the other side of the equation—increasing income by maximizing prices?

Effective immediately, the corporate financial group is being assigned the task of determining the organization necessary to effectuate this policy. Someone in each profit center *must* be made responsible for pricing! He must be familiar with markets, products, costs, and so forth, but since there are few published prices in our industries, this person must primarily operate by trial and error in the initial stages. He must arbitrarily increase prices until he is *positive* he is quoting the highest price! Only after following this policy consistently over a period of time will the competition understand we are sincere in our determination to quote the highest price. A normal competitive structure will then evolve with us in the lead price-wise, but also continuing to get our share of the market. This will take courage, but it can be done if the price czar in each profit center is backed up by the manager of the division.

Obviously the czar must also creatively study every conceivable method of maximizing income from pricing. Leasing, rental, contractual service agreements, and any number of other variants should be considered when applicable. But in all cases *we must be the highest price.* And these prices must be fixed. They cannot

774

EXHIBIT 2 (concluded)

be "negotiable in the field" or the field salesmen, the customer, *and* the competition will know we are susceptible to an "auction." And the end result of an auction is bankruptcy rather than industry leadership!

D. A. Gaudion

Source: Memorandum dated 8/11/65 written by Mr. Donald A. Gaudion, president of Ritter Pfaudler Corporation (predecessor to Sybron Corporation).

Price leadership was justified in terms of basic requirements for long-term growth:

[Price cutting can] so deteriorate an industry that no money is available for the product development, organization development, and product promotion needed for long-term growth.

Efforts by Mr. Gaudion to get divisions to implement this philosophy had taken a variety of forms, including periodic memoranda on pricing and frequent jawboning about price leadership. During the winter of 1971, Mr. Gaudion's price leadership crusade focused on the company's recent annual operating results, which showed shipments up 8 percent and earnings down 9 percent from the preceding year. (See Exhibit 3 for full text of recent memorandum on the subject.) While this "volume-profit relationship" was still better than for U.S. manufacturing firms in general,[7] it nevertheless indicated to Mr. Gaudion that divisions were emphasizing volume to the detriment of profits, and pointed to an overall failure to implement his price leadership policy:

The hard, cruel fact is that our figures show our shipments, incoming orders, and backlog up over last year. If they were off, we might at least have a reasonable excuse for our poor earnings performance. But this shows we do *not* have control of our prices! We *must* learn to manage our businesses in an inflationary economy.

o   o   o   o   o

We must *not* let volume absorb the inexorable inflationary cost creep. We must generate the "flywheel" effect of higher volumes into earnings gains of much greater proportions.

o   o   o   o   o

We *cannot* hide behind the fact that the United States may or may not be in a depression or recession. This is an internal management control problem! We can't overemphasize its critical nature.

---

[7] Which had shown a 12 percent decline to earnings accompanying a 3 percent increase in shipments for the first three quarters of 1970, according to the Quarterly Financial Reports for Manufacturing Corporations prepared by the Federal Trade Commission.

EXHIBIT 3
Management to management letter*

Donald A. Gaudion, president
Sybron Corporation

Subject: The cardinal sin of management—
Volume increases without greater proportionate increase in profit

Our annual report to shareholders shows our shipments for 1970 to be up 8 percent and our pretax earnings down 9 percent.

As all of you know, our long-range plans are (and have been for the past decade or more) predicated on building specialty, proprietary positions in carefully selected markets in which we have enough control of our prices to make sure we can cover the increasing costs of an inflationary economy. Obviously, 100 percent of our product lines do not fall into this category. But hopefully the preponderant do.

Our price leadership policy is based on the assumption that if we price ourselves out of the market on individual product lines, they are "bleeders," and we don't belong in those markets anyway. We are not at all "volume oriented." On most of our product lines the price leadership policy will give us the gross margins necessary to keep the outstanding product and market development people and programs which, in turn, will give us the proprietary positions necessary to maintain price leadership. And, in turn, our financial performance will give us the "blue-chip" market image that will keep our PE multiple up, and therefore our cost of capital competitively down, and our stock options valuable enough to keep top-quality people, and so on. In other words, it can be self-fulfilling or, as we have said, a "bootstrapping" method of obtaining and holding market leadership positions that spiral upward rather than downward.

WE ARE IN DANGER OF LOSING THIS HARD-FOUGHT BATTLE! Last year was the fourth year that our earnings have been essentially plateaued.

Yes, the papers are full of the fact that the United States is in a recession. So what are we complaining about? The hard, cruel fact is that our figures show our shipments, incoming orders, and backlog up over the same period last year. If they were off, we might at least have a reasonable excuse for our poor earnings performance. But this shows we do *not* have control of our costs and prices! And, therefore, credibility is developing on the image we have been slowly building. We *must* learn to manage our businesses in an inflationary economy.

When the markets of the 70s really get rolling, as we're sure they will, we must begin to show earnings per share gains of 50 percent or more. We did in the middle 60s in order to get back on our 15 percent compounded trend line. We can do it again. But we must *not* let volume absorb the inexorable inflationary cost creep. We must generate the "fly-wheel" effect of higher volumes into earnings gains of much greater proportions.

We *cannot* hide behind the fact that the United States may or may not

* Written by Mr. Gaudion, president, dated 1/27/71, and distributed to all division presidents.

EXHIBIT 3 (continued)

be in a depression or recession. This is an internal management control problem! We can't overemphasize its critical nature.

Corrective action taken now can hopefully still help in the current year. But what we're even more concerned with is learning lessons for the future from our problems of the current year. For example, we hope you'll have this experience firmly in mind as we move into budgeting this fall.

In the vernacular, we have all put a lot of blood, sweat, and tears getting to where we are today. Let's not blow it!

While Mr. Gaudion had met formally with PCD management only on infrequent occasions since the 1968 merger, he had nevertheless followed its pricing practices and in particular the AL–4 pricing situation with great interest, mainly through his routine relations with Mr. Fraser. He discussed this interest to the casewriter in early 1971 as follows:

I normally do *not* get involved in pricing decisions. Obviously, I am too remote at the present time from the pressure of the marketplace. On the other hand, I am constantly jawboning the necessity for our divisions to keep their prices ahead of the inflationary cost creep.

The reason I am more intimately involved in the Taylor matter is that they are a relatively new member of the family and we have not yet completely "Sybronized" them into our basic philosophies. Therefore, I have been hammering them on specific products as symbolic of the total pricing philosophy.

I have been undertaking this brainwashing program with Taylor in the past year or so since obviously they are a very important segment of our total earnings. I am afraid, like so many in American business, they are not used to managing a company in an inflationary economy of 6 percent to 8 percent or more. When inflation was in the Schlichter area of 2 percent or 3 percent, it was possible to grind out productivity improvements as an offset and it wasn't as necessary to think of regular annual price increases.

As part of his corporate-wide price leadership program, on April 2, 1971, Mr. Gaudion had sent to Mr. Billings, president of PCD, for circulation throughout the division a study of the chemical industry made by a leading investment banking firm, adding the following comment at the top of the study:

Because the study is such a classic analysis of an industry which has had phenomenal growth in volume and an excellent "new product" record and yet has continually declined in earnings, I thought you would be interested.

Portions of the study which were underlined by Mr. Gaudion are reprinted below:

Physical output of industrial chemicals, plastics, and fibers has increased at an average annual rate of 10.2 percent over 20 years, a performance unmatched by any comparably sized industry grouping. In spite of buoyant volume, the profit growth of the industry has been quite unsatisfactory. Industry pretax profit margin has declined almost continuously for 17 years, and, relative to all manufacturing concerns, for 10 years. Pretax profits for 15 major chemical companies in 1969 were only 22.7 percent greater than they were in 1959, although sales were up by 128 percent.

○   ○   ○   ○   ○

The decline in profitability that produced the poor market performance of chemical stocks has not been due to any reduction in growth in demand for chemical products. Rather, it has been the inability of the industry to transform good growth in demand into earnings growth. This, in turn, has been due in no small measure to the lack of control over the prices of large volume products, particularly those that are growing most rapidly.

○   ○   ○   ○   ○

Another aspect of the situation was the delegation of pricing decisions by management to marketing personnel fairly far down in the chain of command. With the emphasis on sales volume and market share, these people made or met prices without a direct appreciation of the effects on profitability.

○   ○   ○   ○   ○

The decline in prices was continuous and painful. It is worth noting that even when supply and demand were in good balance, producers were reluctant or unable to raise prices because of fear of antagonizing customers and losing business during an ensuing (and usually visible) period of overcapacity.

A few days later, Mr. Bruner offered his rebuttal to this price leadership philosophy in a memorandum addressed to Mr. Billings. (See Exhibit 4 for full text.) In commenting on the chemical industry analysis, Mr. Bruner acknowledged that "a very similar analysis could be made of the instrument industry," which he agreed had suffered declining profits for the same reason as the chemical industry: (1) overcapacity and (2) certain companies "who are dedicated to growth regardless of profit," that is, to price cutting. His solution to the dilemma appeared to be diametrically opposed to the price leadership strategy being espoused at the corporate level, however. He advised that as a competitor you "either play the game or lose your position" while naturally attempting "to be smarter in your cost controls, which includes more effective production from both engineering and factory dollars spent."

PRICE LEADERSHIP AND THE AL-4

Whether or not as a result of corporate pressure, PCD had instituted several across-the-board price increases in recent months: approximately 5

778

EXHIBIT 4
Memorandum dated April 14, 1971, written by Mr. Bruner, vice president of marketing, Process Control Division, to Mr. Billings, president of Process Control Division

Subject: Smith Barney & Company
Chemical Industry Analysis

I have read carefully this introductory report, and I think I can understand why Don Gaudion was anxious to circulate the article. I have a nagging feeling that any chemical company that didn't want to play the game could have passed out of existence, resulting in a substantial loss to the owners. Probably the only way this sad record could have been changed would be for the companies to collaborate and adjust prices, which would be in violation of the principles of the free enterprise system.

A very similar analysis could be made of the instrument industry. As an industry, we have had good growth in volume and new products, but profits have not grown proportionately. There have been a number of reasons, and one of the reasons is new companies with new plants and new investment attempting to invade the industry, creating overcapacity. I could mention two, such as Motorola and GE's present effort. In addition to these new companies with substantial resources attempting to carve out for themselves a position in the market, we have other companies who are dedicated to growth regardless of profit; these factors seem to dictate that you either play the game or lose your position.

I suppose that the only answer is to be smarter in your cost controls which includes more effective production from both engineering and factory dollars spent. Although Mr. Gaudion underlined that part of the report which refers to delegating the pricing to marketing management, I don't believe that marketing management in either the chemical or the instrument industry have a free hand; there is such a thing as price competition, and you can price yourself out of business either by being too low or too high. There are at least two things that we have to learn how to do. One is to do it right the first time, and I don't think our record has been too good in this area; and second, be sensitive to the competitive situation in the marketplace from both product performance and price.

I suppose the reason I have taken the time to make these comments is that it's frustrating to be on the receiving end of this constant barrage on price leadership without ever having the opportunity to make any counter statements. One of the other things that I did over the weekend was read the article you circulated on the organization and control of conglomerates.* I suppose it was because I wanted to, but one of the principal characteristics of successful conglomerates is, according to this article, the right for the lower echelons in the corporation (Division Level) to confront the corporate management. I will stop, not because I don't believe that there is much more that could be said, but because saying what I have said so far doesn't seem to have relieved my frustrations very much.

* Written by Mr. Gaudion.
Source: Company records.

EXHIBIT 5

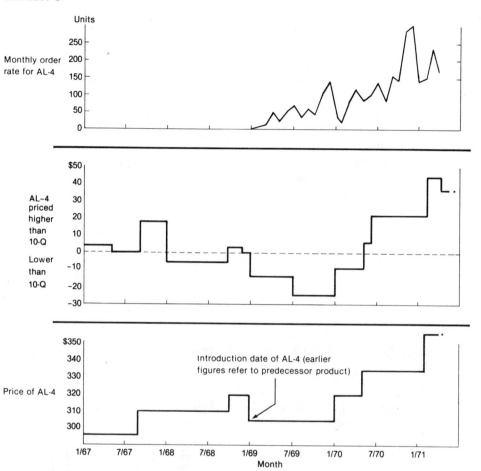

* As of April 19, 1971, prior to vote to lower price on the AL–4.
Source: Company records.

percent in December 1969, 5 percent in May 1970, and 7 percent in January 1971. Anchor had generally followed suit with proportionate though somewhat smaller increases for most competing products. An exception had been the 10–Q. As Exhibit 5 indicates, by April 1971 the AL–4 was priced $38 above the equivalent 10–Q model. While this differential did not yet appear to have seriously undermined the order rate for AL–4s, field sales reports were registering increasingly loud customer complaints. Excerpts from two such reports appear below:

> [Customer A] told me today, "We do think you have a better instrument than Anchor, but not $40 better."

*   *   *   *   *

We lost out this week on getting the annual stock supply business with [Customer B] and [Customer C]. That last 7 percent price increase is really killing it for us.

A further problem involved the whole issue of discounts. Anchor and several other competitors extended to a number of large customers what were referred to in the industry as "National Discounts" of up to 7 percent, constituting blanket discounts on all purchases, whether big or small, throughout the year. PCD had traditionally resisted pressure to discount. With the growing price differential between the AL–4 and the 10–Q, however, customers were increasingly requesting and demanding discounts even for small quantity purchases in order to yield an effective AL–4 price nearer to the 10–Q. A top PCD marketing executive described the danger of this situation as follows:

We've been known and respected in the industry as a one-price, no-bargain house. However, the pressure to discount the AL–4 has been mounting recently to such a level where we might have to yield on this point if we still want to stay in business. Yielding here might well increase our vulnerability to discounting in other product lines as well.

ARGUMENTS FAVORING PRICE REDUCTION

In light of growing customer dissatisfaction, PCD management had come increasingly to favor a price reduction on the AL–4, despite a continuing healthy order rate for the AL–4 and the price leadership philosophy espoused at the corporate level.

During mid-April 1971, about a week before the PCD management committee vote to reduce the price on the AL–4, the casewriter had an opportunity to discuss the AL–4 situation with various members of PCD management. A number of arguments for price reduction were made. For instance, Mr. Billings justified price reduction less on order rate figures than on intuitive feel for the industry:

I don't care what the figures show. I just don't feel it's in the cards for us to maintain any kind of volume over the long haul with a $40 price differential. We tend to be more influenced on this by comments of our customers than by the figures.

*   *   *   *   *

Our feeling is that your product's price simply has to be in line with your competitors'. There's just no way to get $2 for a $1 article.

He went on to clarify his position in light of PCD's overall pricing strategy:

Our basic philosophy is to give the customer the most for his dollar, keep our price down as much as we can, and grow.

This philosophy had apparently been modified somewhat since merger with Sybron, however:

I think in general we have been more aggressive at pricing since joining Sybron. This has naturally improved our margins somewhat. The argument has been that if we price aggressively we can pull the rest of the industry up with us. While this has been true in a number of instances, what do you do when a competitor lowers his price at the same time you're raising yours?

Mr. Bruner favored a price reduction mainly on product grounds:

I know that Mr. Gaudion feels our big mistake was originally pricing the AL–4 *below* instead of *above* competition. The trouble is, the AL–4 is really *not* a new idea; it is simply a *redo* of existing ideas. The product is just not worth $40 more than competition because it is not basically an innovative product. I do feel it's worth 3–4 percent above competition, however.

By contrast, Mr. Fraser based his position mainly on marketplace dynamics:

In a competitive economy, simply raising prices is not the way to make money. You can have all the formulas for pricing you want, but in the end you must finally set price based on what the market will bear, and the signals we've been getting from our customers since our 7 percent price increase in January indicate that the AL–4 is clearly out of line on price. We've put a lot of money into developing this product, and we want to make sure we don't sour its market early in the game by too high a price.

He went on, however, to acknowledge the value of price leadership in an industry such as instrumentation:

Several years ago a Yale professor of economics who had studied our industry in depth told us flatly, "You are throwing away your seed corn" by low-margin pricing. This is really what Don (Mr. Gaudion) has been saying, and I think we've gradually come to agree, at least to some extent. We've been feeling our way with this whole price leadership concept, hoping competition would follow. In general they have. However, in the case of the AL–4, while we think we do have a better instrument than competition, it's not $40 better. We just don't have enough features to warrant that kind of price differential.

While the link between price leadership and proprietary products seemed to be widely recognized at Sybron, there appeared to be some question as to whether PCD's products were in fact proprietary. A PCD salesman voiced his concern as follows:

We've been hearing a lot about proprietary design and price leadership from the corporate office. The trouble is I'm just not sure how valid these concepts are for our industry. For most of our products, the customer simply lines up our offering with those of two or three of our major competitors and picks off the one with the lowest price tag.

Mr. Von Berg, executive vice president, countered this argument by pointing out that proprietariness went considerably beyond product features alone.

> If our service is better than competition's, we have a proprietary edge. If our salesmen understand the customers' problems better than competition, this gives us a proprietary advantage. Our entire strategy, in fact, rests on our being stronger than competition in all these areas, and on being in the kind of business where customers are willing to pay for the benefits we can provide.

DECISION FACING MR. GAUDION

It was, therefore, in light of a complex set of market factors affecting the AL–4, as well as fundamental differences in pricing philosophy at different levels of the company, that PCD's management committee had met on the afternoon of April 19 and voted to reduce the price on the AL–4. Mr. Gaudion was naturally disappointed by the message just given him by Mr. Fraser, since the PCD vote went directly counter to a pricing philosophy which he had been expending a great deal of energy trying to sell to divisions, particularly to Instrument Group divisions. This disappointment was increased by the fact that the Instrument Group, which represented a very significant portion of Sybron's current business and was expected to constitute an even more significant contribution to future sales, had performed well below corporate norms during the three-year period since joining Sybron.

With such considerations in mind and with Mr. Fraser silent at the other end of the telephone line, Mr. Gaudion was wondering just what to say.

Sybron Corporation (C)

During the spring of 1971 Mr. Granger, president of the Permutit Division, one of about 50 divisions of Sybron Corporation, was trying to decide what tactics to employ to secure the resources he felt were needed to develop an instrumentation capability for his division. In his opinion, Permutit, an established name in the design, manufacture, and assembly of industrial and municipal water and waste treatment systems with total annual sales of about $15 million, required such capability in order to bolster its position in the municipal water treatment market.

Several alternatives appeared open to Mr. Granger. First, Permutit might make further attempts to solicit the assistance of Sybron's Process Control Division (PCD), which clearly possessed a closely related capability, since it was the third largest U.S. manufacturer of industrial process control instrumentation. Mr. Granger acknowledged that this alternative presented some difficulties, however. Ever since the former Taylor Instrument Company had become Sybron's Instrument Group through merger of the two companies in early 1968, Permutit had made repeated attempts to get PCD, the Instrument Group's largest division, to cooperate on a variety of projects ranging from joint development of a new product and then a new technology to arrangements for substantially increasing product transfers between the two divisions. Despite these efforts, cooperation between the two divisions by the spring of 1971 was limited to a minor amount of interdivisional product transfers.

A second alternative was to seek corporate help in securing the needed capability. In Mr. Granger's opinion there were at least two ways to go about this. One was to try to gain direct support from Mr. Gaudion, the corporate president. According to Mr. Granger:

> When Don (Gaudion) gets interested in something, things happen; when he doesn't, nothing happens. If he were really convinced that Sybron as a company would benefit from water instrumentation, he would see to it that Permutit obtained the needed capability, either by mandating that PCD

cooperate with us, or by acquiring the capability outside the company and placing it under our management.

Another way was to work through the corporate planning staff. Since this group had acknowledged on a number of occasions that water instrumentation provided an important opportunity for Sybron as a whole, it might be expected, with a little encouragement from Permutit, to work to convince top management to either develop or acquire the needed capability.

A final alternative was of course to simply give up trying to secure instrumentation capability and move on to other less attractive opportunities facing the division.

THE PERMUTIT DIVISION

Permutit designed and assembled, partly from self-manufactured (20 percent) and partly from purchased (80 percent) components, a variety of custom-designed water treatment systems for both industrial and municipal users as well as waste treatment systems for industrial users. Water treatment equipment represented over 90 percent of division sales, with almost 80 percent going to industrial customers. Sales were made direct to industrial customers and through agents as well as direct to municipal customers. Permutit estimated that it commanded the following approximate shares of the markets it served: industrial water treatment, 17 percent; municipal water treatment, 9 percent; and industrial waste treatment, 4 percent.

Permutit had regularly performed well below corporate return on assets and earnings growth targets since becoming a part of Sybron in 1957. One corporate staff executive attributed Permutit's difficulties mainly to competitive pressures within its markets:

> There's been so much talk about pollution control in the past several years that many new firms have entered Permutit's markets recently, largely through acquisition. In a number of cases there have been substantial companies willing to take losses for several years in order to build strong positions in what is increasingly touted to be a burgeoning industry with tremendous long-range potential. All this has naturally depressed profits of many firms traditionally operating in the field.

One Permutit manager felt that part of the division's problems could be attributed to low morale at Permutit:

> In a sense, the history of Permutit since its merger with Sybron has been one of continuing failure, and this has demoralized division management. In 1962 Permutit's most profitable product line, ion-exchange resins, was spun off as a separate division, becoming the nucleus of what is now the fastest growing and most profitable group in Sybron, Specialty Chemicals. The effect on Permutit, however, was catastrophic. Since each water treatment system requires an essentially different custom design, there is no such thing

as standard products or even components in this business. In fact, ion-exchange resins was the closest thing Permutit ever had to a product line in the sense that our designs always incorporated ion-exchange technology utilizing this in-house resin source. With our resin source taken away, the only thing we were left with really was design expertise—experience and brains.

Several subsequent product development failures, involving first a home water softener and then a home fluoridator (for fluoridation of home water to reduce tooth decay), together with continued low profits depressed the division's morale to the point where in the mid-60s there began a substantial exodus of personnel to competitors. Partly to stem this tide and to demonstrate Sybron's long-term commitment to the pollution field, several million dollars in capital funds were appropriated for a new research center in late 1967, at just about the time Lee (Granger) took over as division president. While quite a few department managers have been replaced since, a number of the conservative old guard, essentially demoralized by this long series of events, are still here.

OPPORTUNITIES IN THE MUNICIPAL WATER TREATMENT MARKET

In light of this long history of reverses, Permutit had looked forward with much anticipation to Sybron's 1968 merger with the Taylor Instrument Company since Taylor was perceived as possessing resources potentially valuable to Permutit's markets. In a statement made to the press at the time of the merger, Mr. Shumway, chairman, expressed this feeling as follows:

> The combination of the two companies will bring together technology in both equipment and instrumentation which should strengthen each company in the markets which it serves.

For Permutit the combination was felt to present a unique opportunity for improving its declining position in the municipal water treatment market, which represented about 12 percent of divisional sales at the time of the merger. Approximately half these sales were of water flow measurement systems marketed under the trade name Flow-tap,[1] whose sales and market share had declined steadily in recent years. In a memorandum written shortly after the Taylor merger, Mr. Mertens, assistant to the president of the Permutit Division, described as follows the potential benefits to Flow-tap of the new combination:

> There is a large and growing market for municipal water instrumentation and control. It is a somewhat unique market requiring that a substantial portion of the instruments and controls be specially designed to accommodate the peculiarities of the waterworks field. It has traditionally been a most conservative and technically backward market. However, it

---

[1] Disguised name.

has been changing rapidly and is adopting modern techniques. While telemetry[2] and supervisory control have been used for years, a rapid expansion of their use is anticipated as larger systems are built and more remote operations required.

Permutit is in this market with Flow-tap, but its position is feeble. In truth, we have gradually been going out of the business over the years as our market share has been diminishing and we have done virtually nothing to maintain the line. Flow-tap has in fact been an orphan in industrially oriented Permutit.[3]

The merger with Taylor presents an opportunity, if properly exploited, to regain a strong position in this market. The fundamentals are there. While feeble, Flow-tap does have a basic position, particularly in the primary elements and those controls unique to the municipal water business and also in its long tradition in the marketplace. In addition, Permutit's extensive industrial water treatment capability provides a strong technological base from which to expand in the municipal market. PCD has a modern line of pneumatic and electronic instruments currently being supplied to the industrial market. With a little adaptation, these could presumably be made suitable for the municipal market. Most importantly, PCD has a strong technical organization in instrumentation. Flow-tap's most critical needs are in the technical area, basically, modernizing and expanding its products and designing and developing advanced control systems involving telemetry and supervisory control.

An alternative to improving Flow-tap's capability through a joint development effort with PCD would of course be acquiring such capability outside the company.

Mr. Mertens went on to justify allocating resources to Flow-tap despite generally lower profits on municipal than on industrial sales of instrumentation, and despite the fact that Permutit's performance measured by either return on assets or earnings growth had consistently been below that of PCD:

> While municipal water instrumentation is generally viewed as being less profitable than general industrial instrumentation, it is also considered to be more profitable than water treatment equipment. It is a field in which Sybron is currently involved through Permutit, and the proposed strategy is fundamentally one of expanding existing corporate positions and strengths. From this point of view, the strategy can be a lucrative one for the company as a whole. Hopefully, the combination of strengths, which would be unique in the field, would ultimately provide a strong enough position to improve profitability substantially.

The corporate planning staff had consistently supported Permutit in its campaign for a joint Permutit-PCD approach to this market. The industrial

---

[2] Techniques for transmitting signals over long distances.

[3] Over 80 percent of Permutit's sales were made to industrial rather than municipal customers.

water market was also felt to present considerable opportunity for joint effort. In the opinion of Mr. Feeley, corporate planning director, such cooperation was in the interest of Sybron as a whole for several reasons. First, as recently completed studies of the market served by the two divisions revealed, the water and waste treatment field represented a large and rapidly growing market. Statistics drawn from these studies appear as Exhibit 1.

EXHIBIT 1
Water and waste treatment market

	Municipal		Industrial		General industrial instrumentation market*
	water	waste	water	waste	
Current size of market ($ millions):					
Instrumentation	40	14	50	25	480
Equipment	40	65	65	35	
Projected growth rate of market:					
Instrumentation	12%		14%		9%
Equipment	12		14		
Recent profitability of market:†					
Instrumentation	6		7		9
Equipment	2		3		
Current market share for Sybron:					
Instrument (PCD)	‡	‡	‡	‡	10
Equipment (Permutit)	9%	‡	17%	4%	

* PCD's current market.
† Return on assets.
‡ Less than 1 percent.

Perhaps more important, Sybron was perceived as possessing a combination of capabilities uniquely suited to the needs of this field. Mr. Feeley commented on this situation as follows:

> Our analysis of the water and waste treatment industry indicates an increasing emphasis on complex, highly automated systems requiring integration of Permutit's type of equipment with instrumentation and controls such as those manufactured by PCD. Since no other company combines these capabilities, we have consistently felt that Sybron has a really unique position here.
>
> We're naturally disappointed that two years have gone by since our merger with Taylor without producing any significant cooperation between the two divisions.

THE PROCESS CONTROL DIVISION

Sybron's Instrument Group was the third largest worldwide manufacturer of process control instrumentation. Its Process Control Division, with

1970 sales in the $40–$50 million range, manufactured and sold direct, mainly to industrial customers, a complete instrument line including recorders, controllers, and various devices for sensing process parameters such as flow, pressure, level, temperature, and humidity. PCD commanded significant market shares, ranging from 20 to 50 percent in the food, chemical, paper, rubber, textile, and mining industries. Its share of the total industrial instrument market in 1970 was estimated at about 10 percent.

While the industry as a whole was growing at about 7–8 percent per year, certain segments, such as analytic instruments and digital computer control systems, were thought to be growing at double the average rate. Presumably in the interest of gaining an early lead in these high-growth segments, several major competitors had been spending unusually large amounts for R&D in recent years. One PCD executive commented as follows on the difficulties this situation created for the division:

> We've been keeping a close watch on the R&D efforts of competitors, who in several instances are spending considerably more than we are as a percent of sales. Fortunately, none of them has yet come out with any really significant breakthroughs. In fact, the combination of a large R&D budget plus severe price cutting throughout the industry created such a profit decline for one major competitor that they passed a quarterly dividend this year for the first time in several decades. Whether their big R&D outlays are going to pay off for them in the future or not we don't know. We're keeping our fingers crossed while at the same time trying to increase our own R&D efforts to put us a little more in line with others in the industry. Given our relatively low margins and Sybron's ambitious profit goals, finding enough R&D funds within the division to do this is certainly not an easy task, however.

All research and development for the entire Instrument Group was conducted by PCD and charged out to other divisions in the group on the basis of sales. These charges had ranged from 3 to 6 percent of sales in recent years.[4] Manufacturing costs for PCD products were thought to be about one-third variable, two-thirds fixed. Shipments in recent years had averaged between 60 percent and 80 percent of total manufacturing capacity. While performing considerably below corporate norms for return on assets and earnings growth since joining Sybron, PCD had nevertheless outperformed Permutit by a substantial margin.

PERMUTIT'S ATTEMPTS TO OBTAIN WATER INSTRUMENTATION CAPABILITY

Permutit had made repeated attempts since 1968 to get PCD to cooperate on a joint attack on the water treatment market. These had taken place

---

[4] Selected divisional data have been disguised.

in three major phases: (*a*) efforts to get PCD to develop and manufacture a line of flow indicating devices specially designed for the municipal water market, (*b*) attempts to negotiate lower transfer prices on standard PCD products purchased by Permutit, and (*c*) efforts to interest PCD in joint development of telemetry capability spanning the market needs of both divisions.

Phase 1: Flow indicating device.   In September 1968 Permutit had proposed that PCD develop and manufacture a flow indicating device to be sold through Permutit to the municipal water treatment market. Permutit at the time was purchasing approximately $125,000 annually of a similar device, at $480 per unit, from a competitor of PCD.[5] The device was used in conjunction with a Permutit Venturi tube (a section of pipe with a gradual, carefully machined internal diameter constriction) to measure water flow, and was marketed by Permutit through agents under the trade name Flow-tap. Due in large part to the increasingly obsolete nature of the product, Flow-tap's sales had declined steadily in recent years to approximately $600,000 by 1968.

According to Permutit management, Flow-tap's chief deficiency lay in the area of reliability and accuracy of the signal transmitted between the Venturi tube and the flow indicating device. A Permutit executive confessed that the whole area of signal transmission involved "a very complex technology which is frankly beyond the internal capability of our division." A major motive in having PCD supply the flow indicating device was therefore the hope that they would also supply enough signal transmission technology to improve Flow-tap's overall level of reliability.

Permutit's proposal to PCD was based on a design developed in 1965 for Permutit by Aero Chem, another division in the Process Equipment Group. The design work by Aero Chem had cost Permutit approximately $35,000. Several meetings, mainly between technical personnel of PCD and Permutit, had followed the original proposal. A full technical review of the design had been undertaken by PCD's engineering department, which in turn had proposed an alternate desgn and had drawn up detailed manufacturing cost estimates for both the original and the revised designs. These estimates were both substantially above the price Permutit was paying its outside supplier for the device currently in use. Furthermore, PCD had maintained that substantial additional engineering work, at an estimated cost of $2–$3 million, would be required prior to commercialization of the device, and that PCD itself would not be in a position to underwrite even a portion of these costs. Finally, because of its own heavy existing R&D commitments, PCD had claimed that it would not be able to begin development work on the device for at least two years even if Permutit decided to go ahead on the project.

---

[5] Selected divisional data have been disguised.

Mr. Granger, president of Permutit, explained that PCD's unexpectedly high estimates for engineering work resulted from a fundamental difference in product philosophy between the two divisions.

> What we wanted was simply a product to replace the unit we were purchasing on the outside, largely to get us out of the technical problems plaguing us in the field. PCD, on the other hand, as a matter of policy, apparently wants to develop only full lines of products with many sizes and options, suitable for application across many industries. To do this for the flow device would have involved considerably more engineering work than we were prepared to underwrite.

The two divisions had had no significant discussions on the subject since the November 1968 meeting. By 1971, Permutit was still purchasing all Flow-tap flow measuring devices from outside sources.

Phase 2: Product transfers. Starting in December 1968 Permutit had begun to initiate proposals aimed at increasing the amount of product transferred between the two divisions. While virtually no products were being transferred from Permutit to PCD at the time, Permutit was purchasing approximately $50,000 annually from PCD at the same discounts which PCD extended to its EOM customers and to other divisions in the Instrument Group.[6] As the resulting price was in general well above PCD's variable costs, Permutit had hoped to negotiate a lower price. With this object in mind, Mr. Mertens had proposed the following in a letter to PCD's treasurer:

> As I indicated to you in our phone conversation a few minutes ago, the following is a proposal as to the approach we should take in establishing transfer prices between our two divisions. It seems to me just common sense that since we both contemplate buying from the other, whatever formula we agree to should be something that can be applied both ways. I would suggest that we follow this overall approach:
>
> 1. We should recognize that in large measure transfers between us would involve incremental business and that the underlying formula should recognize this.
> 2. We will want to agree on some overall cost relationships as expressed in some broad, well-documented source such as the 1969 budget.
> 3. The formula that we agree on should be easily administered and require a minimum of interpretation on individual transfers. The formula approach that I am proposing is as follows:
>
>   Transfer price = Out-of-pocket cost, plus some contribution to fixed and nonvariable cost, plus a fair return on assets employed
>
> This formula recognizes the marginal aspect of our transaction. What it does is to allow sellers in each case to recover their variable or out-of-

---

[6] Fifteen percent to 20 percent below list price, depending upon the particular product line involved.

pocket cost, to make some contribution to fixed overhead, and to make a fair return on the assets employed.

PCD had responded by requesting a detailed list of products and quantities desired. Permutit's reply had indicated an interest in purchasing a total of approximately $400,000 annually from PCD, contingent upon a more favorable price. In a series of verbal exchanges which followed, PCD had shown sustained reluctance to lower the current transfer price, however. Permutit had then countered with a variety of arguments (see Exhibit 2 for some of these). PCD's final reply had come during February 1969 in a letter from Mr. Lockwood, sales manager of PCD:

> After receiving your recent letter listing quantities of instruments desired, we reviewed the quantities, looked at our profitability picture, examined our conscience, and came to the conclusion that the quantities which you propose would not materially affect our overall budgets, nor, in our opinion, warrant special consideration for Permutit or Flow-tap over and above the consideration which we give to other divisions in the Instrument Group. We propose therefore that you be treated just as any other division of the Instrument Group, which would mean a 20 percent discount on all pneumatic instruments and a 15 percent discount on all electronic instruments. We propose further that on those few occasions where an extraordinary quantity is involved, either you or your designated agent contact me to discuss any other action which might be appropriate.

About a year later one PCD executive commented as follows on this decision:

> After considering Permutit's proposals we decided we just couldn't make a decent profit if we gave Permutit a better price than we give other divisions in our group. Furthermore, it wouldn't be fair to our own divisions to do so. The trouble is, of course, that after Permutit pays its jobbers 8 percent and extends its usual customer discounts, it ends up making very little if any profit on sales of products purchased from us. I'm afraid that a rigid profit center structure is simply not very conducive to synergism of the kind Permutit is after. Customers don't want to pay two profits on what they buy. We just haven't yet found a way to combine profit centers and yet have the customer pay a single profit.

Another PCD executive commented as follows on the more general issue of synergy:

> Synergy with Sybron so far has been a flop as far as we're concerned. Other divisions either want to sell us a service we don't want or get us to sell a product at a price where we can't make any money. This beautiful idea of a diversified company coming up with synergism is great, but if you have individual profit centers where each person is looking out for his own welfare, synergism just isn't going to work.

In the face of this impasse, Permutit purchases of PCD products had increased only slightly, to an annual level of about $100,000, by early 1971.

EXHIBIT 2
Arguments why Process Control Division should give Permutit preferential prices vis-à-vis OEMs & other Instrument Group divisions

---

A. *Marginal income argument*
   1. We are considering here only business that comes into the company *through the efforts and market position of Permutit.*
   2. Any such business is essentially *incremental business* to the company. By this we mean that no significant additional overhead will be required of PCD to support the business.
   3. The full *variable profit* (selling price less variable costs) will *accrue to Sybron.*
   4. The split of this profit between PCD and Permutit will depend upon the intracompany transfer price. If the price is that determined by PCD's intragroup discount (which is essentially equivalent to what Permutit gets from outside suppliers), then *all of the incremental profit will flow to PCD and Permutit will get none.*
   5. For Permutit to participate in this profitability, it *must have a discount greater than* that given to PCD's OEM customers and other Instrument Group divisions.

B. *Comparability with Instrument Group divisions' argument*
   1. *Transfer price* to other Instrument Group divisions is *arbitrarily based* on U.S. OEM discount price, and not on an incremental cost calculation.
   2. Other Instrument Group divisions are simply *filling overall PCD line,* not expanding coverage into new markets.
   3. Permutit instrumentation sales require *additional noninstrumentation costs* to design PCD into water and waste treatment applications.
   4. Permutit has *alternative sources of instrument supply,* while other Instrument Group divisions necessarily must use PCD equipment.
   5. Since PDC and other Instrument Group divisions are *all in the same group,* some price pressure is relieved; price is important but less critical than for transfers across groups.

C. *Other arguments*
   1. Instrumentation for Permutit is a start-up situation—needs added incentive.
      a. Permutit will incur *incremental costs in pushing instrumentation.*
      b. Permutit will also incur *added costs in terminating old relationships* with former instrument suppliers.
   2. Permutit will have to incur the substantial *costs of designing systems* into which PCD instruments will be placed.
   3. *Permutit's margins and overall profitability are so low* that it can't support water and waste treatment instrumentation effort at a no-profit basis.

Source: Memorandum (with slight deletions) dated February 3, 1969, from Mr. Mertens, assistant to the president of the Permutit Division, to the treasurer of the Process Control Division.

Phase 3: Joint acquisition. By early 1969 Permutit had renewed its search for ways of strengthening Flow-tap, whose sales had continued to decline throughout 1968 and 1969. Since efforts to get PCD to cooperate had not been successful, Permutit this time had turned to the corporate level for assistance, proposing that Sybron acquire a small telemetry firm possessing the capability Permutit required. Corporate's reply had been that it might favor such an acquisition if PCD felt it would also benefit from the move. PCD, which like Permutit was virtually without telemetry capability, had expressed some initial interest in the proposal, considering it a possible means of improving its own position in oil production and gas transmission markets, which were demanding increasingly sophisticated telemetering systems for communicating flow data over the long distances separating field locations from central control stations. A fundamental difference in telemetry requirement appeared to present a problem, however.

Dr. Tatsig, PCD's director of research and development, discussed this a year later with the casewriter as follows:

> Permutit's telemetering needs are a great deal more basic and less expensive to develop than ours. What they need is simple "pulse duration" communication involving a very basic electronic counting technique. Pipeline or oil field applications, on the other hand, where numerous remote locations are tied to a central control station, require "coded" communication which is inherently a lot more expensive to develop than the simple "pulse duration" type. The underlying technologies are fundamentally different enough, we feel, that work on one would provide little spin-off for the other, and vice versa.

Recognizing this potential incompatibility of need, Permutit's original written proposal had recommended that Sybron acquire a company possessing telemetry capability broad enough to span the interests of both divisions:

> We are not looking for a specific product "fix" but rather for a broad technical base from which to develop telemetry capability suitable to the needs of both divisions.

Permutit had then proceeded to identify and evaluate in a preliminary way several acquisition candidates. Following considerable discussion between the two divisions at both the technical and management levels, PCD had finally decided that sufficient community of interest did not exist to warrant a joint effort. By early 1971 telemetry discussions between the two divisions had ceased, no telemetry acquisition had been made, and Flow-tap sales were continuing to decline. PCD in the meantime had hired one telemetry engineer who was proceeding in a modest way to develop PCD's own capability for oil field and gas transmission applications.

SITUATION IN THE SPRING OF 1971

Apparently undaunted by these repeated failures, both the Permutit Division and the corporate planning staff in early 1971 appeared to be still strongly in favor of a joint Permutit-PCD effort in the municipal water market. PCD management cited a number of disadvantages to such a joint effort, however. First, it was felt to benefit Permutit more than PCD:

> The real problem is that Permutit really hasn't got much of a package to offer us. They have a very small manufacturing operation and virtually no product line. Most of their work is simply assembly of products purchased

794

on the outside. I just don't see how we stand to benefit much from working on a joint project with them.

Second, PCD apparently placed higher priorities on opportunities existing within their own markets:

> I must admit I feel a little guilty about not doing more with Permutit. The trouble is, a person has just so much time and money and naturally gravitates towards the most profitable opportunities first.

Third, Permutit's offer to enter a new market was felt to conflict with a major tenet of PCD's strategy:

> Our strategy has become one of intensification rather than diversification. You just can't be all things to all people. That's why we've decided to concentrate on the industrial markets we're already serving.

Fourth, municipal and industrial markets were perceived as requiring quite different skills and resources:

> Selling to municipalities is a very different sort of business from the one we're used to. It requires a different kind of selling: working through city councils, taxpayer groups, sealed bids, and so on. We don't want government business. Our business is to produce industrial instrumentation aimed at lowering cost and increasing the quality of our customers' products. Since we save a customer money, the customer is willing to pay us for this. Municipal customers are being forced to buy because of statutes, not because the equipment helps them increase their profits. This inevitably makes them "hard" buyers looking only at price.

Fifth, supplying components on a subcontract basis was not thought to be a very attractive business to be in:

> All of Permutit's proposals so far have been aimed at putting us in a supplier relationship to them, since we would become their subcontractor for instruments which they in turn would sell to the final customer. Unfortunately, this is just the kind of arrangement we don't want to get into. It's very important to us to deal directly with the final customer in order to get to know this customer better so that we can really understand his problems and needs. Otherwise, it is very difficult for us to provide the service and backup upon which our reputation has been built over the years.

While showing very little interest in cooperating with Permutit in a joint attack on the water and waste treatment market, PCD had not neglected this field altogether. A specialist had recently been hired by PCD to bid on water and waste business for the division, and as a result PCD had already submitted instrumentation bids on several industrial jobs for which Permutit had bid to supply the underlying equipment.

THE DECISION FACING MR. GRANGER

With his division facing intense competition in industrial markets and a continuing decline in sales to municipalities, Mr. Granger was understandably eager to pursue any avenue of potential opportunity. The municipal water field was perceived to be the most significant of these, but success in this market required an instrumentation capability which his division lacked the internal resources to develop. Therefore, the opportunity could be realized only by securing such capability outside of the division itself:

> As you know, we began by looking to PCD for the required capability. As you also know, this has not been very successful, to say the least. I'm wondering whether it isn't time now to shift emphasis from PCD to the corporate level. In other words, if I can't convince Billings (president of PCD), maybe my next move should be to try to convince Don (Gaudion). I know this isn't going to be easy, though. I have talked with Don many times about this, but he invariably ends up saying that divisions must settle this kind of difference between themselves. I don't see how he can really say this, though, since he in the end is the one who really gets things moving in this company. When he gets interested, things happen. When he doesn't, they don't. Take Sybron's chemicals business, for instance. One of the main reasons we're big in this area today is that Don got so interested in chemicals in the early 60s that he took Ionac right out of Permutit and set it up as a separate division. Ionac of course became the nucleus of what is now the Chemicals Group, one of the most profitable and fastest growing segments of the company. This shows that Don is certainly aware that organizations sometimes do need redirecting. As far as I'm concerned, this water instrumentation merry-go-round is a prime example of this. After all, we have spent a great deal of time and money so far on this effort with very little to show for it. Something certainly needs to be done soon.

case 35

Sybron Corporation (E)

BACKGROUND

Sybron in 1954 was an old, reasonably profitable company (Pfaudler) with a 70 percent market share of a cyclical, slow-growth, and technologically vulnerable industry (glass-lined steel tanks for the chemical and process industries). They were concerned about their future (only $16 million in sales, limited internal growth opportunities, and attractive balance sheet and cash flow), but rather than accept a "friendly take-over" by General Dynamics at a substantial premium, they decided to strike out on their own to build a growth company.

Sixteen years and many acquisitions later, Sybron consisted of 25 domestic and 25 international divisions, with sales over $300 million. The stock price had increased by a factor of 13 during the period, and was eight times more than it would have been if the original General Dynamics merger offer had been accepted. During the last five years earnings per share had been relatively flat, however, and the stock price had suffered in the 1968 market break (see Exhibit 1).

Donald Gaudion, who was a young vice president of sales for Pfaudler in 1954, was the principal proponent of the growth strategy and the president of the company since the mid-50s. As of 1970 the principal products of Sybron, with percentage of total sales and profits, respectively, were as follows:

1. *Instruments*—24 percent, 19 percent—third largest U.S. manufacturer (Taylor Instrument Division), also four foreign divisions.
2. *Health*—41 percent, 37 percent—a major factor in dental equipment and supplies, also in hospital products.
3. *Process, water, and waste treatment equipment*—23 percent, 27 percent—of sales.
4. *Specialty chemicals*—12 percent, 17 percent—most profitable and fastest growing segment.

EXHIBIT 1

Historical financial data (per share amounts)

	1954	1955	1956	1957	1958	1959	1960	1961	1962	1963	1964	1965	1966	1967	1968	1969	1970
Net sales	16	14	18	39	33	38	51	50	51	54	59	134	165	187	265	300	333
Net income (after tax)	0.7	0.6	0.9	1.5	1.4	1.7	2.0	2.1	2.2	2.3	2.9	8.0	10.5	12.4	14.8	16.7	16.1
Income per share (after tax)	0.34	0.30	0.44	0.48	0.44	0.52	0.59	0.61	0.64	0.66	0.84	1.15	1.30	1.44	1.35	1.45	1.38
Long-term debt ..	1	1	1	1	2	3	3	8	8	6	6	12	10	17	28	54	60
Common equity ..	8	8	9	14	15	17	18	20	21	23	25	59	72	87	124	134	140
Approximate price range of stock	1–3	2–3	3–4	3–5	4–5	5–6	5–9	9–18	7–13	9–10	10–15	12–17	18–26	20–42	32–44	27–38	20–45

Source: Financial data for Sybron are as reported in annual reports of Sybron Corporation and its successor companies, without retroactive restatement for pooling of interest of acquired companies. Per share amounts have been adjusted to reflect all subsequent stock dividends and splits. All dollar figures are in millions except for per share figures which are in dollars.

Operations outside the United States accounted for 35 percent of Sybron's total worldwide sales of $378 million.

This case focuses on a number of issues currently considered by Mr. Gaudion, the president, to be of importance to the long-run growth and profitability of the company.

> Of course I have to concern myself with the current operations and performance of our divisions, but I cannot afford to let the daily and seemingly more pressing problems divert too much of my time from broader and longer term issues. Unfortunately, the current problems and issues have a way of continually intruding on the time of any executive, for the very good reason that there are usually people directly concerned with the problems and pressing for their resolution. Nobody is beating down my door to get a resolution of what Sybron should aspire to for the year 2000, though, so I have to make sure I devote sufficient attention to such issues myself, as well as get others interested in them.
>
> Perhaps the best way to explain to you the issues I am most concerned with is to give you some discussion memoranda I have written during the past year. I simply distributed these to our corporate executives and our division managers in the hopes they would stimulate their thinking. Perhaps we should provide for some more systematic attention to defining these issues, establishing some priorities for attacking them, and coming to some conclusions about them, but we have not done that as yet.

Three of Mr. Gaudion's memoranda are reproduced (with minor deletions) in Exhibits 2, 3, and 4. They deal principally with three interrelated questions:
1. What growth goals should the company establish?
2. What businesses should the company seek to be in?
3. How much coordination and integration of businesses should be attempted?

As may be seen, Mr. Gaudion was becoming more and more convinced that size was beginning to bring significant disadvantages as well as advantages, and that many other larger companies seemingly had not found a very effective way to deal with these disadvantages.

EXHIBIT 2

The Seventies—The Case for No Biggerness

Donald A. Gaudion
February 4, 1970

Almost two decades ago (1954) we wrote an outline of some of the advantages of corporate size, entitled "The Case for Bigness." Among other things it was proposed that several Rochester companies band together to avoid being taken over by the conglomerators and raiders of the 50s. At that time most of us were in

EXHIBIT 2 (continued)

the $10–$15 million category. In the ensuing period we have followed this policy with the result that we are now in the $350 million size, with a five-year plan taking us to the half-billion-dollar mark, even without any sizable acquisitions.

The question is now, should we continue our aggressive, though highly selective, acquisition program? Or should we stick to largely internal development, with perhaps an even more selective policy of a very limited number of "niche-fillers." (Basically, the purchase of "product lines" that supplement existing product lines?) It should be clearly stated, contrary to the title of this paper, that this internal development would be expected to generate a 10 percent to 15 percent per share annually *earnings* growth. We are *not* building a case for "no bigger-ness" in earnings.

We have largely achieved the element of bigness outlined in the 1954 report. We have a NYSE listed stock rapidly achieving investment status. We have minimized our capital goods cyclical image, diversified our fields of interest to where market and product obsolescence is not likely to have significant impact, built an organization of generalists and specialists in depth, developed over $100 million of volume overseas, with solid organizations in the "developed" areas and at least skeleton organizations in the LDCs (less developed countries). Furthermore, we have built the necessary team to analyze, screen, negotiate, and operate a multinational, multidivisional organization that currently numbers over 50 segments.

Analysis of our acquisition program will indicate that the earnings growth rate of our acquisitions exceeds that of the base companies from which we began. In other words, we have successfully "boot-strapped" our way into areas of higher growth. With "minimum disruption" of the basic momentum of the companies we merged, we have developed dynamic management teams at the divisional level. The budgetary, long-range planning, manpower inventory, goal setting performance reviews, reporting and control disciplines have been instituted and continue to develop.

Then why not let the program continue to develop, adding additional divisions and further diversification as long as they meet our increasingly stringent requirements?

Basically, we are now concerned with the problems of "giganticism."

First, let's look at the case histories of some of the giants. The "blue chips" of the pre–1950 era, such as the motors, the large chemicals (Du Pont, Monsanto, Dow, Carbide, Cyanamid, etc.), AT&T did pretty well with earnings growth in the decade following World War II. But somewhere around 1957–58 they began to soften and their performance in the 60s has been dismal. The conglomerators of the 50s, such as General Dynamics, Brunswick, GPE, AMF, and so on, developed massive cases of indigestion during the 60s even though some of them, such as Brunswick (based on leisure time and health), seemed to be soundly conceived. They would now be termed "concept" stocks.

As we all know, these painful problems of indigestion were no deterrent to the merger and acquisition trend in the 60s as companies like Litton, Gulf and Western, Kidde, Teledyne, Whittaker, "Automatic" Sprinkler, LTV, and dozens of others sprang up. And with the magic of PE multiple leverage (as long as massive doses of new leverage were added), they looked like the "wave of the future."

EXHIBIT 2 (continued)

With their multimarket diversification, decentralized global operations they were predicted to be best able to cope with our rapidly changing world. Yet, following mysteriously similar timing to those of the 50s, they all fell out of bed in the last couple of years of the 60s.

Let me quickly say at this point *I* believe most of them *will* survive and they will go on into the 70s being basically sound companies with good growth in volume. But what I am concerned about is their *earnings* growth rate. We know that much of their earnings growth during the 60s was due to financial leverage rather than "internal" development. That cannot go on due to its nonrecurring nature and what I believe will be relatively permanent higher interest rates. And, as will be discussed later, I am concerned about the diminishing rate of return brought on due to the management problems of size alone. So, history seems to indicate that the "billion-dollar club" is made up of affluent members as far as volume of sales and stability are concerned. *But* the club lapel pins showing the PE multiples are not going to be worn nearly as proudly since the rate of earnings growth will be lower than the "lean and hungry" bourgeoisie trying to get into the club.

Why, with all the prestige of size, can't they outdistance their smaller rivals in earnings growth rate?

Obviously, the answer is complex. I believe it is a blend of the management problems of size combined with the government pressures to prevent monopoly.

I can quickly dispose of the government factor by saying that if we had true laissez-faire, size via monopoly *would* be unbeatable. General Motors and AT&T, for example, *would* run out their competition and then raise prices to whatever extent necessary to give them the optimum and necessary earnings growth rate and stock price. We have long since passed the point of questioning government regulation of monopoly, and now only try to keep it reasonably livable and then try to adapt to it. We then address ourselves to the question of management of the billion-dollar-plus corporation. Obviously, the billion-dollar bench mark is symbolic—it may be high or it may be low, depending, probably, on the complexity of the product line. But somewhere in this range the problems of keeping a profit-conscious organization become increasingly difficult. It will be noted, I have said "increasingly difficult" and *not* "impossible." Perhaps by spelling out and analyzing some of the reasons for failure, the organizational techniques for correcting these problems may be devised.

Simple arithmetic, or "the trees don't grow to the sky" theories, account for much of the problem. The dynamic new company, *if it survives babyhood,* is likely to be "lean and hungry"; has a small group of highly motivated, entrepreneurial people; probably has a strong, authoritarian leadership; ruthlessly eliminates people who do not contribute in an above-average way to its objectives; has few communications problems since the group is small. But, of course, it also has a *much* higher degree of risks as the people who play the "new issue" game know.

By decentralized (almost fragmented) divisional management we have *tried* to keep alive the entrepreneurial spirit of these small companies and yet add the stability and attributes of size—"The Case for Bigness." By and large, we have achieved much of this objective in our development to date, and our growth rate in earnings per share *has* been substantially above average, as outlined in the be-

EXHIBIT 2 (continued)

ginning of this report. And, although the figure seems to be difficult to come by, not over a quarter (and perhaps less) of our 10–15 percent compounded earnings growth rate has come about through "Chinese money"—acquisition leverage in the first year of merger.

The problem of size seems to center around motivation and communications. Movement alone breeds excitement and attracts the type of management that likes a fast-moving, fluid (almost chaotic) atmosphere. "Success breeds success." So we have been blessed with an ability to hire and keep the profit-oriented, entrepreneurial types. In many cases we have acquired companies that are still being managed by the entrepreneur who fought them up from scratch.

Then, from a motivation point of view, why change course? For one reason, as the number of these units increases, the percentage contribution of the single unit to the total becomes automatically smaller and, therefore, the management gets an increasing feeling that they have little to do with overall performance. Yet their stock options, bonus, and so on, are tied strongly to corporate performance. Why not tie then to divisional performance? Then we develop even greater fragmentation than we have now, *no* synergism (although there isn't much now) and essentially become a closed-end investment trust.

Closely allied to this element is the averaging down problem. Ideally *all* of the divisions would end up every year exactly on the corporate target for return on assets employed, earnings growth rate, and so on. Actually it is a spectrum with rather wide variation. Theoretically, we would chop off, in one way or another, all those below the corporate norm. In a large sense, we try to do this by building the weaklings up. If performance shows no chance of meeting the norm, it will be eliminated, but this takes time. In the meantime the high performers tend to be demotivated.

Another aspect of motivation has to do with "executive perks," capital expenditures, paper work, corporate airplanes, and so on. How do these all get lumped together? When one division gets a brand new plant, or has a new fringe benefit, or a new control procedure, others want it. Yes, controls *are* in effect to make sure that every item is checked out in terms of its effect on profit, but paper controls are a poor substitute for the "hard-driving, penny-pinching manager." And also who knows when the "h–d–p–p* manager" is "milking" the operation—showing excellent short-run performance but leaving a shell to his successor. This type of subjective evaluation is always the source of much disagreement in the company. Quantitative analysis we have. But how do we do on qualitative analysis? It probably takes a decade to *really* arrive at a provable qualitative judgment on many of these factors. And by then we may be in catastrophic trouble.

Again, the problem of span of control. The man at the top of the pyramid is finally responsible for making these qualitative, subjective judgments. Over how large an organization can he do this successfully?

This leads into the question of communications. The airplane has facilitated the man-to-man confrontations around the world necessary to make such judgments and to make sure the "party line" is understood, with all of its refinements and innuendoes. But the human body has not been improved enough to maintain

---

* Hard-driving, penny-pinching.

EXHIBIT 2 (concluded)

such a schedule without wearing out at an early age. And we must hire only bachelors or risk ending up with broken family lives throughout the company.

Trying to pulse the point of diminishing returns is extremely difficult. Perhaps that statement in itself indicates we are beyond it? I hope not. But there are red flags, or at least yellow ones, flying here and there in the organization. And, if nothing else, we should devise a control mechanism which will gauge this point. How serious are our communications and motivation problems? Are the measurable advantages of size and momentum continuing to offset the known deteriorating entrepreneurial spirit? In the final analysis, a slowing of the EPS growth rate is the certain signal. I don't want to be around when that signal flashes!

In the meantime (and in order *not* to end on a dismal note) we *must* continue to explore new techniques of organization, motivation, and control. This, again, requires a never-ending search for innovative people. It also necessitates continuing study of the experience of others. So far, the innovations of people like Jimmy Ling (e.g., spinning off segments of the whole in order to motivate their managers) have not looked too exciting. Perhaps we can devise some better ones.

In the meantime, I feel no great urge to rush into membership in the billion-dollar club except through internal growth and very carefully "screened niche-fillers."

EXHIBIT 3

The Seventies—Can We Repeal the Law of the S Curve?

Donald A. Gaudion
February 23, 1970

We are all familiar with the almost inexorable law of the S curve as it applies to the life cycle of a new product. The new product is usually slow to get started, but as it gains market acceptance its volume growth speeds up. Then as competitors find an attractive market they copy it, work around its patents, and begin to tap the lucrative market. The product growth curve begins to shoulder off and, if there are no improvements, eventually goes into a decline. The trick, of course, is to either constantly improve the product ahead of competition or bring out other new products that are in the base of the S-curve phase of development.

In earlier memos on "The Seventies," we have implied that corporate growth tends to follow the same pattern—at least, perhaps, growth in earnings per share, if not volume. As we tried to get at the reason for this we felt it revolved around motivation of management and communications, rather than anything more fundamental since theoretically a fully decentralized divisional operation should be essentially the same as an independent small company.

Since we were talking mostly about *earnings growth rates*, as opposed to volume growth, let's analyze another interesting element. John Kenneth Galbraith, in his *New Industrial State*, makes a very plausible case for the fact that *big* business had already, in cooperation with *big* government and *big* labor, taken over

EXHIBIT 3 (continued)

society, with the implication that it could do whatever it wishes. If this is so, why can't big business develop an earnings growth rate that will give it the 25 plus PE multiple necessary to keep its capital cost in line?

As summarized in "Business and the Consumer,"[*] this reasons "that the American economy consists of two quite different economic systems:

> "The 'entrepreneurial economy' of over 11 million enterprises, largely controlled by owners and working in a competitive system to 'maximize profits' which will accrue to these owners; and,
>
> "A 'mega-economy' of a few hundred super-corporations dominating the whole economy and all aspects of our lives and shaping a future in which the whole society must live.
>
> "Under this view, the two economic systems are totally different: the competitive one, virtually helpless in a marketplace which it cannot greatly influence or control—and threatened by government, labor, competitors, and the whims of consumers; while the mega-economy is controlled by a bureaucratic and managerial group—referred to as 'the technostructure'—which seeks power along with profits.
>
> "Galbraith and his followers claim that the latter system generally has been successful in creating an autonomous area of such power that it can plan its own prices, production, and growth and has either neutralized or allied with the government, its competitors and outside financiers, so that it can pass higher costs, including taxes and wages, and even the burden of dividends on to the public by raising prices."

If we look at the post–World War II period of vastly increased costs for such items as wages, a variety of fringes such as pension costs, which alone now equal 10 percent or more of the payroll, Blue Cross, constantly rising social security taxes, and so on, all of which are ground into increasing material costs, it would seem that industry *has* been capable of "passing these costs on to the consumer." In effect, industry, in the case of increased local, state, and federal taxes, is just the collection agent for the government and, I believe, probably a more efficient one than many of others involved in the intricate system of amassing the 38–40 percent of the gross national product being used to run our governments. So, as long as these taxes (and other costs) are being assessed equally to all competitors, they eventually *are* passed along in the form of higher prices.

Then, coming back again to our fundamental question, why have the *shareholders* of these "mega-corporations" *not* fared well? As we know, the aftertax profits of industry tend to average out around 5 percent of the sales price. In an average company, therefore, an increase in prices of 1 percent (assuming, for the moment, other costs remain the same) would increase aftertax profits by ½ percent which, of course, is a 10 percent increase in earnings. A 2 percent increase in prices equals a 20 percent increase in earnings, and so on.

The only point of this exercise is to dramatize the fact that a very small (compared to our inflationary price increases of recent years) increase in prices would

[*] U.S. Chamber of Commerce.

EXHIBIT 3 (continued)

make a great increase in percentage earnings. Parenthetically, as all Sybron people know, it is one of the baffling phenomena of large companies *to me* to know how we will take in some $350 million this year on the basis of thousands of different pricing decisions in over 50 different autonomous divisions and end up in December each year worrying about meeting or missing budget by a few cents per share, each aftertax cent of which equals a little over $100,000 (1 cent on 11 million shares). It would appear that we *are* able to pass on all of our cost increases on a *very precise* basis!

This ability to pass on increased costs *has* been true of all of the "mega-corporations," the "blue-chip" companies that we discussed in earlier memos. None of them, to my knowledge, has gone bankrupt. Most of them have shown average earnings. Few have cut dividends. They just haven't grown at above average rates.

Then let's talk about the *cost* of capital as opposed to the costs of wages, materials, taxes, and so on. We are seeing interest costs practically doubling in a very short span of years. We are also witnessing companies increasing their debt-equity ratios. Since this is a fixed cost ground into the profit and loss statement before taxes, I predict the mega-corporations will pass it on to their customers in the form of higher prices. It therefore becomes just another contributor to the inflationary cycle. There *will* be loud screaming about the cost-profit squeeze, and it *will* take time, but eventually it will be recognized as a relatively permanent cost increase that we're not going back to 4–5 percent interest rates, and it will be built into costs.

If the increased cost of debt is about to be recognized and built into the cost-price system, why not the increased profits needed to maintain the equity market, the price of the stock? As we all know, traditionally profit (or loss) is what is left over after all the bills have been paid. Therefore, return on the shareholders' equity has *not* been considered a "cost" such as interest on debt.

What I believe has happened is that the professional management (as opposed to entrepreneurial owner-managers) have tended to forget the stockholder in their financial control systems. Thus, they have passed on fantastic cost increases in wages, materials, taxes, and so on (or in the case of the large chemical companies, they had such volume and productivity increases that they could hold prices and still absorb inflationary costs), *but* they have *not* worried enough about the amount left over for the shareholder.

Many factors have contributed to this, a few of which can be mentioned. The government jawboning against "inordinate" profits of the business giants has made them feel self-righteous in "passing on our productivity increases to our customers in the form of lower prices, if possible."

Admittedly in a highly competitive economy with costs going up, price increases are hard to fight through. It is much easier to explain the necessity for increases "to cover the higher cost of labor" or "the higher cost of interest," and so on, than to argue for the necessity for "higher profits." Profit is still a scare word. *But* it is interesting to note that as we said earlier, few, if any, of the giants have gone bankrupt. They *have* passed on enough costs to remain afloat.

EXHIBIT 3 (concluded)

"Professional management" salaries are set generally on the basis of the size of the company rather than on its PE multiple. Thus, the personal incentive, whether it is at the sales and manufacturing manager level or at the top-management level, is on volume rather than profit.

In addition to the tangible fringes, the "psychic" income of being in the management of a corporate giant that is a "household word" is important to many people. Their leadership is called for in a variety of noncorporate functions. They are large buyers of goods and services, they give employment to thousands, and they get a feeling they are making large contributions to the welfare of mankind by creating masses of material goods.

Cutting through all of this negative thinking to a positive conclusion, then, I believe we may see a change *forced* on the mega-corporations in the 70s. They may be *forced* into giving the shareholders a higher priority in their allocation of resources.

I cannot *really* believe that an industry like the chemical industry, which when I was graduated from business school in 1938 was *the* glamour industry, will be content with its 10 PE multiple instead of its traditional 20 to 30, or more. Granted all of its "commodity product" pricing problems, its management and employee motivation problems, its government pressures, it will still be driven by the necessity of getting capital for its 10 to 15 percent compounded annual volume growth needs. And, if Dow, Du Pont, Monsanto, Cyanamid, Carbide, and so on, start grinding a better profit growth record into their prices (and as we saw earlier, it is a small percentage versus the cost increases they have recovered), the public will have to pay. So I believe a change in their management thinking may be in the cards for the 70s or else the management will be fired by the shareholders.

Translated into policy for Sybron, I believe we must continue our efforts to obtain, or maintain, preeminence in our present fields of effort in spite of the problems of size. We must do this with internal development and through "niche-filling" acquisitions *that enhance* our *proprietary positions.*

My hang-ups with this course of action revolve around management techniques and organization for self-renewal and, in turn, motivation and communications as we get larger. Also, of course, the definition of "niche-fillers" and "enhancement of proprietary position" as opposed to further diversification and size for the sake of size. As we move out into higher technology, for example, in the health or instrumentation fields are we enhancing our proprietary position or diversifying further? This becomes even fuzzier as we look at our chemical business. These are the policies that we must continue to refine as we plan our way into the 70s.

EXHIBIT 4

The Seventies—The Illusory Search for Perpetual Above Average Growth in Earnings per Share

Donald A. Gaudion
February 10, 1970

Is it inevitable that a corporation must eventually return to an average trend line growth rate? Or can it perpetually stay above average if it maintains an above-average management team that continually moves the company into new areas as the environment changes?

First, as we have frequently pointed out, the obvious, but frequently overlooked, difference is between the management of a diversified company and the management of a diversified investment portfolio. The portfolio manager can quickly buy and sell into new industries, and companies within those industries, as the outlook for them changes. The management of a diversified company cannot quickly buy and sell divisions of the company as there are changes in the external environment. We must, of necessity, be into them for the longer pull.

Therefore, as we analyze an industry for long-term growth potential we are talking about "what we want to look like as a company in the year 2000." We have to avoid "Wall Street Fads," or situations that are obviously catch-up. And this avoidance of catch-up situations is extremely complex.

We are not talking about such easily identified fad situations as hulahoops or other consumer promotions. They are at one end of the fad spectrum. What we are concerned about is the life expectancy of more fundamental markets.

For example, there is unquestionably a large accumulated market vacuum to be filled in such areas as pollution and health care, to use a couple in which Sybron has a vital interest. We identified the pollution problem in the middle 50s and merged with the leading company at that time, Permutit. Our experience in the ensuing period has not been reassuring even though recognition of the problem has grown tremendously. More recently we have cast our lot with "health care." When will that really take off and how long will it take to catch up in hospital building? Or has it already passed its peak as the public rebels at the skyrocketing cost of health care?

As this point we have to remind ourselves that we are primarily concerned with growth in earnings per share. This adds an additional complication to the growth equation. Plastics development in the chemical industry is our favorite example of a high technology, effective new product introduction, 15 percent compounded annual unit volume growth rate situation which developed into a "commodity priced" product with no growth in earnings per share.

We have seen similar, but less spectacular, developments in consumer fields such as black-and-white TV, then a hiatus and finally a rapid growth in color TV, the timing of which baffled the consumer research experts. During the past couple of decades we have watched Wall Street move in and out of atomic power, various elements of electronics (e.g., transistors, printed circuits, etc.), air transport, office machines, public utilities, and dozens of other "waves of the future." It is extremely difficult to find a situation that over a long period of time will exceed the basic rate of growth in population, and this may be slowing down.

EXHIBIT 4 (continued)

But then we have the Xeroids, the unique "one product" developments that quickly capture a new market with a patented technological and/or marketing breakthrough. Xerox, Polaroid, Technicon, IBM, Avon Products fall into this category. During the 50s we dreamed of such a potentiality. Our management approach to it has been to search the world for new ideas in our fields and "crap shoot" with a certain amount of money in their development (always keeping the amount gambled in manageable proportions to our earning power so that it did not sink the ship). Our record with Nuclear Safeguard, Fluoridator, Audiac, high-temperature coatings, and many others of lesser significance has not been impressive to say the least. Cyberail is, of course, our largest current gamble, and the returns are not yet in. I visualize no great change in our policy of continually searching out this type of opportunity. However, I feel that we should continue to discount the effect of this on our future and look upon any success as merely "velvet."

To try to determine a growth vehicle that will carry over several decades, rather than a few years, requires a much more fundamental analysis, in my opinion. Flexible, above-average, "far-seeing," globally oriented management is really the *only* answer. And, as we have frequently pointed out, they must be trained to "live out into the future" rather than be hung up with the myths of the past.

Somewhat parenthetically, this is why I believe in our current efforts to build social orientation into our management team. I believe this type of mind is the one capable of riding with the tumult of our revolutionary world changes and hopefully keeping ahead of them (or at least abreast of them since even this may be above average). The precise, methodical, make-no-mistakes type of mentality will probably get overwhelmed in the speed of change. Controlled entrepreneurs will survive. Apart from the need for genius management, are we able to make any generalizations at all to guide us in this illusory search for "perpetual" above-average earnings per share growth?

The Leisure Group, Inc.

The Leisure Group, Inc., a once-bustling Los Angeles conglomerate that produced a wide range of products for leisure time use, had grown from sales of $10 million in 1965 to sales of $66 million in 1970. But in 1971 The Leisure Group (TLG) suffered a financial crisis which resulted in losses of $31 million on sales of $58 million. TLG common, which traded over-the-counter for as much as $36 in 1969, sank to $1¼ by the end of 1971 and subsequently declined to 6 cents per share by the end of 1974. Exhibit 1 shows TLG's past ten years' sales and the price range of its common stock since it became a public company in 1968 (see Exhibit 2).

Merle Banta and Stephen Hinchliffe, the founders and co-chief executive officers, controlled about 10 percent of TLG's 3.2 million outstanding shares of common stock. Miraculously enough, they were not only still managing TLG but had managed to show $1 million in profits on $27 million in sales for 1974. Now, however, confident that they had pulled TLG out of the crisis, they both felt they were faced with a new challenge:

> The biggest risk now is in doing nothing. We could sit back, draw a salary, and grow modestly; but that is most risky. We would still be unable to really grow or raise new capital since after three years of survival management, the bankers feel we are resourceful and can do without additional funds. But the truth is that the operations are lean—the rabbits coming out of the hat are awfully thin. There are limits to being resourceful, and we're approaching them. We must now go on the attack instead of defense.

BACKGROUND

In 1964 Hinchliffe and Banta left McKinsey and Company, a large management consulting firm, to look for a company they could buy and manage. After five months of search, they bought Thompson Manufacturing Company, a manufacturer of lawn and garden sprinklers in Los Angeles, using only $8,000 of their own money and borrowing $550,000. With that heavily mortgaged base, they set about showing the business world how a couple of bright young MBAs could achieve fame and fortune while constructing a dynamic business enterprise around the concept of leisure. Hinchliffe and Banta subsequently broadened product lines and acquired other businesses, combining the various activities into The Leisure Group, Inc. By 1969 they were self-made millionaires.

The period from 1965 to 1970 was one of rapid growth for TLG in the manufacturing and marketing of leisure time products. It also represented an aggressive acquisition strategy which had led to the integration of 12 firms into the TLG management system and growth from 2 to 17 factories accounting for an increase in employees from 120 in 1965 to 2,600 in 1969.

Their goals for 15 percent increased annual sales through internal growth had been met except in 1968 when they had cut back their Planet Junior farm and garden product line. Their goal of 50 percent annual sales growth through acquisitions had also been met except for 1967 when management efforts were devoted to integrating the Ben Pearson product line. They surpassed their goal of 25 prcent increase in earnings per share each year. The major problems had been in meeting their goal of 6 percent aftertax profit. Management time and cost of integrating new acquisitions was making it difficult to achieve profit targets. Exhibit 3 gives a summary of TLG performance to those goals through 1969, as reported.

STRATEGY

TLG's business strategy had been to sell leisure time products through mass-merchandising channels. With professional management, TLG was

EXHIBIT 1
Sales and stock price

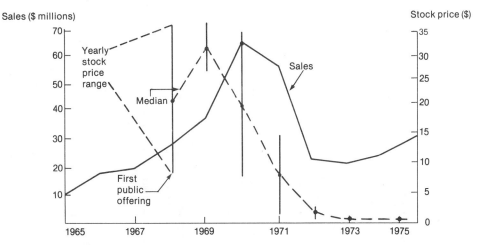

EXHIBIT 2

THE LEISURE GROUP, INC
Selected Ten-Year Operating Results
($000)

	1974	1973	1972	1971	1970	1969	1968	1967	1966	1965
Operating results:*										
Net sales	$26,952	$21,911	$23,713	$57,702	$66,480	$39,694	$30,427	$22,161	$19,069	$10,234
Gross margin	8,345	6,727	6,912	3,002	12,612	10,528	7,572	5,403	4,051	2,068
Operating expenses	5,608	5,294	7,426	15,561	9,438	6,111	4,755	3,756	3,239	1,659
Interest	1,718	1,404	2,023	3,297	2,900	1,308	717	550	423	128
Net income	1,019	222	(7,727)	(31,399)	219	1,678	1,053	571	191	89
Earnings per share	0.13	0.03	(2.46)	(10.16)	0.08	0.73	0.54	0.36	0.14	0.10
Average shares outstanding (000)	3,123.4	3,143.7	3,143.7	3,092.0	3,087.2	2,387.2	2,241.0	n.a.	n.a.	n.a.
Financial position:										
Working capital	2,946	2,531	3,770	5,942	11,504	9,339	5,883	2,777	2,328	489
Net property, plant, and equipment	5,562	6,976	8,072	13,818	20,879	15,060	8,026	3,635	3,326	1,479
Shareholders' equity	6,427	5,453	5,231	8,957	30,705	13,841	8,989	1,723	1,037	521
Retained earnings	(34,145)	(35,164)	(35,386)	(27,659)	3,740	3,300	1,622	n.a.	n.a.	n.a.
Total debt	12,447	14,860	21,072	38,510	43,152	25,801	15,711	n.a.	n.a.	n.a.
Short term†	5,379	5,287	8,695	20,559	24,179	10,369	8,058			
Long term	7,068	9,573	12,377	13,951	9,973	9,342	7,653			
7% convertible subordinated notes	—	—	—	4,000	9,000	6,000	—			
Current assets	12,778	11,533	17,958	32,636	50,953	30,583	20,581	n.a.	n.a.	n.a.
Other information:										
Number of plants	7	8	10	14	19	17	7	4	3	2
Number of employees	1,000	1,000	1,000	1,500	3,300	2,600	1,700	700	530	120
Space occupied (square feet)	492,000	527,000	593,000	1,128,000	2,075,000	1,370,000	750,000	491,000	281,000	50,000

n.a. = not available.   * As stated in annual reports of 1969–74.   † Includes current position of long-term debt.

EXHIBIT 3

TLG five-year performance compared to financial goals

	Goal	Performance (percent)				
		1969	1968	1967	1966	1965
15%	Internal sales growth*	17	3	21	25	9
50%	Acquisition sales growth†	82	68	32	175	84
6%	Aftertax profit‡	4.3	5.5	5.6	3.2	6.3
25%	Increase in EPS§	35	42	90	74	—

* Sales of product lines owned by TLG for the entire year divided by sales of such product lines for most recent prior audited fiscal year whether or not owned by TLG for that entire year (starting one year after acquisition in the case of new product lines).

† Sales during most recent audited fiscal year of product lines acquired during year divided by sales of product lines owned by TLG at beginning of year.

‡ Aftertax profits as reported.

§ EPS compared with prior fiscal year as reported.

Source: 1969 annual report.

concentrating on acquisitions of recognized brands which could be integrated into TLG's new merchandising channels.

Sales. By 1966 Banta and Hinchliffe had zeroed in on the growing demand for leisure products and on new opportunities to mass market them through large outlets rather than small specialty shops. They recognized that with shorter workweeks, younger families, rising incomes, and higher levels of education, Americans were becoming more involved in free-time activities. This trend, coupled with increasingly sophisticated promotional techniques for mass merchandising and self-service, provided the impetus for TLG's strategy of capitalizing on the opportunities by marketing various leisure time products through a single sales force. As Banta commented in 1969:

> This choice is more significant than might seem to be the case at first glance. The most obvious result is, of course, the economies of selling effort spread over several products. Because the products are not highly technical, one salesman can handle the various lines. Equally significant, however, is an ability to provide the buyers at large distributors with facts and data quickly and concisely. What we are working toward is a two-tiered sales force: (1) a small number of expert salesmen who can provide the benefits of our centralized information on several product groups, and (2) a larger number of "retail detail" people who stock shelves, handle promotional material, and so on, at the various retail outlets. The result is that we are able to overpower most of our competitors in dealing with buyers; these competitors are still organized as though they were selling to a network of small retailers. In fact, over 50 percent of the sales of products such as ours are sold through mass merchandisers.

Stephen Hinchliffe also commented in 1969 on their long-run strategy:

> In terms of where we hope to take TLG, we are really still in Phase I. Our present lines can easily be handled by one sales force. The questions I

812

grapple with are what happens when sales of our present groups (and acquisitions to be made in these existing lines) reach $100 million or more and we move into fields such as travel, education, or entertainment. We might have to leave TLG at that time as a separate organization and start almost from scratch with the added services. You know, we can go a long way under the umbrella "leisure time" and "recreation."

Acquisitions. TLG's acquisition strategy was aimed basically at achieving economies of scale through integration of all products into a common sales channel of mass merchandisers. To make this work, it was felt that "brand leadership" was essential for marketing with a single nationwide sales force handling all products. As a result, an acquired firm's operating performance or size was of less importance than its position of product leadership or brand image.

This acquisition policy had led TLG to market leisure-related products in three principal areas: *youth recreation* toys, play equipment, and snow play equipment and sleds; *lawn and garden* sprinklers, sprayers, indoor plant care, and power mower products; and *sporting goods* including firearms, archery equipment, camping equipment, toboggans, trophies, and camouflage hunting wear. (See Exhibit 4 for acquisitions.) The product list had expanded to 10,500 items by 1970.

In analyzing operations of potential acquisitions, TLG concentrated on three major areas: cost of goods sold, manufacturing methods, and technologies that capitalize on the company's design know-how. These areas, more than earnings history, were particularly pertinent because of TLG's policy of total integration of acquired companies.

1. Cost of goods sold: TLG preferred operations with high manufacturing overhead and a high labor content as they represented the greatest potential for improved gross margins.
2. Manufacturing methods: Acquisitions which had not applied professional management techniques in the area of inventory control, production planning, work simplification, and value engineering, provided the best opportunity for TLG to make significant improvement.
3. Design and manufacturing technologies: TLG considered plants as a center of specific manufacturing capability and was interested in acquiring new technologies that might subsequently be applied to existing product lines.

Stephen Hinchliffe described the acquisition process in 1969:

We've had enough experience at making acquisitions to have distilled a few generalizations. The process can be visualized in four stages.

First, Merle and I evaluate the opportunity in the context of our established strategy. Does this situation fit? Can it take us where we want to go? Next we enter a period of negotiating with the present owners as to the value of the firm. Being human, these owners generally want more than a firm is worth; sometimes they seem to expect us to pay them for value we intend to introduce by making changes.

The third stage is probably the most critical: that is to arrange for integrating an acquisition into The Leisure Group, Inc. We take a *task force* into the new firm; usually someone from marketing, operations, and control. Each of these men analyzes the situation he finds and is responsible for developing an "action plan." This plan should tell us, in specific language, what has to be done to turn this company into a contributor to the company. We spend quite a bit of time as a task unit, preparing changes we believe necessary.

The action plans indicated what types of inputs TLG expected to inject into an acquisition, both in the immediate future and over the long term. In most cases to date the immediate emphasis was on reducing general overhead expenses and instituting cost control measures in the plants. More significant were the sophisticated marketing ideas and techniques which TLG brought to bear; products were added and others discontinued to strengthen the line; some products were altered and improved to be more attuned to changes in the markets; and more emphasis was placed on providing retail outlets with data helpful in making their decisions as to product mix and space allocations.

Professional management.   The key element of TLG's concept was the integration of product lines into a single professionally managed organization which would enhance these product lines. Advanced techniques for gathering and analyzing information, establishing objectives; and measuring performance against goals were critical to TLG's management system.

In developing a professionally managed organization, by 1970 TLG had employed 30 men with MBAs from leading business schools. Of the 37 members of the executive staff, 40 percent were under 30 years of age; 58 percent had been employed by corporations in the *Fortune* 500; 30 percent had been with TLG over two years; and, of those, 90 percent had been promoted at least once, had stock options, and had earned incentive bonuses. TLG preferred candidates with past experience in leading packaged goods companies, with successful records, and high motivation towards rapid advancement.

In addition to semiannual salary and stock option reviews, performance bonuses accounted for 10 to 40 percent of salary. Additional motivations were derived from (1) interaction with higher level managers and the chief executive officers; (2) task force assignments to select, negotiate, and integrate acquisitions; and (3) exposure to the financial and business communities. Advancement was based on performance as was compensation.

ORGANIZATION

TLG's organization had been in a constant state of transition, and no formal organization charts were available. (Exhibit 5 is the casewriter's de-

EXHIBIT 4
Acquisitions

Date of acquisition (divestiture)	Former name (location)	Business description (product group)	Approximate terms (accounting method)
1964 (October 1973)	Thompson Mfg. Co. (Los Angeles, Cal.)	Small area sprinklers for lawns and gardens (Lawn and Garden Products)	$555,000 in cash and $350,000 in notes (purchase)
July 1965	Hayes Spray Gun Co. (Los Angeles, Cal.)	Hose and garden sprayers for insecticides and fertilizers (Lawn and Garden Products)	$505,000 in cash and $470,000 in notes (purchase)
February 1966 (November 1971)	Ben Pearson, Inc. (Pine Bluff, Ark.)	Archery equipment [and a line of mechanical harvesting equipment which was disposed of in 1967] (Sporting Goods Products)	$3 million in cash (pooling of interests) [sold in 1971 for $3,289,000 plus $380,000 in liabilities]
September 1967 (May 1971—Planet Junior) (February 1973)	S. L. Allen & Co., Inc. (Philadelphia, Pa.)	Flexible Flyer and Yankee Clipper sleds; Planet Junior farm and garden tools (Youth Recreation Products)	$1,760,000 in notes and common stock (purchase)
November 1967 (October 1973)	Rain Spray Sprinkler, division of Abfo Mfg. Co., Inc. (Los Angeles, Cal.)	Underground lawn and garden sprinklers (Lawn and Garden Products)	$63,000 in cash and $127,000 in notes (purchase)
March 1968	Black Magic, Inc. (Los Angeles, Cal.)	Indoor plant care products (Lawn and Garden Products)	$193,872 in common stock (purchase)
June 1968	The High Standard Mfg. Corp. (New Haven, Conn.)	Sporting fire arms (Sporting Goods Products)	$5,300,000 in cash (purchase)
October 1968 (June 1973)	Werlich Industries Ltd. (Preston, Ontario, Canada)	Toboggans, sleds, and snow saucers (Youth Recreation Products)	$460,000 in cash and $690,000 in notes (purchase)

Date	Company (Location)	Product	Terms
March 1969	Sierra Bullets, Inc. (Santa Fe Springs, Cal.)	Bullets for target and hunting rifles (Sporting Goods Products)	$4.5 million in cash (purchase)
July 1969 (February 1973)	Blazon, Inc. (Jamestown, Pa., and West Point, Miss.)	Play gyms and hobby horses. Sales: $12.5 million (Youth Recreation Products)	$4.5 million in common stock (pooling of interests)
September 1969 (February 1973)	Mascon Toy Co., division of Masco Corp.	Toy telephones and toys for young children [sales: $3 million] (Youth Recreation Products)	$800,000 in cash and $2 million in notes (purchase)
September 1969	The Lyman Gun Sight Corp. (Middlefield, Conn.)	Gunsights and accessories for sporting firearms (Sporting Goods Products)	$2 million in cash (purchase)
September 1969 (October 1973)	Himalayan Industries (Monterey, Cal.)	Backpacks (Sporting Goods Products)	$480,000 in common stock (pooling of interests)
February 1970 (November 1971)	Yard-Man Incorporated (Jackson, Mich., and Sullivan, Ill.)	Powered lawn, garden, and yard maintenance equipment [Sales: 9 months, $22.9 million] (Lawn and Garden Products)	$15.5 million in common stock (purchase resulting in cost of $10.2 million in excess of net asset valuation) [sold for $9 million in notes to be paid over five years]
October 1970	Dodge Trophy (Crystal Lake, Ill.)	Manufacturer of sporting trophies, awards (Oscar, Emmy), trophy cases, plaques, etc. [sales: $6 million] (Sporting Goods Products)	$937,167 in common stock (purchase)
October 1970	Kamo	Camouflage hunting wear [sales: $1.4 million] (Sporting Goods Products)	$210,000 in common stock (pooling of interests)

EXHIBIT 5
Organization chart, 1970

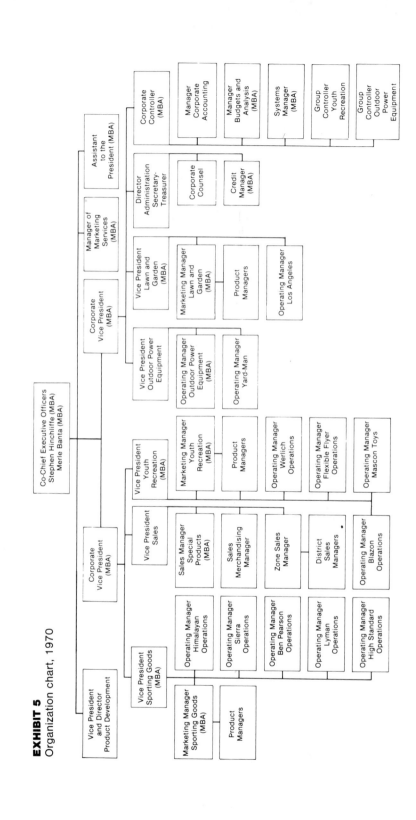

scription developed from TLG's 1970 profile.) In 1970 TLG reorganized from a purely functional organization to concentrate efforts in specific market areas. The product groups, reporting to two corporate vice presidents, had marketing and operations responsibility. The functional areas of sales, product development, and control were all centralized to achieve greater efficiencies. These functional activities had to be coordinated with the product groups to achieve corporate goals. This coordinating function was explained in TLG's 1970 profile:

> Two TLG vice presidents handle coordination of all functional activities, in addition to their specific product line responsibilities. This organizational structure has two objectives: (1) it permits effective coordination and integration of acquisitions into functional areas, and (2) strengthens the entrepreneurial spirit at all TLG management levels by allowing freedom of access by the co-chief executives to all managerial employees, regardless of organizational relationships.

Planning. TLG's management system was a continual cycle of gathering and analyzing information, establishing objectives, and monitoring operations. More and more functions were being centralized at the corporate level so as to develop relevant data and controls. However, data processing facilities were still being "debugged" in 1969, and operations people and product managers were not getting timely data. This problem was forcing consideration of having plant controllers report to their respective plants, instead of to the corporate controller, to provide managers with more responsive information.

For purposes of financial control and planning, a computer model was developed to project sales and expenditures for each manufacturing operation and functional department. Resulting operating statements, balance sheets, cash flows and pertinent ratios were reviewed by the corporate staff to correct possible plan variances.

Stephen Hinchliffe explained in 1969 why there was an emphasis on planning at TLG:

> Given our backgrounds, it's not hard to understand why we are so thorough in our planning efforts around here. Merle and I were consultants, exposed to a broad range of situations where we could observe a number of different planning systems. Most of our marketing organization comes from companies like General Foods, Procter & Gamble, and Xerox—so we have the benefit of knowing how these rather sophisticated firms went about it. And most of us are MBAs, so I'm sure we're all still recovering from the pounding of "planning is a way of life."

He continued:

> Detailed emphasis on planning fits integrally with the style of Merle and myself here at TLG. We both believe it is possible to make certain types of decisions once, and then disseminate procedures for how these recurring

problems should be handled. We have seen so many examples of rather simple decisions being made over and over, each time with a new analysis. In this vein, we are convinced that a strong emphasis on planning forces our people to think in strategic terms. With well-thought-out plans, the everyday events can be interpreted in the context of the larger plan. Planning also contributes to setting goals and specific action routes to accomplishing these goals.

Because TLG was essentially a marketing organization, planning began with the individual product managers. These men were responsible for the preparation of marketing programs derived from five major interrelated marketing plans:

1. Annual product plan: Specified strategies and action for achieving goals by setting long- and short-term profit, market share, and sales goals by specific product group.
2. Product line introduction report (annual): Detailed every product in the line, along with selling prices, cost factors, and the resulting "merchandising profit."
3. Sales forecast: Set product unit sales estimates and sets targets against which all other departments coordinate their programs.
4. Annual budget: Listed all expenditures for product support, including specific promotions, advertising, publicity, packaging, research, advertising allowances, and related expenses.
5. Annual promotion plan: Supplied detail on actions to be taken throughout the year and describes timing, theme, strategy, and implementation of each program.

The bottom line figure for product managers was one which measured sales dollars minus all marketing expenses controllable by PMs, such as advertising and promotion. PMs were held entirely responsible for their product lines.

The managers of operations were given full responsibility for the plant or plants under their supervision. They were responsible for translating marketing forecasts into production quotas and for monitoring ongoing operations to assure they met these goals.

In discussing the internal functioning of TLG's organization, Steve Hinchliffe explained in 1969:

> Clearly the most general fact is our informal communications and the access everyone has to everyone else. Being MBAs, Merle and I expect these men to have an orientation broad enough to fit their job into the more general picture. We also expect them to be problem oriented: to go where they have to and speak to whomever they need, to solve their particular problem.
>
> Secondly, our detailed emphasis on planning and review allows each unit to operate without being totally dependent on other functional units.

Once our annual plans are established, the product and operating managers practically live with each other, going across the functional boundaries. And since product managers have responsibility meeting sales forecasts, they have what I believe to be a very strong incentive to keep in touch with everyone necessary to do so, everyone being other managers at TLG, the sales force, customers, suppliers.

Last, Merle and I have mentioned our belief that a lot of decisions in any firm can be procedurized. We hope to have made the process easier for our people by disseminating procedures and criteria. This provides a framework within which our managers can work.

1970 OPERATING RESULTS

While the results for fiscal 1970 were satisfactory in terms of sales and acquisitions of new product lines, it was a disappointing year for profits and earnings per share. Compared with 1969, sales went from $41 million to $66 million; but net income fell from $1.7 million to $219,000, a drop from 75 cents to 8 cents in earnings per share.

The increase in 1970 sales was from acquisitions of Kamo camouflage hunting wear, Dodge Trophy, a manufacturer of trophies, and Yard-Man outdoor power equipment. Yard-Man accounted for almost $23 million of the $26 million sales increase in 1970.

Part of the problem had come from a 4 percent decline in sales of product lines owned more than one year. This sales slump was seen as a consequence of the economic climate, but the more significant profit decline was caused by the failure to adequately plan for and control changes initiated in operating facilities of acquired product lines. The 1970 annual report listed the major failures as:

Unanticipated labor and overhead costs associated with the consolidation of Blazon play gyms and hobby horse manufacturing and administrative activities from four sites into a single location.

Direct labor, scrap, and manufacturing overhead costs significantly higher than budget in the Flexible Flyer sled plant.

Lower than planned sales of Blazon outdoor play equipment.

A decline in sales of certain High Standard sporting firearms below 1969 levels.

Higher than planned marketing and sales costs, due in part to significant price competition experienced in 1970.

Blazon plant consolidation. The managers of Youth Recreation Products explained in the 1970 annual report that the unanticipated decline in Blazon gross margins was in large part a function of cost overruns in labor, materials, and manufacturing overhead and in lower than planned sales.

As part of the action plan to integrate and consolidate Blazon operations into TLG, it was decided to close three warehouses and three manufacturing plants, while expanding the remaining Mississippi plant. Reduced over-head costs and production efficiencies were estimated to more than offset increased transport costs. However, estimates for the time required to close facilities, transfer equipment and personnel, negotiate with union employ-ees, and institute accounting and control procedures was longer than ex-pected. As explained:

> The net effect was a failure to meet planned manufacturing cost stan-dards. Concurrently, the cost system in use at Blazon plants combined with changes in personnel, manufacturing methods, and locations resulted in a significant portion of these cost overruns being accounted for as "inven-tory." Because of the numerous changes taking place at the operations level throughout 1970, physical inventories were not taken until year-end, and the difference between book and actual inventory was not identified until November 1970.

Flexible Flyer sled manufacturing. The second major factor affecting Youth Recreation Products' gross margins was also explained:

> This plant was constructed in 1969, and substantial plant start-up costs were incurred. The start-up problems resulted in late shipments of sleds in 1969, and, accordingly, attention was directed toward avoiding similar de-livery and customer service problems in 1970.
>
> A combination of failure to develop an adequate inventory mix of sales and an unanticipated increase in sled orders created serious production ca-pacity problems in late 1970. In an effort to meet our customer's delivery requirements, we placed the Medina plant on three-shift operation, six days a week with maintenance and limited production on Sundays. The labor and cost inefficiencies resulting from the influx of new and inadequately trained employees, shift and overtime premiums, and insufficient supervi-sion caused actual manufacturing costs to exceed standard.
>
> Failure to meet standard manufacturing costs and the expensing of ear-lier labor, overhead, and material costs incurred in 1970 and associated with bringing the Medina plant on-stream, added over $1 million to the de-cline in Youth Recreation Products' gross margins.

Financial problems

In January 1970, TLG acquired Yard-Man for common stock valued at $15.5 million. As part of the integration program of Yard-Man into TLG, approximately 50 separate capital programs were planned for prod-uct-line engineering, development, and appearance changes. These pro-grams, plus the added working capital requirements of Yard-Man, led TLG to open a $26 million revolving short-term loan agreement with a group of six banks. This financing arrangement, requiring a minimum of $10.5 mil-lion in working capital, eventually led to the crisis of "Black Wednesday."

Merle Banta explained how the situation developed:

In February of 1971 we needed $26 million to finance operations. We needed $10 million in working capital for Yard-Man plus an additional $16 million in working capital for the other product lines. We had already issued a "Red Herring"[1] to raise additional captial, but the day before we were to meet with the Boston investment community, Nixon invaded Cambodia. Few analysts showed up at the meeting since the brokers were all concerned about the effects of the invasion on the market and were watching their stocks. Well, the Dow Jones dropped sharply, and TLG's stock price fell from $24 to $16. We decided not to go through with the issue. However, that meant that we had no cushion in case anything went wrong.

1971 OPERATING RESULTS

In early 1971, sales of lawn and garden products, principally Yard-Man lawn mowers, dropped substantially and continued to decline through the summer of 1971. At the same time, anticipated improvements in shipping levels and operating efficiencies at Blazon and High Standard plants were not achieved. The combination of lower sales and higher operating costs resulted in a pretax operating loss at nine months of approximately $4.3 million, which placed the company in default under its bank line of credit. Merle Banta explained the default:

> Since our lead bank had a legal loan limit of $6 million, we ended up with a consortium of six banks. Then in our third quarter (May, June, and July), we missed our sales forecast of $18 million with actual sales of $12 million. Had it been just Yard-Man the banks would have understood, but it was across the board—sales were down in sprayers, archery, and 15 other product lines. The banks lost confidence in the management and in the lead bank. They panicked and wanted out.

TLG was required to begin reducing its outstanding bank loans in August. This severely curtailed operating cash at the time of peak seasonal requirements for production and shipping. For several weeks in September and October production at virtually all TLG plants was essentially suspended until interim short-term financing was arranged. Merle Banta explained the events that followed:

> When the banks panicked, we were under the gun. We had proposed to sell some businesses, but the banks felt that would take too long. We had tremendous back orders in archery, shotguns, sleds, and so on, but the banks extracted $10 million in working capital, and we couldn't produce the products. We had a commitment for an additional $3 million in long-term debt, but the new lender would not fund if the banks were going to continue to pull down the working capital line.
>
> On September 28, 1971, we arranged a meeting with the banks in Detroit, but our lead banker didn't attend. The meeting was a debacle and cut

---

[1] Preliminary prospectus.

off any hope for additional funds. On September 29, "Black Wednesday," we closed all 19 plants and laid off all 3,000 employees. We contacted our bank, but couldn't get any help from the loan officer or their assigned "work out" officer. We finally went to the bank's president, whom we knew, and found he didn't know much about our problem. We showed him our back orders and said we wanted financing to enable us to ship until December. Using half the collateral we had left and the president's faith in us, we ended up with an additional $750,000. The $750,000 wouldn't go very far—by the time we paid past-due utilities, rents, taxes, expenses, and salaries, we would have enough to keep only three people per plant for one week. It seemed rather hopeless. Nevertheless, we got the money on Monday, and it kept us alive for one more week. During that period, other senior officers of the participating banks focused on the problem and brought in a team of consultants to assess the situation. Based on the outside advice and the judgments of the new senior officers, the banks reversed their position. They commenced funding again at minimal levels. By November, we had sold Yard-Man and Ben Pearson as we had originally proposed in August, and the crisis started to fade.

As a result of these conditions, many orders could not be shipped in time to meet seasonal schedules. Accordingly, sales in the fourth quarter, ending October 31, 1971, were substantially below forecast with pretax operating losses of $11,580,000, bringing the operating loss for the full year to $15,886,000.

Financial program. TLG's inability to finance its production requirements for the fourth quarter of fiscal 1971 made necessary a new financial program. This plan included the aforementioned sale of Yard-Man and Ben Pearson, renegotiation of existing indebtedness, the conversion of long-term debt to equity, and the establishment of a new line of credit for working capital.

The sale of Yard-Man to Montgomery Ward and Ben Pearson to Brunswick resulted in special charges of $1.5 million plus another $12 million in good will associated with the sale of Yard-Man to be written off. The sale of Planet Junior farm implements in May had also resulted in a $942,000 loss. Total losses resulting from the sale of these divisions, including refinancing costs, were $15,515,000.

The cash and notes received from the sale of Yard-Man and Ben Pearson were used to reduce bank borrowings to about $2 million from $16 million and allowed TLG to obtain an additional one-year agreement with its banks. Past-due trade debt of over $10 million was consolidated into long-term debt through agreement with TLG creditors.

As part of TLG's refinancing program, holders of $9.5 million in 7 percent Convertible Subordinated Notes exchanged their debt for $7 Noncumulative Junior Convertible Preferred Stock. The remaining $4 million of Subordinated Notes was converted in 1973 to Noncumulative Senior Convertible Preferred Stock which had priority over the Junior preferred stock in case of liquidation or dividends. (See Exhibit 6 for details.)

EXHIBIT 6
Shareholders' equity

Preferred stock

The Board of Directors has established the rights and preferences of 150,000 shares of the authorized preferred stock, of which 110,000 shares are $7 Noncumulative Convertible Preferred Stock (Junior Preferred Stock), 95,000 shares of which were issued in November 1971, and 40,000 shares are $7 Noncumulative Senior Convertible Preferred Stock (Senior Preferred Stock) which were issued in April 1973. These shares have an aggregate mandatory redemption and liquidation value of $13,500,000. The Board of Directors has the authority to establish the rights and preferences of the remaining 350,000 shares of authorized but unissued preferred stock.

Holders of Junior Preferred Stock have the same voting rights as holders of the Company's common stock, have votes equal to the shares of common stock they would receive upon conversion, and are entitled to a $7 per share noncumulative annual dividend, commencing February 1, 1974, when and as declared by the Board of Directors. Such dividends are payable before dividends may be paid on the common stock. The Junior Preferred Stock is redeemable at the Company's option at $100 per share, plus a premium of $6.30 per share, such premium reducing annually through 1991. Redemption cannot occur prior to November 1, 1976, unless the market price of common stock is equivalent to at least 150 percent of the per share conversion price. Beginning in 1982, the Company is required to redeem, at $100 per share, 10 percent of the then outstanding Junior Preferred Stock each year through 1991. In the event of involuntary liquidation, holders of Junior Preferred Stock are entitled to $100 per share. Each share of Junior Preferred Stock is convertible into common stock at any time prior to November 1, 1991, on the basis of $2.74 per common share (subject to antidilution adjustments) divided into the redemption price of $100.

The rights and preferences of the holders of the Senior Preferred Stock are the same as the Junior Preferred Stock, except (1) they have preference with respect to dividends and in liquidation, (2) they may convert into common shares on the basis of $3 per common share (subject to antidilution adjustments) divided into the redemption price of $100, and (3) they may preclude the Company from selling a substantial portion of the business or its assets.

Common stock

In 1971 the Company issued seven-year warrants to purchase 670,000 shares of the Company's common stock at $2 per share and 27,671 shares at $2.50 per share. In February 1974 the holders of warrants to purchase 697,671 shares returned them to the Company for cancellation.

In May 1974, 45,000 shares of the Company's stock were received from the former owner of an acquired business in connection with a settlement relating to the acquisition. Accordingly, "cost of purchased businesses in excess of net assets acquired" has been reduced by the stated value of the returned shares.

At October 31, 1974, 4,800,000 shares of common stock were reserved for conversion of $7 Noncumulative Senior and Junior Preferred Stock, and 290,780 shares were reserved for exercise of employee stock options. At October 31, 1974, 51,810 options were exercisable.

To obtain needed flexibility in meeting seasonal production require-ments, a credit line of $3,750,000 was negotiated with a commercial finance company. The resulting interest rates were 6 percent over prime rate.

A summary of the total restrictions on TLG resulting from the various debt agreements is listed in Exhibit 7.

EXHIBIT 7
TLG debt restrictions

THE LEISURE GROUP, INC., AND SUBSIDIARIES
Notes to Consolidated Financial Statements
October 31, 1974

In 1974 and 1973 the Company negotiated repayment schedules and certain other conditions and features of substantially all of its major debt agreements and exchanged $4 million of 7 percent Convertible Subordinated Notes for $7 Noncu-mulative Senior Convertible Preferred Stock. These negotiations resulted in for-giveness of indebtedness and accrued interest which has been reflected as an extraordinary credit to income in the accompanying financial statements but did not result in any obligation to issue additional common stock.

The following summarizes the components of long-term debt:

	1974	1973
Working capital term loan, bearing interest at 6% over prime rate, payable in equal monthly installments to July 15, 1978	$1,470,000	$ 2,798,000
Subordinated bank loans, bearing interest at 1½% over prime rate, payable in equal quarterly in-stallments to October 31, 1983	1,055,000	1,175,000
Extended unsecured trade debt, bearing interest at 7¾%, payable in equal monthly installments to October 15, 1980	2,218,000	2,535,000
Other long-term debt, bearing interest at rates to 6% over prime rate with installments to December 1987:		
Secured	1,275,000	2,058,000
Unsecured	2,214,000	2,647,000
Other	319,000	447,000
	$8,551,000	$11,660,000
Less: Current portion	1,483,000	2,087,000
	$7,068,000	$ 9,573,000

Minimum principal payments due on long-term debt in the next five years are $1,483,000 in 1975, $1,659,000 in 1976, $1,784,000 in 1977, $1,453,000 in 1978, and $1,004,000 in 1979.

All of the Company's assets are collateral for the working capital, bank, and other secured loans. Many of the agreements containing cross-default provisions may be terminated if the lender shall reasonably determine that it is insecure with respect to payment of its loans or may be declared due and payable if a material adverse change in the financial position or results of operations of the Company occurs.

EXHIBIT 7 (continued)

The Company's working capital agreement, with a commercial finance company, provides for short-term loans equal to 80 percent of eligible accounts receivable plus $850,000, bearing interest at 6 percent over prime rate. During 1974, outstanding short-term borrowings averaged $4,559,000 (borrowings ranged from $3,458,000 to $5,264,000) with interest rates averaging 16¾ percent.

The Company's various debt agreements place certain restrictions on the Company with respect to mergers, divestitures, borrowings, leasing, and other activities, and restricts the Company from paying dividends or purchasing or retiring shares of its capital stock.

Under the most restrictive covenants of its debt instruments, the Company must maintain the following financial ratios and conditions, all of which were met at October 31, 1974: (a) A minimum working capital of $1 million; at October 31, 1974, working capital was $2,946,000. (b) A minimum consolidated net worth of $4.5 million; at October 31, 1974, consolidated net worth was $6,427,000. (c) A tangible net worth as defined, of not less than $1 million; at October 31, 1974, tangible net worth as defined, was $1,973,000. (d) Maintain inventories of not less than $4 million; at October 31, 1974, inventories were $7,258,000.

NEW DIRECTIONS: 1973 AND BEYOND

After the 1971 crisis, TLG's operations were reorganized to decentralize product management. In order to improve customer coordination and communication, and to improve the profitability of each operation, the previously centralized general management, sales, and marketing functions were transferred to the operating headquarters of each product division.

The decentralization and reorganization in January 1972 restructured TLG into six divisions. By 1975 two more divisions had been sold for financial reasons and four divisions remained, including the following (see Exhibit 8):

1. Sporting Firearms Products, which had responsibility for High Standard sporting firearms and Kamo products.
2. Reloading Products, having responsibility for Lyman and Sierra products.
3. Trophy Products, responsible for Dodge Trophy products.
4. Lawn and Garden Products, responsible for Black Magic plant care products and Hayes spray guns.

The reduction in the size of TLG's corporate staff obtained through the reorganization and decentralization of operations had reduced corporate general and administrative expenses from $4.6 million in 1971 to $1.3 million in 1974. TLG's professional staff at corporate included seven members in 1975, down from 37 in 1971.

EXHIBIT 8
Organization chart, 1975

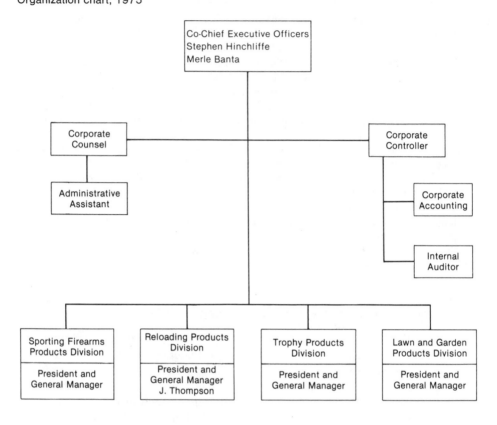

Growth in sales of sporting goods, including firearms, reloading, and trophy products, increased from $14.5 million in 1971 to $20.9 million in 1974. Lawn and Garden accounted for the remaining $1 million in 1971 and $6.1 million in 1974, as seen in Exhibit 9.

EXHIBIT 9
Five-year sales results

	1974	1973	1972	1971	1970
Sales by product class ($000):					
Sporting goods	$20,900	$17,900	$17,250	$14,550	$11,500
Others	6,100	4,000	3,250	1,050	4,200
	$27,000	$21,900	$20,500	$15,600	$15,700
Discontinued operations	—	2,200	14,000	42,100	50,800
	$27,000	$24,100	$34,500	$57,700	$66,500

Management philosophy

Division management. James (Mace) Thompson, president of Reloading Products Division, was one of the few managers who remained through the turnaround. He joined TLG in June 1968, as product manager for High Standard. In November 1969 he became marketing manager for High Standard, Sierra Bullets (acquired May 1969), and Lyman products (acquired October 1969). Mace Thompson related in 1975 his early precrisis experience of integrating the new acquisitions:

> After acquiring a self-sufficient company, we would split it into three units. The operations manager would report to the vice president of operations who reported to Merle Banta. The product manager reported to the vice president of marketing who reported to Steve Hinchliffe. And the sales manager reported to the national sales manager who reported to the vice president of marketing.
>
> There was a functional organization, but the operations manager was located at the factory, the product manager was in Los Angeles, and sales were all over the United States.
>
> An integrating team would go into the company and decide on the changes. The strong-willed MBAs would tend to win any argument, and the acquired companies felt like a herd of elephants ran over them—young guys running in, canning people, changing policy, asking penetrating questions—and morale would be bad until the TLG operations man came in to try and pull it together.

By June 1970 Mace Thompson had additional product responsibilities as marketing manager of Sporting Goods, with product, not sales, responsibility. Products added were Ben Pearson archery, Himalayan back packs, Werlich toboggans, and Dodge Trophy. In December 1970 he was appointed general manager of Shooting and Sports Products with product and operating responsibilities, but not sales. He explained in 1975 some of the difficulties he had:

> Was there really synergy in a common sales force? We were mistaken in what we thought our strengths were. We had 50 salesmen who could make five calls per day and sell x units, and so on, but the mix was wrong, the selling features were different, the sales methods were different. Product managers had no authority over sales. Having sales and marketing report to a vice president may be all right for Procter & Gamble who use a common channel and a "pull" strategy, but not for a sales force calling on back pack, reloading, gun, lawn and garden, and toys customers—they are all different.
>
> Management controls and MIS were ineffective and not available in a given company or to a sales manager. We were flying by the seat of our pants, and good decisions were still based on bad data. We were moving too fast in acquiring new companies—reality was lost.
>
> Forecasts were bad. Backlogs on seasonal products were added to forecasts. But once it was budgeted, there was no turning back—you couldn't

cut back on inventories and get financing as fast as you could change a forecast. Management had a "can do" attitude that didn't allow for much change. Once the backlog was so high, advertising was cut substantially.

The company was reorganized after the crisis, but true decentralization occurred in January 1972, when sales responsibility was given back to the divisions. Mace Thompson explained in 1975 the importance of this move:

> Decentralization! This is the key as to why we're in business today and why we almost weren't in 1971. We had lost our control over receivables, collections, and sales. We had lost the intimacy of an individual company.
>
> In the gun market, for example, you needed to know guns. When I was product manager I wrote a product knowledge manual for salesman training. There was no way we could expect salesmen to be able to sell guns without knowing anything about them. We were also vulnerable to competition since we weren't in some segments and weren't number one in others. For example, target pistols, where we are strong, had little growth, so market share was important. We weren't even in the rim fire segment. Shotguns were the key market, but we were private branding and didn't even have a position. We couldn't expect 15 percent sales increase across the board, we had to look at segments.
>
> By 1971 people were getting dissatisfied unless they were moving rapidly. The corporate group was on a "high"; they were working so hard they lost touch with reality. Salesmen didn't know what to do—missing goals was a deflating experience. It was an invigorating environment as long as you could cope with it, but it tore up a lot of good people. I'm sure they have changed their goals since then. You adopt your personal policy to the environment you're in. For me it was a stimulating, invigorating experience—"doing the impossible dream." I enjoyed it!

A major reduction in corporate overhead expenses came from the shift of responsibilities to the divisions. In addition to moving sales, marketing and general management back to the divisions, the control and administrative functions were also decentralized. Now, accounts receivable, credit, collections, and data processing were divisional responsibilities. TLG's headquarters' functions were basically reduced to that of financial management. Merle Banta describes the change in management's methods.

> We made a 180-degree flip from centralization to decentralization. We now have four divisions which report to Steve or me. They each have a president, controller, marketing staff, and sales force. The divisions run independently though we have mini-board meetings with the division management where we require more than just numbers by digging into what they are doing and why. Cash is also managed centrally. All collections come into corporate headquarters and are then disbursed to fund divisions on a weekly basis. We also set policy on borrowing and allocation of funds, logos, insurance, salaries, hiring and firing, lease agreements, and budgets. Any capital expenditures over $5,000 come to us for authorization.

In elaborating the changes in business philosophy and management methods, Merle Banta explained the shift to a more conservative business approach and the emphasis on experience rather than education.

Though it's not company policy, the 30-year-old, bright MBA hasn't been hired since Black Wednesday. Having an MBA is not in itself a sufficient criterion for success. This became obvious in the Blazon plant consolidation where the chain of command responsible for that project was five MBAs, four of whom had graduated with honors. We now look for mature, experienced people from the appropriate industry or functional area. Many of the people hired since 1971 have been over 40 and wouldn't know a button-down-collared MBA if they were bitten by one.

We've become extremely cautious and even conservative. We've been so close to the brink that our budgets, plans, and forecasts have had to be more realistic.

We're more concerned about the long term. In the 60s, people saw themselves growing fast and weren't in a job over six months. You couldn't evaluate them because they would change jobs too often—never looked at long-term consequences of decisions. Today we are most conscious in marketing—we had really damaged our image when deliveries weren't made. We have good relations now and make long-term decisions first priority.

Motivation is different now, and harder. In the 60s, TLG was a glamorous and exciting company—people clamored to come to work even at a pay cut—it was the "in" place to be. Now that's not the case, especially for the kind of people we want to hire—experienced, tough-minded managers. They report to us, but we don't tell them what to do the way we used to—now we discuss it in much greater depth.

We review objectives quarterly now instead of annually. We sit down with managers and assign their bonus target and set qualitative and quantitative objectives. We started this in 1972 to restore employee confidence and make certain they were working in the right direction.

Morale seems to be good now, but it has been bad during periods of tight cash. Any sales slump would cut receivables, and low cash resulted in a need to delay paying vendors. Everyone has been a part of it.

MBAs are not as salable today as they were in the 60s. They have the image of not being the type who wants to plug away over the long run. That isn't the kind of a guy we want.

The leisure industry.   There had also been a change in TLG's concept of the leisure industry and the approach that would be taken in entering new product areas.

In the 60s we saw it as manufactured products, branded, and sold by mass merchandisers. Now we see it as anything that people do or use during leisure, not necessarily sold by mass merchandisers, manufactured, or branded. The Atlantic Braves could be an example. Being practical, we'll probably stay in areas related to what we have now.

We didn't care before if a product was in a good or bad industry, whether the firm was profitable or not, or whether it was a growing or dying market. Flexible Flyer was a good brand but a dying market. Today we are more traditional—we want a profitable, growing product, unique technology, or manufacturing, and so on—we want some advantage. We would also operate them independently unless it made sense to fold it in with an existing division.

Much of the change in management philosophy had come from a recognition of the fundamental importance of "cash flow" as reflected in the attitudes of "Wall Street" and the increasing importance of "financial institutions." Merle Banta explained in 1975 this shift and its impact on TLG:

> Running a growth business today is totally different from the 60s. Then you had a market that thrived on optimism. Our youth, the MBA and McKinsey background, the excitement of leisure time markets—all sounded great to the young analysts of Wall Street. By 1972 it was a different market, all the hard-assed bankers wanted to see was the cash flow.
>
> During the 60s, you needed earnings growth, a sexy story like leisure time, MBAs, and acquisitions. Now the bankers require a profitable business with good cash flow—we've had to deal with the cash flow to survive. We've had to watch day-to-day working capital while we regained trade creditors' confidence. We went from cash in advance to C.O.D, but now we're at 30–90 days' credit. We've reduced our long-term debt from $40 million to $7 million. Our short-term borrowings were $25 million; now they are $4 million. Our profits plus depreciation exceed the required debt amortization, so we have a positive cash flow! (See Exhibits 10 and 11 for recent financial data.)

In reflecting about the problems that TLG had incurred and rethinking what might have been done differently to have avoided the crisis, Merle Banta felt that the major problem had been in TLG's handling of its banking relations. When asked what they would do differently if they could do it over again, Banta replied:

> Our approach would be similar, but we would avoid the mistakes. We went too fast. We uprooted acquisitions and tried to integrate them in 30 days—now we would take six months or six years, if necessary. The loss of coordination caused by short-term upheavals must be minimized to achieve long-term integration. We would meld the aggressive MBA with the old-time experienced manager. Maybe this change in attitude comes from age—I was 31 when we started The Leisure Group, and you couldn't have anyone older than yourself, could you?
>
> The major difference would be in the way we put together our financing. It was our policy to use the best: auditors—Arthur Andersen; we went to O'Melveny & Myers for counsel; Blyth and Company underwriters. But our lead bank was not a major bank. Moreover, we leaned too heavily—and successfully—on them for short-term financing to avoid further dilution by

EXHIBIT 10

THE LEISURE GROUP, INC.
Consolidated Statements of Operations
For the years Ended October 31, 1974, and 1973

	1974	1973
Continuing operations:		
Net sales	$26,952,000	$21,911,000
Cost of sales	18,607,000	15,184,000
Gross margin	$ 8,345,000	$ 6,727,000
Selling, general, and administrative expenses excluding corporate expenses	4,397,000	4,444,000
Income from continuing operations before corporate expenses	$ 3,948,000	$ 2,283,000
Loss from discontinued operations before corporate expenses	—	(753,000)
Corporate expenses:		
General, administrative, and other expenses	1,211,000	850,000
Interest (including $756,000 and $583,000 on short-term obligations in 1974 and 1973)	1,718,000	1,404,000
Income (loss) before income taxes and extraordinary items	$ 1,019,000	$ (724,000)
Provision for income taxes	519,000	—
Income (loss) before extraordinary items	$ 500,000	$ (724,000)
Extraordinary items	519,000	946,000
Net income	$ 1,019,000	$ 222,000
Income (loss) per share:		
Assuming full dilution:		
Income (loss) before extraordinary items	$0.06	$(0.09)
Extraordinary items	0.07	0.12
Net income	$0.13	$0.03

going to the equity market. In other words, we were too heavily leveraged with too small a bank. As a result, when the crunch came there was no cushion and no real strength leading the bank group. When we go back to the banks, after leaving the Commercial Finance Company, we'll seek a large commercial bank.

Once TLG was caught in the crisis of "Black Wednesday," both Merle Banta and Steve Hinchliffe felt a responsibility to the employees of the acquired companies and were determined to do whatever was possible to work it out. However, by late 1975, their basic entrepreneurial spirit was beginning to come alive again. Banta and Hinchliffe both felt it was necessary to begin looking for new opportunities for growth and had begun looking around for potential acquisitions. Merle Banta explained:

We got everyone into the mess, and we were responsible for getting them out. But as we go on now, it is the chance for economic opportunity

EXHIBIT 11

THE LEISURE GROUP, INC.
Consolidated Balance Sheets
October 31, 1974, and 1973

Assets	1974	1973
Current assets:		
Cash	$ 330,000	$ 267,000
Accounts receivable, less reserves of $586,000 in 1974 and $430,000 in 1973	4,861,000	4,397,000
Receivable from sales of discontinued operations	—	466,000
Federal income tax refunds	—	282,000
Notes receivable	13,000	138,000
Inventories, at the lower of cost (first-in, first-out) or market	7,258,000	5,758,000
Prepaid expenses	316,000	294,000
Total current assets	$12,778,000	$11,602,000
Property, plant, and equipment (at cost):		
Land	$ 562,000	$ 804,000
Buildings and improvements	2,638,000	3,558,000
Machinery and equipment	4,920,000	4,728,000
Office furniture and fixtures	482,000	486,000
	$ 8,602,000	$ 9,576,000
Less: Accumulated depreciation and amortization	3,040,000	2,600,00
Total property, plant, and equipment	$ 5,562,000	$ 6,976,000
Other assets:		
Cost of purchased businesses in excess of net assets acquired	$ 4,454,000	$ 4,499,000
Long-term receivables	218,000	629,000
Cash surrender value of life insurance policies and deposits	315,000	322,000
Total other assets	$ 4,987,000	$ 5,450,000
Total assets	$23,327,000	$24,028,000

Liabilities and Shareholders' Equity	1974	1973
Current liabilities:		
Loan payable	$ 3,896,000	$ 3,202,000
Current portion of long-term debt	1,483,000	2,087,000
Accounts payable	1,904,000	1,286,000
Accrued liabilities	2,549,000	2,427,000
Total current liabilities	$ 9,832,000	$ 9,002,000
Long-term debt:		
Secured	$ 3,800,000	$ 6,031,000
Unsecured	4,432,000	5,182,000
Other	319,000	447,000
	$ 8,551,000	$11,660,000
Less: Current portion included above	1,483,000	2,087,000
Total long-term debt	$ 7,068,000	$ 9,573,000
Commitments and contingencies		
Shareholders' equity (See Exhibit 6):		
Preferred stock, $5 per value: Authorized—500,000 shares Outstanding—135,000 shares, stated at	$13,500,000	$13,500,000
Common stock, no par value: Authorized—10,000,000 shares Outstanding—3,098,684 shares in 1974 and 3,143,684 shares in 1973, stated at	3,099,000	3,144,000
Capital surplus	23,973,000	23,973,000
Retained earnings (deficit)	(34,145,000)	(35,164,000)
Total shareholders' equity	$ 6,427,000	$ 5,453,000
Total liabilities and shareholders' equity	$23,327,000	$24,028,000

that is the motivating factor. I don't have to do more—the economic opportunity line has taken over and that's the motivation. We're basically the same as before—looking for a chance to respond to environmental opportunities. We'll break out of the gate at first chance. Our managerial skills of the 60s are 500 percent better today though our basic beliefs are the same.

Index of Cases

Sybron Corporation (E), 796
Tensor Corporation, 360
Zurn Industries, Inc., 614

This book has been set in 10 and 9 point Caledonia, leaded 2 points. Part numbers are 18 point Helvetica Medium and part titles are 18 point Helvetica, section and chapter numbers are 14 point Helvetica Light, section titles are 14 point Helvetica, and chapter titles are 18 point Helvetica Medium. The size of the type page is 27 by 45½ picas.